T0348401

Credit Engineering for Bankers

Credit Engineering for Bankers
A Practical Guide for Bank Lending, 2nd Edition

Morton Glantz and Johnathan Mun

Amsterdam • Boston • Heidelberg • London • New York • Oxford
Paris • San Diego • San Francisco • Singapore • Sydney • Tokyo

Academic Press is an imprint of Elsevier

Academic Press is an imprint of Elsevier
30 Corporate Drive, Suite 400, Burlington, MA 01803, USA
525 B Street, Suite 1900, San Diego, CA 92101-4495, USA
84 Theobald's Road, London WC1X 8RR, UK
Radarweg 29, PO Box 211, 1000 AE Amsterdam, The Netherlands

First edition 2003
Second edition 2011

Notice
No responsibility is assumed by the publisher for any injury and/or damage to persons or
property as a matter of products liability, negligence or otherwise, or from any use or operation
of any methods, products, instructions or ideas contained in the material herein. Because
of rapid advances in the medical sciences, in particular, independent verification of diagnoses
and drug dosages should be made

Library of Congress Cataloging-in-Publication Data
Credit engineering for bankers: a practical guide for bank lending/edited by Morton Glantz and
Johnathan Mun.
   p. cm.
  ISBN 978-0-12-378585-5
  1. Bank loans–Management. 2. Credit–Management. 3. Asset-liability management.
4. Financial risk management. 5. Bank management. I. Glantz, Morton. II. Mun, Johnathan.
HG1641.C665 2011
332.1'753–dc22

                    2010033503

British Library Cataloguing in Publication Data
A catalogue record for this book is available from the British Library

ISBN: 978-0-12-378585-5

For information on all Academic Press publications visit
our website at books.elsevier.com

Printed and bound in the USA

11 12 13   10 9 8 7 6 5 4 3 2

Working together to grow
libraries in developing countries

www.elsevier.com | www.bookaid.org | www.sabre.org

ELSEVIER   BOOK AID
               International   Sabre Foundation

Models discussed in chapters 5, 6, 10, 11, 20 are located on the companion website to this book and can be located at: www.ElsevierDirect.com

Models discussed in chapters 7, 8, 12, 14, 15, 16, 17, 18 can be downloaded from the Real Options Valuation website: http://www.realoptionsvaluation.com/download.html for the software applications and models, and http://www.realoptionsvaluation.com/creditengineeringbook.html for the software licenses and other models

Contents

Part Two   Credit Administration   309

Dedication

This book is dedicated to my grandson Landon Kissell, my greatest treasure in life, my best friend forever.

– Morton Glantz

To my wife Penny and son Jayden, for their unconditional love and support.

– Johnathan Mun

Dedication

Foreword

When I wrote the foreword for the first edition of this book in 2002, we had just exited the "tech wreck" and a shallow U.S. recession. I emphasized then that "the new economy did not arrive in the way some pundits predicted at the end of the last century. Instead of perpetual economic growth and the death of business cycles, we are in the midst of rapidly evolving markets and rapidly changing corporate structures." The global economy has only become more unstable.

The demise of Lehman Brothers in 2008 marked the return of the business cycle with a vengeance. This time around, banks and governments were at the center of both the crisis and the cleanup. Managing bank risk has become a key priority for both bank executives and regulators. As of the time of writing the second edition of this book, we are still in fragile economic circumstances; managing bank risk remains difficult. It is the pace at which companies appear and disappear that continues to be the hallmark of our new (old) economy. We find economists and policymakers mining history to tell us something about what is new. While asset-based lending dominated in recent years, the fallout from the crisis has forced banks to go back and relearn how to do cash-flow-based analysis. That said, more recently developed tools to support asset-based lending continue to be part of the financial landscape. The ideas described in this book reflect an expanded repertoire of risk analysis approaches for navigating the postcrisis world. Bank executives and risk managers will find that using these approaches will make it much easier to adapt to the changing financial environment. Never has a book on managing bank risk been more relevant.

We are now a few years into the implementation of Basel II in most countries. Despite the time and effort invested in this new regulatory capital framework, systemic crisis appeared again. The most recent crisis has given birth to Basel III proposals. (Nothing like adding more regulation when the existing changes did not seem to make the world safer.) We still lack clarity as to how Basel II and III will continue to change the financial markets. One objective of Basel II focused on removing regulatory arbitrage, which had been the primary motivation for the creation of collateralized loan obligations (CLO). As the market developed, CLOs became an increasingly important financing tool. Before the crisis, assets were placed in a CLO and by virtue of a magical agency rating, the capital requirement decreased. Many wish the magic could have lasted. In fact, the ratings obfuscated actual risk, making transactions possible without real risk transfer. Theoretically, the assets placed into the CLO moved off the bank's balance sheet. We discovered two uncomfortable facts during the most recent crisis: the rating methodologies used to assign risk ratings to CLO tranches turned out to be wildly optimistic, and when a deal starts to unravel, the assets seem to find their way back onto the original bank's balance sheet. Risk appears not to have been transferred. CLOs in particular and collateralized debt obligations (CDOs) in general are now demonized, and market liquidity in these instruments has evaporated. This market implosion highlighted how credit, market, and liquidity risk can mix together in ways not always anticipated. The underlying credit risk of many instruments placed in CDOs deteriorated rapidly, the market risk associated with volatile changes in spreads forced many investors (many of whom were banks) to mark down substantially what they thought were investment-grade CDO tranches, and then liquidity disappeared as everyone questioned the real underlying risk of these instruments. The need for risk transfer and risk trans-formation continues, but we must learn from this debacle. If there is a second life for CDOs, simpler structures with transparent risk ratings and transparent transaction motivation will be essential. Regardless of whether we ever see the return of CDOs, a bank must now, more than ever, develop the internal capability to evaluate and price risk without relying only on an outside agency. Otherwise, the seeds of the next disaster will be easily sown.

In addition to redefining what can be counted as capital (i.e., instrument with loss-absorbing characteristics), Basel III targets leverage and liquidity. While the proposals will likely result in unintended negative consequences, the focus on liquidity is indicative of more focus on funding risk. The interaction of credit and liquidity risk has shifted from a question of academic debate to a question of practical interest. Correlation across risk types is just one area where the most recent crisis has illuminated "hidden" risks that require better and more innovative risk modeling as described in this book.

We are still not out of this most recent crisis. The debates concerning rating agencies, the role of banks, the role of the governments in financial markets, the structure of banks, the structure of financial markets, credit default swaps (CDS), and collateralized debt obligations (CDOs) continue without convergence to a common set of policy or management recommendations. In the midst of this mess, banks still have to be managed.

Returning to first principles, we still need banks to transform short-term liquid deposits into long-term illiquid loans. Bank portfolios should still be managed, and most historical bank crises arise from portfolio concentrations to one segment or another (e.g., large U.S. corporates, Japanese real estate, U.S. residential mortgages). In fact, regulatory overemphasis on derivatives and complicated collateralized structures may inadvertently create an environment for new crises if banks become too dependent on regulatory capital (which does not reflect a portfolio's actual concentration risk) and redirect their business to just a handful of market segments and asset classes (thus forgetting about diversification). The result will be bank failures arising from concentration. Many of the demonized instruments can be quite helpful in minimizing this risk. CDSs and CDOs do not always lead to financial destruction.

CDSs and CDOs are double-edged swords because they can facilitate sensible diversifying trades or lead unsuspecting banks into the realm of money-losing complexity. A less well-known fact during the most recent financial crisis is that some large banks who prudently used models to decide how to improve their portfolios diversification with CDS and CDOs not only came through crisis unscathed, but they actually improved their market position. Bank risk can be better managed with these tools.

Unfortunately, these tools can also lead a bank to destruction. Consider the analogy of another tool that facilitates global economic growth: the airplane. With the advent of modern, global airplanes, businesses can more quickly grow and business trans-actions can be completed more quickly. In fact, the modern economy would grind to a halt without air travel. But in the wrong hands, such as an inexperienced pilot or a terrorist, an airplane can wreak destruction on a large scale. Similarly, in the right hands, tools that facilitate risk and portfolio management can do much to improve the strength, growth, and stability of the financial system. These same tools directed toward simpleminded speculation with no checks on leverage or riskiness can lead to large-scale destruction. The key lies in understanding. This book provides a good chunk of this understanding.

Banks continue to face the specter of concentration risk. Bank crises arise from concentrated segments in a bank's portfolio suffering from an economic downturn. Often this concentration risk arises from underlying correlations that may be "hidden" from bank executives without systems focused on portfolio risk. For example, several of the large U.S. banks that faced difficulties in the most recent financial crisis had substantial concentration risk arising from exposure to both U.S. residential mort-gages and large companies whose fortunes rose and fell with the U.S. housing market. This underlying correlation across retail and institutional portfolios could have been tracked and managed with available correlation models. But many failed banks chose to ignore the signs. An economy growing on the back of excessive consumer borrowing becomes heavily dependent on rising house prices as homes became the collateral of choice. Once the process reversed and the high loan-to-value ratios came back to bite consumer borrowers, not only did residential mortgage portfolios take a hit, but corporate loan portfolios with borrowers such as home builders, auto makers, appliance makers, business services, and realtors (just to name a few) also faced trouble at the same time. Large U.S. banks tended to have exposure to both residential mortgages and corporate borrowers; few of these banks recognized the correlation risk across these portfolios. This process became turbo-charged given that asset-backed securities had facilitated a degree of leverage and credit expansion not ever seen before. While many executives and policy makers want to blame the crisis on the complexity of the instruments and the arcane models that supported them, the risk management issues are much more mundane. Concentration risk can kill. The models and approaches highlighted in Professor Glantz's and Dr. Mun's book are straightforward applications for avoiding the fallout from the next crisis, which will again likely be concentration risk dressed up in new clothes.

Bank executives must worry not just about concentration risk in their loan portfolio but also concentration risk among derivative counterparties and sources of funding. While funding (liquidity) risk has always been lurking in the background, the surprising failure of Northern Rock (a British mortgage lender mostly funded through the wholesale credit market) due to its inability to maintain funding when money market funds stopped lending it money and the general breakdown of the interbank lending market in the weeks that followed Lehman's failure placed a spotlight on an area of risk typically relegated to infrequent, hypothetical stress liquidity planning. It turns out that diversification in funding sources is as important as diversification in a credit portfolio.

As the credit markets have evolved, nonbank financial institutions have become an important part of credit markets. Sometimes these institutions (e.g., AIG, large insurance companies, large money market funds, etc.) are said to constitute a shadow banking system. In the previous edition's foreword, I wrote, "Technology and deregulation have enabled nonbank financial institutions to enter the credit markets in unprecedented ways." The good news is that shadow banks add to the market's liquidity. The bad news is that shadow banks—with AIG at the center—are also not immune to failure arising from concentration risk. Shadow banks suffer from the same kinds of systemic ailments as the regular banking system. We discovered in this latest crisis that concentration risk can develop anywhere banking-type activities are undertaken. We now understand how important it is for analysts and regulators to track nonbank financial institutions. Executives of these institutions will also benefit from learning and implementing the tools discussed in this book.

When the first edition of the book was published, I highlighted how market-observable data are playing a more important role in credit modeling. Equity, debt, and CDS markets can be sources of data in the evaluation of credit risk. Sudden market breaks and general disappearance of market liquidity made these approaches less reliable in certain market environments. That said, these tools still belong in the risk management toolkit of any well-managed bank. We have learned, however, that other tools that rely on behavioral scorecards, cash-flow forecasting, and rigorous integration qualitative assessments from subject matter experts should also be part of that toolkit. We have also learned the importance of macroeconomic-based stress testing and the development of credit portfolio management functions that do not just trade credit assets but also advise originators and provide input to development of bank strategy. It is all too easy to readily dismiss market-based tools and what, at first, appear to be hard-to-understand risk systems. If anything, the crisis has taught us that systematic storage of data, investment in systems that synthesize and distill that data in useful ways, and a focus on transparency and straightforward communication of a bank's risk are even more important. Investing the time to understand the concepts described in this book will pay large dividends.

While stress testing and capital management have become a required part of a bank's risk discipline, regulator and investor pressure to disclose more information makes it all the more important to read the latest thinking on risk evaluation. Transparency into the underlying analytics has become an essential part of good risk governance. Books like this one assist in unraveling the myriads of interlocking concepts.

Almost a decade beyond the first edition of this book, my recommendation that "narrowly focused, simplistic stand-alone credit analysis is no longer enough" is true in a more comprehensive way than before. "To stay competitive, financial institutions must look to more sources of information and adapt sophisticated tools: cash-flow computer modeling, time series/regression, simulation analytics, stochastic optimization, and interactive credit risk ratings." This second edition provides a broader and deeper view of many of these tools that might have been new in 2002 but are now increasingly well established within well-managed financial institutions. Some commentators have asserted that no one saw the current financial crisis coming. This statement is empirically false. Among the dozens of financial institutions with which I have firsthand knowledge of their risk systems, many identified cracks in the financial system well before it was apparent to regulators, the media, the majority of bank executives, and the general public. A select few acted on the output from these systems (note that the best systems coherently combine both quantitative and qualitative analyses; the reader should not assume that blindly implementing an algorithmic risk system eliminates the need for oversight and overrides from experienced risk professionals) and skated through the crisis with minor losses. Many failed banks actually had the information within their institutions to act in time. As in the concentration risk example just described, the underlying correlation across mortgage portfolios and corporate loan portfolios exposed to similar macroeconomic factors flashed red well before the crisis and should have been a signal to dramatically change the portfolios return/risk profile as early as 2005. Many banks failed to act because the right information did not make it to the right decision makers, and/or internal incentives encouraged ignoring recommended hedges or reduction in the size of profitable businesses. Blaming the models and systems redirects honest evaluation of organizations and incentives. The concepts, techniques, and tools described in this book provide both an introduction to neophytes and a guide to veterans to better appreciate risk models and system output to avoid the next crisis.

My concluding paragraph in the foreword to the last edition is almost more relevant today: "The market is an ocean of powerful waves that can harass or be harnessed. Institutions without this market focus will capsize or be rescued, as has been particularly apparent in the bank failures and bank consolidations during the past decade [this referred to 1990 to 2000 and has turned out be even more apropos during 2000 to 2010]. We will continue to see tidal waves of change in the financial industry. The ideas and strategies described in this book can be a compass for navigating these challenging currents." I may be straining the analogy a little too much, but today a compass may need to give way to a global positioning system (GPS). Much as a GPS combines underlying sophistication with an easy-to-understand interface, the challenges today require banks to move to systems with easy-to-understand output fed by underlying models that are necessarily complex. I recommend this book as a users' guide to grasp this complexity.

Dr. Jeffrey R. Bohn
CEO, Soliton Financial Analytics

Introduction

Since 2007, U.S. banks have suffered significant losses brought on by one of the deepest crises ever to hit financial services. As a result, risk and loan management, loan valuation methods, and governance structures are being shaken top to bottom. McKinsey and Company[1] suggests that after two years the fallout from the financial crisis continues to afflict most banks, particularly those with significant levels of illiquid and difficult to sell securities—so-called toxic assets—collateralized mortgage and debt obligations, and credit default swaps. With toxic assets on bank balance sheets, banks are finding it difficult to raise funds from traditional capital suppliers. In response, many institutions are starting to exit capital-intensive, structured deals in an effort to deleverage and, notably, move away from international operations to concentrate on domestic business.

The debt crisis began when loan incentives coupled with the acceleration in housing prices encouraged borrowers to assume mortgages they believed they could refinance at favorable terms. Once prices started to drop, refinancing became difficult. Defaults and foreclosures increased dramatically, as easy terms expired, home prices failed to go up, and interest rates reset higher. Foreclosures accelerated in late 2006, triggering a global financial crisis. Loan activities at banks froze, while the ability of corporations to obtain funds through commercial paper dropped sharply.

Alan Greenspan termed the debt crisis a *perfect storm*, a once in a hundred years event. The CEO of Lehman Brothers said the firm, too, was the victim of "the perfect storm," yet Lehman did not resist the lure of profits, leveraged balance sheets, and cheap credit. At Goldman Sachs, credit swaps created $4 billion profits. The financial modeling that helped produce results at these two investment banks was cutting edge, yet it appears that Lehman, AIG, and other profit takers amassed scant few algorithims to preserve (Value at Risk) capital protection against unexpected macroeconomic collapse.

On the government side, the debt crisis started with the notion that home ownership was a right. Fannie Mae was founded as part of Roosevelt's New Deal both to purchase and securitize mortgages so cash would be available to lend to home buyers. In 1970, a Republican Congress created Freddie Mac to purchase mortgages on the secondary market and pool and sell the mortgage-backed securities. Social and

---

[1] McKinsey & Company is a global management consulting firm that focuses on solving issues of concern to senior management.

political pressure expanded the pool of home owners, mostly to low- and middle-income families. The Equal Credit Opportunity Act enacted in 1974 prohibited institutional discrimination against minorities, while the Community Investment Act of 1977 addressed discrimination in lending and encouraged financial institutions to lend to all income brackets in their communities.

In the early 1980s, the passage of the Alternative Mortgage Transaction Parity Act preempted state laws by prohibiting adjustable rate mortgages, balloon payments, and negative amortization, while allowing lenders to make loans with terms that obscured the loan's cost. The Tax Reform Act enacted in 1986 prohibited taxpayers from deducting interest payments on consumer loans such as auto loans and credit cards but permitted them to deduct interest on mortgages, which sent homeowners by the millions to refinance mortgages and apply for home equity loans. As a result, household debt increased to 134% from 60% of disposable income. The elimination of Regulation Q was partially responsible for the Savings and Loan Crisis, resulting in $40 billion taxpayer loss. Despite the closing of hundreds of thrifts, lawmakers continued to deregulate the industry.

The Federal Housing Enterprises Financial Safety and Soundness Act of 1992 required Freddie Mac and Fannie Mae to devote a higher percentage of loans to support affordable housing. Banks were encouraged to do business across state lines, creating the megabanks we have today. Community banks that had traditionally kept loans in neighborhoods dwindled along with local loans. Behind the scenes, the banking lobby worked to repeal the Glass-Steagall Act of 1932 that had separated commercial and investment banking. Gramm-Leach-Bliley, known also as the Financial Services Modernization Act of 1999, repealed Glass-Steagall and allowed financial institutions to operate as commercial and investment banks and as insurance companies.

It comes, then, as no surprise that regulators agree that financial institutions must rethink credit policies and the risks they take. Credit analysis is and always has been an assessment of fundamentals: willingness and ability to repay, financial reporting, forensic cash flow, stochastic projections, sustainable growth, corporate governance, multivariate ratios, workout, capital adequacy, pricing, risk rating, portfolio optimization, and management of default risk. We recall Basel II ideals: (1) instill best practices and risk management procedures; (2) increase the quantification of risk, specifically operational risk; (3) instill effective ways to track, calculate, monitor, analyze, and report risks; (4) ensure data integrity and reporting; (5) effectively integrate multiple risk types; and (6) promote safety and soundness in the financial industry.[2]

As we sort through the various credit structures covered in the following chapters, we are mindful that a good many financial institutions ignored or misappropriated Basel II (capital) guidelines in their race for profits. Yet, Basel regulators are now preparing new capital requirements and other changes that will impose significant new burdens on banks. Industry-wide, the chicken has come home to roost.

---

[2] "Principles for the Management of Credit Risk," July 1999, consultative paper issued by the Basel Committee on Banking Supervision, Bank for International Settlements.

Overview of Chapters

To address the essential aspects of credit engineering, the book is arranged in two distinct parts, each providing a specific focus: Part I, New Approaches to Fundamental Analysis, and Part II, Credit Administration.

Part I New Approaches to Fundamental Analysis

- Chapter 1 includes a discussion of the PRISM credit systematizing model that helps bankers explore fundamental credit concepts and arrive at prudent credit decisions.
- Chapter 2 reviews international financial reporting standards, the auditor's role, revenue realization, off-balance sheet financial reporting,
- Chapter 3 deals with multivariate ratio analysis; how ratios provide tools to measure size, trend, and quality of financial statements; the extent and nature of liabilities; and detecting shenanigans.
- Chapter 4 sheds light on the challenging business of seasonal lending—modus operandi, risks, signals, defensive measures, temporary versus structural problems, break-even analysis, cash budgets, and overdraft facilities.
- Chapter 5 considers basic axioms of asset-based lending, regulatory audit guidelines, loans secured with accounts receivables, formula-based loans (receivables and inventories), borrowing-based facilities, and asset-based financing models, including acceptance versus rejection cost.
- Chapter 6 introduces forensic cash flow analysis, decomposing and restructuring techniques, and retracing the firm's operating, financing, and investing activities.
- Chapter 7 goes into the nuts and bolts of quantitative risk analysis as it pertains to making business decisions in a bank. As part of credit risk analysis and credit engineering, the general underlying principles of risk analysis remains the same as in general business risk. For instance, credit risk analysis may require applying Monte Carlo simulation for forecasting and backtesting the accuracy of a credit scoring model, testing scenarios and sensitivities on a credit portfolio, integrating and accounting for correlations in a basket of credit issues and vehicles, and so forth. Therefore, this chapter provides the fundamentals of quantitative risk analysis, which is required knowledge and a prerequisite for more advanced applications in banking and credit risk.
- Chapter 8 deals with comprehensive forecast analysis. We explore different methods of predicting (the borrower's) financial condition and identifying future funding needs. Most modern forecasting tools in the financial literature are brought under study: Monte Carlo simulations that work with a range of results and confidence levels; probability distributions; constricting uniform, normal, lognormal, triangular, binomial, and geometric distributions; comparing distributions; rank correlation; and determining the expected default frequency. We become familiar with data diagnostics, econometrics, correlations, and multiple regression modeling; exponential J-growth curves; forecasting manual computations; linear interpolation; logistic S-growth curves; Markov chains; multiple regression; nonlinear extrapolation; stochastic processes and yield curves; time-series analysis; time-series ARIMA; Greeks; tornado and sensitivity charts (linear and nonlinear); and Risk Simulator demos and videos.
- Chapter 9, which deals with sustainable growth, brings our analysis to a special branch of financial leverage: the sustainable growth model and the due diligence process that, if successful, will put a restriction on exposures to rapid growth, highly leveraged firms.

- Chapter 10 concentrates on specialized lending exposures employing the Bank for International Settlements supervisory rating grades for project, object, and commodity finance, and high-volatility commercial real estate exposures. Computerized rating models for each class of specialized exposures generate loss given default and loan loss provisions.
- Chapter 11 moves our discussion to the recognition, diagnosis, and response to troubled loans, first by exploring the best methodology to recognize and diagnose troubled loans, including design of financial distress models, deciding when troublesome loans are candidates for classification, major sources and causes of problem credits, procedures on auditing loan documents, and debtor-in-possession financing, and short- and long-term restructuring objectives. Computer models include accounts receivable audit worksheets, borrowing-based facilities, acceptance versus rejection cost receivable model, inventory audit worksheet, break-even inventory model, and problem loan cash budgets.
- Chapter 12 introduces a cutting edge financial technology: real options. We learn how real options become the tool of choice for bankers exploring innovative, opportunity-producing deals. Real options are similar to financial options in that firms with discretionary investment opportunities have the right—but are under no obligation—to acquire expected cash flows by making an investment on or before the date that the (investment) opportunity ceases to exist.

In addition, we explore why traditional analytical methods such as net present value, internal rate of return, and economic profit measures have been responsible for systematic investment undervaluation. The Real Options Super Lattice Software modules explored in the chapter are highly powerful and customizable binomial and multinomial lattice solvers and can be used to solve many types of options. For bankers, the power of this software is its ability to create and financially engineer customized options.

Part II Credit Administration

- Chapter 13 deals with capital adequacy. We review Basel II accords, risk weights, tier capital, capital ratios, and models designed to determine capital allocation value-at-risk.
- Chapter 14 concentrates on applied analytical techniques for modeling, default probability, loss given default, economic capital, value-at-risk, hurdle rates, and rates of return.
- Chapter 15 expands loan portfolio optimization, employing methodologies that include the use of continuous versus discrete integer optimization, as well as static versus dynamic and stochastic optimizations. Several optimization models are examined to illustrate how the optimization process works. The first is the application of continuous optimization under uncertainty for a simple project selection model, where the idea is to allocate 100% of an individual's investment among several different asset classes (e.g., different types of mutual funds or investment styles: growth, value, aggressive growth, income, global, index, contrarian, momentum, and so forth).

Next we discuss discrete integer optimization, where the idea is to look at several competing project choices, each with a different return, risk, and cost profile. The job of the banker here is to find the best combination of projects that will satisfy the firm's budget constraints while maximizing the portfolio's total value. The chapter continues with running a portfolio investment efficient frontier by applying some of the advanced settings in Risk Simulator, followed by a stochastic optimization model, where simulation is iteratively combined with optimization methods. Next, the efficient frontier is discussed, together with a case on applying the optimal pricing structure on various goods and services by examining the price elasticity of demand.

- Chapter 16 employs option theory to extract credit information embedded in equity markets. Bankers use option pricing models to determine dynamically expected default frequencies and migration matrices affecting loan values and appropriate facility yields: binary digital instruments, inverse floater bond lattice maker, options adjusted spreads on debt, and options on debt.
- Chapter 17 continues coverage of options by extending analysis to include exotic options and credit derivatives: American call option on foreign exchange, barrier, binary digital options, commodity options, currency (foreign exchange) options, perpetual options, inverse floater bond, and credit derivatives.
- Chapter 18 introduces applications of credit and debt valuation and analysis concentrating on computations of credit spread or the risk premium that should be charged beyond a standard interest rate, depending on the obligor's probability of default; valuing the effects of credit spreads on bond and debt prices; simulating and computing credit spreads of a firm; creating a credit shortfall risk and risk ratings table; running a cost-benefit analysis on new credit issues; determining the market value of risky debt; generating a debt amortization table; and valuing the price and yield on risky debt where the underlying interest rates are mean-reverting and stochastic, using the Merton and Vasicek models.
- Chapter 19 covers credit administration policies/procedures by exploring integrated global information/exposure systems A global exposure system is a mandatory tool for credit administration, providing bankers with detailed databases used to track portfolio decay and other risk exposure monitoring activities.
- Chapter 20 provides the necessary building blocks enabling us to structure stochastic risk-adjusted return on capital (RAROC) and return on asset (ROA) pricing models. RAROC is an important performance tool that administrators employ to measure return on economic capital. RAROC considers three types of risk: business, credit, and operational risk. Bankers taking a proactive role managing their portfolios regard RAROC as a major benchmark in pricing and credit decisions.

About The Authors

Professor Morton Glantz is an internationally renowned educator, author, and banker. He serves as a financial consultant, educator, and adviser to a broad spectrum of professionals, including corporate financial executives, government ministers, privatization managers, investment and commercial bankers, public accounting firms, members of merger and acquisition teams, strategic planning executives, management consultants, attorneys, and representatives of foreign governments and international banks. Professor Morton Glantz is a principal of Real Consulting and Real Options Valuation, firms specializing in risk consulting, training, certification, and advanced analytical software in the areas of risk quantification, analysis, and management solutions.

As a senior officer of JP Morgan Chase, Professor Glantz built a progressive career path specializing in credit analysis and credit risk management, risk grading systems, valuation models, and professional training. He was instrumental in the reorganization and development of the credit analysis module of the Bank's Management Training Program—Finance, which at the time was recognized as one of the foremost training programs in the banking industry.

A partial list of client companies Professor Glantz has worked with includes Institutional Investor, The US Government Federal Financial Institutions Examination Council, Development Bank of Southern Africa, CUCORP, Canada, Access Bank, Nigeria, The Bank of China, GE Capital, Cyprus Development Bank, Oracle, Misr Iran Development Bank (Cairo), Bank of the Bahamas, Gulf Bank (Kuwait), United Arab Bank, Abu Dhabi, Institute for International Research, (Dubai), Inter-American Investment Corporation, Ernst & Young, UAL Merchant Bank (Johannesburg), Euromoney, ICICI Bank (India), Council for Trade and Economic Cooperation (Russia), BHF Bank, and IBM Credit Corporation.

Professor Glantz is on the finance faculty of the Fordham Graduate School of Business. He has appeared in the Harvard University International Directory of Business and Management Scholars and Research, and has earned Fordham University Deans Award for Faculty Excellence on three occasions. He is a Board Member of the International Standards Board, International Institute of Professional Education and Research (IIPER). The IIPER is a global institute with partners and offices around the world, including the United States, Switzerland, Hong Kong, Mexico, Portugal, Singapore, Nigeria, and Malaysia.

Professor Glantz is widely published in financial journals and has authored seven books published internationally, including *The Bankers Handbook: Implementing*

Basel II; Credit Derivatives: Techniques to Manage Credit Risk for Financial Professionals, (with Erik Banks and Paul Siegel), McGraw-Hill, 2006; *Optimal Trading Strategies*, AMACOM, 2003 (co-author: Dr. Robert Kissell); *Managing Bank Risk: An Introduction to Broad-Base Credit Engineering*, Academic Press/Elsevier, 2002 (RISKBOOK.COM Award: Best Finance Books of 2003); *Scientific Financial Management*, AMACOM 2000; and *Loan Risk Management*, McGraw-Hill (1995).

Prof. Dr. Johnathan C. Mun is the founder, Chairman and CEO of Real Options Valuation, Inc. (ROV), a consulting, training, and software development firm specializing in strategic real options, financial valuation, Monte Carlo simulation, stochastic forecasting, optimization, and risk analysis located in northern Silicon Valley, California. ROV currently has partners in California, New York, Chicago, Mexico, Chile, Colombia, Switzerland, Australia, Korea, Japan, and a local subsidiary in Shanghai, China. He is also the Chairman of the International Institute of Professional Education and Research (IIPER), an accredited global organization providing the Certified in Risk Management (CRM) designation among others, staffed by professors from named universities from around the world. He is also the creator of the following 12 advanced analytical software applications: Risk Simulator, Real Options Super Lattice Solver, Modeling Toolkit, Employee Stock Options Valuation, ROV Modeler, ROV Optimizer, ROV Compiler, ROV Risk Extractor and Evaluator, ROV Dashboard, ROV BizStats, ROV Quantitative Data Miner as well as the risk analysis Training DVD and he holds public seminars on risk analysis and Certified in Risk Management (CRM) programs. He has authored 12 books including Modeling Risk: Applying Monte Carlo Simulation, Real Options, Optimization, and Forecasting, First and Second Editions (Wiley 2010, and Wiley 2006), Real Options Analysis: Tools and Techniques, First and Second Editions (Wiley 2003, and Wiley 2005), Basel II Handbook on Credit and Market Risk (Elsevier 2008), Credit Engineering (Elsevier 2011), Advanced Analytical Models: 800 Applications from Basel II to Wall Street and Beyond (Wiley 2008), Real Options Analysis Course: Business Cases (Wiley 2003), Applied Risk Analysis: Moving Beyond Uncertainty (Wiley 2003), Valuing Employee Stock Options (Wiley 2004), and others. His books and software are being used at top universities around the world (including the Bern Institute in Germany, Chung-Ang University in South Korea, Georgetown University, ITESM in Mexico, Massachusetts Institute of Technology, Harvard, U.S. Naval Postgraduate School, New York University, Stockholm University in Sweden, University of the Andes in Chile, University of Chile, University of Pennsylvania Wharton School, University of York in the United Kingdom, and Edinburgh University in Scotland, among others).

Dr. Mun is also currently a finance and economics professor and has taught courses in financial management, investments, real options, economics, and statistics at the undergraduate and the graduate M.B.A. levels. He is teaching and has taught at universities all over the world, from the U.S. Naval Postgraduate School (Monterey, California) and University of Applied Sciences (Switzerland and Germany) as full professor, to Golden Gate University (California) and St. Mary's College (California), and has chaired many graduate research thesis committees. He also teaches risk analysis, real options analysis, and risk analysis for managers' public courses where participants can obtain the Certified in Risk Management (CRM) designation upon completion of the week-long program. He also holds the position of the EU President of the American Academy of Financial Management and sits on the Global Board of Standards at the AAFM. He was formerly the Vice President of Analytics at Decisioneering, Inc. where he headed up the development of options and financial analytics software products, analytical consulting, training, and technical support, and where he was the creator of the Real Options Analysis Toolkit software, the older predecessor of the Real Options Super Lattice software. Prior to joining Decisioneering, he was a Consulting Manager and Financial Economist in the Valuation Services and Global Financial Services practice of KPMG Consulting and a Manager with the Economic Consulting Services practice at KPMG LLP. He has extensive experience in econometric modeling, financial analysis, real options, economic analysis, and statistics. During his tenure at Real Options Valuation, Inc., Decisioneering, and at KPMG Consulting, he had taught and consulted on a variety of real options, risk analysis, financial forecasting, project management, and financial valuation issues for over 100 multinational firms (former and current clients include 3M, Airbus, Boeing, BP, Chevron Texaco, Financial Accounting Standards Board, Fujitsu, GE, Microsoft, Motorola, Pfizer, State of California, Timken, U.S. Department of Defense, U.S. Navy, Veritas, and many others). His experience prior to joining KPMG included being Department Head of financial planning and analysis at Viking Inc. of FedEx, performing financial forecasting, economic analysis, and market research. Prior to that, he did financial planning and freelance financial consulting work.

Dr. Mun received his Ph.D. in Finance and Economics from Lehigh University, where his research and academic interests were in the areas of Investment Finance, Econometric Modeling, Financial Options, Corporate Finance, and Microeconomic Theory. He also has an M.B.A. in business administration, an M.S. in management science, and a B.S. in Biology and Physics. He is Certified in Financial Risk Management (FRM), Certified in Financial Consulting (CFC), and is Certified in Risk Management (CRM). He is a member of the American Mensa, Phi Beta Kappa Honor Society, and Golden Key Honor Society as well as several other professional organizations, including the Eastern and Southern Finance Associations, American Economic Association, and Global Association of Risk Professionals. Finally, he has written many academic articles published in the Journal of the Advances in Quantitative Accounting and Finance, the Global Finance Journal, the International Financial Review, the Journal of Financial Analysis, the Journal of Applied Financial Economics, the Journal of International Financial Markets, Institutions and Money, the Financial Engineering News, and the Journal of the Society of Petroleum Engineers. Finally, he has published dozens of internal articles and white papers with the U.S. Department of Defense on strategy, risk and analytics (these confidential articles are not available for public circulation).

Part One

New Approaches to Fundamental Analysis

1 Introduction to Loan Decision Making: The PRISM Model

Unlike Mark Twain's cat that once sat on a hot stove lid and would never again sit even on a warm one, bankers should always be careful to get from an experience just the wisdom that is in it—no more, no less. Banks need a sense of caution in a liberal credit environment, but they also need the courage and wisdom to take reasonable risks when credit is tight. Financial institutions succeed as long as the risks they assume are prudent and within defined parameters of portfolio objectives. Policies and procedures should be in place that ensure that exposures are properly identified, monitored, and controlled, and that safeguards against nonperformance or default match the risk levels to which banks commit.

By and large, bank failures are caused by lax credit standards, ineffectual portfolio risk policies, and risks taken in excess of capital constraints. In addition, blame is due to lenders who neglect technological advances in the field. While recent bank failures owe much to the collapse of the housing market, sloppy lending practices contributed to it at least in part—that is, in spite of regulators' dire warnings of the consequences slack underwriting standards would have in the wake of sharp industry/economic meltdowns.

Credit Engineering for Bankers. DOI: 10.1016/B978-0-12-378585-5.10001-6

As it turned out, liberal credit came on the heels of a robust economy, intense competition to turn deals, pursuit of the bottom line, and the misguided notion that good things—capital adequacy in particular—last forever. Credit meltdown can be something of a paradox, given that regulators have always championed sound, diversified credit portfolios and formal credit evaluation and approval processes—procedures whereby approvals are made in accordance with written guidelines and granted by appropriate levels of management. *There also should be a clear audit trail confirming that the approval process was complied with, identifying line lenders and/or committee(s) influencing (lending) decisions or actually making the credit decision.*[1]

It turned out that the banks that experienced such failures often lacked adequate credit review processes. Solid, tight credit reviews not only help detect poorly underwritten credits, but they largely prevent weak proposals from being approved since credit officers are likely to be more diligent if they know their work will be subject to review. *An effective evaluation process establishes minimum requirements for the information on which the analysis is to be based. There should be policies in place regarding the information and documentation needed to approve new credits, renew existing credits, and/or change the terms and conditions of previously approved credits. The information received will be the basis for any internal evaluation or rating assigned to the credit, and its accuracy and adequacy is critical to management making appropriate judgments about the acceptability of the credit.*[2]

The review process starts with a comprehensive appraisal of the obligor's creditworthiness, calling for a thorough understanding of the strength and quality of an obligor's cash flows and capital structure. Credit analysis is multifaceted. It blends traditional core assessment with quantitative processes: incorporating historical-based models, forward-looking models (the theme of this book), and fundamental analysis. Both historical and forward-looking analytics are integral to gaining an understanding of risks but used in isolation, they are weak tools. To improve the credit analysis process and to understand an obligor's business, we blend historical and projection analyses with qualitative factors brought to the fore by a well-organized and insightful credit analysis covering sustainability and quality of cash flows, debt capacity, asset quality, valuation growth drivers, management, and industry. Management issues such as strategic direction and execution, optimal capital structure, accounting methodologies, aptitude for innovation, labor relations, management changes, and experience go a long way in defining credit quality.

The credit review process lies at the core of PRISM, an acronym for *perspective, repayment, intention, safeguards,* and *management.* In this chapter, we begin our examination of the PRISM components with *management,* which centers on the big picture: what the borrower is all about, including history and prospects. Next we cover *intention,* or loan purpose, which serves as the basis for *repayment.* Repayment focuses on internal and external sources of cash. Internal operations and asset sales produce internal cash, whereas new debt and/or equity injections provide external

---

[1] Paraphrased from "Principles for the Management of Credit Risk," consultative paper issued by the Basel Committee on Banking Supervision, Bank for International Settlements, Basel, July 1999.
[2] Ibid.

cash sources. We learn how conversion of balance sheet temporary assets provides the primary payment source of short-term loans, while long-term loans are paid from internally generated cash flow. *Safeguards,* likewise, have internal and external sources: Internal safeguards originate from the quality and soundness of financial statements, while collateral guarantees and loan covenants provide external safeguards. We consider *perspective,* which pulls together the deal's risks and rewards, and the operating and financing strategies that are broad enough to have a positive impact on shareholder value while enabling the borrower to repay loans. Finally, bankers render a decision and price the deal.

Management

Business Operations

Certain business attributes provide bankers with an image of their borrowers. These qualities result from several factors: the number of years a firm has been in business, reputation and performance record, and, of course, willingness and ability to repay debt. Longevity means staying power and is very important to customers, vendors, competitive markets, and financing sources. Long business life also imparts reputation and, for some, that is the most important attribute of all. In this context, past performance is a good indicator of future success. We begin the information flow with gathering company and industry information.

PRISM: MANAGEMENT
1. Business Operations
2. Management
3. Bank Relationship
4. Financial Reporting

Company Information

- History of the business, including any predecessor companies, changes in capital structure, present capitalization, and any insolvency proceedings.
- Description of products, markets, principal customers, subsidiaries, and lines of business.
- Recent product changes and technological innovation.
- Customer growth, energy availability, and possible ecological problems.
- List of the company's principal suppliers, together with approximate annual amounts purchased, noting delinquencies in settlement of suppliers' accounts.
- Market segmentation by customer type, geographic location, product, distribution channels, pricing policy, and degree of integration.
- Strategic goals and track record meeting or missing goals.
- Number and types of customers broken down by percentage of sales/profit contribution. Note the extent the borrower is overdependent on one or a few customers.
- Government contracts.
- Capital equipment requirements and commitments.

Industry Information

- Industry composition and, in particular, recent changes in that composition.
- Image of the company and its products and services compared to industry leaders.
- Number of firms included in the industry and whether that number has been declining or increasing.
- Borrower's market share and recent trends.
- Recent industry merger, acquisition, and divestiture activities, along with prices paid for these transactions.
- Recent foreign entrants.
- Suppliers' versus buyers' power.
- Bases of competition.
- Industry's rate of business failure.
- Industry's average bond rating.
- Degree of operating leverage inherent in the industry.
- Industry reliance on exports and degree of vulnerability.
- Names of the bank industry specialists whom you should contact for help in developing projections and other industry analysis.
- Trade organizations, consultants, economists, and security analysts who can help you with forecasts.
- Adverse conditions reported by financial, investment, or industry analysts.
- Extent that litigation might affect production of or demand for the industry's products (case in point, Firestone Tires).
- The effects of government regulations and environmental issues on the industry.
- If publicly traded, the exchanges on which the stock is traded, the dealer-making markets for over-the-counter stock, institutional holdings, trading volume, and total market capitalization.

For additional information, the banker typically examines details of company operations. Each type of business has its own idiosyncrasies that set it apart from other industries. How economically sensitive is the business to new products, competitors, interest rates, and disposable income? How has the borrower fared in good markets as well as bad when benchmarked against the rest of the industry? Is the company seasonal?

Management Basics

Banks need to understand to whom they are granting credit. Therefore, prior to entering into any new credit relationship, a bank must become familiar with the borrower or counterparty and be confident that it is dealing with an individual or organization of sound repute and creditworthiness. In particular, strict policies must be in place to avoid association with individuals involved in fraudulent activities and other crimes. This can be achieved through a number of ways, including asking for references from known parties, accessing credit registries, becoming familiar with the individuals responsible for managing a company, and checking their personal references and financial condition. However, a bank should not grant credit simply because the borrower or counterparty is familiar to the bank or is perceived to be highly reputable.[3]

---

[3] Ibid.

Who are the key players and what contributions are they making? It's a good idea to prepare a brief biographical summary for each senior manager so you are better able to evaluate overall management philosophy. The human factor in decision making is hugely significant, and because it is, a single error in judgment can mean serious and unpredictable problems.

Integrity deals with communication as well. Since the majority of information comes from management, lenders must have confidence in *that* information. The amount and quality of information you obtain from management will depend on the deal's requirements and, of course, information that management is willing to supply. Keep this simple rule in mind: The lower the credit grade, the more information management is asked to supply. Think about the following:

- List of officers and directors, along with affiliations, ages, and number of years in office.
- Names, addresses, and contacts of the company's professional advisers, including attorneys, auditors, principal bankers at other banks, and investment bankers.
- Number of people employed and major areas of activity.
- Strategies management is using to increase market share and profitability.
- The intelligence demonstrated in taking advantage of changes in the marketplace and environment.
- Overview of management's problem-solving and decision-making abilities, and whether the right decisions are made at the appropriate level.
- Management's basic philosophy—for example, is management entrepreneurial?
- The work environment.
- How management and subordinates work as an effective team. Management can be smoothly intergraded or crisis prone.
- Ratio of officer salaries to net revenues (Robert Morris Statement Studies). Is compensation reasonable when compared to results?
- Determine if executives prevent problems from arising or use valuable time to work out the same problems over and over.
- The reputation of present owners, directors, management, and professional advisers gathered from industry journals, periodicals, and a good Internet browsing.
- Adequacy of quantitative and statistical information, including strategic and tactical plans, effective policies and procedures, adequate management information systems, budgetary control and responsibility accounting, standards of performance and control, and management and manpower development.
- Obtain an organization chart and business plans, both short-term and long-range.
- Evaluate if business objectives and strategies are well thought out and represent genuine management tools or if they have been presented for show.

Bank Relationship

If the relationship is an existing one, how solid has it been? Obviously, a loyal customer with a strong history receives better treatment than someone who walks through the door for the first time.

Financial Reporting

Naturally, banks evaluate the accounting firms that are preparing the financial statements. Reputation is important. Are the financials liberal or conservative? Do they provide an accurate picture of the borrower's condition? Here are a few good pointers:

- Obtain audited financial statements, including registration statements (if they exist) and comparative financial results by major division.
- Procure recent unaudited quarterly statements, including sales backlog information and a description of accounting practices.
- If you can obtain them, secure tax returns for the last five years, IRS reports, and schedules of unused loss and investment credit carryforwards.
- Ask the client to submit projected operating and financial statements.
- Obtain any SEC filings and a shareholder list, if available.
- Form an opinion about the overall credibility and reliability of financial reporting. Check if an independent accounting firm audited the books, and investigate the accountant's reputation.
- Check bank records. Auditors who submitted falsified reports on other deals will end up in the database.
- Review the adequacy and sophistication of the client's internal auditing systems.
- Find out what the auditor's major recent findings were and the company's disposition of those findings. Determine to whom the internal auditing department reports.
- Assess the adequacy of internal accounting controls along with the company's attitude toward strong controls, making sure of the extent earnings were managed.
- Assess the strength of the financial management and controllership function.
- Determine how often internal reports are issued, how soon after the end of the period the reports are available and if they are used, and whether the internal reporting timetable and content are consistent with the auditor's monthly closing requirements.
- Find out whether subsidiaries have autonomous accounting departments that may not be functioning uniformly and, if so, how overall control is exercised.
- Check to see if long-range plans reflect competitive reactions and include alternative strategies.
- Check if objectives are described so achievement can be monitored.

Intention (Purpose)

"Banks must operate under sound, well-defined credit-granting criteria. These criteria should include a thorough understanding of the borrower or counterparty, as well as the purpose and structure of the credit, and its source of repayment."[4] First, pin down what the loan's real intention is—whether it is real as opposed to fanciful. "Fanciful" is what troubled clients offer as the reason they would like the bank to believe, and such intentions may be flat-out fabrications. Second, be aware that behind intention are three reasons why firms borrow. The first deals with asset purchases—short term, to support seasonality, and long term, to support growth. Loans to acquire seasonal assets are repaid once inventory is worked down and

[4] Ibid.

receivables collected. Long-term loans support fixed-asset purchases along with nonseasonal current assets.

The second reason is that firms borrow to replace other creditors. For example, management usually anticipates suppliers' 2/10 net 30-day terms to take advantage of trade discounts. On the one hand, short-term loans approved to replace creditors may be symptomatic of problems if (agency) reports, such as Dun and Bradstreet, reveal tardiness. Late payments to suppliers often point to slow-moving inventory or receivable problems. On the other hand, loan requests to replace creditors (recycling debt) may, perhaps, simply mean that another financial institution is offering better rates or service.

Finally, the third reason is that firms borrow to replace equity—stock buybacks (e.g., buying up a partner's share in the business, acquisitions, leveraged buyouts, employ stock option plans, and so on. Equity replaced with debt can easily dislodge the debt-to-equity ratio and cash flow coverage, putting the remaining equity at risk. One reason lenders prepare *pro forma* (what if) financial statements is to ensure that the equity is not impaired.

Repayment

Firms can raise cash primarily in two ways: internally, through business activities, and externally, via new monies from debt and equity sources. Asset liquidations bring in cash as well, but normally as a secondhand source.

Internal Repayment Sources: Short-Term Loans

The conversion/contraction process influences short-term *internal* repayment sources. Say a company borrows to support its seasonal manufacturing operations. Assets and liabilities increase spontaneously. The seasonal high point begins as inventory is sold, creating receivables. When receivables convert to cash, the balance sheet contracts and the company retires its debt. As a result, the seasonal conversion process becomes the primary source of repayment.

Short-Term Loans Facilities

Own paper borrowing: This implies that lenders evaluate each request on its own merit and includes short-term, unsecured borrowings not falling under a line of credit. *Lines of credit:* Unlike own paper borrowings, credit lines are usually established with a bank letter stating the approved advances and maximum amount allowed. The amount borrowed may be repaid and reborrowed up to the line limit. While banks are not legally obligated to honor loan requests against lines of credit, arbitrarily canceling lines is the fastest way to alienate customers and lose business. Hence, lines are generally limited to high-quality customers with little chance of failing.

REPAYMENT

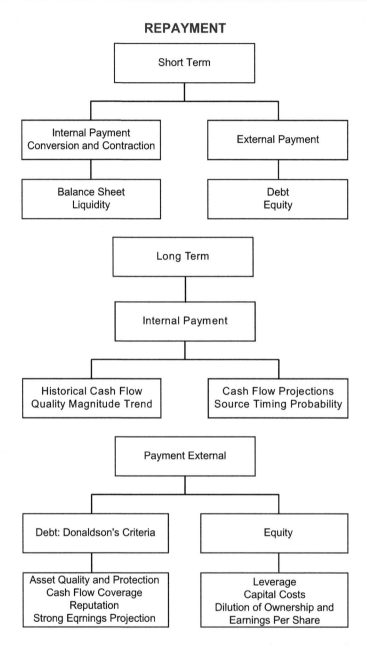

Seasonal loans provide for the short-term working capital needs of eligible small businesses by financing the seasonal increases in the trading assets (receivables and inventory), the liquidation of which repays the loan at the end of each season. A seasonal loan is taken out only for seasonal needs and is repaid when inventory and receivables are partially converted into cash at the end of the seasonal upsurge. It is, then, a self-liquidating loan, with its repayment dependent on the conversion of other current assets into cash.

For many small and medium-size firms, the true essence of seasonal lending emerges as an infusion of working capital to support operating activities stimulated by demand. Companies classified as seasonal in nature are traditionally undercapitalized, requiring short-term financing to support temporary current assets. In a broader sense, however, any short-term loan supporting temporary levels of accounts receivable or inventory is referred to as a seasonal loan if it is satisfied through the conversion of these assets.

Commercial banks grant short-term loans with the understanding that loans are retired at the low point of the season or the end of the cash conversion cycle. During the fiscal year, a seasonal company's balance sheet goes through expansion and contraction. At the high point, or most active part of the period, debt and assets increase to support seasonal activity, thus expanding the balance sheet. During this phase, sales emulate the manufacturing cycle; the result of which is the conversion of inventory into accounts receivables. At the low point, or least active part of the period, the manufacturing cycle has ebbed, leaving the firm with the responsibility to "clean up" outstanding short-term debt. This is accomplished through the conversion of accounts receivables to cash or deposits. Once all short-term debt has been satisfied, the firm's balance sheet will contract back to its normal level. Any excess cash on hand is usually designated for temporary current asset investments in the next season.

External Repayment Sources: Short-Term Loans

If the balance sheet fails to fully convert, a company may seek external sources to cover exposures in the form of new outside debt or equity injections. Thus bankers evaluate a borrower's debt capacity. The key attributes to acquiring new monies are the borrower's reputation, existing capital structure, asset quality, profit-generating abilities, and economic value.

Intermediate-Term Loans

Unlike confirmed lines of credit, revolving commitments/credits (R/Cs) and term loans (T/Ls) involve a *legal commitment* on the part of the issuing bank. The loans (commitments) are made under a written loan agreement that sets down the terms and conditions of advances. Commitment fees are computed on the average daily unused portion of line, generally ¼% to ½%. Commitments require a loan agreement containing restrictive covenants.

R/Cs authorize discretionary borrowing up to a specific amount for periods of at least one year. R/Cs typically convert into term loans at the end of a specific period, as specified in the agreement. R/Cs are useful financing vehicles for new projects not expecting to produce immediate cash flows. The expiration of R/Cs (and conversion to a T/L) can be timed to coincide with the project's expected cash flow, matching cash inflows and outflows.

T/Ls are nonrevolving commitments with maturities beyond one year. These loans generally contain periodic (annual, semiannual, or quarterly) amortization provisions. T/Ls involve greater risk than do short-term advances, because of the length of time the credit is outstanding. Because of the greater risk factor, T/Ls are sometimes secured loan agreements on such credits and normally contain restrictive covenants during the life of the loan. These loans have assumed increasing importance in recent years. T/Ls generally finance capital expenditures needed by the firm to maintain low production costs and improve its competitive superiority. T/Ls also finance new ventures and acquisitions, such as new product procurement or vertical/horizontal mergers.

Internal Repayment Sources: Long-Term Loans

The main question to be answered is: Does the company have the cash flow to support fixed asset investment(s)? Internal repayment of long-term loans is directly related to historical and projected cash flow quality, magnitude, and trend. Historical cash flow analysis provides a track record of the company's past performance.

The quality of historical cash flow is analyzed by looking at the firm's gross operating cash flow (net income plus noncash charges less noncash credits). If the gross operating cash flows are comprised of primarily noncash items, such as depreciation, deferred taxes, or asset write-downs, with a relatively small amount of cash being generated on the income statement, the quality of the operating cash flow may not be sufficient to repay credit. As stated earlier, profits and the sale of assets play a major role in retiring debt requirements, so it is imperative that the bank analysts identify what accounts for the firm's cash flow.

The magnitude of historical cash flow relative to growth plans will help to identify the external financing requirements facing the firm. The smaller the cash flow, the greater the debt load required to support long-term growth plans. If, for example, the income statement is not producing enough cash flow to service its loans year after year, the firm is in jeopardy of defaulting on its loans and going bankrupt. Astute loan officers should question why funds are being funneled into a company in the first place if it can't buy assets to produce a decent level of profits to pay back debt.

Historical cash flow trends enable the creditor to determine if the firm's cash flows support the decision to go for growth. This is decided by evaluating the company's viability. A healthy company is able to fund a good part its expansion internally. On the other hand, a company suffering from declining cash flows requires the helping hand of debt to expand.

Projections are not intended to predict the future perfectly but to see how the borrower will perform under a variety of situations. It is up to the lender to ascribe an expected probability to each set of projections and to determine a most likely scenario on which to evaluate the borrower's *repayment* ability. Projections quantify expectations but can never replace a banker's judgment and experience; the mental ability to perceive and distinguish relationships is naturally a PRISM hallmark.

External Repayment Sources: Long-Term Loans

Let's look at *external* repayment of long-term (e.g., cash flow) loans. Repayment often depends on whether funding sources are readily available. Consider these questions: What will be the company's comfort level of debt? To what degree will operating cash flow protect debt service? Will the borrower continue to generate good asset quality to attract debt? Will the company sustain its overall reputation?

Some credit wells run dry during downturns. If the bank's approval depends solely on an external takeout, beware. Consider what Federal Reserve examiners have to say:[5]

> *Overreliance on continued ready access to financial markets on favorable terms can come in many ways, including:*

1. Explicit reliance on future public market debt or equity offerings, or on other sources of refinancing, as the ultimate source of principal repayment, which presumes that market liquidity and appetite for such instruments will be favorable at the time that the facility is to be repaid;

2. Ambiguous or poorly supported analysis of the sources of repayment of the loan's principal, together with implicit reliance for repayment on some realization of the implied market valuation of the borrower (e.g., through refinancing, asset sales, or some form of equity infusion), which also assumes that markets will be receptive to such transactions at the time that the facility is to be repaid;

3. Measuring a borrower's leverage and cash coverage ratios based solely on the market capitalization of the firm without regard to "book" equity, and thereby implicitly assuming that currently unrealized appreciation in the value of the firm can be readily realized if needed; or

4. More generally, extending bank loans with a risk profile that more closely resembles that of an equity investment and under circumstances that leave additional bank credit or default as the borrower's only resort should favorable expectations not be met.

Safeguards

What *safeguards* or protection does the bank have against default? If a bank is to extend credit to a firm, the level of risk influences the degree of protection lenders generally require. Safeguards can be internal, external, or a combination of both. Internal safeguards refer to financial analysis, while collateral, personal guarantees, and loan covenants provide external protection. Although external safeguards are popular, they usually are not considered before internal protection. Internal protection relates to the borrower's cash power depending on whether the *intention* of the loan is short term or long term.

Recall that the primary source of internal repayment of short-term loans is balance sheet liquidity, the result of the season's cash conversion cycle. Internal safeguards of

---

[5] From Federal Reserve Bank memo.

SAFEGUARDS

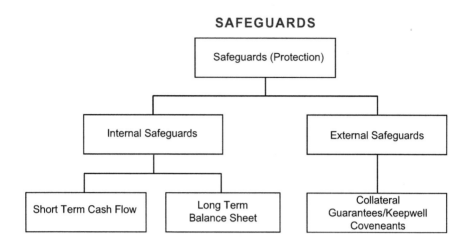

seasonal loans relate to the quality magnitude and trend of cash flows/income statements. The bank just wants to make sure that a seasonal *temporary* problem does not become a *structural* cash flow problem in the years ahead. External safeguards can come from a variety of sources: collateral, guarantees, covenants, and syndications and participations.

Collateral

Collateral is defined as property pledged as security for the satisfaction of a debt or other obligation. Credit grades assigned to secured loans depend on, among other things, the degree of coverage, the economic life cycle of the collateral versus the term of the loan, possible constraints of liquidating the collateral, and the bank's ability to skillfully and economically monitor and liquidate collateral. What is its value compared to credit exposure? What is its liquidity, or how quickly may its value be realized and with what certainty? What presumed legal right does the borrower have to the collateral?

Guarantees

A guaranty is a written contract, agreement, or undertaking involving three parties. The first party, the *guarantor*, agrees to see that the performance of the second party, the *guarantee*, is fulfilled according to the terms of the contract, agreement, or undertaking. The third party is the *creditor*, or the party to benefit from the performance.

Covenants

Covenants of a loan agreement lay the framework for the financial plan jointly agreed on by the borrower and the lender. The number and detail of the covenants will largely depend on the financial strength of the enterprise, management's aptitude, and the length of the proposed loan.

Perspective

What is the deal's perspective or "conclusion(s)"? The perspective section considers the following:

1. Risk/reward analysis.
2. Operating and financing strategies that the banker believes might improve performance and go a long way toward adding to shareholder value and, from the banker's perspective, preserve credit quality.
3. Finally, we render a decision and recommend pricing.

2 International Financial Reporting Standards

Chapter Outline

Credit Engineering for Bankers. DOI: 10.1016/B978-0-12-378585-5.10002-8

"Banks should have methodologies that enable them to quantify the risk involved in exposures to individual borrowers or counterparties. Banks should use measurement techniques that are appropriate to the complexity and level of the risks involved in their activities, based on robust data, and subject to periodic validation."[1]

As global banking, bank clients, and capital markets become increasingly integrated and Basel II compliance–oriented, many countries are adopting International Financial Reporting Standards (IFRS). For example, in the European Union, companies with publicly traded shares or debt on a European exchange must use IFRS for their financial reporting as of January 1, 2005. IFRS refer to the entire body of the International Accounting Standards Board's (IASB) pronouncements, including standards and interpretations approved by the IASB and International Accounting Standards (IAS), and Standing Interpretations Committee (SIC)[2] interpretations approved by its predecessor, the International Accounting Standards Committee (IASC). The scope of IFRS includes the following:[3]

- All IAS and interpretations issued by the former IASC and SIC continue to be applicable unless and until they are amended or withdrawn.
- IFRS apply to general purpose financial statements and other financial reporting by profit-oriented entities—that is, those engaged in commercial, industrial, financial, and similar activities, regardless of their legal form.
- Entities other than profit-oriented business entities may also find IFRS appropriate.
- General purpose financial statements are intended to meet the common needs of shareholders, creditors, employees, and the public at large for information about an entity's financial position, performance, and cash flows.
- Other financial reporting includes information provided outside financial statements that assists in the interpretation of a complete set of financial statements or improves users' ability to make efficient economic decisions.
- IFRS apply to individual company and consolidated financial statements.
- A complete set of financial statements includes a balance sheet; an income statement; a cash flow statement; a statement showing either all changes in equity or changes in equity other than those arising from investments by, and distributions to, owners; a summary of accounting policies; and explanatory notes.
- If an IFRS allows both a "benchmark" and an "allowed alternative" treatment, financial statements may be described as conforming to IFRS, whichever treatment is followed.
- In developing standards, IASB intends not to permit choices in accounting treatment. Further, IASB intends to reconsider the choices in existing IAS with a view to reducing the number of those choices.

---

[1] Principle 11, in "Principles for the Management of Credit Risk," July 1999, consultative paper issued by the Basel Committee on Banking Supervision, Bank for International Settlements.

[2] Standing Interpretations Committee. The board of the International Accounting Standards Committee (IASC) formed the Standing Interpretations Committee (SIC) in 1997. It was founded with the objective of developing interpretations of International Accounting Standards (IAS) to be applied where the standards are silent or unclear.

[3] *IFRS Digest,* "What U.S. Practitioners and Entities Need to Know Now," available at AICPA website, http://www.aicpa.org.

- IFRS will present fundamental principles in boldface type and other guidance in nonbold type (the black-letter/gray-letter distinction). Paragraphs of both types have equal authority.
- The provision of IAS 1 that conformity with IAS requires compliance with every applicable IAS, and interpretation requires compliance with all IFRS as well.

Under the IASCF Constitution, the four main objectives of the IASB are as follows:

1. To develop, in the public interest, a single set of high-quality, understandable, and enforceable global accounting standards that require high quality, transparency, and comparable information in financial statements and other financial reporting to help participants in the world's capital markets and other users make economic decisions.
2. To promote the use and rigorous application of those standards.
3. In fulfilling the objectives associated with (1) and (2), to take account of, as appropriate, the special needs of small- and medium-size entities and emerging economies.
4. To bring about convergence of national accounting standards, IAS, and IFRS to high-quality solutions.

Readers can obtain IASB publications in the following formats:

- Individual copies of its standard
- An annual bound volume of all existing standards and interpretations
- Electronic IFRS (eIFRS)
- A CD ROM with standards and interpretations

Publications and subscriptions may be ordered on IASB's website, www.isab.org.

The use of a single set of accounting standards makes it easier for bankers to arrive at credit decisions (far easier than working through differing sets of national accounting standards). Without a single set of accounting standards, bankers must spend a lot of time, cost, and effort to understand borrowers' financial statements. In addition, when borrowers provide lenders with financial information that varies substantially depending on which set of accounting standards is employed, confusion arises about actual financial results (bankers are outsiders and are not usually privy to investment budgets and so on) and results in a correspondingly adverse effect on the lender's confidence in the actual fiscal reporting. In this chapter, we burrow to the core level of IFRS, which deals with the auditor's role and the significance of solid financial information.

The Tie Between Bankers and Auditors

The Auditor's Role

Publicly traded companies must issue financial statements, including a balance sheet, a cash flow statement, and an income statement. To ensure financials are within the framework of generally accepted accounting principles (GAAP), they are audited and certified by an independent accountant. The accountant's role centers around preparation of independent reports based on properly conducted audits and supported by all tests necessary to verify the accuracy of data under scrutiny. The accountant who certifies financial statements must follow the outlines provided by GAAP. Investors can use the certified financial statements with confidence when evaluating a company. When financial statements have been certified, they have been reviewed to ensure the information is correct, true, and reliable.

Financial statements that have been reviewed by an outside accountant are referred to as *certified financial statements*. However, financial statements are often released that have not been certified, and those are known as *compiled financial statements*. Since certification takes time, especially for large public firms, it is often necessary for timely information to be disseminated before official audits can be drawn.

Compiled financial statements (unaudited statements) are not audited adequately, and no opinion on the quality of the financial statements is rendered. Statements about the accuracy of such financial documents are below the level of certified financial statements. Accountants who compile a company's financial statements do not have to confirm the records or analyze financials for accuracy. In the event the auditor discovers misleading, incorrect, or incomplete information, he or she will inform management and will likely walk away from any involvement with the audit.

While credit decisions can never be based solely on financial reports, they play a major role within a much broader context called *lending due diligence*. To understand the borrower's true situation, bankers need plenty of ancillary information. As we described in Chapter One, credit decisions are founded on real values, such as the earning power of assets, and never *just* on historically based financial reports. Real values are generally absent from auditors' reports. That said, few documents are more crucial to the art of lending than good old-fashioned financial statements. In today's complex lending environment set against elaborate accounting standards, the significance of the auditor's work and its impact on the usefulness and credibility of financial statements cannot be overstated.

The auditor bears greater responsibility for fostering the usefulness of financial statements, now more than ever. Through standards adopted by the accounting profession, as well as those imposed by both government and private business sources, members of the accounting profession seek to perform their work with one primary objective: to increase the reliability and usefulness of audits.

Auditors are members of independent accounting firms meeting prescribed professional standards and are licensed to practice in the clients' country or state. The auditor, on the basis of his or her independent judgment formed against the background of appropriate accounting standards and procedures, attests to the fairness of financial statements presented by management. Auditors are responsible to the reader for the proper exercise of judgment in two main areas: statements that are presented fairly in accordance with generally accepted accounting principles and adequate disclosure.

While auditors undertake assignments for fees, it is the accountant's responsibility, not management's (no matter how prodigious the fee), to decide on the information—good or bad—to be disclosed. However, the terms of an accountant's engagement determine to a large degree the extent of the audit, the number and detail of schedules, and the amount of verification work completed. Also, the adequacy of the audit, and the experience and reputation of the accountant, is weighed against the size and financial condition of the borrower. Nonetheless, accountants have a fiduciary responsibility to *clarify all data that bankers want clarified* and included in audits of publicly traded companies. If stock is privately held, banks requiring additional schedules, exhibits, or other information withheld from publication will usually need the borrower's permission before accountants can release the desired information.

A caveat: In spite of the development of the accounting profession internationally, there appears to be a lack of uniformity in both training and experience. Those who rely on the certificates produced by auditing firms must know more about the firms performing audits, including about the license the individual auditor or firm holds and the requirements necessary to obtain the license. Familiarity is essential because even the professional organizations of certified public accountants (CPAs) do not claim equivalence of competence for their respective members (the same can be said for professional organizations of lawyers or doctors).

How, then, does a lender judge an auditor? The best call is an objective appraisal that comes with a banker's knowledge of requirements the auditor has met in securing his or her professional title; second best is a subjective appraisal arrived at through personal knowledge and reputation, which usually entails personal acquaintance. Information about auditors can also come from direct dealings through discussions relative to specific borrowers' financial statements, bank reference files denoting experience with different auditors, CPA files,[4] discussions with other bankers who have knowledge of the particular auditor's work, and the local or national reputation of the auditor. In any case, bankers should judge auditors against the *highest standards* of the profession and consider only auditors that have at least the following:

- Possession of the CPA certificate
- Membership in state and national associations
- Interest in the profession implied by active participation in professional organizations

It is impossible, of course, to document every area in which differences of interpretation or disagreement in opinions can arise between the banking and accounting professions. After all, financial reports are dynamic, breathing documents. And because (good) audits are precursors to credit and breathe life into the banking profession, the arts of credit and accounting operate as different sides of the same coin, in much the same way pharmaceuticals relate to the art of doctoring. Most loan officials do not view financial statements as inanimate, repetitive, or detached objects. As for the rest, such bankers have only themselves to blame when their deals hit the fire and the Office of the Comptroller of the Currency uses its authority to close up their shops.

Accounting Conventions

Financial reports are expected to present fairly, clearly, and completely the borrower's economic, financial, and operating conditions. In preparing financial reports, it is

---

[4] Data mining software is a wonderful tool to accumulate CPA experience via a CPA central file.

perhaps naive to think that accounting (like any communication process) is immune to threats of bias, misinterpretation, error, and evasiveness. To minimize these dangers and to render financial statements that are industry comparable and consistent period-to-period, the (accounting) profession has developed a body of conventions that is both generally accepted and universally practiced. Without this body of accounting conventions, each auditor or chief financial officer would have to develop a unique theory structure and individualistic set of practices. In this hypothetical, and some-what ridiculous, setting, bankers would be required to know every company's anomalous accounting method, an almost impossible task.

Today there is almost universal adoption of a common set of accounting concepts, standards, and procedures under the heading of GAAP and IAS. For example, IAS 1, *Disclosure of Accounting Policies,* includes the following guidelines for financial reports:

- Fair presentation
- Accounting policies
- Going concern
- Accrual basis of accounting
- Consistency of presentation
- Materiality and aggregation
- Offsetting
- Comparative information

IAS 1 also prescribes the minimum structure and content, including certain information, required on the face of the financial statements:

- Balance sheet (current/noncurrent distinction is not required)
- Income statement (operating/nonoperating separation is required)
- Cash flow statement (IAS 7 sets out the details)
- Statement showing changes in equity; various formats are allowed:[5]
  - The statement shows (a) each item of income and expense, gain or loss, which, as required by other IASC Standards, is recognized directly in equity, and the total of these items (examples include property revaluations (IAS 16, *Property, Plant and Equipment*), certain foreign currency translation gains and losses (IAS 21, *The Effects of Changes in Foreign Exchange Rates*), and changes in fair values of financial instruments (IAS 39, *Financial Instruments: Recognition and Measurement*)) and (b) net profit or loss for the period but no total of (a) and (b). Owners' investments and withdrawals of capital and other movements in retained earnings and equity capital are shown in the notes.
  - Same as number 1, but with a total of (a) and (b) (sometimes called "comprehensive income"). Again, owners' investments and withdrawals of capital and other movements in retained earnings and equity capital are shown in the notes.
  - The statement shows both the recognized gains and losses that are not reported in the income statement and owners' investments and withdrawals of capital and other movements in retained earnings and equity capital. An example of this would be the traditional multicolumn statement of changes in shareholders' equity.

---

[5] IAS 1, *"Presentation of Financial Statements."* The objective of this Standard is to prescribe the basis for presentation of general purpose financial statements to ensure comparability both with the entity's financial statements of previous periods and with the financial statements of other entities.

Although accounting standards and principles have provoked debate and healthy criticism, international business recognizes this far-reaching body of theories, methods, and practices as the fundamental bonding of finance and banking. There is little to substitute in the way of conventional auditing standards, as the alternatives are often quite bleak.

Auditor's Opinions

The report of an independent accountant may be a complete detailed audit implying attempts to verify all items and transactions or simply a book audit, concerned only with the maintenance of mathematical accuracy in transferring the general ledger's other schedules onto reported statements. Between these extremes are special purpose audits and limited audits. In the latter, the auditor's report usually indicates that some items are incorporated with insufficient verification because of restrictive circumstances or because of management's insistence that certain figures be accepted without complete checking. For a book audit in such cases, accountants protect themselves and avoid misleading users as to the extent of the verification by noting in the report's certificate any limitations imposed on the examination. Accounting standards are governed by "reporting thresholds," called *opinions*. Auditors sometimes render qualified or adverse opinions, or they can disclaim an opinion. Let's examine the underlying principles behind accountants' opinions.

Qualified Opinion

A qualified opinion stipulates that overall the financial statements provide a fair representation of the firm's condition, but certain items need qualification. Exceptions outlined in this opinion are not serious enough to negate the report. If so, the audit would contain an adverse opinion. The events that result in opinions other than the standard unqualified short-form include the following:

- Limited scope of the examination or constraints placed on the audit.
- Financials depart from that required to present fairly the firm's financial position or its results of operations due to a digression or lack of conformity with GAAP and standards or inadequate disclosure.
- Accounting principles and standards are not consistently applied.
- Unusual uncertainties exist concerning future developments, the effects of which cannot be reasonably estimated or otherwise resolved satisfactorily.

Adverse Opinion

An adverse opinion is required in any report in which the exceptions of fair presentation are so significant that, in the independent auditor's judgment, a qualified opinion is not justified. Adverse opinions are rare, because most enterprises change their accounting to conform to the auditor's desires.

Following is an adverse opinion that raised substantial doubt about the company's ability to continue as a going concern:

Board of Directors and Shareholders
The Great American Golf Works, Inc.
We have audited the accompanying balance sheets of The Great American Golf Works, Inc. (a Delaware corporation) as of December 31, 1999 and 1998 and the related statements of operations and comprehensive income, changes in shareholders' equity, and cash flows for each of the years then ended. These financial statements are the responsibility of the Company's management. Our responsibility is to express an opinion on these financial statements based on our audits.

We conducted our audits in accordance with generally accepted auditing standards. Those standards require that we plan and perform the audits to obtain reasonable assurance about whether the financial statements are free of material misstatement. An audit includes examining, on a test basis, evidence supporting the amounts and disclosures in the financial statements. An audit also includes assessing the accounting principles used and significant estimates made by management, as well as evaluating the overall financial statement presentation. We believe that our audits provide a reasonable basis for our opinion.

In our opinion, the financial statements referred to above present fairly, in all material respects, the financial position of The Great American Golf Works, Inc., as of December 31, 1999 and 1998, and the results of its operations and its cash flows for each of the years then ended, in conformity with generally accepted accounting principles.

The accompanying financial statements have been prepared assuming that the Company will continue as a going concern. As discussed in Note A to the financial statements, the Company is dependent upon its majority shareholder to maintain the corporate status of the Company and to provide all nominal working capital support on the Company's behalf. **Because of the Company's lack of operating assets, its continuance is fully dependent upon the majority shareholder's continuing support. This situation raises a substantial doubt about the Company's ability to continue as a going concern.** *The majority shareholder intends to continue the funding of nominal necessary expenses to sustain the corporate entity. The financial statements do not include any adjustments that might result from the outcome of this uncertainty.*

S. W. HATFIELD, CPA
Dallas, Texas

Disclaimer

A disclaimer of an opinion is normally issued for one of two reasons: Either the auditor has gathered so little information on the financial statements that no opinion can be expressed or the auditor concludes on the basis of the evaluation that the ability of the company to continue on a going-concern basis is highly questionable because of financing or operating problems.

Letter of Transmittal

The letter of transmittal in which the accountants report the results of an audit is termed the *certificate*. The certificate may be a relatively brief "short form," or it may be a more expansive "long form" document. The short-form certificate commonly describes the scope of the work in general terms, noting exceptions to usual practices or procedures and expressing the opinion that the schedules were prepared fairly and correctly present the results of operations for the period reported and the actual financial condition of the concern on the date of the statement. The long-form letter refers to all material assets (and liabilities), besides including standard phrases used in the short certificate. Bankers almost always deal with the short certificate. The short certificate covering a detailed audit usually assures the client and the creditors of the audited firm of the following:

1. The firm's accounting records were audited for the period indicated.
2. The examination was made in accordance with generally accepted auditing standards.
3. Such tests of the accounting records and other auditing procedures were made as were necessary under the circumstances.
4. The major assets and liabilities were confirmed or checked, with exceptions noted if there were any.
5. In the opinion of the auditor, the facts and figures reported fairly present the affairs of the firm and were arrived at in conformity with GAAP, which were applied in a manner consistent with that of the preceding year.

The importance of the last statement is such that its absence from the report of an independent accountant should invariably be questioned. This phrase gives assurance that, in the absence of notice to the contrary, no changes have been made from one year to another in the method of evaluation or in determining depreciation charges and reserves and that income statement items have not been shifted from one category to another.

Compilation

A compilation is actually management's report. For a compilation, a CPA prepares monthly, quarterly, or annual financial statements. However, he or she offers no assurance as to whether material, or significant, changes are necessary for the statements to be in conformity with GAAP (or another comprehensive basis of accounting, such as the cash or tax basis). During a compilation, the CPA arranges the data in a conventional financial statement format and does not probe beneath the surface unless he or she becomes aware that the information management provided is in error or is incomplete. A compilation is sufficient for many private companies. However, if a business needs to provide some degree of assurance to outside groups that its financial statements are reliable, it may be necessary to engage a CPA to perform a review.[6]

[6] "Understanding Compilation Review and Audit," The CPA. Never Underestimate the Value. American Institute of Certified Public Accountants, http://www.tscpa.com/publicinfo/SBarticles/understanding_compilations.aspx.

A Review of Accounting Principles

In view of the basic assumptions of accounting, what are the principles or guidelines that the accountant follows in recording transaction data? The principles relate basically to how assets, liabilities, revenues, and expenses are to be identified, measured, and reported.

Historical Cost

Historical costs are real and, once established, are fixed for the life of the asset or as long as the asset remains on the company's books. For example, when a company purchases a building, the purchase price, or historical cost, is recorded on the company's balance sheet. However, if that building appreciates in value, the asset is still recorded at the historical cost, less depreciation. This accounting practice often results in assets that are carried at significantly off-market prices. Bankers should note that historical costs might overstate or understate asset value.

In a slightly different context, the (accounting) principal of recording assets at historical cost may lend itself to manipulation. A company with a trading position that is out-the-money (money is lost if the position is closed) may be inclined to roll over that position and either postpone recognizing the loss or hope the market changes and turns the position into a gain.

Accounting Standards as Applied to Revenue Realization

This is one facet of reporting practice to which lenders pay particular attention. Revenues (i.e., cash received for merchandise sold or services rendered) are generally recorded at the time of sale or completion of the service. However, two conditions must be met before revenue can be recorded. First, the earnings process must be substantially complete, and second, the collectibility of the revenue must be estimated. The earnings process is *not* substantially complete under the following conditions:

- The seller and buyer have not agreed on the price of the merchandise or service.
- The buyer does not have to pay the seller until the merchandise is resold.
- The merchandise is stolen or physically destroyed, and the buyer does not have to pay the seller.
- The transactions are intercompany—that is, the buyer and seller are related parties.
- The seller must continue to provide substantial performance or services to the buyer or aid in reselling the product. If, however, substantial performance has occurred and the collectibility of the revenue can be estimated, the sale of the product or service can be recorded.

Revenue recognition, while consistent with applicable accounting standards, may be derived from sources other than operating cash flows. For example, some firms turn retiree medical plans into a source of profit. Financial Accounting Standard 106, introduced in the early 1990s, requires companies to report their total anticipated retiree health care coverage costs. Companies were given two incentives to overstate their anticipated costs: Excessive costs provided a rational basis to reduce employee benefits, and if the excessive costs proved to be wrong—that is, too excessive—then the companies could recognize a paper gain by reducing their retiree liability. For example, "in its latest fiscal year, Procter & Gamble's retiree medical program boosted corporate pretax income by $336 million. Altogether, since 1994 the retiree medical plan has contributed $909 million to pretax income."[7] As another example, Walt Disney took a $202 million pretax charge to reflect retiree health liability after its 1993 change in accounting standards. With its large liability, Disney dramatically reduced by more than half its related expenses in the following year. As the estimate of the benefit liability began to be excessive, the company began to book paper gains—$90 million from 1995 through 1998.[8]

The Matching Principle

The popularity of the calendar year as a fiscal period is partly due to the collection of federal income taxes on a calendar-year basis. However, the Internal Revenue Service permits filing tax returns on the basis of a business year instead of a calendar year. GAAP recognizes the concept of matching under the accrual method. The intention is to determine revenue first and then match appropriate costs against revenue. If a financial statement is prepared on another basis of accounting, a statement must be made that the presentation is not in conformity with GAPP. Many small businesses have chosen this method. By preparing their financial statements on an income tax basis, many of the complexities, such as calculating deferred taxes, are avoided.

Consistency

While consistency means applying identical methods fiscal to fiscal, firms are free to switch from one method of accounting to another, but with restrictions. Firms and their accountants need to demonstrate to bankers and investors that the newly adopted principle is preferable to the old. In addition, the nature and effect of the accounting change, as well as the justification for it, must be disclosed in the financial statements for the period in which the change is made.

Disclosure

Adequate disclosure calls for revealing facts that are considered significant enough to influence the judgment of a knowledgeable reader. Sufficient disclosure includes more descriptive explanations, acceptable presentation, and succinct but meaningful footnotes. For example, detailed disclosure of financial obligations, current accounts such as inventory breakdown and method of pricing, and whatever additional disclosure is required to prevent the audit from becoming a guessing game should be provided. Auditors can add one or more paragraphs to an unqualified report if they

---

[7] Ellen Schultz and Robert McGough, "Health Advisory: Investors Should Do a Checkup on Firms That Use Medical Plans to Lift Profits," *The Wall Street Journal,* October 25, 2000, pp. C1 and C21.

[8] Ellen Schultz, "This Won't Hurt: Companies Transform Retiree-Medical Plans into Source of Profits," *The Wall Street Journal,* October 25, 2000, pp. A1 and A14.

feel that the information is important for the reader to know. This addition is known as the *emphasis of a matter* paragraph and is usually added before the standard opinion paragraph of an unqualified report. Obviously, the paragraph should not include mention of the emphasized matter but should, instead, refer to the footnotes.

Objectivity

Notwithstanding an audit disclaimer, it is imperative that bankers be assured the information in financial reports is factual and impartial. While no disclosure is totally objective, the process must be based on the auditor's sound judgment, diagnostic good sense, and an irrefutable background. Reliable estimates must be made of depreciation charges, deferrals, and accruals of cost, along with revenue items, equity earnings, restructuring charges, and deferred tax credits. Estimates are deemed objective if the audit process is founded on adequate information and data that can be authenticated by independent parties. Most importantly, if there is any doubt, objectivity should favor conservatism. Howard M. Schilit suggests that financial statement readers favor firms that present conservative accounting policies:

> *Companies that fail to use conservative accounting methods might demonstrate a lack of integrity in their financial reporting process. Indeed, many analysts place a premium on companies that use conservative accounting policies. In searching for excellent companies, for example, the widely respected analyst and shenanigan buster Thornton O'Glove offers the following advice: "Look for companies that use very conservative accounting principles. In my experience, if a company does not cut corners in its accounting, there's a good chance it doesn't cut corners in its operations. You know you've got your money with a high-quality management."*[9]

Financial Reports

Frequency of Statements

Annual Statements

For purposes of credit analysis, the date of the annual statement is important in order to relate the figures to the stage or level of seasonal operations and to the closing date of the income tax statement. The date of the statement filed with the income tax return occasionally differs from that published for trade use. Bankers usually consider this when observing the provisions for income taxes.

Interim Statements

The Securities and Exchange Commission (SEC) requires filing of quarterly sales data by all concerns listed on an exchange. Many of these concerns issue midyear and even

---

[9] *Financial Shenanigans,* Howard M. Schilit, McGraw-Hill, NY, 1993.

quarterly statements for the benefit of creditors, investors, and potential stock subscribers. Some small cap firms, attempting to comfort suppliers and other credit sources, issue quarterly statements or trial balance figures covering very short-interim periods, including monthly. Since the trial balance serves as a source of valuable interim information, its use in credit analysis is increasing. (Analysis of the trial balance is discussed in Chapter Four.) Interim reports are unaudited or are at most subjected to a limited review. Short-term lenders may request cash budgets prepared by the borrower's financial team and completed with only peripheral help from accountants.

Footnotes

An astute lender can be no less an astute auditor.

Smart lenders read their client's annual report cover to cover, paying heed to the fine print. After all, there is more to a financial report than just numbers. We find the chairman's optimistic statement, a historical record of three or more years, pictures of smiling employees, the latest hot products, charts that Andy Warhol would proudly remake into museum quality, and wonderfully vivid graphs. Of course, footnotes also appear—where *real* information is to be found.

Footnotes are integral to financial statements but are often overlooked because they tend to be somewhat technical and frequently appear in small print. However, they are the accountant's way of disclosing details of crucial data. Restrictions imposed by footnotes provide bankers with a wealth of information for assessing the financial condition of borrowers and the quality of reported earnings. Schilit reminds us that the footnotes detail such issues as *"(1) accounting policies selected, (2) pending or imminent litigation, (3) long-term purchase commitments, (4) changes in accounting principles or estimates, (5) industry-specific notes, and (6) segment information showing healthy and unhealthy operations."*[10]

On the whole, credit analysts see footnote disclosure as a step above core financial data. Kenneth Fisher Forbes writes, "The back of the report, the footnotes, is where they hide the bad stuff they didn't want to disclose but had to. They bury the bodies where the fewest folks find them—in the fine print." The Accounting Principles Board (APB)[11] in Opinion No. 22, "Disclosure of Accounting Policies," concluded that "information about the accounting policies adopted and followed by a reporting entity is essential for financial-statement users in making economic decisions."[12]

---

[10] Ibid.

[11] The Accounting Principles Board (APB) is the former authoritative body of the American Institute of Certified Public Accountants (AICPA). It was created by the American Institute of Certified Public Accountants in 1959 and issued pronouncements on accounting principles until 1973, when it was replaced by the Financial Accounting Standards Board (FASB).

[12] The focus of APB Opinion No. 22 is on the disclosure of accounting policies. This information is important to financial statement readers in determining (1) whether accounting policies are consistently applied from year to year; (2) the value of obsolete items included in ending inventory; (3) net income for the year; and (4) whether the working capital position is adequate for future operations. Read more at http://www.justanswer.com/questions/3hokn-the-focus-of-apb-opinion-no-22-is-on-the-disclosure-of-accounting#ixzz0pKJQ18aR.

Contingent Liabilities

As an integral part of financial reports, a statement identifies accounting policies adopted and followed by the reporting entity. The APB believes disclosure should be given in a separate *Summary of Significant Accounting Policies* preceding the notes to the financial statements or as the initial note. After perusing the disclosure of accounting policies, wise bankers look for information that may negatively impact borrowers, such as contingencies. The complete disclosure of material contingencies is an important property (of financial statements) according to IAS guidelines because of the uncertainties that may exist at the conclusion of each accounting period.[13]

For example, standards governing accounting for loss contingencies require accrual and/or note disclosure when specified recognition and disclosure criteria are met. Gain contingencies generally are not recognized in financial statements but can be disclosed. Reporting criteria centers around the high probability that a change in the estimate will occur in the near term. Following are examples of the types of situations that may require disclosure in accordance with Statement of Position (SOP) 94-6:[14]

- Specialized equipment subject to technological obsolescence
- Valuation allowances for deferred tax assets based on future taxable income
- Capitalized motion picture film production costs
- Inventory subject to rapid technological obsolescence
- Capitalized computer software costs
- Deferred policy acquisition costs of insurance enterprises
- Valuation allowances for commercial and real estate loans
- Environmental remediation-related obligations
- Litigation-related obligations
- Contingent liabilities for obligations of other entities
- Amounts reported for long-term obligations like pensions
- Expected loss on disposition of a business or assets
- Amounts reported for long-term contracts

Under Financial Accounting Standards Board (FASB) Statement No. 5, an estimated loss from a loss contingency must be charged against net income as soon as the loss becomes probable and estimable. In addition, now that the use of prior period adjustments has been extremely narrowed by FASB Statement No. 16, *Prior Period Adjustments,* almost all such loss accruals must be charged against current income. Another impact of FASB Statement No. 5 on earnings is that accrual of contingency losses is prohibited unless it is probable that an asset has been impaired or a liability has been incurred and that the loss is estimable. This means that firms cannot provide reserves for future losses through yearly income statement adjustments. The reason is to prevent earnings volatility, the result of guesswork.

---

[13] Financial Accounting Standards Board Statement No. 5, *Accounting for Contingencies.*

[14] The Accounting Standards Executive Committee issued Statement of Position (SOP) 94-6, Disclosure of Significant Risks and Uncertainties, December 19, 1995, that requires disclosures about the nature of operations, the use of estimates in the preparation of financial statements, certain significant estimates, and current vulnerabilities due to concentrations.

Classification of Contingencies

FASB Statement No. 5 defines the different levels of probability as to whether future events will confirm the existence of a loss as follows:

1. Probable—The future event or events are likely to occur.
2. Reasonably possible—The chance of the future event or events occurring is more than remote but less than likely.
3. Remote—The chance of the future event or events occurring is slight.

Professional judgment is required to classify the likelihood of the future events occurring. All relevant information that can be acquired concerning the uncertain set of circumstances needs to be obtained and used to determine the classification.

While some contingencies are disclosed in footnotes, bankers should recalculate certain balance sheet ratios in figuring possible losses. That's because creditors focus on possible accounting loss associated with financial instruments, including losses from the failure of another party to perform according to contract terms (credit risk), the possibility that future changes in market prices may render financial instruments less valuable (market risk), and the risk of physical loss.

Likewise, a financial instrument has off-balance sheet risk if the risk of loss exceeds the amount recognized as an asset or if the obligation exceeds the amount recognized in the financial statements. Bankers are particularly watchful of general loss contingencies.

General Loss Contingencies

General loss contingencies may arise from the risk of exposure to the following:

- Product warranties or defects
- Pending or threatened litigation
- Risk of catastrophe (losses)
- Direct guarantees (guarantor makes payment to creditor if debtor fails to do so)
- Claims and assessments
- Preacquisition contingencies

Financial Instruments with Off-Balance Sheet Risk

While management may claim that off-balance sheet financial instruments reduce risks, these instruments can function as speculative tools. Borrowers anticipating a harsh fiscal environment may capitalize on positive changes in the value of financial instruments to improve results—results unattainable through normal operating activities. The market crash of 1987 suddenly revealed some large, sophisticated companies that had taken inordinately large (that is, beyond the size required for risk management) derivative positions that resulted in significant losses. Under extraordinary circumstances these derivative positions can weaken a credit. Lenders tend to find out about these positions. Financial instruments with off-balance sheet risk include the following:

- A recourse obligation on receivables or bills receivables (B/Rs) sold
- Interest rate and currency swaps, caps, and floors
- Loan commitments and options written on securities; futures contracts

- Obligations arising from financial instruments sold short
- Synthetic asset swap that might result in an unwind if the bond goes into default
- Obligations to repurchase securities sold

Product Warranties or Defects

A warranty (product guarantee) is a promise—for a specific time period—made by a seller to a buyer to make good on a deficiency of quantity, quality, or performance in a product. Warranties can result in future cash outlays, *frequently significant additional outlays.* Although the future cost is indefinite as to amount, due date, and even customer, a liability—an estimate of costs incurred after sale and delivery associated with defect correction—does exist, and experienced lenders ask accountants or management to quantify the downside effect.

Litigation Contingencies

Publicly traded companies are required to disclose litigation contingencies when eventual loss from a lawsuit is possible. Studies were done on the classification of predisposition years (refers to years before the year of court adjudication or settlement). In one study, it was found that 47.6% of surveyed companies showed unsatisfactory disclosure with no mention of the litigation in financial statements, or that a strong disclaimer of liability did not accompany mention of the litigation. Legal action includes antitrust, patent infringement, fraud or misrepresentation, breach of contract, and other noninsurable suits. That survey represents a banker's bona fide red flag, if ever there was one.

Contingencies such as product lawsuits losses can show up from out of nowhere, are often explosive, and can finish off an otherwise profitable company in the process. The best hedge against litigation contingencies is preparation that often means a present value analysis, which places values on material lawsuits by determining present value. Minor lawsuits, in comparison, are usually irrelevant; an adverse opinion will not impact on equity, debt service, or the borrower's sustainable cash flows. However, if we have a Firestone on our hands, can litigation be settled? If so, when and for how much? Such a situation brings up other questions:

- If litigation cannot be settled, when will the court hear the case?
- What are the probabilities the court will render an adverse opinion?
- If the opinion is adverse, will there be grounds for appeal?
- If so, when will the appeal be heard?
- What are the probabilities the appeal will collapse?
- Given the time value of money and the joint probabilities of adverse opinions, including appeals, what is the expected present value of the product lawsuit (use face amounts, not expected reduced awards)?
- With pro forma expected losses on fiscal spreadsheets, is the financial structure strong enough to absorb expected losses?
- Related to the preceding, how do adjusted (pro forma) debt and cash flow coverage ratios stack up against the industry or benchmarks? Has the borrower's industry quartile ranking deteriorated? What is the anticipated impact on bond ratings and/or the bank's credit grade?

Environmental Contingencies

Environmental protection laws pose many dangers for unwary lenders. To avoid potentially unlimited liability that may result from environmental violations, prudent bankers try to extrapolate expected present values and adjust financials accordingly. Environmental trouble spots include, but are not restricted to, the following:

- Transportation and disposition of hazardous substances
- Real property
- Manufacturing processes that involve use, creation, or disposition of hazardous wastes
- Petroleum or chemicals stored on the premises
- Underground storage tanks
- Equipment used to transport hazardous materials
- Pipes leading to waterways

CIT Corporation, once a leading commercial finance company, prepared a checklist for a client regarding environmental contingencies:

1. Are toxic or otherwise hazardous or regulated materials, such as used machine oil, handled at any stage of the production process?
2. Request a copy of the borrower's EPA plan, if any.
3. Does the client have above- or below-ground tanks, and when were they last inspected for environmental impact purposes?
4. Are there paint shops on the property?
5. What was the previous use of the property prior to our client owning it, and how long has our client been at this property?
6. Have there been any past or are there present EPA violations against the property? If so, provide copies of those violations to our marketing representative.
7. Are there any waterways on or near the property? If so, where are they located in proximity to the property?
8. What is the specific use of the property—in other words, what kind of process or processes are being done on the property?
9. Does our prospective client stock drums of solvents or fluids on the property? If so, what is the exact nature of those solvents or fluids, and where are they located?
10. What is the nature of the uses on adjoining and neighboring properties? Do they appear to create environmental risk?

Extraordinary Losses

Two criteria must be met to classify a gain or loss as an extraordinary item (both criteria must be met before a company can classify a gain or loss as "extraordinary"):

1. *Unusual*: An event that is unrelated to the typical activities of the business.
2. *Nonrecurring*: An event that management does not expect to occur again.

Natural disasters meet the definition of unusual (unrelated to the typical activities of the business). For example, on the one hand, a corn farmer in Kansas hit by a drought would not classify the loss as nonrecurring, and thus it could not be considered extraordinary. On the other hand, a flood in Phoenix would give rise to an extraordinary loss. The criteria of "unusual" and "nonrecurring" must be considered from the standpoint of the firm's geographical location and its type of business.

Direct and Indirect Guarantees

Direct guarantees, representing a direct connection between creditor and guarantor, warrant that the guarantor will make payment to the creditor if the debtor fails to do so. In an indirect guarantee, the guarantor agrees to transfer funds to the debtor if a specified event occurs. Indirect guarantees connect directly from the guarantor to debtor, but they benefit the creditor indirectly.

FASB No. 5 requires that the nature and amount of the guarantee be disclosed in the financial statements. Guarantees to repurchase receivables or related property, obligations of banks under letters of credit or *standby agreements,* guarantees of the indebtedness of others, and unconditional obligations to make payments are examples of the types of guarantee contingencies that must be disclosed even if they have a *remote* possibility of materializing.

Recourse Obligations on Receivables or Bills Receivables Sold

A widely used method of financing transactions involving small, high-ticket items, notably furs and fine jewelry, has been the presentation of B/Rs, or notes receivables, for discount or as security to demand loans. A B/R is an unconditional order in writing addressed by one person (or firm) to another, signed by the person giving it, requiring the person to whom it is addressed to pay on demand or at a fixed or determinable future time a sum certain in money to order or to bearer. A B/R evidences indebtedness arising out of the sale of goods by the bank's customer in the normal course of business. B/Rs are endorsed over to the bank with *full recourse* to the bank's customer. These are off-balance sheet contingencies and should be pro forma back on the balance sheet by an amount equal to the expected loss.

Asset Securitization

If an asset can generate cash flow, it can be securitized. When a company securitizes its assets, those assets are sold as a "true sale" and are no longer assets of the company. In fact, many times that is precisely the reason many companies securitize assets: to get them off their balance sheet to improve their profitability ratios. However, some have argued that securitization may inadvertently cause adverse selection for the company's remaining assets; that is, the company securitizes its best assets (the assets most marketable and easiest to securitize) and retains its poorer assets, thereby causing an adverse selection.

Creditors face little risk in the event of bankruptcy because assets can be quickly liquidated. In exchange, however, the creditor receives a lower return on its investments. In addition, if these creditors liquidate the securitized assets, the company will be further unable to recover from a financial crisis and will put its general creditors at even greater risk. Other risks beside credit/default include maturity mismatch and prepayment volatility. As a side note, bankers and investors can reduce contingency risks by using computer software that provides models and structural and analytical data for asset securitizations, including commercial loan securitizations, whole—loan and senior—subordinated securities, as well as home equity loans.[15]

Futures Contracts

A commodity such as copper used for production may be purchased for current delivery or for future delivery. Investing in commodity futures refers to the buying or the selling of a contract to deliver a commodity in the future. In the case of a purchase contract, the buyer agrees to accept a specific commodity that meets a specified quality in a specified month. In the case of a sale, the seller agrees to deliver the specified commodity during the designated month. Hedging against unexpected increases in raw material costs is a wise move; speculating in commodity futures, with the bank's money, is another story. There is a large probability that the firm will suffer a loss on any particular purchase or sale of a commodity contract.

Management may purchase a contract for future delivery or take a long position in which the firm will profit if the price of the commodity—say, copper—rises. Management may also enter into a contract for future delivery (short position). These long and short positions run parallel to the long and short positions in security markets.

Pensions

Pension expense represents the amount of money management should invest at the end of the year to cover future pension payments that will be made to employees for this additional year's service. Accounting records reflect management's best guess as to real pension costs. Accountants try to measure the cost of these retirement benefits at the time the employee earns them, rather than when the employee actually receives them. A multiplicity of pension assumptions needs to be compiled to come up with the required pension amount, including the following:

- Interest the invested funds are expected to earn
- Number of years an employee is expected to live after retirement
- Salary of employee at retirement
- Average years of service of an employee at retirement

Beware of unfunded projected benefit obligations, since this liability indicates that pension investments fall short of future pension benefits. Borrowers that continuously fund less than current pension expense or incorporate unrealistic assumptions in their pension plan could find themselves embedded in a thicket of thorns in the not too distant future.

Companies with defined benefit pension plans must disclose three items: the pension discount rate, the expected rate of future compensation increases, and the projected long-term rate of return on pension assets. Understanding what these figures

---

[15] Ron Unz, "New Software Can Provide Risk Models," *American Banker,* August 25, 1992, vol. 157, no. 164, p. 12A (1).

mean provides insight into, for example, whether a merger candidate's pension liabilities make it worth less than meets the eye and how companies use perfectly legal (but fairly sneaky) accounting gimmicks to inflate profits.

Discretionary Items

Some expenditures are discretionary, meaning they fall under management's control, including the following:

- Repair and maintenance of equipment
- Research and development (R&D)
- Marketing and advertising expenditures
- New product lines, acquisitions, and divestitures of operating units

Management might forgo timely equipment repairs in order to improve earnings, but the policy could backfire over the longer term.

Research and Development

In its Statement of Financial Accounting Standards No. 2, "Accounting for Research and Development Costs" (October 1974), the FASB concludes, "All research and development costs encompassed by this Statement shall be charged to expense when incurred." The FASB (Statement No. 2) and the SEC (ASR No. 178) mandated all companies to expense R&D outlays. The Board reached its conclusion as a result of a reasoning process in which several preliminary premises were accepted as true:

- Uncertainty of future benefits. R&D expenditures often are undertaken whereby there is a small probability of success. The Accounting Board mentioned that the high degree of uncertainty of realizing the future benefits of individual R&D projects was a significant factor in reaching this conclusion.
- Lack of a causal relationship between expenditures and benefits.
- R&D does not meet the accounting concept of an asset.
- Matching of revenues and expenses.
- Relevance of resulting information for investment and credit decisions.

An incontrovertible solution for avoiding problems dealing with overstating R&D expenditures is to expense costs associated with the acquisition of assets where some significant probability exists that the asset will be worth less than cost. This so-called conservative approach is consistent with guidelines dealing with expensing R&D.

3 Multivariate Ratio Analysis

Chapter Outline

Credit Engineering for Bankers. DOI: 10.1016/B978-0-12-378585-5.10003-X

The Role of Ratios

While ratios help creditors evaluate financial position and irregularities that may affect repayment, they do not tell the whole story; ratios offer clues, not complete answers. It is unreasonable to expect that mechanical calculation of one ratio or a group of ratios will automatically yield definitive information concerning a complex business. Bankers must look behind the numbers to judge credit quality.

Ratios are relative measures and are used to (1) clarify the relationship between items appearing on financial reports (structural analysis); (2) match borrowers' performance against historical levels (time-series analysis); and (3) compare performance with benchmarks or industry averages (cross-sectional analysis). Ratios filter absolute numbers down to a common scale. On the one hand, for example, a borrower may have expanded markets over the past few periods, so comparing gross profit, an absolute number, to historical levels will not be particularly useful. On the other hand, ratios eliminate the problem of trying to extract meaning through the vacuum of absolute numbers—gross profit, debt level, or revenue.

We can track a firm's historical performance, evaluate its present position, and obtain a relative value to compare with industry averages. Does the company earn a fair return? Can it withstand downturns? Does it have the financial flexibility to attract additional creditors and investors? Is management adroit in its efforts to upgrade weak operations, reinforce strong ones, pursue profitable opportunities, and push the value of common stock to the highest possible levels?

Limitations of Ratios

Time-series and cross-sectional analysis can easily be distorted by inflation or an unusual business climate such as the recent recession. Furthermore, because financial statements are routinely prepared for special purposes, such as reports to shareholders and bankers, financials may be more liberal than realistic. The bank's overall assessment of even the most detailed financial reports is important and should be standard practice before the first ratio is calculated. In this chapter, we proceed on the following assumptions:

1. Ratios apply to manufacturers, wholesalers, retailers, and service companies. Different ratios are used to analyze banks, utilities, insurance, and finance companies. Divergent asset quality and capital structure make it necessary to employ other ratios.
2. Ratios concentrate on the past.
3. Some firms "window-dress" their financial statements to make them look better for credit analysts—for example, by selling a corporate aircraft for cash just before issuing a quarterly statement.

4. Benchmarks or industry leaders are better targets than published industry averages. The idea is to match customers against the solid performers; averages are not necessarily good measures in economic downturns.

5. The quality and availability of data affect the usefulness of ratios.

6. Ratios come from raw numbers derived from accounting data. International Accounting Standards along with generally accepted accounting principles (GAAP), as applied in Chapter Two, allow flexibility and, therefore, varied interpretation. It is fact, not fiction, that different accounting methods distort intercompany comparison, so many bankers will employ various methods to interpret the following:

   a. *Revenue recognition:* Certain types of companies—for example, contractors—may recognize revenue on a percentage of the completion method for major projects to closely match the timing of costs and profits earned.

   b. *Inventory valuation:* LIFO versus FIFO accounting usually influences liquidity ratios. FIFO signifies first-in, first-out inventory, meaning the oldest inventory items are recorded as sold first. LIFO denotes last-in, first-out inventory—that is, the most recently purchased items are recorded as sold first. Since the 1970s, U.S. companies have tended to use LIFO, which lowers their income taxes in times of inflation and correspondingly reduces inventory recorded on the balance sheet.

   c. *Depreciation:* Even under GAAP, there is considerable latitude for depreciation schedules for various asset classes. Firms with large capital equipment requirements may benefit from accelerating depreciation to minimize taxes.

   d. *Bad debts:* Although GAAP requires that companies establish a reserve account or provision for doubtful accounts, there is room for interpretation on what percentage of problem accounts should be recognized or when a bad debt should be charged off. A good example of this leeway was the banking industry a few years ago. Federal regulators viewed banks as underreserved with respect to potential problem loans, particularly real estate. Regulators encouraged banks to make huge additions to reserves, resulting in large losses for the banks.

   e. *Capitalization of costs:* GAAP allows computer software companies to capitalize certain developmental costs over the expected life of the software. This technique can significantly affect a company's perceived profitability and cash flow.

   f. *Pension fund costs (PFCs):* PFCs represent a special long-term liability: the pension fund. For many companies, this is a very large liability and is usually not captured on the balance sheet but, rather, appears as a type of off-balance sheet financing. Pension fund accounting is complicated, and the footnotes are often lengthy. Bankers need to understand a few basics in order to know the most important questions to ask an obligor with a large pension fund, particularly if the fund is underfunded. A pension plan has two primary elements: the future liabilities, or benefit obligations, created by employee service, and the pension fund, or plan assets, used to pay for retiree benefits. Funded status equals plan assets minus projected benefit obligation. If plan assets fall below projected benefit obligations, the plan is underfunded

   g. *Cost versus equity accounting for investments:* How an investment (e.g., in another company) is recognized on the balance sheet can greatly impact the financial statements. Investments at cost remain on the balance sheet at the lower of cost or market. Provided that the value of the investment does not depreciate below cost, there will be no change in the carrying value of the investment.

   Under the equity method of accounting for investments, the company is required to reflect its percentage share of the profit or losses from the investment in each period. Suppose Company A owns 35% of Company B. Company A is required to report 35% of

Company B's profit or losses in each period on Company A's financial statements, though these are noncash events to Company A.

h. *Seasonality and different fiscal years:* Borrowers affected by seasonal variation need to measure this variation to plan for temporary increases or decreases in seasonal assets: labor requirements, raw material purchases, production, and periodic maintenance. Fiscal audits are planned at the low point in the seasonal cycle. Ratio analysis will be distorted if fiscal ratios are measured against interim ratios.

i. *Mergers and acquisitions (M&A):* Mergers, acquisitions, divestitures, consolidations, and international market expansion have become important strategic objectives for value actualizing borrowers. Time-series ratio analysis will be affected by M&A activities and call for careful due diligence.

Peer Group or Industry Comparisons

Under certain circumstances, we might question the validity of comparative ratios, especially when we compare ratios to industry norms without knowing a firm's history. We question comparative ratio analysis when the business cycle differs from that of the rest of the industry. This often creates an illusion when, for example a borrower with a high current or quick ratio may be viewed as liquid, when in reality high ratios can mask inefficient use of resources or, worse, stale current assets. In addition, it may be difficult to measure a diversified firm's financials compared to industry averages because we may not be comparing like numbers; the firm's ratios may be drawn from figures of consolidated heterogeneous operations/industries. Before jumping to conclusions about quality, magnitude, and ratio trends, we measure companies individually (asking for consolidating financials may not be a bad idea). Is the ratio composed of the "right stuff"?

In 2005, for example, a comparison of Cisco with Airtight Networks would not have easily yielded accurate information. Cisco was so much larger than Airtight at the time that the two firms had separate and diverse financial statements, while both were in the same industry. Consider Cognizant Technology Solutions. Cognizant has a few very expensive mainframe systems listed on its balance sheet and could greatly influence comparisons if management disposed of one mainframe system just before or after the end of a fiscal period.

The type of assets leads to different levels of quality in the ratios. R. J. Reynolds, with its diverse number of divisions and product lines, could distort ratios. Similarly, RKO owns radio and television stations, makes movies, bottles soda, runs hotels, and holds a large stake in an airline company. If only the total business income figure is available for this conglomerate, there is no way to tell from the consolidated data the extent to which the differing product lines contribute to profitability and risk.

In the highly volatile capital markets industry, we might find it especially hard to establish a meaningful set of comparative industry averages because of its various methods of classifying assets and liabilities. Companies that specialize in niche markets and cater to specialized markets pose still another problem. The Concorde jet, for example, was the sole product in the market, and there were no other originating firms to compare it against.

Companies that vary in size within an industry could distort ratios, and some firms may straddle more than one industry. Some industries, such as biotechnology, are extremely volatile. Similarly, each firm has diverse contingencies such as patents, litigation, licensing agreements, and joint ventures affecting comparisons. Additional problems arise with the use of industry averages. Norms only represent the center, and, therefore, the actual position of the company within its peer group is often not clear. For example, Microsoft has a very large bearing on the benchmark within its industry.

Geographic differences can also affect companies in the same industry. For example, how can you compare two home public transport companies? One firm may do business on the East Coast, while the other may operate on the West Coast. Both firms are grouped together into one broad industry group: regional transport services. Because of differences in local economies, cultures, and demographics, the East Coast transporter can have drastically different financial ratios compared to the West Coast transporter.

Another problem surfaces when we analyze a youthful firm or industry. New businesses, such as clean energy storage firms, lack history, thus making it difficult to track historical trends. Another industry that comes to mind from the not so distant past is information technology, and the telecommunication industry research and development firms further illustrate the difficulty in establishing meaningful benchmark comparisons for industries in their infancy.

Different accounting practices also sometimes distort ratio comparisons: FIFO versus LIFO, leasing versus financing, accounts receivable provisions, capitalized expenses, differing depreciation methods, and research and development costs accounting. Since comparative financial ratios are based on accounting numbers, the possibility of different firms or even different divisions within a company using different accounting can lead us down the wrong path. Sometimes ratios are calculated that do not reflect ongoing operations, which might confound lenders when they compare the net margin to industry averages. Also, some firms use different year-ends, and this practice may alter financials and distort comparisons. Another difficulty lies in comparing international firms or foreign-owned companies. One area of benchmark comparisons where ratio analysis is simply not enough is the seasonal business. Because the flows and contractions of seasonal businesses do not always coincide, lenders might find it hard to peg an industry average. Industry averages for seasonal businesses will, of course, depend on whether we calculate ratios before or after the peak season.

Substantial size differences of firms might make it hard to canvass an industry and pick the right benchmarks. Large firms tend to operate efficiently because of economies of scale and their high operating leverage. For example, Sony is more efficient than many smaller flat-screen TV producers, which may make comparisons within the industry inaccurate, since Sony has a sizable bearing on the benchmark.

When bankers work with ratio comparatives, they should ensure that it is reasonable to rank two companies—the company to the industry, and the "industry" to the "industry." There may be unique characteristics that cause differences in the comparison, meaning that we should know enough about an industry to select an appropriate benchmark. Industry averages should be replaced by specific benchmarks, if possible. If a lender feels conformable with averages, he or she should at least confirm that ratios fall within one standard deviation of the median. Above all, lenders should talk with those who are familiar with the industry: accountants, consultants, suppliers, or industry specialists.

Ratio Trends

Are financial trends consistent historically, or do ratios reveal an unreasonable departure from trends? A seasonal amusement park operator who was historically cash rich during the tourist season needed to borrow in the off-season to pay expenses. Patterns in the interim reports depicted the expansion and contraction process. A newly assigned account officer noticed that the company's loan was fully extended in the middle of August and began to ask questions. The finding: The borrower diverted cash normally used to repay the bank loan into a new fledgling enterprise and couldn't repay the credit line.

Several categories of financial ratios—liquidity ratios, activity or performance ratios, profitability ratios, leverage or capital structure ratios, and growth and valuation ratios—are covered in this chapter. Specific examples of each ratio discussed are based on the information presented in the case study, Trudy Patterns, Inc.

Case Study: Trudy Patterns, Inc.

The loan officer at First Central Bank was recently alerted to the deteriorating financial position of their client, Trudy Patterns, Inc. If any ratio falls significantly below industry averages provided by *RMA Annual Statement Studies: Financial Ratio Benchmarks,* we raise red flags. Loan terms require that certain ratios be maintained at specified minimum levels. When an analysis was run on Trudy Patterns three months earlier, the firm's banker noticed that key ratios continued to trend down, falling below industry averages. The banker sent a copy of the computer output to management, together with a note voicing concern.

Initial analysis indicated that problems were developing, but no ratio was below the level specified in the loan agreement between the bank and the borrower. However, the second analysis, which was based on the data given in Table 3.1, showed that the current ratio was below the 2.0 times specified in the loan agreement.

The loan agreement specifies that the bank can call for immediate payment of the entire bank loan, and if payment is not forthcoming within 10 days, the bank can call the loan, forcing Trudy Patterns, Inc., into bankruptcy. The banker has no intention of actually enforcing loan covenants at this time, but instead intended to use the loan agreement to encourage management to take decisive action to improve the firm's financial condition.

Trudy Patterns manufactures a line of costume jewelry. In addition to its regular merchandise, Trudy creates special holiday items for the respective seasons. Seasonal

Table 3.1 Trudy Patterns, Inc., Ratio Trends

Ratio	2008	2009	2010	Industry
Current Ratio	3.05	2.67	1.75	2.50
Quick Ratio	1.65	1.08	0.73	1.00
Average Collection Period	37 Days	37 Days	55 Days	32 Days
Inventory Turnover	7.1X	4.5X	3.6X	5.7X
Fixed Asset Turnover	11.7X	12.0X	12.1X	12.1X
Working Capital Turnover	6.2X	5.3X	5.6X	4.5X
Total Asset Turnover	3.0X	2.5X	2.0X	2.8X
Average Settlement Period	18 Days	26 Days	44 Days	35 Days
Gross Profit Margin	19.9%	17.7%	13.8%	18.0%
Selling, General, and Administration Expenses	8.7%	10.2%	13.8%	9.3%
Net Profit Margin	5.5%	3.4%	0.39%	2.90%
Return on Total Assets	16.8%	8.9%	0.7%	8.8%
Return on Net Worth	28.3%	16.7%	2.0%	17.5%
Dividend Payout Rate	25.3%	23.8%	13.5%	7%
Debt Ratio (Debt/Assets)	40.6%	46.5%	59.87%	50.0%
Times Interest Earned	15.8X	7.9X	1.4X	7.7X

working capital requirements are financed by a $300,000 line of credit. In accordance with standard banking practices, however, the loan agreement requires repayment in full at some time during the year—in this case by February 2011.

Higher raw material costs together with increased wages led to a decline in the firm's profit margin the last half of 2009, as well as during most of 2010. Sales increased during both of these years, however, due to the firm's aggressive marketing program and in spite of competition from shell and turquoise jewelry makers.

The company received a copy of the banker's ratio analysis along with a letter informing management that the bank would insist on immediate repayment of the entire loan unless the firm submitted a business plan showing how operations could be turned around. Management felt that sales levels could not improve without an increase in the bank loan from $300,000 to $400,000, since payments of $100,000 for construction of a plant addition would have to be made in January 2011. While the firm had been a loyal customer for over 50 years, management questioned whether the bank would continue to supply the present line of credit, let alone approve facility increases

The banker examined exigent ratios with the client, centering on strengths and weaknesses revealed by the ratio analysis derived from the accompanying balance sheet. He wanted to know specifically the amount of internal funds that could have been available for debt payment if fiscal performance were at industry levels, with particular focus on the two working capital accounts: receivables and inventory. After meeting with management, the bank reviewed alternatives and arrived at a credit decision, which is revealed at the end of this chapter.

Trudy Patterns, Inc., Balance Sheet, Year Ended December 31 ($ Thousands)

	Assets	1998	1999	2000
1.	Current Assets			
2.	Cash and Cash Items	$15,445	$12,007	$11,717
3.	Accounts and Notes Receivable, Net	$51,793	$55,886	$88,571
4.	Inventories	$56,801	$99,087	$139,976
5.	Current Assets	$124,039	$166,980	$240,264
6.	Property, Plant, and Equipment	$53,282	$60,301	$68,621
7.	Accumulated Depreciation	($8,989)	($13,961)	($20,081)
8.	**Net Fixed Assets**	**$44,294**	**$46,340**	**$48,539**
9.	**Total Assets**	**$168,333**	**$213,320**	**$288,803**
	Liabilities and Equities	**2008**	**2009**	**2010**
10.	Current Liabilities			
11.	Short-Term Loans	$10,062	$15,800	$55,198
12.	Accounts Payable	$20,292	$31,518	$59,995
13.	Accruals	$10,328	$15,300	$21,994
14.	Current Liabilities	$40,682	$62,618	$137,187
15.	Long-Term Bank Loans	$19,125	$28,688	$28,688
16.	Mortgage	$8,606	$7,803	$7,018
17.	Long-Term Debt	$27,731	$36,491	$35,706
18.	Total Liabilities	$68,413	$99,109	$172,893
19.	Common Stock (No Par Value)	$69,807	$69,807	$69,807
20.	Retained Earnings	$30,113	$44,404	$46,103
21.	Stockholders Equity	$99,920	$114,211	$115,910
22.	Total Liabilities and Equity	$168,333	$213,320	$288,803

Income Statement, Year Ended December 31 ($ Millions)

		2008	2009	2010
23.	Net Sales	$512,693	$553,675	$586,895
24.	Cost of Goods Sold	$405,803	$450,394	$499,928
25.	**Gross Profit**	**$106,889**	**$103,281**	**$86,967**
	Cost and Expenses:			
26.	Selling, Administration, and General Expenses	$50,643	$38,369	$46,034
27.	Depreciation	$4,781	$4,973	$6,120
28.	Miscellaneous Expenses	$6,082	$10,672	$17,174
29.	**Total Costs and Expenses**	**$49,233**	**$61,678**	**$73,937**
30.	**Earnings Before Interest and Taxes (EBIT)**	**$57,658**	**$41,602**	**$13,030**
	Less Interest Expense:			
	Interest on Short-Term Loans	$956	$1,683	$5,470
	Interest on Long-Term Loans	$1,913	$2,869	$2,869
	Interest on Mortgage	$779	$707	$636
31.	Total Interest Expense	$3,648	$5,258	$8,974
32.	**Earnings Before Taxes**	**$54,010**	**$36,343**	**$4,056**
33.	Income Taxes	$26,068	$17,589	$2,091
34.	Net Income	$27,943	$18,754	$1,965
35.	Dividends on Stock	$7,062	$4,463	$266
36.	Additions to Retained Earnings	$20,883	$14,291	$1,699

Liquidity Ratios

Liquidity ratios measure the quality and capability of current assets to meet maturing short-term obligations as they come due. Acceptable liquidity levels depend on economic and industry conditions, the predictability of cash flow, and the quality of assets making up liquidity ratios.

Current Ratio

Defined as current assets divided by current liabilities, this ratio is a commonly used measure of short-term solvency and debt service. Per the case study, Trudy Patterns' current ratio at year-end 2000 is:

Current Ratio = Current Assets/Current Liabilities
$$= \$240,264/\$137,187 = 1.75X$$

2008	2009	2010	Industry Average
3.05X	2.67X	1.75X	2.50%

The borrower's current ratio declined over the preceding three years, falling below the industry average. An account receivables buildup points to worsening aging in addition to increased possibilities of bad debt write-offs. Furthermore, inventory has increased. While some financial writers maintain that "high is best," the current ratio's magnitude means little if receivable and inventory qualities fall below acceptable levels.

Current Assets	
Cash	$11,717
Accounts Receivables	$88,571
Inventories	$139,976
Current Assets	$240,264
Current Liabilities	
Short-Term Loans	$55,198
Accounts Payable	$59,995
Accruals	$21,994
Current Liabilities	$137,187

Quick Ratio

A more conservative liquidity measure, the quick ratio (also know as the "acid test") depicts the borrower's short-term repayment ability. This ratio is generally considered to be a more accurate assessment of liquidity than the current ratio, since inventory reliance is lower. Here is Trudy Patterns' quick ratio:

Quick Ratio = Cash and Accounts Receivable/Current Liabilities
$$= (\$11,717 + \$88,571)/\$137,187 = 0.73X$$

2008	2009	2010	Industry Average
1.65X	1.08X	0.73X	1.00X

The firm's quick ratio has also declined over the preceding three years, dropping below the industry.

Activity or Turnover Ratios

Activity ratios, known also as efficiency or turnover ratios measure a firm's ability to convert different balance sheet accounts into cash or sales.

Average Collection Period

The average collection period (ACP) measures the time it takes to convert receivables into cash. Accounts receivable policy is closely allied to inventory management, since these represent the two largest current asset accounts. Of approximately equal magnitude, together they comprise almost 80% of current assets and over 30% of total assets for manufacturing industries. The ACP is influenced partly by economic conditions and partly by a set of controllable factors, which are called *internal* (management) factors. Internal factors include credit policy variables (liberal, balanced, or conservative credit policy), credit terms, sales discounts, and collection. From the case study, we have the following:

$$\mathbf{ACP} = (\mathbf{Accounts\ Receivables/Sales}) \times 365$$
$$= (\$88,571/\$586,895) \times 365 = 55\ \mathbf{days}$$

2008	2009	2010	Industry Average
37 days	37 days	55 days	32 days

Trudy Patterns' ACP has increased and is well above the industry. A short ACP generally equates to acceptable receivable quality, but only a receivables aging will confirm this outcome. In any case, the banker will determine the role management plays in influencing this ratio. For instance, if receivables slowed due to a sluggish economy, the industry average would be higher. This is not the case here.

Bad Debt Expense/Sales

The bad debt expense/sales ratio measures overall accounts receivable quality.[1]
* Is allowance for bad debt reasonable?
* Request that the borrower furnish specific client information.
* Compare the ratio over time. It may be that receivable problems are related to lax customer screening or the weak financial condition of your borrower's customers.

[1] We have not determined this ratio and a number of other ratios for Trudy Patterns, Inc., since not enough information was provided in the fiscal statements.

Inventory Turnover

How well does management control inventory? The inventory turnover measures the number of times inventory turns over fiscal to fiscal and is always benchmarked to the industry. Inventory control is essential to the overall cycle of cash flows and debt service, since redundant inventory points to unproductive investments carrying unacceptable returns.

Inventory control (and analysis) presumes a basic understanding of the interrelationship between raw materials, work in process, and finished goods. Investments in raw materials depend largely on anticipated production, seasonality, and reliability of suppliers. If raw material inventories are salable and commodity-like, inventory is more liquid than, say, work-in-process inventory. However, a buildup indicates price increases and/or shortages.

Work-in-process inventory deals with the length of the production cycle. Particulars include equipment efficiency factors, engineering techniques, and maintenance of highly skilled workers. Bankers watch for production slowdowns and manufacturing inefficiencies.

Finished goods involve coordinating production with anticipated sales. A buildup here is especially worrisome. If the consumer market avoids production output, how will loans be repaid? Again, referring to the Trudy Patterns example:

$$\textbf{Inventory Turnover (Cost)} = \textbf{Cost of Goods Sold/Inventory}$$
$$= \$499,928/\$139,976 = 3.6X$$

$$\textbf{Inventory Turnover (Sales)} = \textbf{Sales/Inventory} = \$586,895/\$139,976 = 4.2X$$

2008	2009	2010	Industry Average
7.1 X	4.5 X	3.6 X	5.7 X
9.0 X	5.6 X	4.2 X	7.0 X

(Cost and sales, respectively.)

The company's inventory turnover is substantially below the industry average and trending downward, suggesting (1) too much inventory is on hand, (2) actual liquidity may be worse than indicated (by the current ratio), and (3) inventory is obsolete and may have to be written off.

The Fixed Asset Turnover

Directing the firm's capital equipment policies is central to management's goal of maximizing shareholder's wealth. Investment in fixed assets decreases cash flow in the periods investments are made. As a result, cash generated by productive assets must offset initial investment outflows, producing a positive net present value. In other words, this ratio influences the sustainability of the firm's cash flow. For Trudy Patterns:

Fixed Asset Turnover = Sales/Net Fixed Assets = $\$586,895/\$139,976 = 12.1X$

2008	2009	2010	Industry Average
11.7X	12.0X	12.1X	12.1X

Trudy Patterns' fixed asset turnover is level with the industry. Let's review some clues that point to efficient fixed asset management. Large ratios suggest the following:

- The firm's efficient use of property, plant, and equipment has resulted in a high level of operating capacity.
- Merger and divestment activity has changed the composition and size of fixed assets on the consolidated balance sheet.
- The firm has increased its plant capacity, utilizing more of the machines already in place.
- Management has planned expansion programs, carefully using up-to-date capital budgeting techniques.
- Fixed assets required to maintain a degree of operating leverage and production efficiency were divested.

Working Capital Turnover

Working capital as defined by the literature is the excess of current assets over current liabilities—that is, cash and other liquid assets expected to be consumed or converted into cash within the accounting period over obligations due within the same period. It is a general measure of liquidity and represents the margin of protection short-term creditors expect. Working capital is essential for a company to meet its continuous operational needs. Its adequacy influences the firm's ability to meet its trade and short-term debt obligations, as well as to remain financially viable. From the case study, we see that Trudy Patterns' working capital turnover ratio is:

$$\textbf{Working Capital Turnover = Sales/Working Capital}$$
$$= \$586,895/\$103,077 = 5.6X$$

2008	2009	2010	Industry Average
6.2%X	5.3X	5.6X	4.5X

Total Asset Turnover

The total asset turnover ratio suggests how efficiently borrowers utilize capital or how many dollars of turnover are generated by each dollar of investment. Trudy Patterns' ratio is calculated as:

Total Asset Turnover = Sales/Total Assets = $\$586,895/\$288,803 = 2.0X$

2008	2009	2010	Industry Average
3.0X	2.5X	2.0X	2.8X

In 2010, asset turnover dipped significantly below the industry, implying that the borrower employed more assets per sales dollars versus the industry. A decline in this ratio points to lower asset productivity. With *fixed* assets turnover equal to the industry, problems in this business can be traced to poor current asset management and planning.

The Average Settlement Period

The average settlement period (ASP) ratio measures the length of time a company takes to pay creditors, or the number of times trade payables turn over in one year. It is figured as:

Average Payment Period $=$ Accounts Payable / Average Purchases Per Day

The higher the ratio, the shorter the time period between purchase and payment. If, for example, the firm's payables turned slower than the industry, some likely causes would be disputed invoices, received extended terms, deliberately expanded trade credit, or cash flow problems.

The ASP, or the day's payable, ratio is the payables measure typically utilized by bankers because sufficient information is available on fiscal statements. In most case, the choice of ratio will depend on the information available:

Accounts Payable Turnover $=$ Cost of Goods Sold/Accounts Payable

From the case study:

$$\text{Average Settlement Period (ASP)} = (\text{Accounts Payable/Cost of Goods Sold})$$
$$\times 365 = (\$59,995/\$499,928) \times 365 = 44 \text{ days}$$

2008	2009	2010	Industry Average
18 days	26 days	44 days	35 days

Profitability Ratios

Management's success in expense control, the ability to counter economic and industry downturns, plus a number of hybrid factors—quality, trend, and magnitude of the ratio's residual components—make up the important group of profitability ratios.

The Gross Profit Margin

The gross profit margin measures production success and is an integral part of the lending toolbox because it is especially adept at differentiating between temporary and structural problems. Were higher production costs successfully passed to consumers? Are raw material costs adequately controlled? Is the labor/machine mix optimal? Do production policies and methods measure favorably against benchmark firms? What is the degree of operating leverage? Operating leverage is an important constituent of this ratio. For example, to a physicist, *leverage*, implies raising a heavy object with a small force using a lever. In business, a high degree of operating leverage implies that relatively small changes in sales result in large changes in operating income.

In general, gross profit is calculated as:

Gross Profit = Net Sales − Cost of Goods Sold

where

Net Sales = Gross Sales − Returns, Allowances, Discounts

and

Cost of Goods Sold = Beginning Inventory + Purchases + Factory Labor +
Labor + Factory Depreciation + Freight In − Ending Inventory

Thus, from the case study, Trudy Patterns' gross profit margin is figured as:

Gross Profit Margin = Gross Profit/Net Sales = $80,847/$586,895 = 13.8%

2008	2009	2010	Industry Average
19.9%	17.7%	13.8%	18.0%

Obviously, its gross margin has fallen sharply and is significantly below the industry. The cause may be the result of a weak pricing policy, high production costs, or a combination of both. Gross profit troubles can usually be traced to poor asset management policies and operating leverage problems, which is very likely the case here.

Selling, General, and Administration Expenses/Sales

The ratio derived from selling, general, and administration expenses divided by sales measures management's ability to control costs not associated with production. Expenses that are higher than historical levels may be justified if accompanied by strong product demand. For example, outlays for advertising, promotion, and research expenditures promote sustainability of cash flows and thus directly influence share-holder value. Trudy Patterns' ratio turns out to be:

(Selling, General, Administration + Miscellaneous Expenses)/Net Sales
= ($50,643 + $17,174)/$586,895 = 11.5%

2008	2009	2010	Industry Average
8.7%	10.2%	13.8%	9.3%

Its expenses, including miscellaneous expenses, to sales are much higher than the industry norm. The firm's accountant included interest cost, meaning that this borrower's failure to reduce short-term debt has resulted in higher miscellaneous expenses.

Effective Tax Rate

The provision for income taxes excludes excise, Social Security, and sales taxes. You may want to compare this rate to the statutory tax rate and to the prior year's effective tax rate. For our Trudy Patterns example:

Effective Tax Rate = Income Taxes/Pretax Income = $2,091/$4056 = 51%

2008	2009	2010
48.3%	48.4%	51%

The Net Margin

An important yardstick of success, the net margin depicts the percentage of each sales dollar remaining after all expenses and taxes have been deducted. Trudy Patterns' net margin works out to be:

Net Margin = Net Income/Net Sales = $1,965/$586,895 = 0.35%

2008	2009	2010	Industry Average
5.5%	3.4%	0.39%	2.90%

The borrower's low margin reflects rising costs accompanied by lower than proportional increases in revenue. As a first step toward improving profitability, Trudy Patterns should attempt to increase revenue and/or decrease costs. If demand would allow higher prices, profitability could be increased through selective price increases. Otherwise, the firm would have to attempt to cut costs. The relatively high inventory might be responsible for greater storage costs, larger losses from trend changes, and other factors. Operating expenses might also be cut back. In addition, the low turnover indicates that this borrower is not utilizing assets efficiently. If higher sales cannot be produced to bring current assets into line, the firm should consider reducing assets, particularly inventory, which is twice as large as the industry average.

Return on Net Worth

Return on net worth provides the per dollar yield on investment to the equity holder. This ratio can be expressed as a function of the return on assets, the profit margin, and leverage. If returns are consistently below the risk-free rate of return, one would have to wonder why the business is operating. For Trudy Patterns:

$$\textbf{Return on Net Worth} = \textbf{Reported Net Income/Average Net Worth}$$
$$= \$1,965/\$115,910 = 1.7\%$$

2008	2009	2010	Industry Average
28.3%	16.7%	2.0%	17.5%

The firm's return to shareholders has fallen significantly and far below the average for the industry. The lower the ratio, the harder it will be for Trudy Patterns, Inc., to attract new funds. Investors are most interested in investing in companies with a strong ability to deliver on investments. Otherwise, why invest in Trudy Patterns when a treasury bill produces a higher return with no risk? Companies that generate low returns relative to new worth (or equity) are companies that fail to pay their owners even marginally, creating poor-quality asset levels for each dollar invested.

Return on Total Assets

Also called return on investment, or ROI, the return on total assets (ROTA) ratio measures how effectively a company employs its total assets. While the ratio calculates profitability of assets, it ignores asset composition and quality, and debt to equity mix. Using Trudy Patterns from the case study, we find:

$$\textbf{ROTA} = \textbf{Reported Net Income/Total Assets}$$
$$= \$1,965/\$288,803 = 0.68\%$$

2008	2009	2010	Industry Average
16.8%	8.9%	0.7%	8.8%

The ROTA ratio shows how much profit the firm made for every $1 invested in assets. The firm's results are disappointing. Poor current asset productivity, as evidenced by weak and deteriorating ACP and inventory turnover, is the primary cause of a continuously deteriorating ROTA.

Dividend Payout Ratio

The dividend payout ratio indicates the percentage of earnings paid out in dividends. For Trudy Patterns:

$$\textbf{Dividend Payout Ratio} = \textbf{Total Cash Dividends/Net Income}$$
$$= \$266/\$1965 = 13.5\%$$

2008	2009	2010	Industry Average
25.3%	23.8%	13.5%	27%

Dividends affect the relationship between debt and shareholder equity. Leverage will increase if a high dividend payout rate is financed by large debt infusions. Because dividends represent a use of cash (we see how this works in Chapter Six), bankers target this ratio when debt levels become too high. For example, a historically profitable borrower serving the entertainment industry began paying large dividends financed by bank loans. When the inevitable recession hit, the firm lacked the cash reserves and debt capacity to survive. The firm reduced its dividend but perhaps should have withheld distribution until liquidity and operating problems were resolved.

Leverage Ratios

The family of leverage ratios depicts the relationship between shareholders' funds (and reserves) and the total value of loans made to it. The higher the leverage (or gearing), the greater the proportion of borrowed money to the firm's "own" money. Highly leveraged borrowers, depending on industry demographics, face greater risk if profits abruptly dissipate, since interest and principle must be paid whether or not profits are there. How high leverage may increase without undermining the borrower's financial structure depends on numerous factors, including asset quality, cash flow coverage (of debt service), debt mix (short term versus long term), and sustainable operating and financial factors such as revenue growth and equity market values.

Unlike activity and profitability ratios, financial leverage is not something management necessarily wants to maximize, though asset returns or tax benefits may run higher. Strategic plans, at least the sound ones, aim at striking the right balance between the benefits of debt and the cost of risk.

Debt to Equity and Debt to Total Assets Ratios

The debt to equity ratio (also known as *debt ratio*) determines the relative use of borrowed funds. Debt levels vary according to the industry. For example, it is not uncommon for firms with highly liquid assets, like banks, to boast 9:1 debt to equity. In contrast, manufacturers tend to position leverage below 100%. Using the information from the case study, we find:

Total Debt/Stockholders Equity $= \$172,893/\$115,910 = 149.1\%$

Total Debt/Total Assets $= \$172,893/\$288,803 = 59.9\%$

2008	2009	2010	Industry Average
40.6%	46.5%	59.87%	50.0%

Trudy Patterns' debt levels have increased to above the industry. Taken in isolation, this occurrence is usually not a concern. However, this borrower's questionable asset quality together with an apparent imbalance between current and noncurrent liabilities, weak cash flow coverage, and unquestioned low equity value (in real terms) may well have pushed leverage beyond acceptable tolerance levels.

For another example, take the case of Bijou Furniture, a borrower that consolidated operations with a competitor to broaden market share. Based on (sales) projections, Bijou was able to finance the acquisition with loans. When sales dropped unexpectedly, the firm defaulted on its loans and was forced to sell assets at liquidation value to meet partial payments. The firm's banker might have avoided this headache had he considered the underlying mechanics of leverage ratios in general and the interdependence of leverage, return, and productively allied to this acquisition.

Times Interest Earned

The times interest earned ratio measures how far earnings drop before interest is not covered. This ratio is a weaker measure of debt coverage than the fixed charge and cash flow coverage ratios that follow. For Trudy Patterns, we calculate:

$$\textbf{Times Interest Earned} = \textbf{Earnings Before Interest and Taxes/Interest}$$
$$= \$13,030/\$8,973 = 1.4\text{X}$$

2008	2009	2010	Industry Average
15.8%	7.9%	1.4%	7.7X

The firm covers interest costs with only 1.4 times earnings. It appears that profits will not be available to make much of a dent paying down principle.

The Fixed Charge Coverage Ratio

The fixed charge coverage ratio is very similar to times interest earned. Adding the cost of annual long-term lease obligations to EBIT and dividing this number by the sum of interest charges plus lease obligations produces the result:

$$\textbf{Fixed Charge Coverage Ratio} = \textbf{EBIT}/(\textbf{Interest} + [\textbf{Principal Payment} +$$
$$\textbf{Lease Payments} + \textbf{Preferred Stock Dividend}])$$

This ratio can be particularly important for bankers that are lending to companies that negotiate long-term leases, since lease payments are both fixed and long term.

Debt Affordability Ratio

Cash inflows and outflows are two important determinants of debt affordability. Cash inflows equal operating income plus noncash expenses, while cash outflows pertain to financing costs.

Table 3.2 Simulation Result Trudy's Debt Service Coverage

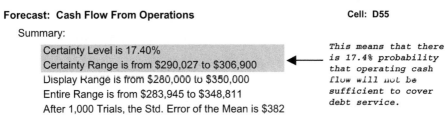

Forecast: Cash Flow From Operations   **Cell: D55**

Summary:

Certainty Level is 17.40%

Certainty Range is from $290,027 to $306,900

Display Range is from $280,000 to $350,000

Entire Range is from $283,945 to $348,811

After 1,000 Trials, the Std. Error of the Mean is $382

This means that there is 17.4% probability that operating cash flow will not be sufficient to cover debt service.

Debt Affordability Ratio = Cash Inflows/Cash Outflows

When debt affordability falls below 1, the firm might have taken on too much debt.

Cash Flow Coverage

One of the most important ratios in credit analysis, cash flow coverage describes the number of times operating cash flows cover debt service. Debt service includes interest and principle. The following example illustrates how computer simulations and cash flow coverage work together.

A builder took his construction plans to Hanover Multifactor Bank requesting $3 million of permanent financing at 9% interest for a 12-year term with a balloon payment due at the end. The constant payment including interest and principal would be 10.23%. The bank stipulated that the building's *operating cash flow* must be sufficient to cover *debt service* of $306,900 with *no less than a 98% probability*. While the builder's net worth statement revealed some liquidity, the bank did not feel comfortable that enough external funds were available to supplement the project's expected cash flow coverage ratio. Extracting the cash flow coverage section from the simulation output, Table 3.2 shows the bank determined that because cash flow coverage was good to only an 82.6% probability, short of the 98% required by Hanover Multifactor Bank, collateral and an escrow deposit were required. The customer agreed to the conditions, and the bank approved the loan.

We explore simulations in Chapters Seven and Eight, where we discuss the Monte Carlo simulation, working with a range of results and confidence levels. The principle behind the Monte Carlo process is the simulation of real-world situations involving elements of uncertainty that are too complex to be solved analytically.

Growth Ratios

While strong sales and profit growth rates are generally comforting to lenders, they may well be chimeric. Is growth "real" or illusionary? Are inflationary factors or noncash credits propelling fiscal results? Are revenues sustainable?

Sales Growth Rate

$$\text{Sales Growth Rate} = (\text{Sales}_t - \text{Sales}_{t-1})/\text{Sales}_{t-1}$$
$$= (\$586,895 - \$553,675)/\$553,675 = 6.0\%$$

2009	2010	Industry Average
8.0%	6.0%	9.5%

Profit Growth Rate

$$\text{Profit Growth Rate} = (\text{Profit}_t - \text{Profit}_{t-1})/\text{Profit}_{t-1}$$
$$= (\$586,895 - \$553,675)/\$553,675 = 6.0\%$$

2009	2010	Industry Average
-32.9%	-89.5%	11.5%

Valuation Ratios

Valuation ratios extend beyond historical cost-based accounting and offer a more realistic depiction of the real value of borrowers.

Book Value per Share/Market Range

If shares trade far below book, a new equity offering may well result in dilution of existing shares. The questions arise: "Why is market perception of the worth so low? Are assets overstated in terms of their true net worth?"

$$\text{Book Value per Share} = \text{Common Equity}/\text{Number of Common Shares Outstanding}$$

The market range is disclosed in annual reports, in newspapers, or on the Internet.

Price/Earnings

The price/earnings (P/E) ratio divides the stock price by the previous four quarters' earnings. For instance, if a firm was trading at $10 a share, and $1.00 in trailing earnings per share, P/E is 15X:

$$\$15 \text{ share price}/\$1.00 \text{ training EPS} = 15 \text{ P/E}$$

The P/E ratio is an important loan ratio because a borrower's stock price centers on the market's perception of future performance, whereas reported earnings are tied to the past and are influenced by opinions of auditors. There are many permutations of P/Es using forecasted or trailing 12 months' earnings.

Borrowers may report low earnings yet produce impressive values because they are engaged in extensive research and product development or are recent entrants into high-growth industries. It may be a good idea to establish industry homogeneity, since industry distortions can and do occur.

Price/Sales

The price/sales ratio takes the current market capitalization of firms and divides the result by the last 12 months' trailing revenues. The market capitalization is the current market value of a company, arrived at by multiplying the current share price by the shares outstanding.

Liquidation Valuation Approach

One of the most important measures in any banker's ratio toolbox, the market value/liquidation value ratio focuses on the relationship between book/market equity value and liquidation/cash flow values. Management's decision to divest a business unit can often be tied to these spreads. A. C. Hax and N. S. Majluf are proponents of the market value/liquidation value ratio.[2] They suggest that business units destroy value if liquidation value falls below ongoing cash flow value, and corporate resources could be better served elsewhere. These operations represent "cash traps" that end up draining resources from other more successful business segments. Under such conditions, divestiture might be the most logical choice if the bank's exposure is to be salvaged.

Statistical Analysis of Ratios: Decomposition Analysis

Decomposition analysis builds on the theory that little in finance is left to chance. Management is constantly faced with exogenous forces tugging at their firms, and it must continuously shift assets and financial resources to counter these forces and preserve cash flow equilibrium. It is the extent, or magnitude, of statistical "shifting around" that corroborates decomposition.[3] Equilibrium relationships in business organizations, suggested Baruch Lev, are usually the result of economic optimality criteria designed to improve efficiency and maximize value. Thus, for every level of activity there exists "optimal relationships between labor and capital inputs, inventory and sales, cash and short-term securities, debt and equity capital."[4] Management

---

[2] Arnoldo C. Hax and Nicolas Majluf, *Strategic Management: An Integrative Perspective*, Prentice Hall, 1984.

[3] Baruch Lev, "Decomposition Measures for Financial Analysis," *Financial Management*, Vol. 2, No. 1 (Spring 1973), pp. 56–63. See also Lev's *Financial Statement Analysis: A New Approach*, Prentice Hall, 1974.

[4] Ibid.

allocation decisions in the face of exogenous economic and market forces are reflected in financial statements.

Decomposition made it possible to measure the degree of stability that firms have been able to sustain in an often volatile marketplace—inherent in the mix and volatility of their financial statements over time. Variations over time in the relationship among financial statements items shadow significant business events, planned and unplanned, and are thus crucial to lenders engaged in assessing future performance. Lev studied the application of decomposition analysis to a wide range of administration and social science areas, including economics, sociology, psychology, and accounting. Statistical decomposition of financial reports is especially suited for the analysis of mass data such as large computer files of financial statements.

Decomposition Analysis of Trudy Patterns, Inc., Balance Sheet

The application of decomposition analysis to Trudy Patterns' balance sheet is discussed here.

	Absolute Value			Relative Value		
	2008	2009	2010	2008	2009	2010
Cash and Cash Items	$15,445	$12,007	$11,717	0.092	0.056	0.041
Accounts Receivable	$51,793	$55,886	$88,571	0.308	0.262	0.307
Inventories	$56,801	$99,087	$139,976	0.337	0.464	0.485
Net Fixed Assets	$44,294	$46,340	$48,539	0.263	0.217	0.168
Total Assets	$168,333	$213,320	$288,803	1.000	1.000	1.000

Lev designates the earlier relative values by pi, where $i = 1 \ldots n$. In Trudy's case for 2009, p1 (cash) $= .056$, p2 (receivables) $= .262$, and so on, and $n = 4$. The corresponding values of a later financial statement are qi, where q1 $= .041$, q2 $= .307$, and so on. The asset composition measure is defined by Lev as:

$$IA = n \sum i = I, \text{ qi log qi/pi}$$

Trudy Patterns' decomposition measure for 2009/2010 was calculated as follows:

$$IA = .041 \log e .041/.056 + .307 \log e .307/.262 + .485 \log e .385/.464 +$$
$$.168 \log e .368/.217 = 0.01252 \text{ nits}^5$$

Asset Decomposition Measures (in 10^{-4} nits)

	2006/2007	2007/2008	2008/2009	2009/2010
Trudy Patterns	352	392	372	**125**
Industry Average (Assumed)	125	165	140	**153**

---

[5] Lev's term meaning "decomposition units."

The instability of assets during 2009/2010 reflects, once again, Trudy's serious inventory and accounts receivable problems. That decomposition measures reflect the occurrence of important events worthy of investigation is supported by several studies, which empirically established an association between certain key business events and decomposition measures. The point remains, according to some studies, financially distressed firms had, for at least five years before bankruptcy, substantially larger balance sheet decomposition measures (shifts) than those of comparable solvent firms.

First Central Bank's Credit Decision Re: Trudy Patterns, Inc.

While Trudy Patterns, Inc., has been a customer of the bank for some years, the operations have deteriorated over the last three years. If the trend continues, the company could end up insolvent, with First Central Bank writing off its investment. The bank would not retreat to a status quo position of inaction but instead cajoled Trudy Patterns' management into correcting operating and liquidity problems.

Trudy Patterns has the potential for raising an additional $37,118 by liquidating redundant accounts receivables and $52,269 through reduction of inventories. Reductions in these working capital accounts could not be achieved overnight, but assuming inventories are salable and the accounts receivable collectible, it should be possible for the firm to generate cash from these sources and reduce the bank's exposure.

First Central first estimated the dollar amount of "over-the-limit" receivables by (1) setting the ACP (in the formula) equal to the industry average, (2) including the firm's fiscal sales, and (3) solving for accounts receivable. The result: pro forma receivables, assuming collections had been industry efficient. The difference between year-end and pro forma receivables represents additional cash that could have been used to pay down the loan as depicted by the following accounts receivable pro forma analysis:

1. Determine the additional cash inflows likely by reducing the ACP.
2. ACP = (Accounts Receivable/Sales) × 365
3. Insert industry collection period, 32 days, into the formula: 32 = (Accounts Receivable)/ $586,895) × 365
4. Solve for accounts receivables in (3): (Accounts Receivables/586,895) × 365; Accounts Receivables = $51,453
5. Determine pro forma cash available:

Fiscal Accounts Receivable	$88,571
minus Pro Forma Accounts Receivable	$51,453
Cash Available by Reducing Collection Time Industry Average	**$37,118**

If inventories could be reduced to the average level for the industry, this reduction would provide the firm with approximately \$52,269 in receivables and/or cash as seen in the following inventory pro forma analysis:

$$\textbf{Fiscal Inventory Turnover (Cost)} = \textbf{Cost of Goods Sold/Inventory}$$
$$= \$499,928/\$139,976 = 3.6$$

Industry Average: 5.7

1. Set the inventory turnover to the industry average; include Trudy Patterns' sales and solve for inventory:

$$\textbf{Industry Inventory Turnover (Cost)} = \textbf{Cost of Goods Sold/Inventory 5.7}$$
$$= \$499,928/\text{Inventory};$$

Pro Forma Inventory = \$87,707

2. Solve for inventory to obtain pro forma inventory:

Fiscal Inventory	\$139,976
Receivable and Cash Available to Gem If Inventory Converted as Fast as Industry	\$87,707
Additional Cash or Accounts Receivable Available	**\$52,269**

The bank decided to extend the full amount of the credit but placed a lien on receivables and enforced a tight repayment plan. Trudy Patterns, Inc., agreed to reduce inventories and accounts receivable to inventory levels over the next 12 months. The plan called for selling off inventories by cutting sale prices and increasing advertising expenditures while at the same time cutting back production. The company agreed to follow a "get-tough" policy on collecting tardy receivables, and improved production control measures were enacted immediately to help the gross profit margin recover. These practices paid off, and the company met the scheduled loan payments.

4 Credit Analysis of Seasonal Businesses: An Integrated Approach

Lenders deciding to approve or renew seasonal loans weigh the obligor's financial condition, bank relationship (including deposit balances), and payment history. Most seasonal loans are unsecured; risks include the borrower's inability to meet scheduled maturities, the loss of principal and interest, and the possibility of conversion to "evergreen credit," which locks the bank into the credit for many years.

Seasonal loans are self-liquidating and provide short-term working capital (WC) needs by financing seasonal increases in receivables and inventory (see Chapter Five: Asset-Based Lending). The liquidation, or cash conversion/contraction, process retires the loan at the season's end, which is one good reason banks actively seek seasonal loans. Seasonal firms typically finance seasonal WC by purchasing raw materials on credit from suppliers, creating accounts payable and thus easing cash needs.

Types of Seasonal Businesses

The following are some examples of "seasonal" businesses:

- Jewelry retailers, bookstores, and toy distributors increase sales markedly just before the holiday season. Retail department stores and candy retailers follow the same pattern. Garden

Credit Engineering for Bankers. DOI: 10.1016/B978-0-12-378585-5.10004-1

outlets, sporting goods stores, and home lumber dealers experience peak sales during the warm spring and summer months.

- Retail businesses use seasonal loans to support swings in sales activity. Clothing stores anticipate increases in volume in the spring and again in the fall as new lines arrive. Retail firms borrow heavily during the Christmas and Easter seasons to carry increased inventories and accounts receivable.
- Steel operations on the Great Lakes usually build iron ore inventories during the summer months to supply their needs through the winter when lake freighters cannot transport raw materials because of inclement weather.
- Swimsuit manufacturers start producing bathing suits in the fall for spring distribution to retailers. During the manufacturing phase, inventories build, along with labor, overhead, and other product costs. In the spring, swimsuits are sold. Shortly thereafter, receivables fall due, with proceeds providing the annual (loan) cleanup.
- Building contractors achieve higher levels of production when the weather is favorable.
- Forest products producers build substantial log inventories to keep production plants supplied with raw materials during the seasons when logging operations are limited.
- Coal and fuel oil dealers build inventories during the summer months, running them off steadily in the fall and winter to a low point by early spring.
- Food processors use short-term credit lines to finance crops grown and shipped during specific seasons. Short-term financing supports fertilizer and other production costs and the distribution and marketing of crops during the harvesting season.
- Fish canneries require high seasonal inventory to complete processing.

Successful and Unsuccessful Seasonal Cycles

Typical seasonal companies go through five stages (Figure 4.1):

1. *Buildup Period:* During buildup, cash deposits drop, whereas loan balances, trade payables, and inventory increase. The balance sheet begins to expand.
2. *High Point:* As the season reaches its high point of activity, inventory, bank debt, and trade payables peak. Liquidity bottoms out and receivables remain low. The balance sheet reaches expansion limits.

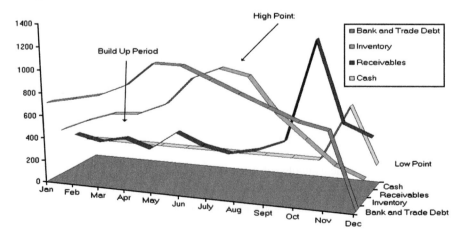

Figure 4.1 Successful Seasonal Conversion.

3. *Conversion Cycle Begins:* At the beginning of the conversion cycle, inventory decreases and receivables increase as demand strengthens. Payables and bank debt remain steady or decline slightly. The balance sheet moves in tandem with the reduction in liabilities.

4. *Conversion Cycle Intensifies:* As the conversion cycle intensifies, shipments accelerate, causing inventory to decline quickly and receivables to build further. Demand deposits rise but at a slower rate as some receivables convert to cash. Payables and short-term loans begin to fall faster as collections are converted into cash. Balance sheet contraction moves in tandem with cash conversion.

5. *Conversion Cycle Subsides:* As the seasonal low point approaches, the conversion cycle subsides. Firms ship very little merchandise. Inventory is already at low levels, and receivables decline quickly because the conversion process causes deposits to swell. The balance sheet fully contracts to its low point as trade payables and bank debt are retired or cleaned up. After the "traditional 30 days" have passed, renewed debt replenishes the account in preparation for the next season.

Sometimes things go wrong for a seasonal business and its inventories have not been sold. At season's end these obligors may not have the cash available to zero out credit lines. The process generally follows a repetitive pattern in which the conversion cycle ultimately fails (Figure 4.2):

1. *Buildup Period:* During buildup, demand deposits drop and loan balances, trade payables, and inventory increase. The balance sheet starts expanding. So far, so good.

2. *High Point:* As the firm reaches its high point, inventory, bank debt, and trade payables peak. Liquidity requirements abate, receivables remain low, and the balance sheet reaches expansion limits. Still no signs of problems.

3. *Conversion Cycle Fails:* Canceled bookings, goods that are shipped late, production breakdowns, and the evaporation of consumer demand all mark failed seasons and the failure of the conversion cycle. As a result, inventory is stuck at high levels, and receivables and cash bottom out. With low cash balances, seasonal borrowers find it difficult or impossible to repay suppliers and short-term lenders.

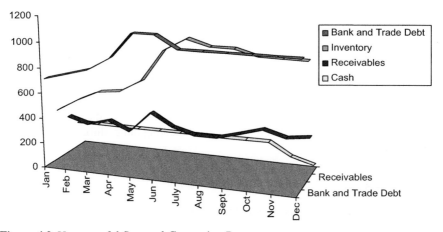

Figure 4.2 Unsuccessful Seasonal Conversion Process.

An Example of a Successful Season

In part due to heavy inventory requirements during peak season, seasonal borrows are traditionally undercapitalized. Morton Toy Company typically receives orders for the bulk of its sales during the summer months. Shipments of orders are expected in October, November, and December—just in time for the start of the holiday rush. Since Morton manufactures most of its product line before the shipping period, short-term bank loans are used to finance raw material buildup. As toys are delivered to retailers during the fall months, the firm experiences higher receivable levels as inventory is sold. After the holiday season has ended, inventory and receivables decline as deposits increase. Cash is used to pay down short-term bank loans and payables. As long as the firm sells inventory, debt and equity levels normalize by fiscal close, and the firm's short-term undercapitalized position is only that: *temporary*.

Another Example of a Successful Season

Gem Lawn Furniture closes its books on August 31. During late summer and fall, Gem purchases raw materials, the bulk of which are forest product derivatives, and seasonal borrowing begins. Labor and other manufacturing costs increase in late fall and early winter, pushing borrowings to a high point. By late winter, demand accelerates with products shipped from warehouses to distribution channels. Inventories reduce, while receivables increase. With production at or near a low point, Gem's credit line levels off. By early summer, receivables and bank debt begin running off, the result of cash collections. At the close of books on August 31, inventories and receivables are reduced to their annual low point, and seasonal debt is retired.

The successful conversion/contraction flow experienced by Gem may not have occurred if short-term debt were used to finance long-term, or core, assets (as opposed to WC assets) because the firm would be forced to use cash to pay two short-term loans simultaneously. Long-term, or core, assets should be financed with long-term debt (match funding) to preserve the WC required for the annual seasonal cleanup. Core assets (nonseasonal) are, in actuality, a firm's nerve center in that they are its most direct route to sustainable cash flows and shareholder value. Again, core assets should be supported by liabilities of similar duration; short-term debt used to finance core assets could easily result in seasonal liquidity problems.

Techniques for Evaluating Seasonal Lending

Seasonal loan techniques are central to lending due diligence. They mean investigation/ analysis into relevant facets of the credit, that is – "thinking things through" and "doing one' homework".

Cash Budgets

One of the most effective tools used to derive peak short-term financing requirements is the cash budget. Cash budgets usually span short periods—monthly, quarterly, semiannually, annually—but management will also use cash budgets to help focus on long-term horizons—2, 5, or 10 years. Short-term budgets pinpoint both borrowings required and timing of repayments. Cash budgets do the following:

- *Provide lenders with a way to monitor seasonal activity.* For example, if *actual* cash receipts fall below *planned* receipts, bankers may assume that management either missed revenue targets or that the goals were unrealistic to begin with.
- *Help determine appropriate credit lines or loan ceilings.* Lenders typically set credit lines roughly equal to the highest cash deficit revealed in the budget.
- *Spot months in which bankers can reasonably expect loan reductions.* If additional draw-downs replace loan repayments, inventory likely did not move satisfactorily.
- *Identify wayward deployment of seasonal advances.* For example, if a borrower suffered a fiscal loss and plans excessive dividends, the loan may be used to line investors' pockets and *not* placed to finance seasonal WC. Firms have also been known to fund the activities of affiliates or management-sponsored investments out of loans the bankers intended for the purchase of inventory.
- *Work as quasi-marketing tools.* For instance, capital expenditures normally call for large outlays during the budget period. If banks spot anticipated outlays early enough, they might encourage term loans or other facilities before clients approach competing banks or leasing companies.

A cash budget (Table 4.1) can be prepared by following these steps:

1. Set up a matrix that includes both historical and forecast sales by month. Data can be extracted from the obligor's projected sales budget, which projects the expected monthly sales in units and selling price per unit.
2. Next, calculate credit sales as a percentage of total sales. From Table 4.1, we see that Acme sells $80% on credit.
3. Subtract credit sales from total sales to arrive at credit sales.
4. Next, develop an accounts receivable aging from historical experience and expectations. For example, in Table 4.1, Acme expects 25% of the present month's credit sales will be collected in the current month, as well as 5% of the prior month's credit sales to be collected in the current month.
5. Enter the expected collections in the budget you developed from the aging.
6. Enter total cash inflows.
7. Develop the cash disbursement for purchases schedule following the same method used to find cash receipts from sales.
8. Enter total cash inflows.
9. Juxtapose total cash inflows with outflows.
10. Complete a Cumulative (Financial Needs) Surplus Zero Balance Account Matrix. This schedule assumes that the firm keeps no minimum balance and that First City Bank will automatically finance all overdrafts.
11. Complete the cash budget assuming Acme requires a minimum $900 transactions cash in its demand deposit account at all times.

Trial Balance and Break-Even Inventory

Trial balances take snapshots of general ledger accounts for assets, liabilities, and owner's equity during any point in the season. To detect liquidity problems that stem

Table 4.1 Acme's Cash Budget

Acme Toy Company
Cash Budget
31-Mar-94
(in 000's up to decimal point)

		Actual Sales			**Forecasted Sales**					
		December	*January*	*February*	*March*	*April*	*May*	*June*	*July*	*August*	*September*
Total Sales		900.00	900.00	1,800.00	2,250.00	2,700.00	3,600.00	5,400.00	5,400.00	2,700.00	1,800.00
Credit Sales		45.00	63.00	90.00	180.00	225.00	450.00	1,575.00	1,575.00	135.00	45.00
Cash Sales						2,475.00	3,150.00	3,825.00	3,825.00	2,565.00	1,755.00
First Month (A)						56.25	112.50	393.75	393.75	33.75	11.25
Second Month (B)						9.00	11.25	22.50	78.75	78.75	6.75
Third Month(C)						36.90	73.80	92.25	184.50	645.75	645.75
Fourth Month (D)						5.67	8.10	16.20	20.25	40.50	141.75
Total Cash Receipts Forecasted from Sales						2,582.82	3,355.65	4,349.70	4,502.25	3,363.75	2,560.50
and Collections											
(A) Percent of Current Month's Credit Sales	25.00%										
(B) Percent of Prior Month's Credit Sales	5.00%										
(C) Percent of Second Prior Month Credit Sales	41.00%										
(D) Percent of Third Prior Months Credit Sales	9.00%										
Total Cash Receipts Forecasted from Sales and Collections						2,582.82	3,355.65	4,349.70	4,502.25	3,363.75	2,560.50
Cash Dividends Received						45.00			45.00		
Disposals								540.00			
Interest						9.00	9.00	9.00	9.00	9.00	9.00
Total Cash Inflow						2,636.82	3,364.65	4,898.70	4,556.25	3,372.75	2,569.50
Cash Disbursements for Purchases											
		Actual Purchases				**Forecasted Purchases**					
		December	*January*	*February*	*March*	*April*	*May*	*June*	*July*	*August*	*September*
Total		2,700.00	2,700.00	1,350.00	900.00	900.00	900.00	450.00	225.00	225.00	270.00
Credit		1,800.00	1,800.00	1,350.00	900.00	900.00	900.00	225.00	45.00	45.00	90.00
Cash						0.00	0.00	225.00	180.00	180.00	180.00
Payment											
First Month (A)						225.00	225.00	56.25	11.25	11.25	22.50
Second Month (B)						558.00	558.00	558.00	139.50	27.90	27.90
Third Month (C)						148.50	99.00	99.00	99.00	24.75	4.95
Fourth Month (D)						27.00	20.25	13.50	13.50	13.50	3.38
Total Cash Disbursements Forecasted from Purchases						958.50	902.25	951.75	443.25	257.40	238.73
(A) Percent d Current Month's Credit Purchases	25.00%										
(B) Percent of Prior Month's Credit Purchases	62.00%										
(C) Percent of Second Prior Month's Credit Purchases	11.00%										
(D) Percent d Third Prior Months Credit Purchases	1.50%										
Total Cash Disbursements						*April*	*May*	*June*	*July*	*August*	*September*
Selling Expenses						958.50	902.25	951.75	443.25	257.40	238.73
General and Administration Expenses						765.00	900.00	1,080.00	1,080.00	540.00	360.00
Taxes: Income						1,350.00	1,620.00	1,530.00	1,350.00	1,350.00	1,350.00
Taxes: Witholding						126.00			126.00		
Pensions						90.00	90.00	90.00	90.00	90.00	90.00
Dividends						45.00		45.00		45.00	
Funded Debt Payments						63.00			63.00		
Total Cash Outflow						450.00			450.00		
						3,847.50	3,512.25	3,696.75	3,602.25	2,282.40	2,038.73
Juxtaposing Total Cash Inflows to Total Cash Outflows:											
						April	*May*	*June*	*July*	*August*	*September*
Total Cash In						2,636.82	3,364.65	4,898.70	4,556.25	3,372.75	2,569.50
Total Cash Out						3,847.50	3,512.25	3,696.75	3,602.25	2,282.40	2,038.73
Net Cash Available						(1,210.68)	(147.60)	1,201.95	954.00	1,090.35	530.78
Cummulative Cash Available						(1,210.68)	(1,358.28)	(156.33)	797.67	1,888.02	2,418.80

Thus, Acme Toy Company will require $1,210,680 in cash in April and $147,600 in May, looking
to its own cash and marketable securities account. This assumes that the cash and marketable
securities account on March 31, is $900 and the firm needs $900 in cash to operate. It is
obvious that the firm does not need a credit line of $7.5 million originally as requested. A credit
line of $1.5 million to 2 million appears to satisfy the requirements of the budget. ATC needs
to borrow from utside sources as follows:

						April	*May*	*June*	*July*	*August*	*September*
Net Cash Available						(1,210.68)	(147.60)	1,201.95	954.00	1,090.35	530.78
Cash Balance Available (Balance March 31)						900.00	(310.68)	(458.28)	743.67	1,697.67	2,788.02
Cummulative (Financial Needs) Surplus Zero Balance Account						(310.68)	(458.28)	743.67	1,697.67	2,788.02	3,318.80
Minimum Cash Balance						900.00	900.00	900.00	900.00	900.00	900.00
Cummulative (Fancial Needs) Minimum Balance Account						(1,210.68)	(1,358.28)	(156.33)	797.67	1,888.02	2,418.80

from inventory devaluations (write-downs) and compromise repayment, lenders use the break-even inventory method derived from a trial balance. Trouble can surface quickly—two or three months down the season—often on the heels of disappointing bookings. At this point in time, inventory value usually falls below recorded book value.

Trial balances are associated with the *periodic* inventory method—inventory counted and valued at the lower of cost or market periodically—as opposed to the *perpetual* inventory system, whereby inventory is counted and valued frequently. Because ending inventory determines the cost of goods sold and, ultimately, profits, bankers should know the inventory value *throughout* the season. Examples of perpetual inventory include items scanned into the computer a shopper sees at the checkout and high-ticket items painstakingly monitored. Of the two methods, periodic inventory is more uncertain, rendering seasonal analysis indefinable at best, if not nigh impossible unless break-even techniques are effectively employed.

Though accountants have not appraised inventory value, assuming *periodic* inventory, management certainly has; otherwise, how could they not know if inventory is reduced to fire-sale values? Thus, lenders derive break-even inventory by first asking management for estimated *lower of cost or market inventory* values. They then figure spreads between the two: break-even and estimated. For example, if the inventory *required* to break even is $700,000 and management's *estimated* inventory is $300,000, a net loss for the period is derived at $400,000. *Interim losses caused by large devaluations reduce the chances of a debt cleanup.* What is the logic? Write-downs follow production problems, poor strategic planning, stockpiling, canceled orders, overly optimistic sales projections, and flawed cash budgets.

Seasonal Ratio Analysis

Seasonal ratios are analyzed on a comparative basis and summarized in what is referred to as the "write-up" (see the case study at the end of this chapter). The ratios include the following:

> *(Cash + Accounts Receivable)/(Short-Term Bank Debt + Trade Payables).* Near the seasonal low point, cash and receivables should be sufficient to reduce short-term debt and trade payables.
>
> *Returns and Allowances/Gross Sales.* High returns and allowances to gross sales ratios may be due to merchandise allowances, defective lines, or missed seasons. Have returns been reshipped on a timely basis? Holdover goods postseason are usually written down.
>
> *Purchases/Sales.* A high purchases to sales ratio points to saturated inventory, or it may just be the result of normal gearing up in anticipation of strong orders.

Break-Even Shipments

The break-even shipments (BES) technique derives shipments (gross sales) needed to break even. Shipments must be sufficient to cover production and operating expenses for both shipping (forecast) periods and buildup (historical) months in order for the obligor to produce fiscal profits. BES is best used a few months before the season's end because minimal sales occur early in the cycle. Some successful seasons are chronicled by late, brief selling, culminating in excellent shipping months just prior to fiscal. Christmas ornament manufacturers, for example, ship very late in the season, with profits during these months offsetting losses that come with production. The following equation derives BES:

$$S_b = E_i/(G_i)(1 - R_i)$$

S_b must be compared to S_e, the value of shipments the company expects to ship (the estimated shipments) over the period being analyzed. If $S_e > S_b$, results will be profitable; if $S_e < S_b$, losses will result; and if $S_e = S_b$, break even is achieved.

Example of Break-Even Shipments

A firm provides the following information for the month of April:

> Estimated gross profit margin is 35%.
> Estimated shipments are $500,000.
> Returns allowances and discounts are 10% of gross sales.
> Expected expenses are $200,000.

Can we expect a profit or loss based on the data given?
   Solution

$$S_b = E_i/(G_i)(1 - R_i) = \frac{200,000}{(.35)(1 - .10)} = \$634,900$$

Compare S_b to S_e. Since the estimated shipments (S_e) of $500,000 fall below break even (S_b) of $634,900, the firm can expect a loss during the month of April.

Early Warning Signs of Trouble

While storm signals come in all shapes and sizes, the big question is, are problems temporary or structural? You be the judge:

- Slow in-house orders in comparison to corresponding periods in previous years.
- Factory operating well below capacity.
- Changes in the manner payables are paid.
- Owners no longer take pride in their business.
- Frequent visits to the customer's place of business reveal deteriorating general appearance of the premises. For example, rolling stock and equipment have not been properly maintained.
- Loans to or from officers and affiliates.
- Management does not know what condition the company is in and the direction in which it is headed.
- The lender did not examine the obligor's cash budget and consequently overestimated seasonal peaks and valleys, resulting in approval of an excessive loan.
- Inability to clean up bank debt or cleanups affected by rotating bank debt.
- Unusual items in the financial statements.
- Negative trends such as losses, weak gross margins, slowness in accounts receivable, and decrease in sales volume.
- Intercompany payables/receivables are not adequately explained.

- Cash balances reduce substantially or are overdrawn and uncollected during normally liquid periods.
- Management fails to take trade discounts because of poor inventory turnover.
- Cash flow problems resulting in very low probabilities of operating cash flows covering debt service.
- Withholding tax liability builds as taxes are used to pay other debt.
- Frequent "downtiering" of financial reporting sparked in an effort to bring on a more "liberal" accountant.
- Changes in financial management.
- Totals on receivables and payables aging schedules do not agree with amounts shown on the balance sheet of the same date.
- At the end of the cycle, creditors are not completely paid out. The bank sometimes can be paid out when the borrower leans on the trade. (This action often gives bankers a false sense of security, but the company may be unable to borrow from the trade for the next buildup of inventory.)
- Sharp reduction in officers' salaries brings a lower standard of living home and might suggest a last-ditch effort to save a distressed business. Alternatively, reduced salaries might signal a concerted effort to make headway.
- Erratic interim results signaling a departure from normal and historical seasonal patterns.
- The lender does not allow enough cushion for error. If the seasonal loan is not repaid and there is no other way out but liquidation of the collateral, the lender is taking possession of collateral at the worst possible time. It is the end of the season, and if the obligor cannot sell, how will the bank?
- Financials are submitted late in an attempt by management or their accountants to postpone unfavorable news.
- Unwillingness to provide budgets, projections, or interim information.
- Suppliers cut back terms or request Cash on Delivery.
- Changes in inventory, followed by an excessive inventory buildup or the retention of obsolete merchandise.
- The borrower changes suppliers frequently, or transient buying results in higher raw materials costs.
- Increased inventory to one customer or perilous reliance on one account.
- Changing concentration from a major well-known customer to one of lesser stature, pointing to problem inventory. A good mix of customers is the best defense against "seasonal shock therapy."
- The lender permits advances on the seasonal loan to fund other purposes, notably payments on the bank's own term debt. Indeed, the term debt is handled as agreed, but the seasonal loan goes up and stays up.
- Company loses an important supplier or customer.
- Concentrations in receivables and payables. Failure to get satisfactory explanations on these concentrations. Failure to conduct investigations on the creditworthiness of larger receivables.
- The lender finances highly speculative inventory whereby the borrower is trying for a "home run."
- Intangible signals such as failure to look the banker in the eye, letting the condition of the business deteriorate, or taking longer to return calls.
- Management orders three-pound lobsters during a banker's lunch because the bank is picking up the check and because in the coming days they won't be able to afford such a meal themselves; the firm has just gone off a cliff.

Defensive Measures

Prudently structured credits fall back on a second way out, or, as the literature defines it, a good exit strategy. The bank may decide to restructure the credit—that is, extend a term loan or revolver to be repaid over the next few years out of operating cash flows. A loan agreement, by virtue of its covenants and events of default, will give the bank greater control over the credit. Consider these important factors:

- *Cash Flow.* Strong cash flows are crucial to debt service. If an established seasonal borrower boasts a solid track record, the bank can afford to be generous. This year's temporary problems may be corrected with strong cash flow returning over the next year or two. However, if cash flow expectations are bleak, the banker can expect a series of chronic structural problems.
- *Equity Injection.* Owners may be asked to inject cash in the form of subordinated debt or straight equity if profits cannot sustain the capital structure or if assets are poorly utilized.
- *Formula-Based Advances.* Owners may be required to make formula-based advances against confirmed orders, or asset liens may work on a temporary basis.
- *Credit Insurance.* Insurance against excessive losses may be assigned to the bank. However, if the business is in trouble, credit insurance will be unavailable or prohibitively expensive.

Working Capital as a Defensive Measure

Broadly defined, *working capital* is the excess of current assets over current liabilities. It is cash and other assets expected to be consumed or converted into cash over the accounting period less obligations due during the same period. WC is a generic measure of liquidity acting as the margin of protection that short-term creditors look to behind conversion of current assets (the primary source of payment). In short, a basic understanding of WC mechanics (and cash flow) provides lenders with a way to differentiate between temporary and structural problems.

Cash Flow versus Working Capital Analysis

A cash flow is more refined than a WC analysis and should always be used to evaluate loans with maturities beyond one year. However, WC concepts are much more direct and perfectly suited for seasonal ("what's my second way out?") analysis.

Mechanics of Working Capital

Simple, very useful WC math crystallizes the flow funds approach and points the way to the second way out of the credit. Table 4.2 lists the seven equations needed to prove that WC concepts lie beyond simple differences between current assets and liabilities.

From Equation (6) we see that subtracting the noncurrent accounts of two balance sheets is equal to WC. Thus, increases in noncurrent liabilities, increases in equity, and reductions in noncurrent assets represent sources of funds. Conversely, decreases

Table 4.2 The Arithmetic of Working Capital (WC)

Equation	Equation Defined	Explanation
1	Assets = Liabilities + Equity	Basic accounting equation.
2	WC = Current Assets − Current Liabilities	Traditional definition of WC.
3	Current Assets + Fixed Assets = Current Liabilities + Fixed Liabilities + Equity	Equation (1) expanded.
4	Current Assets − Current Liabilities = Fixed Liabilities + Equity − Fixed Assets	Rearrange current accounts to the left of the equals sign and noncurrent accounts to the right.
5	WC = Fixed Liabilities + Equity − Fixed Assets	Substitution: Equation (2) equals Equation (4).
6	ΔWC = ΔFixed Liabilities − ΔFixed Assets − ΔEquity	Increases in WC are a function of increases in fixed liabilities, increases in equity, and decreases in fixed assets.
7	WC + Fixed Assets = Fixed Liabilities + Equity	Equation (5) rearranged with Fixed Assets moved to the left side of the equals sign.

in noncurrent liabilities, decreases in equity, and increases in noncurrent assets serve as uses of WC.

Equation (7) is the core of WC liquidity analysis, helping to define problems as either temporary or structural. The right side of Equation (7) —long-term liabilities (generally funded debt) plus equity—is the firm's capital structure (or permanent financing). Equation (7) easily confirms that the capital structure supports both fixed assets *plus* the firm's entire WC position. For example, suppose you lent money to a business only to find out that because of structural problems (competitive pressures, eroding gross profit margin, etc.), the obligor will at best break even. Assuming no new stock is issued, the equity component of the capital structure decreases or stays constant.

Next, since a major attractor of debt capacity is continuous expansion of the equity base, the firm may find it difficult to attract debt capital. The right side of Equation (7) will decrease or remain unchanged at best. Let's assume capital expenditures are bottlenecked; the major part of the capitol expansion program the bank financed has been poorly deployed. If the fixed asset component—Equation (7)—balloons upward while the capital structure stagnates or falls, lenders will likely not have liquidity protection—or find the proverbial second way out of the credit.

Alternatively, suppose the borrower promises strong, quality profits over the next few years. The firm will likely prosper and draw on its long-term financing sources. The capital structure will, indeed, expand. In addition, if fixed assets are maintained at efficient levels, the WC component in Equation (7) expands nicely. Liquidity flows into the business to finance innovative product lines; reduce debt levels; help fund acquisitions; and position the balance sheet for high-yield restructuring, leveraged buyouts, treasury stock purchases, and so on.

Equation (7) provides a straightforward methodology to WC (funds) analysis. Its mathematics point to three factors that produce liquidity levels that short-term lenders look to for protection:

1. Before you approve a seasonal loan, evaluate exit strategies. The best one is to have a surefire second way out: *Equation (7) liquidity.* Make sure strong (high-quality) profits are attainable—and sustainable—and that sufficient profits are retained to fund debt service.
2. Encourage borrowers to borrow long term if funds are used to expand core assets (capital expenditures).
3. Ask for a capital budget, evaluate and authenticate it, and confirm that capital outlays produce industry-acceptable internal rates of return.

Case Study: Finn Coat

On October 15, 2008, Finn Coat Manufacturing reported its results for the previous nine months (Exhibit 4.1).

(1) Only partial comparatives were available.

After reviewing the figures, you place a call to J. Smith, who informs you of the following details:

- Inventory (cost or market) as of today (10/18/08) is worth a good $650.
- Due to an increase in foreign imports, coupled with temporary shortages, profit margins have been squeezed. However, margins should increase slightly in December, and by next June the gross profit will approach the 12/31/07 fiscal gross profit margin of 36%. (Fiscal 12/31/07 net sales were $4,700.)
- Delivery and production schedules indicate that $400 will be shipped in October and $200 in November.
- Expenses in October and November are expected to be $110 and $130, respectively.
- Returns, allowances, and discounts to gross sales are expected to continue unchanged from the trial balance date.
- The credit file indicates that more than 50 trade inquiries were received over the past two months versus historical levels of approximately 20 during the same time period.

Steps to Complete a Finn Coat Manufacturing Analysis

1. Derive a break-even income statement and balance sheet. Compare break-even inventory with management's estimates. Determine the magnitude of profit or loss. Determine the interim gross profit margin.
2. Calculate seasonal ratios, and complete a trial balance analysis.
3. Derive break-even shipments BES.
4. Write up Finn Coat's interim results incorporating break-even and ratio analysis.
5. Plan to meet with Finn Coat's management to discuss the results. What issues should you consider as a result of your analysis?

Step 1: Derive a break-even income statement and balance sheet (Exhibit 4.2), comparing break-even inventory with management's estimate of inventory value (on the basis of cost or market, whichever is lower). If break even is higher than estimated

Account	9/30/08	9/30/07 (1)
Cash	15	125
Sales (Gross)	3,080	3,600
Accruals	1,180	
Purchases	560	
Prepaid Expenses	735	
Net Plant and Equipment	7,111	
Discounts on Sales	187	200
Intangibles	140	
Equity	2,900	
*Factory Labor	490	
*Freight In	80	
Short-Term Bank Debt	1,000	200
Long-Term Debt	6,000	6,000
*Factory Depreciation Expense	30	
Officer Salaries	28	70
Returns and Allowances	153	135
Other Assets	1,875	
*Fiscal (Beginning) Inventory	840	
Accounts Receivable	1,100	1,150
Accounts Payable	680	775
*Factory Overhead	650	
Administration Expense	280	
Selling Expense	536	
Estimated Tax Expense	30	

*Cost of Goods Sold items.

Exhibit 4.1 Finn Coat Manufacturing 9/30/2008 Nine-Month Results, Prepared by J. Smith, Treasurer.

inventory, a nine-month loss results as measured by the difference between the two inventory values. In addition, determine the interim gross profit margin.

Since Finn's estimated inventory is below break even, the firm suffered a nine-month loss. The banker surmises the loss is due to an inventory write-down—just the thing to affect liquidity and seasonal ratios. Seasonal ratio analysis along with basic trial balance analysis will corroborate Finn's poor year.

Step 2: Calculate seasonal ratios and complete a trial balance analysis per the following:

Ratio	2008	2007
(Cash + Accounts Receivable)/Short-Term Debt + Accounts Payable	.66	1.3
Returns and Allowances/Gross Sales	.049	.038
Short-Term Debt/Accounts Payable	1.5	.26

Finn Coat Manufacturing Break-Even Income Statement (9/30/2008) and Break-Even Inventory

Steps to Derive Break-Even Inventory	**Trial Balance Information**		
Step 4: Include Sales *given*	Sales		3,080
Steps 5 and 6: Returns and Allowances and			
Discounts given	Returns and Allowances	(153)	
	Discounts	(187)	(340)
Step 7: *Derive* Net Sales	Net Sales		2,740
Step 8: *Calculate* Break-Even Cost of Goods Sold	B/E Cost of Goods Sold		1,866
Step 3: Let Gross Profit = Expenses	B/E Gross Profit		874
Step 2: Include Expenses *given*	Officers' Salaries		(28)
	Administration Expenses		(280)
	Selling Expenses		(536)
	Estimated Taxes		(30)
Step 1: Profits Assumed to *Break Even*	B/E Profit		0

Finn Coat Break-Even Inventory Position	
Break-EvenInventory:	
Plus (Fiscal) Beginning Inventory	840
Plus Purchases	560
Plus Labor	490
Plus Freight In	80
Plus Depreciation	30
Plus Overhead	650
Less:	
Break-Even CGS	(1,866)
Equal Break-Even Inventory	784

Profit//Loss Estimate:	
Management's Estimated Inventory	650
Less Break-Even Inventory	784
Equals Interim Loss	(134)

Exhibit 4.2 Finn Coat Manufacturing Break-Even Income Statement (9/30/2008) and Break-Even Inventory.

Finn Coat Interim Gross Profit Margin	
Cost of Goods Sold:	
Fiscal Inventory	840
Purchases	560
Factory Labor	490
*Freight In	80
Depreciation	30
Overhead	650
Less	
Mgt. Estimated Inventory	
= Actual Cost of Goods Sold	2,000

Measure actual interim gross profit margin:

= Gross Profit/Sales

= (Net Sales − Actual Cost of Goods Sold)/Net sales

= (2,700 − 2,000)/2740

= 27%

Finn Coat Break-Even Balance Sheet***			
9/30/08			
Cash	15	Accruals	1,180
A/R	1,100	A/P	680
*B/E Inventory	784	S/T Debt	1,000
Prepaid Expenses	735	L/T/D	6,000
Fixed Assets	7,111	**Fiscal Equity	2,900
Other Assets	1,875		
Intangibles	140		
Total Assets	**11,760**	**Liabilities and Equity_11,760**	

* Plug or balancing figure

** Equity remains unchanged from fiscal—that is, break even.

***Notice that the break-even balance sheet produces the same inventory as the break even derived on the income statement.

Exhibit 4.2 (*continued*).

Basic trial balance analysis reveals the following:

- Officer Salaries declined to $42 from $70.
- Nine-month gross sales declined 14%.
- Liquidity is low compared to last year.
- Short-term debt and payables have not reduced.
- Receivables increased substantially relative to sales.

Step 3: Determine shipments required to break even for the forecast months October and November 2008. Make sure to:

- Compare each month's BES to management's estimates of shipments.
- Determine if the firm will be profitable during each of the two months.
- Use the actual interim gross profit to find BES.
  $S_b = E_i/(G_i)(1 - R_i)$
  $S_{Oct} = 110/(.27)(1 - .11) = 457 > 300 - Loss$
  $S_{Nov} = 130/(.27)(1 - .11) = 540 > 200 - Loss$

Step 4: Write up Finn Coat's interim results incorporating break-even and ratio analysis. The banker's seasonal write-up, as a matter of record, will be placed in the credit file. The write-up serves as the basis for a meeting between the banker (relationship manager) and client.

Nine months' 2008 gross sales declined 14% to $3080M from the corresponding period in the previous year. Returns and Allowances increased slightly to 4.9%. The Gross Profit Margin, derived at 27%, was weak and reflected the high cost of linings associated with temporary shortages. Break-Even Inventory of $784 was well over management's estimate of $650M, suggesting an interim loss of around $134M.

The poor interim performance affected liquidity, as cash and receivables were only 66% of Bank and Trade Debt versus 1.3X during the corresponding period last year. Accounts receivables declined to $1100M but moved faster than sales. Increased reliance on bank lines was evidenced by Bank to Trade debt of 1.5X versus .26, while two-month trade inquiries jumped to 50, a considerable increase over historical periods. Noteworthy was the decline in officers' salaries to $42M from $70M.

The firm's weak interim performance is not expected to improve over the next few months, as only $400M and $200M will be shipped in October and November, respectively, which is significantly below the break-even level of $457M and $540M.

Step 5: Plan to meet with Finn Coat's management to discuss the results. What issues should you consider as a result of your analysis?

Before the meeting, you, the account officer, should prepare a cash budget to pinpoint the inflow and outflow of funds. Loan documentation should be checked also to ensure that it is current and in order.

Then consider whether the problem is minor and expected to be temporary. If it is, the banker may merely waive this year's cleanup. If the problem is more acute, other steps may have to be taken. The bank may decide to restructure Finn Coat's loan— that is, create a loan to be repaid from internally generated cash flow over months or years (presuming that future cash flows are expected). The loan agreement, by virtue of its covenants and events of default, will give the bank greater control over the borrower. Loans may also be put on a demand basis, although the effect on the borrower is largely psychological. Also consider defensive measures: (1) *cash flow* (strong cash flows are crucial!); (2) *equity injections*; (3) *formula-based advances, including accounts receivable financing*; and (4) *collateral.*

Many firms that are unsuited for unsecured seasonal borrowings may meet financing needs by securing assets or changing over to accounts receivable financing. In Chapter Five, collateral and accounts receivable financing are discussed in relation to the risk characteristics of the borrower, advantages to the borrower and the bank, credit and collateral analysis, documentation, and safeguards to ensure the authenticity and collectibility of assigned collateral. Collateral will not automatically ensure payment; the bank will need to judge the overall risks of the credit by evaluating the quality and magnitude of collateral, the borrower's financial condition, management's strategic plans, cash flow, and debt servicing ability. But most important to good decision making are the internal controls, policies, practices, and procedures of the bank itself.

5 Asset-Based Lending

Chapter Outline

Credit Engineering for Bankers. DOI: 10.1016/B978-0-12-378585-5.10005-3

"Banks can utilize collateral and guarantees to help mitigate risks inherent in individual credits, but transactions should be entered into primarily on the strength of the borrower's repayment capacity. Collateral cannot be a substitute for a comprehensive assessment of the borrower or counterparty, nor can it compensate for insufficient information. It should be recognized that any credit enforcement actions (e.g., foreclosure proceedings) typically eliminate the profit margin on the transaction. In addition, banks need to be mindful that the value of collateral may well be impaired by the same factors that have led to the diminished recoverability of the credit. Banks should have policies covering the acceptability of various forms of collateral, procedures for the ongoing valuation of such collateral, and a process to ensure that collateral is, and continues to be, enforceable and realizable. With regard to guarantees, banks should evaluate the level of coverage being provided in relation to the credit quality and legal capacity of the guarantor. Banks should only factor explicit guarantees into the credit decision and not those that might be considered implicit, such as anticipated support from the government."[1]

Firms that are unable to borrow unsecured generally find themselves unable to do so for the following reasons:

- Business life cycle new and unproven
- Questionable ability to service unsecured debt
- Year-round financing in amounts too large to justify unsecured credit
- Working capital and profits insufficient to periodic cleanup of short-term loans
- Working capital inadequate for sales volume and type of operation
- Previous unsecured borrowings no longer warranted because of various credit factors
- Loan amounts falling beyond a borrower's unsecured credit limit

Secured borrowers can be categorized into two broad market segments: short term and long term.

Market Segments

Short-Term Secured Borrowers

- Commodities
- Middle markets and micro-businesses
- Finance companies

---

[1] "Principles for the Management of Credit Risk," consultative paper issued by the Basel Committee on Banking Supervision, Bank for International Settlements, Basel, July 1999.

- High net worth individuals
- Market segments

Long-Term Secured Borrowers

- Real estate
- Project finance
- Transportation and shipping
- High net worth individuals
- Leasing
- Corporate finance

When evaluating collateral, banks take into account the degree of coverage; the economic life cycle of the collateral versus the term of the loan; constraints on liquidating the collateral; the bank's ability to monitor and liquidate collateral— namely, collateral values matched to credit exposures; liquidity, or how quickly value can be realized; and the legal rights to pledged assets. Companies finance against receivables when existing credit facilities cannot finance expanding needs or when requirements fluctuate beyond acceptable norms.

Secured financing is advantageous to the borrower for several reasons:

- It is an efficient way to finance expanding operations because borrowing capacity expands along with sales.
- It permits borrowers to take advantage of purchase discounts because cash is received immediately upon sales, thus permitting prompt payment to suppliers, which earns the company a good enough reputation to reduce the cost of purchases.
- It ensures a revolving, expanding line of credit.

It is advantageous to the bank for the following reasons:

- Collateral loans generate relatively high yields.
- It results in depository relationships.
- It permits a continuing banking relationship with long-standing customers whose financial condition no longer warrants unsecured credit.
- It generates new business.
- It minimizes potential loss because loans are structured as formula-based facilities whereby advances are made against a percentage of acceptable collateral.

Basic Axioms of Asset-Based Lending

Bankers generally look at collateral as cake frosting, with cash flow being the cake. As we saw in Chapter One, collateral, within the PRISM lending model, acts as a secondary means of repayment, with cash flow or asset conversion being the primary source. Borrowers are, after all, going concerns; they should not be in liquidation or restructuring, nor should they be likely candidates for either at the time the bank considers taking collateral.

As such, banks should establish lending standards governing asset-based loans before obtaining collateral. These standards should be derived from well-defined loan policies and procedures. For example, Peter Larr offers the following guidelines for successful asset-based lending:[2]

Financial Analysis. A due diligence PRISM top to bottom—a thorough financial analysis, with analytic standards equal to those used for unsecured deals—is a must.

Seniority. The bank should have seniority—that is, priority on obligor assets over other creditors via a legally protected claim on specific collateral, or be senior on unsecured claims against an asset pool to which no other creditor has a claim.

Protection. The bank should have protection, which is defined as the net realizable value of the specific assets such that, on liquidation, the collateral should be adequate to cover a risk exposure (principal, accrued interest, and collection costs). Collateral protection includes at least five attributes:

1. *Value.* Value is associated with market price. How a market price is obtained depends on the nature of the collateral. Price quotations taken from a newspaper or from an electronic feed to a production system for listed securities are quite different from an appraiser's opinion of the value of a painting. Valuations of real estate present complexities because they are affected by capitalization rates and projected cash flow assumptions regarding leasing or sellout rates.

2. *Margin.* Margins should be sufficient to include coverage of the borrower's overhead for the period of time necessary for the borrower to liquidate the collateral on behalf of the lender. This qualification is realistic, since the borrower, even in financial distress, would likely be able to dispose of collateral faster, more easily, and more cheaply than the lender can.

3. *Vulnerability.* Event risk and inherent volatility make up the risk of vulnerability.

4. *Marketability.* The ease and timeliness of liquidation, which can affect value and margin, are part of the marketability concept.

5. *Insurance.* Assets taken as collateral must be properly insured to protect value. If collateral is not fully insured, at least the value and the margin should be reassessed.

6. *Control.* Poor collateral control can lead to loss. If a bank is unable to ensure internal quality control, then the institution should not encourage collateralized exposures. Collateral monitoring requires resources devoted to the management of both operations and systems supporting collateral. Thus, trained personnel must administer the collateral loan book to ensure that collateral retains acceptable values.

Security Interest

A security interest in loans arises when lenders receive something from borrowers that is more tangible than traditional promises of repayment. Any asset allowing title transfer acts as a pledge to secured credit, and on default, banks have rights, senior to other creditors, to claim assets pledged.

If a borrower defaults on a secured loan and the collateral is sold for less than the loan amount, the bank becomes a general or unsecured creditor for the balance. The last thing a secured lender wants is an unsecured loan position, since collateral was required to approve the deal in the first place. Therefore, banks want collateral with market values comfortably over loan exposures (i.e., the loan to value ratio is minimized) and pledged assets with durability (life span) in excess of loan terms.

---

[2] Mr. Larr was a senior vice president and risk asset review executive at Chase Manhattan.

Secured loans require documentation generally known as *security agreements*. A bank's security interest in collateral is formalized with a security agreement signed by the bank and the borrower (the *parties*) and filed with a public office (usually the secretary of state) in the state in which the collateral is located. This filing gives public notice to interested parties that the lender has prior claim to the collateral. Before approving loans, lenders search public records to determine if pledged assets are secured elsewhere. The *Uniform Commercial Code* (UCC) deals with lender protection on security interests. Bankers should be familiar with the *Code* before they obtain a security interest in collateral.

Under Article 9 of the UCC, the bank must create a valid and enforceable security interest and "perfect" that interest. Once enforceable security interest is created, the secured party can always enforce it, on default, against the debtor, provided there is no superior third-party interest. If the holder of a valid and enforceable Article 9 interest takes the additional steps required under Article 9 "to perfect," it will defeat most such third parties. Sections 9-203 and 9-204 of the UCC require that the parties take four steps to create a valid and enforceable security interest:

1. Enter into a security agreement.
2. Reduce as much of that agreement to writing as is necessary to satisfy Section 9-203 (which also requires that the debtor sign this writing), or the creditor have possession of the collateral.
3. Have the debtor acquire rights in the collateral.
4. Have the secured party give value.

Section 9-302(10) provides for automatic perfection, without filing a financing statement, when any or all assignments to the bank do not transfer a significant part of the outstanding accounts of the borrower. However, in all other accounts receivable security interests, the bank must file a financing statement to perfect its security interest. The law of the jurisdiction in which the debtor is located governs the perfection of the security interest. Location is determined by place of business, executive office, or residence if the debtor has no place of business in the state.

The Federal Reserve also provides guidelines concerning the collateral used to secure loans. The following questions from its *Commercial Bank Examination Manual* should be considered before entering into a security agreement:[3]

1. Is negotiable collateral held under joint custody?
2. Has the customer obtained and filed for released collateral and signed a receipt?
3. Are securities and commodities valued and margin requirements reviewed at least monthly?

---

[3] From the *Commercial Bank Examination Manual,* Division of Banking Supervision and Regulation, The Board of Governors, Federal Reserve System. December, 2008. The manual *"Presents examination objectives and procedures that Federal Reserve System examiners follow in evaluating the safety and soundness of state member banks. Intended as guidance for planning and conducting bank examinations. The goal of the Commercial Bank Examination Manual is to organize and formalize longstanding examination objectives and procedures that provide guidance to the examiner, and to enhance the quality and consistent application of examination procedures."*

4. When the support rests on the cash surrender value of insurance policies, is a periodic accounting received from the insurance company and maintained with the policy?

5. Is a record maintained of entry to the collateral vault?

6. Are stock powers filed separately to bar negotiability and to deter abstraction of both the security and the negotiating instrument?

7. Are securities out for transfer, exchange, and so on controlled by prenumbered temporary vaultout tickets?

8. Has the bank instituted a system that ensures that (1) security agreements are filed, (2) collateral mortgages are properly recorded, (3) title searches and property appraisals are performed in connection with collateral mortgages, and (4) insurance coverage (including loss payee clause) is in effect on property covered by collateral mortgages?

9. Are acknowledgments received for pledged deposits held at other banks?

10. Is an officer's approval necessary before collateral can be released or substituted?

11. Does the bank have an internal review system that reexamines collateral items for negotiability and proper assignment, checks values assigned to collateral when the loan is made and at frequent intervals thereafter, determines that items out on temporary vaultout tickets are authorized and have not been outstanding for an unreasonable length of time, and determines that loan payments are promptly posted?

12. Are all notes assigned consecutive numbers and recorded on a note register or similar record? Do numbers on notes agree with those recorded on the register?

13. Are collection notices handled by someone not connected with loan processing?

14. In mortgage warehouse financing, does the bank hold the original mortgage note, trust deed, or other critical document, releasing only against payment?

15. Have standards been set for determining the percentage advance to be made against acceptable receivables?

16. Are acceptable receivables defined?

17. Has the bank established minimum requirements for verification of the borrower's accounts receivable and established minimum standards for documentation?

18. Have accounts receivable financing policies been reviewed at least annually to determine if they are compatible with changing market conditions?

19. Have loan statements, delinquent accounts, collection requests, and past due notices been checked with the trial balances that are used in reconciling subsidiary records of accounts receivable financing loans with general ledger accounts?

20. Have inquiries about accounts receivable financing loan balances been answered and investigated?

21. Is the bank in receipt of documents supporting recorded credit adjustments to loan accounts or accrued interest receivable accounts? Have these documents been checked or tested subsequently?

22. Are terms, dates, weights, description of merchandise, and so on shown on invoices, shipping documents, delivery receipts, and bills of lading? Are these documents scrutinized for differences?

23. Were payments from customers scrutinized for differences in invoice dates, numbers, terms, and so on?

24. Do bank records show, on a timely basis, a first lien on the assigned receivables for each borrower?

25. Do loans granted on the security of the receivables also have an assignment of the inventory?

26. Does the bank verify the borrower's accounts receivable or require independent verification on a periodic basis?

27. Does the bank require the borrower to provide aged accounts receivable schedules on a periodic basis?

Loans Secured with Accounts Receivables

Illustrative Example: Borrowing Base Facility
Location: Models are available on the Elsevier Website www.ElsevierDirect.com
Brief Description: Applies accounts receivable borrowing base analysis, auditing procedures, acceptance/rejection cost modeling, and cash budget analysis to the approval process.

Accounts receivables financing is an arrangement whereby a bank or finance company either advances funds by *purchasing* invoices or accounts receivables outright over a period of time (*factoring*) or lending against receivables—using an assignment on receivables as primary collateral. Factoring is conducted on a notification basis (the client's customer is notified that the factor purchased receivables), whereas straight receivable financing is practiced on a nonnotification basis

Although accounts receivable loans are collateralized, bankers analyze the borrower's financial statements as if the loans were unsecured. Even if collateral quality is solid and well in excess of the loan, borrowers must demonstrate that they are viable as repayment through collateral liquidation as an exit strategy of last resort (there may be court claims against collateral if the firm is in financial distress and the banker books the loan with prior knowledge of the borrower's condition).

Trade reports are reviewed, and agings of receivables and payables are scrutinized. Banks take only *acceptable receivables:* those accounts that are current or not more than a given number of days past due. The entire amount of receivables may be unacceptable if a certain percentage (e.g., 10%) is 90 days or more delinquent. Also, a limit is placed on the maximum dollar amount due from any one account debtor, since there is always the possibility of unforeseen and undisclosed credit failure or a return of merchandise. A common benchmark is to have no more than 20% of assigned receivables from one customer. To verify authenticity of pledged collateral, banks institute a program of direct confirmation. This procedure is particularly important if receivables are pledged on a nonnotification basis, since the bank does not have the same control of the debtor accounts as it does when the receivables are pledged on a notification basis.

The following factors should be considered in evaluating the quality of receivables pledged:[4]

- The turnover of the receivables pledged and the borrower's credit limit. If the turnover is decreasing, the quality of receivables may be deteriorating.
- Aging of accounts receivable. The bank should obtain a monthly aging of the accounts receivable pledged. The examiner should note the percentage of accounts delinquent in relation to the total accounts pledged, concentrations if any, and those accounts having past due balances that also have current amounts due.
- Concentration of debtor accounts. A lender may be vulnerable to loss if a large percentage of the dollar amount of receivables assigned is concentrated in a few accounts. A list of concentrations should be prepared periodically showing the largest accounts.

[4] Ibid.

- Ineligible receivables. The examiner should be aware of receivables, which, by their nature, should be excluded from the lending formula. The following receivables are examples:
  - Due from affiliated companies. Although such receivables might be valid, the temptation for the borrower to create fraudulent invoices would be great.
  - Receivables subject to a purchase money interest, such as floor plan arrangements. The manufacturer will frequently file financing statements when merchandise is delivered to the borrower. That filing usually gives the manufacturer a superior lien on the receivable. An alternative would be to enter into an agreement with the manufacturer where rights to the receivables are subordinated to the bank.

Formula-Based Loans

Formula-based loans are established on a borrowing base formula. The formula determines which assets will be loaned against, the minimum acceptable quality of those assets, and the amount of cushion required to reduce exposure risks. Losses are rare if there is more than enough strong collateral to cover outstanding loans.

Newly created receivables feed into a pool, while reductions flow from payments on account, returns and allowances, bad debts, and the charge off of serious past due accounts. Rates are quoted as a spread over the prime lending rate. In addition to charging interest—at two or three percentage points above prime—it is customary to impose a service charge amounting to 1% or 2% of the borrower's average loan balance.

The quality of financed receivables is influenced by a number of important factors, including the following:

1. The credit standing of the borrower's customers
2. Age and size of the receivable
3. Merchandise quality
4. Number of returns due to missed season and/or faulty merchandise
5. General competitive positive of the borrower
6. The amount of funds continuously generated in the account
7. Credit policies

The Loan Agreement

Important items usually covered by a loan agreement for accounts receivable financing include the following:

- Duration of the lending arrangement.
- Right of the bank to screen the accounts presented to it by the borrower to determine which are acceptable as security.
- Procedure by which accounts held by the bank are to be replaced or the loan reduced if they become past due.
- Percentage that the bank will loan against the face amount of the receivables.
- Maximum dollar amount of the loan.
- Reports required from the borrower to indicate amounts owed by each customer. As additional sales are made, the borrower may be required to submit copies of invoices or other evidence of shipment.

- The responsibility of the borrower to forward directly to the bank payments received on assigned accounts.
- Authorization for the bank to inspect the borrower's books and to verify the accounts receivable through confirmation by a public accounting firm or other agency.
- Reports required from the borrower to indicate amounts owed by each customer. As additional sales are made, the borrower may be required to submit copies of invoices or other evidence of shipment.
- Responsibility of the borrower to forward directly to the bank payments received on assigned accounts.
- Authorization for the bank to inspect the borrower's books and to verify accounts receivable through a public accounting firm.

Loan Formula Certificate

The bank usually requires a loan formula certificate that has been signed by an official of the borrowing company. This certificate, which is completed by the client, includes total receivables, eligible receivables, total inventory, eligible inventory, loan amount outstanding, and the amount of debt that is over or under allowed borrowings. Additional advances may be made if sufficient collateral is available. The debt is to be reduced if it is over the amount allowed as shown by the loan formula certificate.

Exposure Percentage

Except in special circumstances, advances are limited to 75% or 80% of eligible accounts receivable. Ineligible receivables include accounts more than 90 days past due, those that are intercompany or from related businesses, and those that have offsetting payables or prepayments. To derive the exposure percentage, divide accounts receivable advances into net collateral. *Net collateral* represents assigned receivable plus blocked cash accounts, less dilution and 90 days past dues. Via computer, this information is plotted against the borrower's records. While minor differences are ignored, ledger accounts may reveal major discrepancies, such as unreported receipts.

The Loan Officer's Responsibilities

The loan officer's responsibilities follow designated policies and procedures to ensure the safety and integrity of assigned receivables. The affairs of the borrower together with the status of the loan are policed on a regular basis. The loan also must see to it that public filings are recorded properly and that state statutes are followed with regard to locale and number of filings needed to ensure a proper lien.

The Audit: Scope and Details

To verify information supplied by the borrower, the bank will usually send bank personnel to the borrower's place of business to audit its books; if the bank is small, however, the lender will sometimes commission the audit to outside financing agents. If this is the case, the cost of borrowing on the security of accounts receivable tends to be higher than the cost of an unsecured loan. The audit should occur several times a year, and it is usually performed on a quarterly basis. The scope of such an audit should include preparation of balance sheets and profit and loss statements; working capital analysis; agings of payables and receivables; an inspection of inventory and related records; and a determination that the debtor's accounts are properly marked on the books as assigned to the bank. The audit also should include procedures to ascertain that all significant credit memos have been properly issued and reported by the borrower to the bank. If a bank decides to take a security interest in a company's seasonal collections, it requires a judicious and thorough audit of the financial statements.

Following is a step-by-step approach to auditing accounts receivable as a security:

Step 1: Financial Statements

Current information fundamental to a sound audit includes trial balances, interim statements, cash budgets, invoice copies, and ledger computer printouts. In all probability, a trial balance may be required if inventory is not valued on a perpetual basis (see Chapter Four).

Step 2: Receivables (Overview)

Banks conduct a credit check on large positions. The three main sources of credit information include agency reports, banks, and trade debtors. Ratings are evaluated and recorded on the audit report and then classified as acceptable or not acceptable. Some minor accounts, while not considered prime paper, may be classified as acceptable due to their small size. Other measures of receivable quality, or lack of it, include the collection period, proximity to economically depressed areas, diversification, and the balance of the portfolio.

Receivable concentrations are watched carefully—the danger of control looms large. For example, the client's customer may end up dictating unfavorable terms or threaten to cancel orders at the slightest provocation. Key points to consider when securing a portfolio of concentrated receivables include the following:

- Evaluate these receivables thoroughly in terms of account classification and aging. An aging schedule is discussed in Step 3.
- Credit reports and checkings are obtained on the largest accounts. Sources of information include agency reports, banks, trade journals, suppliers, and credit reporting agencies. Information is evaluated and recorded in the audit report. Verify receivables with trade debtors, and compute the collection period for each account.
- Accounts are classified into acceptable and unacceptable categories.
- Other measures of viability to consider include collection period, delinquency ratio (past due receivables over credit sales), and bad debt ratio (write-offs over net receivables).
- Files of past due accounts are checked for recent correspondence and collection effort. Large positions are reviewed.

Step 3: Accounts Receivable Aging

A Dun and Bradstreet code (if rated) depicts approximate net worth. Receivables are listed as 1–30 days, 31–60 days, 61–90 days, and accounts over 90 days past due. Levels of concentration are measured by dividing the sum of the largest accounts receivable into total receivables. Accounts over 90 days are usually discarded from the net collateral figure.

Aging Schedule of Accounts Receivable

Number of Days Outstanding	Amount	Percent
0–30	$45,000	66.3%
30–45	$11,300	16.6%
45–60	$6,500	9.6%
60–90	$3,200	4.7%
90 or more	$1,900	2.80%
Total	$67,900	100.0%

Concentration is tested by (1) acceptable receivables to total receivables and (2) the average of the five largest receivables summed to total receivables. The average size of accounts is calculated to determine expense allocation. The larger the account, the more work that is involved and the more the bank should be compensated.

Step 4: Credit and Collection Policies

Review the following:
1. *Terms of sale.* Policies regarding terms of sale can vary by industry, and they range from cash before delivery to extended seasonal dating.
2. *Credit approval.* Firms having strict credit approval policies have fewer receivables exposed.
3. *Collection.* Optimal collection policies maximize collection while maximizing customer goodwill. They should be convincing without being harsh.
4. *Average collection period.* Analyze trends alongside the inventory. Interim Average collection period (ACP) should be annualized and compared to similar periods, particularly seasonal operations.

Step 5: Analysis of Delinquencies

Instead of supplying the borrower with additional funds as new sales are made, bankers may substitute new receivables for those no longer acceptable as collateral— that is, until delinquencies are corrected. If delinquent receivables are large, the borrower is faced with the prospect of having to operate without funding from either customers or the bank.

Step 6: Evaluation of Sales

A detailed analysis of the client's sales record is required in the initial audit. More than a few banks and commercial finance companies fail to appreciate the value of sales analysis, not realizing that omitting this step often leads to weak forecasting results. Valuable sales information is frequently buried in invoice files. There is no single method to analyze sales data. Typical methods will reduce sales into categories that include geographic analysis where sales are separated by location. The lender must determine the geographical distribution of sales and the concentration of the client's sales, while keeping the following factors in mind:

- Product analysis; size of package and grade
- Class of trade
- Price
- Method: mail, telephone, and direct selling
- Terms: cash or charge
- Order size

It is important to keep in mind that although proper compliance with the UCC, in most instances, creates a valid and enforceable first lien, it does not insulate the bank from the need to police its collateral. By filing a lien, the bank establishes its right to collect on receivables to it, provided the following factors hold:

- The sales are legitimate.
- The merchandise has been delivered.
- The merchandise is as ordered.
- The sales were made without warranties.
- The merchandise was not shipped on consignment.
- The merchandise is not subject to offset—that is, contra-accounts or liens.
- The receivable has not already been paid to the borrower.

Step 7: Product Analysis and Product Policies

Analysis of products and product policies should be directed to product planning where specific product objectives and policy are outlined. Also, since products have life cycles, it is essential that the product be defined in terms of its life cycle.

The start-up phase—the first phase of a product's life cycle—generally requires large-scale promotion in order to "get the product off the ground" and could cause enough of a cash drain to put the capital structure at risk. Following start-up, assuming initial success, a firm may grow rapidly and start to earn profits (phase two). However, the small increment to equity generated by earnings retention is often too small to finance the insatiable appetite for new assets required by rapid growth firms. Risk of default is highest during the rapid growth phase. Phase three of a product's typical life cycle is known as the mature or stable growth phase in which product price and earnings are consistent with economic growth.

In the mature or stable phase, the entrance of new competitors often causes product demand to decline, while acceptance of new or improved competitive products triggers phase four, the decline phase. These concepts are developed further in Chapter Nine on sustainable growth.

Product policies should be reviewed and generally include the following:

- Sales volume
- Type and number of competitors
- Technical opportunity
- Patent protection
- Raw materials required
- Production load
- Value added
- Similarity to major businesses
- Effect on other products

Step 8: Inventory

If the audit includes an examination of inventory, lenders determine the amount and condition of inventory and the breakdown of inventory, including raw materials, work in progress, and finished goods. Merchandise quality is important, since the higher the inventory quality, the fewer the returns and refusals to pay. The returns to gross sales ratio can effectively monitor inventory quality.

Economic order quantity models might easily identify order or carrying cost problems. Decomposing each inventory segment is important to identify inventory buildup problems. This is accomplished by dividing each component of inventory as a percentage of total inventory. Here are a few examples:

- *Check raw material inventory.* A large raw material inventory may mean stockpiling raw material.
- *Watch work in process inventory.* If out of line, this category could mean a production problem. Worse still, partially manufactured merchandise cannot be shipped to customers. Bankers should check order backlogs. If order backlogs have jumped, the increase in disappointed customers waiting for past due deliveries can easily turn into sharply reduced orders, and a weakened borrowing base.
- *Finished goods inventory* that climbs too fast may reveal demand problems. If inventory is not moved out on a timely basis, the borrower may liberalize credit standards, which may well reduce the quality of the bank's lien on receivables.

Step 9: Fixed Assets

This phase of the examination includes evaluation of fixed assets and the depreciation methods in use.

Step 10: Analysis of Accounts Payable and Purchases

An absence of diversity is almost as risky as receivable concentrations. Payables represent purchases. Slow payables are a drag on the client's major supply sources, which could be cut off without warning. Without supplier support, goods cannot be produced. Bankers isolate large payable(s) and work out a payable concentration ratio of large payable to total payables.

An accounts payable audit typically includes the following:

- Classification according to creditor

- Dates of each payable
- Amount and maturity date
- Payables aging compared to the receivables aging
- Listing of large or unusual payables

Step 11: Subordination Agreements

Creditors review subordination agreements often enough since the funds generated by these agreements boost working capital and the firm's capital structure.

Step 12: Analysis of Deposits in Cash Account

Analysis of the cash account can spot unauthorized sales of encumbered assets, withdrawal of funds for personal use, or fraudulent practices, such as unauthorized multiple assignments of receivables. Cash position determines if remittances have been diverted. Differences in unreported credits are recorded and explained.

Step 13: Bank Statement Audit

This section of the auditing procedure serves as a reminder to scrutinize the borrower's bank statement. Note the following:

- Confirm that collections have been earmarked to reduce loan balances.
- Checks payable to subsidiaries (representing advances) should be watched very closely since they represent a cash drain from the core business. In addition, the principals may be devoting excessive time to an outside venture unrelated to the core business.
- Bank statements and checks are also reviewed for large items and stale or unusual checks.
- Diversion of credits to other uses may easily create an untenable cash position at some future date and drive the company out of business. It is, therefore, reasonable to deduce that any prudent lending officer will question any large withdrawal, which usually shows up as a large item check.
- Federal withholding and Social Security taxes are recorded, and paid checks are cited to verify that remittance to governmental agencies has indeed been made. Nonpayment of these obligations might easily jeopardize the bank's collateral position. Paid checks are also reviewed to ensure that subordinated indebtedness remains intact.
- Bank accounts at other financial institutions are examined for updated credit stories. However, most bank checkings will yield account information only and confirm that the relationship is satisfactory.

Step 14: Analysis of Loans, Collateral, and Statistics

Secured lenders review outstandings, collateral position, and other statistics reported as part of the loan audit on at least a monthly basis. These data help to gauge the firm's peak requirements and cash needs.

Step 15: Prebillings

Prebilling represents the assignment of invoices before goods are actually shipped. The prebilling audit involves matching invoice and delivery dates. Forwarding invoices prior to shipment date is a warning sign. Bankers spot prebillings by comparing shipment dates to the assigned invoice dates. Prebilling practices should be strongly discouraged, since invoices should not be forwarded to lenders before shipment.

Step 16: Check for Fraud

All accounts appearing in the general ledger should be of sufficient quality to minimize the risk of fraud. Lenders should be cognizant of two areas of concern regarding deceptive practices: The nature of accounts receivable financing provides opportunities for dubious practices and the variety of fraud possibilities, which provide opportunities for deceiving lenders. The varieties of fraud include the following:

- Assignment of fictitious accounts, accompanied by forged shipping documents,
- Duplicate assignment of the same account
- Diversion of collections to client's use—otherwise known as personal withdrawals beyond a reasonable amount
- Failure to report charge backs (returns and allowances)
- Submission of false financial information
- Forged shipping documents

Step 17: Record Comparisons and Ledgering Accounts

Lenders compare the borrower's records with those of the bank(s). Ledger accounts may reveal credit allowances and/or contra items, such as bills receivable discounted. Major discrepancies must be noted, explained, and corrected.

In ledgering the accounts, the lender receives duplicate copies of the invoices together with the shipping documents and/or delivery receipts. On receipt of satisfactory information, the bank advances the agreed percentage of the outstanding receivables. The receivables are usually pledged on a notification basis. Under this method, the bank maintains complete control of all funds paid on all accounts pledged by requiring the borrower's customer to remit directly to the bank. The same application of payments is then used as under the blanket assignment method.

Loans Secured by Inventories

Illustrative Example: Loans Secured by Inventory
Location: Models are available on the Elsevier Website www.ElsevierDirect.com
Brief Description: Illustrates inventory audit worksheets and checklists, inventory break-even analysis, and acceptance/rejection cost modeling.

If a borrower is considered a poor or questionable risk, lenders may insist on a blanket lien against inventory—*assuming suppliers have filed no prior liens and will continue to ship behind the bank's lien.* While blanket liens provide security against all inventories, borrowers are free to dispose of inventory as long as funds are earmarked to reduce outstandings. The downside risk of using inventory as collateral includes declining stock values or severe markdowns by borrowers in a panic.

Marketability

Marketability means that pledged inventory can sell at prices at least equal to book value or replacement cost, such as most auto tires, hardware goods, and footwear, as opposed to high-tech items, where a real chance of obsolesce exists. Marketability is associated with the inventory's physical properties, as well. A warehouse full of frozen turkeys may be marketable, but the cost of storing and selling the turkeys may be prohibitive.

Price Stability and Physical Properties

Standardized and staple durables are desirable as collateral, since these ticket items have stable prices, ready markets, and no undesirable physical properties. *Perishable* items create problems for sellers and lenders for obvious reasons, as do *specialized* items. Specialized inventories are problematic if markets are thin—for example, special purpose machinery, fresh produce, and advertising materials. Large high-ticket items may not be desirable collateral if the expenses associated with storage and transportation are high.

Commodities and products such as grain, cotton, wool, coffee, sugar, logs, lumber, canned foods, baled wood pulp, automobiles, and major appliances are acceptable collateral, whereas refrigerators-in-process are usually worthless.

Trust Receipts

A trust receipt is an instrument acknowledging that the borrower holds goods in trust for the lender. The lien is valid as long as the merchandise is in the borrower's possession and properly identified. When lenders advance funds, borrowers convey a trust receipt for the goods financed.

Goods can be stored in a public warehouse or held on the premises. The borrower receives merchandise, with the lender advancing anywhere from 80% to 100% of the cost. The lender files a lien on the items financed. Documents include a list of each item along with its description and serial number. The borrower is free to sell the secured inventory but is "trusted" to remit to the lender *immediately* earmarked funds, which are used to repay advances plus accrued interest. In return, the lender releases the lien. The lender conducts periodic checks to ensure that the required collateral is still "in the yard." Inventory financing under trust receipts, for retail sale, is commonly called *floorplanning*. For example, an automobile dealer may have arranged to finance the purchase of new cars with trust receipts.

Warehouse Receipts

Like trust receipts, field warehouse financing employs inventory as collateral. A warehouse receipt allows the lender to obtain control over pledged collateral, providing the ultimate degree of security. The costs of these loans are high due to the high cost of hiring third parties (warehouse firms) to maintain and guard inventory collateral. In addition to the interest charge, the borrower must absorb the costs of warehousing by paying the warehouse fee, which is generally between 1% and 3% of the loan.

Terminal Warehouse

A terminal warehouse is located within the borrower's geographical area. It is a central warehouse used to store the merchandise of various customers. The lender generally uses a terminal warehouse when secured inventory is easily and cheaply transported to the warehouse. When goods arrive at the warehouse designated by the lender, the *warehouse official* "checks-in" the merchandise, listing each item on a *warehouse receipt*. Noted on the *check-in list* are the quantity, the serial or lot numbers, and the estimated value. After officials check in merchandise, the receipt is forwarded to the lender, who advances a specified percentage of the collateral value to the borrower and files a lien on all the items listed on the receipt.

Field Warehouses

Field warehouse financing is usually economical; the warehouse is established on the borrower's premises. Under a field warehouse arrangement, a lender hires a reputable field warehousing company to set up a warehouse on the borrower's premises or lease part of the borrower's warehouse. The warehousing company, as the lender's agent, is responsible for seeing that the collateral pledged is actually in the warehouse. There have been instances when warehousing companies have fraudulently issued receipts against nonexistent collateral. If this happens, and the borrower defaults, the lender ends up being an unsecured creditor.

Once inventory is isolated, it is registered with the warehouse receipt being forwarded to the lender. The lender advances a specified percentage of collateral value and files a lien on the pledged security. A field warehouse may take the form of a fence around a stock of raw materials, a roped-off section of the borrower's warehouse, or a warehouse constructed by the warehousing company on the borrower's premises.

Regardless of whether a terminal or field warehouse is established, the warehousing company employs a security official to guard inventory. The guard or warehouse official is not permitted to release collateral without prior authorization, since lenders have total control over inventory. Only on written approval of the lender can any portion of the secured inventory be released.

Although most warehouse receipts are nonnegotiable, some are *negotiable*, meaning that the lender may transfer them to other parties. If the lender wants to remove a warehouse receipt loan from its books, it can sell a negotiable warehouse receipt to another party, who then replaces the original lender in the agreement. In some instances, the ability to transfer a warehouse receipt to another party may be desirable.

Negotiable warehouse receipts are used to finance inventories in which trading is active, such as corn, cotton, and wheat. The major disadvantage of negotiable warehouse receipts is that they are easily transferred, are usually in large denominations, and must be presented to the warehouse operator each time a withdrawal is made. Therefore, banks prefer the use of nonnegotiable receipts issued in the name of the bank for the simple reason that they provide better control of the pledged inventory.

Example of a Field Warehouse Loan Transaction

A canner of exotic fruits determines that the firm's major requirements for bank financing are during the canning season. To get the required seed capital to purchase and process an initial harvest of fruit, the canner can finance approximately 20% of its operations during the season.

As cans are put into boxes and placed in storerooms, the canner realizes that additional funds are needed for labor and raw material to make the cans. Without these funds, operations will come to a grinding halt. A seasonal pattern clearly forms here. At the beginning of the fruit harvest and canning season, cash needs and loan requirements increase and reach a maximum at the termination of the canning season. Because of the canner's modest worth and substantial seasonal financing needs, the firm's bank insists on acceptable security for the funds needed to meet those needs. The services of a field warehouse company are obtained, and a field warehouse is set up.

The field warehouse company notifies the bank that the boxes of canned fruit have been shipped and checked in. At this point, the bank is assured of control over the canned goods on which loans are based and can establish a line of credit from which the canner can draw funds. As the canner receives purchase orders, it sends them to the bank. The bank then authorizes the warehouse custodian to release the boxes of canned fruit associated with the purchase orders. When the high point of the season is over, the line of credit diminishes as checks from the canner's distributors are received by the canner. This stage results in a borrowing low point, putting the canner in the low debt position necessary before a new seasonal buildup occurs.

In certain instances, banks may permit outstanding seasonal loans to the canner to reach an amount many times the amount of the canner's own equity capital. The fruit growers, the canner, the canner's distributors, the field warehouse company, and the bank all join forces in working out a successful distributive process to everyone's advantage. If the runoff of cash is not enough to retire seasonal loans and the canner's financial structure is sound, the bank will likely carry over the loan(s) until next season. This carryover should give the canner enough time to clean up the debt. The primary consideration for this arrangement is the fact that canned fruit is easily salable.

Loans Secured by Marketable Securities

A loan secured directly or indirectly by any stock or convertible security falls under Regulation U. This regulation governs extension of credits by banks for purchasing and carrying margin securities. Margin stock is defined as follows:

- Listed or unlisted stock
- Securities convertible into a margin stock
- Most over-the-counter stock
- Rights or warrants
- Mutual fund certificates

Following are suggested guidelines for advances against the market value of securities:

Collateral	Advance
Stocks listed on major exchanges	70%
Over-the-counter stocks	50%
Listed bonds	80%
Unlisted bonds	function of quality
U.S. government securities	90–95%
Municipal bonds	function of quality
Convertible securities	80% of call value and 50–70% of premium
Mutual funds	70%
Stocks selling below $5	Nominal advance
Stock inactively traded	Nominal advance

Definitions and Final Points to Keep in Mind When You Lend Against Marketable Securities

- Unregistered stock is sold as a block to a private investor and does not fall under the usual regulations. Letter stock cannot be broken up and is not passed through the market. The security represents a source of funds to the firm, and it can be more flexible concerning dividends, since it is off market and nonvoting.
- Bearer instruments should not secure advances unless the lender is convinced that the borrower owns the securities. Proof of ownership must be established by canceled checks, delivery tickets, and the like unless the borrower is well known at the bank.
- When *hypothecated* collateral (collateral owned by someone else) secures advances, use extra caution. Hypothecated collateral may cause problems in liquidation. The best way to preserve collateral integrity is to obtain a new hypothecation agreement when the loan is renewed.
- Stock splits involve the division of capital stock into a larger number of shares. The lender should ensure that additional shares are obtained, since the stock may fall to undermargined levels.
- Bond quotations should be reviewed regularly. Bond prices are inversely related to interest rates and might fall to undermargined levels during periods of rising interest rates.

Collateral Module in Risk Rating

A large international bank broke down collateral into three categories for the purpose of risk grading the collateral module:

Classification I: Highly Liquid and Readily Attainable Collateral with Difference Secured by Other Less Liquid Assets

1. Cash
2. Bankers' acceptances or commercial paper
3. Top investment grade bonds

Classification II: Independent Audit/Valuation Required

1. Highest accounts receivable quality/liquid and diversified
2. Highest inventory quality/liquid and diversified
3. Fixed assets—prime and readily marketable
   a. Real estate: commercial, collateral
   b. Easily accessible by assignees or participants
   c. Voting rights on collateral not abridged

Classification III: Other Collateral (No Impact on Credit Grade)

1. Leasehold improvements
2. Stock of subsidiaries
3. Stock on pink sheets
4. Receivables: concentrated/questionable quality
5. Inventory: concentrated/questionable quality
6. Real estate: questionable quality and marketability

6 Cash Flow Analysis

Credit Engineering for Bankers. DOI: 10.1016/B978-0-12-378585-5.10006-5
Copyright © 2011 Elsevier Inc. All rights reserved.

Cash flow analysis may well be the most important tool used by commercial and investment bankers to evaluate loans and value companies. Cash flow is, literally, the cash that flows through a company during the course of a quarter or the year after adjusting for noncash, nonoperating events. Lenders rely on cash flow statements because cash flows reveal both the degree by which historical and future cash flows cover debt service and borrowers' chances for survival.

Cash flow is the firm's lifeblood. The greater and more certain the cash flows, the lower the default probabilities. Volatile cash flow is associated with weak bond ratings and higher default rates. There really is no substitute for in-depth knowledge of the firm, the industry in which the borrower operates, and the quality of management. In the final analysis, historical cash flows are simply offerings set by accounting information and guidelines, and they come to life only through the diligence, alertness, and the creativity of the minds that perceive them.

Bankers should always read financials carefully. For example, a clothing manufacturer may make several large shipments of finished products shortly before the end of the fiscal year. The anticipated payment for these goods is booked as a debit to accounts receivable and a credit to revenue. While this transaction is recorded on the company's income statement, the goods shipped may be subject to returns. Returns result in the manufacturer shipping out a "make good" in a subsequent period. In another case, if the goods are acceptable but the customers are marginal credit risks, a substantial portion of the payments may never be realized and may be written off. In both instances, accrued revenue may not bring cash to the company, resulting in an artificially inflated fiscal disclosure.

After reporting healthy profits for years, Enron imploded; the disaster was fueled in part by illusionary earnings in energy services. The firm supplied power to customers at fixed rates and then would make rosy projections on electricity and natural gas prices for the full term of the deal, which could last as long as 10 years. In short, those prices would decline enough to produce substantial profits. Under generally accepted accounting principles (GAAP), Enron was required to "mark to market" the value of its energy trades. However, this is difficult to do when no active market exists on "energy paper," as with stocks or bonds. Companies like Enron were allowed to use their own simulation models to estimate profits and thus marked-to-model the results that management thought Wall Street wanted to see.

To complicate matters, many contracts dealt with customers in states that had not yet deregulated their power markets. Enron forecasted when states would deregulate those markets and then projected what prices would be under the currently nonexistent deregulated market. Then, based on its projections, Enron would calculate its total profit over the life of the contract. After discounting that figure to account for the risk its customer would default and the fact that it would not receive most payments for years, Enron would book the profit immediately.

Introduction to Analysis

Statements of Financial Accounting Standards (SFAS) No. 95[1] (U.S. accounting standards) and International Accounting Standards (IAS) No. 7 mandate that cash flow statements be included in annual reports. Following is a summary from IAS 7:

- The cash flow statement is a required basic financial statement.
- It explains changes in cash and cash equivalents during a specified period.
- Cash equivalents are short-term, highly liquid investments subject to insignificant risk of changes in value.
- Cash flow statements should break down changes in cash and cash equivalents into operating, investing, and financial activities.
    - *Operating:* Cash flows may be presented using either the direct or indirect methods. The direct method shows receipts from customers and payments to suppliers, employees, government (taxes), and so on. The indirect method begins with accrual basis net profit or loss and adjusts for major noncash items.
    - *Investing:* The following should be disclosed separately: cash receipts and payments arising from acquisition or sale of property, plant, and equipment (PP&E); acquisition or sale of equity or debt instruments of other enterprises (including acquisition or sale of subsidiaries); and advances and loans made to, or repayments from, third parties.
    - *Financing:* The following should be disclosed separately: cash receipts and payments arising from an issue of shares or other equity securities; payments made to redeem such securities; proceeds arising from issuing debentures, loans, and notes; and repayments of such securities.
- Cash flows from taxes should be disclosed separately within operating activities, unless they can be specifically identified with one of the other two headings: financing or investing activities.
- Investing and financing activities that do not give rise to cash flows (a nonmonetary transaction such as acquisition of property by issuing debt) should be excluded.

From a banker's perspective, SFAS No. 95 and IAS No. 7 mandated that cash flow statements should be completed in sufficient enough detail to make it easier for analysts to measure the impact cash and noncash investments have on financial position, external financing requirements, reasons for variances between payments and income, and the ability to fund dividends and meet obligations. Earlier accounting standards (specifically, Accounting Principles Board [APB] Opinion 19) allowed businesses to disclose information on either a working capital or cash basis. However, there are significant problems with accepting working capital as a proxy for cash. For example, working capital reports fail to take into account the composition of working capital. While absolute working capital may increase, liquidity could actually be compromised due to buildups of stale inventory.

---

[1] In 1987, FASB Statement No. 95 (FAS 95) mandated that firms provide cash flow statements. While SFAS No. 95, IAS No. 7, and updates represent primary sources, the authors reference the *Miller GAAP Guide,* an excellent reference tool. Researching GAAP can be time consuming because of the multiple sources for pronouncements.

The section on operating activities may be disclosed using either direct or indirect methods. Under either method, a reconciliation of net cash flow from operations to net income is required, and either method should result in the same cash flow from operations. The direct method focuses on cash and the impact cash inflows/outflows have on the borrower's financial condition. By checking numbers carefully and comparing cash-based numbers to accrual results, bankers walk away with a better understanding of their client's cash flow. The indirect basis starts off with net income but makes the necessary adjustments to pull out noncash and nonoperating revenue and expenses to arrive at the correct operating cash flow.

Indirect Method of Cash Reporting: The Banker's Cash Flow

Most reported cash flow statements commingle working (capital) assets/liabilities with gross operating cash flow (GOCF), which is weak disclosure at best. Net operating cash flow should break out working capital and not combine income statement accounts. GOCF represents the income statement's ability to provide the primary internal cash required for future growth. Two cash sources are available to finance growth: internal and external. We associate external financing with debt or equity injections, while internal sources originate from within firms themselves— namely, from profits and net asset disposals.

For purposes of the banker's cash flow, internal cash flow or cash from the income statement is classified as GOCF. Thus, GOCF is introduced to the cash flow format. GOCF is usually compared to cash provided by debt financing activities. This comparison allows the lender to check for any imbalance in internal versus external financing and to make comparisons in financial leverage trends (Figure 6.1).

Direct Method of Reporting Cash

To form a better understanding of the intricacies of the cash flow statement, let's take a look at each section individually.

Investing Activities

The *Miller GAAP Guide*[2] summarizes investing activities as including the following:

> *Making and collecting loans and acquiring and disposing of debt or equity instruments and property, plant, and equipment and other productive assets—that*

---

[2] Jan R. Williams and Joseph V. Carcello, *Miller GAAP Guide (Level A)*, CCH, Inc., 2009 edition (October 1, 2008). *GAAP Guide Level A* analyzes authoritative GAAP literature contained in Level A of the GAAP hierarchy, established by the Statement on Auditing Standards No. 69, including FASB Statements and Interpretations, as well as APB Opinions and Accounting Research Bulletins. In clear language, each pronouncement is discussed in a comprehensive format that makes it easy to understand and apply. Practical illustrations and examples demonstrate and clarify specific accounting principles. The 2009 edition covers up to FAS-163.

COMPANY X
For the Year Ended December 31, 2010

Increase (Decrease) in Cash and Cash Equivalents		
Cash flows from operating activities:		
Net income	3,040	
Adjustments to reconcile net income to net cash provided by operating activities.		
Depreciation and amortization	1,780	
Provision for losses on accounts receivable	800	
Gain on sale of facility	(320)	
Undistributed earnings of affiliate	(100)	
Gross operating cash flow*		**5,200**
(Inc.) Dec. accounts receivable	(860)	
(Inc.) Dec. inventory	820	
(Inc.) Dec. prepaid expenses	(100)	
Operating cash needs*		**(140)**
Inc. (Dec.) accounts payable and accrued expenses	(1,000)	
Inc. (Dec.) interest and income taxes payable	200	
Inc. (Dec.) deferred taxes	600	
Inc. (Dec.) other current liabilities	200	
Inc. (Dec.) other adjustments	400	
Operating cash sources*		**400**
Net cash provided by operating activities		**5,460**
Cash flows from investing activities:		
Proceeds from sale of facility	2,400	
Payment received on note for sale of plant	600	
Capital expenditures	(4,000)	
Payment for purchase of Company S, net of cash acquired	(3,700)	
Net cash used in investing activities		**(4,700)**
Cash flows from financing activities:		
Net borrowings under line of credit agreement	1,200	
Principal payments under capital lease obligation	(500)	
Proceeds from issuance of long-term debt	1,600	
Net cash provided by debt financing activities*		**2,300**
Proceeds from issuance of common stock	2,000	
Dividends paid	(800)	
Net cash provided by other financing activities		**1,200**
Net increase in cash and cash equivalents		**4,260**
Cash and cash equivalents at beginning of year	2,400	
Cash and cash equivalents at end of year	6,660	

*Category added to complete Bankers' Cash Flow format.

Figure 6.1 Revised Bankers Cash Flow.

is, assets held for or used in the production of goods or services by the enterprise (other than materials that are part of the enterprise's inventory).

Investment activities include advances and repayments to subsidiaries, securities transactions, and investments in long-term revenue-producing assets. Cash inflows from investing include proceeds from disposals of equipment and proceeds from the sale of investment securities (Figure 6.2). Cash outflows include capital expenditures and the purchase of stock of other entities, project financing, capital and operating leases, and master limited partnerships

Property, Plant, and Equipment

Cash flows associated with PP&E activities include fixed assets purchased through acquisitions and equipment purchases, capital leases, and proceeds from property disposals. Noncash transactions include translation gains and losses, transfers, depreciation, reverse consolidations, and restatements.

Lenders do not usually require borrowers to break out property expenditures into expenditures for the maintenance of existing capacity and expenditures for expansion into new capacity, though this would be ideal disclosure, since maintenance and capital expenditures are nondiscretionary outlays. However, due to the difficulty (and subjectivity) involved in differentiating between maintenance outlays from expansion, amounts assigned to maintenance accounts would likely prove unreliable.

Unconsolidated Subsidiaries

When companies acquire between 20% and 50% of outside stock, the purchase is denoted an "investment in unconsolidated subsidiary" and is listed as an asset on the acquiring firm's balance sheet. Cash inflows/outflows include dividends, advances, repayments, and stock acquisitions and sales. Noncash events include equity earnings and translation gains and losses.

Investment Project Cash Flows and Joint Ventures

These include investments in joint ventures or separate entities formed for the purpose of carrying out large projects. Typically, new entities borrow funds to build plants or projects supported with debt guarantees furnished by companies forming the new

Cash flows from investing activities:

Proceeds from sale of facility	2,400	
Payment received on note for sale of plant	600	
Capital expenditures	(4,000)	
Payment for purchase of Company S, net of cash acquired	(3,700)	
Net cash used in investing activities		**(4,700)**

Figure 6.2 Example of Investment Reconciliation.

entity. Cash flows generally are remitted (upstreamed) to owner firms as dividends. Bankers typically receive a through-and-through disclosure of the project's future cash flows, because endeavors such as construction projects are governed by explicit accounting rules. Thus, it is often difficult for bankers to untangle cash flows hidden beneath noncash events such as equity earnings. In addition, the project's projections may not be useful if cash streams are masked in joint ventures while the loan that financed the project to begin with is disclosed on the borrower's consolidated balance sheet.

Financing Activities

According to the *Miller GAAP Guide,* financing activities include the following:[3]

> *Obtaining resources from owners and providing them with a return on, and return of, their investment; borrowing money and repaying amounts borrowed, or otherwise settling the obligation; and obtaining and paying for other resources obtained from creditors on long-term credit.*

Cash inflows from financing activities include new equity infusions, treasury stock sales, and funded debt such as bonds, mortgages, notes, commercial paper, and short-term loans. Cash outflows consist of dividends, treasury stock purchases, and loan payments (Figure 6.3).

Long-Term Debt

Debt proceeds represent the amount a company actually receives from a debt issue, while increases and reductions in long-term debt include amortization of debt discounts and premiums. Amortization of a debt discount reduces earnings (noncash charge), while the debt's book value increases accordingly. No cash was received or paid out via the bookkeeping entry, yet debt levels were adjusted on financial statements. Thus, debt discounts are subtracted from debt increases to determine "true" debt increases. The amortization of a debt premium is subtracted from long-term debt reductions to determine the "actual" reductions.

Keep in mind that the traditional interest-bearing bond is composed of the principal portion, which will be repaid to the holder of the bond in full at maturity, and the interest portion of the bond, which consists of coupon payments that the holder of the bond receives at regular intervals, usually every six months. In comparison, zero coupons pay "zero" coupons, deferring the interest to maturity. The amortization required, because it is so large, increases reported debt levels, but no cash payout is made until maturity. Hence, the only time cash flow is affected is at maturity when payment is due to investors. Bankers should always keep this in mind when evaluating disparate debt issues. Conversion of debt to equity normally results in a substantial noncash transaction. However, conversion eliminates interest payments while

[3] Ibid.

Cash flows from financing activities:

Net borrowings under line of credit agreement	1,200	
Principal payments under capital lease obligation	(500)	
Proceeds from issuance of long-term debt	1,600	
Net cash provided by debt financing activities		**2,300**
Proceeds from issuance of common stock	2,000	
Dividends paid	(800)	
Net cash provided by equity financing activities		**1200**
Cash flows from financing activities		**3,500**

Figure 6.3 Example of Financing Activities.

reducing financial leverage. Financing activities also include preferred and common stock issues plus treasury stock inflows/outflows and options.

Dividends

Businesses grow by reinvesting current earnings. If stockholders withdraw earnings to support a lavish lifestyle, they put the cart before the horse. Most businesses experience cycles of good and bad times, growth and retraction. Without accumulating a "war chest," firms may not survive recessions or be liquid enough to repay obligations. Further, without reinvesting earnings, management cannot exploit opportunities by financing expansion internally.

Operating Activities

Figure 6.4 is an example of the most important source of internal cash flow: operating activities.

The *Miller GAAP Guide* defines operating activities as follows:[4]

> *All transactions and other events not defined as investing or financing activities. Operating activities generally involve producing and delivering goods and providing services. Cash flows from operating activities are generally the cash effects of transactions and other events that enter into the determination of income.*

Gross Operating Cash Flow

GOCF, an important feature of the cash flow statement, equals net income plus noncash charges, less noncash credits, plus or minus nonoperating events. This section depicts cash generated by operating income, routinely the borrower's dominant source of internal financing. Noncash charges represent reductions in income not calling for cash outlays. Depreciation and amortization, provision for deferred taxes,

---

[4] Ibid.

Cash flows from operating activities

Net income	$3,040	
Adjustments to reconcile net income to net cash		
provided by operating activities:		
Depreciation and amortization	1,780	
Provision for losses on accounts receivable	800	
Gain on sale of facility	(320)	
Undistributed earnings of affiliate	(100)	
Gross operating cash flow		**$5200**
Increase in accounts receivable	$(860)	
Decrease in inventory	820	
Increase in prepaid expenses	(100)	
Operating cash needs		**(140)**
Decrease in accounts payable and accrued expenses	$(1,000)	
Increase in interest and income taxes payable	200	
Increase in deferred taxes	600	
Increase in other liabilities	200	
Other adjustments	400	
Operating cash sources		**400**
Net cash provided by operating activities		**5,460**

Figure 6.4 Operating Activities.

asset write-downs, and amortization of bond discounts, provisions, reserves, and losses in equity investments are familiar examples of noncash charges. Noncash credits increase earnings without generating cash and include equity earnings in unconsolidated investments, amortization of bond premiums, and negative deferred tax provisions. Nonoperating charges and earnings such as restructuring gains/charges and gains and losses on the sale of equipment are adjusted as well, representing further refinements to reported earnings.

A typical interpretative problem area for lenders is disclosure of unconsolidated entities where cash inflows depend on dividend streams returned by projects or investment divestitures. Noncash profits can easily be managed by selecting liberal accounting methods or by simply manufacturing income. In one such case, Enron, which was involved in a joint venture with Blockbuster, reported large profits even though the venture never attracted more than a few customers (see Enron cash flow, available on the website).

Cash generated from nonrecurring items may artificially inflate the borrower's profits, but it usually cannot be depended on to provide cash flow to support long-term financing. Included are gains and losses from the sale of business units, judgments awarded to the company, and other one-time cash inflows. One-time extraordinary expenses usually have little impact on long-term cash flows. For example, if XYZ Company settles a lawsuit over patent infringement that results in a one-time cash payout, the long-term health of the company may not be affected—that is, if XYZ Company can afford the settlement. On the other hand, consider a pharmaceutical company that loses a product liability suit, resulting in a cash settlement along with the recall of its best-selling drug. If the product is crucial to long-term survival, the borrower may end up financially distressed. Lenders should review nonrecurring items and their impact on credit decisions, since it is core earnings that pay off loans, not phantom events or extraordinary income. Indeed, borrowing or capital stock issues may provide more funds than operations, but bankers count on business operations to provide the funds to finance ongoing operations, repay obligations, and distribute dividends.

Equity Earnings

Equity earnings show up on the income statement as increases to earnings. These often illusory earnings end up included in retained earnings, and because they are noncash items, leverage and coverage ratios are sometimes distorted. What's the story behind equity earning? Suppose your borrower owns between 20% and 50% of another firm's stock. Accountants say your borrower "influences" the firm's operations and so must include the prorated share of earnings into its financial statements. Thus, if the firm makes $1,000,000 profit, 25% of those profits (or $250,000) is included as equity earnings.

Suppose your borrower, Company A, originally invested $1 million in Company B in year 0, obtaining a 25% equity stake. By year 5, the value of this 25% stake may have grown to $2.5 million. The equity earnings from this investment would have been reflected on your borrower's (Company A) income statement over the five-year period, but no cash has been received from the investment (assuming no dividends)—cash that might have paid loans. To adjust for the income statement distortion, banks pull this noncash credit from cash flows. The investment may be perfectly circumspect in a number of ways, but there is the danger that the investment could pay out ill-timed dividends or otherwise set the stage for financial maneuvering—siphoning funds, for example.

Deferred Tax Credits

Deferred tax credits cause earnings to increase but may not provide cash or offer a sustainable source of cash. Deferred tax credits often come about when previous provisions for deferred taxes are reversed.

Operating Cash Needs

Of approximately equal magnitude, accounts receivable and inventory typically constitute almost 80% of current assets for manufacturing industries. With such a large, relatively volatile working capital investment, operating cash needs deserve special attention. Accounts receivable and inventory levels reflect the borrower's marketing abilities and credit policies. Revenue from sales may have been reported for the period, but cash may not have been received. A rise in receivables represents a use of cash and is usually financed. A decrease in receivables is associated with cash inflows.

Operating Cash Sources

The right side of the balance sheet supports assets. Large increases and decreases in current accounts represent substantial inflows and outflows of cash. Operating cash sources generally include non-interest-bearing current liabilities that tend to follow sales increases. Accounts payable represents inventory purchases on credit. Increases in accounts payable are a source of cash in the sense that they delay cash outflows into the future. While the borrower has use of this cash, it can utilize it for daily needs as well as for investment purposes. Eventual payment to creditors decreases accounts payable, converting them into a use of cash. Generally, decreases from one period to the next represent an amount paid to suppliers in excess of purchases expensed. Increases in accruals and taxes payable represent sources of cash, because items such as salaries, taxes, and interest are expensed but not paid out. Thus, cash is conserved for a limited period. A decrease in accruals arises from payments in excess of costs expensed. In the current period, therefore, the decrease is subtracted from the cash flow as a use of cash.

Net Operating Cash Flow

Net operating cash flow denotes the cash available from GOCF to internally finance a borrower's future growth (after demands on working capital are satisfied). One of the great things about the structure of the cash flow format is how pieces of information surface to offer compelling insights about company operations. For example, if GOCF is often lower than net cash flow from operations, traditional sources of working capital, accounts payable, and accruals have completely covered traditional working capital uses, accounts receivable, inventory, and so on. As a result, precious operating cash income need not be diverted to support working capital levels and can thus be rerouted to finance "growth" strategies included in investment activities—the lifeblood of shareholder value.

Cash Flow Workshop

The cash flow analysis is not a stand-alone document. It is used in conjunction with the balance sheet and income statement. As discussed earlier, cash flow is the sum of cash flowing in and out of firms. Before beginning our workshop, we consider transactions making up sources and uses of cash and how each is derived. The statement of cash flow is directly related to the balance sheet. To illustrate, behind two fiscal balance sheets are underlying transactions that make up all operating, investment, and financing activities. Subtracting two balance sheets will make it relatively easy to classify transactions that, indeed, end up on the banker's cash flow statement. Let's start with the basic accounting equation given in Figure 6.5. Later in the chapter, we move the technique further along by decomposing and recreating the cash flow of Gem Furniture, a firm requesting a $2 million line of credit.

Equations 4 and 5 in Figure 6.5 show that changes in cash are exactly equal to differences between cash sources and uses. Note that assets, defined as uses of cash, depict negative deltas ($-\Delta$) preceding balance sheet changes, while liabilities and

DERIVATION OF CASH FLOW	NOTES
Equation 1: Assets = Liabilities + Equity	Basic accounting equation
Equation 2: Cash + Accounts receivable + Inventory + Net fixed assets+ Investments in unconsolidated subsidiaries = Accounts payable + Accruals + Short-term debt + Current portion long-term debt + Long-term debt + Equity	Extrapolate the basic accounting equation
Equation 3: Cash = Accounts payable + Accruals + Short-term debt + Current portion long-term debt + Long-term debt + Equity − Accounts receivable − Inventory − Net fixed assets − Investments in unconsolidated subsidiaries	Solve for cash
Equation 4: Δ Cash = Δ Accounts payable + Δ Accruals + Δ Short-term debt + Δ Current portion long-term debt + Δ Long-term debt + Δ Equity − Δ Accounts receivable − Δ Inventory − Δ Net fixed assets − Δ Investments in unconsolidated subsidiaries	Multiply both sides of Equation 3 by delta Δ
Equation 5:− Δ Cash = − Δ Accounts payable − Δ Accruals − Δ Short-term debt − Δ Current portion long-term debt − Δ Long-term debt − Δ Equity + Δ Accounts receivable + Δ Inventory + Δ Net fixed assets + Δ Investments in unconsolidated subsidiaries	Multiply both sides of Equation 4 by minus 1

Figure 6.5 Steps to Derive Cash Flow Equation.

equity accounts, traditional sources of cash, are preceded by positive deltas (Δ). For example, if a borrower—say, Company A—manufactures product X and sells it but has not paid for raw materials used in production, cash is conserved. The result is increases in accounts payable, a source of cash. Conversely, if the firm sells on terms, no cash is received at the time of the sale, resulting in the expansion of receivable, a use of cash.

Cash sources and uses include the following:

Sources of cash include	Uses of cash include
Decreases in assets (−Δ)	Increases in assets (−Δ)
Increases in liabilities (+Δ)	Decreases in liabilities (−Δ)
Increases in equity (+Δ)	Decreases in equity (−Δ)

Now let's work with a simple example, Gem Furniture Corp. Download the Gem Furniture case—both the Excel worksheet and the solution from the Elsevier website www.ElsevierDirect.com. Now we can build up its cash flow from scratch. Four steps are involved:

1. Develop a control sheet.
2. Prepare reconciliations arising from your control sheet.
3. Complete the cash flow statement.
4. Develop your analysis

Gem Furniture Corporation Deal Analysis

Scenario

It is February 2009. Landon Smith, vice president of Mason National Bank (MNB) of Atlanta's largest corporate banking center, was delighted when Nancy Brown, the new Gem Furniture Corporation Chief Financial Officer (CFO), approached him stating that Gem was ready to start transferring the firm's banking relationship at City Bank Group (CBG) to MNB. MNB had been soliciting the Gem account for 15 years, but in spite of intensive efforts, it never succeeded in dislodging the relationship away from CBG.

Smith wanted to move quickly to accommodate Gem's CFO and win the bank this business. As a "groundbreaker," Ms. Brown is requesting approval of a $2 million short-term credit line to supplement the firm's $50 million short-term credit line at City Bank Group, fully utilized. Brown mentioned that over a reasonable time Gem will drop the CBG business altogether and lodge the entire relationship with MNB. In addition to the line, the firm owes $35 million on a three-year revolver used to finance an acquisition, which is expected to be reduced in two years.

Business Summary

Gem Furniture Corporation, a private firm located in Atlanta, runs a furniture-making empire. The company ranks as one of the top U.S. makers of residential furniture. Gem Furniture's subsidiaries offer a lineup of nationally recognized brands. Gem Furniture distributes its products through a network of furniture centers, independent dealers, national and local chains, and department stores.

The firm operates about 20 plants in South Carolina, North Carolina, and Georgia. It has been looking for ways to diversify. In mid-2008, Gem Furniture announced plans to expand its licensing program. The Allison brand has already extended its reach beyond furniture into residential flooring, lighting, and kitchen cabinetry. The company is looking to license its Bobby, Heritage, Monaha, and Henry Stellar brands.

To better focus on the residential rather than business furnishings market, Gem Furniture sold its business furniture division, Robbins Business Furniture (RBF), to Zarchen Corp. for about $75 million in 2007. Gem Furniture also is refocusing its distribution efforts. Thomasville and Heritage are expanding their network of branded stores, both company- and dealer-owned, while Broyhill and Lane are focusing on distributing to traditional furniture retailers and mass merchants. Gem closed or announced the closing of more than 35 domestic manufacturing facilities since 2001. It has also boosted its manufacturing capacity in Indonesia to capitalize on the low manufacturing costs. In addition, it owns and operates several offshore plants in the Philippines and Indonesia.

Gem's Chief Executive Officer (CEO) informed Mr. Smith that while fiscal profits fell to a disappointing $2 million due mostly to the U.S. economic downturn, profits will not fall below present levels within a five-year projection horizon. Pointing to a savings of some $20 million a year, Gem Furniture hopes to ride out the economic downturn as consumers begin to spend more on outfitting their homes. Thus, income should actually return to normal levels "when things improve." To help weather the recession, in December 2008, Gem laid off some 15% of its domestic workforce, amounting to about 1,400 jobs, which included both management and hourly employees. It made further cuts in May 2009 by laying off 250 plant workers. The cuts have primarily affected manufacturing centers in North Carolina and Georgia.

Finally, because strategic efforts combined with the economic downturn put pressure on working capital, the firm's working capital position will likely not normalize for at least three years—hence the need for additional short-term bank lines.

The Four-Step Approach

Let's proceed from the point of view that you are the senior vice president in charge of MNB's Atlanta banking center. You just received a memo from VP Landon Smith recommending approval of the proposed $2 million credit line. Smith cited in his recommendation memo (1) Gem's successful history, (2) MNB's intensive and previously unsuccessful solicitation efforts, and (3) the firm's excellent fiscal performance record. In response to Smith's recommendation, you write a memo (paragraph) to Smith expressing your thoughts and, of course, your decision.

FINANCIAL INFORMATION: OPEN MG GEMCF ANSWER EXCEL.XLS ON THE ELSEVIER WEBSITE www.ElsevierDirect.com

The 2008 fiscal statement for Gem Furniture, shown here, was audited by Deloitte. In the accountant's opinion, the fiscal statements give a true and fair view of the company's financial position and performance.

First Step: Develop the Control Sheet for Gem Furniture (Range: F5:H29)

Simply subtract Gem's fiscal 2008 balance sheet from fiscal 2007. Figure 6.6 shows the result.

1. Calculate year-to-year balance sheet changes.
2. Decide whether an item is a source or use of cash. For example, Gem's accounts receivable increased by $32,683, a use of cash.
3. Total the columns to identify the cash change. The change in cash is equal to the difference between sources and uses of cash.

We must break out reconciliation accounts, deriving transactions that contributed to change. One of the most important benefits of reconciliations is that they determine so-called information gaps, or differences between derived and ending balances on important reconciliations.

Decide what in the control sheet needs to be reconciled. Some reconciliations are nondiscretionary, while others are discretionary. Nondiscretionary reconciliations include net fixed assets, equity, long-term debt, investments in unconsolidated subsidiaries, deferred taxes, minority interest, and, most important, any bizarre or unusual item that appears on the balance sheet. Discretionary reconciliations include goodwill and intangibles.

Gem Furniture Company
Balance Sheet (000's)

Assets	12/31/2006	12/31/2007	12/31/2008
Cash	15,445	12,007	11,717
Accts Receivable Net	51,793	55,886	88,571
Inventory (1)	56,801	99,087	139,976
Total Current Assets	124,039	166,980	240,264
Plant & Equipment	53,283	60,301	68,621
Accumulated Deprec	(8,989)	(13,961)	(20,082)
Net Plant & Equip.	44,294	46,340	48,539
Total Assets	168,333	213,320	288,803
Short Term Borrowings	9,562	15,300	54,698
Accounts Payable	20,292	31,518	59,995
Accruals	10,328	15,300	21,994
Curr Portion Debt	500	500	500
Total Current Liabilities	40,682	62,618	137,187
Senior Long Term Debt	27,731	36,491	35,706
Total Liabilities	68,413	99,109	172,893
Common Stock	69,807	69,807	69,807
Retained Earnings	30,113	44,404	46,103
Total Owner's Equity	99,920	114,211	115,910
Total Liabilities and Equity	168,333	213,320	288,803

Gem Furniture Company
Income Statement (000's)

	12/31/2006	12/31/2007	12/31/2008
Net Sales	512,693	553,675	586,895
Cost of Goods Sold	(405,803)	(450,394)	(499,928)
Depreciation Expense	(4,781)	(4,973)	(6,120)
Gross Profit	102,109	98,308	80,847
S G & A Expense	(38,369)	(46,034)	(50,643)
Miscellaneous Expenses	(6,082)	(10,672)	(17,174)
Net Operating Profit	57,658	41,602	13,030
Interest Expense	(3,648)	(5,258)	(8,974)
Pre Tax Profit	54,010	36,344	4,056
Tax Expense	(26,068)	(17,589)	(2,091)
Net Profit	27,942	18,755	1,965

Inventory Footnote 1

Percent of Total Inventory	2006	2007	2008
Raw Materials	33%	35%	24%
Work In Progress	18%	45%	63%
Finished Goods	49%	20%	13%
Total	100%	100%	100%
Order Backlogs	15	135	297

ASSUME FISCAL 2008 FOOTNOTES REVEAL	
Capital Expenditures	8319
Dividends	266
Long Term Debt Increase	0
Long Term Debt Decrease	785

Figure 6.6 Gem Furniture's December 31, 2008, Control Sheet.

	Increase	Decrease
Cash		**(290)**
	Source	**Use**
Accts Receivable Net		32,685
Inventory		40,889
Net Plant & Equipment		2,199
Short-Term Borrowings	39,398	
Accounts Payable	28,477	
Accruals	6,694	
Current Portion Debt	0	
Senior Long-Term Debt		785
Retained Earnings	1,699	
Total	**76,268**	**76,558**
Change in cash and marketable securities	**(290)**	

Figure 6.6 *(Continued).*

Second Step: Expand Gem's Control Sheet for Gem Furniture with Asset Reconciliations

Net Fixed Asset Reconciliation

Included in this category are capital expenditures, depreciation, acquisitions, capital leases, proceeds from disposals of property, unrealized translation gains and losses, and transfers. Adding book gains or subtracting book losses derives proceeds from disposals. Translation gains and losses (FASB 52) earmark currency holding gains and losses. They are included so bankers can distinguish between realized and unrealized fixed asset transactions. Figure 6.7 provides an example of what is generally included in a fixed asset reconciliation, and Figure 6.8 shows the fixed asset reconciliation prepared for Gem Furniture.

Equity Reconciliation

Comprehensive equity reconciliations are frequently organized in annual report footnotes and the cash flow statement. The equity reconciliation is completed as follows:

- Equity accounts and opening balances appear as headings, with total equity as the last column.
- Listed down the columns are transactions corresponding to their respective equity account. Totals for each transaction along the row are recorded in the total equity column.
- After the transactions are recorded, each column is totaled, identifying the ending balance for each equity account. The ending balance equals year-end account balances.
- The total equity column should reconcile to the sum of the account balances across the bottom, thus maintaining the self-proving nature of the system.

Net Property Plant and Equipment	(prior period)
Less: Depreciation and amortization of net fixed assets	(current period)
Less: Proceeds from disposals	(current period)
Less: Losses on sale of fixed assets	(current period)
Plus: Gain on sale of fixed assets	(current period)
Plus: Capital expenditures	(current period)
Plus: Acquired fixed assets	(current period)
Plus/(Less) Translation Gains (Losses)	(current period)
= Derived Net Property Plant and Equipment	(current period)
Less: Actual Net Property Plant and Equipment	(current period)
= Increase/Decrease Net Property Plant and Equipment	(current period) INFORMATION GAP

Figure 6.7 An Example of the Fixed Asset Reconciliation.

Property Plant and Equipment	Amount	Information	Source/Use	Cash Flow Category
Beginning: Balance 2006	46,340	Balance Sheet		
Less: Depreciation 2007	(6,120)	Cash Flow Statement	Source	Gross Operating Cash Flow
Plus: Capital Expenditures 2007	8,319	Cash Flow Statement	Use	Investment Activities
Derived Ending Balance 2007	48,539			
Balance Sheet Ending Balance	48,529	Balance Sheet		
(Inc)Dec Fixed Assets	0			No Information Gap

Figure 6.8 Gem Furniture's Fixed Asset Reconciliation (Range: A56:B62).

• Transactions not affecting cash cancel out, so no number is carried to the total column, and it will not appear on the cash flow statement.

Examples of accounts that belong in equity include net income, cash dividends, proceeds from stock sale, exercise of stock options, cumulative translation adjustments, and purchases and sales of treasury stock. Cash transactions affecting equity are carried to the cash flow statement. Equity transfers, like stock dividends, are excluded. The Gem equity reconciliation appears in Figure 6.9 and in Excel worksheet A65:D72.

The long-term debt reconciliation (Figure 6.10) for Gem Furniture appears in Figure 6.11 and in cells A65:D72 of the Excel worksheet.

	Common Stock	Retained Earnings	Total
Equity Accounts			
Beginning Balance	69,807	44,404	114,211
Net Income (Loss)		1,965	1,965
Cash Div.		(266)	(266)
Ending Balance	69,807	46,103	115,910

Figure 6.9 Gem Furniture's Reconciliation of Equity Accounts.

Current portion	(prior year)
Plus: Noncurrent portion	(prior year)
Plus: Increase in long-term debt (current year derived from the issue-by-issue breakdown in the footnotes)	(current year)
Less: Noncurrent portion	(current year)
= Reductions in long-term debt	(current year)

Figure 6.10 Long-Term Debt Reconciliation.

		Source/(Use)	Bankers Cash Flow
Current Portion Long-Term Debt 2006	500		
Noncurrent Long-Term Debt 2007	36491		
Plus: New Debt Issue	0	Neutral	Financing Activity
Less Current Portion Long-Term Debt 1993	(500)	Use	
Less: Noncurrent Long-Term Debt 1993	(35706)		
= Long-Term Decreases 1993	785	Use	Financing Activities

Figure 6.11 Gem Furniture's Long-Term Debt Reconciliation.

Third Step: Complete the Cash Flow Statement for Gem Furniture

Gem's cash flow statement is constructed from scratch. At the end of this exercise the cash flow statement you complete will look exactly like Figure 6.12 and in cells A82:C107 of the Excel worksheet.

To complete the cash flow statement for Gem Furniture, first set up labels as follows, leaving enough space to include transfers from the control sheet and cash flow reconciliations you derived:

1. Gross Operating Cash Flow
2. Operating Cash Needs
3. Operating Cash Sources
4. Net Cash Flow From Operations

Gem Furniture Company		
Cash Flow Fiscal December 31, 2008		
Cash Flow Accounts		
Net Income	1,965	
Plus/Less: Noncash Items		
Depreciation	6,120	
GROSS OPERATING CASH FLOW		**8,085**
(Inc.)/Dec. Net A/R	(32,685)	
(Inc.)/Dec. Inventory	(40,889)	
Operating Cash Needs		**(73,574)**
(Inc.)/Dec. Net A/P	28,477	
(Inc.)/Dec. Accruals	6,694	
Operating Cash Sources		**35,171**
Net Cash Provided By		
Operating Activities		**(30,318)**
Capital Expenditures	(8,319)	
Net Cash Used In Investing Activities		(8,319)
Long-Term Debt Increases	0	
Long-Term Debt Payments	(785)	
Short-Term Debt	39,398	
Cash Flows From Interest Bearing Debt		**38,613**
Cash Dividends	(266)	
Cash Flows From Equity		**(266)**
NET CHANGE IN CASH ITEMS		**(290)**

Figure 6.12 Cash Flow Statement for Gem Furniture.

	2006	2007	2008
Quick Ratio	0.2	0.1	0.1
Current Ratio	3.0	2.7	1.8
Inventory Turnover	7.1	4.5	3.6
Average Collection Period	36.9	36.8	55.1
Fixed Asset Turnover	11.6	11.9	12.1
Total Asset Turnover	3.0	2.6	2.0
Return on Total Assets	16.6%	8.8%	0.7%
Return on Net Worth	28.0%	16.4%	1.7%
Debt Ratio (Debt/Assets)	0.41	0.46	0.60
Net Profit Margin	5.45%	3.39%	0.33%
GPM	19.92%	17.76%	13.78%

Figure 6.13 Gem Furniture's Key Ratios.

5. Investment Activities
6. Financing Activities
7. Change in Cash

Next, transfer directly to the cash flow all control sheet items that did not require a reconciliation: accounts receivable, inventory, and so on. Transfer them exactly as they appear on the control sheet: A source of cash on the control sheet is a source of cash on the banker's cash flow statement. Then transfer all items within the reconciliations and determine whether the items about to be transferred are sources or uses of cash. Finally, sum the cash flow and make sure you have included subtotals. The change in cash should prove to the difference between the sources and uses of cash.

Fourth Step: Develop Your Analysis

As we shall see, ratios and cash flow are integrated to help us better understand the potential risks this deal presents to the bank (Figure 6.13).

What ratios should be integrated into the cash flow? Let's review Gem's cash flow in Figure 6.14. If weaknesses occur, ratios will help us understand why.

Decision

While most bankers would not approve this loan proposal as submitted, there are exceptions. What is your decision? Write a paragraph or two supporting your position.

Other Important Reconciliations Bankers Consider

Investment Reconciliation

Equity investment transactions include equity earnings, dividends from subsidiaries, advances, repayments, purchase and sale of securities, translation gains/losses,

Cash Flow	Meaning
Gross operating cash flow(GOCF) > net income.	Normal, since noncash charges produce this result. Bankers should be cautious if GOCF < net income because noncash credits (i.e., equity earnings or deferred tax credit) likely have inflated earnings. Fiscal net income of 1,965 was lower than GOCF of 8,085. This means noncash credits were not a factor. Noncash credits increase earnings but did not produce cash and inflate the income statement. Gem passed this first test.
Net cash flow from operating < GOCF.	Net cash flow from operations represents internal cash flow available for investment activities. Because Gem's net cash from operations is below GOCF, operating cash needs may be cannibalizing the income statement's ability to finance investments internally. Accounts receivable, inventory, and other operating current assets likely are increasing too quickly. Ratios (average collection period and inventory turnover) will determine if increases in receivables and inventory are normal or represent a serious problem.
Net cash flow from operations is negative.	Gem's net cash from operations is negative 30,318. This is disturbing, since the firm has no internal cash flow available to finance investment activities. Financing is nondiscretionary.
Dividends < income.	Acceptable under normal conditions but questionable here because net cash flow from operations is negative.
Liquidity ratios are deteriorating.	Disturbing. While the actual changes seem relatively small, pro forma analysis will show that the changes will have a strong negative impact on the firm's ability to finance it.
Operating Cash Needs Analysis: Substitute last year's ACP and solve for accounts receivable pro forma (receivables that should have appeared on Gem's balance sheet had Gem been as efficient as last year collecting them). See Figure 6.15, Operating Cash Needs Pro Forma Analysis (Worksheet A112:B140). Pro forma, or "what if," analysis calculates fiscal 2008 accounts receivable and inventory that *would have* appeared on the	Figure 6.15 (cells A112:B140) indicates that a change in the average collection period to 55 days, fiscal 2008, from 37 days resulted in a pro forma increase in receivables. Thus, excessive accounts receivables were 29,332 (cell B125). In addition to excessive receivables, Gem's fiscal 2008 inventory was excessive. We substitute 2007 inventory turnover and solve for inventory that would have appeared on the Gem's 2008 fiscal balance sheet had the firm been as efficient as industry average at controlling inventory. Excessive inventory was 29,991 (cell B139).

balance sheet had the firm been as efficient as collection receivables and controlling inventory as industry average levels. Differences between fiscal and pro forma receivables and inventory represent internal cash flow lost or compromised because of problems in operating current assets.	
Analyze components of fiscal 2008 inventory and order backlogs (Figure 6.16); cells A142:D150.	We found excessive inventory is 29,991. Most inventories are a work in progress, which is disturbing because order backlogs increased significantly. Many disappointed customers who will not receive finished goods shipments as planned may turn to other vendors, compounding the problem next year.
Compare net cash flow from operations of (30,310) to excess inventory and receivables of 59,323.	Net cash flow from operations would have been positive if inventory and receivables were in control. The short-term loan financed redundant current assets, not capital improvements.

Figure 6.14 (*continued*).

consolidations, and divestitures. A summary financial statement may be included in the footnotes if the auditor determines that a more detailed explanation is warranted. Equity earnings are sometimes netted out against dividends. Dividends can be pulled out as the difference between undistributed equity and equity earnings. Project finance activities can also show up in investment schedules. Figure 6.17 shows an example of the unconsolidated investment reconciliation.

Deferred Tax Reconciliation

Tax expense includes both current and deferred taxes. Deferred taxes arise because of so-called timing differences—for example, when income/expenses reported on financial statements differ from taxes reported to the IRS. Some common factors causing timing dissimilarities include different depreciation methods for financial statement and tax purposes and recognition of income in different periods for book and tax purposes. If taxable income exceeds book income (this occurs when prepaid cash is booked, such as a subscription), deferred taxes are recorded as an asset. A negative provision increases income and reduces the deferred tax liability. Information on deferred tax is usually found in the tax footnote. Figure 6.18 shows the deferred tax reconciliation.

Intangible Reconciliation

Goodwill and intangible reconciliations (Figure 6.19) are required when amortization of goodwill or intangibles are disclosed in the annual report.

Analysis of receivables

Accounts receivable 2007	55,886
Accounts receivable 2008	88,571
Sales 2007	553,675
Sales 2008	586,895
Average collection period 2007	37
Average collection period 2008	55

Substitute 2009 Average Collection Period
(ACP); solve AR Pro forma
Accounts receivable 2008 pro forma = 37*586895/365

Accounts receivable 2008 pro forma	59,239
Accounts receivable 2008 actual	<u>88,571</u>
Excess accounts receivables	**29,332**

DRAIN ON Net Cash Flow From Operations

Analysis of Inventory

Inventory 2007	99,087
Inventory2008	139,976
Cost of sales 2007	450,394
Cost of sales 2008	499,928
Inventory turnover 2007	4.55
Inventory turnover 2008	3.57

Substitute 2007 turnover; solve for inventory pro forma

Inventory pro forma 2008 = 499928/4.56	109,985
Inventory 2008	<u>139,976</u>
Excess Inventory	**29,991**

Or, inventory that failed to convert to receivables

Figure 6.15 Gem Furniture's Operating Cash Needs Pro Forma Analysis.

FINANCIAL STATEMENTS REVEAL

Percent of Total Inventory	2006	2007	2008
Raw Materials	33%	35%	24%
Work In Progress	18%	45%	63%
Finished Goods	<u>49%</u>	<u>20%</u>	<u>13%</u>
Total	**100%**	**100%**	**100%**
Order Backlogs	15	135	297

Figure 6.16 Components of Fiscal 2008 Inventory and Order Backlogs.

Investment in Unconsolidated Subsidiaries	(prior period)
Plus: Equity earnings	(current period)
Less: Cash dividends from subsidiaries	(current period)
Plus: Advances to subsidiaries	(current period)
Less: Repayment of loans	(current period)
Plus: Translation gains (FASB 52)	(current period)
Less: Translation losses (FASB 52)	(current period)
= Derived Investment in Unconsolidated Subsidiaries	(current period)
Less: Actual Investment in Unconsolidated Subsidiaries	(current period)
= Inc./Dec. Investment in Unconsolidated Subsidiaries *(Information Gap)*	(current period)

Figure 6.17 Example of the Unconsolidated Investment Reconciliation.

Deferred taxes	(prior period)
Plus: Deferred tax provision	(current period)
Less: Deferred tax credits	(current period)
= Derived deferred taxes	(current period)
Less: Actual deferred taxes	(current period)
= Increase/decrease deferred taxes *(Information Gap)*	(current period)

Figure 6.18 Deferred Tax Reconciliation.

Balance sheet beginning balance	(prior year)
Plus: Amortization of intangibles	(current year)
Plus: Acquired intangibles	(current year)
Derived intangibles	(current year)
Balance sheet ending balance	(current year)
Inc./Dec. Intangibles *(Information Gap)*	(current year)

Figure 6.19 Intangible Reconciliation.

Balance sheet beginning balance	(prior year)
Plus: Minority interest in earnings	(current year)
Less: Dividends to minority interest	(current year)
Derived minority interest	(current year)
Inc. (Dec.) in minority interest	(current year)

Figure 6.20 Minority Interest Reconciliation.

Minority Interest Reconciliation

Claims on the parent's income by minority shareholders are recognized as minority interest in earnings (income statement) and minority interest (balance sheet). Figure 6.20 shows the minority interest reconciliation.

Cash Flow Analysis: Generic Points

- Cash flow statements retrace all financing and investment activities of a firm for a given period of time, including the extent to which cash has been generated and absorbed.
- Today more and more lenders rely on the statement of cash flows as a measure of corporate performance because it "images" the probability distribution of future cash flows in relation to debt capacity.
- The greater and more certain the cash flows, the greater the debt capacity of the firm.
- SFAS 95 mandates segregating the borrower's business activities into three classifications: operating, financing, and investing activities. The operating activities section may be presented using either a direct or indirect presentation.
- The direct method focuses on cash and the impact of cash on the financial condition of the business.
- Investing activities involve making and collecting loans and acquiring and disposing of debt or equity instruments and PP&E, and other productive assets—that is, assets held for or used in the production of goods or services by the enterprise.
- Cash flows from unconsolidated subsidiaries include dividends from subsidiaries, advances and repayments, and the acquisition or sale of securities of subsidiaries. Noncash transactions include equity earnings, translation gains and losses, and consolidations.
- Prudent bankers must obtain a full disclosure concerning the project's future cash flows since construction projects may report noncash earnings—construction accounting or equity earnings.
- Investing activities involve obtaining resources from owners and providing them with a return on, and return of, their investment; borrowing money and repaying amounts borrowed or otherwise settling the obligation; and obtaining and paying for other resources obtained from creditors on long-term credit.
- Operating activities include all transactions and other events that are not defined as investing or financing activities. Operating activities generally involve producing and delivering goods and providing services. Cash flows from operating activities are generally the cash effects of transactions and other events that enter into the determination of income.

- GOCF is often the most important line in the cash flow statement, representing net income plus all noncash charges less all noncash credits, plus or minus all nonoperating transactions.
- Cash generated from nonrecurring items may artificially inflate earnings for a period, but it cannot be depended on to provide cash flow to support long-term financing.
- Net income must be the predominant source of a firm's funds in the long run.
- For the most part, current assets represent more than half the total assets of many businesses. With such a large, relatively volatile cash investment connected to optimizing shareholder value, current assets are deserving of financial management's undivided attention.
- Net operating cash flow denotes the cash available from GOCF to internally finance a firm's future growth after working capital demands have been satisfied.
- Sources of cash include decreases in assets, increases in liabilities, and increases in equity. Uses of cash include increases in assets, decreases in liabilities, and decreases in equity.
- The control sheet shows that the change in the cash account is always equal to the difference between sources and uses of cash.
- Sources and uses of cash are usually net changes, meaning the end result of many different transactions. Thus, reconciliations lie at the core of cash flow analysis.
- The quality, magnitude, and trend of operating cash flow must be examined carefully since it should contribute a reasonable amount to financing. These features are readily determined by the composition of the GOCF.
- When depreciation expenses consistently exceed capital expenditures over time, this occurrence is an indication of a business in decline. Eventually, it will lead to a reduction in earnings and profitability.
- If investment in unconsolidated subsidiaries represents a large item on the balance sheet, lenders should ask for financial statements of the unconsolidated subsidiary—or at least a full financial summary.

Cash Flow Analysis: Constituent Points

Gross Operating Cash Flow

- Merchandise is sometimes shipped out at the end of the year to window-dress the financials. Be on the lookout for the following warning signs: unearned income; shifting sales to future periods via reserves; income-smoothing gimmicks; creating gains and losses by selling or retiring debt; hiding losses inside discontinued operations; selling assets after pooling; moving current expenses to later periods by improperly capitalizing costs; amortizing costs too slowly; and failing to write off worthless assets.
- Analyze the quality, magnitude, and trend of earnings. Check quality of earnings in such areas as adequacy of reserves, nonrecurring items, and cash versus accrual-based income.
- When you analyze earnings trends, pay particular attention to the contribution of income to overall financing. If income is contributing less and less to overall financing, go back and check the strategic plans.
- Compare net income and dividends to each other. Are dividends large in proportion to net income? If so, why are they upstreamed?
- Compare depreciation with capital expenditures. If depreciation is greater than capital expenditures, assets may be running below optimal levels.
- Although reserves and write-downs such as inventory are add-backs to GOCF, they should be fully investigated.

Operating Cash Uses

- Beware of the following red flags: large overdue receivables; excessive dependence on one or two customers; related-party receivables; slow receivables turnover (annualize this frequently); right of return exists; changes in terms, credit standards, discounts, or collections; or creating receivables through distortive accounting. For example, Enron issued its common stock in exchange for notes receivable. The company then increased both notes receivable and shareholder's equity in recognition of these transactions. However, accounting convention requires that notes receivable culminating from transactions containing a company's capital stock be presented as deductions from stockholder's equity and not as assets, which is not how Enron and its auditor, Arthur Andersen, had booked the transactions.
- If the average collection period (ACP) has increased, determine the reason(s). The ACP measures the time it takes to convert receivables into cash. Accounts receivable policy is closely allied to inventory management, since these represent the two largest current asset accounts. Of approximately equal magnitude, together they comprise almost 80% of current assets and over 30% of total assets for manufacturing industries. The ACP is influenced partly by economic conditions and partly by a set of controllable factors, which are called *internal* (management) *factors*. Internal factors include credit policy variables (liberal, balanced, or conservative credit policy), credit terms, sales discounts, and collection.
- Be extra cautious if you notice large increases in inventory when sales are flat; slow inventory .... turnover; faddish inventory; inventory collateralized without your signature; watch unjustified LIFO to FIFO changes; insufficient insurance; change in divisional inventory valuation methods; increase in the number of LIFO pools; unreasonable intercompany profits; inclusion of inflation profits in inventory; large, unexplained increase in inventory; gross profit trends bad but no markdowns; inclusion of improper costs in inventory; capitalized instead of flow-through.
- Analyze ratios and develop a pro forma analysis to figure out the cash loss resulting from poor receivable management. The difference between receivables borrowers should have on their fiscal statements and actual receivables represents the loss in cash flow bankers now must replace.

Operating Cash Sources

- The spread between loan pricing and an annualized 37% return associated with anticipating 2/10 net 30 terms multiplied by the payable is nothing to sneeze at. Check to see if the payables manager takes advantage of trade discounts.
- Operating cash flow should be compared with accounts payable. A "bulge" in payables may indicate late payments, particularly if GOCF is not making an adequate contribution to investment activities or the operating unit is highly leveraged.
- Determine if the cash conversion cycle contributes to increased payables balances and late payments.

Net Cash Provided by Operating Activities

- Net cash provided by operating activities is the line in the cash flow statement that provides cash to primary expenditures after working capital coverage.
- Working capital requirements can pull large amounts of cash from the business. This drain of cash can cut into capital expansion programs, particularly if operating cash flow falls significantly below expectations.

- Keep in mind that one of the best ways to check the quality of earnings is to compare net income to net cash flow from operations. A case in point: If earnings consistently reach high levels but little remains to cover investment activities, then the question arises—what good is net income availability to pay debt service? For example, has net income been distorted and/or cannibalized by noncash credits, uncollectible receivables, or increases in unsalable inventory? If so, little income will be left to finance both new investments and loan reductions.

Investment Activities

- Companies with volatile cash flow histories tend to invest less on average than firms with smoother cash flows. They may also face stiffer costs when seeking funds from external capital markets.
- For firms with volatile cash flow patterns, business decisions are complicated by a higher tendency to have periods of low internal cash flows that can distract managers and cause them to throw out budgets, delay debt repayments, and defer capital expenditures.
- Categorize investment activities into two groups: discretionary and nondiscretionary. Nondiscretionary investment activities refer to outlays required to keep a healthy gross margin on the operating-unit level. Say, for example, you determine that nondiscretionary investments are covered by the borrower's internal cash flow. From this you can assume that financing activities are discretionary and the firm has better control of its capital structure.
- Assets require continuous replacement and upgrading to ensure efficient operations. When depreciation expenses consistently exceed capital expenditures over time, this is an indication of a declining operation. Eventually, this situation will lead to a fall in earnings and profitability. Capital expenditures represent major nondiscretionary outlays.
- Watch out for outdated equipment and technology, high maintenance and repair expenses, a declining output level, inadequate depreciation charges, changes in depreciation methods, a lengthening depreciation period, a decline in the depreciation expense, and a large write-off of assets. Also watch out for distortions regarding currency translations.
- Check to see if deferred taxes are running off. Deferred taxes usually increase when capital expenditures accelerate. Download the most recent capital budgeting schedule. Focus on project cost, net present values (NPVs), and internal rate of return (IRR).
- Check to see if fixed asset turnover (sales/net fixed assets) increases sharply. This ratio measures the turnover of plant and equipment in relation to sales. The fixed asset/turnover ratio is really a measure of cash flow efficiency, since it indicates how well fixed assets are being utilized.
- Determine if backlogs are increasing without a large pickup in sales. Unresolved backlogs usually happen only once, and then customers go elsewhere.
- Determine if work-in-progress inventory ties into a sharply deteriorating inventory turnover.
- Make sure the gross margin has not trended down over the past few years due to increased labor costs and decreased operating leverage.
- Utilize real options tools when applicable.

Investment Project Cash Flows and Joint Ventures

- Once the financial merits of a project have been examined, it must be discerned whether the project's cash flow is reasonably understood. For example, if XYZ division fails to maintain PP&E, a series of problems could easily ensue. The unit's aging or outmoded machinery would increasingly experience longer periods of downtime, and the goods produced could be defective. The operating unit will begin to fall behind its competitors from both a technological and opportunity cost standpoint. Worse, customers may perceive its products as inferior, of lower quality, or old fashioned compared to its competitors.

- From a summary of IAS 31, a joint venture is a contractual arrangement subject to joint control. The three types of joint ventures are jointly controlled operations, jointly controlled assets, and jointly controlled entities.
- The venture should recognize jointly controlled operations by including the assets and liabilities that it controls, the expenses that it incurs, and its share of the income that it earns from the sale of goods or services by the venture. Jointly controlled assets should be recognized on a proportional basis, and jointly controlled entities should be recognized in consolidated financial statements.
- The cost of capital should be appropriate. If it is artificially low, the project's NPV will be inflated.
- Look for a slow amortization period, a lengthening amortization period, a high ratio of intangibles to total assets and capital, and a large balance in goodwill even though profits are weak.
- Make sure the time frame to complete the project is realistic, rather than a "pie in the sky" scenario. Projects that take longer than projected to complete will invariably cost more than budgeted. This overage will lower the project's NPV and may lead to an eventual cash crunch for the company.
- Determine what, if any, contingencies have been made by the company in the event that the project costs or completion time exceeds the original estimate. The ability of the business to raise additional capital without difficulty is a very positive factor from a lender's point of view.
- Watch for switching between current and noncurrent classifications, investments recorded in excess of costs, and investments.
- Determine the real value of projects and not just book values.
- Increases in long-term debt should always be examined on a specific issue basis to ensure optimal financing.
- Optimal financing means financing that minimizes the cost of capital, maximizes equity value, and may prevent your borrower's credit grade or bond rating from downtiering.
- Make sure you distinguish real debt increases from accounting debt increases on the cash flow statement. For example, amortization of bond discount results in debt increases, but no cash inflow is involved.
- Decreases in long-term debt should be matched against increases in long-term debt along with the magnitude of GOCF. For example, in an expanding business, increases in long-term debt may exceed reductions. As long as leverage is within acceptable levels, internal cash flow is probably contributing its fair share to the overall financing of the business.
- Amortization of bond premiums distorts actual debt reductions. Find cash decreases by separating bond premiums from debt payments.
- Look for long-term debt conversions to equity. Conversion to equity may represent a substantial noncash exchange.
- Finally, savvy bankers should never cease questioning clients on off-balance sheet projects not fully understood. Enron's Raptor partnerships were used to exaggerate profits by $1 billion over a period of months. Perhaps aggressive cash flow due diligence by bankers would have extracted this shenanigan from its Alice in Wonderland milieu.

Equity and Other Financing Activities

- Review dividends to determine whether they are tied to income or are relatively constant.
- Examine financial leverage as well to verify that dividends are reasonable in light of future prospects. Determine whether an established partner exists in the business's capital expenditure program.

Conclusion

Those of us who have studied cash flow and cash flow analysis no doubt understand the correlation between the flow of numbers and probabilities that loans will not be repaid. To those readers new to cash flow, the authors hope this chapter has shown that the whole is much more the sum of parts, the parts being an array of numbers, and the whole, enlightened credit judgment. Consider that at any given concert of Beethoven's *Eroica,* the power and intensity of the music will visibly shake people. If, at the concert's conclusion, you stroll by the orchestra pit and peek at the sheet music, you will likely think the score of this most towering work is a jumble of scribbles and scrawls. But to a musician, the scribbles come alive and resonate both in mind and soul. A musician actually *hears* Beethoven's rich, organic sounds by simply looking at the score. Bars, clefs, keys, sharps, and flats are more than a short collection of scrawls on paper.

Like the *Eroica* score, a well-crafted cash flow and analysis is much more than a collection of bars, clefs, and keys. Rather, like many a great work, cash flow realizes subtle interactions beyond the obvious.

Beautiful mathematics is, indeed, much like an elegant movement in a symphony.

7 A Primer on Quantitative Risk Analysis

Credit Engineering for Bankers. DOI: 10.1016/B978-0-12-378585-5.10007-7

This chapter gets into the nuts and bolts of quantitative risk analysis as it pertains to making business decisions in a bank. As part of credit risk analysis and credit engineering, the general underlying principles of risk analysis remain the same as in general business risk. For instance, credit risk analysis may require applying Monte Carlo simulation for forecasting and backtesting the accuracy of a credit scoring model, testing scenarios and sensitivities on a credit portfolio, integrating and accounting for correlations in a basket of credit issues and vehicles, and so forth. Therefore, this chapter provides the fundamentals of quantitative risk analysis that are required knowledge and prerequisite for more advanced applications in banking and credit risk. The chapter starts off with an interesting historical perspective of risk, followed by discussions of the basic characteristics of risk and the nature of risk versus returns. It then provides detailed hands-on applications of running quantitative Monte Carlo risk simulations using the Risk Simulator software. Finally, the chapter wraps up with two hands-on exercises for using the software on running risk simulations and understanding the diversification effects of correlations on risk.

A Brief History of Risk: What Exactly Is Risk?

Since the beginning of recorded history, games of chance have been a popular pastime. Even in biblical accounts, Roman soldiers cast lots for Christ's garments. In earlier times, chance was something that occurred in nature, and humans were simply subjected to it as a ship is to the capricious tosses of the waves in an ocean. Even up to the time of the Renaissance, the future was thought to be simply a chance occurrence of completely random events and beyond the control of humans. However, with the advent of games of chance, human greed propelled the study of risk and chance to ever more closely mirror real-life events. Although these games were initially played with great enthusiasm, the players rarely sat down and actually figured out the odds. Of course, the individual who understood and mastered the concept of chance was bound to be in a better position to profit from such games of chance. It was not until the mid-1600s that the concept of chance was properly studied and the first such serious endeavor can be credited to Blaise Pascal, one of the fathers of modern choice, chance, and probability. Fortunately for us, after many centuries of mathematical and statistical innovations from pioneers such as Pascal, Bernoulli, Bayes, Gauss, LaPlace, and Fermat, our modern world of uncertainty can be explained with much more elegance through methodological applications of risk and uncertainty.

To the people who lived centuries ago, risk was simply the inevitability of chance occurrence beyond the realm of human control. Albeit many phony soothsayers profited from their ability to convincingly profess their clairvoyance by simply stating the obvious or reading the victims' body language and telling them what they wanted to hear. We modern-day humans—ignoring for the moment the occasional seers among us—with our fancy technological achievements are still susceptible to risk and uncertainty. We may be able to predict the orbital paths of planets in our solar system with astounding accuracy or the escape velocity required to shoot a man from Earth to the moon, but when it comes to predicting a firm's revenues the following year, we are at a loss. Humans have been struggling with risk our entire existence, but through trial and error, and through the evolution of human knowledge and thought, we have devised ways to describe, quantify, hedge, and take advantage of risk.

Clearly, the entire realm of risk analysis is vast and would most probably be intractable within the few chapters of a book. Therefore, this book is concerned with only a small niche of risk—namely, *applied business risk modeling and analysis.* Even in the areas of applied business risk analysis, the diversity is great. For instance, business risk can be roughly divided into the areas of operational risk management and financial risk management. In financial risk, one can look at market risk, private risk, credit risk, default risk, maturity risk, liquidity risk, inflationary risk, interest rate risk, country risk, and so forth. This book focuses on the application of risk analysis in the sense of how to adequately apply the tools to identify, understand, quantify, and diversify risk such that it can be hedged and managed more effectively. These tools are generic enough that they can be applied across a whole spectrum of business conditions, industries, and needs. Finally, understanding this text, together with *Real Options Analysis,* Second Edition (Wiley 2005), *Modeling Risk*, Second Edition (Wiley 2010), and the associated Risk Simulator and Real Options SLS software are required for the Certified Risk Management or CRM certification (see www. realoptionsvaluation.com for more details).

Risky ventures are the norm in the daily business world. The mere mention of names such as George Soros, John Meriweather, Paul Reichmann, and Nicholas Leeson, or firms such as Long Term Capital Management, Metallgesellschaft, Barings Bank, Bankers Trust, Daiwa Bank, Sumimoto Corporation, Merrill Lynch, and Citibank brings a shrug of disbelief and fear. These names are some of the biggest in the world of business and finance. Their claim to fame is not simply for being the best and brightest individuals, nor are they the largest and most respected firms, but they are renown for bearing the stigma of being involved in highly risky ventures that turned sour almost overnight.

George Soros was and still is one of the most respected names in high finance; he is known globally for his brilliance and exploits. Paul Reichmann was a reputable and brilliant real estate and property tycoon. Between the two of them, nothing was impossible, but when they ventured into investments in Mexican real estate, the wild fluctuations of the peso in the foreign exchange market caused nothing short of a disaster. During late 1994 and early 1995, the peso hit an all-time low, and their ventures went from bad to worse. The one thing that they did not expect, however, was that the situation would become a lot worse before it was all over and that billions would be lost as a consequence.

Long Term Capital Management was headed by Meriweather, one of the rising stars in Wall Street, with a slew of superstars on its management team, including several Nobel laureates in finance and economics (Robert Merton and Myron Scholes). The firm was also backed by giant investment banks. A firm that seemed indestructible literally blew up with billions of dollars in the red, shaking the international investment community with repercussions throughout Wall Street as individual investors started to lose faith in large hedge funds and wealth-management firms, forcing the eventual massive Federal Reserve bailout.

Barings was one of the oldest banks in England. It was so respected that even Queen Elizabeth II herself held a private account with it. This multibillion-dollar institution was brought down singlehandedly by Nicholas Leeson, an employee halfway around the world. Leeson was a young and brilliant investment banker who headed up Barings's Singapore branch. His illegally doctored track record showed significant investment profits, which gave him more leeway and trust from the home office over time. He was able to cover his losses through fancy accounting and by taking significant amounts of risk. His speculations in the Japanese yen went south, he took Barings down with him, and the top echelons in London never knew what hit them.

Had any of the managers in the boardrooms at their respective headquarters bothered to look at the risk profile of their investments, they would surely have made a very different decision much earlier on, preventing what became major embarrassments in the global investment community. If the projected returns are adjusted for risks—that is, finding what levels of risk are required to attain such seemingly extravagant returns—it would be sensible not to proceed.

Risks that do not require investments in the multimillions are common. For instance, when would one purchase a house in a fluctuating housing market? When would it be more profitable to lock in a fixed-rate mortgage rate rather than keep a floating variable rate? What are the chances that there will be insufficient funds at retirement? What about the potential personal property losses when a hurricane hits? How much accident insurance is considered sufficient? How much is a lottery ticket actually worth?

Risk permeates all aspects of life, and we can never avoid taking or facing risks. What we can do is to understand risks better through a systematic assessment of their impacts and repercussions. This assessment framework must also be capable of measuring, monitoring, and managing risks; otherwise, simply noting that risks exist and moving on is not optimal. This book provides the tools and framework necessary to tackle risks head-on. Only with the added insights gained through a rigorous assessment of risk can we actively manage and monitor risk.

Risks permeate every aspect of business, but we do not have to be passive participants. What we can do is develop a framework to better understand risks through a systematic assessment of their impacts and repercussions. This framework must also be capable of measuring, monitoring, and managing risks.

The Basics of Risk

Risk can be defined as any uncertainty that affects a system in an unknown fashion whereby the ramifications are also unknown but bear with them great fluctuation in value and outcome. In every instance, for risk to be evident, the following generalities must exist:

- Uncertainties and risks have a time horizon.
- Uncertainties exist in the future and will evolve over time.
- Uncertainties become risks if they affect the outcomes and scenarios of the system.
- These changing scenarios' effects on the system can be measured.
- The measurement has to be set against a benchmark.

Risk is never instantaneous. It has a time horizon. For instance, a firm engaged in a risky research and development venture will face significant amounts of risk but only until the product is fully developed or has proven itself in the market. These risks are caused by uncertainties in the technology of the product under research, uncertainties about the potential market, uncertainties about the level of competitive threats and substitutes, and so forth. These uncertainties will change over the course of the company's research and marketing activities; some uncertainties will increase, while others will most likely decrease through the passage of time, actions, and events. However, only the uncertainties that affect the product directly will have any bearing on the risks of the product being successful. That is, only uncertainties that change the possible scenario outcomes will make the product risky (e.g., market and economic conditions). Finally, risk exists if it can be measured and compared against a benchmark. If no benchmark exists, then perhaps the conditions just described are the norm for research and development activities, and thus the negative results are to be expected. These benchmarks have to be measurable and tangible—for example, gross profits, success rates, market share, time to implementation, and so forth.

Risk is any uncertainty that affects a system in an unknown fashion whereby its ramifications are unknown but may bring great fluctuation in value and outcome. Risk has a time horizon, meaning that uncertainty evolves over time, which affects measurable future outcomes and scenarios with respect to a benchmark.

The Nature of Risk and Return

Nobel Laureate Harry Markowitz's groundbreaking research into the nature of risk and return has revolutionized the world of finance. His seminal work, which is now known all over the world as the *Markowitz Efficient Frontier*, looks at the nature of risk and return. Markowitz did not look at risk as the enemy but as a condition that should be embraced and balanced out through its expected returns. The concept of risk and return was then refined through later works by other Nobel Laureates such as William Sharpe, who stated that a heightened risk necessitates a higher return, as elegantly expressed through the *capital asset pricing model* (CAPM), where the required rate of return on a marketable risky equity is equivalent to the return on an equivalent riskless asset plus a beta systematic and undiversifiable risk measure multiplied by the market risk's return premium. In essence, a higher-risk asset requires a higher return. In Markowitz's model, one could strike a balance between risk and return. Depending on the risk appetite of an investor, the optimal or best-case returns can be obtained through the efficient frontier. Should the investor require a higher level of returns, he or she would have to face a higher level of risk. Markowitz's work carried over to finding combinations of individual projects or assets in a portfolio that would provide the best *bang for the buck*, striking an elegant balance between risk and return. In order to better understand this balance, also known as *risk-adjustment* in modern risk analysis language, risks must first be measured and understood.

Uncertainty versus Risk

Risk and uncertainty are very different-looking animals, but they are of the same species; however, the lines of demarcation are often blurred. A distinction is critical at this juncture before proceeding and worthy of segue. Suppose I am senseless enough to take a skydiving trip with a good friend, and we board a plane headed for the Palm Springs desert. While airborne at 10,000 feet and watching our lives flash before our eyes, we realize that in our haste we forgot to pack our parachutes on board. However, there is an old, dusty, and dilapidated emergency parachute on the plane. At that point, both my friend and I have the same level of uncertainty: the uncertainty of whether the old parachute will open and, if it does not, whether we will fall to our deaths. However, being the risk-adverse, nice guy I am, I decide to let my buddy take the plunge. Clearly, he is the one taking the plunge and the same person taking the risk. I bear no risk at this time, while my friend bears all the risk. However, we both have the same level of uncertainty as to whether the parachute will actually fail. In fact, we both have the same level of uncertainty as to the outcome of the day's trading on the New York Stock Exchange—which has absolutely no impact on whether we live or die that day. Only when he jumps and the parachute opens will the uncertainty become resolved through the passage of time, action, and events. However, even when the uncertainty is resolved with the opening of the parachute, the risk still exists as to whether he will land safely on the ground below.

Therefore, risk is something one bears and is the outcome of uncertainty. Just because there is uncertainty, there could very well be no risk. If the only thing that bothers a U.S.-based firm's CEO is the fluctuation in the foreign exchange market of the Zambian kwacha, then I might suggest shorting some kwachas and shifting his portfolio to U.S.-based debt. This uncertainty, if it does not affect the firm's bottom line in any way, is only uncertainty and not risk. This book is concerned with risk by performing uncertainty analysis—the same uncertainty that brings about risk by its mere existence as it impacts the value of a particular project. It is further assumed that the end user of this uncertainty analysis uses the results appropriately, whether the analysis is for identifying, adjusting, or selecting projects with respect to their risks, and so forth. Otherwise, running millions of fancy simulation trials and letting the results "marinate" will be useless. By running simulations on the foreign exchange market of the Zambian kwacha, an analyst sitting in a cubicle somewhere in downtown San Francisco will in no way reduce the risk of the kwacha in the market or the firm's exposure to the same. Only by using the results from an uncertainty simulation analysis and finding ways to hedge or mitigate the quantified fluctuation and downside risks of the firm's foreign exchange exposure through the derivatives market could the analyst be construed as having performed risk analysis and risk management.

To further illustrate the differences between risk and uncertainty, suppose we are attempting to forecast the stock price of Microsoft (MSFT). Suppose MSFT is currently priced at $25 per share, and historical prices place the stock at 21.89% volatility. Now suppose that for the next five years, MSFT does not engage in any risky ventures and stays exactly the way it is, and further suppose that the entire economic and financial world remains constant. This means that *risk* is fixed and unchanging—that is, volatility is unchanging for the next five years. However, the price uncertainty still increases over time. That is, the width of the forecast intervals will still increase over time. For instance, Year 0's forecast is known and is $25. However, as we progress one day, MSFT will most probably vary between $24 and $26. One year later, the uncertainty bounds may be between $20 and $30. Five years into the future, the boundaries might be between $10 and $50. So, in this example, *uncertainties increase,* while *risks remain the same.* Therefore, risk is not equal to uncertainty. This idea is, of course, applicable to any forecasting approach whereby it becomes more and more difficult to forecast the future even though the risk remains the same. Now if risk changes over time, the bounds of uncertainty get more complicated (e.g., uncertainty bounds of sinusoidal waves with discrete event jumps).

In other instances, risk and uncertainty are used interchangeably. For instance, suppose you play a coin-toss game—bet 50 cents, and if heads come up, you win $1, but if it's tails, you lose everything. The risk here is you lose everything because the risk is that tails may appear. The uncertainty here is that tails may appear. Given that tails appear, you lose everything; hence, uncertainty brings with it risk. Uncertainty is the possibility of an event occurring, and risk is the ramification of such an event occurring. People tend to mistakenly use these two terms interchangeably.

In discussing uncertainty, there are three levels of uncertainties in the world: the *known,* the *unknown,* and the *unknowable.* The known is, of course, what we know will occur and are certain of its occurrence (contractual obligations or a guaranteed event); the unknown is what we do not know and can be simulated. These events will become known through the passage of time, events, and action (the uncertainty of whether a new drug or technology can be developed successfully will become known after spending years and millions on research programs; it will either work or not, and we will know this in the future), and these events carry with them risks, but these risks will be reduced or eliminated over time. However, unknowable events carry both uncertainty and risk such that the totality of the risk and uncertainty may not change through the passage of time, events, or actions. These are events such as when the next tsunami or earthquake will hit, or when another act of terrorism will occur around the world. When an event occurs, uncertainty becomes resolved, but risk still remains (another one may or may not hit tomorrow). In traditional analysis, we care about the known factors. In risk analysis, we care about the unknown and unknowable factors. The unknowable factors are easy to hedge—get the appropriate insurance! That is, do not do business in a wartorn country, get away from politically unstable economies, buy hazard and business interruption insurance, and so forth. Risk analysis will provide the most significant amount of value for the unknown factors.

Risk Simulation Applications

This chapter continues by providing the novice risk analyst an introduction to the Risk Simulator software for performing Monte Carlo simulation, and a 30-day trial of this software is included as part of this book. To claim the necessary license, follow these instructions:

Visit www.realoptionsvaluation.com/creditenginneringbook.html or www.rovdown loads.com/creditenginneringbook.html and click on the Downloads link, scroll down to the Risk Simulator software section, review the system requirements, and then download and install the software. Make sure your system has all the required prerequisites listed on this webpage (e.g., Windows XP, Windows Vista, Windows 7 or later; Excel 2003, 2007, 2010, or later; and that you have administrative rights to install software). Follow the instructions on this webpage to install your free extended trial license of the software.

We continue the chapter by illustrating what Risk Simulator does and what steps are taken in a Monte Carlo simulation, as well as some of the more basic elements in a simulation analysis. The chapter then continues with how to interpret the results from a simulation and ends with a discussion of correlating variables in a simulation, as well as applying precision and error control. As software versions with new enhancements are continually released, be sure to review the software's user manual for more up-to-date details on using the latest version of the software.

Risk Simulator is a Monte Carlo simulation, forecasting, optimization, and risk analytics software. It is written in Microsoft .NET C# and functions together with Excel as an add-in. When you have the software installed, simply start Excel and you will see a new menu item called Risk Simulator. If you are using Excel 2007 or Excel 2010, you will see a new tab called Risk Simulator as well as some large icons that you can access. The examples used throughout this book use Risk Simulator version 2010 and above, with the following languages: English, Chinese, Japanese, Korean, Spanish, French, Italian, German, and Portuguese.

Monte Carlo risk simulation is used very heavily in credit risk analysis and credit engineering. Applications may include perturbing certain input variables (e.g., interest rates and yield curves) to determine the effects on outputs (e.g., creditworthiness, credit spreads), where thousands of economic scenarios can be run and sensitivity analyses can be performed to identify the credit impact of a specific credit vehicle and so forth. The results from such risk simulations may include Value at Risk, worst-case scenarios, probability of defaults, probability of losses, exposure at default, and so forth.

This software is also compatible and often used with the Real Options SLS (Super Lattice Solver) software, both developed by the author. The different functions or modules in both software applications are briefly described in the list that follows. Note that there are other software applications such as the ROV Basel II Modeling Toolkit, ROV Employee Stock Options Valuation Toolkit, ROV Compiler, ROV Risk Extractor and Evaluator, ROV BizStats, ROV Modeler, ROV Valuator, ROV Dashboard, and ROV Quantitative Data Mining created by Real Options Valuation, Inc., the same company that developed Risk Simulator introduced in this book. You can get more information on these tools by visiting www.realoptionsvaluation.com, where you can also view some free modeling videos and obtain whitepapers, case studies, and other free models. In fact, it is *highly recommended* that you first watch the Getting Started videos on the webpage or attempt the step-by-step exercises at the end of this chapter *before* reading the text in this chapter. The videos and exercises will get you started immediately, whereas the text in this chapter focuses more on the theory and detailed explanations of the properties of simulation. You can view the videos online at www.realoptionsvaluation.com/risksimulator.html.

- The *Simulation* module allows you to run simulations in your existing Excel-based models, generate and extract simulation forecasts (distributions of results), perform distributional fitting (automatically finding the best-fitting statistical distribution), compute correlations (maintain relationships among simulated random variables), identify sensitivities (creating tornado and sensitivity charts), test statistical hypotheses (finding statistical differences between pairs of forecasts), run bootstrap simulation (testing the robustness of result statistics), and run custom and nonparametric simulations (simulations using historical data without specifying any distributions or their parameters for forecasting without data or applying expert opinion forecasts).
- The *Forecasting* module can be used to generate automatic time-series forecasts (with and without seasonality and trend), multivariate regressions (modeling relationships among variables), nonlinear extrapolations (curve fitting), stochastic processes (random walks, mean-reversions, jump-diffusion, and mixed processes), Box-Jenkins ARIMA (econometric forecasts), Auto ARIMA, basic econometrics and auto-econometrics (modeling relationships and generating forecasts), exponential J curves, logistic S curves, GARCH models and their multiple variations (modeling and forecasting volatility), maximum likelihood models for limited dependent variables (logit, tobit, and probit models), Markov chains, trendlines, spine curves, and others.
- The *Optimization* module is used for optimizing multiple decision variables subject to constraints to maximize or minimize an objective and can be run either as a static optimization, as dynamic and stochastic optimization under uncertainty together with Monte Carlo simulation, or as a stochastic optimization with Super Speed simulations. The software can handle linear and nonlinear optimizations with binary, integer, and continuous variables, as well as generate Markowitz efficient frontiers.
- The *Analytical Tools* module allows you to run segmentation clustering, hypothesis testing, statistical tests of raw data, data diagnostics of technical forecasting assumptions (e.g., heteroskedasticity, multicollinearity, and the like), sensitivity and scenario analyses, overlay chart analysis, spider charts, tornado charts, and many other powerful tools.
- The Real Options Super Lattice Solver is another stand-alone software that complements Risk Simulator, and it is used for solving simple to complex real options problems.

The following sections walk you through the basics of the *Simulation Module* in Risk Simulator, while subsequent chapters provide more details on the applications of other modules. To follow along, make sure you have Risk Simulator installed on your computer to proceed.

Running a Monte Carlo Simulation

Typically, to run a simulation in your existing Excel model, the following steps have to be performed:

1. Start a new simulation profile or open an existing profile.
2. Define input assumptions in the relevant cells.
3. Define output forecasts in the relevant cells.
4. Run simulation.
5. Interpret the results.

If desired, and for practice, open the example file called *Basic Simulation Model* and follow along with the examples provided here on creating a simulation. The example file can be found by first starting Excel and then clicking on *Risk Simulator | Example Models | 02 Basic Simulation Model.*

1   Start a New Simulation Profile

To start a new simulation, you must first create a simulation profile. A simulation profile contains a complete set of instructions on how you would like to run a simulation—that is, all the assumptions, forecasts, run preferences, and so forth. Having profiles facilitates creating multiple scenarios of simulations; using the same exact model, several profiles can be created, each with its own specific simulation properties and requirements. The same person can create different test scenarios using different distributional assumptions and inputs, or multiple persons can test their own assumptions and inputs on the same model.

1. Start Excel and create a new model or open an existing one (you can use the *Basic Simulation Model* example to follow along).
2. Click on *Risk Simulator | New Simulation Profile.*
3. Specify a title for your simulation, as well as all other pertinent information (Figure 7.1).
   - *Title.* Specifying a simulation title allows you to create multiple simulation profiles in a single Excel model. Using a title means that you can now save different simulation scenario profiles within the same model without having to delete existing assumptions and changing them each time a new simulation scenario is required. You can always change the profile's name later (*Risk Simulator | Edit Profile*).
   - *Number of trials.* This is where the number of simulation trials required is entered. That is, running 1,000 trials means that 1,000 different iterations of outcomes based on the input assumptions will be generated. You can change this number as desired, but the input has to be positive integers. The default number of runs is 1,000 trials. You can use precision and error control to automatically help determine how many simulation trials to run (see the section on precision and error control later in this chapter for details).

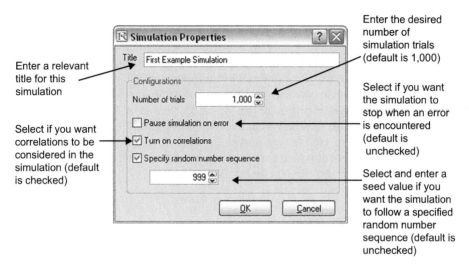

Enter a relevant title for this simulation

Select if you want correlations to be considered in the simulation (default is checked)

Enter the desired number of simulation trials (default is 1,000)

Select if you want the simulation to stop when an error is encountered (default is unchecked)

Select and enter a seed value if you want the simulation to follow a specified random number sequence (default is unchecked)

Figure 7.1 New Simulation Profile.

- *Pause simulation on error.* If checked, the simulation stops every time an error is encountered in the Excel model. That is, if your model encounters a computation error (e.g., some input values generated in a simulation trial may yield a divide by zero error in one of your spreadsheet cells), the simulation stops. This feature is important to help audit your model to make sure there are no computational errors in your Excel model. However, if you are sure the model works, then there is no need for this preference to be checked.
- *Turn on correlations.* If checked, correlations between paired input assumptions will be computed. Otherwise, correlations will all be set to zero and a simulation is run assuming no cross-correlations between input assumptions. As an example, applying correlations will yield more accurate results if, indeed, correlations exist and will tend to yield a lower forecast confidence if negative correlations exist. After turning on correlations here, you can later set the relevant correlation coefficients on each assumption generated (see the section on correlations and precision control later in this chapter for more details).
- *Specify random number sequence.* Simulation, by definition, will yield slightly different results every time a simulation is run. Different results occur by virtue of the random number generation routine in Monte Carlo simulation; this characteristic is a theoretical fact in all random number generators. However, when making presentations, if you require the same results (such as especially when the report being presented shows one set of results and during a live presentation you would like to show the same results being generated, or when you are sharing models with others and would like the same results to be obtained every time), then check this preference and enter in an initial seed number. The seed number can be any positive integer. Using the same initial seed value, the same number of trials, and the same input assumptions, the simulation will always yield the same sequence of random numbers, guaranteeing the same final set of results.

Note that once a new simulation profile has been created, you can come back later and modify these selections. In order to do this, make sure that the current active profile is the profile you wish to modify; otherwise, click on *Risk Simulator | Change Simulation Profile*, select the profile you wish to change, and click OK (Figure 7.2 shows an example of multiple profiles and how to activate a selected profile). Then, click on *Risk Simulator | Edit Simulation Profile* and make the required changes. You can also duplicate or rename an existing profile. When creating multiple profiles in the same Excel model, make sure to give each profile a unique name so you can tell them apart later on. Also, these profiles are stored inside hidden sectors of the Excel *.xls file, and you do not have to save any additional files. The profiles and their contents (assumptions, forecasts, etc.) are automatically saved when you save the Excel file. Finally, the last profile that is active when you exit and save the Excel file will be the one that is opened the next time the Excel file is accessed.

2 Define Input Assumptions

The next step is to set input assumptions in your model. Note that assumptions can only be assigned to cells without any equations or functions (i.e., typed-in numerical values that are inputs in a model), whereas output forecasts can only be assigned to cells with equations and functions (i.e., outputs of a model). Recall that assumptions and forecasts cannot be set unless a simulation profile already exists. Do the following to set new input assumptions in your model:

1. Make sure a Simulation Profile exists, open an existing profile, or start a new profile (Risk Simulator | New Simulation Profile).
2. Select the cell you wish to set an assumption on (e.g., cell G8 in the Basic Simulation Model example).
3. Click on Risk Simulator | Set Input Assumption, or click on the set input assumption icon in the Risk Simulator icon toolbar.

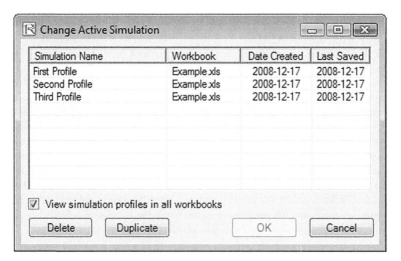

Figure 7.2 Change Active Simulation.

4. Select the relevant distribution you want, enter the relevant distribution parameters (e.g., select Triangular distribution and use 1, 2, and 2.5 as the minimum, most likely, and maximum values), and hit OK to insert the input assumption into your model (Figure 7.3).

Note that you can also set assumptions by selecting the cell you wish to set the assumption on and, using the mouse right-click, access the shortcut Risk Simulator menu to set an input assumption. In addition, for expert users, you can set input assumptions using the Risk Simulator *RS Functions*: select the cell of choice, click on Excel's *Insert, Function,* select the *All Category,* and scroll down to the *RS* functions list (we do not recommend using RS functions unless you are an expert user). For the examples going forward, we suggest following the basic instructions in accessing menus and icons.

Notice that in the Assumption Properties (Figure 7.4), there are several key areas worthy of mention:

- *Assumption Name.* This is an optional area that allows you to enter in unique names for the assumptions to help track what each of the assumptions represents. Good modeling practice is to use short but precise assumption names.
- *Distribution Gallery.* This area to the left shows all of the different distributions available in the software. To change the views, right-click anywhere in the gallery and select large icons, small icons, or list. More than two dozen distributions are available.
- *Input Parameters.* Depending on the distribution selected, the required relevant parameters are shown. You may either enter the parameters directly or link them to specific cells in your worksheet. Hard coding or typing the parameters is useful when the assumption parameters are assumed not to change. Linking to worksheet cells is useful when the input parameters need to be visible or are allowed to be changed (click on the link icon to link an input parameter to a worksheet cell).

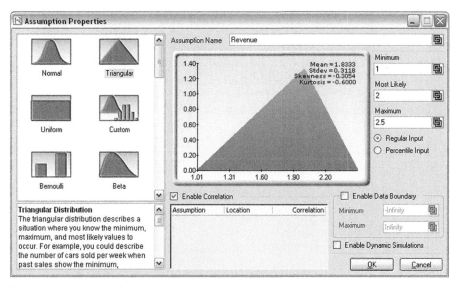

Figure 7.3 Setting an Input Assumption.

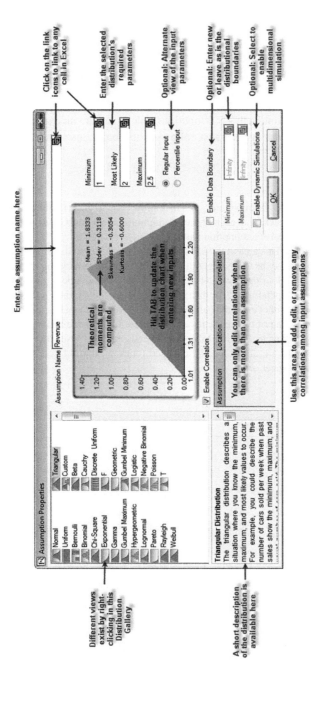

Figure 7.4 Assumption Properties.

- *Enable Data Boundary.* This feature is typically not used by the average analyst; it exists for truncating the distributional assumptions. For instance, if a normal distribution is selected, the theoretical boundaries are between negative infinity and positive infinity. However, in practice, the simulated variable exists only within some smaller range, and this range can then be entered to truncate the distribution appropriately.
- *Correlations.* Pairwise correlations can be assigned to input assumptions here. If assumptions are required, remember to check the *Turn on Correlations* preference by clicking on *Risk Simulator | Edit Simulation Profile.* See the discussion on correlations later in this chapter for more details about assigning correlations and the effects correlations will have on a model. Notice that you can either truncate a distribution or correlate it to another assumption, but not both.
- *Short Descriptions.* These exist for each of the distributions in the gallery. The short descriptions explain when a certain distribution is used, as well as the input parameter requirements.
- *Regular Input and Percentile Input.* This option allows the user to perform a quick due diligence test of the input assumption. For instance, if setting a normal distribution with some mean and standard deviation inputs, you can click on the percentile input to see the corresponding 10th and 90th percentiles.
- *Enable Dynamic Simulation.* This option is unchecked by default, but if you wish to run a multidimensional simulation (i.e., if you link the input parameters of the assumption to another cell that is itself an assumption, you are simulating the inputs, or simulating the simulation), then remember to check this option. Dynamic simulation will not work unless the inputs are linked to other changing input assumptions.

Note: If you are following along with the example, continue by setting another assumption on cell G9. This time use the *Uniform* distribution with a minimum value of 0.9 and a maximum value of 1.1. Then proceed to defining the output forecasts in the next step.

3   Define Output Forecasts

The next step is to define output forecasts in the model. Forecasts can only be defined on output cells with equations or functions. The following describes the set forecast process:

1. Select the cell on which you wish to set an assumption (e.g., cell G10 in the Basic Simulation Model example).
2. Click on Risk Simulator and select Set Output Forecast, or click on the set output forecast icon on the Risk Simulator icon toolbar.
3. Enter the relevant information and click OK.

Note that you can also set output forecasts by selecting the cell on which you wish to set the assumption and, using the mouse right-click, access the shortcut Risk Simulator menu to set an output forecast.

Figure 7.5 illustrates the set forecast properties:

- *Forecast Name.* Specify the name of the forecast cell. This is important because when you have a large model with multiple forecast cells, naming the forecast cells individually allows you to access the right results quickly. Do not underestimate the importance of this simple step. Good modeling practice is to use short but precise assumption names.

Figure 7.5 Set Output Forecast.

- *Forecast Precision.* Instead of relying on a guesstimate of how many trials to run in your simulation, you can set up precision and error controls. When an error-precision combination has been achieved in the simulation, the simulation will pause and inform you of the precision achieved, making the number of simulation trials an automated process and eliminating guesses on the required number of trials to simulate. Review the section on precision and error control later in this chapter for more specific details.
- *Show Forecast Window.* This property allows the user to show or not show a particular forecast window. The default is to always show a forecast chart.

4 Run Simulation

If everything looks right, simply click on *Risk Simulator | Run Simulation,* or click on the *Run* icon on the Risk Simulator toolbar, and the simulation will proceed. You may also reset a simulation after it has run to rerun it (*Risk Simulator | Reset Simulation* or the reset simulation icon on the toolbar) or to pause it during a run. Also, the *step* function (*Risk Simulator | Step Simulation* or the step simulation icon on the toolbar) allows you to simulate a single trial, one at a time, which is useful for educating others on simulation (i.e., you can show that at each trial all the values in the assumption cells are being replaced and the entire model is recalculated each time). You can also access the run simulation menu by right-clicking anywhere in the model and selecting *Run Simulation.*

Risk Simulator also allows you to run the simulation at extremely fast speed, called Super Speed. To do this, click on *Risk Simulator | Run Super Speed Simulation,* or use the *Run Super Speed* icon. Notice how much faster the Super Speed simulation runs. In fact, for practice, click on *Reset Simulation* and then *Edit Simulation Profile,* change the *Number of Trials* to *100,000,* and click on *Run Super Speed.* It should only take a few seconds to run. However, be aware that Super Speed simulation will not run if the model has errors, VBA (Visual Basic for Applications), or links to external data sources or applications. In such situations, you will be notified, and the regular speed simulation will be run instead. Regular speed simulations are always able to run even with errors, VBA, or external links.

5 Interpret the Forecast Results

The final step in Monte Carlo simulation is to interpret the resulting forecast charts. Figures 7.6 through 7.13 show the forecast charts and the corresponding statistics generated after running the simulation. Typically, the following features are important in interpreting the results of a simulation:

- *Forecast Chart.* The forecast chart shown in Figure 7.6 is a probability histogram that shows the frequency counts of values occurring in the total number of trials simulated. The vertical bars show the frequency of a particular *x* value occurring out of the total number of trials, while the cumulative frequency (smooth line) shows the total probabilities of all values at and below *x* occurring in the forecast.
- *Forecast Statistics.* The forecast statistics shown in Figure 7.7 summarize the distribution of the forecast values in terms of the four moments of a distribution. You can rotate between the histogram and statistics tab by depressing the space bar.
- *Preferences.* The preferences tab in the forecast chart (Figure 7.8) allows you to change the look and feel of the charts. For instance, if *Always Show Window On Top* is selected, the forecast charts will always be visible regardless of what other software are running on your computer. *Histogram Resolution* allows you to change the number of bins of the histogram, anywhere from 5 bins to 100 bins. Also, the *Data Update* section allows you to control how fast the simulation runs versus how often the forecast chart is updated. That is, if you wish to

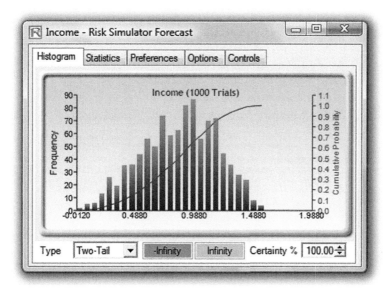

Figure 7.6 Forecast Chart.

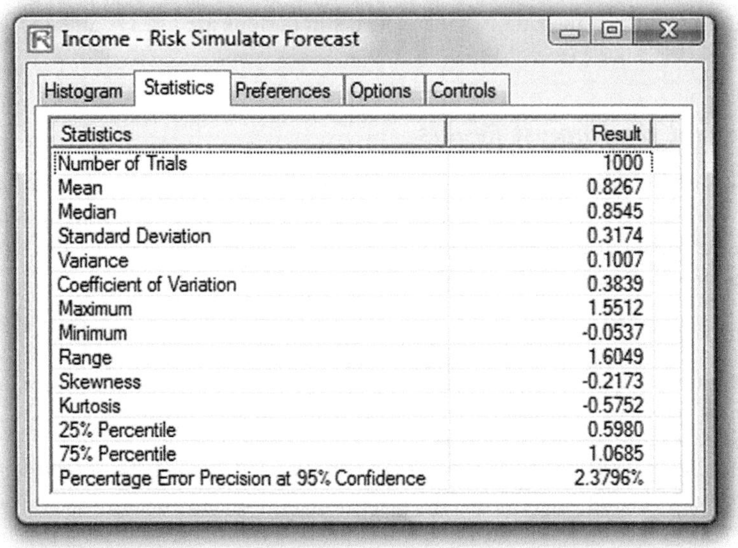

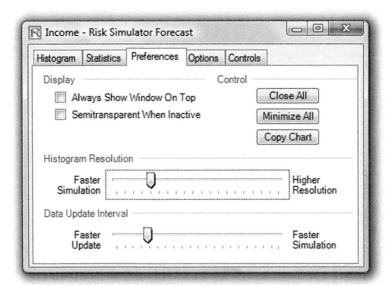

Figure 7.7 Forecast Statistics.

see the forecast chart updated at almost every trial, this feature will slow down the simulation as more memory is being allocated to updating the chart versus running the simulation. This option is merely a user preference and in no way changes the results of the simulation, just the speed of completing the simulation. To further increase the speed of the

Figure 7.8 Forecast Chart Preferences.

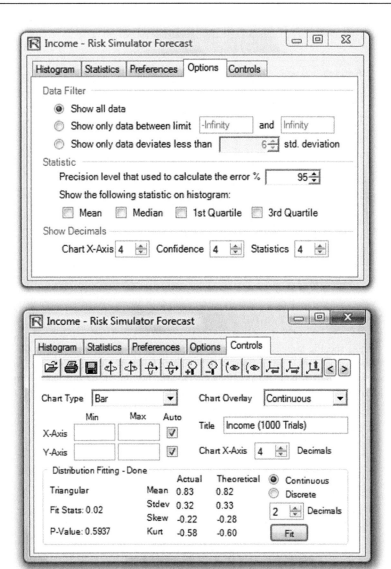

Figure 7.9 Forecast Chart Options and Control.

simulation, you can minimize Excel while the simulation is running, thereby reducing the memory required to visibly update the Excel spreadsheet and freeing up the memory to run the simulation. The *Clear All* and *Minimize All* selections control all the open forecast charts.

- *Options.* The forecast chart options (Figure 7.9, top) for showing data allow you to show all the forecast data or to filter in/out values that fall within some specified interval you choose or within some standard deviation you choose. Also, the precision level can be set

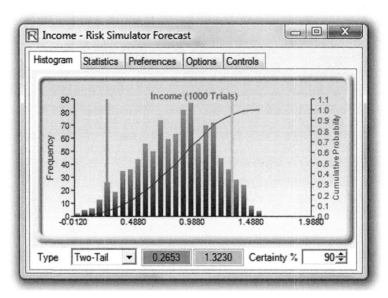

Figure 7.10 Forecast Chart Two-Tail Confidence Interval.

here for this specific forecast to show the error levels in the statistics view. See the section on precision and error control later in this chapter for more details. *Show the following statistic on histogram* is a user preference as to whether the mean, median, first quartile, and fourth quartile lines (25th and 75th percentiles) should be displayed on the forecast chart.

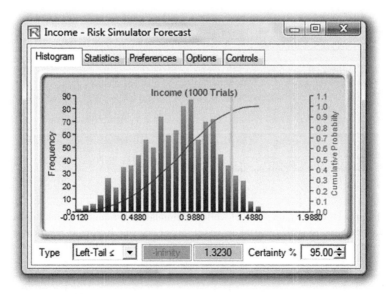

Figure 7.11 Forecast Chart One-Tail Confidence Interval.

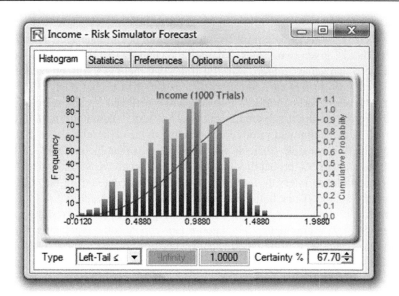

Figure 7.12 Forecast Chart Probability Evaluation.

- *Controls*. This tab (Figure 7.9, bottom) has all the functionalities in allowing you to change the type, color, size, zoom, tilt, 3D, and other things in the forecast chart, as well as providing overlay charts (PDF, CDF) and running distributional fitting on your forecast data (see the Data Fitting sections in the user manual for more details on this methodology).

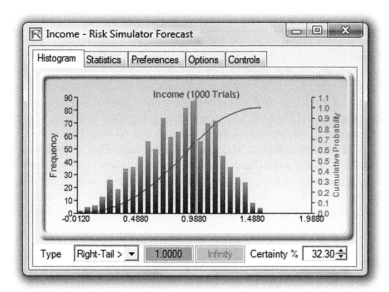

Figure 7.13 Forecast Chart Probability Evaluation.

Using Forecast Charts and Confidence Intervals

In forecast charts, you can determine the probability of occurrence, called *confidence intervals*. That is, given two values, what are the chances that the outcome will fall between these two values? Figure 7.10 illustrates that there is a 90% probability that the final outcome (in this case, the level of income) will be between $0.2653 and $1.3230. The two-tailed confidence interval can be obtained by first selecting *Two-Tail* as the type, entering the desired certainty value (e.g., 90), and hitting *TAB* on the keyboard. The two computed values corresponding to the certainty value will then be displayed. In this example, there is a 5% probability that income will be below $0.2653 and another 5% probability that income will be above $1.3230. That is, the two-tailed confidence interval is a symmetrical interval centered on the median or 50th percentile value. Thus, both tails will have the same probability.

Alternatively, a one-tail probability can be computed. Figure 7.11 shows a *Left-Tail* selection at 95% confidence (i.e., choose *Left-Tail* ≤ as the type, enter 95 as the certainty level, and hit *TAB* on the keyboard). This means that there is a 95% probability that the income will be at or below $1.3230 or a 5% probability that income will be above $1.3230, corresponding perfectly with the results seen in Figure 7.10.

Forecast charts and forecast statistics can be used to determine the Credit Value at Risk of your credit issue or portfolio of credit instruments (e.g., Value at Risk for a one-tail 99.95% confidence for a 10-day holding period), as well as determine the risk characteristics of your portfolio (e.g., looking at the fourth moment of the distribution or kurtosis to determine if there are extreme value events or catastrophic events that may have a high probability of occurrence, potentially wiping out the profits of your portfolio). You can also determine the probability that your engineered credit vehicle will be profitable and compare one vehicle or instrument with another in terms of risk and return characteristics.

In addition to evaluating the confidence interval (i.e., given a probability level and finding the relevant income values), you can determine the probability of a given income value (Figure 7.12). For instance, what is the probability that income will be less than or equal to $1? To do this, select the *Left-Tail* ≤ probability type, enter 1 into the value input box, and hit *TAB*. The corresponding certainty will then be computed (in this case, there is a 67.70% probability income will be at or below $1).

For the sake of completeness, you can select the *Right-Tail* > probability type, enter the value 1 in the value input box, and hit *TAB* (Figure 7.13). The resulting probability indicates the right-tail probability past the value 1—that is, the probability of income exceeding $1 (in this case, we see that there is a 32.30% probability of income exceeding $1). The sum of 32.30% and 67.70% is, of course 100%, the total probability under the curve.

Some Tips
- The forecast window is resizable by clicking on and dragging the bottom right corner of the forecast window. It is always advisable that before rerunning a simulation, the current simulation should be reset (*Risk Simulator | Reset Simulation*).

- Remember that you will need to hit *TAB* on the keyboard to update the chart and results when you type in the certainty values or right- and left-tail values.
- You can also hit the *spacebar* on the keyboard repeatedly to cycle among the histogram, statistics, preferences, options, and control tabs.
- In addition, if you click on *Risk Simulator | Options,* you can access several different options for Risk Simulator, including allowing Risk Simulator to start each time Excel starts or to start only when you want it to (by going to *Start | Programs | Real Options Valuation | Risk Simulator | Risk Simulator*), change the *cell colors* of assumptions and forecasts, or turn *cell comments* on and off (cell comments will allow you to see which cells are input assumptions and which are output forecasts, as well as their respective input parameters and names). Do spend some time experimenting with the forecast chart outputs and the various bells and whistles, especially the *Controls* tab.

Correlations and Precision Control

The Basics of Correlations

The correlation coefficient is a measure of the strength and direction of the relationship between two variables, and it can take on any values between -1.0 and $+1.0$. That is, the correlation coefficient can be decomposed into its sign (positive or negative relationship between two variables) and the magnitude or strength of the relationship (the higher the absolute value of the correlation coefficient, the stronger the relationship).

The correlation coefficient can be computed in several ways. The first approach is to manually compute the correlation r of two variables x and y using:

$$r_{x,y} = \frac{n \sum x_i y_i - \sum x_i \sum y_i}{\sqrt{n \sum x_i^2 - (\sum x_i)^2} \sqrt{n \sum y_i^2 - (\sum y_i)^2}}$$

The second approach is to use Excel's *CORREL* function. For instance, if the 10 data points for x and y are listed in cells A1:B10, then the Excel function to use is *CORREL (A1:A10, B1:B10)*. The third approach is to run Risk Simulator's *Multi-Fit Tool*, and the resulting correlation matrix will be computed and displayed.

It is important to note that correlation does not imply causation. Two completely unrelated random variables might display some correlation, but this does not imply any causation between the two (e.g., sunspot activity and events in the stock market are correlated, but there is no causation between the two).

Correlations affect risk, or the second moment of the distribution, and when multiple credit instruments are placed in a portfolio, correlations are critical in determining the credit concentration or credit diversification effects that one instrument may offset another. Some credit instruments have linear correlations to other credit instruments and are nonlinearly correlated to their underlying assets (e.g., probability of default, exposure at default) and exogenous economic variables (e.g., interest rates, inflation, foreign exchange exposures).

The two general types of correlations are *parametric* and *nonparametric*. Pearson's correlation coefficient is the most common correlation measure, and it is usually referred to simply as the correlation coefficient. However, Pearson's correlation is a parametric measure, which means that it requires both correlated variables to have an underlying normal distribution and that the relationship between the variables is linear. When these conditions are violated, which is often the case in Monte Carlo simulation, the nonparametric counterparts become more important. Spearman's rank correlation and Kendall's tau are the two nonparametric alternatives. The Spearman correlation is most commonly used and is most appropriate when applied in the context of Monte Carlo simulation; there is no dependence on normal distributions or linearity, meaning that correlations between different variables with different distribution can be applied. To compute the Spearman correlation, first rank all the x and y variable values and then apply the Pearson's correlation computation.

In the case of Risk Simulator, the correlation used is the more robust nonparametric Spearman's rank correlation. However, to simplify the simulation process, and to be consistent with Excel's correlation function, the correlation inputs required are the Pearson's correlation coefficients. Risk Simulator will then apply its own algorithms to convert them into Spearman's rank correlation, thereby simplifying the process. However, to simplify the user interface, we allow users to enter the more common Pearson's product-moment correlation (e.g., computed using Excel's *CORREL* function), while in the mathematical codes, we convert these simple correlations into Spearman's rank-based correlations for distributional simulations. See Exercise 2: Correlation Effects Model at the end of this chapter for more details on these linear parametric and nonlinear nonparametric correlations.

Applying Correlations in Risk Simulator

Correlations can be applied in Risk Simulator in several ways:
- When defining assumptions (*Risk Simulator | Set Input Assumption*), simply enter the correlations into the correlation matrix grid in the Distribution Gallery.
- With existing data, run the Multi-Fit Tool (*Risk Simulator | Tools | Distributional Fitting | Multiple Variables*) to perform distributional fitting and to obtain the correlation matrix between pairwise variables. If a simulation profile exists, the assumptions fitted will automatically contain the relevant correlation values.
- With existing assumptions, you can click on *Risk Simulator | Tools | Edit Correlations* to enter the pairwise correlations of all the assumptions directly in one user interface.

Note that the correlation matrix must be positive definite. That is, the correlation must be mathematically valid. For instance, suppose you are trying to correlate three variables: grades of graduate students in a particular year, the number of beers they consume a week, and the number of hours they study a week. One would assume that the following correlation relationships exist:

Grades and Beer:	– The more they drink, the lower the grades (no show on exams).
Grades and Study:	+ The more they study, the higher the grades.
Beer and Study:	– The more they drink, the less they study (drunk and partying all the time).

However, if you input a negative correlation between Grades and Study, and assuming that the correlation coefficients have high magnitudes, the correlation matrix will be nonpositive definite. It would defy logic, correlation requirements, and matrix mathematics. Nevertheless, smaller coefficients can sometimes still work even with the bad logic. When a nonpositive or bad correlation matrix is entered, Risk Simulator will automatically inform you and offer to adjust these correlations to something that is semipositive definite while still maintaining the overall structure of the correlation relationship (the same signs as well as the same relative strengths).

The Effects of Correlations in Monte Carlo Simulation

Although the computations required to correlate variables in a simulation are complex, the resulting effects are fairly clear. Figure 7.14 shows a simple correlation model (Correlation Effects Model in the example folder). The calculation for revenue is simply price multiplied by quantity. The same model is replicated for no correlations, positive correlation (+0.9), and negative correlation (−0.9) between price and quantity.

The resulting statistics are shown in Figure 7.15. Notice that the standard deviation of the model without correlations is 0.1450, compared to 0.1886 for the positive correlation and 0.0717 for the negative correlation. That is, for simple models, negative correlations tend to reduce the average spread of the distribution and create a tight and more concentrated forecast distribution as compared to positive correlations with larger average spreads. However, the mean remains relatively stable. This result implies that correlations do little to change the expected value of projects but can reduce or increase a project's risk.

Figure 7.16 illustrates the results after running a simulation, extracting the raw data of the assumptions, and computing the correlations between the variables. The figure shows that the input assumptions are recovered in the simulation. That is, you enter +0.9 and −0.9 correlations, and the resulting simulated values have the same correlations.

Precision and Error Control

One very powerful tool in Monte Carlo simulation is that of precision control. For instance, how many trials are considered sufficient to run in a complex model? Precision control takes the guesswork out of estimating the relevant number of trials by allowing the simulation to stop if the level of prespecified precision is reached.

	Without Correlation	Positive Correlation	Negative Correlation
Price	$2.00	$2.00	$2.00
Quantity	1.00	1.00	1.00
Revenue	$2.00	$2.00	$2.00

Figure 7.14 Simple Correlation Model.

Revenue Positive Correlation - Risk Simulator Forecast

Histogram | Statistic | Preferences | Options

Statistics	Result
Number of Trials	1000
Mean	2.0020
Median	1.9992
Standard Deviation	0.1886
Variance	0.0356
Coefficient of Variation	0.0942
Maximum	2.4147
Minimum	1.6278
Range	0.7869
Skewness	0.0788
Kurtosis	-0.9641
25% Percentile	1.8475
75% Percentile	2.1480
Percentage Error Precision at 95% Confidence	0.5839%

Revenue Negative Correlation - Risk Simulator Forec...

Histogram | Statistic | Preferences | Options

Statistics	Result
Number of Trials	1000
Mean	1.9976
Median	1.9961
Standard Deviation	0.0717
Variance	0.0051
Coefficient of Variation	0.0359
Maximum	2.2148
Minimum	1.8197
Range	0.3951
Skewness	0.1040
Kurtosis	-0.3191
25% Percentile	1.9437
75% Percentile	2.0487
Percentage Error Precision at 95% Confidence	0.2224%

Revenue No Correlation - Risk Simulator Forecast

Histogram | Statistic | Preferences | Options

Statistics	Result
Number of Trials	1000
Mean	2.0036
Median	1.9995
Standard Deviation	0.1450
Variance	0.0210
Coefficient of Variation	0.0724
Maximum	2.3907
Minimum	1.6844
Range	0.7063
Skewness	0.0304
Kurtosis	-0.7316
25% Percentile	1.8945
75% Percentile	2.1128
Percentage Error Precision at 95% Confidence	0.4486%

Figure 7.15 Correlation Results.

Spearman's Nonlinear Rank Correlation on Raw Data Extracted from Simulation

Price Negative Correlation	Quantity Negative Correlation	Correlation	Price Positive Correlation	Quantity Positive Correlation	Correlation
676	145	-0.90	102	158	0.89
368	452		461	515	
264	880		515	477	
235	877		874	833	
122	711		769	792	
490	641		481	471	
336	638		627	446	
495	383		82	190	
241	568		659	674	
651	571		188	286	
854	59		458	439	
66	950		981	972	
707	262		528	569	
943	186		865	812	

Figure 7.16 Correlations Recovered.

The precision control functionality lets you set how precise you want your forecast to be. Generally speaking, as more trials are calculated, the confidence interval narrows and the statistics become more accurate. The precision control feature in Risk Simulator uses the characteristic of confidence intervals to determine when a specified accuracy of a statistic has been reached. For each forecast, you can specify the specific confidence interval for the precision level.

Precision and errors in a credit model, as well as calibrating and stress testing a model over time, are important factors to consider as part of doing due diligence.

Make sure that you do not confuse three very different terms: *error, precision,* and *confidence.* Although they sound similar, the concepts are significantly different from one another. A simple illustration is in order. Suppose you are a taco shell manufacturer and are interested in finding out how many broken taco shells there are on average in a box of 100 shells. One way to do this is to collect a sample of prepackaged boxes of 100 taco shells, open them, and count how many of them are actually broken. You manufacture 1 million boxes a day (this is your *population*), but you randomly open only 10 boxes (this is your *sample* size, also known as your number of *trials* in a simulation). The number of broken shells in each box is as follows: 24, 22, 4, 15, 33, 32, 4, 1, 45, and 2. The calculated average number of broken shells is 18.2. Based on these 10 samples or trials, the average is 18.2 units, while based on the sample, the 80% confidence interval is between 2 and 33 units (that is, 80% of the time, the number of broken shells is between 2 and 33 *based on this sample size or number of trials run*). However, how sure are you that 18.2 is the correct average? Are 10 trials sufficient to establish this?

The confidence interval between 2 and 33 is too wide and too variable. Suppose you require a more accurate average value where the error is ±2 taco shells 90% of the time. This means that if you open *all* 1 million boxes manufactured in a day, 900,000 of these boxes will have broken taco shells on average at some mean unit ±2 taco shells. How many more taco shell boxes would you then need to sample (or trials run) to obtain this level of precision? Here, the 2 taco shells is the error level, while the 90% is the level of precision. If sufficient numbers of trials are run, then the 90% confidence interval will be identical to the 90% precision level, where a more precise measure of the average is obtained such that 90% of the time, the error and, thus, the confidence will be ±2 taco shells. As an example, say the average is 20 units; then the 90% confidence interval will be between 18 and 22 units, where this interval is precise 90% of the time, where in opening all 1 million boxes, 900,000 of them will have between 18 and 22 broken taco shells. The number of trials required to hit this precision is based on the sampling error equation of

$$\bar{x} \pm Z\frac{s}{\sqrt{n}}$$

where

$$Z\frac{s}{\sqrt{n}}$$

is the error of 2 taco shells, $\bar{x}$ is the sample average, Z is the standard-normal Z score obtained from the 90% precision level, s is the sample standard deviation, and n is the number of trials required to hit this level of error with the specified precision.

Figures 7.17 and 7.18 illustrate how precision control can be performed on multiple simulated forecasts in Risk Simulator. This feature prevents the user from having to decide how many trials to run in a simulation, and it eliminates all

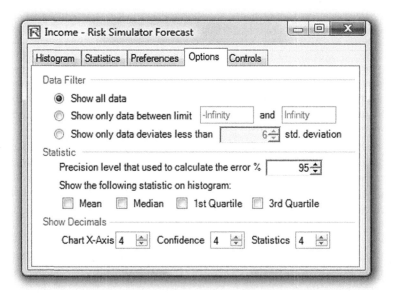

Figure 7.17 Setting the Forecast's Precision Level.

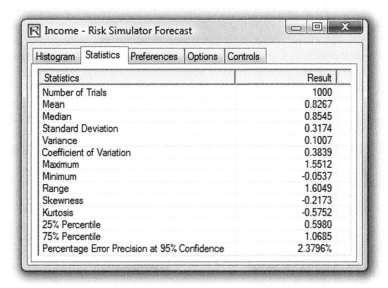

Figure 7.18 Computing the Error.

possibilities of guesswork. Figure 7.17 illustrates the forecast chart with a 95% precision level set. This value can be changed and will be reflected in the *Statistics* tab, as shown in Figure 7.18.

Exercise 1: Basic Simulation Model

This sample model illustrates how to use Risk Simulator for:
1. Running a Monte Carlo risk simulation
2. Using forecast charts
3. Interpreting the risk statistics
4. Setting seed values
5. Running a Super Speed simulation
6. Setting run preferences (simulation properties)
7. Extracting simulation data
8. Creating a simulation report and forecast statistics table
9. Creating forecast statistics using the RS functions
10. Saving a simulation run's forecast charts
11. Creating new and switching among simulation profiles
12. Distributional truncation and multidimensional simulation

Model Background
File Name: Basic Simulation Model.xls
Access: www.ElsevierDirect.com (search for this book, click Companion Site button, click link in Additional Models section)
Access: Risk Simulator | Example Models | 02 Basic Simulation Model

The *Static and Dynamic Model* worksheet illustrates a very simple model with two input assumptions (revenue and cost) and an output forecast (income), as seen in Figure 7.E1.A. The model on the left is a static model with single-point estimates, while the model on the right is a dynamic model on which we will set Monte Carlo input assumptions and output forecasts. After running the simulation, the results can be extracted and further analyzed. In this model we can also learn to set different simulation preferences, run a simulation, set seed values, and much more. To perform these exercises, you will need to have Risk Simulator version 2010 or later installed and working.

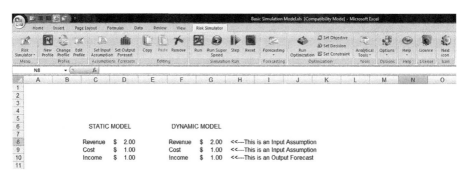

Figure 7.E1.A Basic Simulation Model.

1 Running a Monte Carlo Risk Simulation

Setting up and running a simulation model using Risk Simulator is as simple as 1, 2, 3—that is, (1) create a new profile, (2) set inputs and outputs, and then (3) run. To follow along, open the example Basic Simulation Model and do the following:

1. Select Risk Simulator | New Simulation Profile (or click on the New Profile icon), provide it with a name (e.g., "Practice Simulation"), and leave everything else as is (we come back later and revisit some of these settings).
2. Select cell G8 and click on Risk Simulator | Set Input Assumption (or click on the Set Input Assumption icon), and then select Triangular Distribution and set the Min = 1.50, Most Likely = 2.00, Max = 2.25, and then hit OK (Figure 7.E1.B).
3. Select cell G9 and set another input assumption. This time use Uniform Distribution with Min = 0.85 and Max = 1.25.
4. Select cell G10 and set that cell as the output forecast by clicking on Risk Simulator | Set Output Forecast. You can use the default name "Income" that it picked up from the model.
5. Select Risk Simulator | Run Simulation (or click on the Run icon) to start the simulation.

Figure 7.E1.C shows the simulation run. At the end of the simulation, click OK. There are a few things to notice here. The first is that the resulting model at the end of the simulation run returns the same results as the static model. That is, two dollars minus one dollar is equal to one dollar. However, what simulation does is create thousands of possible outcomes of "around two dollars" in revenue minus thousands of possible outcomes of "around one dollar" cost, resulting in the income of "around one dollar." The results are shown as a histogram, complete with the risk statistics, which we review later in this exercise.

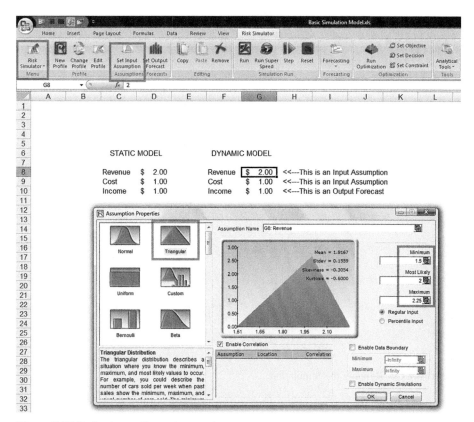

Figure 7.E1.B Setting an Input Assumption.

2 Using Forecast Charts

The forecast chart (Figure 7.E1.D) is shown when the simulation is running. Once simulation is completed, the forecast chart can be used. The forecast chart has several tabs: *Histogram, Statistics, Preferences, Options,* and *Controls.* Of particular interest are the first two: the *Histogram* and *Statistics* tabs. For instance, the first tab shows the output forecast's probability distribution in the form of a histogram, where the specific values can be determined using the certainty boxes.

In the *Histogram* tab, select *Two-Tail,* enter *90* in the *Certainty* box, and hit *TAB* on your keyboard. The 90% confidence interval is shown (0.5269 and 1.1712). This result means that there is a 5% chance that the income will fall below $0.5269, and another 5% chance that it will be above $1.1712. Alternatively, you can select Left-Tail ≤ and enter *1.0* on the input box, hit *TAB*, and see that the left-tail certainty is 76.30%, indicating that there is a 76.30% chance that the income will fall at or below $1.0 (or that there is a 23.70% chance that income will exceed $1.0). Note that your results will *not* be exactly the same as what we illustrate here due to the theoretical fact that we are running a simulation of random numbers. Do not be concerned at this

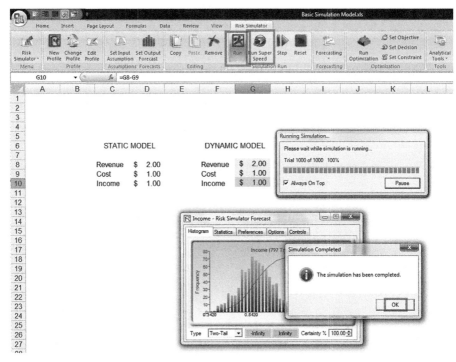

Figure 7.E1.C Running the Simulation.

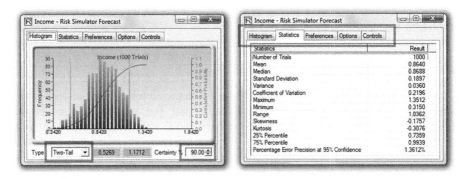

Figure 7.E1.D Simulation Results and Forecast Charts.

point; continue on to the seed value exercise for more details on how to get the same simulation results going forward.

3 Interpreting the Risk Statistics

The *Statistics* tab illustrates the statistical results of the forecast variable. Refer to the Risk Simulator user manual on the basics of risk statistics for more details on how to interpret and use these risk profile statistics in risk analysis and risk management. Note that your results will not be exactly the same as those illustrated here because a simulation (random number generation) was run, and by definition, the results will not be exactly the same every time. However, if a seed value is set (see later section), the results will be identical in every single run.

Optional Exercises

For additional exercise, view the *Preferences, Options,* and *Controls* tabs, and play with some of the settings. Specifically, try the following:

Preferences

1. Try selecting and deselecting the Always Show Windows On Top option. Navigate around different applications that might be open, and notice the behavior of the forecast chart.
2. Run a simulation with at least three forecasts and select Semitransparent When Inactive on all three forecast charts (e.g., use your own model or in cell G11, set it to be =G10, in G12, set it also to be =G10, set these two cells G11 and G12 as output forecasts, and then run a simulation). Then, minimize all other software applications, leaving these three forecast charts visible, overlay one chart on top of another, and then click anywhere on the desktop to deactivate the forecast charts. Notice how you can now compare different forecast charts.
3. Change the Histogram Resolution to different levels and view the histogram to see how the shape changes.
4. Also, if you have multiple forecast charts up and running and you forget to reset the previous simulation (resetting the simulation will clear all the forecast charts and simulated data from temporary memory, allowing you to rerun another simulation), you can Minimize All Charts, Close All Charts, or Copy a specific chart (you can set up the chart any way you like and then copy the chart to clipboard and paste it into another software such as Microsoft Word or Microsoft PowerPoint) from this tab.

Options

1. Play with the Data Filter by showing only limited data such as only 2 standard deviations from the mean or a specific range of values. Go back to the *Histogram* tab and notice the change in the chart; go back to the *Statistics* tab and notice that the computed risk statistics are now based on the truncated data and not the entire data set.
2. You can also select the Statistic to show or the number of Decimals to show in the *Histogram* chart and *Statistics* tabs. This option may come in handy if you wish to obtain higher precision of the results (more decimals) or show fewer decimals for large value results.

Controls

1. From this tab, you can control how the histogram looks by changing the orientation, color, 2D and 3D aspects of the chart, background, type of overlay curve to show (CDF versus PDF), chart types, and many other chart controls. Try out several of these items and see what happens to the *Histogram* chart each time.
2. You can also perform a distributional fitting of the forecast results and obtain the theoretical versus empirical moments of the distribution (see the Distributional Data Fitting exercise for more details on how distribution fitting routines work) or show the fitted distribution's

theoretical curve on top of the empirical histogram (first click on Fit, select either Continuous or Discrete from the Chart Overlay droplist, and then go back to the *Histogram* tab to view the resulting charts).
3. Finally, you can change the Chart Type (bar, cylinder, pyramid, and so forth), Chart Title, Min and Max values of the chart axes, and the Decimals to show on the chart. Try out several of these items and see what happens to the *Histogram* chart each time.

If you are using Risk Simulator 2010 or later, you can click on the Global View link on the top right corner of the forecast chart to view all the aforementioned tabs and functionalities in a single view or click on the Normal View link to return to the tabbed view previously described.

Setting Seed Values

1. Reset the simulation by selecting Risk Simulator | Reset Simulation.
2. Select Risk Simulator | Edit Simulation Profile (Figure 7.E1.E).
3. Select the check box for the random number sequence and enter in a seed value (e.g., 999) and click OK (see Figure 7.E1.E).
4. Run the simulation and verify that the results are the same as the results obtained in Figure 7.E1.E. In fact, run the simulation a few more times, and each time verify that the results are identical.

Note that the random number sequence, or seed number, has to be a positive integer value. Running the same model with the same assumptions and forecasts with an identical seed value and the same number of trials will always yield the same results. The number of simulation trials to run can be set in the same run properties box (see Figure 7.E1.E). Setting a seed value is important, especially when you wish to obtain the same values in each simulation run. Say, for example, that you need the live model to return the same results as a printed report during a presentation. If the results in your live demonstration are slightly off compared to the printed results, questions may arise as to their validity. By having a seed value, the results are guaranteed to always be the same.

Let us now revisit the confidence interval analysis after you have run another simulation with the seed value. Figure 7.E1.F illustrates the results of these manipulations.

1. Select Two-Tail, enter a Certainty of 90, and hit TAB on the keyboard. You will obtain the two-tailed 90% confidence interval of 0.5307 and 1.1739, which means that 90% of the time, the income level will be between these two values, with a 5% chance it will be below 0.5307 and a 5% chance it will be above 1.1739.
2. To verify that 5% result, select Left-Tail <, enter a Certainty of 5, and hit TAB. You will obtain the value of 0.5307, indicating that there is a 5% chance you will receive an income less than 0.5307.
3. Next, select Left-Tail ≤, enter in the value 1, and hit TAB. This time, instead of providing a probability to receive a value, you provide a value to receive the probability. In this case, it states that you have a 74.30% chance that your income will be less than or equal to the 1.000 value that your static single-point model had predicted. In fact, in Figure 7.E1.E, you see that the mean or average income value is 0.8626. In other words, the expected value (mean) is not the same as the value expected (in your original single-point estimate static model).
4. Select Right-Tail >, enter in 1, and hit TAB. Here you can see the complement of the Left-Tail ≤ value. In other words, the value you receive, 25.70%, indicates the probability you

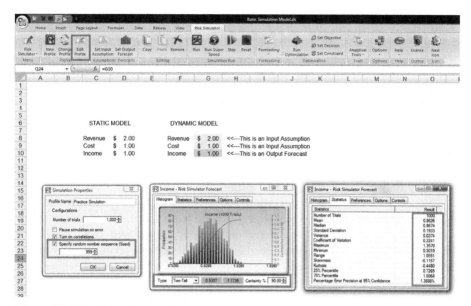

Figure 7.E1.E Using a Seed Value.

will make more than your target of 1.000, and if you take 100% minus 25.70%, you obtain 74.30%, the Left-Tail ≤ value. When doing this exercise, make sure you select the correct inequality signs (less than, less than or equal to, greater than, greater than or equal to).

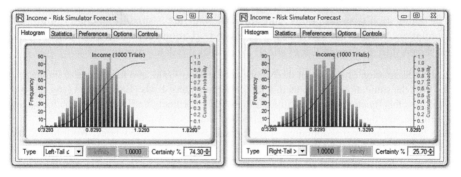

Figure 7.E1.F Left-, Right-, and Two-Tail Probabilities (Simulation Results with Seed Values).

Running Super Speed Simulation

1. Reset the simulation by selecting Risk Simulator | Reset Simulation.
2. Select Risk Simulator | Run Super Speed Simulation (see Figure 7.E1.C).

Notice how much faster the Super Speed simulation runs. In fact, for practice, *Reset the Simulation*, *Edit Simulation Profile*, change the *Number of Trials* to *100,000*, and *Run Super Speed*. It should only take a few seconds to run. However, be aware that

Super Speed simulation will not run if the model has errors, VBA (visual basic for applications), or links to external data sources or applications. In such situations, you will be notified and the regular speed simulation will be run instead. Regular speed simulations are always able to run even with errors, VBA, or external links.

Setting Run Preferences (Simulation Properties)

The run preferences or *Simulation Properties* dialog box that came up when you first created a new profile or edited the current profile (see Figure 7.E1.E) allows you to specify the *Number of Trials* to run in a particular simulation (by default it will be 1,000 trials). In theory, the higher the number of trials, the more precise the results (try rerunning the simulation again, and this time keep an eye on the *Percentage Error Precision at 95% Confidence* value, which should decrease as you increase the number of trials). In addition, *Pause Simulation on Error* can be set up so that the simulation will stop running if a computational error in Excel is encountered (e.g., #NUM or #ERROR), which is a good tool for ascertaining if your model is set up correctly. If this option is not checked, any errors will be ignored, and only the valid results will be used in the forecast charts. Correlations can also be specified between pairs of input assumptions, and if *Turn on Correlations* is selected, these specified correlations will be imputed in the simulation. See Exercise 2: Correlation Effects Model for how to set up correlations and to understand how correlations affect the outcome of your results, the theory of risk diversification, portfolio effects on distributional moments, and others.

Extracting Simulation Data

The simulation's assumptions and forecast data are stored in memory until the simulation is reset or when Excel is closed. If required, these raw data can be extracted into a separate Excel sheet. To extract the data, simply:

1. Edit Simulation Profile, reset the Number of Trials to 1,000, and then Run the simulation.
2. After the simulation is completed, select Risk Simulator | Tools | Extract Data (you can also access this function by clicking on the Next icon repeatedly until you get to the tools icon ribbon, and then click on the Data Extraction icon, as shown in Figure 7.E1.G).
3. Choose the relevant assumptions or forecasts to extract, select New Excel Worksheet as the extraction format, and click OK.

Optional Exercise

The 1,000 simulated revenue and cost values will be extracted, as well as the computed forecast income variable (see Figure 7.E1.G). Note that if you had not first run a simulation, the extracted data report would be empty, as there are no values to extract. Try clicking on the *Select* button a few times to see what happens.

Optional Exercise

Using the extracted data, apply Excel's functions to compute all of the risk statistics— for example, the mean, median, standard deviation, and so forth—and compare to

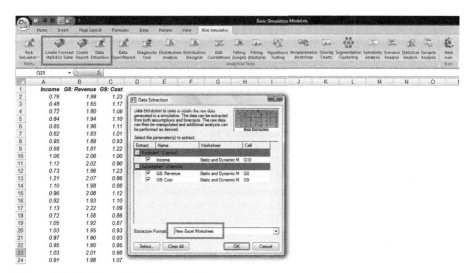

Figure 7.E1.G Extracting Simulation Data.

make sure the results are identical to those obtained in Risk Simulator's forecast statistics tab. *Hint:* Use the following Excel functions for this exercise: AVERAGE(), STDEV(), VAR(), SKEW(), KURT(), MIN(), MAX().

Creating a Simulation Report and Forecast Statistics Table

The simulation's input assumptions and output forecasts, as well as the detailed risk statistics, can also be extracted after a simulation has been run. *Assuming the simulation has already been run,* simply:

1. Select Risk Simulator | Tools | Create Report (you can also access this function by clicking on the Next icon repeatedly until you get to the tools icon ribbon, and then click on the Create Report icon as shown in Figure 7.E1.G). Spend some time reviewing the report that is generated.
2. Select Risk Simulator | Tools | Create Forecast Statistics Table (you can also access this function by clicking on the Next icon repeatedly until you get to the tools icon ribbon, and then click on the Create Forecast Statistics Table icon as shown in Figure 7.E1.G). Here you can select the forecasts you wish to show. In this simple example, we only have one forecast, but in larger models, you can select multiple forecasts at once. We suggest you try creating this statistics table with the other exercises.

Creating Forecast Statistics Using the RS Functions

You can also obtain the forecast statistics not in a report format but in a specific cell by using the Risk Simulator function call. For example, do the following:

1. Save the example file and then exit Excel and click on Start | Programs | Real Options Valuation | Risk Simulator | Tools | Install Functions. When the installation is complete in

a few short seconds, hit the spacebar to close the black console pad and start Excel. *Note:* If you are running Windows Vista or Windows 7, right-click on Install Functions in the Start menu and choose Run As Administrator.

2. Reopen the example at Risk Simulator | Example Models | 02 Basic Simulation Model and run a simulation in Super Speed Risk Simulator | Run Super Speed Simulation.

3. Select cell G12 and click on the FX (insert function) icon in Excel or click on and select the ALL category and scroll down to the RS functions list. Here you see several set input assumption functions for various distributions. The last item on the RS list is RSForecastStatistic. Select this function or you can type this function directly in the cell. For instance, type in =RSForecastStatistic(G10,"Average"), where G10 is the forecast output cell and "Average" is the statistic you wish to obtain. Remember to keep the quotes (" ") and you can replace the Average parameter with any of the following: Average, CoefficientofVariation, Median, Maximum, StandardDeviation, Minimum, Variance, Range, Skewness, Percentile75, Kurtosis, Certainty1.0, Percentile99.9. In fact, you can use "PercentileXX.XX" and "CertaintyXX.XX" and just replace the X with your own number for a left-tail < value. The Percentile parameter means you enter the percentage and receive the value X, whereas for the Certainty parameter, you enter the value X and get the left-tail percentage.

4. Just for practice, reset the simulation, run a regular speed simulation; notice that the statistics will keep changing as you run the simulation and that it stops at the final result when the simulation completes. You can now use this function call as part of your model. One quick note: If you run a Super Speed simulation, the function call will not be updated automatically. You will have to select the cell with the function after the simulation is run, hit F2 on the keyboard, and then hit Enter to update the function calculation.

Saving a Simulation Run's Forecast Charts

Suppose you run a large model and want to save the forecast charts. You can do so in Risk Simulator by saving the results as a Risk Sim file format. Saving the forecast charts allows you to reopen the results without having to rerun the simulation, thereby saving you some time.

1. Run a simulation as usual.
2. Select Risk Simulator | Tools | Data Extraction/Export (you can also access this function by clicking on the Next icon repeatedly until you get to the tools icon ribbon, and then click on the Data Extraction icon). Here you select the Extraction Format as Risk Simulator Data (Risk Sim) file (Figure 7.E1.H). Save the file to the desired location. You can now save and exit Excel.
3. Open Excel and select Risk Simulator | Tools | Data Open/Import (you can also access this function by clicking on the Next icon repeatedly until you get to the tools icon ribbon, and click on the Data Open/Import icon). Select the Risk Sim file you saved previously, and the forecast charts will now reappear.

Creating New and Switching Among Simulation Profiles

The same model can have multiple Risk Simulator profiles. That is, different users of the same model can, in fact, create their own simulation input assumptions, forecasts, run preferences, and so forth. All these preferences are stored in separate simulation

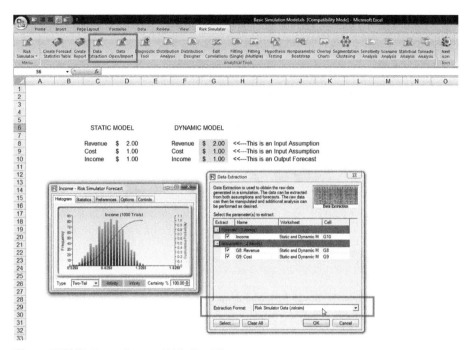

Figure 7.E1.H Extracting to a Risk Sim File.

profiles, and each profile can be run independently. This is a powerful feature that allows multiple users to run the same model their own way or for the same user to run the model under different simulation conditions, thereby allowing for scenario analysis in Monte Carlo simulation. To create different profiles and switch among different profiles, simply:

1. Create several new profiles by clicking on Risk Simulator | New Simulation Profile and provide each new profile with a unique name.
2. Add the relevant assumptions and forecasts, or change the run preferences as desired in each simulation profile.
3. Switch among different profiles by clicking on Risk Simulator | Change Active Simulation.

Note that you can create as many profiles as you wish, but each profile needs to have its own unique name. Also, you can select an existing profile and click on *Duplicate* (Figure 7.E1.I) to duplicate all the input assumptions and output forecasts that are in this profile, which means you do not have to replicate all of these manually. You can then change to this new profile and make any modifications as required. From this user interface, you can also *Delete* any unwanted profiles (but note that you need to have at least one profile active in the model, which means that you can delete any profile you choose, but you cannot delete all of them because one profile must be left in the model). You can also click on a profile, click again on the name of the profile, and rename the profile as required.

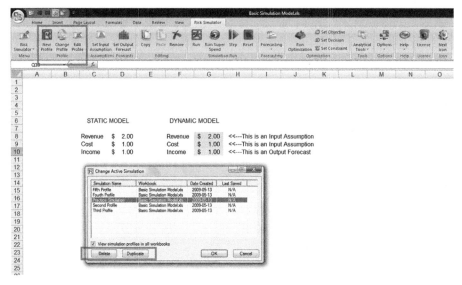

Figure 7.E1.I Multiple Profiles in Risk Simulator.

Finally, as you save the Excel file, you will also save these profiles in the same Excel file. Profiles are stored in a special hidden segment of the Excel file and will be available to you as you open the Excel file in the future. For further practice, try saving the Excel file and then reopening the file again; notice that all your profiles and settings are still available. Just bear in mind that if you have multiple profiles, the last profile used will be the profile that is activated by default when the Excel file is opened the next time. Depending on what you are trying to do, you may need to remember to *Change the Profile* to the one you wish to use before you start running any simulations.

Distributional Truncation, Alternate Parameters, and Multidimensional Simulation

Distributional truncations, or *data boundaries,* are typically not used by the average analyst but exist for truncating the distributional assumptions. For instance, if a normal distribution is selected, the theoretical boundaries are between negative infinity and positive infinity. However, in practice, the simulated variable exists only within some smaller range, and this range can then be entered to truncate the distribution appropriately. Not considering truncation is a major error users commit, especially when using the triangular distribution. The triangular distribution is very simple and intuitive. As a matter of fact, it is probably the most widely used distribution in Risk Simulator, apart from the normal and uniform distributions. Simplistically, the triangular distribution looks at the minimum value, the most probable value, and the maximum value. These three inputs are often confused with the worst-case, nominal-case, and best-case scenarios. This assumption is, indeed, incorrect.

In fact, a worst-case scenario can be translated as a highly unlikely condition that will still occur given a percentage of the time. For instance, one can model the economy as high, average, and low, analogous to the worst-case, nominal-case, and best-case scenarios. Thus, logic would dictate that the worst-case scenario might have, say, a 15% chance of occurrence; the nominal-case, a 50% chance of occurrence; and the best-case scenario a 35% chance. This approach is what is meant by using a best-, nominal-, and worst-case scenario analysis. However, compare that to the triangular distribution, where the minimum and maximum cases will almost never occur, with a probability of occurrence set at zero!

For instance, in Figure 7.E1.J, the worst-, nominal-, and best-case scenarios are set as 5, 10, and 15, respectively. Note that at the extreme values, the probability of 5 or 15 occurring is virtually zero, as the areas under the curve (the measure of probability) of these extreme points are zero. In other words, 5 and 15 will almost never occur. Compare that to the economic scenario where these extreme values have either a 15% or 35% chance of occurrence. Instead, distributional truncation should be considered here. The same applies to any other distribution. Figure 7.E1.K illustrates a truncated normal distribution where the extreme values do not extend to both positive and negative infinities but are truncated at 7 and 13.

Another critical activity is looking at *Alternate Parameters*—that is, looking at the same distribution but through a different set of parameters. For instance, if a *normal distribution* is used in simulating market share, and the mean is set at *55%* with a standard deviation of *45%,* one should be extremely worried. Using Risk Simulator's *Percentile Input* selection in the *Set Input Assumption* user interface, the 10th and 90th percentiles indicate a value of −2.67% and 112.67% (Figure 7.E1.L). Clearly these values cannot exist under actual conditions. How can a product have −2.67% or

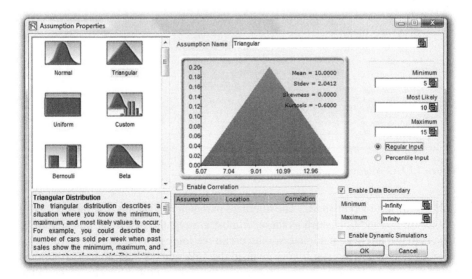

Figure 7.E1.J Sample Triangular Distribution.

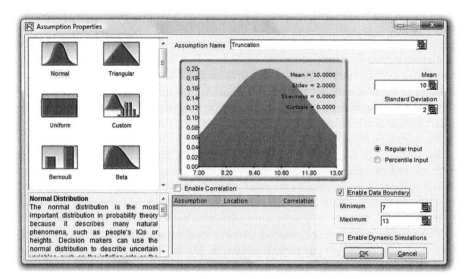

Figure 7.E1.K Truncating a Distribution.

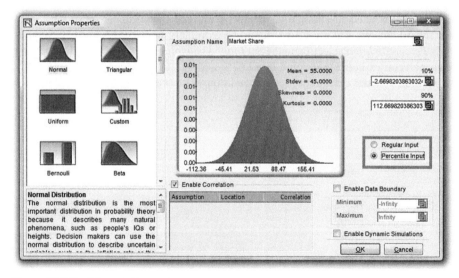

Figure 7.E1.L Alternate Parameters.

112.67% of the market share? The alternate-parameters function is a very powerful tool to use in conditions such as these. Almost always, the first thing that should be done is to use alternate parameters to ascertain the logical upper and lower values of an input parameter. So even if you obtained the 55% and 45% through distributional fitting (which, by the way, is correct, because the fit was probably very strong in the center of the normal distribution), by virtue of a theoretical fitting routine, the entire normal distribution will be fitted, and the normal distribution's tails extend from negative infinity to positive infinity, which is clearly outside the range of the norm for market share. So using the alternate parameters will quickly allow you to visualize the 10th and 90th percentiles, and then you can decide to change the distribution or still use the distribution but apply distributional truncation as discussed previously. See the exercise on distributional analysis tools for obtaining other percentiles for any distribution other than the default 10% and 90% as described here.

Finally, Figures 7E1.M and 7E1.N illustrate how *multidimensional simulation*, or *dynamic simulation*, works. Suppose you have a model like the one shown, and further suppose that you have an input triangular distribution assumption in cell G5, and you used the Link icon to link its input parameters to other cells (H5, I5, and J5 for the minimum, most-likely, and maximum values), as shown in Figure 7.E1.M. Typically, this is a basic assumption, and you are all done. However, what if the minimum, most-likely, and maximum inputs are themselves uncertain? If that is the case, then you can set an input assumption for these inputs (cells H5, I5, J5). In other words, if you have an assumption that is linked to other cells, and these other cells themselves are assumptions, you have just created a two-layer simulation (of course, you can add additional layers where these input cells are again linked to other cells that are simulated and so forth, creating a multidimensional simulation model). If you do this, remember to select the *Enable Dynamic Simulation* checkbox (see Figure 7.E1.M) on the assumption that links to other assumptions. So if you ran a 1,000-trial simulation, instead of having a single triangular distribution and picking random numbers from this single distribution, there are actually 1,000 triangular distributions, where at each trial there will be new parameters for this triangular distribution, and a random number is selected from this distribution, and then on the next trial, you repeat the entire process. This multidimensional simulation approach allows you to simulate uncertain input parameters into the simulation.

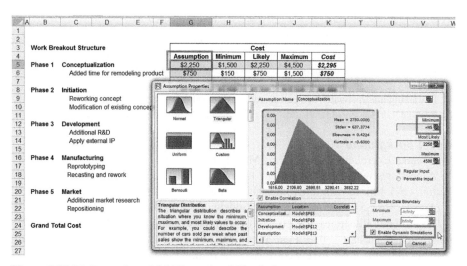

Figure 7.E1.M Dynamic or Multidimensional Simulation.

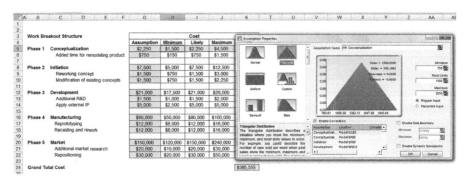

Figure 7.E1.N Input Parameter as an Assumption.

There is one little word of caution: Do not overdo the multidimensional layers because suppose you are using a triangular distribution with Min = A, Most Likely = B, and Max = C. Further suppose A is a uniform distribution with Min = D and Max = E. If C is also another uniform distribution with Min = F and Max = G, all is well as long as E and F do not cross each other. Put another way, if you accidentally set E > F, then there will be times in a random simulation where the random value E is higher than F. This result means that A > C in the original distribution, which violates the input requirements, causing the simulation stop and creating an error (i.e., the maximum value is less than the minimum value in the triangular distribution; this cannot work and the simulation stops). So if you are confused by distributional truncation, it might be best to avoid using it.

Exercise 2: Correlation Effects Model

This sample model illustrates how to use Risk Simulator for:

1. Setting up a simulation's input assumptions and output forecasts
2. Copying, pasting, and deleting simulation assumptions and forecasts
3. Running correlated simulations, comparing results between correlated and uncorrelated models
4. Extracting and manually computing and verifying the assumptions' correlations
5. Pearson's Product Moment Linear Correlation and Spearman's Nonlinear Rank Correlation

Model Background
File Name: Correlation Risk Effects Model.xls
   Access: www.ElsevierDirect.com (search for this book, click Companion Site button, click link in Additional Models section)
   Access: Risk Simulator | Example Models | 04 Correlation Risk Effects Model
   This model illustrates the effects of correlated simulation versus uncorrelated simulation. That is, whether a pair of simulated assumptions is not correlated, positively correlated, or negatively correlated, the results can sometimes be very different. In addition, the simulated assumptions' raw data are extracted after the simulation and

manual computations of their pairwise correlations are performed. The results indicate that the input correlations hold after the simulation.

1 Setting Up a Simulation's Input Assumptions and Output Forecasts

Open the model *Risk Simulator* | *Example Models* | *04 Correlation Risk Effects Model*. Go to the *Correlation Model* worksheet (Figure 7.E2.A). Follow the instructions shown on the following pages to set up and run this model.

Figure 7.E2.A Correlation Model.

2 Copying, Pasting, and Deleting Simulation Assumptions and Forecasts

We replicate the assumptions and forecasts per the instructions on the worksheet by setting the input assumptions for price and quantity, and forecast outputs for revenue. When setting up the input assumptions, you can practice by setting up one assumption at a time, or you can set up a single assumption and then use the Risk Simulator copy and paste technique to replicate the assumptions across multiple cells at once. Follow these steps:

Procedures

1. Create a new profile: Risk Simulator | New Profile (or use the New Profile icon) and give it a name.
2. Select cell D5 for the price without correlation. Click on Risk Simulator | Set Input Assumption (or use the Set Input Assumption icon), select the Triangular distribution, and set the parameters as 1.8, 2.0, and 2.2 as instructed on the worksheet (Figure 7.E2.B). Click OK when done.
3. Select cell D5 again, after the assumption has been set, and click on Risk Simulator | Copy Parameter (or use the Copy icon in the Risk Simulator toolbar). Make sure you do not use Excel's copy or Ctrl+C or right-click Copy because using Excel copy will only copy the cell contents, color, equations, and font. Only by using Risk Simulator's copy can you copy the input assumption and its parameters.

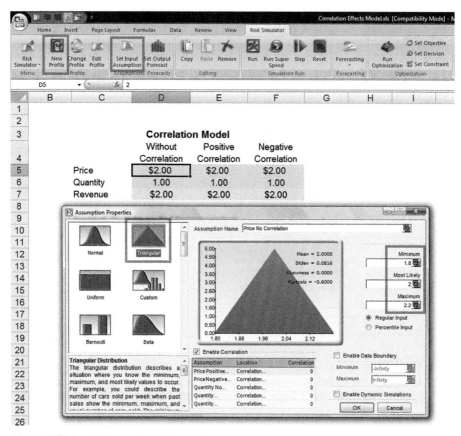

Figure 7.E2.B Setting an Input Assumption.

4. Select cells E5 and F5 and click on Risk Simulator | Paste Parameter (or use the Paste icon in the Risk Simulator toolbar). Again, make sure you do not hit Enter and do not use Excel's paste function or Ctrl+V, as this will only paste the Excel cell contents and not the input assumptions (Figure 7.E2.C).
5. Select cell D6 and repeat the process above, this time using a Uniform distribution with 0.9 and 1.1 as the input parameters. Copy/paste the parameters for cells E6 and F6.
6. Select cell D7 and set it as an output forecast by clicking on Risk Simulator | Set Output Forecast (or use the Set Output Forecast icon), and link the forecast name to cell D4. Then select cell D7 again, copy the parameter, and select cells E7 and F7 to paste the parameters using Risk Simulator copy and paste. Later, remember to review the tip presented in the next section for an important reminder on copy and pasting.
7. Next, set the correlations among the variables. There are two ways to set correlations: You can set correlations one pair of assumptions at a time or set them in a correlation matrix all at once. We explore both approaches as follows:
   a. As cell E5 is supposed to be correlated to cell E6, select cell E5 and click on Risk Simulator | Set Input Assumption (or use the Set Input Assumption icon) once again. This time, look at the pairwise correlation section (Figure 7.E2.D). You may click and

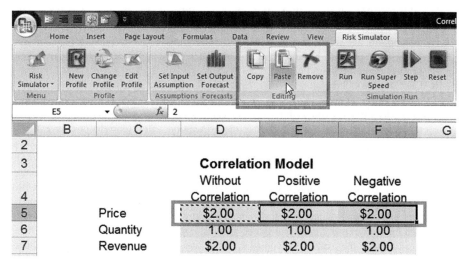

Figure 7.E2.C Simulation Parameter Copy and Paste.

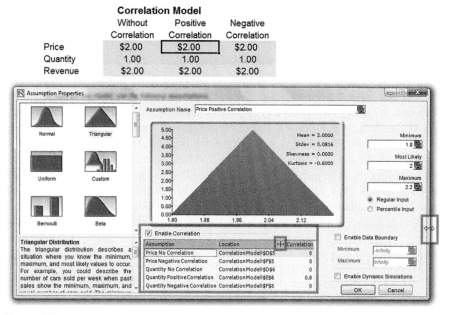

Figure 7.E2.D Pairwise Correlations (Manual).

drag to enlarge the user interface form, as well as to increase the width of the three columns for assumptions, location, and correlation. Find the input assumption for E6, enter the correlation of 0.8 and hit Enter on the keyboard (see Figure 7.E2.D). Remember to hit Enter on the keyboard when you are done entering the correlation, otherwise the software will think that you are still typing in the input box. Click OK when done. For the sake of completeness, select cell E6 and again set an input assumption, and notice that by setting the assumption in cell E5 previously and correlating it to E6, cell E6 automatically correlates back to E5. Repeat the correlation process for cell F5 and F6.

b. Click on Risk Simulator | Tools | Edit Correlations and you will be provided with a correlation tool (Figure 7.E2.E). Select the Show Cell Name checkbox and you can select the variables you wish to correlate or click on Select All to show all of them. In the correlation matrix section, enter the correlation value (correlations have to be between –1 and 1, and zeroes are allowed, of course). Notice that the correlation matrix shown is a full square matrix and the upper triangle mirrors the lower triangle. So all you need to do is enter the correlation on either the upper or lower triangle and hit Enter on the keyboard. The value will be updated in both upper and lower triangles. Click OK when done. Also, note that the user interface allows you to Paste in a correlation matrix. This tool comes in handy if you wish the correlation matrix to be visible in Excel. When you have an existing matrix in Excel, you can copy the matrix and then paste it here (making sure the matrix you copied is square and the upper and lower triangles have identical pairwise correlation values). You are now done with setting correlations. For the sake of completeness, you can select any one of the input assumptions and set assumption again to make sure that the correlations are set up correctly (see Figure 7.E2.D).

8. Run the simulation by clicking on Risk Simulator | Run Simulation (or use the Run Simulation icon) and interpret the results. Proceed to the next section for an interpretation of the results. You can also try running Super Speed Simulation for faster results.

Tip: For the copy and paste in Risk Simulator, this quick tip will come in handy when you are setting inputs and outputs on larger models. When you select a cell and use the Risk Simulator *Copy* function, it copies everything into Windows clipboard, including the cell's value, equation, function, color, font, and size, as well as Risk Simulator's assumptions, forecasts, or decision variables. Then, as you apply the Risk Simulator *Paste* function, you have two options. The first option is to apply the Risk Simulator *Paste* directly, and all cell values, color, font, equation, functions *and* parameters will be pasted, akin to the preceding example. However, the second option is to first click *Escape* on the keyboard, and then apply the Risk Simulator *Paste*. *Escape* tells Risk Simulator that you only wish to paste the Risk Simulator

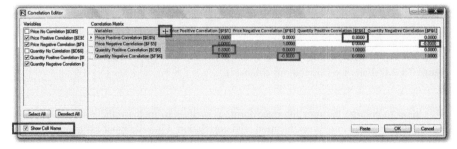

Figure 7.E2.E Pairwise Correlations (Matrix).

assumption, forecast, or decision variable and *not* the cell's values, color, equation, function, font, and so forth. Hitting *Escape* before pasting allows you to maintain the target cell's values and computations, and pastes only the Risk Simulator parameters.

Tip: In Risk Simulator version 2010, you can also click on the View Correlation Charts tool to view sample representations of how different correlation levels look when variables are plotted on a scatter chart You can also use this tool to compute correlations of your raw data.

Tip: In Risk Simulator version 2010, you can select multiple cells with assumptions and forecasts, and use Risk Simulator copy and paste functionalities.

3 Running Correlated Simulations and Comparing Results between Correlated and Uncorrelated Models

The resulting simulation statistics indicate that the negatively correlated variables provide a tighter or smaller standard deviation or overall risk level on the model. This relationship exists because negative correlations provide a diversification effect on the variables and thus tend to make the standard deviation slightly smaller. Therefore, we need to make sure to input correlations when there are, indeed, correlations between variables. Otherwise this interacting effect will not be accounted for in the simulation.

The positive correlation model has a larger standard deviation because a positive correlation tends to make both variables travel in the same direction, making the extreme ends wider and thus increasing the overall risk. Therefore, the model without any correlations will have a standard deviation between the positive and negative correlation models.

Notice that the expected value or mean does not change much. In fact, if sufficient simulation trials are run, the theoretical and empirical values of the mean remain the same. The first moment (central tendency or expected value) does not change with correlations. Only the second moment (spread or risk and uncertainty) will change with correlations (Figure 7.E2.F).

Note that this characteristic exists only in simple models with a positive relationship. That is, a Price × Quantity model is considered a "positive" relationship model (as are Price + Quantity), where a negative correlation decreases the range and a positive correlation increases the range. The opposite is true for negative relationship models. For instance, Price/Quantity or Price – Quantity would be a negative relationship model, where a positive correlation will reduce the range of the forecast variable, and a negative correlation will increase the range. Finally, for more complex models (e.g., larger models with multiple variables interacting with positive and negative relationships and sometimes with positive and negative correlations), the results are hard to predict and cannot be determined theoretically. Only by running a simulation can the true results of the range and outcomes be determined. In such a scenario, tornado analysis and sensitivity analysis would be more appropriate.

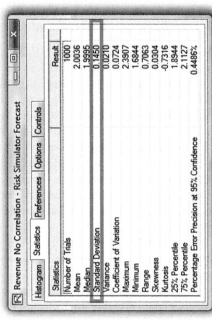

Figure 7.E2.F Risk Effects on Distributional Moments.

4   Extracting and Manually Computing and Verifying the Assumptions' Correlations

For additional exercise, run the simulation and then extract the simulated data. Then run a correlation computation and see if the correlations are similar to what you have entered into Risk Simulator.

Procedures

1. Run the simulation: Risk Simulator | Run Simulation (or use the Run Simulation icon). Click OK when simulation is done.
2. Extract the data: Risk Simulator | Tools | Data Extraction and Export (or use the Data Extraction icon under the Analytical Tools ribbon). Select New Excel Worksheet and you can click the Select All… button repeatedly to select only the forecasts, only the assumptions, or all forecasts and assumptions at once (Figure 7.E2.G). Let's just select all forecasts and assumptions and click OK to extract the data.
3. Go to the extracted data worksheet and use Excel's CORREL function to compute the pairwise correlations of the simulated data. For example, Figure 7.E2.H illustrates that the

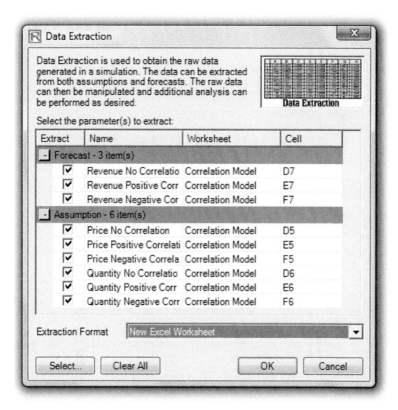

Figure 7.E2.G Data Extraction.

Revenue No Correlation	Revenue Positive Correlation	Revenue Negative Correlation	Price No Correlation	Price Positive Correlation	Price Negative Correlation	Quantity No Correlation	Quantity Positive Correlation	Quantity Negative Correlation
2.08	1.77	2.00	2.08	1.95	1.89	1.00	0.91	1.06
1.83	1.83	2.08	1.89	1.92	1.98	0.97	0.95	1.05
2.10	2.10	2.06	2.05	2.02	1.89	1.03	1.04	1.09
2.19	2.09	1.95	2.04	2.04	1.88	1.08	1.03	1.04
2.07	1.71	1.82	2.04	1.89	1.96	1.01	0.91	0.93
1.92	2.07	1.89	2.09	1.98	2.02	0.92	1.05	0.93
2.01	2.11	2.04	1.92	2.05	2.00	1.05	1.03	1.02
2.05	1.71	1.93	2.05	1.87	1.86	1.00	0.91	1.04
2.04	1.67	1.99	1.93	1.84	1.96	1.06	0.91	1.02
1.95	2.13	1.94	1.95	2.06	1.90	1.00	1.03	1.02
1.98	2.00	2.11	1.98	1.98	1.92	1.00	1.01	1.10
1.80	1.91	2.03	1.91	1.99	2.00	0.94	0.96	1.02
1.92	1.95	2.02	1.88	1.93	1.84	1.03	1.01	1.10
2.11	2.04	2.01	2.17	2.01	1.83	0.98	1.02	1.09
2.05	1.75	1.98	1.97	1.89	1.81	1.04	0.93	1.10
2.13	2.02	2.12	1.94	2.04	2.01	1.10	0.99	1.05
1.92	1.72	2.05	2.03	1.86	1.87	0.94	0.92	1.09
1.79	1.79	1.94	1.92	1.94	1.98	0.93	0.92	0.98
1.93	2.11	1.99	2.03	2.11	1.81	0.95	1.00	1.10
2.07	2.17	1.94	2.10	2.10	2.09	0.98	1.03	0.93
2.17	1.71	2.03	2.13	1.88	1.96	1.02	0.91	1.04
1.84	2.38	2.11	2.05	2.17	1.95	0.90	1.10	1.08
1.99	2.38	1.96	1.96	2.18	2.04	1.01	1.09	0.96

K	Equation
0.03	Equation: =CORREL(D2:D1001,G2:G1001)
0.80	Equation: =CORREL(E2:E1001,H2:H1001)
-0.80	Equation: =CORREL(F2:F1001,I2:I1001)

Figure 7.E2.H Correlation of Simulated Values.

computed correlations are +0.8 and –0.8 for the positive and negative correlation pairs, plus the uncorrelated pair is close to zero (the correlation is never exactly equal to zero because of the randomness effect, and 0.03 is statistically significantly identical to zero in this case). In other words, the correlations we inputted originally are maintained in the simulation model.

5   Pearson's Product Moment Linear Correlation and Spearman's Nonlinear Rank Correlation

Typically, when we use the term *correlation*, we usually mean a linear correlation. And, of course, correlations can take on any value between –1 and +1, inclusive, which means that the correlation coefficient has a sign (direction) and magnitude (strength). The problem arises when there is nonlinearity and we use linear correlations. Figure 7.E2.I illustrates a few scatter charts with pairwise X and Y variables (e.g., hours of study and school grades). If we draw an imaginary best-fitting line in the scatter diagram, we can see the approximate correlation (we show a computation of correlation in a moment, but for now, let's just visualize). Part A shows a relatively high positive correlation coefficient (R) of about 0.7 as an increase in X means an increase in Y, so there is a positive slope and, therefore, a positive correlation. Part B shows an even stronger negative correlation (negatively sloped, an increase of X means a decrease of Y and vice versa). It has slightly higher magnitude because the dots are closer to the line. In fact, when the dots are exactly on the line, as in Part D, the correlation is +1 (if positively sloped) or –1 (if negatively sloped), indicating a perfect correlation. Part C shows a situation where the curve is perfectly flat, or has zero correlation, where, regardless of the X value, Y remains unchanged, indicating that there is no relationship.

The problem arises when there are nonlinear relationships (typically the case in a many real-life situations) as shown in Figure 7.E2.J. Part E shows an exponential relationship between X and Y. If we use a nonlinear correlation, we get +0.9, but if we use a linear correlation, it is much lower at 0.6 (Part F), which means that there is information that is not picked up by the linear correlation. The situation gets a lot worse when we have a sinusoidal relationship, as in Parts G and H. The nonlinear correlation picks up the relationship very nicely with a 0.9 correlation coefficient; using a linear correlation, the best-fitting line is literally a flat horizontal line, indicating zero correlation. However, just looking at the picture would tell you that there is a relationship. *So we must therefore distinguish between linear and nonlinear correlations because as we have seen in this exercise, correlation affects risk, and we are dealing with risk analysis!*

The linear correlation coefficient is also known as the Pearson's product moment correlation coefficient. It is computed by $R = \dfrac{\sum_{i=1}^{n}(X_i-\overline{X})(Y_i-\overline{Y})}{\sqrt{\sum_{i=1}^{n}(X_i-\overline{X})^2(Y_i-\overline{Y})^2}}$ and assumes that the underlying distribution is normal or near-normal such as the t-distribution. Therefore, this is a parametric correlation. You can use Excel's *CORREL* function to compute this effortlessly. The nonlinear correlation is the Spearman's nonparametric rank-based correlation, which does not assume any underlying distribution, making it a nonparametric measure. The approach to Spearman's nonlinear correlation is

Columns (Value)	LOG (VALUE)	RANK (VALUE)
1	0	1
10	1	2
100	2	3
1000	3	4
10000	4	5
100000	5	6

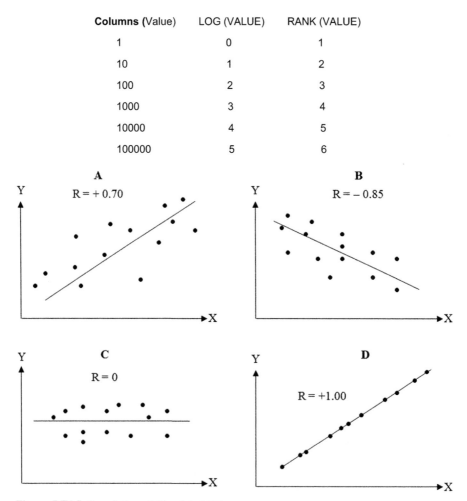

Figure 7.E2.I Correlation of Simulated Values.

very simple. Using the original data we first "linearize" the data and then apply the Pearson's correlation computation to get the Spearman's correlation. Typically, whenever there is nonlinear data, we can linearize it by either using a *LOG* function (or, equivalently, an *LN* or natural log function) or a *RANK* function. The following table illustrates this effect. The original value is clearly nonlinear (it is 10^x, where x is from 0 to 5). However, if you apply a log function, the data becomes linear (1, 2, 3, 4, 5), or when you apply ranks, the rank (either high to low or low to high) is also linear. Once we have linearized the data, we can apply the linear Pearson's correlation. To summarize, Spearman's nonparametric nonlinear correlation coefficient is obtained by first ranking the data and then applying Pearson's parametric linear correlation coefficient.

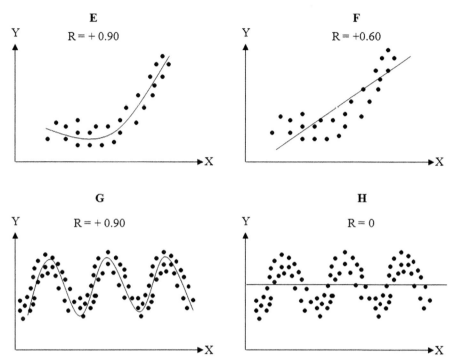

Figure 7.E2.J Correlation of Simulated Values.

Value	LOG(VALUE)	RANK(VALUE)
1	0	1
10	1	2
100	2	3
1000	3	4
10000	4	5
100000	5	6

8 Projections and Risk Assessment

Credit Engineering for Bankers. DOI: 10.1016/B978-0-12-378585-5.10008-9

This chapter covers the fundamental concepts of quantitative forecasting and predictions. In credit engineering, one of the critical tasks is to predict the future based on objective historical data or facts as well as on subjective estimates and assumptions. For instance, a credit instrument is priced based on expectations of how the interest rates will change in the future, as well as how the obligors behave (e.g., forecasted probability of default based on a person's age, income levels, educational level, debt levels, past payment history, etc.). In Basel II requirements, we take these forecasted results and compare them with actuals to do backtesting and stress-testing analyses.

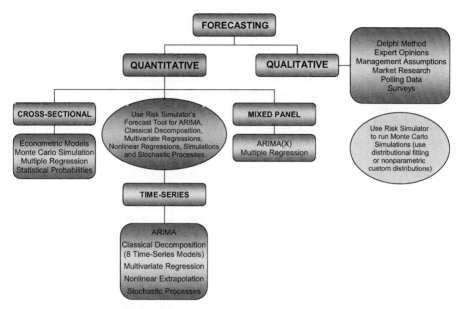

Figure 8.1 Forecasting Methods.

Forecasting is the act of predicting the future, whether it is based on historical data or speculation about the future when no history exists. When historical data exist, a quantitative or statistical approach is best, but if no historical data exist, then a qualitative or judgmental approach is usually the only recourse. Figure 8.1 shows the most common methodologies for forecasting.

Different Types of Forecasting Techniques

Generally, forecasting can be divided into quantitative and qualitative approaches. Qualitative forecasting is used when little to no reliable historical, contemporaneous, or comparable data exist. Several qualitative methods exist such as the Delphi or expert opinion approach (a consensus-building forecast by field experts, marketing experts, or internal staff members) and management assumptions (target growth rates set by senior management), as well as market research or external data or polling and surveys (data obtained through third-party sources, industry and sector indexes, or from active market research). These estimates can be either single-point estimates (an average consensus) or a set of prediction values (a distribution of predictions). The latter can be entered into Risk Simulator as a custom distribution, and the resulting predictions can be simulated—that is, running a nonparametric simulation using the prediction data points as the custom distribution.

For quantitative forecasting, the available data or data that need to be forecasted can be divided into time-series (values that have a time element to them, such as revenues at different years, inflation rates, interest rates, market share, failure rates, etc.), cross-sectional (values that are time-independent, such as the grade point average of sophomore students across the nation in a particular year, given each student's levels of SAT scores, IQ, and number of alcoholic beverages consumed per week), or mixed panel (mixture between time-series and panel data—for example, predicting sales over the next 10 years given budgeted marketing expenses and market share projections, where time-series sales data are used with exogenous variables such as marketing expenses and market share exist to help to model the forecast predictions). Here is a quick review of each methodology (several quick getting started examples are provided at the end of the chapter).

- *ARIMA.* Autoregressive integrated moving average (ARIMA, also known as Box-Jenkins ARIMA) is an advanced econometric modeling technique. ARIMA looks at historical time-series data and performs backfitting optimization routines to account for historical auto-correlation (the relationship of one value versus another in time) and for the stability of the data to correct for the nonstationary characteristics of the data. This predictive model learns over time by correcting its forecasting errors. Advanced knowledge in econometrics is typically required to build good predictive models using this approach, which can be used to forecast variables such as price of commodities.
- *Auto-ARIMA.* The Auto-ARIMA module automates some of the traditional ARIMA modeling by automatically testing multiple permutations of model specifications and returns the best-fitting model. Running the Auto-ARIMA module is similar to running regular ARIMA forecasts. The differences are that the P, D, Q inputs are no longer required and that different combinations of these inputs are automatically run and compared.
- *Basic Econometrics.* Econometrics refers to a branch of business analytics, modeling, and forecasting techniques for modeling the behavior OF or forecasting certain business, economic, finance, physics, manufacturing, operations, and any other variables. Running the Basic Econometrics model is similar to regular regression analysis except that the dependent and independent variables are allowed to be modified before a regression is run.
- *Basic Auto Econometrics.* This methodology is similar to basic econometrics, but thousands of linear, nonlinear, interacting, lagged, and mixed variables are automatically run on the data to determine the best-fitting econometric model that describes the behavior of the dependent variable. It is useful for modeling the effects of the variables and for forecasting future outcomes, while not requiring the analyst to be an expert econometrician.
- *Custom Distributions.* Using Risk Simulator, expert opinions can be collected and a customized distribution can be generated. This forecasting technique comes in handy when the data set is small or the goodness-of-fit is bad when applied to a distributional fitting routine. You can use this approach for historical simulation and forecasting based on qualitative and subject-matter expert opinions.
- *GARCH.* The generalized autoregressive conditional heteroskedasticity (GARCH) model is used to model historical and forecast future volatility levels of a marketable security (e.g., stock prices, commodity prices, oil prices, etc.). The data set has to be a time-series of raw price levels. GARCH will first convert the prices into relative returns and then run an internal optimization to fit the historical data to a mean-reverting volatility term structure, while assuming that the volatility is heteroskedastic in nature (changes over time according to some econometric characteristics). Several variations of this methodology are available in Risk Simulator, including EGARCH, EGARCH-T, GARCH-M, GJR-GARCH, GJR-GARCH-T, IGARCH, and T-GARCH.

- *J-Curve.* The J-curve, or exponential growth curve, is one where the growth of the next period depends on the current period's level and the increase is exponential. This phenomenon means that, over time, the values will increase significantly, from one period to another. This model is typically used in forecasting biological growth and chemical reactions over time.

- *Markov Chains.* A Markov chain exists when the probability of a future state depends on a previous state and when linked together forms a chain that reverts to a long-run steady state level. This approach is typically used to forecast the market share of two competitors. The required inputs are the starting probability of a customer in the first store (the first state) returning to the same store in the next period, versus the probability of switching to a competitor's store in the next state.

- *Maximum Likelihood on Logit, Probit, and Tobit.* Maximum likelihood estimation (MLE) is used to forecast the probability of something occurring given some independent variables. For instance, MLE is used to predict if a credit line or debt will default—probability of default—given the obligor's characteristics (30 years old, single, salary of $100,000 per year, and total credit card debt of $10,000), or the probability a patient will have lung cancer if the person is a male between the ages of 50 and 60, smokes five packs of cigarettes per month or year, and so forth. In these circumstances, the dependent variable is limited (i.e., limited to being binary 1 and 0 for default/die and no default/live, or limited to truncated values or integer values such as 1, 2, 3, etc.) and the desired outcome of the model is to predict the probability of an event occurring. Traditional regression analysis will not work in these situations (the predicted probability is usually less than zero or greater than one, and many of the required regression assumptions are violated, such as independence and normality of the errors, and the errors will be fairly large).

- *Multivariate Regression.* Multivariate regression is used to model the relationship structure and characteristics of a certain dependent variable as it depends on other independent exogenous variables. Using the modeled relationship, we can forecast the future values of the dependent variable. The accuracy and goodness-of-fit for this model can also be determined. Linear and nonlinear models can be fitted in the multiple regression analysis.

- *Nonlinear Extrapolation.* In this methodology, the underlying structure of the data to be forecasted is assumed to be nonlinear over time. For instance, a data set such as 1, 4, 9, 16, 25 is considered to be nonlinear (these data points are from a squared function).

- *S-Curves.* The S-curve, or logistic growth curve, starts off like a J-curve, with exponential growth rates. Over time, the environment becomes saturated (e.g., market saturation, competition, overcrowding), the growth slows, and the forecast value eventually ends up at a saturation or maximum level. The S-curve model is typically used in forecasting market share or sales growth of a new product from market introduction until maturity and decline, population dynamics, and other naturally occurring phenomenon.

- *Spline Curves.* Sometimes there are missing values in a time-series data set. For instance, interest rates for years 1 to 3 may exist, followed by years 5 to 8, and then year 10. Spline curves can be used to interpolate the missing years' interest rate values based on the data that exist. Spline curves can also be used to forecast or extrapolate values of future time periods beyond the time period of available data. The data can be linear or nonlinear and is very useful for forecasting yield curves based on forward rate expectations.

- *Stochastic Process Forecasting.* Sometimes variables are stochastic and cannot be readily predicted using traditional means. These variables are said to be *stochastic*. Nonetheless, most financial, economic, and naturally occurring phenomena (e.g., motion of molecules through the air) follow a known mathematical law or relationship. Although the resulting values are uncertain, the underlying mathematical structure is known and can be simulated using Monte Carlo risk simulation. The processes supported in Risk Simulator include Brownian motion random walk, mean-reversion, jump-diffusion, and mixed processes useful for forecasting nonstationary time-series variables. This approach is useful for forecasting and simulating stock prices, interest rates, inflation rates, and commodity prices such as oil or gold.

*   *Time-Series Analysis and Decomposition.* In well-behaved time-series data (typical examples include sales revenues and cost structures of large corporations), the values tend to have up to three elements: a base value, trend, and seasonality. Time-series analysis uses these historical data and decomposes them into these three elements and recomposes them into future forecasts. In other words, this forecasting method, like some of the others described, first performs a backfitting (backcast) of historical data before it provides estimates of future values (forecasts).

Running the Forecasting Tool in Risk Simulator

In general, to create forecasts, several quick steps are required:

*   Start Excel and enter in or open existing historical data.
*   Select the data and click on *Risk Simulator | Forecasting.*
*   Select the relevant sections (Box-Jenkins ARIMA, Time-Series Analysis, Multivariate Regression, Stochastic Forecasting, or Nonlinear Extrapolation) and enter the relevant inputs.

Figure 8.2 illustrates the *Forecasting* tool and the various methodologies available in Risk Simulator.

The following provides a quick review of each methodology and several quick getting started examples in using the software. The example data files used to create these examples are included in the Risk Simulator software and can be accessed through Excel: *Risk Simulator | Example Models.*

Time-Series Analysis

Theory

Figure 8.3 lists the eight most common time-series models, segregated by seasonality and trend. For instance, if the data variable has no trend or seasonality, then a single moving-average model or a single exponential-smoothing model would suffice. However, if seasonality exists but no discernable trend is present, either a seasonal additive or seasonal multiplicative model would be better, and so forth.

Procedure

*   Start Excel and type in or open an existing spreadsheet with the relevant historical data (the following example uses the *Time-Series Forecasting* file in the examples folder).
*   Make sure you start a new simulation profile or that there is an existing profile in the model if you want the forecast results to automatically generate Monte Carlo assumptions.

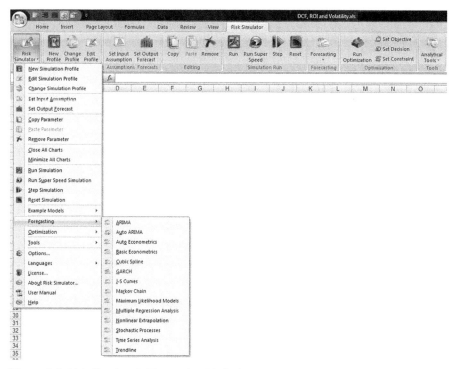

Figure 8.2 Risk Simulator's Forecasting Methods.

	No Seasonality	With Seasonality
No Trend	Single Moving Average	Seasonal Additive
	Single Exponential Smoothing	Seasonal Multiplicative
With Trend	Double Moving Average	Holt-Winter's Additive
	Double Exponential Smoothing	Holt-Winter's Multiplicative

Figure 8.3 The Eight Most Common Time-Series Methods.

Historical Sales Revenues

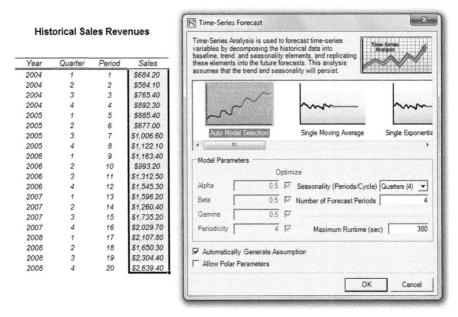

Year	Quarter	Period	Sales
2004	1	1	$684.20
2004	2	2	$584.10
2004	3	3	$765.40
2004	4	4	$892.30
2005	1	5	$885.40
2005	2	6	$677.00
2005	3	7	$1,006.60
2005	4	8	$1,122.10
2006	1	9	$1,163.40
2006	2	10	$993.20
2006	3	11	$1,312.50
2006	4	12	$1,545.30
2007	1	13	$1,596.20
2007	2	14	$1,260.40
2007	3	15	$1,735.20
2007	4	16	$2,029.70
2008	1	17	$2,107.80
2008	2	18	$1,650.30
2008	3	19	$2,304.40
2008	4	20	$2,639.40

Figure 8.4 Time-Series Analysis.

- Select the historical data not including the variable name (data should be listed in a single column).
- Select *Risk Simulator | Forecasting | Time-Series Analysis.*
- Choose the model to apply, enter the relevant assumptions, and click *OK.*

To follow along in this example, choose *Auto Model Selection*, select *Quarters (4)* for seasonality periods per cycle, and forecast for 4 periods (Figure 8.4).

Results Interpretation

Figure 8.5 illustrates the sample results generated by using the *Forecasting* tool. The model used was a Holt-Winters multiplicative model. Notice that in Figure 8.5, the model-fitting and forecast chart indicate that the trend and seasonality are picked up nicely by the Holt-Winters multiplicative model. The time-series analysis report provides the relevant optimized alpha, beta, and gamma parameters; the error measurements; fitted data; forecast values; and forecast-fitted graph. The parameters are simply for reference. Alpha captures the memory effect of the base level changes over time; beta is the trend parameter that measures the strength of the trend; and gamma measures the seasonality strength of the historical data. The analysis decomposes the historical data into these three elements and then recomposes them to forecast the future. The fitted data illustrate the historical data as well as the fitted data using the recomposed model and show how close the forecasts are in the past (a technique called *backcasting*). The forecast values are either single-point estimates

Holt-Winter's Multiplicative

Summary Statistics

Alpha, Beta, Gamma	RMSE	Alpha, Beta, Gamma	RMSE
0.00, 0.00, 0.00	914.824	0.00, 0.00, 0.00	914.824
0.10, 0.10, 0.10	415.322	0.10, 0.10, 0.10	415.322
0.20, 0.20, 0.20	187.202	0.20, 0.20, 0.20	187.202
0.30, 0.30, 0.30	118.795	0.30, 0.30, 0.30	118.795
0.40, 0.40, 0.40	101.794	0.40, 0.40, 0.40	101.794
0.50, 0.50, 0.50	102.143		

The analysis was run with alpha = 0.2429, beta = 1.0000, gamma = 0.7797, and seasonality = 4

Time-Series Analysis Summary

When both seasonality and trend exist, more advanced models are required to decompose the data into their base elements: a base-case level (L) weighted by the alpha parameter; a trend component (b) weighted by the beta parameter; and a seasonality component (S) weighted by the gamma parameter. Several methods exist but the two most common are the Holt-Winters' additive seasonality and Holt-Winters' multiplicative seasonality methods. In the Holt-Winter's additive model, the base case level, seasonality, and trend are added together to obtain the forecast fit.

The best-fitting test for the moving average forecast uses the root mean squared errors (RMSE). The RMSE calculates the square root of the average squared deviations of the fitted values versus the actual data points.

Mean Squared Error (MSE) is an absolute error measure that squares the errors (the difference between the actual historical data and the forecast-fitted data predicted by the model) to keep the positive and negative errors from canceling each other out. This measure also tends to exaggerate large errors by weighting the large errors more heavily than smaller errors by squaring them, which can help when comparing different time-series models. Root Mean Square Error (RMSE) is the square root of MSE and is the most popular error measure, also known as the quadratic loss function. RMSE can be defined as the average of the absolute values of the forecast errors and is highly appropriate when the cost of the forecast errors is proportional to the absolute size of the forecast error. The RMSE is used as the selection criteria for the best-fitting time-series model.

Mean Absolute Percentage Error (MAPE) is a relative error statistic measured as an average percent error of the historical data points and is most appropriate when the cost of the forecast error is more closely related to the percentage error than the numerical size of the error. Finally, an associated measure is the Theil's U statistic, which measures the naivety of the model's forecast. That is, if the Theil's U statistic is less than 1.0, then the forecast method used provides an estimate that is statistically better than guessing.

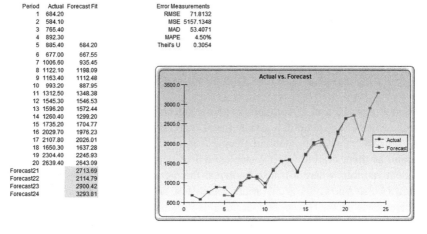

Period	Actual	Forecast Fit
1	684.20	
2	584.10	
3	765.40	
4	892.30	
5	885.40	684.20
6	677.00	667.55
7	1006.60	935.45
8	1122.10	1198.09
9	1163.40	1112.48
10	993.20	887.95
11	1312.50	1348.38
12	1545.30	1546.53
13	1596.20	1572.44
14	1260.40	1299.20
15	1735.20	1704.77
16	2029.70	1976.23
17	2107.80	2026.01
18	1650.30	1637.28
19	2304.40	2245.93
20	2639.40	2643.09
Forecast21		2713.69
Forecast22		2114.79
Forecast23		2900.42
Forecast24		3293.81

Error Measurements

RMSE	71.8132
MSE	5157.1348
MAD	53.4071
MAPE	4.50%
Theil's U	0.3054

Figure 8.5 Example of Holt-Winters Forecast Report.

or assumptions (if the automatically generated assumptions option is chosen and if a simulation profile exists). The graph illustrates the historical, fitted, and forecast values. The chart is a powerful communication and visual tool to see how good the forecast model is.

Notes

This time-series analysis module contains the eight time-series models shown in Figure 8.3. You can choose the specific model to run based on the trend and seasonality criteria or choose the Auto Model Selection, which will automatically iterate through all eight methods, optimize the parameters, and find the best-fitting model for your data. Alternatively, if you choose one of the eight models, you can also deselect the *optimize* checkboxes and enter your own alpha, beta, and gamma parameters. In addition, you would need to enter the relevant seasonality periods if you choose the automatic model selection or any of the seasonal models. The seasonality input must be a positive integer (e.g., if the data are quarterly, enter 4 as the number of seasons or cycles a year, or enter 12 if monthly data, or any other positive integer representing the data periods of a full cycle). Next, enter the number of periods to forecast. This value also has to be a positive integer. The maximum runtime is set at 300 seconds. Typically, no changes are required. However, when forecasting with a significant amount of historical data, the analysis might take slightly longer, and if the processing time exceeds this runtime, the process will be terminated. You can also elect to have the forecast automatically generate assumptions; that is, instead of single-point estimates, the forecasts will be assumptions. However, to automatically generate assumptions, a simulation profile must first exist. Finally, the polar parameters option allows you to optimize the alpha, beta, and gamma parameters to include zero and one. Certain forecasting software allows these polar parameters, while others do not. Risk Simulator allows you to choose which to use. Typically, there is no need to use polar parameters.

Multivariate Regression

Theory

It is assumed that the user is sufficiently knowledgeable about the fundamentals of regression analysis. The general bivariate linear regression equation takes the form of $Y = \beta_0 + \beta_1 X + \varepsilon$, where β_0 is the intercept, β_1 is the slope, and ε is the error term. It is bivariate, as there are only two variables: a Y or dependent variable and an X or independent variable, where X is also known as the *regressor*. (Sometimes a bivariate regression is also known as a univariate regression because there is only a single independent variable X.) The dependent variable is named as such because it *depends* on the independent variable; for example, sales revenue depends on the amount of marketing costs expended on a product's advertising and promotion, making the dependent variable sales and the independent variable marketing costs. An example of a bivariate regression is seen as simply inserting the best-fitting line through a set of data points in a two-dimensional plane, as shown in the left panel in Figure 8.6. In other cases, a multivariate regression can be performed, where there are multiple, or k number, of independent X variables or regressors, where the general regression equation will now take the form of $Y = \beta_0 + \beta_1 X_1 + \beta_2 X_2 + \beta_3 X_3 \ldots + \beta_k X_k + \varepsilon$. In this case, the best-fitting line will be within a $k + 1$ dimensional plane.

However, fitting a line through a set of data points in a scatter plot as in Figure 8.6 may result in numerous possible lines. The best-fitting line is defined as the single unique line that minimizes the total vertical errors—that is, the sum of the absolute distances between the actual data points (Y_i) and the estimated line ($\widehat{Y}$), as shown in the right panel of Figure 8.6. To find the best-fitting unique line that minimizes the

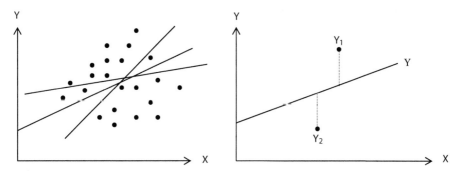

Figure 8.6 Bivariate Regression.

errors, a more sophisticated approach is applied, using regression analysis. Regression analysis therefore finds the unique best-fitting line by requiring that the total errors be minimized, or by calculating:

$$Min \sum_{i=1}^{n} (Y_i - \widehat{Y}_i)^2$$

where only one unique line minimizes this sum of squared errors. The errors (vertical distances between the actual data and the predicted line) are squared to avoid the negative errors from canceling out the positive errors. Solving this minimization problem with respect to the slope and intercept requires calculating first derivatives and setting them equal to zero:

$$\frac{d}{d\beta_0} \sum_{i=1}^{n} (Y_i - \widehat{Y}_i)^2 = 0 \text{ and } \frac{d}{d\beta_1} \sum_{i=1}^{n} (Y_i - \widehat{Y}_i)^2 = 0$$

which yields the bivariate regression's least squares equations:

$$\beta_1 = \frac{\sum_{i=1}^{n} (X_i - \overline{X})(Y_i - \overline{Y})}{\sum_{i=1}^{n} (X_i - \overline{X})^2} = \frac{\sum_{i=1}^{n} X_i Y_i - \frac{\sum_{i=1}^{n} X_i \sum_{i=1}^{n} Y_i}{n}}{\sum_{i=1}^{n} X_i^2 - \frac{\left(\sum_{i=1}^{n} X_i\right)^2}{n}}$$

$$\beta_0 = \overline{Y} - \beta_1 \overline{X}$$

For multivariate regression, the analogy is expanded to account for multiple independent variables, where $Y_i = \beta_1 + \beta_2 X_{2,i} + \beta_3 X_{3,i} + \varepsilon_i$ and the estimated slopes can be calculated by:

$$\widehat{\beta}_2 = \frac{\sum Y_i X_{2,i} \sum X_{3,i}^2 - \sum Y_i X_{3,i} \sum X_{2,i} X_{3,i}}{\sum X_{2,i}^2 \sum X_{3,i}^2 - \left(\sum X_{2,i} X_{3,i}\right)^2}$$

$$\widehat{\beta}_3 = \frac{\sum Y_i X_{3,i} \sum X_{2,i}^2 - \sum Y_i X_{2,i} \sum X_{2,i} X_{3,i}}{\sum X_{2,i}^2 \sum X_{3,i}^2 - \left(\sum X_{2,i} X_{3,i}\right)^2}$$

In running multivariate regressions, great care must be taken to set up and interpret the results. For instance, a good understanding of econometric modeling is required (e.g., identifying regression pitfalls such as structural breaks, multicollinearity, heteroskedasticity, autocorrelation, specification tests, nonlinearities, etc.) before a proper model can be constructed.

Procedure

- Start Excel and type in or open your existing dataset (Figure 8.7 uses the file *Multiple Regression* in the examples folder).
- Check to make sure that the data are arranged in columns, select the data including the variable headings, and click on *Risk Simulator* | *Forecasting* | *Multiple Regression.*
- Select the dependent variable, check the relevant options (lags, stepwise regression, nonlinear regression, and so forth), and click *OK* (see Figure 8.7).

Results Interpretation

Figure 8.8 illustrates a sample multivariate regression result report generated. The report comes complete with all the regression results, analysis of variance results, fitted chart, and hypothesis test results.

Multivariate Regression

Y	X1	X2	X3	X4	X5
521	18308	185	4.041	79.6	7.2
367	1148	600	0.55	1	8.5
443	18068	372	3.665	32.3	5.7
365	7729	142	2.351	45.1	7.3
614	100484	432	29.76	190.8	7.5
385	16728	290	3.294	31.8	5
286	14630	346	3.287	678.4	6.7
397	4008	328	0.666	340.8	6.2
764	38927	354	12.938	239.6	7.3
427	22322	266	6.478	111.9	5
153	3711	320	1.108	172.5	2.8
231	3136	197	1.007	12.2	6.1
524	50508	266	11.431	205.6	7.1
328	28886	173	5.544	154.6	5.9
240	16996	190	2.777	49.7	4.6
286	13035	239	2.478	30.3	4.4
285	12973	190	3.685	92.8	7.4
569	16309	241	4.22	96.9	7.1
96	5227	189	1.228	39.8	7.5
498	19235	358	4.781	489.2	5.9
481	44487	315	6.016	767.6	9
468	44213	303	9.295	163.6	9.2
177	23619	228	4.375	55	5.1
198	9106	134	2.573	54.9	8.6
458	24917	189	5.117	74.3	6.6
108	3872	196	0.799	5.5	6.9
246	8945	183	1.578	20.5	2.7
291	2373	417	1.202	10.9	5.5
68	7128	233	1.109	123.7	7.2
311	23624	349	7.73	1042	6.6
606	5242	284	1.515	12.5	6.9
512	92629	499	17.99	381	7.2
426	28795	231	6.629	136.1	5.8
47	4487	143	0.639	9.3	4.1
265	48799	249	10.847	264.9	6.4
370	14067	195	3.146	45.8	6.7
312	12693	288	2.842	29.6	6
222	62184	229	11.882	265.1	6.9
280	9153	287	1.003	960.3	8.5

Real Options Valuation
www.realoptionsvaluation.com

1. Select the data area including the headers (B5:G55)
2. Click on **Risk Simulator | Forecasting | Multiple Regression**
3. Select the Dependent Variable (in this example, the variable Y) and select any specific modifications as required (Lag Regressors, Nonlinear Regression, Stepwise Regression) and click **OK**. Review the generated regression report for analytical results

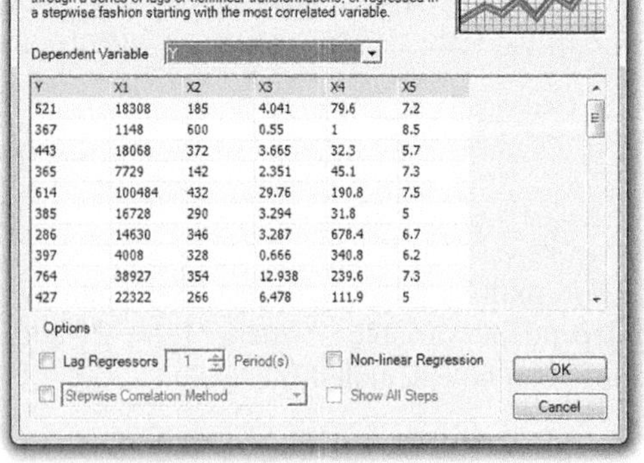

Figure 8.7 Running a Multivariate Regression.

Stepwise Regression

One powerful automated approach to regression analysis is "stepwise regression," which, as its name indicates, is a regression process that proceeds in multiple steps. There are several ways to set up these stepwise algorithms, including the correlation approach, forward method, backward method, and the forward and backward method (these methods are all available in Risk Simulator).

In the correlation method, the dependent variable (Y) is correlated to all the independent variables (X), and starting with the X variable with the highest absolute correlation value, a regression is run. Then subsequent X variables are added until the p-values indicate that the new X variable is no longer statistically significant. This approach is quick and simple but does not account for interactions among variables, and an X variable, when added, will statistically overshadow other variables.

In the forward method, we first correlate Y with all X variables, run a regression for Y on the highest absolute value correlation of X, and obtain the fitting errors. Then, we correlate these errors with the remaining X variables and choose the highest absolute value correlation among this remaining set and run another regression. The process is

Regression Analysis Report

Regression Statistics

R-Squared (Coefficient of Determination)	0.3272
Adjusted R-Squared	0.2508
Multiple R (Multiple Correlation Coefficient)	0.5720
Standard Error of the Estimates (SEy)	149.6720
Number of Observations	50

The R-Squared or Coefficient of Determination indicates that 0.33 of the variation in the dependent variable can be explained and accounted for by the independent variables in this regression analysis. However, in a multiple regression, the Adjusted R-Squared takes into account the existence of additional independent variables or regressors and adjusts this R-Squared value to a more accurate view of the regression's explanatory power. Hence, only 0.25 of the variation in the dependent variable can be explained by the regressors.

The Multiple Correlation Coefficient (Multiple R) measures the correlation between the actual dependent variable (Y) and the estimated or fitted (Y) based on the regression equation. This is also the square root of the Coefficient of Determination (R-Squared).

The Standard Error of the Estimates (SEy) describes the dispersion of data points above and below the regression line or plane. This value is used as part of the calculation to obtain the confidence interval of the estimates later.

Regression Results

	Intercept	X1	X2	X3	X4	X5
Coefficients	57.9555	-0.0035	0.4644	25.2377	-0.0086	16.5579
Standard Error	108.7901	0.0035	0.2535	14.1172	0.1016	14.7996
t-Statistic	0.5327	-1.0066	1.8316	1.7877	-0.0843	1.1188
p-Value	0.5969	0.3197	0.0738	0.0807	0.9332	0.2693
Lower 5%	-161.2966	-0.0106	-0.0466	-3.2137	-0.2132	-13.2687
Upper 95%	277.2076	0.0036	0.9753	53.6891	0.1961	46.3845

Degrees of Freedom		Hypothesis Test	
Degrees of Freedom for Regression	5	Critical t-Statistic (99% confidence with df of 44)	2.6923
Degrees of Freedom for Residual	44	Critical t-Statistic (95% confidence with df of 44)	2.0154
Total Degrees of Freedom	49	Critical t-Statistic (90% confidence with df of 44)	1.6802

The Coefficients provide the estimated regression intercept and slopes. For instance, the coefficients are estimates of the true, population b values in the following regression equation Y = b0 + b1X1 + b2X2 + ... + bnXn. The Standard Error measures how accurate the predicted Coefficients are, and the t-Statistics are the ratios of each predicted Coefficient to its Standard Error.

The t-Statistic is used in hypothesis testing, where we set the null hypothesis (Ho) such that the real mean of the Coefficient = 0, and the alternate hypothesis (Ha) such that the real mean of the Coefficient is not equal to 0. A t-test is is performed and the calculated t-Statistic is compared to the critical values at the relevant Degrees of Freedom for Residual. The t-test is very important as it calculates if each of the coefficients is statistically significant in the presence of the other regressors. This means that the t-test statistically verifies whether a regressor or independent variable should remain in the regression or it should be dropped.

The Coefficient is statistically significant if its calculated t-Statistic exceeds the Critical t-Statistic at the relevant degrees of freedom (df). The three main confidence levels used to test for significance are 90%, 95% and 99%. If a Coefficient's t-Statistic exceeds the Critical level, it is considered statistically significant. Alternatively, the p-Value calculates each t-Statistic's probability of occurrence, which means that the smaller the p-Value, the more significant the Coefficient. The usual significant levels for the p-Value are 0.01, 0.05, and 0.10, corresponding to the 99%, 95%, and 90% confidence levels.

The Coefficients with their p-Values highlighted in blue indicate that they are statistically significant at the 90% confidence or 0.10 alpha level, while those highlighted in red indicate that they are not statistically significant at any other alpha levels.

Figure 8.8 Multivariate Regression Results.

Analysis of Variance

	Sums of Squares	Mean of Squares	F-Statistic	p-Value	Hypothesis Test	
Regression	479388.49	95877.70	4.28	0.0029	Critical F-statistic (99% confidence with df of 5 and 44)	3.4651
Residual	985675.19	22401.71			Critical F-statistic (95% confidence with df of 5 and 44)	2.4270
Total	1465063.68				Critical F-statistic (90% confidence with df of 5 and 44)	1.9828

The Analysis of Variance (ANOVA) table provides an F-test of the regression model's overall statistical significance. Instead of looking at individual regressors as in the t-test, the F-test looks at all the estimated Coefficients' statistical properties. The F-Statistic is calculated as the ratio of the Regression's Mean of Squares to the Residual's Mean of Squares. The numerator measures how much of the regression is explained, while the denominator measures how much is unexplained. Hence, the larger the F-Statistic, the more significant the model. The corresponding p-Value is calculated to test the null hypothesis (Ho) where all the Coefficients are simultaneously equal to zero, versus the alternate hypothesis (Ha) that they are all simultaneously different from zero, indicating a significant overall regression model. If the p-Value is smaller than the 0.01, 0.05, or 0.10 alpha significance, then the regression is significant. The same approach can be applied to the F-Statistic by comparing the calculated F-Statistic with the critical F values at various significance levels.

Forecasting

Period	Actual (Y)	Forecast (F)	Error (E)
1	521.0000	299.5124	221.4876
2	367.0000	487.1243	(120.1243)
3	443.0000	353.2789	89.7211
4	365.0000	276.3296	88.6704
5	614.0000	776.1336	(162.1336)
6	385.0000	298.9993	86.0007
7	286.0000	354.8718	(68.8718)
8	397.0000	312.6155	84.3845
9	764.0000	529.7550	234.2450
10	427.0000	347.7034	79.2966
11	153.0000	266.2526	(113.2526)
12	231.0000	264.6375	(33.6375)
13	524.0000	406.8009	117.1991
14	328.0000	272.2226	55.7774
15	240.0000	231.7882	8.2118
16	286.0000	257.8862	28.1138
17	285.0000	314.9521	(29.9521)
18	569.0000	335.3140	233.6860
19	96.0000	282.0356	(186.0356)
20	498.0000	370.2062	127.7938
21	481.0000	340.8742	140.1258
22	468.0000	427.5118	40.4882
23	177.0000	274.5298	(97.5298)
24	198.0000	294.7795	(96.7795)
25	458.0000	295.2180	162.7820
26	108.0000	269.6195	(161.6195)
27	246.0000	195.5955	50.4045
28	291.0000	364.5004	(73.5004)

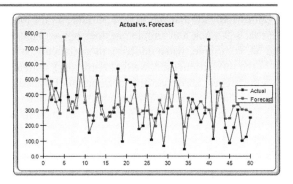

Figure 8.8 (*continued*).

repeated until the p-value for the latest X variable coefficient is no longer statistically significant, at which point we stop the process.

In the backward method, regression with Y on all X variables is run. Then each variable's p-value is reviewed and we systematically eliminate the variable with the largest p-value. Then regression is run again and repeated each time until all p-values are statistically significant.

In the forward and backward method, we apply the forward method to obtain three X variables and then apply the backward approach to see if one of them needs to be eliminated because it is statistically insignificant. Then we repeat the forward method and then the backward method until all remaining X variables are considered.

Stochastic Forecasting

Theory

A stochastic process is nothing but a mathematically defined equation that can create a series of outcomes over time—outcomes that are not deterministic in nature; that is, an equation or process that does not follow any simple discernible rule such as price will increase $X\%$ every year, or revenues will increase by this factor of X plus $Y\%$. A stochastic process is by definition nondeterministic, and one can plug numbers into a stochastic process equation and obtain different results every time. For instance, the path of a stock price is stochastic in nature, and one cannot reliably predict the exact stock price path with any certainty. However, the price evolution over time is enveloped in a process that generates these prices. *The process is fixed and predetermined, but the outcomes are not.* Hence, by stochastic simulation, we create multiple pathways of prices, obtain a statistical sampling of these simulations, and make inferences on the potential pathways that the actual price may undertake given the nature and parameters of the stochastic process used to generate the time series. Four stochastic processes are included in Risk Simulator's Forecasting tool, including geometric Brownian motion or random walk, which is the most common and prevalently used process due to its simplicity and wide-ranging applications. The other three stochastic processes are the mean-reversion process, jump-diffusion process, and a mixed process.

The interesting thing about stochastic process simulation is that historical data are not necessarily required; that is, the model does not have to fit any sets of historical data. Simply compute the expected returns and the volatility of the historical data, estimate them using comparable external data, or make assumptions about these values.

Procedure

- Start the module by selecting *Risk Simulator | Forecasting | Stochastic Processes*.
- Select the desired process, enter the required inputs, click on *Update Chart* a few times to make sure the process is behaving the way you expect it to, and click *OK* (Figure 8.9).

Results Interpretation

Figure 8.10 shows the results of a sample stochastic process. The chart shows a sample set of the iterations, while the report explains the basics of stochastic processes. In addition, the forecast values (mean and standard deviation) for each time period are provided. Using these values, you can decide which time period is relevant to your analysis, and set assumptions based on these mean and standard deviation values using the normal distribution. These assumptions can then be simulated in your own custom model.

Brownian Motion Random Walk Process

The Brownian motion random walk process takes the form of $\frac{\delta S}{S} = \mu(\delta t) + \sigma\varepsilon\sqrt{\delta t}$ for regular options simulation, or a more generic version takes the form of $\frac{\delta S}{S} = (\mu - \sigma^2/2)\delta t + \sigma\varepsilon\sqrt{\delta t}$ for a geometric process. For an exponential version, we simply take the exponentials, and as an example, we have $\frac{\delta S}{S} = \exp[\mu(\delta t) + \sigma\varepsilon\sqrt{\delta t}]$, where we define:

S as the variable's previous value

δS as the change in the variable's value from one step to the next

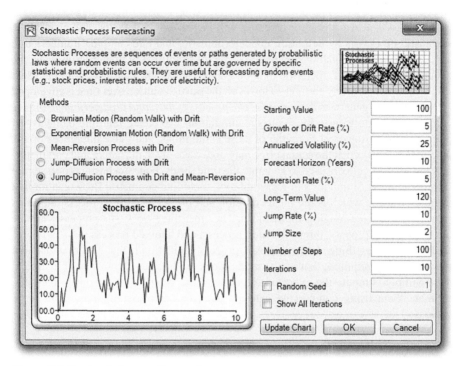

Figure 8.9 Stochastic Process Forecasting.

μ as the annualized growth or drift rate
σ as the annualized volatility

To estimate the parameters from a set of time-series data, the drift rate and volatility can be found by setting μ to be the average of the natural logarithm of the relative returns $ln\frac{S_t}{S_{t-1}}$, while σ is the standard deviation of all $ln\frac{S_t}{S_{t-1}}$ values.

Mean-Reversion Process

The following describes the mathematical structure of a mean-reverting process with drift:

$$\frac{\delta S}{S} = \eta(\bar{S}e^{\mu(\delta t)} - S)\delta t + \mu(\delta t) + \sigma\varepsilon\sqrt{\delta t}$$

In order to obtain the rate of reversion and long-term rate, using the historical data points, run a regression such that $Y_t - Y_{t-1} = \beta_0 + \beta_1 Y_{t-1} + \varepsilon$ and we find $\eta = -\ln[1 + \beta_1]$ and $\bar{S} = -\beta_0/\beta_1$, where we define:

η as the rate of reversion to the mean
$\bar{S}$ as the long-term value the process reverts to
Y as the historical data series

Stochastic Process Forecasting

Statistical Summary

Time	Mean	Stdev
0.0000	100.00	0.00
0.1000	98.53	5.32
0.2000	95.93	10.81
0.3000	98.01	14.42
0.4000	95.98	17.17
0.5000	93.81	18.65
0.6000	88.67	18.21
0.7000	89.82	21.19
0.8000	96.75	26.08
0.9000	91.57	25.54
1.0000	92.43	24.95
1.1000	85.81	21.76
1.2000	86.02	22.45
1.3000	85.56	24.00
1.4000	82.71	24.51
1.5000	84.16	23.19
1.6000	85.91	21.52
1.7000	89.14	23.43
1.8000	88.24	22.72
1.9000	90.66	23.78
2.0000	94.08	23.16
2.1000	93.25	29.43
2.2000	96.75	33.39
2.3000	99.05	34.48
2.4000	103.39	39.69
2.5000	104.63	37.84
2.6000	101.45	36.72
2.7000	106.01	36.66
2.8000	105.38	36.70
2.9000	106.06	35.75
3.0000	104.69	29.02
3.1000	105.99	29.57
3.2000	108.69	32.90
3.3000	112.51	38.44
3.4000	113.39	39.35
3.5000	114.35	41.07
3.6000	109.68	38.28
3.7000	110.24	32.91
3.8000	110.81	33.13
3.9000	111.28	33.83
4.0000	110.64	36.59
4.1000	109.94	42.60
4.2000	107.24	39.76
4.3000	103.55	32.80
4.4000	99.25	34.79
4.5000	101.28	35.24
4.6000	101.22	34.62
4.7000	97.13	32.09
4.8000	96.63	25.88
4.9000	93.08	20.80
5.0000	98.33	21.29
5.1000	100.54	25.46

A stochastic process is a sequence of events or paths generated by probabilistic laws. That is, random events can occur over time but are governed by specific statistical and probabilistic rules. The main stochastic processes include Random Walk or Brownian Motion, Mean-Reversion, and Jump-Diffusion. These processes can be used to forecast a multitude of variables that seemingly follow random trends but yet are restricted by probabilistic laws.

The Random Walk Brownian Motion process can be used to forecast stock prices, prices of commodities, and other stochastic time-series data given a drift or growth rate and a volatility around the drift path. The Mean-Reversion process can be used to reduce the fluctuations of the Random Walk process by allowing the path to target a long-term value, making it useful for forecasting time-series variables that have a long-term rate such as interest rates and inflation rates (these are long-term target rates by regulatory authorities or the market). The Jump-Diffusion process is useful for forecasting time-series data when the variable can occasionally exhibit random jumps, such as oil prices or price of electricity (discrete exogenous event shocks can make prices jump up or down). Finally, these three stochastic processes can be mixed and matched as required.

The results on the right indicate the mean and standard deviation of all the iterations generated at each time step. If the Show All Iterations option is selected, each iteration pathway will be shown in a separate worksheet. The graph generated below shows a sample set of the iteration pathways.

Stochastic Process: Brownian Motion (Random Walk) with Drift

Start Value	100	Steps	100.00	Jump Rate	N/A	
Drift Rate	5.00%	Iterations	10.00	Jump Size	N/A	
Volatility	25.00%	Reversion Rate	N/A	Random Seed	254005543	
Horizon	10	Long-Term Value	N/A			

Figure 8.10 Stochastic Forecast Result.

β_0 as the intercept coefficient in a regression analysis
β_1 as the slope coefficient in a regression analysis

Jump Diffusion Process

A jump diffusion process is similar to a random walk process, but there is a probability of a jump at any point in time. The occurrences of such jumps are completely random, but the probability and magnitude are governed by the process itself.

$$\frac{\delta S}{S} = \eta(\overline{S}e^{\mu(\delta t)} - S)\delta t + \mu(\delta t) + \sigma\varepsilon\sqrt{\delta t} + \theta F(\lambda)(\delta t)$$

for a jump diffusion process where we define

θ as the jump size of S
$F(\lambda)$ as the inverse of the Poisson cumulative probability distribution
λ as the jump rate of S

The jump size can be found by computing the ratio of the postjump to the prejump levels, and the jump rate can be imputed from past historical data. The other parameters are found the same way as shown previously.

Nonlinear Extrapolation

Theory

Extrapolation involves making statistical forecasts by using historical trends that are projected for a specified period of time into the future. It is only used for time-series forecasts. For cross-sectional or mixed panel data (time-series with cross-sectional data), multivariate regression is more appropriate. This methodology is useful when major changes are not expected; that is, causal factors are expected to remain constant or when the causal factors of a situation are not clearly understood. It also helps discourage the introduction of personal biases into the process.

Extrapolation is fairly reliable, relatively simple, and inexpensive. However, extrapolation, which assumes that recent and historical trends will continue, produces large forecast errors if discontinuities occur within the projected time period; that is, pure extrapolation of time-series assumes that all we need to know is contained in the historical values of the series being forecasted. If we assume that past behavior is a good predictor of future behavior, extrapolation is appealing. This makes it a useful approach when all that is needed are many short-term forecasts.

This methodology estimates the $f(x)$ function for any arbitrary x value by interpolating a smooth nonlinear curve through all the x values and, using this smooth curve, extrapolates future x values beyond the historical data set. The methodology employs either the polynomial functional form or the rational functional form (a ratio of two polynomials). Typically, a polynomial functional form is sufficient for well-behaved data, but rational functional forms are sometimes more accurate (especially with polar functions—i.e., functions with denominators approaching zero).

Procedure

- Start Excel and enter your data, or open an existing worksheet with historical data to forecast (Figure 8.11 uses the file *Nonlinear Extrapolation* from the examples folder).
- Select the time-series data and select *Risk Simulator | Forecasting | Nonlinear Extrapolation*.

Year	Month	Period	Sales
	Historical Sales Revenues **Polynomial Growth Rates**		
2004	1	1	$1.00
2004	2	2	$6.73
2004	3	3	$20.52
2004	4	4	$45.25
2004	5	5	$83.59
2004	6	6	$138.01
2004	7	7	$210.87
2004	8	8	$304.44
2004	9	9	$420.89
2004	10	10	$562.34
2004	11	11	$730.85
2004	12	12	$928.43

Year	Month	Period	Income
	Historical Net Income **Sinusoidal Growth Rates**		
2004	1	1	$84.15
2004	2	2	$90.93
2004	3	3	$14.11
2004	4	4	($75.68)
2004	5	5	($95.89)
2004	6	6	($27.94)
2004	7	7	$65.70
2004	8	8	$98.94
2004	9	9	$41.21
2004	10	10	($54.40)
2004	11	11	($100.00)
2004	12	12	($53.66)
2005	1	13	$42.02
2005	2	14	$99.06
2005	3	15	$65.03
2005	4	16	($28.79)
2005	5	17	($96.14)
2005	6	18	($75.10)

Figure 8.11 Running a Nonlinear Extrapolation.

- Select the extrapolation type (automatic selection, polynomial function, or rational function are available, but in this example use automatic selection), enter the number of forecast period desired (see Figure 8.11), and click *OK*.

Results Interpretation

The results report in Figure 8.12 shows the extrapolated forecast values, the error measurements, and the graphical representation of the extrapolation results. The error measurements should be used to check the validity of the forecast and are especially important when used to compare the forecast quality and accuracy of extrapolation versus time-series analysis.

Notes

When the historical data are smooth and follow some nonlinear patterns and curves, extrapolation is better than time-series analysis. However, when the data patterns follow seasonal cycles and a trend, time-series analysis will provide better results. It is always advisable to run both time-series analysis and extrapolation and compare the results to see which has a lower error measure and a better fit.

Nonlinear Extrapolation

Statistical Summary

Extrapolation involves making statistical projections by using historical trends that are projected for a specified period of time into the future. It is only used for time-series forecasts. For cross-sectional or mixed panel data (time-series with cross-sectional data), multivariate regression is more appropriate. This methodology is useful when major changes are not expected, that is, causal factors are expected to remain constant or when the causal factors of a situation are not clearly understood. It also helps discourage introduction of personal biases into the process. Extrapolation is fairly reliable, relatively simple, and inexpensive. However, extrapolation, which assumes that recent and historical trends will continue, produces large forecast errors if discontinuities occur within the projected time period. That is, pure extrapolation of time series assumes that all we need to know is contained in the historical values of the series that is being forecasted. If we assume that past behavior is a good predictor of future behavior, extrapolation is appealing. This makes it a useful approach when all that is needed are many short-term forecasts.

This methodology estimates the f(x) function for any arbitrary x value, by interpolating a smooth nonlinear curve through all the x values, and using this smooth curve, extrapolates future x values beyond the historical data set. The methodology employs either the polynomial functional form or the rational functional form (a ratio of two polynomials). Typically, a polynomial functional form is sufficient for well-behaved data, however, rational functional forms are sometimes more accurate (especially with polar functions, i.e., functions with denominators approaching zero).

Period	Actual	Forecast Fit	Estimate Error		Error Measurements	
1	1.00				RMSE	19.6799
2	6.73	1.00			MSE	387.2974
3	20.52	-1.42	-8.15		MAD	10.2095
4	45.25	99.82	119.36		MAPE	31.56%
5	83.59	55.92	-46.67		Theil's U	1.1210
6	138.01	136.71	14.39			
7	210.87	211.96	1.69		Function Type: Rational	
8	304.44	304.43	-0.41			
9	420.89	420.89	0.01			
10	562.34	562.34	0.00			
11	730.85	730.85	0.00			
12	928.43	928.43	0.00			
Forecast 13		1157.03	0.00			
Forecast 14		1418.57	0.00			
Forecast 15		1714.95	0.00			
Forecast 16		2048.00	0.00			
Forecast 17		2419.55	0.00			
Forecast 18		2831.39	0.00			

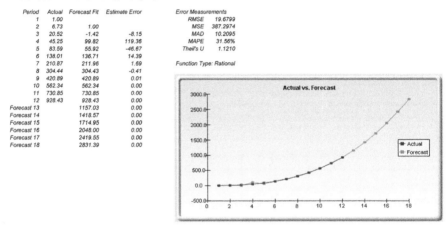

Figure 8.12 Nonlinear Extrapolation Results.

Box-Jenkins Autoregressive Integrated Moving Average (ARIMA) Advanced Time-Series

Theory

One very powerful advanced times-series forecasting tool is the ARIMA or Autoregressive Integrated Moving Average approach, which assembles three separate tools into a comprehensive model. The first tool segment is the autoregressive or "AR" term, which corresponds to the number of lagged value of the residual in the unconditional forecast model. In essence, the model captures the historical variation of actual data to a forecasting model and uses this variation or residual to create a better predicting model. The second tool segment is the integration order or the "I" term. This integration term corresponds to the number of differencing that the time-series to be forecasted goes through to make the data stationary. This element accounts for any nonlinear growth rates existing in the data. The third tool segment is the moving average or "MA" term, which is essentially the moving average of lagged forecast errors. By incorporating this lagged forecast errors moving average, the model in essence learns from its forecast errors or mistakes and corrects for them through a moving average calculation.

The ARIMA model follows the Box-Jenkins methodology, with each term representing steps taken in the model construction until only random noise remains. Also, ARIMA modeling uses correlation techniques in generating forecasts. ARIMA can be used to model patterns that may not be visible in plotted data. In addition, ARIMA models can be mixed with exogenous variables, but make sure that the exogenous variables have enough data points to cover the additional number of periods to forecast. Finally, be aware that ARIMA cannot and should not be used to forecast stochastic processes or time-series data that are stochastic in nature; use the *Stochastic Process* module to forecast instead.

There are many reasons why an ARIMA model is superior to common time-series analysis and multivariate regressions. The common finding in time-series analysis and multivariate regression is that the error residuals are correlated with their own lagged values. This serial correlation violates the standard assumption of regression theory that disturbances are not correlated with other disturbances. The primary problems associated with serial correlation are as follows:

- Regression analysis and basic time-series analysis are no longer efficient among the different linear estimators. However, because the error residuals can help to predict current error residuals, we can take advantage of this information to form a better prediction of the dependent variable using ARIMA.
- Standard errors computed using the regression and time-series formula are not correct and are generally understated. If there are lagged dependent variables set as the regressors, regression estimates are biased and inconsistent, but can be fixed using ARIMA.

Autoregressive Integrated Moving Average or ARIMA(P,D,Q) models are the extension of the AR model that uses three components for modeling the serial correlation in the time-series data. The first component is the autoregressive (AR) term. The AR(p) model uses the p lags of the time-series in the equation. An AR(p) model has the form $y_t = a_1 y_{t-1} + \ldots + a_p y_{t-p} + e_t$. The second component is the integration (d) order term. Each integration order corresponds to differencing the time-series. I(1) means differencing the data once. I(d) means differencing the data d times. The third component is the moving average (MA) term. The MA(q) model uses the q lags of the forecast errors to improve the forecast. An MA(q) model has the form $y_t = e_t + b_1 e_{t-1} + \ldots + b_q e_{t-q}$. Finally, an ARMA(p,q) model has the combined form $y_t = a_1 y_{t-1} + \ldots + a_p y_{t-p} + e_t + b_1 e_{t-1} + \ldots + b_q e_{t-q}$.

Procedure

- Start Excel and enter your data or open an existing worksheet with historical data to forecast (the illustration shown next uses the example file *Time-Series Forecasting*).
- Click on *Risk Simulator | Forecasting | ARIMA* and select the time-series data.
- Enter the relevant p, d, and q parameters (positive integers only), enter the number of forecast periods desired, and click *OK*.

Results Interpretation

In interpreting the results of an ARIMA model, most of the specifications are identical to the multivariate regression analysis. However, there are several additional sets of results specific to the ARIMA analysis, as shown in Figure 8.13. The first is the addition of Akaike Information Criterion (AIC) and Schwarz Criterion (SC), which are often used in ARIMA model selection and identification. That is, AIC and SC are used to determine if a particular model with a specific set of p, d, and q parameters is a good statistical fit. SC imposes a greater penalty for additional coefficients than the AIC but, generally, the model with the lowest AIC and SC values should be chosen.

ARIMA (Autoregressive Integrated Moving Average)

Regression Statistics

R-Squared (Coefficient of Determination)	0.9999	Akaike Information Criterion (AIC)	4.6213
Adjusted R-Squared	0.9999	Schwarz Criterion (SC)	4.6632
Multiple R (Multiple Correlation Coefficient)	1.0000	Log Likelihood	-1005.13
Standard Error of the Estimates (SEy)	297.52	Durbin-Watson (DW) Statistic	1.8588
Number of Observations	435	Number of Iterations	5

Autoregressive Integrated Moving Average or ARIMA(p,d,q) models are the extension of the AR model that use three components for modeling the serial correlation in the time-series data. The first component is the autoregressive (AR) term. The AR(p) model uses the p lags of the time series in the equation. An AR(p) model has the form: $y(t)=a(1)*y(t-1)+...+a(p)*y(t-p)+e(t)$. The second component is the integration (d) order term. Each integration order corresponds to differencing the time series. I(1) means differencing the data once. I(d) means differencing the data d times. The third component is the moving average (MA) term. The MA(q) model uses the q lags of the forecast errors to improve the forecast. An MA(q) model has the form: $y(t)=e(t)+b(1)*e(t-1)+...+b(q)*e(t-q)$. Finally, an ARIMA(p,q) model has the combined form: $y(t)=a(1)*y(t-1)+...+a(p)*y(t-p)+e(t)+b(1)*e(t-1)+...+b(q)*e(t-q)$.

The R-Squared, or Coefficient of Determination, indicates the percent variation in the dependent variable that can be explained and accounted for by the independent variables in this regression analysis. However, in a multiple regression, the Adjusted R-Squared takes into account the existence of additional independent variables or regressors and adjusts this R-Squared value to a more accurate view the regression's explanatory power. However, under some ARIMA modeling circumstances (e.g., with nonconvergence models), the R-Squared tends to be unreliable.

The Multiple Correlation Coefficient (Multiple R) measures the correlation between the actual dependent variable (Y) and the estimated or fitted (Y) based on the regression equation. This correlation is also the square root of the Coefficient of Determination (R-Squared).

The Standard Error of the Estimates (SEy) describes the dispersion of data points above and below the regression line or plane. This value is used as part of the calculation to obtain the confidence interval of the estimates later.

The AIC and SC are often used in model selection. SC imposes a greater penalty for additional coefficients. Generally, the user should select a model with the lowest value of the AIC and SC.

The Durbin-Watson statistic measures the serial correlation in the residuals. Generally, DW less than 2 implies positive serial correlation.

Regression Results

	Intercept	AR(1)	MA(1)
Coefficients	-0.0626	1.0055	0.4936
Standard Error	0.3108	0.0006	0.0420
t-Statistic	-0.2013	1691.1373	11.7633
p-Value	0.8406	0.0000	0.0000
Lower 5%	0.4498	1.0065	0.5628
Upper 95%	-0.5749	1.0046	0.4244

Degrees of Freedom		Hypothesis Test	
Degrees of Freedom for Regression	2	Critical t-Statistic (99% confidence with df of 432)	2.5873
Degrees of Freedom for Residual	432	Critical t-Statistic (95% confidence with df of 432)	1.9655
Total Degrees of Freedom	434	Critical t-Statistic (90% confidence with df of 432)	1.6484

The Coefficients provide the estimated regression intercept and slopes. For instance, the coefficients are estimates of the true; population b values in the following regression equation $Y = b0 + b1X1 + b2X2 + ... + bnXn$. The Standard Error measures how accurate the predicted Coefficients are, and the t-Statistics are the ratios of each predicted Coefficient to its Standard Error.

The t-Statistic is used in hypothesis testing, where we set the null hypothesis (Ho) such that the real mean of the Coefficient = 0, and the alternate hypothesis (Ha) such that the real mean of the Coefficient is not equal to 0. A t-test is is performed and the calculated t-Statistic is compared to the critical values at the relevant Degrees of Freedom for Residual. The t-test is very important as it calculates if each of the coefficients is statistically significant in the presence of the other regressors. This means that the t-test statistically verifies whether a regressor or independent variable should remain in the regression or it should be dropped.

The Coefficient is statistically significant if its calculated t-Statistic exceeds the Critical t-Statistic at the relevant degrees of freedom (df). The three main confidence levels used to test for significance are 90%, 95% and 99%. If a Coefficient's t-Statistic exceeds the Critical level, it is considered statistically significant. Alternatively, the p-Value calculates each t-Statistic's probability of occurrence, which means that the smaller the p-Value, the more significant the Coefficient. The usual significant levels for the p-Value are 0.01, 0.05, and 0.10, corresponding to the 99%, 95%, and 90% confidence levels.

The Coefficients with their p-Values highlighted in blue indicate that they are statistically significant at the 90% confidence or 0.10 alpha level, while those highlighted in red indicate that they are not statistically significant at any other alpha levels.

Analysis of Variance

	Sums of Squares	Mean of Squares	F-Statistic	p-Value	Hypothesis Test	
Regression	38415447.53	19207723.76	3171851.1	0.0000	Critical F-statistic (99% confidence with df of 2 and 432)	4.6546
Residual	2616.05	6.06			Critical F-statistic (95% confidence with df of 2 and 432)	3.0166
Total	38418063.58				Critical F-statistic (90% confidence with df of 2 and 432)	2.3149

The Analysis of Variance (ANOVA) table provides an F-test of the regression model's overall statistical significance. Instead of looking at individual regressors as in the t-test, the F-test looks at all the estimated Coefficients' statistical properties. The F-Statistic is calculated as the ratio of the Regression's Mean of Squares to the Residual's Mean of Squares. The numerator measures how much of the regression is explained, while the denominator measures how much is unexplained. Hence, the larger the F-Statistic, the more significant the model. The corresponding p-Value is calculated to test the null hypothesis (Ho) where all the Coefficients are simultaneously equal to zero, versus the alternate hypothesis (Ha) that they are all simultaneously different from zero, indicating a significant overall regression model. If the p-Value is smaller than the 0.01, 0.05, or 0.10 alpha significance, then the regression is significant. The same approach can be applied to the F-Statistic by comparing the calculated F-Statistic with the critical F values at various significance levels.

Figure 8.13 Box-Jenkins Autoregressive Integrated Moving Average (ARIMA) Forecast Report.

Autocorrelation

Time Lag	AC	PAC	Lower Bound	Upper Bound	Q-Stat	Prob
1	0.9921	0.9921	(0.0958)	0.0958	431.1216	-
2	0.9841	(0.0105)	(0.0958)	0.0958	856.3037	-
3	0.9760	(0.0109)	(0.0958)	0.0958	1,275.4818	-
4	0.9678	(0.0142)	(0.0958)	0.0958	1,688.5499	-
5	0.9594	(0.0098)	(0.0958)	0.0958	2,095.4625	-
6	0.9509	(0.0113)	(0.0958)	0.0958	2,496.1572	-
7	0.9423	(0.0124)	(0.0958)	0.0958	2,890.5594	-
8	0.9336	(0.0147)	(0.0958)	0.0958	3,278.5669	-
9	0.9247	(0.0121)	(0.0958)	0.0958	3,660.1152	-
10	0.9156	(0.0139)	(0.0958)	0.0958	4,035.1192	-
11	0.9066	(0.0049)	(0.0958)	0.0958	4,403.6117	-
12	0.8975	(0.0068)	(0.0958)	0.0958	4,765.6032	-
13	0.8883	(0.0097)	(0.0958)	0.0958	5,121.0697	-
14	0.8791	(0.0087)	(0.0958)	0.0958	5,470.0032	-
15	0.8698	(0.0064)	(0.0958)	0.0958	5,812.4256	-
16	0.8605	(0.0056)	(0.0958)	0.0958	6,148.3694	-
17	0.8512	(0.0062)	(0.0958)	0.0958	6,477.8620	-
18	0.8419	(0.0038)	(0.0958)	0.0958	6,800.9622	-
19	0.8326	(0.0003)	(0.0958)	0.0958	7,117.7709	-
20	0.8235	0.0002	(0.0958)	0.0958	7,428.3952	-

If autocorrelation AC(1) is nonzero, it means that the series is first order serially correlated. If AC(k) dies off more or less geometrically with increasing lag , it implies that the series follows a low-order autoregressive process. If AC(k) drops to zero after a small number of lags, it implies that the series follows a low-order moving-average process. Partial correlation PAC(k) measures the correlation of values that are k periods apart after removing the correlation from the intervening lags. If the pattern of autocorrelation can be captured by an autoregression of order less than k, then the partial autocorrelation at lag k will be close to zero. Ljung-Box Q-statistics and their p-values at lag k has the null hypothesis that there is no autocorrelation up to order k. The dotted lines in the plots of the autocorrelations are the approximate two standard error bounds. If the autocorrelation is within these bounds, it is not significantly different from zero at (approximately) the 5% significance level.

Forecasting

Period	Actual (Y)	Forecast (F)	Error (E)
2	139.4000	139.6056	(0.2056)
3	139.7000	140.0069	(0.3069)
4	139.7000	140.2586	(0.5586)
5	140.7000	140.1343	0.5657
6	141.2000	141.6948	(0.4948)
7	141.7000	141.6741	0.0259
8	141.9000	142.4339	(0.5339)
9	141.0000	142.3587	(1.3587)
10	140.5000	141.0466	(0.5466)
11	140.4000	140.9447	(0.5447)
12	140.0000	140.8451	(0.8451)
13	140.0000	140.2946	(0.2946)
14	139.9000	140.5663	(0.6663)
15	139.8000	140.2823	(0.4823)
16	139.6000	140.2726	(0.6726)
17	139.6000	139.9775	(0.3775)
18	139.6000	140.1232	(0.5231)
19	140.2000	140.0513	0.1487
20	141.3000	140.9862	0.3138
21	141.2000	142.1738	(0.9738)
22	140.9000	141.4377	(0.5377)
23	140.9000	141.3513	(0.4513)
24	140.7000	141.3939	(0.6939)
25	141.1000	141.0731	0.0270
26	141.6000	141.8311	(0.2311)
27	141.9000	142.2065	(0.3065)
28	142.1000	142.4709	(0.3709)
29	142.7000	142.6402	0.0598
30	142.9000	143.4561	(0.5561)
31	142.9000	143.3532	(0.4532)
32	143.5000	143.4040	0.0960
33	143.8000	144.2784	(0.4784)
34	144.1000	144.2966	(0.1966)
35	144.8000	144.7374	0.0626
36	145.2000	145.5692	(0.3692)
37	145.2000	145.7582	(0.5582)
38	145.7000	145.6649	0.0351
39	146.0000	146.4605	(0.4605)
40	146.4000	146.5176	(0.1176)
41	146.8000	147.0891	(0.2891)
42	146.6000	147.4066	(0.8066)
43	146.5000	146.9501	(0.4501)

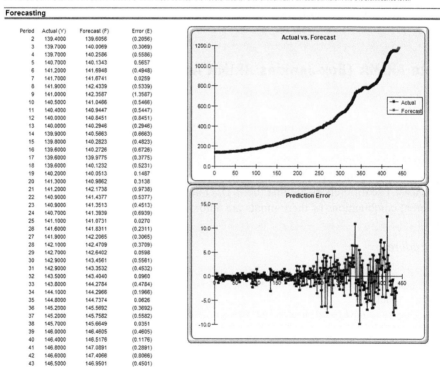

Figure 8.13 (*continued*).

Finally, an additional set of results called the autocorrelation (AC) and partial autocorrelation (PAC) statistics are provided in the ARIMA report.

For instance, if autocorrelation AC(1) is nonzero, it means that the series is first-order serially correlated. If AC dies off more or less geometrically with increasing lags, it implies that the series follows a low-order autoregressive process. If AC drops to zero after a small number of lags, it implies that the series follows a low-order moving-average process. In contrast, PAC measures the correlation of values that are k periods apart after removing the correlation from the intervening lags. If the pattern of autocorrelation can be captured by an autoregression of order less than k, then the partial autocorrelation at lag k will be close to zero. The Ljung-Box Q-statistics and their p-values at lag k are also provided, where the null hypothesis being tested is such that there is no autocorrelation up to order k. The dotted lines in the plots of the autocorrelations are the approximate two standard error bounds. If the autocorrelation is within these bounds, it is not significantly different from zero at approximately the 5% significance level. Finding the right ARIMA model takes practice and experience. These AC, PAC, SC, and AIC results are highly useful diagnostic tools to help identify the correct model specification. Finally, the ARIMA parameter results are obtained using sophisticated optimization and iterative algorithms, which means that although the functional forms look like those of a multivariate regression, they are not the same. ARIMA is a much more computationally intensive and advanced econometric approach than multivariate regression.

Auto ARIMA (Box-Jenkins ARIMA Advanced Time-Series)

Theory

This tool provides analyses identical to the ARIMA module except that the Auto-ARIMA module automates some of the traditional ARIMA modeling by automatically testing multiple permutations of model specifications and returns the best-fitting model. Running the Auto-ARIMA module is similar to running regular ARIMA forecasts. The differences are that the P, D, Q inputs are no longer required and that different combinations of these inputs are automatically run and compared.

Procedure

- Start Excel and enter your data or open an existing worksheet with historical data to forecast (Figure 8.14 uses the example file *Advanced Forecasting Models* in the *Examples* menu of Risk Simulator).
- In the *Auto-ARIMA* worksheet, select *Risk Simulator | Forecasting | Auto-ARIMA*. You can also access the method through the Forecasting icons ribbon or right-clicking anywhere in the model and selecting the forecasting shortcut menu.
- Click on the *Link* icon and link to the existing time-series data, enter the number of forecast periods desired, and click *OK*.

ARIMA and Auto-ARIMA Note

For ARIMA and Auto-ARIMA, you can model and forecast future periods either by using only the dependent variable (Y)—that is, the *Time-Series Variable* by itself—or

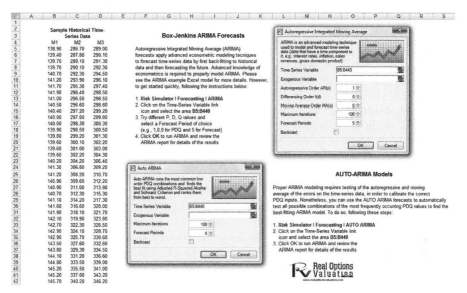

Figure 8.14 Auto-ARIMA Module.

you can insert additional exogenous variables ($X_1, X_2, \ldots, X_n$), just as in a regression analysis where you have multiple independent variables. You can run as many forecast periods as you wish if you only use the time-series variable (Y). However, if you add exogenous variables (X), be sure to note that your forecast periods are limited to the number of exogenous variables' data periods minus the time-series variable's data periods. For example, you can only forecast up to 5 periods if you have time-series historical data of 100 periods and only if you have exogenous variables of 105 periods (100 historical periods to match the time-series variable and 5 additional future periods of independent exogenous variables to forecast the time-series dependent variable).

Basic Econometrics

Theory

Econometrics refers to a branch of business analytics, modeling, and forecasting techniques for modeling the behavior or forecasting certain business, financial, economic, physical science, and other variables. Running the Basic Econometrics models is similar to regular regression analysis except that the dependent and independent variables are allowed to be modified before a regression is run. The report generated is the same as previously shown in the Multiple Regression section and the interpretations are identical to those described previously.

Procedure

- Start Excel and enter your data or open an existing worksheet with historical data to forecast (Figure 8.15 uses the file example file *Advanced Forecasting Models* in the *Examples* menu of Risk Simulator).
- Select the data in the *Basic Econometrics* worksheet and select *Risk Simulator | Forecasting | Basic Econometrics*.
- Enter the desired dependent and independent variables (see Figure 8.15 for examples) and click *OK* to run the model and report, or click on *Show Results* to view the results before generating the report in case you need to make any changes to the model.

Notes

- To run an econometric model, simply select the data (B5:G55) including headers and click on *Risk Simulator | Forecasting | Basic Econometrics*. You can then type in the variables and their modifications for the dependent and independent variables (see Figure 8.15). Note that only one variable is allowed as the Dependent Variable (Y), whereas multiple variables are allowed in the Independent Variables (X) section, separated by a semicolon (;) and that basic mathematical functions can be used (e.g., LN, LOG, LAG, +, −, /, *, TIME, RESIDUAL, DIFF). Click on *Show Results* to preview the computed model and click *OK* to generate the econometric model report.
- You can also automatically generate Multiple Models by entering a sample model and using the predefined *INTEGER(N)* variable as well as *Shifting Data* up or down specific rows repeatedly. For instance, if you use the variable *LAG(VAR1, INTEGER1)* and you set *INTEGER1* to be between *MIN* = 1 and *MAX* = 3, then the following three models will be run: first *LAG(VAR1,1)*, then *LAG(VAR1,2)*, and, finally, *LAG(VAR1,3)*. Also, sometimes you might want to test if the time-series data has structural shifts or if the behavior of the model is consistent over time by shifting the data and then running the same model. For

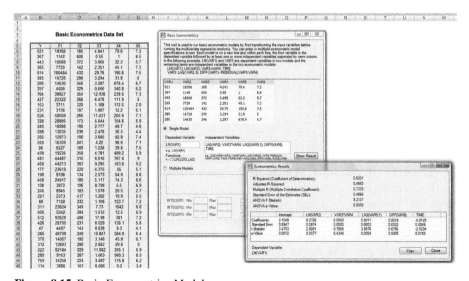

Figure 8.15 Basic Econometrics Module.

example, if you have 100 months of data listed chronologically, you can shift down 3 months at a time for 10 times (i.e., the model will be run on months 1–100, 4–100, 7–100, etc.). Using this *Multiple Models* section in Basic Econometrics, you can run hundreds of models by simply entering a single model equation if you use these predefined integer variables and shifting methods.

J-Curve and S-Curve Forecasts

Theory

The J-curve, or exponential growth curve, is one where the growth of the next period depends on the current period's level and the increase is exponential. This phenomenon means that, over time, the values will increase significantly from one period to another. This model is typically used in forecasting biological growth and chemical reactions over time.

Procedure

- Start Excel and select *Risk Simulator | Forecasting | JS Curves*.
- Select the J- or S-curve type, enter the required input assumptions (see Figures 8.16 and 8.17 for examples), and click *OK* to run the model and report.

J-Curve Exponential Growth Curves

In mathematics, a quantity that grows exponentially is one whose growth rate is always proportional to its current size. Such growth is said to follow an exponential law. This implies that for any exponentially growing quantity, the larger the quantity gets, the faster it grows. But it also implies that the relationship between the size of the dependent variable and its rate of growth is governed by a strict law, of the simplest kind: direct proportion. The general principle behind exponential growth is that the larger a number gets, the faster it grows. Any exponentially growing number will eventually grow larger than any other number which grows at only a constant rate for the same amount of time. This forecast method is also called a J curve due to its shape resembling the letter J. There is no maximum level of this growth curve. Other growth curves include S-curves and Markov Chains.

To generate a J curve forecast, follow the instructions below:

1. Click on **Risk Simulator | Forecasting | JS Curves**
2. Select Exponential J Curve and enter in the desired inputs
   (e.g., Starting Value of 100, Growth Rate of 5 percent, End Period of 100)
3. Click OK to run the forecast and spend some time reviewing the forecast report

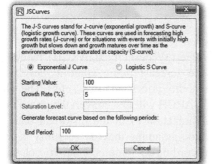

Figure 8.16 J-Curve Forecast.

Logistic S Curve

A logistic function or logistic curve models the S-curve of growth of some variable X. The initial stage of growth is approximately exponential; then, as competition arises, the growth slows, and at maturity, growth stops. These functions find applications in a range of fields, from biology to economics. For example, in the development of an embryo, a fertilized ovum splits, and the cell count grows: 1, 2, 4, 8, 16, 32, 64, etc. This is exponential growth. But the fetus can grow only as large as the uterus can hold; thus other factors start slowing down the increase in the cell count, and the rate of growth slows (but the baby is still growing, of course). After a suitable time, the child is born and keeps growing. Ultimately, the cell count is stable; the person's height is constant; the growth has stopped, at maturity. The same principles can be applied to population growth of animals or humans, and the market penetration and revenues of a product, with an initial growth spurt in market penetration, but over time, the growth slows due to competition and eventually the market declines and matures.

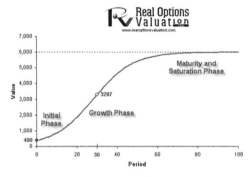

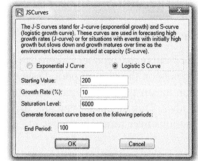

1. Click on **Risk Simulator I Forecasting I JS Curves**
2. Enter in the required inputs (see below for an example)
3. Click **OK** and review the forecast report

Figure 8.17 S-Curve Forecast.

The S-curve, or logistic growth curve, starts off like a J-curve, with exponential growth rates. Over time, the environment becomes saturated (e.g., market saturation, competition, overcrowding), the growth slows, and the forecast value eventually ends up at a saturation or maximum level. The S-curve model is typically used in forecasting market share or sales growth of a new product from market introduction until maturity and decline, population dynamics, growth of bacterial cultures, and other naturally occurring variables. Figure 8.17 illustrates a sample S-curve.

Generalized Autoregressive Conditional Heteroskedasticity (GARCH) Volatility Forecasts

Theory

The generalized autoregressive conditional heteroskedasticity (GARCH) model is used to model historical volatility levels and forecast future volatility levels of a marketable security (e.g., stock prices, commodity prices, oil prices, etc.). The data set has to be a time-series of raw price levels. GARCH will first convert the prices into relative returns and then run an internal optimization to fit the historical data to a mean-reverting volatility term structure, while assuming that the volatility is heteroskedastic in nature (changes over time according to some econometric characteristics). The theoretical specifics of a GARCH model are outside the purview of this user manual.

Procedure

- Start Excel, open the example file *Advanced Forecasting Model,* go to the *GARCH* worksheet, and select *Risk Simulator | Forecasting | GARCH.*
- Click on the Link icon, select the *Data Location,* enter the required input assumptions (Figure 8.18), and click *OK* to run the model and report.

Notes

The typical volatility forecast situation requires P = 1, Q = 1; Periodicity = number of periods per year (12 for monthly data, 52 for weekly data, 252 or 365 for daily data); Base = minimum of 1 and up to the periodicity value; and Forecast Periods = number of annualized volatility forecasts you wish to obtain. There are several

Generalized Autoregressive Conditional Heteroskedasticity (GARCH)

Historical Data

Days	Inputs
1	459.11
2	460.71
3	460.34
4	460.68
5	460.83
6	461.68
7	461.66
8	461.64
9	465.97
10	469.38
11	470.05
12	469.72
13	466.95
14	464.78
15	465.81
16	465.86
17	467.44
18	468.32
19	470.39
20	468.51
21	470.42
22	470.4
23	472.78
24	478.64
25	481.14
26	480.81
27	481.19
28	480.19
29	481.46
30	481.65
31	482.55
32	484.54
33	485.22
34	481.97
35	482.74
36	485.07
37	486.91

To run a GARCH model, enter in the relevant time-series data, then click on **Risk Simulator I Forecasting I GARCH** and click on on the data location *link* icon, select the historical data area (e.g., C8:C2428). Enter in the required inputs (e.g., P 1, Q 1, Daily Trading Periodicity 252, Predictive Base 1, Forecast Periods 10) and click OK. Review the generated forecast report.

GARCH

GARCH or generalized autoregressive conditional heteroskedasticity models are used in forecasting the volatility of financial instruments, using the prices themselves. The GARCH (P,Q) model allows for different positive P and Q integer lag parameters for the mean (news) and variance equations. Note than only positive data values can be used in a GARCH volatility forecast. Periodicity is the number of periods per year (e.g., 12 for monthly data, 252 for daily trading data, 365 for daily data) to annualize the volatility or keep as 1 for periodic volatility. Base is the predictive base periods (this means how many periods back you would like to use as a forecast base to predict future volatility, e.g., enter in 12 if using the past 12 periods). Variance Targeting means if you wish the volatility forecast to revert to an imputed long-run mean over time. Make sure to arrange your raw price data in chronological order (past to present in a single column with multiple rows).

Data Location: C8:C2428

Generate a GARCH (P,Q) model for:

P: 1   Q: 1   Periodicity: 252   Base: 1   Forecast Periods: 10

☐ Apply Variance Targeting

◉ GARCH   ○ GARCH-M   ○ TGARCH
○ TGARCH-M   ○ EGARCH   ○ EGARCH-T
○ GJR GARCH   ○ GJR TGARCH   ○ Run All Models

OK   Cancel

Figure 8.18 GARCH Volatility Forecast.

GARCH models available in Risk Simulator, including EGARCH, EGARCH-T, GARCH-M, GJR-GARCH, GJR-GARCH-T, IGARCH, and T-GARCH.

GARCH models are used mainly in analyzing financial time-series data to ascertain their conditional variances and volatilities. These volatilities are then used to value the options as usual, but the amount of historical data necessary for a good volatility estimate remains significant. Usually, several dozen—and even up to hundreds—of data points are required to obtain good GARCH estimates. GARCH is a term that incorporates a family of models that can take on a variety of forms, known as GARCH(p,q), where p and q are positive integers that define the resulting GARCH model and its forecasts. In most cases for financial instruments, a GARCH(1,1) is sufficient and is most generally used. For instance, a GARCH(1,1) model takes the form of:

$$y_t = x_t \gamma + \varepsilon_t$$

$$\sigma_t^2 = \omega + \alpha \varepsilon_{t-1}^2 + \beta \sigma_{t-1}^2$$

where the first equation's dependent variable (y_t) is a function of exogenous variables (x_t) with an error term (ε_t). The second equation estimates the variance (squared volatility σ_t^2) at time t, which depends on a historical mean (ω), news about volatility from the previous period, measured as a lag of the squared residual from the mean equation (ε_{t-1}^2), and volatility from the previous period (σ_{t-1}^2). The exact modeling specification of a GARCH model is beyond the scope of this book. Suffice it to say that detailed knowledge of econometric modeling (model specification tests, structural breaks, and error estimation) is required to run a GARCH model, making it less accessible to the general analyst. Another problem with GARCH models is that the model usually does not provide a good statistical fit. That is, it is almost impossible to predict the stock market and, of course, just as hard, if not harder, to predict a stock's volatility over time.

Note that the GARCH function has several inputs as follows:

- *Time-Series Data*—The time-series of data in chronological order (e.g., stock prices). Typically, dozens of data points are required for a decent volatility forecast.
- *Periodicity*—A positive integer indicating the number of periods per year (e.g., 12 for monthly data, 252 for daily trading data, etc.), assuming you wish to annualize the volatility. For getting periodic volatility, enter 1.
- *Predictive Base*—The number of periods (the time-series data) back to use as a base to forecast volatility. The higher this number, the longer the historical base is used to forecast future volatility.
- *Forecast Period*—A positive integer indicating how many future periods beyond the historical stock prices you wish to forecast.
- *Variance Targeting*—This variable is set as False by default (even if you do not enter anything here) but can be set as True. False means the omega variable is automatically optimized and computed. The suggestion is to leave this variable empty. If you wish to create mean-reverting volatility with variance targeting, set this variable as True.
- *P*—The number of previous lags on the mean equation.
- *Q*—The number of previous lags on the variance equation.

Table 8.1 Selected GARCH Specifications Used in Risk Simulator

	$z_t \sim$ **Normal Distribution**	$z_t \sim$ **T-Distribution**
GARCH-M Variance in Mean Equation	$y_t = c + \lambda \sigma_t^2 + \varepsilon_t$ $\varepsilon_t = \sigma_t z_t$ $\sigma_t^2 = \omega + \alpha \varepsilon_{t-1}^2 + \beta \sigma_{t-1}^2$	$y_t = c + \lambda \sigma_t^2 + \varepsilon_t$ $\varepsilon_t = \sigma_t z_t$ $\sigma_t^2 = \omega + \alpha \varepsilon_{t-1}^2 + \beta \sigma_{t-1}^2$
GARCH-M Standard Deviation in Mean Equation	$y_t = c + \lambda \sigma_t + \varepsilon_t$ $\varepsilon_t = \sigma_t z_t$ $\sigma_t^2 = \omega + \alpha \varepsilon_{t-1}^2 + \beta \sigma_{t-1}^2$	$y_t = c + \lambda \sigma_t + \varepsilon_t$ $\varepsilon_t = \sigma_t z_t$ $\sigma_t^2 = \omega + \alpha \varepsilon_{t-1}^2 + \beta \sigma_{t-1}^2$
GARCH-M Log Variance in Mean Equation	$y_t = c + \lambda \ln(\sigma_t^2) + \varepsilon_t$ $\varepsilon_t = \sigma_t z_t$ $\sigma_t^2 = \omega + \alpha \varepsilon_{t-1}^2 + \beta \sigma_{t-1}^2$	$y_t = c + \lambda \ln(\sigma_t^2) + \varepsilon_t$ $\varepsilon_t = \sigma_t z_t$ $\sigma_t^2 = \omega + \alpha \varepsilon_{t-1}^2 + \beta \sigma_{t-1}^2$
GARCH	$y_t = x_t \gamma + \varepsilon_t$ $\sigma_t^2 = \omega + \alpha \varepsilon_{t-1}^2 + \beta \sigma_{t-1}^2$	$y_t = \varepsilon_t$ $\varepsilon_t = \sigma_t z_t$ $\sigma_t^2 = \omega + \alpha \varepsilon_{t-1}^2 + \beta \sigma_{t-1}^2$
EGARCH	$y_t = \varepsilon_t$ $\varepsilon_t = \sigma_t z_t$ $\ln(\sigma_t^2) = \omega + \beta \ln(\sigma_{t-1}^2) +$ $\alpha \left[\left\| \frac{\varepsilon_{t-1}}{\sigma_{t-1}} \right\| - E(\|\varepsilon_t\|) \right] + r \frac{\varepsilon_{t-1}}{\sigma_{t-1}}$ $E(\|\varepsilon_t\|) = \sqrt{\frac{2}{\pi}}$	$y_t = \varepsilon_t$ $\varepsilon_t = \sigma_t z_t$ $\ln(\sigma_t^2) = \omega + \beta \ln(\sigma_{t-1}^2) +$ $\alpha \left[\left\| \frac{\varepsilon_{t-1}}{\sigma_{t-1}} \right\| - E(\|\varepsilon_t\|) \right] + r \frac{\varepsilon_{t-1}}{\sigma_{t-1}}$ $E(\|\varepsilon_t\|) = \frac{2\sqrt{v-2}\,\Gamma((v+1)/2)}{(v-1)\Gamma(v/2)\sqrt{\pi}}$
GJR-GARCH	$y_t = \varepsilon_t$ $\varepsilon_t = \sigma_t z_t$ $\sigma_t^2 = \omega + \alpha \varepsilon_{t-1}^2 +$ $r \varepsilon_{t-1}^2 d_{t-1} + \beta \sigma_{t-1}^2$ $d_{t-1} = \begin{cases} 1 & \text{if } \varepsilon_{t-1} < 0 \\ 0 & \text{otherwise} \end{cases}$	$y_t = \varepsilon_t$ $\varepsilon_t = \sigma_t z_t$ $\sigma_t^2 = \omega + \alpha \varepsilon_{t-1}^2 +$ $r \varepsilon_{t-1}^2 d_{t-1} + \beta \sigma_{t-1}^2$ $d_{t-1} = \begin{cases} 1 & \text{if } \varepsilon_{t-1} < 0 \\ 0 & \text{otherwise} \end{cases}$

Table 8.1 lists some of the GARCH specifications used in Risk Simulator with two underlying distributional assumptions: one for normal distribution and the other for the t-distribution.

For the GARCH-M models, the conditional variance equations are the same in the six variations, but the mean equations are different, and assumption on z_t can be either normal distribution or t-distribution. The estimated parameters for GARCH-M with normal distribution are those five parameters in the mean and conditional variance equations. The estimated parameters for GARCH-M with the t-distribution are those five parameters in the mean and conditional variance equations plus another parameter, the degrees of freedom for the t-distribution. In contrast, for the GJR models, the mean equations are the same in the six variations and the differences are that the conditional variance equations and the assumption on z_t can be either a normal distribution or t-distribution. The estimated parameters for EGARCH and GJR-GARCH with normal distribution are those four parameters in the conditional variance equation. The estimated parameters for GARCH, EARCH, and GJR-GARCH with t-distribution are those parameters in the conditional variance equation plus the degrees of freedom for the t-distribution. More technical details of GARCH methodologies fall outside of the scope of this book.

Markov Chains

Theory

A Markov chain exists when the probability of a future state depends on a previous state and when linked together forms a chain that reverts to a long-run steady-state level. This Markov approach is typically used to forecast the market share of two competitors. The required inputs are the starting probability of a customer in the first store (the first state) returning to the same store in the next period versus the probability of switching to a competitor's store in the next state.

Procedure

- Start Excel and select *Risk Simulator | Forecasting | Markov Chain*.
- Enter the required input assumptions (see Figure 8.19 for an example) and click *OK* to run the model and report.

Note

Set both probabilities to 10% and rerun the Markov chain, and you will see the effects of switching behaviors very clearly in the resulting chart as shown at the bottom of Figure 8.19.

Limited Dependent Variables using Maximum Likelihood Models on Logit, Probit, and Tobit

Theory

Limited Dependent Variables describe the situation where the dependent variable contains data that are limited in scope and range, such as binary responses (*0* or *1*), truncated, ordered, or censored data. For instance, given a set of independent variables (e.g., age, income, education level of credit card or mortgage loan holders), we can model the probability of default using MLE. The response or dependent variable *Y* is binary—that is, it can have only two possible outcomes that we denote as *1* and *0* (e.g., *Y* may represent presence/absence of a certain condition, defaulted/not defaulted on previous loans, success/failure of some device, answer yes/no on a survey, etc.)—and we also have a vector of independent variable regressors *X*, which are assumed to influence the outcome *Y*. A typical ordinary least squares regression

Markov Chain Forecast or Markov Process

The Markov Process is useful for studying the evolution of systems over multiple and repeated trials in successive time periods. The system's state at a particular time is unknown, and we are interested in knowing the probability that a particular state exists. For instance, Markov Chains are used to compute the probability that a particular machine or equipment will continue to function in the next time period or whether a consumer purchasing Product A will continue to purchase Product A in the next period or switch to a competitive Product B.

To generate a Markov process, follow the instructions below:

1. Click on **Risk Simulator | Forecasting | Markov Chain**
2. Enter in the relevant state probabilities (e.g., 90 and 80 percents) and click OK
3. Review the forecast report generated

Tip: For an interesting State model, try 10 percent for both probability inputs and see the generated chart.

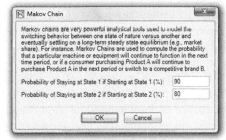

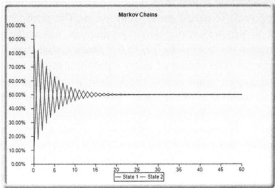

Figure 8.19 Markov Chains (Switching Regimes).

approach is invalid because the regression errors are heteroskedastic and nonnormal, and the resulting estimated probability estimates will return nonsensical values of above *1* or below *0*. MLE analysis handles these problems using an iterative optimization routine to maximize a log likelihood function when the dependent variables are limited.

A logit or logistic regression is used for predicting the probability of occurrence of an event by fitting data to a logistic curve. It is a generalized linear model used for binomial regression, and like many forms of regression analysis, it makes use of several predictor variables that may be either numerical or categorical. MLE applied in a binary multivariate logistic analysis is used to model dependent variables to determine the expected probability of success of belonging to a certain group. The estimated coefficients for the logit model are the logarithmic odds ratios and cannot be interpreted directly as probabilities. A quick computation is first required and the approach is simple.

The logit model is specified as *Estimated Y $= LN[P_i/(1-P_i)]$* or, conversely, $P_i = EXP$ *(Estimated Y)/(1+EXP(Estimated Y))*, and the coefficients β_i are the log odds ratios. So taking the antilog or $EXP(\beta_i)$, we obtain the odds ratio of $P_i/(1-P_i)$. This means that with an increase in a unit of β_i, the log odds ratio increases by this amount. Finally, the rate of change in the probability $dP/dX = \beta_i P_i(1-P_i)$. The standard error measures how accurate the predicted coefficients are, and the t-statistics are the ratios of each predicted coefficient to its standard error and are used in the typical regression hypothesis test of the significance of each estimated parameter. To estimate the probability of success of belonging to a certain group (e.g., predicting if a smoker will develop chest complications given the amount smoked per year), simply compute the *Estimated Y* value using the MLE coefficients. For example, if the model is $Y = 1.1 + 0.005$ (cigarettes), then someone smoking 100 packs per year has an *Estimated Y* of $1.1 + 0.005(100) = 1.6$. Next, compute the inverse antilog of the odds ratio by doing: *EXP(Estimated Y)/[1 + EXP(Estimated Y)]* $= EXP(1.6)/(1+ EXP(1.6)) = 0.8320$. So such a person has an *83.20%* chance of developing some chest complications in his or her lifetime.

A probit model (sometimes also known as a normit model) is a popular alternative specification for a binary response model, which employs a probit function estimated using MLE, and the approach is called probit regression. The probit and logistic regression models tend to produce very similar predictions where the parameter estimates in a logistic regression tend to be 1.6 to 1.8 times higher than they are in a corresponding probit model. The choice of using a probit or logit is entirely up to convenience, and the main distinction is that the logistic distribution has a higher kurtosis (fatter tails) to account for extreme values. For example, suppose that house ownership is the decision to be modeled, and this response variable is binary (home purchase or no home purchase) and depends on a series of independent variables X_i such as income, age, and so forth, such that $I_i = \beta_0 + \beta_1 X_1 + ... + \beta_n X_n$, where the larger the value of I_i, the higher the probability of home ownership. For each family, a critical I^* threshold exists, where, if exceeded, the house is purchased; otherwise, no home is purchased, and the outcome probability (P) is assumed to be normally distributed, such that $P_i = CDF(I)$ using a standard normal cumulative distribution function (CDF). Therefore, use the estimated coefficients exactly like those of a regression model and using the *Estimated Y* value, apply a standard normal distribution (you can use Excel's *NORMSDIST* function or Risk Simulator's Distributional Analysis tool by selecting Normal distribution and setting the mean to be *0* and standard deviation to be *1*). Finally, to obtain a probit or probability unit measure, set $I_i + 5$ (because whenever the probability $P_i < 0.5$, the estimated I_i is negative, due to the fact that the normal distribution is symmetrical around a mean of zero).

The tobit model (censored tobit) is an econometric and biometric modeling method used to describe the relationship between a nonnegative dependent variable Y_i and one or more independent variables X_i. A tobit model is an econometric model in which the dependent variable is censored; that is, the dependent variable is censored because values below zero are not observed. The tobit model assumes that there is a latent unobservable variable Y^*. This variable is linearly dependent on the X_i variables via a vector of β_i coefficients that determine their inter-relationships. In addition, there is a normally distributed error term, U_i, to capture random influences on this relationship. The observable variable Y_i is defined to be equal to the latent variables whenever the latent variables are above zero, and Y_i is assumed to be zero otherwise. That is, $Y_i = Y^*$

Binary Logistic Maximum Likelihood Forecast

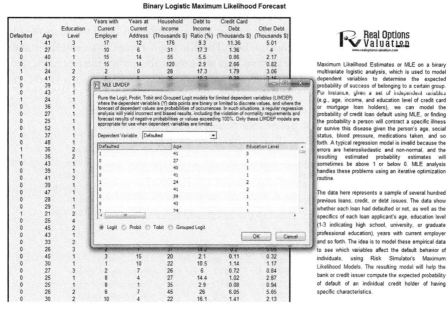

Defaulted	Age	Education Level	Years with Current Employer	Years at Current Address	Household Income (Thousands $)	Debt to Income Ratio (%)	Credit Card Debt (Thousands $)	Other Debt (Thousands $)
1	41	3	17	12	176	9.3	11.36	5.01
0	27	1	10	6	31	17.3	1.36	4
0	40	1	15	14	55	5.5	0.86	2.17
0	41	1	15	14	120	2.9	2.66	0.82
1	24	2	2	0	28	17.3	1.79	3.06
0	41	2			25	10.2	0.39	2.16
0	39	1						
0	43	1						
1	24	1						
0	36	1						
0	27	1						
0	25	1						
0	52	1						
0	37	1						
0	48	1						
1	36	1						
1	36	2						
0	43	1						
0	39	1						
0	41	3						
0	39	1						
0	47	1						
0	28	1						
0	29	1						
1	21	2						
0	25	4						
0	45	2						
0	43	1						
0	33	2						
0	26	3			37	14.2	0.2	5.05
0	45	1	3	15	20	2.1	0.11	0.32
0	30	1	1	10	22	10.5	1.14	1.17
0	27	3	2	7	26	6	0.72	0.84
0	25	1	8	4	27	14.4	1.02	2.87
0	25	1	8	1	35	2.9	0.08	0.94
0	26	2	6	7	45	26	6.05	5.65
0	30	2	10	4	22	16.1	1.41	2.13

Maximum Likelihood Estimates or MLE on a binary multivariate logistic analysis, which is used to model dependent variables to determine the expected probability of success of belonging to a certain group. For instance, given a set of independent variables (e.g., age, income, and education level of credit card or mortgage loan holders), we can model the probability of credit loan default using MLE, or finding the probability a person will contract a specific illness or survive this disease given the person's age, social status, blood pressure, medications taken, and so forth. A typical regression model is invalid because the errors are heteroskedastic and non-normal, and the resulting estimated probability estimates will sometimes be above 1 or below 0. MLE analysis handles these problems using an iterative optimization routine.

The data here represents a sample of several hundred previous loans, credit, or debt issues. The data show whether each loan had defaulted or not, as well as the specifics of each loan applicant's age, education level (1-3 indicating high school, university, or graduate professional education), years with current employer and so forth. The idea is to model these empirical data to see which variables affect the default behavior of individuals, using Risk Simulator's Maximum Likelihood Models. The resulting model will help the bank or credit issuer compute the expected probability of default of an individual credit holder of having specific characteristics.

Figure 8.20 Maximum Likelihood Module.

if $Y^* > 0$ *and* $Y_i = 0$ *if* $Y^* = 0$. If the relationship parameter β_i is estimated by using ordinary least squares regression of the observed Y_i on X_i, the resulting regression estimators are inconsistent and yield downward-biased slope coefficients and an upward-biased intercept. Only MLE would be consistent for a tobit model. In the tobit model, there is an ancillary statistic called *sigma*, which is equivalent to the standard error of estimate in a standard ordinary least squares regression, and the estimated coefficients are used the same way as a regression analysis.

Procedure

- Start Excel and open the example file *Advanced Forecasting Model,* go to the *MLE* worksheet, select the data set including the headers, and click on *Risk Simulator | Forecasting | MLE LIMDEP.*
- Select the dependent variable from the drop list (Figure 8.20) and click *OK* to run the model and report.

Spline (Cubic Spline Interpolation and Extrapolation)

Theory

Sometimes there are missing values in a time-series data set. For instance, interest rates for years 1 to 3 may exist, followed by years 5 to 8, and then year 10. Spline curves can be used to interpolate the missing years' interest rate values based on the data that exist. Spline curves can also be used to forecast or extrapolate values of future time periods beyond the time period of available data. The data can be linear or nonlinear. Figure 8.21 illustrates how a cubic spline is run, and Figure 8.22 shows the resulting forecast report from this module. The Known X values represent the values on the x-axis of a chart (in our example, this is Years of the known interest rates, and, usually, the x-axis are the values that are known in advance such as time or years) and

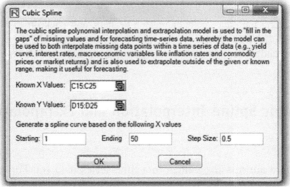

3	**Cubic Spline Interpolation and Extrapolation**
4	
5	The cubic spline polynomial interpolation and extrapolation model is used
6	to "fill in the gaps" of missing spot yields and term structure of interest rates
7	whereby the model can be used to both interpolate missing data points within
8	a time series of interest rates (as well as other macroeconomic variables such
9	as inflation rates and commodity prices or market returns) and also used to
10	extrapolate outside of the given or known range, useful for forecasting purposes.
11	
12	
13	

	Years	Spot Yields	
14			
15	0.0833	4.55%	These are the yields
16	0.2500	4.47%	that are known and
17	0.5000	4.52%	are used as inputs in
18	1.0000	4.39%	the Cubic Spline
19	2.0000	4.13%	Interpolation and
20	3.0000	4.16%	Extrapolation model
21	5.0000	4.26%	
22	7.0000	4.38%	
23	10.0000	4.56%	
24	20.0000	4.88%	
25	30.0000	4.84%	

To run the Cubic Spline forecast, click on **Risk Simulator I Forecasting I Cubic Spline** and then click on the link icon and select C15:C25 as the Known X values (values on the x-axis of a time-series chart) and D15:D25 as the Known Y values (make sure the length of Known X and Y values are the same). Enter the desired forecast periods (e.g., Starting 1, Ending 50, Step Size 0.5). Click OK and review the generated forecasts and chart.

Figure 8.21 Cubic Spline Module.

Cubic Spline Forecasts

The cubic spline polynomial interpolation and extrapolation model is used to "fill in the gaps" of missing values and for forecasting time-series data, whereby the model can be used to both interpolate missing data points within a time series of data (e.g., yield curve, interest rates, macroeconomic variables like inflation rates and commodity prices or market returns) and also used to extrapolate outside of the given or known range, making it useful for forecasting.

Spline Interpolation and Extrapolation Results

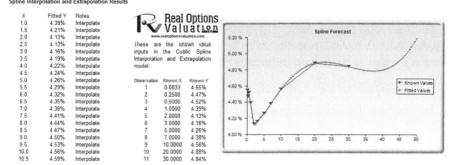

X	Fitted Y	Notes
1.0	4.39%	Interpolate
1.5	4.21%	Interpolate
2.0	4.13%	Interpolate
2.5	4.13%	Interpolate
3.0	4.16%	Interpolate
3.5	4.19%	Interpolate
4.0	4.22%	Interpolate
4.5	4.24%	Interpolate
5.0	4.26%	Interpolate
5.5	4.29%	Interpolate
6.0	4.32%	Interpolate
6.5	4.35%	Interpolate
7.0	4.38%	Interpolate
7.5	4.41%	Interpolate
8.0	4.44%	Interpolate
8.5	4.47%	Interpolate
9.0	4.50%	Interpolate
9.5	4.53%	Interpolate
10.0	4.56%	Interpolate
10.5	4.59%	Interpolate

These are the known value inputs in the Cubic Spline Interpolation and Extrapolation model:

Observation	Known X	Known Y
1	0.0833	4.55%
2	0.2500	4.47%
3	0.5000	4.52%
4	1.0000	4.39%
5	2.0000	4.13%
6	3.0000	4.16%
7	5.0000	4.26%
8	7.0000	4.38%
9	10.0000	4.56%
10	20.0000	4.88%
11	30.0000	4.84%

Figure 8.22 Spline Forecast Results.

the Known *Y* values represent the values on the *y*-axis (in our case, the known Interest Rates). The *y*-axis variable is typically the variable you wish to interpolate missing values from or extrapolate for the values into the future.

Procedure

- Start Excel and open the example file *Advanced Forecasting Model,* go to the *Cubic Spline* worksheet, select the data set excluding the headers, and click on *Risk Simulator | Forecasting | Cubic Spline.*
- The data location is automatically inserted into the user interface if you first select the data, or you can also manually click on the *Link* icon and link the *Known X* values and *Known Y* values (see Figure 8.21 for an example), then enter the required *Starting* and *Ending* values to extrapolate and interpolate, as well as the required *Step Size* between these starting and ending values. Click *OK* to run the model and report (see Figure 8.22).

"Sensitivity" Financial Forecasting

Modified Percent of Sales Method

Historical relationships that held firm generally will not change much, at least into the near term. Finding relationships in historical statements improves forecast accuracy; it is as simple as that. If historical relationships—say, accounts receivables to revenue—were to change significantly, your ability to predict results becomes murky until you identify and justify the new relationship. That is where forecasting financial statements come in—arguably the best way to complement and/or reinforce statistical methods. One widely used method is *modified percent of sales*.

The rationale behind this method is based on the premise that the balance sheet is correlated to changes in sales. Whether a firm restructures or just grows normally, variations in revenue generally require asset/liabilities adjustments. The "sensitivity" approach to forecasting is an efficient method to develop strategic plans. In the process of developing a forecast you will work with two important equations: *Financial Needs Formula (F)* and *Projected Percent of Sales Externally Financed Formula (E):*

(1) $F = A/S(\Delta S) + \Delta NFA - LI/S(\Delta S) - P(S)(1 - d) + R$. The F formula determines the external financing needs of the firm. If used in conjunction with the percent of sales method, both techniques render the same answer.

$$E = (A/S - L1/S) - (P/g)(1 + g)(1 - d) + R/\Delta S$$

For the both the F and E formulas, we have:

F	= Cumulative financial
A	= Projected spontaneous assets
S	= Projected sales
ΔS	= Change in sales
ΔNFA	= Change in net fixed assets
L1	= Spontaneous liabilities
P	= Projected profit margin (%)
D	= Dividend payout rate
R	= Debt maturities
T	= Targeted growth rate
L	= Leverage
g	= Sales growth rate

The E formula identifies the percentage of sales growth requiring external financing. The two equations are interconnected, since they both are derived from the popular IAS and FAS cash flow statement. For example, firms with high growth potential create shareholder value. That aphorism is as old as the hills. Yet, a high-growth firm running on high-octane fixed assets can push the firm to the brink.

Setting Up the Percent of Sales Method: Do Financial Statements Make Sense?

Since balance sheet changes follow the income statement, the income statement is a logical point of departure. Internally generated sources of cash (payables, accruals, retained earnings, etc.) on the balance sheet depend on revenue and margin assumptions. Assets and uses of cash are also tied to the income statement. A good test of income statement credibility is the comparison of pure output variables (POV)—projected pretax margins, aftertax margins, and the return on total assets with historical levels.

Current assets proportional (or spontaneous) to sales include cash, receivables, prepaid expenses, and inventory. For instance, if accounts receivable historically run 30% of sales, and next year's sales are forecasted to be $100 million, accounts receivable will be projected at $30 million. Fixed assets do not generally correlate precisely with sales.

On the right side of the balance sheet, spontaneous liabilities—accounts payable and accruals—move in tandem with sales. Liabilities independent of sales—all the funded ones representing financing activities—are excluded. Equity including

Table 8.2 Input Screen Projection Assumptions

	1999	2000	2001	2002	2003
Cash	2.0%	2.0%	2.0%	2.0%	2.0%
Receivables	15.1%	15.1%	15.1%	15.1%	15.1%
Inventory	23.9%	23.9%	23.9%	23.9%	23.9%
Fixed Assets	8.3%	8.3%	8.3%	8.3%	8.3%
Accounts Payable	10.2%	10.2%	10.2%	10.2%	10.2%
Accruals	3.7%	3.7%	3.7%	3.7%	3.7%
Sales Growth Rate	6.0%	6.0%	6.0%	6.0%	6.0%
Profit Margin	1.0%	1.0%	1.0%	1.0%	1.0%
Dividend Payout	25.0%	25.0%	25.0%	25.0%	25.0%
Loan Amortization	$500.0	$500.0	$500.0	$500.0	$500.0

preferred and common are financing activities and are not directly derived from variations in sales. Retained earnings are calculated by deducting the dividend payout from net profits. Before we go further, another important point to make is that you must also identify and estimate noncritical variables (not included in this exercise). This is accomplished by extrapolating historical patterns or adjusting historical trends. Examples of noncritical variables include various prepaid assets and disposals.

| Boston Widget Co. Inc. |
| Balance Sheet |
| Year Ended December 31 |

Assets	1996	1997	1998
Cash	$15,445	$12,007	$11,717
Receivables	$51,793	$55,886	$88,571
Inventory	$56,801	$99,087	$139,976
Current Assets	$124,039	$166,980	$240,264
Fixed Assets	$44,294	$46,340	$48,539
Total Assets	$168,333	$213,320	$288,803
Liabilities and Equity			
Short-Term Debt	$9,562	$15,300	$54,698
Payables	$20,292	$31,518	$59,995
Accruals	$10,328	$15,300	$21,994
Current Maturities	$500	$500	$500
Current Liabilities	$40,682	$62,618	$137,187
Long-Term Debt	$27,731	$36,491	$35,706
Total Liabilities	$68,413	$99,109	$172,893
Common Stock	$69,807	$69,807	$69,807
Retained Earnings	$30,113	$44,404	$46,103
Total Liability and Equity	$168,333	$213,320	$288,803

As an example, applying the modified sales percentage method to Boston Widget's 1998 financial statements, we see that the ratios have been calculated as a percentage of sales and will be used as projection assumptions for the company's original five-year strategic plan:

Boston Widget Co. Inc.
Projected Statements
Year Ended December 31

This exhibit should be read along with Exhibit 11-6

** Note: calculation carried out 5 decimal places to generate this projection

INCOME STATEMENT:

		1999	2000	2001	2002	2003
Sales	** [Sales 1998(.06)]	$622,108.7	$659,435.2	$699,001.3	$740,941.4	$785,397.9
Profits	[.01 ($622,108.7)]	$6,221.1	$6,594.4	$6,990.0	$7,409.4	$7,854.0
Dividends	[.25 ($6,221.1)]	$1,555.3	$1,648.6	$1,747.5	$1,852.4	$1,963.5

BALANCE SHEET:

		1999	2000	2001	2002	2003
Cash	[.02 ($622,108.7)]	$12,442.2	$13,165.2	$13,955.1	$14,792.4	$15,680.0
Receivables	[.151 ($622,108.7)]	$93,885.3	$99,518.4	$105,489.5	$111,818.8	$118,528.0
Inventory	[.239 ($622,108.7)]	$148,374.6	$157,277.0	$166,713.7	$176,716.5	$187,319.5
Current Assets		$254,702.0	$269,960.6	$286,158.3	$303,327.8	$321,527.4
Fixed Assets	[.083 ($622,108.7)]	$51,451.3	$54,538.4	$57,810.7	$61,279.4	$64,956.1
Total Assets		$306,153.3	$324,499.1	$343,969.0	$364,607.1	$386,483.6

Liabilities, Financial Needs, and Equity

		1999	2000	2001	2002	2003
Short Term Debt	[not tied to sales]	$54,698.0	$54,698.0	$54,698.0	$54,698.0	$54,698.0
Accounts Payables	[.102 ($622,108.7)]	$63,594.7	$67,410.4	$71,455.0	$75,742.3	$80,286.8
Accruals	[.037 ($622,108.7)]	$23,313.6	$24,712.5	$26,195.2	$27,766.9	$29,432.9
Current Maturity	[not tied to sales]	$500.0	$500.0	$500.0	$500.0	$500.0
Current Liab.		$142,106.3	$147,320.8	$152,848.2	$158,707.2	$164,917.8
Long Term Debt	[not tied to sales]	$35,206.0	$34,706.0	$34,206.0	$33,706.0	$33,206.0
Common Stock	[not tied to sales]	$69,807.0	$69,807.0	$69,807.0	$69,807.0	$69,807.0
Ret. Earn	[1998 R/E + $6221.1 - $1555.3]	$50,768.8	$55,714.6	$60,957.1	$66,514.2	$72,404.6
**Financial Needs **	**[Plug]**	**$8,265.2**	**$16,950.6**	**$26,150.7**	**$35,872.8**	**$46,148.2**
Liabilities and Equity		$306,153.3	$324,499.1	$343,969.0	$364,607.1	$386,483.6

Two outcomes occur as a result of applying modified percent of sales: (1) projected liabilities and equity $<$ projected assets produces financial needs (e.g., amount of additional funding required to obtain predicted sales) and (2) projected liabilities and equity $>$ projected assets produce a cash surplus.

You can see that Boston Widget requires additional debt or equity funding to meet sales targets in each of the four years projected. Reintroducing the F and E equations, we can draw conclusions that go beyond the yields provided by a simple accounting projection. Let's begin by first examining the F equation:

$$F = A/S(\Delta S) + \Delta NFA - LI/S(\Delta S) - P(S)(1 - d) + R$$
$$= .4094(35214) + 2912.3 - .1397(35214) - .01(622109)(1 - .25) + 500$$
$$= 8244$$

The results yield exactly the same financial needs as the projected financial statements.

We see the effect independent (X) variables have on Boston Widget's (Y), its financial needs after adjustments. The first test involves changes in spontaneous asset levels. Currently, Boston Widget's asset investments are projected at 49.2% of sales. If, for example, spontaneous assets levels decrease, the overall effect on financial needs, or F, will also decrease. Since inventory and accounts receivable usually make up 80% of current assets, it may be in your best interest to hold the line to minimum levels to maintain optimal levels of working capital. When current assets operate at optimal points, the cash cycle becomes smooth and clean.

The next sensitivity variable is spontaneous liabilities. If Boston Widget's spontaneous liabilities increase from their current level of 14%, financial needs decrease. For example, by increasing accruals (a source of cash), financial needs will decrease as they approach or surpass assets levels. What would be the overall effect if sales decreased? It makes sense that reduced sales projections require less financing and result in reduced external support. The same theory holds true for the dividend rate. By lowering the dividend payout ratio, additional funds will be funneled back into the company (retained earnings). With additional internal funds available to support future needs, cash requirements lower along with unsystematic risk. Stakeholders relax a bit. Now let's look at E:

$$E = (A/S - L1/S) - (P/g)(1 + g)(1 - d) + (R/\Delta S)$$
$$= .492122 - .1397 - .01/.06(1 + .06)(1 - .25) + .014 = .234$$

where:

E = Projected % of sales growth externally financed
g = Growth rate

Thus, 23.4% of Boston Widget's sales growth will be generated by external financing, with 76.6% generated by internal cash flow (.234 × 35,213 = 8244, the same answer as previously calculated for formual F).

Deriving Financial Needs Using The "F" and "E" Equations

Boston Widget Co. Inc.: Base Case Projection

Financial Needs (F): (Note: Fixed Assets are included in A/S)

F = A/S(ΔS)-L₁/S(ΔS)-P(S)(1-d) + R [Program this formula into the HP-19BII calculator]

F = .4094 (35214) + 2912.3 - .1397 (35214) - .01 (622109) (1-.25) + 500 = 8244

	1999	2000	2001	2002	2003
F1 =	8,244.3	8,707.6	9,200.1	9,722.1	10,275.4
F =	8,244.3	16,951.9	26,151.9	35,874.0	46,149.4

	1999	2000	2001	2002	2003
A/S =	49.2%	49.2%	49.2%	49.2%	49.2%
T =	6.0%	6.0%	6.0%	6.0%	6.0%
L₁/S =	14.0%	14.0%	14.0%	14.0%	14.0%
R/ΔS =	1.4%	1.3%	1.3%	1.2%	1.1%
L =	153.9%	158.5%	163.0%	167.5%	171.8%

Percent of Sales Externally Financed:

E = (A/S-L₁/S) - (P/G)(1+G)(1d) + R/ΔS [Program this formula into the HP-19BII]

E = .492122 - .1397 - .01 /.06 (1 + .06)(1-.25) + .014 = .234

	1999	2000	2001	2002	2003
E =	23.4%	23.3%	23.3%	23.2%	23.1%

23.4% of Boston's sales growth will be financed externally.

And so, .23412 (35214) = 8244 which is exactly the financial needs using the "F" formula

PROOF:

	1999	2000	2001	2002	2003
E * ΔS =	8,244.3	8,707.6	9,200.1	9,722.1	10,275.4
CUMULATIVE	8,244.3	16,951.9	26,151.9	35,874.0	46,149.4

As the formula implies, the E equation determines how much sales growth requires external financing. If E reaches 95% in the projection period, only 5% of sales growth will be internally financed—an immediate storm signal, especially if base year leverage is excessive.

Setting E to zero and solving for g, the sales growth rate, will give you a quick reading of the quality and magnitude of cash flows. Say E is set to zero and g falls somewhere in the first industry quartile. This means that the company's financials are not only strong but can be financed with internal cash flow. Let's look at another example. Let's assume that base year leverage is high and you want to reduce leverage by internal financing levels set at 40%. Set the equation at 60% and solve for the capital output ratio required to make your strategy work. If embedded ratios (receivables, inventory, and fixed assets) are below industry or benchmarks, call a meeting of the department heads and read them the riot act.

The Cash Deficit: Identifying the Borrower's Need

The cash deficit is the amount of external cash required from any source, bank or nonbank. The bank reviews the cash deficit to determine its causes. Perhaps the deficit is caused by growth core assets and capital expenditures; nonproductive uses such as dividends and treasury stock purchases; or large debt maturities. Most companies will show a combination of these uses.

Can the Borrower Afford to Grow?

Are leverage, coverage, and liquidity ratios at reasonable levels, even during periods of financial stress? Coverage ratios may indicate that margins are too slim to support increased volume. We can now summarize the approach in Table 8.3.

Table 8.3 Projections Methods Summary

	Method	Advantages	Financial Needs: First Projection Period	Cumulative Financial Needs
Projected Financial Statements	Computer	Provides forecasted financial statements.	$8,244.3	$46,149.4
"F" Equation	Calculator or computer	Derives financial needs quickly and allows you to perform accurate sensitivity analysis on the spot.	$8,244.3	$46,149.4
"E" Equation	Calculator or computer	Used with "F" formula, the "E" equation determines if the firm is generating sufficient internally generated funds.	$8,244.3	$46,149.4

Exercise: Forecasting

This sample exercise illustrates how to use Risk Simulator for running:

1. Autoregressive integrated moving average (ARIMA)
2. Auto-ARIMA
3. Basic econometrics and auto-econometrics
4. Cubic spline
5. Custom distribution
6. GARCH
7. J-curve (exponential curve)
8. Markov chain process
9. Maximum likelihood (logit, probit, tobit)
10. Nonlinear extrapolation
11. Multiple regression
12. S-curve (logistic curve)
13. Stochastic processes (random walk, Brownian motion, mean-reversion, jump-diffusion)
14. Time-series decomposition
15. Trendlines

It is assumed that you have reviewed Chapter Eight for all the technical and usability details of these forecasting methods and are somewhat familiar with what each of them is used for.

1   ARIMA

Autoregressive integrated moving average (ARIMA) forecasts apply advanced econometric modeling techniques to forecast time-series data by first *backfitting* to historical data and then *forecasting* the future. Advanced knowledge of econometrics is required to properly model ARIMA. See the ARIMA example Excel model for more details. However, to get started quickly, follow the instructions given here:

1. Start Excel and open the example model *Risk Simulator | Example Models | 01 Advanced Forecast Models.*
2. Go to the *ARIMA and Auto-ARIMA* worksheet.
3. Select the data area B5:B440 and click on *Risk Simulator | Forecasting | ARIMA* and click *OK* (you can keep the default settings for now). Spend some time reviewing the generated ARIMA report.
4. Next, go back to the worksheet and rerun ARIMA. This time you can try different P, D, Q values and enter a different Forecast Period of choice (e.g., 1,0,0 for P, D, Q, and 5 for Forecast...remember that these inputs have to be 0 or positive integers).
5. Run ARIMA again, but this time, click on the *Link* icon to select the data set B5:B440 on the worksheet for the time-series variable and C5:D445 for the exogenous variables.
   - *Exercise Question:* What does "exogenous variable" mean?
   - *Exercise Question:* What types of variables might be well-suited for ARIMA forecasting?
   - *Exercise Question:* What types of data are appropriate for ARIMA: time-series, cross-sectional, or mixed-panel data?
   - *Exercise Question:* What are the P, D, Q values used for?
   - *Exercise Question:* How does ARIMA compare with multiple regression analysis?

Note: For ARIMA and Auto-ARIMA, you can run as many forecast periods as you wish if you only use the time-series variable (*Y*). If you add exogenous variables (*X*), note that your forecast period is limited to the number of exogenous variables' data periods minus the time-series variable's data periods. For example, you can only forecast up to 5 periods if you have time-series historical data of 100 periods and only if you have exogenous variables of 105 periods (100 historical periods to match the time-series variable and 5 additional future periods of independent exogenous variables to forecast the time-series dependent variable).

2 Auto-ARIMA

Proper ARIMA modeling requires testing of the autoregressive and moving average of the errors on the time-series data in order to calibrate the correct P, D, Q inputs. Nonetheless, you can use the Auto-ARIMA forecasts to automatically test all possible combinations of the most frequently occurring P, D, Q values to find the best-fitting ARIMA model. To do so, follow these steps:

1. Start Excel and open the example model *Risk Simulator | Example Models | 01 Advanced Forecast Models.*
2. Go to the *ARIMA* and *Auto-ARIMA* worksheet.
3. Select the data area *B5:B440*, click on *Risk Simulator | Forecasting | Auto-ARIMA*, and click *OK.* Review the ARIMA report for details of the results.
4. Run ARIMA again, but this time, click on the *Link* icon to select the data set *B5:B440* on the worksheet for the time-series variable and *C5:D445* for the exogenous variables.
   - *Exercise Question:* What is the difference between ARIMA and Auto-ARIMA?
   - *Exercise Question:* What additional information is provided in the report, and what input parameters are no longer required?

3 Basic Econometrics and Auto-Econometrics

To run an econometric model, follow these instructions:

1. Start Excel and open the example model *Risk Simulator | Example Models | 01 Advanced Forecast Models.*
2. Go to the *Basic Econometrics* worksheet.
3. Select the data area *B5:G55*, click on *Risk Simulator | Forecasting | Basic Econometrics*, and then type in the variables and their modifications for the dependent and independent variables:
   a. Dependent Variable: VAR1
   b. Independent Variables: VAR2; VAR3; VAR4; VAR5; VAR6
4. Click on *Show Results* to preview the computed model, and click *OK* to generate the econometric model report.
5. Go back to the data and rerun Basic Econometrics. This time, set up the model:
   a. Dependent Variable: LN(VAR1)
   b. Independent Variable: LN(VAR2); VAR3*VAR4; LAG(VAR5,1); DIFF(VAR6); TIME
6. Go back to the data one more time and rerun Basic Econometrics. This time, select the *Multiple Models* option. Run the initial model with *VAR1* as the dependent variable and *LAG*

(VAR5,INTEGER1); VAR3 VAR4* as the independent variable, set *INTEGER1* to be between *1* and *3*, Sort by Adjusted R-Square, Shift Data 1 Row Down 5 Times, and click *OK*.

- *Exercise Question:* What happens when you perform a shift to multiple econometric models?
- *Exercise Question:* How do you model linear, nonlinear, interacting, lag, lead, log, natural log, time-series, difference, and ratios?

7. Go back to the data, select *Risk Simulator | Forecasting | Auto Econometrics,* this time select *Linear and Nonlinear Interacting,* and then click OK. Review the generated report.

Note: Only one variable is allowed as the Dependent Variable (*Y*), whereas multiple variables are allowed in the Independent Variables (*X*) section, separated by a semi-colon (;), and basic mathematical functions can be used (e.g., *LN, LOG, LAG,* $+, -, /, *,$ *TIME, RESIDUAL, DIFF*). You can also automatically generate *Multiple Models* by entering a sample model and using the predefined '*INTEGER(N)*' variable as well as *Shifting Data* up or down specific rows repeatedly. For instance, if you use the variable *LAG(VAR1, INTEGER1)* and you set *INTEGER1* to be between *MIN* = 1 and *MAX* = 3, then the following three models will be run: *LAG(VAR1,1)*, then *LAG(VAR1,2)*, and, finally, *LAG(VAR1,3)*. Using this *Multiple Models* section in Basic Econometrics, you can run hundreds of models by simply entering a single model equation if you use these predefined integer variables and shifting methods.

4 Cubic Spline

The cubic spline polynomial interpolation and extrapolation model is used to "fill in the gaps" of missing values in that it can be used to both interpolate missing data points within a time-series (e.g., interest rates as well as other macroeconomic variables such as inflation rates and commodity prices or market returns) and to extrapolate outside of the given or known range, useful for forecasting purposes.

To run the Cubic Spline forecast, follow the instructions given here:

1. Start Excel and open the example model *Risk Simulator | Example Models | 01 Advanced Forecast Models.*
2. Go to the *Cubic Spline* worksheet.
3. Select the data area *C15:D25* and click on *Risk Simulator | Forecasting | Cubic Spline* (check to make sure C15:C25 is set as the *Known X* values and D15:D25 is set as the *Known Y* values). Enter the desired forecast periods *Starting = 1, Ending = 50, Step Size = 0.5,* and click *OK*. Review the generated forecasts and chart.
   - *Exercise Question:* How do you know which variable should be set as the Known *Y* versus the Known *X*?
   - *Exercise Question:* What is a spline curve supposed to do?
   - *Exercise Question:* Is this methodology appropriate for time-series data, and can it be used for cross-sectional data sets with missing intermediate values?

5 Custom Distribution

To create a custom distribution assumption, follow these instructions:

1. Start Excel and open the example model *Risk Simulator | Example Models | 01 Advanced Forecast Models.*

2. Go to the *Custom Distribution* and *Delphi* worksheet.

3. Create a new profile by clicking on *Risk Simulator | New Simulation Profile*.

4. Select the data area *B14:C24* and click on *Edit |Copy* in Excel, or use *CTRL+C* to copy the data into temporary clipboard memory and then select any empty cell in the worksheet.

5. Click on *Risk Simulator | Set Input Assumption,* select *Custom Distribution,* and then click on *Create Distribution.* Then in the custom distribution designer interface, just click on and follow each of the four steps: *1 Paste, 2 Update Chart, 3 Apply,* and *4 Close.* Finally, back in the *Set Assumptions Properties,* click *OK* to set the assumption.

6. Click on the Step Simulation icon a few times to see the value in the cell changing, and you will see that it is randomly selecting the numbers from the original data set, where numbers that have the highest probability of occurrence or that are repeated more often in the original data set are selected more often, of course.

- *Exercise Question:* Why is the custom distribution considered a nonparametric simulation?
- *Exercise Question:* Is it better to use data fitting to find the best-fitting distribution to run a simulation or to use a custom distribution?
- *Exercise Question:* What is the p-value for the distributional fitting if we were to apply a hypothesis test to see what the goodness-of-fit is for a custom distribution?

6   GARCH

To run a GARCH model, follow the instructions given here:

1. Start Excel and open the example model *Risk Simulator | Example Models | 01 Advanced Forecast Models.*

2. Go to the *GARCH* worksheet.

3. Select the data area *C8:C2428* and click on *Risk Simulator | Forecasting | GARCH* (you can also click on the *Data Location Link* icon to select the historical data area or preselect the data area before starting the GARCH routine). Enter in the required inputs as *P = 1, Q = 1, Daily Trading Periodicity = 252, Predictive Base = 1, Forecast Periods = 10,* and click *OK.* Review the generated forecast report and chart.

- *Exercise Question:* What variables are most appropriate for running a GARCH model?
- *Exercise Question:* Can cross-sectional data be used to run GARCH, or is it only restricted to time-series data?
- *Exercise Question:* What does GARCH forecast?
- *Exercise Question:* Briefly describe what GARCH is used for.
- *Exercise Question:* Why is number of days set to 252? Why is it not 365?

7   J-Curve (Exponential Curve)

In mathematics, a quantity that grows exponentially is one whose growth rate is always proportional to its current size. Such growth is said to follow an exponential law. This law implies that for any exponentially growing quantity, the larger the quantity gets, the faster it grows. But it also implies that the relationship between the size of the dependent variable and its rate of growth is governed by a strict law: direct proportion. This forecast method is also called a J-curve due to its shape resembling the letter J. There is no maximum level of this growth curve.

To generate a J-curve forecast, follow these instructions:

1. Start Excel and open the example model *Risk Simulator | Example Models | 01 Advanced Forecast Models.*
2. Go to the *J-Curve* worksheet.
3. Click on *Risk Simulator | Forecasting | JS Curves,* click on *J-Curve,* and use *Starting Value = 100, Growth Rate = 5 percent, End Period = 100.* Then click *OK* to run the forecast and spend some time reviewing the forecast report.
   - *Exercise Question:* Can J-curves be used to forecast cross-sectional data, or are they only appropriate for time-series data?

8 Markov Chain Process

The Markov process is useful for studying the evolution of systems over multiple and repeated trials in successive time periods. The system's state at a particular time is unknown, and we are interested in knowing the probability that a particular state exists. For instance, Markov chains are used to compute the probability that a particular machine or equipment will continue to function in the next time period, or whether a consumer purchasing Product A will continue to purchase Product A in the next period or switch to a competitive Product B.

To generate a Markov process, follow these instructions:

1. Start Excel and open the example model *Risk Simulator | Example Models | 01 Advanced Forecast Models.*
2. Go to the *Markov* worksheet.
3. Click on *Risk Simulator | Forecasting | Markov Chain,* enter in *10%* for both state probabilities, and click *OK* to create the report and chart. Review the chart and see what happens when the probability is low.
4. Rerun the Markov chain, and this time set the probabilities to both be at *90%*.
   - *Exercise Question:* What is the difference between a stochastic process forecast and a Markov chain forecast?
   - *Exercise Question:* What happens when the state probabilities are small? Why are there such high levels of switching back and forth on the chart as compared to a much lower fluctuation level with high probabilities?

9 Limited Dependent Variables using Maximum Likelihood Models on Logit, Probit, and Tobit

The Limited Dependent Variables models are solved using a Maximum Likelihood Estimate, or MLE, which is a set of binary multivariate logistic analysis used to model dependent variables to determine the expected probability of success of belonging to a certain group. For instance, given a set of independent variables (e.g., age, income, and education level of credit card or mortgage loan holders), we can model the probability of credit loan default using MLE, or we can determine the probability a person will contract a specific illness or survive this disease given the person's age, social status, blood pressure, medications taken, and so forth. A typical regression model is invalid because the errors are heteroskedastic and nonnormal, and the resulting estimated probability estimates will sometimes be above 1 or below 0. MLE analysis handles these problems using an iterative optimization routine. The data here represent a sample of several hundred previous loans, credit, or debt issues. The data show whether each loan had defaulted or not, as well as the specifics of each loan applicant's age, education level (1–3 indicating high school, university, or graduate professional education), years with current employer, and so forth. The idea is to model these empirical data to see which variables affect the default behavior of individuals, using Risk Simulator's Maximum Likelihood Models. The resulting model will help the bank or credit issuer compute the expected probability of default of an individual credit holder having specific characteristics.

To run the analysis, follow the instructions given here:

1. Start Excel and open the example model *Risk Simulator | Example Models | 01 Advanced Forecast Models.*
2. Go to the *MLE* worksheet.
3. Select the data area including the headers or cells *B4:J504* and click on *Risk Simulator | Forecasting | MLE LIMDEP.* Select *the Dependent Variable as Defaulted* and click *OK.* Review the generated forecasts and charts.
   - *Exercise Question:* What does "limited dependent variable" mean?
   - *Exercise Question:* What types of dependent variable data can be used in this logit, probit, and tobit model?
   - *Exercise Question:* Follow the preceding instructions to compute the expected probability of default of an individual with the following information:

Age	35
Education Level	2
Years with Current Employer	10
Years at Current Address	10
Household Income (Thousands $)	50
Debt to Income Ratio (%)	0
Credit Card Debt (Thousands $)	0
Other Debt (Thousands $)	0

10 Nonlinear Extrapolation

Nonlinear extrapolation involves making statistical projections by using historical trends that are projected for a specified period of time into the future. It is only used for time-series forecasts. Extrapolation is fairly reliable, relatively simple, and inexpensive. However, extrapolation, which assumes that recent and historical trends will continue, produces large forecast errors if discontinuities occur within the projected time period.

To run the nonlinear extrapolation model, follow these steps:

1. Start Excel and open the example model *Risk Simulator | Example Models | 01 Advanced Forecast Models.*
2. Go to the *Nonlinear Extrapolation* worksheet.

3. Select the data area excluding the headers or cells *E13:E24* and click on *Risk Simulator | Forecasting | Nonlinear Extrapolation*. Input the number of periods to forecast as *3*, use the *Automatic Selection* option, and click *OK*. Review the report and chart that are created.
   - *Exercise Question:* What is a polynomial function versus a rational function?
   - *Exercise Question:* How many periods into the future may be considered a reasonable forecast assuming there are 12 periods of historical data?
   - *Exercise Question:* Would this model be appropriate for cross-sectional data?

11 Multiple Regression

To run the multiple regression analysis, follow these steps:

1. Start Excel and open the example model *Risk Simulator | Example Models | 01 Advanced Forecast Models.*
2. Go to the *Regression* worksheet.
3. Select the data area including the headers or cells *B5:G55* and click on *Risk Simulator | Forecasting | Regression Analysis*. Select the *Dependent Variable* as the variable *Y*, leave everything else alone, and click *OK*. Review the generated report.
   - *Exercise Question:* Which of the independent variables are statistically insignificant, and how can you tell? That is, which statistic did you use?
   - *Exercise Question:* How good is the initial model's fit?
   - *Exercise Question:* Delete the entire variable columns of data that are insignificant and rerun the regression (i.e., select the column headers in Excel's grid, right-click, and delete). Compare the *R-Square* and *Adjusted R-Square* values for both regressions. What can you determine?
   - *Exercise Question:* Will R-square always increase when you have more independent variables, regardless of their being statistically significant? How about adjusted R-square? Which is a more conservative and appropriate goodness-of-fit measure?
   - *Exercise Question:* What can you do to increase the adjusted R-Square of this model? *Hint:* Consider nonlinearity and some other econometric modeling techniques.
   - *Exercise Question:* Run an Auto-Econometric model on this dataset and select the nonlinear and interacting option and see what happens. Does the generated model better fit the data?

12 Logistic S-Curve

A logistic function or logistic curve models the S-curve of growth of some variable *X*. The initial stage of growth is approximately exponential; then, as competition arises, the growth slows, and at maturity, growth stops. These functions find applications in a range of fields, from biology to economics. For example, in the development of an embryo, a fertilized ovum splits, and the cell count grows: 1, 2, 4, 8, 16, 32, 64, and so on. This is exponential growth. But the fetus can grow only as large as what the uterus can hold, so other factors start slowing down the increase in the cell count, and the rate of growth slows (but the baby is still growing, of course). After a suitable time, the child is born and keeps growing. Ultimately, the cell count is stable; the person's height is constant; and the growth has stopped, at maturity. The same principles can be applied to population growth of animals or humans, as well as the market penetration and revenues of a product, with an initial growth spurt in market penetration, but over time, the growth slows due to competition and eventually the market declines and matures.

To generate an S-curve forecast, follow the instructions given here:

1. Start Excel and open the example model *Risk Simulator | Example Models | 01 Advanced Forecast Models*.
2. Go to the *S-Curve* worksheet.
3. Click on *Risk Simulator | Forecasting | JS Curves* and click on *S-Curve*. Use *Starting Value = 200, Growth Rate = 10 percent, Saturation Level = 6000, End Period = 100,* and click *OK* to run the forecast. Spend some time reviewing the forecast report.
   - *Exercise Question:* Can S-curves be used to forecast cross-sectional data, or are they only appropriate for time-series data?
   - *Exercise Question:* How would one obtain the value of the saturation level? What does "saturation level" mean?

13 Stochastic Processes (Random Walk, Brownian Motion, Mean-Reversion, Jump-Diffusion)

A stochastic process is a sequence of events or paths generated by probabilistic laws. That is, random events can occur over time but are governed by specific statistical and probabilistic rules. The main stochastic processes include random walk or Brownian motion, mean-reversion, and jump-diffusion. These processes can be used to forecast a multitude of variables that seemingly follow random trends, but yet are restricted by probabilistic laws. We can use Risk Simulator's Stochastic Process module to simulate and create such processes. These processes can be used to forecast a multitude of time-series data including stock prices, interest rates, inflation rates, oil prices, electricity prices, commodity prices, and so forth.

To run this forecast method, follow these instructions:

1. Start Excel and open the example model *Risk Simulator | Example Models | 01 Advanced Forecast Models*.
2. Click on *Risk Simulator | Forecasting | Stochastic Processes*.
3. Enter a set of relevant inputs or use the existing inputs as a test case. Then you can select the relevant process to simulate. Click *Update Chart* several times to view the updated computation of a single path each time. When ready, click *OK* to generate the process.
4. Rerun the stochastic process module and try out other processes. Using the default sample inputs, modify some of them and see what happens to the sample generated path as you click *Update Chart* repeatedly. For instance, select the mean-reversion process and change the reversion rate from 5% to 1%, and then to 10% to see what happens to the chart when you click on *Update Chart* a few times. Be very careful with your choice of inputs because sometimes large values will invalidate the process and it will not run.
   - *Exercise Question:* How does a mean-reversion process compare to a Brownian motion random walk process?
   - *Exercise Question:* What types of variables might be best suited for a random walk process versus a mean-reversion process versus a jump-diffusion process?

14   Time-Series Decomposition

Time-series forecasting decomposes the historical data into the baseline, trend, and seasonality, if any. The models then apply an optimization procedure to find the alpha, beta, and gamma parameters for the baseline, trend, and seasonality coefficients and then recompose them into a forecast. In other words, this methodology first applies a "backcast" to find the best-fitting model and best-fitting parameters of the model that minimize forecast errors, and then proceeds to "forecast" the future based on the historical data that exist. This process, of course, assumes that the same baseline growth, trend, and seasonality hold going forward. Even if they do not—say, when there exists a structural shift (e.g., company goes global, has a merger or spin-off, etc.)—the baseline forecasts can be computed and then the required adjustments can be made to the forecasts.

To run these forecast models, follow these steps:

1. Start Excel and open the example model *Risk Simulator | Example Models | 01 Advanced Forecast Models*.
2. Go to the *Time-Series Decomposition* worksheet.
3. Create a new profile at *Risk Simulator | New Simulation Profile* if you wish the software to automatically generate assumptions for the forecast. Otherwise, if you do not need the assumption, a new profile is not required.
4. Select the data excluding the headers or cells *E25:E44*.
5. Click on *Risk Simulator | Forecasting | Time-Series Analysis* and choose *Auto Model Selection*, set *Forecast = 4, Periods and Seasonality = 4 Periods*. Note that you can only select *Create Simulation Assumptions* if an existing Simulation Profile exists. Click *OK* to run the analysis. Review the generated report and chart.
   - *Exercise Question:* What do the alpha, beta, and gamma mean or represent?
   - *Exercise Question:* What are the three elements that a time-series analysis decomposes into?
   - *Exercise Question:* Can time-series analysis be used to forecast cross-sectional data? How about for panel data?
   - *Exercise Question:* How accurate are the forecast results? How can you tell? What does each of the error measures represent in the report?
   - *Exercise Question:* How is heteroskedasticity modeled in this forecast method? *Hint:* Look at each of the input assumptions automatically set up in the report.

15   Trendlines

To run trendlines analysis, follow the steps given here:

1. Start Excel and open the example model *Risk Simulator | Example Models | 01 Advanced Forecast Models*.
2. Go to the *Time-Series Decomposition* worksheet.
3. Select the data excluding the headers or cells *E25:E44*.
4. Click on *Risk Simulator | Forecasting | Trendlines*, select the trendlines you wish to run or leave everything checked by default, and click *OK* to run. Review the generated report.
   - *Exercise Question:* Is a low p-value or a high p-value a better fit?
   - *Exercise Question:* Would you rather have a low or high R-squared value, and what does R-square here represent?

9 Sustainable Growth and Credit Risk Management

Chapter Outline

Growth is important to financial health, but it can be too rapid for an obligor's own good. Too rapid sales expansion can put excessive pressure on a firm's financial structure. In addition, the more accelerated the growth rate, the greater the requirement for funds to support growth—particularly if the growth is exponential and the borrower is saddled with high operating leverage. The resulting high debt ratios could end in financial turmoil, leaving the firm with few suppliers or customers. The sustainable growth model can help bankers and customers alike bring the capital structure into equilibrium with targeted sales.

The *sustainable growth rate* is the maximum growth rate in sales (over the foreseeable future) that a firm can achieve without placing excessive strain on its financial structure. In simple terms, operations need money to make money. Sustainable growth solutions center on boosting equity when volume accelerates, thus maintaining the right balance between liabilities and equity. Industry benchmarks act as points of reference—and reflect the cumulative decisions of management, lenders, suppliers, customers, and competitors. Whenever the relationship between liabilities and net worth is significantly below industry standards, questions arise about management's competence and the firm's unsystematic risk control. Just look at the spreads between treasuries and the rates charged on corporate issues sitting in the lowest quartile of their respective industry.

Credit Engineering for Bankers. DOI: 10.1016/B978-0-12-378585-5.10009-0

The *sustainable growth model* is a special case cash flow model that measures the probability that increases (in sales) of high leveraged, rapid growth companies stress out the financial structure. The model helps identify the proportion of growth fueled through internal versus external cash flow. The results are set to different degrees of tolerance by manipulating specific variables to determine various levels of risk. Thus, sustainable growth acts as a telescope focused on the projected cash flow statement. For example, if the model reveals that 90% of sales growth targeted for the foreseeable future will be financed externally while the borrower is currently debt saturated, the situation could get out of hand, and fast.

We determine the sustainable growth rate by setting up (X) variables, including projected sales, assets, profit margin, dividend payout, and spontaneous liabilities, and solving for (Y), the sustainable growth rate. Again, sustainable growth runs are singularly important for highly leveraged, rapid growth operations since their cash flows are often volatile and unpredictable. These units operate in an environment that is much riskier than any other period in a typical four-phase industry life cycle since unsystematic (company-specific) default risks are unique and difficult to analyze. Let's see how the rapid growth phase works in terms of the industry life cycle:

Phase 1: Start-Up. Firms starting out face a high risk of financial distress, and higher risks require special financing: venture capital. Venture capital investment companies structure deals with convertibles, warrants, or stock, or may extend credit calling for substantial risk premiums.

Phase 2: Rapid Growth. Following inception, a successful firm with good growth potential will enter phase two of its life cycle. The firm has achieved initial success, may grow rapidly, and start to earn profits. However, the small increment to equity generated by earnings retention is often too inconsequential to finance the insatiable appetite for new assets required by rapid growth firms. Creditors advancing funds at relatively low-risk premiums do not often know if loans represent down payments for accelerating credit demands—until the firm implodes—or whether loans can be successfully amortized through internal cash flow, which is the aftereffect of slower growth.

If rapid growth continues for long, the situation may further deteriorate, making it abundantly clear from the bank's standpoint that equity injections are required. Unsystematic risk (debt to equity ratio) will exceed judicious limits, yet the firm may be reluctant to bring in outside capital because owners are unwilling to share control, give up tax benefits (of debt financing), or dilute earnings. The sustainable growth model helps bankers understand phase-two default risk.

Phase 3: Mature or Stable Growth. The mature phase of a firm's (or industry's) life cycle is one in which growth rates for price, book value, earnings, and dividends are approximately the same and are consistent with general economic growth. In the mature phase, operating activities throw off more cash, while growth requirements diminish sufficiently to lower investing activities—particularly in capital expansion areas. Financing requirements drop as more cash is generated than absorbed. The firm reduces debt levels with more ease while raising dividend payout.

Phase 4: Decline. Sales declines—the result of heightened competition or changes in consumer demand—force down profits, Operating cash cannot cover working capital and capital expenditures, and reduced investment activities provide limited cash flow. At this stage, the firm should be paying down substantial amounts of debt and may engage in stock repurchases to further shrink its size. The firm may seek out growth acquisitions to provide a longer lease on life.

The Sustainable Growth Model

Successful firms move assets through operations efficiently; product lines produce healthy profits; and equity base, along with the rest of the capital structure, strengthens. For companies in the rapid growth stage of the business cycle, this success is a somewhat difficult goal to attain. Characteristically, companies in this phase experience rapid expansion in sales along with receivables, inventory, and fixed assets. Financial problems accelerate when a borrower's insatiable appetite for core assets and capital expansion overwhelms modest profit contributions to equity. As is shown in Chapter Eight, the standard forecast model that follows considers this.

$$F = A_1/S \, (\Delta S) + \Delta NFA - L_1/S \, (\Delta S) - P(S + \Delta S)(1 - d) + R$$

$$E = (A/S - L_1/S) - (P/G)(1 + G)(1 - D) + R$$

$$g^* = \frac{P(1-D)(1+L)}{A/S-P(1-D)(1+L)}$$

$$L^* = T[(A/S) - P(1 - D)] - P(1 - D)/[P(1 - D)(1 + T)]$$

where:

A = total assets projected
A_1 = projected spontaneous assets
D (or d) = dividend payout rate
E = projected percent of sales growth externally financed
F = projected financial needs (–F = cash surplus)
g^* = sustainable growth rate
L = maximum leverage (to retain financial solvency)
L_1 = spontaneous liabilities
L^* = equilibrium leverage
P = projected profit margin
R = projected debt maturities
S = projected sales
ΔS = change in sales
T = projected sales growth rate (targeted growth rate)
ΔNFA = change in net fixed assets

Consider the historical financial statements of Landon Inc. for the fiscal period ending December 31, 2010. This young growth company is a producer of cable for the computer industry and is requesting a $50 million loan for plant expansion. The expansion program is needed to raise operating leverage, reduce labor costs, improve production efficiency, and increase the gross profit margin. Management presented the following historical and projected financial statements to their bankers in support of their request for a loan:

Landon Inc. Historical Balance Sheet 12/31/10 (in Thousands $)

Cash	2,000	.02
Accounts Receivable	4,000	.04
Inventories	54,000	.54
Net Plant and Equipment	60,000	.60
Total Assets	120,000	1.20
Accounts Payable	20,000	.20
Accruals	6,000	.06
Long-Term Debt	44,000	Constant*
Capital Stock	10,000	Constant*
Paid in Capital	10,000	Constant*
Retained Earnings	30,000	Earnings Retention
Total Liabilities and Equity	120,000	

*Financing decision; does not vary with sales.

Landon Inc. Historical Income Statement 12/31/10 (in Thousands $)

		Percent of Sales
Net Sales	100,000	1.00
Cost of Goods Sold	75,000	.75
Gross Margin	25,000	.25
Expenses (including Taxes)	23,000	.23
Net Income	2,000	.02
Projected Sales 2011:	150,000	

Landon Inc. Projected Balance Sheet 12/31/11 (in Thousands $)

Cash	3,000	.02
Accounts Receivable	6,000	.04
Inventories	81,000	.54
Net Plant and Equipment	90,000	.60
Total Assets	180,000	1.20
Accounts Payable	30,000	.20
Accruals	9,000	.06
Long-Term Debt	44,000	Constant
Capital Stock	10,000	Constant
Paid in Capital	10,000	Constant
Retained Earnings	33,000*	Earnings Retention
Available Capitalization	136,000	
Financial Needs	*44,000*	*Derived*
Total Liabilities and Equity	180,000	

*$30,000 + .02($150,000) – 0 = $33,000

Landon Inc. Forecast Income Statement 12/31/11 (in Thousands $)

		Percent of Sales
Net Sales	150,000	1.00
Cost of Goods Sold	112,500	.75
Gross Margin	37,500	.25
Expenses (including taxes)	34,500	.23
Net Income	3,000	.02

The firm's financial needs can also be derived from:

$$F = A/S(\Delta S) - L_1/S(\Delta S) - P(S + \Delta S)(1 - d)$$

Thus:

$$F = 180,000/150,000(50,000) - 39,000/150,000(50,000) - .02(150,000)$$
$$(1 - 0) = 44,000$$

The percent of sales increase that needs to be externally financed can be found by:

$$E = (A/S - L_1/S) - P/G(1 + G)(1 - D)$$

Thus:

$$E = [(180,000/150,000) - (39,000/150,000)] - .02/.5(1 + .5)(1 - 0) = .88$$

Eighty-eight percent of sales growth will be financed externally. If Landon were leveraged at fiscal, the projection period adds to leverage due to the imbalance between internal and external financing. Since sales growth is 50% in the first projection period, $.88(50,000) = 44,000$, as before. While the "E" formula is efficacious for mature firms, we need a more powerful equation for Landon Inc. We shall use the sustainable growth model to help us understand this lending deal.

As we can see from the sustainable growth equation, a firm's financial needs increase if asset efficiency, profits, or the retention rate $(1 - d)$ decline. In contrast, reliance on trade credit and/or accruals will reduce external financing requirements. The sustainable growth model's powerful logic rests with the notion that the financial structure of a fast-growing, highly leveraged firm is already near a fixed saturation point. Increasing leverage beyond that point causes loan risk premiums to skyrocket following the change in unsystematic risk. The sustainable growth rate is estimated:

$$g^* = \Delta S/S = \frac{P(1 - d)(1 + L)}{A/S - P(1 - d)(1 + L)}$$

We can easily derive the sustainable growth rate from the financial needs equation starting with a set of four standard sustainable growth assumptions:

1. No equity issues permitted while the company is in the sustainable growth mode
2. Constant dividend payout
3. Stable financial structure
4. Constant capital output ratio

In effect, we take a snapshot of the capital structure—stopping time in a mathematical manner of speaking. By withholding equity, we determine how the capital structure looks without equity injections; that is, can the firm sustain its financial health without additional equity inflows? Also, dividend payout, profit margin, and the debt to equity ratio are held constant as well—requirements to set the math in place. We now rework the equation:

$$F = A/S(\Delta S) - L_1/S(\Delta S) - P(S + \Delta S)(1 - d)$$

by adding a lag variable $(S + \Delta S)$ and rearranging terms assuming no equity financing except retained earnings:

$$A/S(\Delta S) = [F + L_1/S(\Delta S)] + P(S + \Delta S)(1 - d)$$

where $A/S(\Delta S)$ = incremental spontaneous assets; $F + LI/S(\Delta S)$ = incremental external financing (all debt); and $P(S + \Delta S)(1 - d)$ = profit retention. The expression $F + L_1/S(\Delta S)$ contains the redundant variable F, financial needs, which we eliminate (Table 9.1).

Simplifying the term $F + L1/S(\Delta S)$ with the given assumption of stable capital structure, we have D/E = D/E and $\Delta D = \Delta E(D/E)$, where D/E = L, or leverage. We can now substitute: $\Delta D = \Delta E/(L)$. That is to say, an increase in equity (from retained earnings—remember our assumption!) is followed by a proportional increase in debt. We see from the preceding that since ΔE can only come about as $P(S + \Delta S)(1 - d)$, we substitute for that term and obtain:

$$\Delta D = P(S + \Delta S)(1 - d)L$$

Setting this back into the equation, we obtain:

$$A/S(\Delta S) = P(S + \Delta S)(1 - d)L + P(S + \Delta S)(1 - d)$$

Simplifying:

$$S(\Delta S) = [P(S + \Delta S)(1 - d)L]/A + [P(S + \Delta S)(1 - d)]/A$$
$$= [P(S + \Delta S)(1 - d)(1 + L)]/A$$
$$= [P(S)(1 - d)(1 + L)]/A + [P\Delta S(1 - d)(1 + L)]/A$$

Table 9.1 Derivation: Eliminating the Variable F

This Year's Balance Sheet	From Equation (1)	Next Year's Balance Sheet	Assumptions
Assets	$A/S(\Delta S)$	Last year's assets plus the change in assets	
Debt	$F + LI/S(\Delta S)$	Last year's debt plus the change in debt	Financial needs: all debt plus incremental accounts payable and accruals (operating cash sources). See assumption (1).
Equity	$P(S + \Delta S)(1 - d)$	Last year's equity plus the change in equity	Earnings retention only. See assumption (1).

$$\Delta S/S = [P(S + \Delta S)(1 - d)(1 + L)]/A$$
$$= [P(S)(1 - d)(1 + L)]/A + [(P\Delta S)(1 - d)(1 + L)]/A$$

Thus:

$$\Delta S/S^2 = [P(1 - d)(1 + L)]/A + [(\Delta S/S)(P(1 - d)(1 + L)]/A$$

Finally, sustainable growth rate falls out:

$$g^* = \Delta S/S = \frac{P(1 - d)(1 + L)}{A/S - P(1 - d)(1 + L)}$$

The model may be adjusted to derive equilibrium leverage (L), given the firm's targeted growth rate (T), when T is substituted for the sustainable growth rate (g*).

The Two Conditions for "L": the Debt/Equity Ratio

The sustainable growth rate (g*) shows if the company is inundated with too much debt. If the sustainable growth rate falls below the targeted growth rate (T), excessive leverage will likely prevent the company from achieving its growth objectives. This result is readily seen with three cases:

Case One: Set L, the debt/equity ratio, at the maximum levels allowable. The ratio may be set at the industry unsystematic risk maximum, "bankruptcy" leverage, or simply at the lender's tolerance level.

Case Two: Set g* equal to the targeted growth rate and solve for L to secure the debt/equity ratio in equilibrium with the borrower's targeted growth rate. The question is, simply: If the borrower continues its growth pattern, how high will leverage climb assuming the firm raises no new equity?

Formula:

$$T = \frac{P(1 - d)(1 + L)}{A/S - P(1 - d)(1 + L)}$$

Example Case One

Here we see that the sustainable growth model identifies asset management, dividend payout, and operating and leverage imbalance. Landon's lenders asked for new projections, citing that sales growth of 50% in the first projection period (just examined) was far too optimistic. Consequently, the firm met again with its bankers and presented a set of projections (Figure 9.1). They insist that while sales were pegged too high, improved manufacturing techniques will boost productivity and increase the net profit margin to 7%. Ratios were extracted from the new projections, including the net profit margin, dividend payout rate, assets to sales, and targeted growth rate. Projections include the plant expansion program related to the loan request.

Solving for the sustainable growth rate where:

A = Projected assets
D = Dividend payout rate

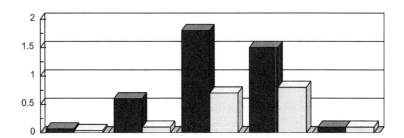

	Profit Margin	Dividend Payout	Capital Output	Leverage Limit	Target Growth
■ High Risk	7.0%	60.0%	180.0%	150.0%	10.0%
☐ Industry	4.0%	10.0%	70.0%	80.0%	10.0%

Figure 9.1 Summary of Landon's Projected Ratios versus the Industry Average.

g* = Sustainable growth rate
L = Maximum leverage allowable by the bankers.
S = Projected sales

we get:

$$g^* = \frac{P(1-d)(1+L)}{A/S - P(1-d)(1+L)} = \frac{.07(1-.6)(1+1.50)}{1.8 - .07(1-.6)(1+1.50)} = .04$$

This firm can sustain a 4% growth rate without increasing its debt/equity ratio above 150%. However, Landon's sales growth rate is targeted at 10%. If the company grows at a higher rate than the sustainable growth rate, the firm's current debt to equity ratio will increase beyond the 150% leverage ceiling set by the lenders.

A 10% growth rate has a negative affect on cash flow. Without adequate cash availability, operating leverage tends to increase as additional debt is raised to cover cash shortfalls. A high degree of both operating leverage and financial leverage may place the firm in jeopardy. If a firm has a significant degree of operating leverage, a high level of sales must be attained to reach its break-even point. Any changes in the sales level will have a substantial impact on earnings before interest and taxes (EBIT). Changes to EBIT directly affect net income, return on equity, and earnings per share. Financial leverage influences profits in much the same way: The higher the leverage, the higher the break-even point for sales and the greater the effect on profits from fluctuations in sales volume. Therefore, if Landon Inc. has a significant degree of both operating leverage and financial leverage, even minute changes in the level of sales will create wide fluctuations in net income, return on equity, and earnings per share. This potential for increased volatility is something the firm cannot afford.

Will the firm need to revert to increased borrowings to finance differences between internal and external financing? Here we are concerned with the effect recessions have on a company's financial condition. During a period of economic slowdown, sales may decrease sufficiently to cause cash flow streams to run dry. Such a situation means more money must be spent on new asset purchases, requiring a corresponding increase in sales and internal cash flow to match the purchases of the assets. The firm's bankers are well aware that without an adequate source of cash, the areas where debt funds are used (debt payments, etc.) run the risk of being in default, therefore putting the bank's investment in jeopardy. Landon's creditors can determine that an imbalance between internal and external cash flow will occur by comparing the firm's sustainable growth rate to its targeted growth rate.

Example Case Two

Set g* equal to the targeted growth rate, T, and solve for L to obtain the debt/equity ratio in equilibrium with the borrower's targeted growth rate:

$$g^* = T = \frac{P(1-d)(1+L)}{A/S - P(1-d)(1+L)}$$

$$.10 = \frac{.07(1-.6)(1+L)}{1.8 - .07(1-.6)(1+L)}$$

$$L = 4.84$$

Solving for L leaves a value of 4.84. Thus, leverage must increase to 484% for the sales growth and the financial structure to join in equilibrium. The firm's growth must be tied to its financial structure. Since the maximum allowable debt/equity ratio that the firm's lenders originally set was 150%, the deal, as presented, will not be approved. While high leverage might provide high returns for shareholders, this possibility is not the bank's major concern. Levels of acceptable leverage are proportional to the reliability of Landon's projected cash flow. The characteristics of both the company and its industry, along with specifics of the transaction, are essential when management and its creditors set acceptable or tolerance leverage; leverage tolerance levels will be governed by sets of very specific factors that decide unsystematic risk.

For example, certain debt structures such as having a layer of mezzanine capital subordinate to other creditor claims might justify a higher tolerance level. Then again, if the company is in a very cyclical industry subject to rapid technological obsolescence making cash flow more difficult to predict, creditors might set a higher leverage tolerance. Landon's profit margin is influenced by this firm's overall performance and its relationship to the industry. Within the analysis, operating trends will be carefully examined, as well as the company's position in the industry.

Solving Sustainable Growth Problems

Sustainable growth problems are resolved by equity infusions, reducing the capital output ratio (asset/sales), reducing dividends, and increasing profits. Pruning profits, which might include such strategies as selling off unprofitable divisions, is another solution to sustainable growth problems. Knowing when rapid growth levels off, as generally occurs when the mature phase begins, is interpreted as a solution, as well. Once the firm is in the mature phase of its company life cycle, cash inflows pick up, overall financial and operating risk decreases, and working capital becomes more predictable.

If selling new equity is not feasible, a firm may cut the dividend payout ratio or simply increase leverage. A cut in dividend payout increases the sustainable growth rate by increasing the portion of earnings retained in the business, while increasing leverage raises the amount of debt the firm can add for each dollar of retained profits. As we noted, however, there are limits to the use of debt financing. All firms have a creditor-imposed debt capacity that restricts the amount of leverage the company can use. As leverage increases, the risks carried by owners and creditors rise, as do the costs of securing additional capital.

The most conservative solution to resolving sustainable growth problems is to simply reduce growth to a level that is compatible with the company's current dividend or financing policies. These solutions must be approached prudently.

Issue Equity

As a potential solution to sustainable growth problems, the timing of equity issues should be well planned so serious share dilution is avoided. If a firm is willing and able to raise new equity capital by selling shares, its sustainable growth problems simply disappear. Note the following pitfalls of this approach:

- This may be difficult to do in a small firm with limited access to the venture capital market.
- Most countries do not have active, developed equity markets.
- New equity is expensive, it dilutes ownership, and it is likely to reduce earnings per share.

Define the Targeted Growth Period

When actual growth exceeds sustainable growth, the first step is to determine just how long the situation is likely to continue. If Landon's growth rate is likely to decline in the near term as the firm reaches maturity, the problem is temporary and can probably be solved by increasing leverage to feasible levels. Later, when actual growth falls below the sustainable growth rate, cash is generated, not absorbed, and loans can be repaid. The key, then, is to know with some degree of precision when rapid growth will end and a slower period expansion will take place will reduce a sustainable growth problem.

Improve the Capital/Output Ratio (Assets/Sales)

The assets to sales ratio is an important benchmark for measuring sustainable growth problems. The ratio is set (in the equation) to represent the base (before profit retention) on which an appropriate and sustainable growth rate is calculated. If this rate exceeds a tolerable level, we know leverage will rapidly increase. Management largely decides capital output, as its policies give rise to expansion. Analyzing the effectiveness of these policies, we easily find a tolerable growth rate (for g^*), set projected debt levels for L, and calculate an equilibrium assets/sales ratio. Covenants might be written to ensure management administers the firm's asset portfolio to sustainable growth guidelines. If they fail, problems show up in projections.

As shown previously, unmanaged growth forces a firm to borrow from external sources with little restraint because the appetite for funds is enormous—resulting in a rising debt ratio. A high debt level reduces loan protection, since it effectively blocks external equity infusions. In addition, as leverage increases within the sustainable growth universe, cash flows need to be channeled to debt service, cannibalizing operating cash flows. As mentioned before, a company cannot sustain high financial and operating leverage. The upshot of all of this is that with cash flow volatility comes increased credit risk.

If a firm's leverage is already too high, rather than using actual leverage in the model, use an industry average debt level and the same tolerable growth rate for g^*. The derived equilibrium assets to sales ratio should be compared to the actual ratio of that firm to again decide the appropriateness of asset management policies.

An asset to sales ratio that is in line with or lower than the industry norm depicts strong asset management practices. We can assume that asset utilization ratios provided in support of the loan agreement are being used efficiently and are growing at a pace that equity capital can support. In this case, if borrowers retire older debt uniformly and regularly, and cash flows are predictable, then credit risk is under control.

The most basic reason the capital output ratio is critically important is that it examines the level of assets required to produce a level of sales. In today's ultracompetitive environment, the left side of the balance sheet is managed aggressively to allow for sustainable growth. "Just in time" (JIT) inventory is one example of this type of management. Often, JIT inventory requires an expensive investment in technology. For instance, JIT can require scanners at the point of sale that transmit information directly to the supplier, who then ships additional items; this type of arrangement eliminates some cost of carrying inventory. Firms not leveraged to the hilt, with strong debt capacity and cash flow, are in a better position to finance sophisticated asset management systems.

However, Landon is in no position to bargain and may need to make hard decisions to reduce debt levels. For example, the firm may decide to contract out its production assignments to other vendors to reduce raw materials and work in progress inventory. This is not a sweet pill to swallow, as this activity will reduce profit margins as well, because goods will cost more to produce.

Increase Profit Margins

Improved profit margins reflect strategic operating and financing decisions. Strategies involve critically important decision areas, such as choice of product market areas in which the firm conducts its operations, whether to emphasize cost reduction or product differentiation, and whether to focus on selected product areas or seek to cover a broad range of potential buyers.

Reduce the Dividend Payout Ratio

Increases in both dividends and debt to equity ratios are potentially alarming because dividends reduce cash flow. In contrast, earnings retention indicates a reinvestment commitment.

Pruning Profits

When a firm spreads its resources across many products, it may not be able to compete effectively in all of them. It is better to sell off marginal operations and plow the proceeds back into the remaining businesses. Profit pruning reduces sustainable growth problems in two ways. It generates cash directly through the sale of marginal businesses, and it reduces actual sales growth by eliminating some sources of the growth. Profit pruning is also viable for a single-product company. The firm could prune out slow-paying customers or slow-turning inventory. This strategy lessens sustainable growth problems in three ways. It frees up cash, which can be used to support new growth; it increases asset turnover; and it reduces sales. The strategy reduces sales because tightening credit terms and reducing inventory selection will drive away some customers.

As shown earlier, Landon's g* is equal to 4%, and the company can grow at 4% without increasing leverage over 150%. However, Landon is forecasting a sales increase of 10%. Since the company is growing at a higher rate than the sustainable growth rate, the firm's current debt to equity ratio exceeds the 150% maximum level set by the firm's lenders. By setting the targeted growth rate at 10%, and solving for L, the lenders realize that leverage of 484% equates with the firm's 10% growth rate— much too high.

Landon Inc., not unlike most firms, will see its sales growth rate as the overriding issue to long-run financial planning. But in the search for more profit dollars, some managers ignore the relationship between sales growth and debt levels borrowers can support. Financial planning establishes guidelines for changes in the firm's financial structure.

The sustainable growth model depends on the major elements of the firm's financial planning. Landon's financial planning should include the following:

· Identifying financial goals.
· Analyzing the differences between these goals and the current financial status.
· A statement of actions needed to achieve financial goals.

The financial policies associated with growth and profitability include the following:

· The degree of financial leverage management chooses to employ.
· Dividend policy.
· Available investment opportunities now and into the future.

Landon's sales will be influenced by several factors. The prevailing economic conditions at a given time affect separate industries differently. For example, automobiles and home construction contracts fall during a recession, whereas food sales would tend to be stable. In analyzing the potential cash flows and credit risks of this firm, the prevailing market conditions will need to be considered first. These are factors that will affect an industry as a whole. You can analyze an individual company by finding its market share compared with its industry. Innovative firms with strong programs in research and development often achieve a competitive edge. Confirmed orders reveal future sales and production requirements, but projecting sales is sometimes difficult in emerging industries because the *predictability* horizon is so short.

While growth in leverage ratios also increases the sustainable growth rate, debt composition is also important. If an emerging company uses too much short-term debt, it may increase exposure to volatile and rising yield curves that may drastically impact the cost of funds and may also limit financing flexibility. In addition, other creditors may be skeptical of the company's future cash flows and may not want to increase exposures. Asset quality should be part of leverage evaluation because higher-quality assets provide space to increase debt prudently. Analysis of Landon's cash flow coverage ratios should be measured and trended over a period to decide if the leveraged company is experiencing current or near-term problems covering interest expense and satisfying debt payments.

A New Strategy: The Solution

Management, with guidance from its lenders, understood the company was experiencing the "too much, too soon" syndrome—the danger of growing too quickly in terms of its capital structure. While the founding entrepreneurs built a successful company, they attempted to create a challenge beyond their experience and capital capacity. As a result, cash flow shortages would soon occur, expenses would begin to exceed revenues at an increasing pace, and the company would begin to hemorrhage. Growth for the sake of growth alone, or believing anything will work, is dangerous and likely to result in wasted capital and financial distress. Thus, management will implement the following strategies, with results presented in Figure 9.2:

1. Landon Inc. will not issue new equity, preserving ownership control. Instead, as agreed, subcontractors will produce and ship to Landon's customers. Because the use of subcontractors will squeeze profit margins, sales will continue to grow at 10%, since Landon will absorb the higher costs of production.
2. Using subcontractors will lower inventory levels and reduce capital spending.

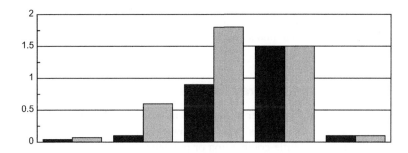

	Profit Margin	Dividend Payout	Capital Output	Leverage Limit	Target Grwoth
■ Revised Strategy	4.0%	10.0%	90.0%	150.0%	10.0%
▫ Original Strategy	7.0%	60.0%	180.0%	150.0%	10.0%

Figure 9.2 Results of the Revised Strategy.

3. Landon consents to tight control of receivables.
4. Dividends must be reduced.
5. Leverage will not transcend the ceiling imposed by the firm's lenders.

We enter the results in the sustainable growth equation:

$$g^* = \frac{P(1-d)(1+L)}{A/S - P(1-d)(1+L)} = \frac{.04(1 - .1)(1 + 1.50)}{.90 - .04(1 - .1)(1 + 1.50)} = .11$$

The previous condition was:

$$g^* = [.07 \, (1 - .6)(1 + 1.50)] / [1.8 - .07(1 - .6)(1 + 1.50)] = .04$$

The sustainable growth rate is 11%. Thus, the firm can expand at 11% a year over the foreseeable future without increasing leverage beyond 150%, the leverage ceiling. Since the business's 10% targeted growth rate is less than its 11% sustainable growth rate, leverage will fall below the maximum level permitted by the business's creditors. Poor asset management combined with an aggressive dividend policy—as we readily see—and an increase in the sustainable growth rate while profits declined caused the business's cash flow problems.

Curve Fitting

We all may have tried to draw a straight line through a maze of data plotted on an X–Y grid. The line, you hoped, would give you the general trend from the data and enable you to predict a Y value when you knew the X value. Although drawing lines to predict trends is easy, you can never be sure how well the lines fit the data. When Y depends on multiple sets of X, the problem becomes far too complex for hand-drawn lines.

Linear regression analysis and multiple regression analysis are the most well-known methods of finding trends, predicting the near future, and calculating dependent or unknown values. Linear regression analysis uses a set of X and Y data to calculate a line with the least amount of error. Multiple regression analysis uses multiple sets of data to find a multidimensional plane with the least amount of error in predicting Y.

Exponential Growth Regression Curve and the Sustainable Growth Model

Rapid growth rates, whether in nature or in business, usually can be described with an exponential curve. This type of growth happens in animal populations with plentiful food and little competition or predation. Such growth, we have seen, often occurs in the initial stages of rapidly expanding businesses. The *exponential curve fit* is an excellent tool for examining rapid or initial growth rates. We use it to examine growth rates as diverse as sales volume and tissue cultures. The key point is: The sustainable model's capacity to red flag thinly capitalized financial structures expands in proportion to the R square correlation score of growth rates and its regression line.

Logarithmic Regression Curve and the Sustainable Growth Model

Industries and animal populations often grow rapidly at first and then decline with time. Limited resources, competition, or predation causes the slowdown. Populations (whether industry or animal) that are approaching the saturation point grow along a *logarithmic curve*. The logarithmic curve illustrates a rapid growth, followed by a gradual decrease in growth rate. After growth and resources balance out, growth may continue at the same rate at which resources increase. When industries grow, they eventually reach the saturation point; from that point on, replacements or population growth accounts for most new sales. Growth rates for industries that have reached this level are nearly straight lines.

The sustainable growth model teaches us that both quantitative and qualitative analyses call for judgment. Combined with the qualitative factors we consider, the objective of growth/leverage mathematics (i.e., sustainable growth) is to offer an infrastructure for lending decisions, pricing, and tight loan agreements.

10 Specialized Lending Risk Rating

In October 2001, the Basel Committee's Models Task Force first proposed to treat specialized lending differently from other corporate loans under the internal ratings-based (IRB) approach. In its "Working Paper on the Internal Ratings Based Approach to Specialized Lending Exposures," the Task Force defined *specialized lending* (SL) products as including project finance (PF) loans, income-producing real estate (IPRE) loans, object finance (e.g., vessels, aircraft, and rolling stock), and commodities finance transactions. In this chapter, we deal specifically with the risk ratings of these SL products in context with Basel II Accord Section 249.[1]

---

[1] The authors acknowledge that much of the information in this chapter is drawn from the Basel Committee on Banking Supervision guidelines on *The Internal Ratings-Based Approach to Specialized Lending Exposures and Bank for International Settlements*. The risk rating systems themselves, "Supervisory Slotting Criteria for Specialized Lending," were presented in hard text and set in Excel by the authors so models could be applied in practice. Since SL risk ratings are acknowledged as a fundamental capital issue with regulators, much of the important source text remains in original form with the proper acknowledgement to the true experts/authors at the Bank for International Settlement and the Basel Committee on Banking Supervision.

The regulations specify that capital assigned against SL exposures is computed using one of three approaches:

1. *Standardized approach*—banks must allocate exposures into buckets of credit quality, and a capital percentage is assigned to each bucket.
2. *Foundation IRB approach*—lenders are able to use their own models to determine their regulatory capital requirement. Under the foundation IRB approach, lenders estimate a probability of default (PD), while the supervisor provides set values for loss given default (LGD), exposure at default (EAD), and maturity of exposure (M). These values are plugged into the lender's appropriate risk weight function to provide a risk weighting for each exposure or type of exposure.
3. *Advanced IRB approach*—lenders with the most advanced risk management and risk modeling skills are able to move to the advanced IRB approach, under which the lender estimates PD, LGD, EAD, and M. In the case of retail portfolios, only estimates of PD, LGD, and EAD are required, and the approach is known as *retail IRB*.

Banks that do not meet the requirements for the estimation of PD under the foundation approach for their SL assets are *required to use the standardized approach and map their internal risk grades to five supervisory categories, each of which is associated with a specific risk weight.*[2]

The characteristics that define the supervisory categories, and the probabilities of defaults associated with each category, have been developed to express the same degree of default risk across the four SL product lines: project, object, commodity finance, and real estate. As such, a PF exposure slotted in the "strong" PF supervisory category would be associated with the same PD as a real estate exposure that is slotted into the "strong" category. The supervisory default probabilities estimates are set out below. The values are based on industry consultation on the comparable riskiness of different SL exposure types, anecdotal and empirical evidence on the quality distribution of banks' SL portfolios, and analysis of default data from banks and external rating agencies.

Supervisory Slotting Class	1-Year PD	Approximate Correspondence to External Debt Rating rating
Strong	0.5%	BBB– or better
Fair	2.5%	B+ to BB+
Weak	12.5%	B or worse
Default	100%	D

SL encompasses exposures whereby the obligor's primary repayment source depends on the cash flow generated by financed assets rather than the financial strength of a business. Such exposures are embedded with special characteristics:

- Loans are directed to special purpose vehicles (SPVs) or entities created specifically to operate or finance physical assets.

[2] Basel II Accord Sections 244 to 269. The five supervisory categories associated with a specific risk weight are "Strong," "Good," "High Satisfactory," "Low Satisfactory," and "Weak."

- The borrowing entity has little, if any, material assets or does not conduct any other business activity, and thus no independent cash flow or other sources of payment except the specific assets financed; that is, the cash flow generated by the collateral is the loan's sole or almost exclusive source of repayment.
- The primary determinant of credit risk is the variability of the cash flow generated by the collateral rather than the independent capacity of a broader commercial enterprise.
- The loan represents a significant liability in the borrower's capital structure.
- Financing terms provide lenders with complete asset control and domination over the flow of funds the asset generates.

Corporate exposures are generally expressed as the debt obligations of corporations, partnerships, or single-entity businesses (proprietorships).

SL internal credit ratings play an important role not only as a "first step" in the credit risk measurement process but also as an important stand-alone risk management tool. Credit ratings are a basis for regular risk reports to senior management and boards of directors. Internal rating systems are also the basis for a continuous loan review process, under which large corporate credits generally are reviewed and regarded at least annually in order to focus attention on deteriorating credits well before they become "criticized" by examiners or external auditors.

Project Finance

Illustrative Example Project Finance Risk Rating System
Location: Models are available on the Elsevier Website www.ElsevierDirect.com
Brief Description: Supervisory slotting BIS risk rating system developed in Excel by the authors—from primary financial measures to security modules, Moody's-KMV, S&P default rates, project expected default frequency (EDF), loan loss provisions.

The International Project Finance Association (IPFA) defines this as the financing of long-term infrastructure, industrial projects, and public services based on a nonrecourse or limited recourse financial structure where project debt and equity used to finance the project are paid back from the cash flow generated by the project. This type of financing is usually for large, complex, and expensive installations that might include, for example, power plants, chemical processing plants, mines, transportation infrastructure, environment, and telecommunications infrastructure. Usually, a PF structure involves a number of equity investors, known as sponsors, as well as a syndicate of banks that provide loans to the operation. In such transactions, the lender is usually paid solely or almost exclusively out of the funds generated by the contracts for the facility's output, such as the electricity sold by a power plant. The borrower is usually a special purpose entity (SPE) that is not permitted to perform any function other than developing, owning, and operating the installation. Project lenders are given a lien on all of these assets and are able to assume control of a project if the project company has difficulties complying with the loan terms.

Generally, an SPE is created for each project, thereby shielding other assets owned by a project sponsor from the detrimental effects of a project failure. As an SPE, the project company has no assets other than the project. Capital contribution commitments by the owners of the project company are sometimes necessary to ensure that the project is financially sound. PF is often more complicated than alternative financing methods. Traditionally, PF has been most commonly used in the mining, transportation, telecommunication, and public utility industries. More recently, particularly in Europe, PF principles have been applied to public infrastructure under public–private partnerships (PPP) or, in the United Kingdom, Private Finance Initiative (PFI) transactions.[3]

Risk identification and allocation is a key component of PF. A project may be subject to a number of technical, environmental, economic, and political risks, particularly in developing countries and emerging markets. Financial institutions and project sponsors may conclude that the risks inherent in project development and operation are unacceptable. To cope with these risks, project sponsors in these industries (such as power plants or railway lines) are generally made up of a number of specialist companies operating in a contractual network with one another that allocates risk in a way that allows financing to take place. The various patterns of implementation are sometimes referred to as "project delivery methods." The financing of these projects must also be distributed among multiple parties, so as to distribute the risk associated with the project while simultaneously ensuring profits for each party involved. A complex PF structure may incorporate corporate finance, securitization, options, insurance provisions, or other types of collateral enhancement to mitigate unallocated risk.

Example[4]

A bank finances an SPV that will build and operate a project. If the bank is exposed to the key risks in the project—construction risk (the risk that the project will not be completed in a timely and/or cost effective manner), operational/technology risk (the risk that the project will not operate up to specifications), or market/price risk (the risk that the demand and the price of the output will fall and/or that the margin between output prices and input prices and production costs will deteriorate)—then the project should be classified as SL. Also, if a circular relationship exists between the end user's and the project's financial strength, the project should be classified as SL. This would be the case when an end user has limited resources or capacity to generate revenues apart from those generated by the project being financed, so that the end user's ability to honor its off-take contract depends primarily on the performance of the project.

We will explore an Excel version of Annex 4 Supervisory Slotting Criteria for Specialized Lending: Table 1_Supervisory Rating Grades for Project Finance Exposures. Rating components consist of a comprehensive set of building blocks that determines LGD, the project's risk grade, and the appropriate loan loss reserve.

---

[3] Wikipedia: Project Finance.

[4] Basel Committee on Banking Supervision, Working Paper on the Internal Ratings-Based Approach to Specialized Lending Exposures, October 2001, p. 2.

Basic Structure

1. Project ratings:
   a. S&P/Moody's credit assessment
   b. S&P/Moody's assessment 20-year average of 3-year cumulative default rates (CDRs)
   c. Basel proposed 3-year benchmarks monitoring level
   d. Basel proposed 3-year CDR benchmarks trigger level
2. Individual and cumulative grades within each rating module. The cumulative grades are determined by a weighting system and weights assigned by project bankers and project managers in analysis.
3. Modules include **Project Financial Measures** (market conditions, financial ratios, stress analysis, financial structure, currency risk); **Political and Legal Environment** (political risk, force measured risk, government support, legal and regulatory environment stability, support acquisition, and contract enforceability); **Transaction Characteristics** (design and technology risk, construction risk, completion guarantees, contractor track record, operating risk, off-take risk (1), off-take risk (2), supply risk, and real options); **Security Package** (assignment of contracts, pledge of assets, lender's control over cash flow, strength of the covenant package, and reserve funds); and **Composite** (each module's composite rating, final project grade before and after overrides, LGD, dollar exposure risk, S&P/Moody's assessment 20-year average 3-year cumulative default risk, and reserve for project write-off). Weighted and cumulative average default and recovery rates on PF loans measured against corporate finance loans are shown in Figure 10.1 and Version 2 Basel PF 6A/Recovery Rates. Recovery rates were 74.3% extracted from a sample of observations, while 311 observations of senior unsecured debt indicated a recovery rate of 46.2%.

Criteria

- *Market conditions*: It is important that the bank consider whether the project has a durable advantage in location, the cost, if there are few competing suppliers, and if demand is strong and growing.
- *Financial ratios*: Banks must determine and interpret financial measures considering the level of project risk. Project financial ratios include *cash available for debt service; debt service reserve account; earnings before interest and taxes plus depreciation and amortization; free cash flow; cost of debt; interest and debt service coverage ratios (DSCRs); minimum and average DSCR; loan life coverage ratio; cost-to-market price; and loan-to-value ratio.*
- *Stressed conditions*: Unexpected macroeconomic shocks can easily undermine a project. Banks must determine if the project can meet its financial obligations under the most severely stressed conditions.
- *Financial structure*: If the useful life of the project falls significantly below the tenure of the loan, risks may be significant.
- *Currency risk*: There may be risk of devaluation and/or inconvertibility of local currency into another currency. Banks must consider the risk that local currency will depreciate, whether revenue and cost streams are mismatched, or if there exists a substantial risk of currency inconvertibility.
- *Political risk*: This includes transfer risk taking into consideration project type and mitigants.
- *Government support*: In some countries, a key question is: What is a project's importance for the particular country over the long term? Lenders should verify that the project is of

DESCRIPTIVE STATISTICS ON RECOVERY RATES BY ASSET TYPE

Asset Type	Number of Observations	Mean	Median	Standard Deviation	Maximum	Minimum	Kolmogurnv Test	Rank Sum Test	Kruskal-Wallis Statistic
Project Finance	43	75.30%	100.00%	34.90%	100.00%	0%			
Leveraged Loans	203	78.03	95.26	29.56	151.01	0	1	0	0.7424
Secured Debt	339	68.55	75.56	32.68	111.49	0	1	0	0.0829
Senior Debt	814	67.33	78.05	34.19	12/5/1923	0	1	0	0.0567
Senior Unsecured	311	46.20	40.38	36.27	125.23	0	1	1	0

DESCRIPTIVE STATISTICS ON RECOVERY RATES: PROJECT FINANCE VS. LEVERAGED LOANS

Project Finance	43	75.39%	100.00%	34.90%	100.00%	0%			
Leveraged Loans	203	78.03	98.26	29.56	151.01	0	1	0	0.7421
LL. Rank 1	182	61.66	100.00	26.55	15111	0	1	0	0.8574
LL. Rank 2	19	51.29	50.85	34.33	104.36	0	I	1	0.0074
Not Classified	2	n/a	n/a	n/a	n/a	n/a	n/a	Na	n/a

Recovery rate greater than 100% can occur when a bank receives equity as part of a loan restructuring and the equity subsequently appreciates. Defaults with 100% account for less than 1% of the total number of observations.
A value of 1 indicates the distribution of recovery rates for this type of loon is significantly different from the distribution for project finance loans
A value near 0 indicates that the distribution for this type of loan is significantly different from the distribution for project finance loans
Leveraged loan contain second and unsecured corporate leans of companies with over $50 million in debt at the time of default

DEFAULT RATES ON PROJECT FINANCE AND CORPORATE FINANCE LOANS

	Project Finance Loans				Corporate Finance Loans	
	Default-Broadly Defined a.		Default - Narrowly Defined b.		Default-Broadly Defined	
Year	Weighted Avg. Marginal Default rates c.	Cumulative Average Default Rates d.	Weighted Avg. Marginal Default Rates c.	Cumulative Average Default Rate$_d$	Weighted Avg. Marginal Default Rates c.	Cumulative Average Default Rate$_d$
1	1.52%	1.52%	63%	0.63%	1.49%	149%
2	1.61	3.13	0.69	1.32	1.49	2.98
3	1.27	4.40	0.59	1.91	1.32	4.30
4	1.19	5.58	0.54	2.46	1.08	5.38
5	1.07	6.65	0.53	2.99	0.90	6.27
6	0.44	7.09	0.14	3.14	0.79	7.06
7	0.21	7.30	0.21	3.35	0.69	7.75
4	0.33	7.63	0.33	3.68	0.59	8.34
9	0.00	7.63	0.00	3.68	0.54	8.67
10	0.00	7.63	0.00	3.68	0.51	9.38

a. Borrower was unable to make a contractually scheduled payment of principal and/or interest This Includes disrupt payment, including default within the grace period. consensual restructuring, amendment of the credit repayment term and/or refinancing of the facility with the original lenders in order to give the *borrower* more
b. Excludes loans restructured. with no accounting loss but with change of amortization or extension of loans paid during the cure period (cure period is period borrow is allowed to remedy a default under a contract).
c. The weighted average of all static pool defaults in years 1. 2, etc.
d. Sum of weighted average marginal default rates.

Figure 10.1 Weighted and Cumulative Average Default and Recovery Rates.

strategic importance (preferably export oriented) and enjoys strong support from government.

- *Legal and regulatory environment*: The bank must carefully evaluate the legal and regulatory environment and risk of frequent changes in the law. Current or future regulatory issues may affect the project.
- *Support acquisition*: This means acquisition of all necessary supports and approvals for relief from local content laws.
- *Contract enforceability*: The bank must assure that contracts are enforceable—particularly contracts governing collateral and security—and the necessary permits are obtained. If there are major unresolved issues dealing with enforcement of contracts, they must be cleared.

- *Design and technology risk:* Unproven technology and design pose a significant project risk. An effort must be made to obtain the appropriate report or studies.
- *Construction risk:* Permits need to be obtained, and the bank should verify that no adverse conditions are attached. If some permits are still outstanding, their receipt should, at the least, be very likely.
- *Completion guarantees:* Completion should be assured and substantial liquidated damages paid, supported by the financial substance of sponsor. The bank should verify the sponsor's financial standing and track record.
- *Operating risk:* Operating and maintenance contracts should be strong and long term, backed by the operator's expertise, track record, and financial strength. The contracts should provide incentives and/or reserves. Banks should determine if the local operator is dependent on local authorities.
- *Off-take risk:* An off-taker is the purchaser of a project's output, while in an off-take agreement, the off-taker agrees to purchase all or a substantial part of the product produced by a project, which typically provides the revenue stream for a project's financing. Two possibilities exist: (1) if there is a take-or-pay or fixed-price off-take contract (the off-taker is the purchaser of a project's output) and (2) if there is no take-or-pay or fixed-price off-take contract (take-or-pay contract requires buyer to take and pay for the good or service only if it is delivered). If condition (1) applies, the bank should determine the creditworthiness of the off-taker, whether strong termination clauses exist, and if the tenure of the contract comfortably exceeds the maturity of the debt. If off-take risk (2) exists, the bank should verify that the project produces essential services or offers a commodity sold widely on a world market whereby the output can easily be absorbed at projected prices or, conservatively, even at lower than historic market growth rates.
- *Supply risk*: The bank should ensure that the supply contract is not short term. A long-term supply contract should not be completed with a financially weak supplier. Also check if the degree of price risk definitely remains and if the project relies to some extent on potential and undeveloped reserves.
- *Assignment of contracts and accounts and pledge of assets:* The assignment of contracts should be fully comprehensive. The bank should check to see if they have obtained first (perfected) security interest in all project assets, contracts, permits, and accounts necessary to run the project.
- *Lender's control over cash flow:* The lender's control over cash flow is improved by the use of independent escrow accounts and cash sweeps. An *independent escrow account* involves the right to hold funds in escrow—that is, a deposit held in trust by a third party to be turned over to the grantee on specified conditions. In PF, an escrow account is often used to channel funds needed to pay debt service. During a *cash sweep,* the entire cash flow available for debt service is used to repay principal and interest. Stand-alone cash sweep analysis is used to calculate the amount of time it takes to repay the project debt in full.
- *Strength of the covenant package:* The bank must have a sound process to monitor mandatory prepayments, payment deferrals, and payment cascade and dividend restrictions. The covenant package should be strong for the project because the project may issue unlimited additional debt to secure the bank's position.
- *Reserve funds:* It is imperative that the bank employ robust procedures to control debt service, operating and maintenance, renewal and replacement, and unforeseen events. Shorter than average coverage periods should be watched, as well as reserve funds funded from operating cash flows.

Object Finance

Illustrative Example Object Finance Risk Rating System

Location: Models are available on the Elsevier Website www.ElsevierDirect.com

Brief Description: Supervisory slotting Object finance BIS risk rating system developed in Excel by the authors—from primary financial measures to security package, suggested EDF, loan loss provisions.

Object finance refers to a method of funding the acquisition of physical assets (e.g., ships, aircraft, satellites, and railcars), where the repayment of the exposure is dependent on the cash flows generated by the specific assets that have been financed and pledged or assigned to the lender. A primary source of these cash flows might be rental or lease contracts with one or several third parties. In contrast, if the exposure is to a borrower whose financial condition and debt-servicing capacity enables it to repay the debt without undue reliance on the specifically pledged assets, the exposure should be treated as a collateralized corporate exposure. As a matter of principle, LGDs should reflect a bank's own loss experience, tempered with some conservatism.

Examples[5]

1. *A charter airline with an established business plan, many aircraft, and diversified service routes finances the purchase of additional aircraft to be used in its own operations. The airline establishes an SPV to own the subject aircraft. The bank lends to the SPV and takes a security interest in the aircraft. The SPV enters into a long-term lease with the airline. The lease's term exceeds the term of the underlying loan. The lease cannot be terminated under any condition. This exposure would be placed in the corporate exposure class because the repayment of the loan depends on the overall operations of the airline and is not unduly dependent on the specific aircraft as the primary source of repayment.*
2. *Same example as the preceding, except that (a) the lease term can be cancelled by the airline without penalty at some time before the end of the loan term, or (b) even if the lease is non-cancellable, the lease payments do not fully cover the aggregate loan payments over the life of the loan. This loan should be classified as object finance, given that the airline/lessee is not fully committed to a lease sufficient to repay the loan, so pass-through treatment is inappropriate.*

Rating component consists of a comprehensive set of building blocks that determines LGD, the asset's risk grade, and the appropriate loan loss reserve.

Basic Structure

1. Asset credit assessment using estimated default statistics.
2. Individual and cumulative grades within each rating module. The cumulative grades are determined by a weighting system and weights assigned by bankers evaluating the financing.
3. Modules include **Object Financial Measures** (market conditions, financial ratios, stress analysis, financial structure); **Political and Legal Environment** (political risk, legal and regulatory risk); **Transaction Characteristics** (financial terms compared to the economic

---

[5] Basel Committee on Banking Supervision, Working Paper on the Internal Ratings-Based Approach to Specialized Lending Exposures, October 2001, p. 4.

life of the asset); **Operating Risk** (permits licensing, scope and nature of operation and maintenance (O&M) contract, operator's financial strength); **Asset Characteristics** (configuration, size, design, and maintenance; resale value; sensitivity of the asset value and liquidity to economic cycle); **Strength of Sponsor** (operator's financial strength, sponsor's track record and financial strength); **Security Package** (asset control, rights and means at the lender's disposal to monitor, insurance against damages); and **Composite** (as with the PF system, each module's composite rating, final asset grade before/after overrides, estimated LGD, dollar exposure risk, and reserve for asset write-off).

Criteria

- *Market conditions:* The bank should ascertain that demand is strong and growing for the asset financed, and whether there exist strong entry barriers, low sensitivity to changes in technology, and a strong economic outlook for the asset.
- *Financial ratios:* Ratios are important determinates of the asset's financial potential and include DSCR and loan-to-value ratios. Financial ratios should be evaluated in context of the level of project risk.
- *Stress analysis:* A viable asset will enjoy stable long-term revenues capable of withstanding severely stressed conditions through an economic cycle.
- *Financial structure:* Asset liquidity should be evaluated as residual value provides lenders with degree of protection in the event cash flow is insufficient to retire loans.
- *Political risk, including transfer risk:* Banks should watch excessive exposures with no or weak mitigation instruments.
- *Legal and regulatory risks:* In the event the asset's debt service fails, banks will need to enforce contracts. Thus, jurisdiction is favorable to repossession and enforcement of contracts.
- *Transaction characteristics:* Financing tenure should be shorter than the economic life of the asset.
- *Asset characteristics:* The configuration, size, design, maintenance, and age (e.g., a plane or boat) should be checked against other assets in the same market. The criteria: strong advantage in design and maintenance and that the object meets a liquid market.
- *Resale value:* The bank should ensure that resale value does not fall below debt value.
- *Sensitivity of the asset value and liquidity to economic cycles:* Asset value and liquidity are relatively insensitive to economic cycles.
- *Asset control:* Legal documentation provides the lender effective control (e.g., a first perfected security interest, or a leasing structure including such security) on the asset, or on the company owning it.
- *Rights and means at the lender's disposal to monitor location and condition of the asset:* The lender is able to monitor the location and condition of the asset, at any time and place (regular reports, possibility to lead inspections).
- *Insurance against damages:* Strong insurance coverage including collateral damages with top quality insurance companies.

Commodities Finance

Commodities finance is defined as short term financing for the acquisition of readily marketable commodities that are to be resold and the proceeds applied to loan repayment.

Open Commodity Finance Risk Rating

The structured nature of the commodities finance is designed to compensate for the weak credit quality of the borrower. The exposure's rating reflects the self-liquidating nature of the transaction and the lender's skill in structuring the transaction rather than going through a traditional credit analysis. Basically, commodities finance deals with structured short-term lending to finance reserves, inventories, or receivables of exchange-traded commodities, such as crude oil, metals, and crops, whereby exposures are repaid from the proceeds of the sale of the commodity and the obligor operates no other activities, owns no other material assets, and thus has no independent means to satisfy the obligation.

Examples[6]

1. The bank extends short-term documentary trade credit to a small independent trading company that acts as an intermediary between producers and their customers. The trader specializes in a single commodity and a single region. Each commodity shipment handled by the trader is financed and secured separately. Credit is extended upon delivery of the commodity to the trader, who has already contracted for the resale of the commodity shipment. A trustworthy third party controls the shipment of the commodity, and the bank controls payment by the customer. This loan would be classified as a commodity finance exposure in the SL exposure class, since repayment depends primarily on the proceeds of the sale of the commodity.
2. The bank extends short-term documentary trade credit to a small trader. The circumstances are the same as in the preceding case, except that the trader has not yet contracted for the resale of the commodity. This loan would be classified as a corporate exposure, since it may not be self-liquidating, given that the trader has not hedged the transaction's market risk. The bank's credit exposure is primarily to the nonhedged trader taking a long position on the commodity.
3. The bank provides an unsecured nontransactional working capital loan to a small trader, either separately or as part of a transactional credit facility. Such an unsecured loan would be classified as a corporate exposure, since its repayment depends on the trader rather than on the revenues generated by the sale of any specific commodity shipment being financed.

Basic Structure

1. Asset credit assessment using estimated default statistics.
2. Individual and cumulative grades within each rating module. The cumulative grades are determined by a weighting system and weights assigned by bankers evaluating the financing.
3. Modules include **Financial Measures** (degree of overcollaterization); **Political and Legal Environment** (country risk, mitigation of country risks); **Asset Characteristics** (liquidity and susceptibility to damage); Strength of Sponsor (financial strength of trader; track record; including ability to manage the logistic process, trading controls, and hedging policies; quality of financial disclosure); and **Security Package** (asset control, insurance against damages).

---

[6] Basel Committee on Banking Supervision, Working Paper on the Internal Ratings-Based Approach to Specialized Lending Exposures, October 2001, p. 7.

Criteria

- *Degree of overcollateralization:* Should be strong. Loan value of collateral must be no greater than the current fair market value of the collateral at the time of drawing. Commodity collateral should be marked-to-market frequently and promptly whenever there is any indication of material depreciation in value or any default by the borrower. In the case of material depreciation of value, the commodity collateral must be revalued by a professional appraiser and not assessed by references to statistical methods only. These procedures must be fully reflected in the underlying loan agreement.
  - There must be liquid markets for the collateral to facilitate disposal and existence of publicly available market prices.
  - Periodic valuation revaluation process must include physical inspection of the collateral.
- *Country risk:* Strong exposure to country risk (in particular, inland reserves in an emerging country).
- *Mitigation of country risks:* Very strong mitigation, strong offshore mechanisms, strategic commodity, first class buyer.
- *Legal enforceability of physical collateral:* Banks must confirm enforceability and priority under all applicable laws with respect to the bank's security over the commodity collateral. Also, bankers must confirm security interests are properly and timely perfected, and, in line with this, the bank must continuously monitor the existence of priority liens, particularly governmental liens associated with unpaid taxes, wage withholding taxes, or social security claims.
- *Asset control:* The agreement must ensure that the bank can take command of collateral soon after default.
- *Asset characteristics:* Commodity is quoted and can be hedged through futures or OTC instruments. Commodity is not susceptible to damage.
- *Financial strength of trader:* Very strong, relative to trading philosophy and risks.
- *Track record, including ability to manage the logistic process:* Extensive experience with the type of transaction in question. Strong record of operating success and cost efficiency.
- *Trading controls and hedging policies:* Watch if trader has experienced significant losses on past deals.
- *Quality of financial disclosure:* All documentation related to credit-risk mitigation must be supported by legal opinions in all relevant jurisdictions in addition to documentation pertaining to the security interests themselves.
- *Asset control:* First perfected security interest provides the lender the legal control of the assets at any time if needed.
- *Insurance against damages:* The bank must ensure that the collateral is adequately insured against loss or deterioration, in that it has strong insurance coverage including collateral damages with top-quality insurance companies.

Income-Producing Real Estate, High-Volatility Commercial Real Estate Exposures, and Real Estate Projects Under Construction

Illustrative Examples: Risk Rating Complete Stabilized Property; Risk Rating Property Under Construction

Location: Models are available on the Elsevier Website www.ElsevierDirect.com
Brief Description: Supervisory slotting IPRE developed in Excel by the authors.

Income-Producing Real Estate

IPRE refers to a method of providing funding to real estate (such as office buildings to let, retail space, multifamily residential buildings, industrial or warehouse space, office parks, supermarkets, shopping centers, and hotels) where the prospects for repayment and recovery on the exposure depend primarily on the cash flows generated by the asset. The primary source of these cash flows would generally be lease or rental payments or the sale of the asset. The borrower may be, but is not required to be, an SPE, an operating company focused on real estate construction or holdings, or an operating company with sources of revenue other than real estate. The distinguishing characteristic of IPRE versus other collateralized corporate exposures is a strong positive correlation between the prospects for repayment of the exposure and the prospects for recovery in the event of default, with both depending primarily on the cash flows generated by a property.

Examples[7]

1. *A bank makes a loan to an SPV to finance the construction of an office building that will be rented to tenants. The SPV has essentially no other assets and has been created just to manage this office building. The office building is pledged as collateral on the loan. This loan should be classified in the IPRE product line of SL, given that the prospects for repayment and recovery depend primarily on the cash flow generated by the asset.*
2. *A bank makes a loan to a large, well-diversified operating company to finance the construction of an office building that will be primarily occupied by the company. The office building is pledged as collateral on the loan, and the loan is a general obligation of the company. The loan is small relative to the overall assets and debt service capacity of the company. This loan should be classified as a corporate exposure since repayment depends primarily on the overall condition of the operating company, which does not, in turn, depend significantly on the cash flow generated by the asset.*
3. *A bank makes a loan to an operating company to finance the construction or acquisition of an office building that will be let to tenants. The office building is pledged as collateral on the loan, and the loan is a general obligation of the company. The company has essentially no other assets. The bank underwrites the loan using its corporate procedures. Despite the fact that the borrower is an operating company and the bank uses its corporate underwriting procedures, this loan should be classified in the IPRE product line of SL. The motivation is that the prospects for repayment and recovery both depend primarily on the cash flow generated by the asset. Although there is legal recourse to the project sponsor, which is an operating company, the overall condition of the project sponsor depends primarily on the cash flow generated by the asset. Therefore, in the event of project failure, the sponsor will have essentially no ability to meet its general obligations.*

[7] Basel Committee on Banking Supervision, Working Paper on the Internal Ratings-Based Approach to Specialized Lending Exposures, October 2001, pp. 3, 4.

4. *This is the same as example 3, except that the loan is unsecured. Again, the loan should be classified as IPRE. The fact that the office building is not pledged as collateral on the loan does not override the fact that the loan shares the risk characteristics common to IPRE loans in the SL portfolio.*

5. *A bank makes a loan to an SPV to finance the acquisition of an office building that will be primarily leased to a large, well-diversified operating company under a long-term lease. The SPV has essentially no other assets and has been created just to manage this office building. The lease is at least as long as the loan term and is noncancellable, and the lease payments completely cover the cash flow needs of the borrower (debt service, capital expenditures, operating expenses, etc.). The loan is amortized fully over the term of the lease with no bullet or balloon payment at maturity. In classifying this loan, the bank may look through the SPV to the long-term tenant, treating it as a corporate loan. This is because the prospects for repayment and recovery depend primarily on the overall condition of the long-term tenant, which will determine the cash flow generated by the asset.*

6. *Same as example 5, except that (1) the lease term can be cancelled at some time before the end of the loan term, or (2) even if the lease is noncancellable, the lease payments do not fully cover the aggregate loan payments over the life of the loan. This loan should be classified in the IPRE product line of SL because the tenant is not fully committed to the lease sufficient to repay the loan, so pass-through treatment is inappropriate.*

High-Volatility Commercial Real Estate

Open Real Estate Risk Rating Complete but Unstabilized Property

Lending in the category of high-volatility commercial real estate (HVCRE) represents the financing of commercial real estate that exhibits higher loss rate volatility (i.e., higher asset correlation) compared to other types of SL. Transactions involving HVCRE include the following characteristics:

- Commercial real estate exposures secured by properties of types that are categorized by the national supervisor as sharing higher volatilities in portfolio default rates.
- Loans financing any of the land acquisition, development, and construction phases for properties of those types in such jurisdictions.
- Loans financing any other properties where the source of repayment at origination of the exposure is either the future uncertain sale of the property or cash flows whose source of repayment is substantially uncertain (e.g., the property has not yet been leased to the occupancy rate prevailing in that geographic market for that type of commercial real estate), unless the borrower has substantial equity at risk.

Rating components consist of a comprehensive set of building blocks that determines LGD, the real estate financing risk grade, and the appropriate loan loss reserve.

Basic Structure

1. Individual and cumulative grades within each rating module. The cumulative grades are determined by a weighting system and weights assigned by project bankers and project managers in analysis.
2. Modules include **Real Estate Financial Measures** (market conditions financial ratios; stress analysis; *cash flow predictability for complete and stabilized property, for complete*

but not stabilized property, and for construction phase;[8] **Asset Characteristics** (location, design and condition, property is under construction [if applicable]); **Strength of Sponsor/Developer** (financial capacity and willingness to support the property, reputation and track record with similar properties, relationship with relevant real estate actors); **Security Package** (nature of lien, assignment of rents for projects leased to long-term tenants, quality of the insurance coverage); and **Composite** (each module's composite rating, final project grade before and after overrides, LGD, dollar exposure risk, estimated 20-year average of 3-year cumulative default risk, and reserve for real estate project write-off).

Criteria

- *Management experience:* The bank should verify that management is experienced and the sponsors' quality is high and beyond reproach.
- *Management reputation:* Management should have a solid reputation and a lengthy, successful record with similar properties.
- *Competitive properties:* Competitive properties coming to market should be lower than demand.
- *Ratios:* Lenders should ensure that the property's debt service coverage ratio is strong (not relevant for the construction phase), while loan-to-value ratio is low given its property type.
  - The loan-to-value is the ratio of the fair market value of an asset to the value of the loan that will finance the purchase. Loan-to-value tells the lender if potential losses due to nonpayment may be recouped by selling the asset.
  - The ratio between an asset's indebtedness and its market value is a strong predictor of its level of credit risk. An asset's loan-to-value is closely related to its DSCR.
  - Due to the relationship between a project's DSCR and its loan-to-value, these two assessments should work together in identifying property cash flows that are deteriorating and improving. The DSCR represents the relationship between an asset's cash flow and its debt service requirement and is a strong predictor of financial capacity.
- *Stress testing should be undertaken.* Stress testing will generally show how a project's cash flows and debt coverage ratios respond to an extreme scenario. The stress-testing process is important for real estate projects, particularly high-volatility projects as it looks at the "what if" scenarios to flag vulnerabilities.
  - Regulators globally are increasingly encouraging the use of stress testing to evaluate capital adequacy. There have also been calls for improved stress testing and scenario analysis, *particularly in the wake of the 2008 banking crisis, when it quickly became clear that something had gone badly wrong with the banks' stress-testing regimes.*
- The property's leases should be long term with creditworthy tenants and maturity dates scattered. The bank should ensure that the property has a track record of tenant retention on lease expiration and that the vacancy rate is low. Also, if expenses (maintenance, insurance, security, and property taxes) are predictable, project risk is more manageable.
- If the property is under construction, lenders should check to see if the property is entirely preleased through the tenure of the loan or presold to an investment-grade tenant or buyer, or the bank has a binding commitment for take-out financing from an investment-grade lender.

---

[8] Income producing real estate IPRE and HVCRE are similar except for cash flow predictability,

- Property location should be desirable and convenient to services tenants desire. The bank should also ensure the property is appropriate in terms of its design, configuration, and maintenance, and is competitive with new properties.
- If the property is under construction, the bank should confirm that contractors are qualified and the construction budget they submit is conservative, while technical hazards are limited.
- If the sponsor/developer made a substantial cash contribution to the construction or purchase of the property and has substantial resources combined with limited direct and contingent liabilities, the bank may consider reducing the project's loan loss reserves. Lenders should also check whether the sponsor/developer's properties are spread out geographically and diversified by property type.
- Property and casualty insurance is a must, and banks should check policies carefully to ensure that the quality of insurance coverage is appropriate. Insurance protects lenders by providing coverage not only against fire damage (bank has lien on property) but protects cash flow coverage by offering protection for all business-related tangible and intangible assets including money, accounting records, inventory, furniture, and other related supplies.

Riga Deal Analysis: Financing a Residential Complex and Shopping Mall

Illustrative Example Bankers Construction Budget
Location: Models are available on the Elsevier Website www.ElsevierDirect.com
Brief Description: Construction budget of residential property and large shopping mall, cash flow and investment analysis, simulation analysis.

Illustrative Example Riga Project Feasibility Study
Location: Models are available on the Elsevier Website www.ElsevierDirect.com
Brief Description: Feasibility study of large residential property and shopping mall construction project.

The Riga construction project workbook *Bankers Construction Budget* and the feasibility study *Riga Project Feasibility Study PPT* files reinforce the premise of this chapter by applying stochastic analytical capabilities to the credit analysis of large construction projects. Stochastic credit analysis helps improve due diligence and goes a long way in reinforcing risk rating—in this case, IPRE and construction projects. It is not required that you fully understand the deal; rather, you are welcome to use the comprehensive construction workbook and feasibility study file as templates for framing your own credit analyses and, thus, improving your SL risk-rating capabilities.

Deal: The Riga Project, Riga Latvia.
Loan: US$48 million, 7–10 year 10% conventional construction and/or take-out loan (mortgage).
Security: (1) Mortgage of land and improvement to be executed by the builder; (2) full guarantee of initial drawdown; (3) performance and payment (subcontractors and suppliers) bond.
Construction: Construction of commercial Western-world standard "mall" area that will house retail commercial establishments. A large department store selling midrange goods

priced to be affordable, and a large auto showroom will serve as anchor tenants. Upscale restaurants, a general-purpose hall, aboveground parking, a gas station, and a 13- to 14-story office/residential apartment tower are to be included. With a tentative list of viable, interested parties, tenant commitments will grow quickly once the project receives a conditional commit.

Construction budget, residences: Excavation, foundation and structural system, civil works, garage foundation and structural system, garage civil works, civil works finishing, fixed furniture and decoration, electric and electromechanic works, passenger lifts, sanitary system, and heating system.

Construction budget, shopping center: Excavation, foundation and structural system, civil works course, civil works finishing, fixed furniture and decoration, electric and electromechanic works, passenger lift and escalator, and sanitary system.

Lender's primary source of payment: Cash flow. Conservative projections geared to test the viability of the project to protect construction (and/or take-out lender) in terms of (1) ability of the project to generate operating cash flows over debt service, (2) probabilities that the project requires additional equity over $7 million, and (3) whether, after debt service, returns are available to service equity participants. Given conservative projections, it appears the project is solid and sound in terms of full lender payout.

Select input variables: Contractor's submitted budget, monthly draws, cumulative contractor's draws required, initial equity, interest during construction, monthly construction costs, years to complete construction project, construction loan rate, mortgage take-out assumption, commercial rents, tax abatement, vacancy rate, capital cost recovery allowance, renovation rate, depreciation, cost of capital in projection period, cost of capital in residual period, and mall operating expenses.

Select output statistics: Operating profit before depreciation allowance, income before interest and taxes, after-tax income, net cash flows, stochastic debt service coverage (probabilities operating cash flows cover debt service), project's equity recovery, present value of cash flows, investment value, and project IRR.

Select simulation statistics: Net cash flows at a 95% confidence interval, number of data points, mean, median, standard deviation, variance, coefficient of variation, range, percentile error precision, skewness, kurtosis, correlation matrix, nonlinear rank correlation, percent variation explained, scenario analysis, and tornado analysis.

11 Recognition, Diagnosis, and Response to Troubled Loans

In addition to management incompetence, the origins of many financial problems are infused in the fundamental changes that have occurred in an obligor's business,

Credit Engineering for Bankers. DOI: 10.1016/B978-0-12-378585-5.10011-9

marketplace, economy, or industry—months or even years prior to failure. They may be as systemic as the recent debt crisis or changes in economic/industry demographics (the demise of shirt manufacturing in the United States, for instance), or they may be company specific: shifts in consumer purchases, loss of major contracts, expansion into consumer-adverse markets, accelerated growth without support of adequate capital, loss of key employees and customers, or an acquisition gone sour. Can bankers detect signs of financial distress early enough so they can initiate a proper course of action before things get out of hand? They can if they know what to look for. These are some early signs of distress:

- Slow in-house orders in comparison to corresponding periods in previous years.
- Factory operating well below capacity.
- Changes in the manner payables are paid.
- Owners no longer take pride in their business.
- Frequent visits to the customer's place of business reveal deteriorating general appearance of the premises. For example, rolling stock and equipment have not been properly maintained.
- Unusual items in the financial statements.
- Negative trends such as losses or lower gross and net profits.
- Slowness in accounts receivable.
- Decrease in sales volume.
- Intercompany payables/receivables are not adequately explained.
- Cash balances reduce substantially or are overdrawn and uncollected during normally liquid periods.
- Management fails to take trade discounts because of poor inventory turnover.
- Withholding tax liability builds as taxes are used to pay other debt.
- Frequent "downtiering" of financial reporting.
- Changes in financial management.
- At the end of the cycle, creditors are not completely paid out.
- Sharp reduction in officers' salaries.
- Erratic interim results.
- Financials are late.
- Unwillingness to provide budgets, projections, or interim information.
- Suppliers cut back terms or request COD.
- Changes in inventory, followed by an excessive inventory buildup or the retention of obsolete merchandise.
- The borrower changes suppliers frequently.
- Increased inventory to one customer.
- Changing concentration from a major well-known customer to one of lesser stature.
- The lender permits advances on the seasonal loan to fund other purposes.
- Company loses an important supplier or customer.
- Concentrations in receivables and payables.
- Failure to get satisfactory explanations from the company on these concentrations.
- Loans to or from officers and affiliates.
- The principals of the company do not know what condition the company is in and the direction in which it is headed.
- The lender overestimates the peaks and valleys in the seasonal loan, thereby setting up a seasonal loan that is excessive.

- Inability to clean up bank debt or cleanups affected by rotating bank debt.
- Failure to conduct investigations on the creditworthiness of larger receivables.
- The lender finances a highly speculative inventory position in which the owner is trying for a "home run."
- Change in product demand.
- Obsolete distribution and/or production methods.
- Overexpansion without adequate working capital.
- Dependency on troubled customers and/or industries.
- Changes in senior management.
- Nonparticipating board of directors.
- Unbalanced administrative team.
- Lack of management depth.
- Management performing functions that should be delegated to others.
- Weak financial controls.
- Improper pricing.
- Excessive investment in fixed assets.
- Unusual or extraordinary litigation and events not customarily encountered in the industry.
- Asset sales used to fund working capital needs.
- Borrowing against remaining unsecured assets.
- Sales of profitable division.
- Key personnel resignations.
- Large sales discounts and/or significant sales returns.
- Inability to make timely deposits of trust funds such as employee withholding taxes.
- Surprise losses and significant variances from expected or projected results to actual for the last several years without adequate explanation.
- Regular borrowing at or near the credit limit or increased credit lines and borrowing inquiries.
- Suppliers requesting credit information late in the selling season or creditors unwilling to advance credit.
- Noncompliance with financial covenants or excessive renegotiation of broken loan covenants.

Financial Distress Models

Statistical distress models are usually associated with regression and discriminant analysis. Regression utilizes historical data to forecast future events, while discriminant analysis classifies observations into one of several a priori groupings.

Altman's Z Score

Bankers, auditors, management consultants, the legal profession, and a host of other users employ database systems to predict distress, An example is the popular Altman Z Score. E. I. Altman's original data sample drew from 66 sample firms, half of which filed for bankruptcy. All businesses in the database were manufacturers. The formula is:

$$Z = 1.2X + 1.4X_2 + 3.3X_3 + 0.6X_4 + 1.0X_5$$

where:

X = working capital/total assets (in %)
X_2 = retained earnings/total assets (in %)
X_3 = EBIT/total assets (in %)
X_4 = market value of equity/book value of debt (in %)
X_5 = sales/total assets (times)

A company with a score of $Z > 2.99$ is classified as financially sound, while one with where $Z < 1.81$ is classified as financially distressed.

The issue here involves a *domino-multiplier effect* and the *asset management effect*. The *domino-multiplier effect* holds for high (operating) leverage manufacturing firms. A high degree of operating leverage implies that relatively small changes in sales result in large changes in net operating income. For example, airlines operate with high operating leverage, requiring seating in excess of a break-even load factor to cover fixed costs. Similarly, firms borrowing to expand their fixed asset base run the risk of not being able to cover overhead if sales unexpectedly drop. The domino effect is propagated by large capital expenditures followed by disappointing sales. Therefore, lenders should be extra cautious when considering financing high operating leveraged borrowers until they are convinced projected sales will occur.

The asset management effect indicates high probabilities of distress if assets such as inventory, receivables, and equipment build up out of control. It is interesting that total assets make up the denominator of four out of five of the Z-score variables, meaning distressed companies hold excessive assets relative to operating requirements. The consequences that redundant assets bring to lenders are readily seen in sustainable growth rates, too.

Sustainable growth and Altman models are two fruits from the same tree. The sustainable growth rate compares a company's sustainable growth rate with its targeted growth rate to determine if the capital structure and growth are in equilibrium. Recall that the sustainable growth rate is defined thus:

$$g^* = \Delta S/S = \frac{P(1-d)(1+L)}{A/S - P(1-d)(1+L)}$$

As the denominator implies, asset inefficiency causes the capital output ratio (A/S) to rise, increasing pressure on the sustainable growth rate. As we noted, if the sustainable growth rate drops below the targeted growth rate, the company is likely impairing its capital structure. The connection between assets and sales is an important efficiency measuring benchmark; it is positioned in the equation to represent the base (before profit retention) on which an appropriate and sustainable growth rate is calculated. If this rate exceeds a tolerable rate, we know that leverage can rapidly increase. The assets to sales ratio is largely decided by management, as management policies give rise to asset expansion.

Let's take another look at a compelling variable in the financial needs formula (see Chapter Eight):

$$F = A/S(\Delta S) + \Delta NFA - L_1/S(\Delta S) - P(S + \Delta S)(1 - d) + R$$

Table 11.1 Components of Altman's Z Score

Coefficient Relative Values	Domino-Multiplier Syndrome	Explanation
$3.3X_3$ EBIT/Total assets	$1.0X_5$ Sales/Total assets	Sales reductions force down the Z-score. Sales declines also drive down X_3 (EBIT/Assets) due to the negative effects of operating leverage.
$1.4X_2$ Retained earnings/Total assets	$3.3X_3$ EBIT/Total assets	A drop in X_3 (EBIT/Assets) knocks over a domino by driving down $1.4X_2$ (Retained earnings/Assets) as losses flow through.
$1.2X_1$ Working capital/Total assets	$1.4X_2$ Retained earnings/Total assets	Retained earnings are a component of working capital (along with increases in long-term obligations and reductions in fixed assets). Thus, X_2 (Retained earnings/Total assets) links to X_1 (Working capital/Total assets)
$1.0X_5$ Sales/Total assets	$1.2X_1$ Working capital/ Total assets	And what effect will our dominos have on X_4 (Market value of equity/ Book value of debt)? Investors start dumping shares in panic selling, fearing that the firm's weak liquidity (caused by operating losses) makes it difficult or nigh impossible to reduce debt.
$0.6X_4$ Market value of equity/ Book value of debt	$0.6X_4$ Market value of equity/ Book value of debt	Financial leverage reaches dangerous levels as the domino effect crosses its zenith.

Here, A/S determines the effect of low asset productivity; increased assets without corresponding increases in sales could easily lead to excessive borrowings and strained capital. Cash flow, financial needs, sustainable growth, and Altman's financial distress equation are members of the same family.

From Altman's Z-score formulas, we can see it is not so much the coefficients that produce Altman's Z-score (though they, too, provide a great deal of different meaning), but it is the model's connective attributes. Observing the "operating leverage domino effect" and taking each variable in order of importance, we have the explanations shown in Table 11.1.

The following example depicts the income statement and balance sheet for The Specialty Group, a publicly traded manufacturer of specialty steel products, for the year ending December 31, 2010. These abbreviated financial statements provide the data needed to use the discriminant Z function.

The Specialty Group
Fiscal Year Ending
31-Dec-10

Net Sales	281,242
Cost of Sales	(261,130)
Gross Profit	20,112
Operating Expenses	(980)
Depreciation	(18,711)
Earnings Before Interest, Taxes	421
Interest Expense	(21,717)
Taxes (Credit)	6,058
Net Loss	(15,238)
Dividends.	808

Assets		Liabilities	
Cash	8,714	Notes Payable	20,681
Investments	3,865	Current Debt	8,892
Accounts Receivable	37,141	Accts Payable	27,342
Tax Refund	4,825	Accruals	16,359
Inventories	62,397	Income Taxes	151
Other Current Assets	17,159	**Current Liabilities**	73,425
Current Assets	134,101	Long Term Debt	184,180
Net Property	186,468	Deferred Taxes	12,900
Other Assets	18,510	Common Stock	47,353
Total Assets	**339,079**	Paid In Capital	100
		Retained Earnings	21,121
		Total	**339,079**

Using the data from the preceding statements, the five key financial ratios required for function Z can be calculated. The Z value for The Specialty Group as of fiscal 2010 is:

Altman Variables	Ratio	Z	Ratio X Z
x_1 = Working capital/Total assets:	0.1789	1.2	0.2147
x_2 = Retained earnings/Total assets:	0.0623	1.4	0.0872
x_3 = EBIT/Total assets	0.0012	3.3	0.0041
x_4 = Market value of equity/Book value of deb	0.0012	0.6	0.0007
x_5 = Sales/Total assets:	0.8294	0.999	0.8286
Z Value			1.1354

$$Z = 1.2(.2147) + 1.4(.0872) + 3.3(.0041) + .6(.0007) + .999(.8286) = 1.14$$

Recall that the failure benchmark Z value is 1.81; the firm's 1.14 Z-score falls below benchmark, meaning the firm might be financially distressed.

Other Models

Several researchers influenced by the work of Altman on the application of discriminant analysis explored ways to develop more reliable financial distress prediction models. Logit analysis, probit analysis, and the linear probability model are the most commonly used techniques as alternatives. J. S. Ohlson utilized the logit and probit analysis to estimate the probability of bankruptcy.[1] The adjustments of estimation bias resulting from oversampling, such as weights based on prior probabilities in the estimation process and optimal cutoff point, are discussed by M. E. Zmijewski.[2] The problems of pooling data due to a small number of samples are addressed by C. Zavgren and M. Dugan.[3]

Models that distinguish between financially distressed firms that survive and financially distressed firms that ultimately go bankrupt have been investigated as well. Sample firms were classified into bankrupt or nonbankrupt, with classification probabilities estimated by the multinomial logit technique.

J. Wilcox, A. Santomero, J. Vinso, and others have adapted a gambler's ruin approach to bankruptcy prediction.[4] Here, bankruptcy is probable when a company's net liquidation value becomes negative. Net liquidation value is defined as total asset liquidation value less total liabilities. From period-to-period, net liquidation values were increased by cash inflows and decreased by cash outflows. Wilcox combined cash inflows and outflows, defining them as "adjusted cash flow." All other things being equal, the probability of failure increased; the lower the beginning net liquidation value, the smaller the company's adjusted (net) cash flow, and the larger the variation of the company's adjusted cash flow. Wilcox uses the gambler's ruin formula to show that a company's risk of failure is dependent on both the preceding factors and the size of the company's adjusted cash flow "at risk" each period (i.e., the size of the company's bet).

---

[1] J. S. Ohlson, "Financial Ratios and the Probabilistic Prediction of Bankruptcy," *Journal of Accounting Research* 18(1):109–131 (1980).

[2] M. E. Zmijewski, "Essays on Corporate Bankruptcy," Ph.D. dissertation. State University of New York at Buffalo, 1983; and "Methodological Issues Related to the Estimation of Financial Distress Prediction Models," *Journal of Accounting Research* (Supplement) 22:59–86.364C (1984)

[3] M. Dugan and C. Zavgren, "How a Bankruptcy Model Could Be Incorporated as an Analytical Procedure," *CPA Journal* (May), 64–65 (1989).

[4] Wilcox's gambler's ruin formula can be used to estimate the liquidation value of a company. It is likely to be significantly less than the book value because of the "fire sale" nature. See J. Wilcox, "A Gambler's Ruin Prediction of Business Failure Using Accounting Data," *Sloan Management Review,* 12(3):1–10 (Spring 1971); "A Prediction of Business Failure Using Accounting Data," *Journal of Accounting Research*, 11:163–179 (1973); and "The Gamblers Ruin Approach to Business Risk," *Sloan Management Review* 18(1):33–46 (Fall 1976). Also see Christine V. Zavgren, "Assessing the Vulnerability to Failure of American Industrial Firms: A Logistic Analysis," *Journal of Business Finance and Accounting* 12 (1):19–46 (1985). Anthony M. Santomero, Ph.D. is Richard King Mellon Professor Emeritus of Finance at the Wharton School, University of Pennsylvania. Dr. Santomero served as president of the Federal Reserve Bank of Philadelphia from July 2000 to April 2006. He served as senior advisor of McKinsey & Company from July 2006 to January 2008 and as a long-standing advisor of the Swedish Central Bank. Finally, refer to Joseph D. Vinso's article "A Determination of the Risk of Ruin, *Journal of Financial and Quantitative Analysis*, 14:77–100 (1979).

Moody's KMV RiskCalc Private Model is a web-based program that estimates the probability that a private firm will default on a loan. Moody's uses a database of 28,000 private firms' financial statements and 1600 private firms' loan defaults to isolate attributes common to distressed borrowers. A majority of private companies with $100,000 to $100 million of assets are not covered by private debt-rating firms, so there is no standard measure of their debt's risk level. There is no secondary market for that debt because without such benchmarking, securitization is impossible.

Another approach to distress prediction is founded on neural networks. Neural networks are computer systems and programs designed to process information parallel to the way the human brain works. These systems retain data in patterns and are able to learn from their processing experience.

Loan Classification

The Financial Accounting Standards Board Statement No. 114, "Accounting by Creditors for Impairment of a Loan" (FAS 114), as amended by Statement No. 118, "Accounting by Creditors for Impairment of a Loan—Income Recognition and Disclosures" (FAS 118), sets forth standards for estimating the impairment of a loan for general financial reporting purposes.[5] Regulators are instructed to follow FAS 114 *to the letter* in assessing the portion of the allowance for loan and lease losses established for impaired loans in determining the amount of capital impairment (if any) and adequacy of the loan loss allowance. FAS 114, as amended by FAS 118 with regard to income recognition, establishes generally accepted accounting principles (GAAP) for use by banking organizations and other creditors when accounting for the impairment of certain loans.

According to FAS 114, a loan is "impaired" when, based on current information and events, it is probable that a creditor will be unable to collect all amounts due (principal and interest) according to the contractual terms of the loan agreement. The purpose of a loan review is, of course, to identify troubled loans, document findings, update credit grades, and, when necessary, criticize or classify exposures. Loan review includes discussing degrees of risk along with the likelihood of reorganization/liquidation with higher-level lenders, including those assigned to workout areas and in-house attorneys. The worst thing bankers can do is bury problems under the rug.

Criticized assets fall into five categories:[6] specially mentioned loans, substandard assets, doubtful assets, loss assets, and partially charged-off loans.

---

[5] FAS 114 is effective for fiscal years beginning after December 15, 1994, and earlier application was permitted. FAS 118 is effective concurrently with FAS 114.

[6] Sources: FRB's *Commercial Bank Examination Manual,* 1995, Section 2060.1; Accounting, Reporting, and Disclosure Issues—Nonaccrual Loans and Restructured Debt Section 2065.1; Interagency policy statements and guidance, issued on March 1, 1991; March 10, 1993; and June 10, 1993, clarified supervisory policies regarding nonaccrual assets, restructured loans, and collateral valuation; SR-95-38; the reporting instructions for the bank call report and the FR-Y-9C, the consolidated bank holding company report; Division F Banking Supervision and Regulation SR 99-24 (SUP) September 29, 1999—Subject: Loan Write-Up Standards for Assets Criticized During Examinations.

Specially Mentioned Loans

Loans in this category are inherently weak. The Federal Reserve Bank (FRB) defines these exposures as constituting an "undue and unwarranted" credit risk but not to the point of justifying a classification of substandard. Credit risks may be relatively minor yet may involve unwarranted risk. Credit risks may represent exposures the bank may be unable to properly supervise due to an inadequate loan agreement. In addition, they may include the poor condition or control over collateral, failure to obtain proper documentation, or other deviations apart from prudent lending practices. Future economic or market conditions may produce an adverse operating trend or cause imbalanced positions on balance sheets but will likely not reach a point where collateral liquidation is jeopardized.

Loans secured by assets carry certain risk, but to criticize these loans, it must be evident that the risks are increased beyond a point where otherwise the original loan would not have been granted—that is, crossing a credit grade threshold. Rapid increases in receivables, for example, without the bank knowing causative factors; concentrations lacking proper credit support; lack of on-site audits; or other similar matters could lead auditors to rate the loan as special mention. Assets in which actual weaknesses are significant are candidates for more serious criticism.

A notable exception exists: An additional allowance on impaired loans may be necessary based on consideration of institution-specific factors, such as historical loss experience compared with estimates of such losses and concerns about the reliability of cash flow estimates, the quality of an institution's loan review function, and controls over its process for estimating its FAS 114 allowance.

Substandard Assets

A substandard asset is inadequately protected by the obligor's financial condition or collateral pledged. Assets so classified must have well-defined weaknesses that jeopardize liquidation of the debt. They are characterized by the distinct possibility that the bank will sustain some loss if deficiencies are not corrected. Loss potential, while existing in the aggregate amount of substandard assets, does not have to exist in individual assets classified as substandard.

Doubtful Assets

An asset classified "doubtful" has all the weaknesses inherent in one that is classified "substandard," with the added characteristic that weaknesses make collection or liquidation in full highly questionable. In some cases, auditors will determine a reasonable carrying value for a distressed asset and request a write-down through a charge to the loan loss reserve or to the operating expenses, or they may look for an additional capital allocation. In addition, any portion of loan balances on collateral-dependent loans that exceeds fair market value of the collateral and that can be identified as uncollectible is generally classified as a loss and promptly charged off.

While possibility of loss is extremely high, certain important factors may work to strengthen the credit, deferring the downgrade classification to estimated loss at least temporarily. The borrower may be in the process of restructuring, an acquisition may be likely, or capital injections may be forthcoming; also, the bank may be in a position to obtain additional collateral.

As far as collateral-dependent loans are concerned, these loans are structured whereby repayment is predicated solely on the value of underlying collateral (no other reliable sources of repayment are available). Regulators do not automatically require additional allowances for credit losses for impaired loans over and above what is required on these loans under FAS 114. In addition, a collateralized loan that becomes impaired is not considered "collateral dependent" if repayment is available from reliable sources other than the collateral. Thus, any impairment on such a loan may, at the bank's option, be determined based on the present value of the expected future cash flows discounted at the loan's effective interest rate or, as a practical expedient, on the loan's observable market price.

Loss Assets

Banks are required to promptly charge off identified losses. Loans classified as losses are considered uncollectible and of such little value that their continuance as bankable assets is not warranted. This classification does not mean that the asset has absolutely no recovery or salvage value, but rather that it is not practical or desirable to defer writing off what is clearly appraised as basically worthless. Losses are taken in periods during which this classification is acknowledged.

Partially Charged-Off Loans[7]

Exposures may have well-defined weaknesses that jeopardize collection in full, but a portion may be reasonably expected to be collected. When the bank has taken a charge-off in an amount sufficient that the remaining balance is being serviced and reasonably assured of collection—for example, with loans secured by readily marketable collateral—there may be no need to write down the remaining exposure.

Just a word about income recognition: FAS 118 amended FAS 114 to eliminate its income recognition provisions, and, thus, no Financial Accounting Standards Board (FASB) standard exists for income recognition on impaired loans. Since full collection of principal and interest is generally not expected for impaired loans, income accrual should normally be discontinued on such loans at the time that they first become impaired.

The Classified Loan Write-Up

Bank examiners file reports on classified exposures. As shown here, these write-ups are often a lender's moment of truth, providing detail sufficient to support a bank (or auditor's) classification.[8]

---

[7] FRB's *Commercial Bank Examination Manual,* 1995, Section 2060.

[8] FRB memos and reports.

1. A general description of the obligation:
   a. Amount of exposure (both outstanding and contingent or undrawn)
   b. Location of obligor and type of business or occupation
2. Description and value of collateral.
3. Notation if borrower is an insider or a related interest of an insider.
4. Guarantors and a brief description of their ability to act as a source of repayment, especially if their financial strength has changed significantly since the initial guarantee of the credit facility.
5. Amounts previously classified.
6. Repayment terms and historical performance, including prior charge-offs, and current delinquency status.
7. A summary listing of weaknesses resulting in classification or special mention treatment.
8. A reference to any identified deficiencies dealing with loan administration or violation comments elsewhere in the report.
9. If management disagrees with the classification, a statement to that effect along with management's rationale.
10. A concise description of management action taken or planned to address weakness in the exposure.

Workout

The goals of workout are twofold: to explain why the credit is not performing as agreed and to develop an analytical foundation for thinking about solutions to the problem. Generally, two choices are open to workout: loan restructuring or liquidation. We examine these alternatives more fully later in the chapter. For now, we assume a "go-ahead" mode aimed at loan restructuring so the concepts might be more succinctly developed.

Loan problems, spotted both through monitoring systems, such as risk grading, or by "traditional" PRISM analysis should be summarily classified (as defined in the previous sections) and forwarded to loan workout. While line bankers know the borrower better than anyone at the bank, the workout department has more experience solving credit problems. Workout officers make decisions fast, usually without conferring with other departments (the legal department being the notable exception). The objective of the workout group is to correct problems that can be corrected and return the company to a traditional banking relationship. If that is not feasible, then the secondary objective is to maximize the potential for ultimate collection of outstandings. These actions, if accomplished in a way consistent with prudent lending principles, can improve prospects for collection.

When a loan is transferred to workout, the relationship officer and workout officer meet to review all information dealing with the relationship. After reviewing the file, the workout officer schedules a meeting with the borrower and relationship officer. Legal council may also be present. The function of the meeting is to define the specific role of the workout group and its interaction with the borrower. The borrower will be informed that the new account officer is the workout officer.

The workout officer notes any additional sources of repayment or collateral that could be available from the customer. Arrangements are made for the workout banker to visit the company as soon as possible. Sound workout programs begin with full disclosure of relevant information and are based on a realistic evaluation of the abilities of both the borrower and workout officer to resolve problems. The two parties should agree on the strategy aimed at resolving financial and operating problems, the course of which starts with a series of questions:

1. Are 90-day cash budgets positive or negative?
2. Will the firm be able to extend trade terms?
3. Can the company file for an expedited tax refund to provide a quick injection of cash?
4. Can outside consultants be of assistance (accountants, investment bankers, turnaround specialists, outside counsel)?
5. Are there other sources of cash, such as guarantors or new equity?
6. Is the company or any part of it viable so restructuring is a viable alternative?
7. Does the firm plan alternative legal moves, preventing restructuring?
8. If a move is not made quickly, will delay cause a partial or full dissipation of assets, actions by other creditors, or increased carrying costs for the bank?
9. How should the bank treat new loans (new money)? Do advances enhance collateral value?
10. Is there a plan to repay new money within a reasonable time frame, and will a portion of the imbedded debt be repaid with it?
11. Will new money be LIFO and senior to embedded debt? (Rule of thumb: New money should not exceed more than one-third of embedded debt.)

Follow-Up Procedures and Documentation

Obtain a Properly Signed Note

Obtaining a properly signed note that has been checked against borrowing resolutions is essential to preserving the bank's position. It is also a good idea to make a copy of the note, since the distressed borrower may claim there was never a properly executed note to begin with.

Review Subordination Agreements

One of the worst things that can happen to a lender is finding out that the subordination agreement executed by the principals has expired when it is most needed. This occurs when the documentation is not specific to continuing the subordination agreement past cleanup. In one case, the borrower signed a subordination agreement stating explicitly that the $1,000,000 lent to the business by the principles would not be paid until the loan was paid up. The borrower cleaned up the $500,000 outstanding loan for one day, immediately signing a new note for the same amount and withdrawing the $1,000,000 under the subordination agreement. This action stripped the firm of underlying equity, causing it to go bankrupt shortly thereafter. The banker simply "forgot" to get a new subordination, or it failed to when the loan was being rolled over.

Maintain a Complete Credit File

Workout officers will refer to memorandums of past meetings with borrowers, loan offering proposals, visits to companies, analysis of financial information, and ongoing records of due diligence and follow-up. It should be stressed that the loan officer's documentation in the file details both the original transaction and subsequent renewals. It is important, after learning that the financial condition has deteriorated, to write up credit file memos spelling out exactly what the bank officer's perception of the deterioration was along with a planned course of action. If the loan represents an initial transaction or renewal, the banker should write out who requested the loan, the individual's position in the company (making sure proper authorizations specified in the corporate resolution are in place, and on file at the bank), and, most importantly, *if the guarantor, if any, approved it in writing*. The officer should also indicate who completed the signing of the note, the guarantee, the collateral, and the date.

The workout area requires complete and objective credit files to develop insight into projection assumptions; cash flows and cash budgets; and, if the borrower is a public firm, records of rating downgrades from agencies. It is not uncommon for financially distressed borrowers to inflate reality to appease the relationship manager and the workout group.

Make Sure Guarantees Are in Order and Completely Understood

The guarantor must have both the financial capacity and willingness to provide support for the credit. Also, the nature of the guarantee should be worded so it provides support for repayment, in whole or in part, during the loan tenure. Guarantees must be unconditional, uncontested, and legally enforceable. In a distress situation, the bank must have sufficient information in the credit file supporting the guarantor's financial condition, liquidity, cash flow, contingent liabilities, and other relevant factors (including credit ratings, when available).

The bank will also note the number and amount of guarantees extended by a guarantor to determine if the guarantor has the financial capacity to fulfill the contingent claims that exist. If the guarantor was called on in the past to honor the agreement, information dealing with its ability and willingness to fulfill previous obligations should be available. In this case, the bank will note whether a previously required performance under a guarantee agreement was voluntary or the result of legal or other actions taken by the lender to enforce the guarantee.

Review Uniform Commercial Code (UCC) Filings

UCC filings should be reviewed to ensure that they have been properly filed and are up-to-date. In one case, the borrower gave the bank a security interest in receivables. The borrower asked the bank not to record the lien for 45 days. The account officer foolishly agreed, and the firm went bankrupt shortly thereafter. The failure to file a properly recorded lien caused the bank to lose its lien status in Chapter 7 bankruptcy proceedings.

Check for Unencumbered Assets

- Accounts receivable
- Inventory: Placing liens can scare off trade credit.
- Fixed assets: Is there equity value?

- Patents, trademarks, intellectual property
- Stock of a subsidiary that is relatively debt free.

Check That Proper Documentation for All Collateral Is in Order

- Security agreements
- Mortgages
- UCC filings
- Stock/bond powers
- Federal filings (aircraft, intellectual property)

A Lender's Liability Help Line

Because of the need for immediate and often tough action, the loan workout officer should not be unreasonably limited by committee and staff approvals. An open and frank relationship with the customer is of utmost importance at this point. Both relationship and workout officers should let the customer know how the situation is viewed and the actions they feel are necessary. Customers should be encouraged to be equally open and frank. Loan workout is not the time to make enemies, as the disagreeable alternative might be a lender liability suit. We look at this possibility now with a few pointers on how to avoid this hornet's nest.

Lenders could avert lawsuits, or mitigate their effects, if they follow a few basic, precautionary steps. These steps include avoiding any types of oral understandings with borrowers that are not in the loan documentation; avoiding intrusion by the lender into the day-to-day operation of the borrower's business; avoiding any act or conduct that might lend support to a legal claim of malice or ill will; and giving borrowers as much advance written notice as possible should the lender decide to terminate a loan or refuse further credit.[9] The proliferation of actions against lenders only underscores the importance of lenders to use guidelines such as these (and those prescribed in the chapter) and follow the basic precepts of caution and common sense in their lending and workout policies.

We offer here a brief introduction to lender's liability, along with a few of one bank's "pearls of wisdom." An old friend, Phil Z., an executive in the loan workout section of a major bank, compiled a Lender Liability Help Line. Phil's colorful direct manner has been left intact, and he would be the first to assert that no guide can replace the sound advice of legal counsel!

Compliance with Agreements

1. Did the lender act in full compliance with the express terms of the documents governing the loans?
2. Were the terms of the document modified or waived by the subsequent writings, statements, or conduct?

[9] Loeb Granoff, "Emerging Theories of Lender Liability: Flawed Applications of Old Concepts," *Bank. L. Journal* (1987).

3. Do loan documents unambiguously give the lender the right to terminate funding or to demand payments? Is this right consistent with the other terms of the loan?
4. Did the borrower breach any of the contractual covenants or conditions precedents contained in the documents?
5. If so, can such breach be established by objective criteria?

Compliance with Duty of Good Faith and Fair Dealing

1. Assuming the lender terminated funding, did the lender give the borrower reasonable notice of its intent?
2. Was the borrower afforded a reasonable opportunity to obtain alternative financing?
3. Was the lender's action supported by objective criteria?
4. Was the lender's action consistent with its institutional policies for terminating funding?
5. Did the lender cause the borrower to believe that additional funds would be forthcoming? Did the borrower act in reasonable reliance and to its detriment on the anticipated financing?
6. Has a relationship of trust or confidence been established between the lender and borrower? Did the lender routinely offer advice or suggestions to the borrower? Is there a disparity of sophistication or bargaining power between the parties?

Domination and Control

1. If the terms of the loan give the lender broad power with respect to management and operations of the debtor, did the lender actually exercise such control in an improper fashion?
2. Has the lender's involvement merely consisted of its legitimate right to monitor the debtor's business and to collect its debt, or has the lender, in effect, been running the debtor's operations?
3. Is the lender actively participating in the day-to-day management of the business, or does the lender merely possess "veto power" over certain business decisions?
4. Is the lender the sole or primary source of credit for the lender?
5. Did the lender wrongfully use threats in an attempt to control the borrower's conduct?
6. Does the lender have control over a substantial amount of stock of the debtor?
7. Do all factors indicative of control, taken together, constitute sufficient control to rise to the level of domination for the purpose of the instrumentality rule or the doctrine of equitable subordination?
8. If so, can the lender satisfy the higher standard of care required of fiduciaries?

Minimize Risks of Lawsuits

1. Prepare memos to the file properly, leaving out epithets, vulgarisms, and threats.
2. Make sure any deal struck is clearly understood by the parties, avoiding side agreements and oral "explications," if possible. It can be helpful to write a self-serving memo to the file, outlining the specifics.
3. Use appropriate documentation, reflective of the actual transaction.
4. Avoid the imposition of excessively harsh terms not intended for use (such as waiver of jury trial? management control provisions?).
5. Review loan manuals of the bank and the borrower's credit evaluations, remembering either or both may be read to the jury.

6. Avoid personality conflict, immediately removing officers who could be accused of acting prejudicially or unfairly.
7. Pack up your troubles in an old kit bag, and leave them with the attorneys.

AND, when you do find a problem loan, before it's too late:

1. Review the file for all the facts.
2. Audit all loan documents.
3. Interview all the personnel involved.
4. Assess your borrower's motivation to settle rather than to sue.
5. Look for enforcement alternatives to suit. Will giving a little in a restructure gain a lot, such as collateral? New guarantees? Time to overcome adverse courses of conduct?
6. Review all waivers the bank might possibly have given, whether in writing or orally.
7. Provide ample notice of bank action (including demand, setoff) when that is at all practical. If working toward deadlines, make sure they are clearly understood by the borrower. Put them in writing, if possible. When the deadlines are extended or modified, correspondence to the borrower should detail the new terms and conditions now applicable.
8. Work with good attorneys, who are called in as soon as practicable. Reliance on advice of counsel may demonstrate good faith, adding to your chances of a successful defense.
9. Never (*never!*) sue for small sums or just for spite: consider the advisability of suing when the borrower can't pay.
10. Always be businesslike, avoiding abusive language, harshness, and table pounding.
11. Management changes can be effected, when necessary, but they require care to accomplish without liability.
12. Let the borrower and its advisers be the source of business plans, not the bank.

Loan Restructuring: A Workout Decision

For a formally restructured loan, focus is on the ability of the borrower to repay the loan vis-à-vis any modified terms. Classification follows a formally restructured loan if, after restructuring, weaknesses occur that threaten to jeopardize repayment set by modified terms. Clearly, a period of sustained performance is important in determining whether reasonable assurance of repayment exists. Due diligence might reveal an improvement in the borrower's condition that helps chances of repayment. The borrower might win a sizable contract that significantly improves cash flow, financial leverage, and debt-service coverage. The loan may return to an accrual status (from a restructured basis), reasonably ensuring full repayment.

If nonfinancial factors are strong within the company, there may be viable alternatives to liquidation: trademarks, brand reorganization, and viable operating units liberated from the weak consolidated form. Underperforming, outdated business units will be liquidated, along with possibly the management team that got the company in trouble in the first place. Workout specialists will bring in their team of experts to run the business. From the standpoint of workout, short-term workout strategies include plans to get the firm past its next season; stop the bleeding, stabilize the firm, and return it to health so long-term goals are achievable: a potential buyout by another company to attract investors to replace existing turnaround management.

"Stop the bleeding" means fast action. New turnaround management must ensure that an acceptable percentage of supplies and customers stick with the firm. Without supplier and customer support, the firm may be deemed not viable, and steps will be put in place to liquidate.

The following models will help bankers track the turnaround. You may download these models available on http://www.elsevierdirect.com/companion.jsp?ISBN= 9780123785855

- Workout: Accounts receivable audit worksheet
- Workout: Borrowing-based facility
- Workout: Acceptance versus rejection cost receivable model
- Workout: Inventory audit worksheet
- Workout: Break-even inventory model
- Workout: Economic Order Quantity (EOQ) model
- Workout: Problem loan cash budget
- Turnaround diagnostics: the turnaround specialist's role; the bank's role in a workout
- Short- and long-term restructuring objectives
- Performance checks using valuation models and simulation

Corporate Valuation Model: A View of Liquidation versus Restructuring Decisions

Illustrative Example Valuation Appraisal Model
Location: Models are available on the Elsevier Website www.ElsevierDirect.com
Brief Description: This is the Corporate Valuation Model used for developing financial statements, as well as for enterprise valuation, and computing the total enterprise value, earnings per share, economic profit, and other financial metrics.

The decision to liquidate or continue the workout may be quantified by spreads between market value and liquidation value. Why is a low ratio significant in workout? It could mean a firm is likely to see more value liquidating than trying to stay in business. For example, if the company wins a new contract, what effect does the new business have on the turnaround firm's value and changes in the ratio market value/liquidation value? The Modeling Toolkit software includes several valuation models that can be used to perform valuation appraisals of clients. For instance, under Modeling Toolkit | Valuation | Valuation Appraisal Model, you will see the valuation appraisal model. The cells in boxes are the required inputs, and the results are displayed throughout various worksheets in the model. The corporate valuation model presented in Figure 11.1 is used for developing financial statements, as well as for evaluating an enterprise and computing the total enterprise value, earnings per share, economic profit, and other financial metrics. The inputs are the boxed cells. You can extend the model to additional years by first entering the Years to Forecast and typing in the various required values in these future years (the boxes will automatically appear).

The model returns a set of financial statements such as the balance sheet, income statement, and statement of cash flows, as well as the resulting computations of NOPAT (net operating profits after taxes), which is then used in the computation of free cash flows to the firm and the resulting economic profit analysis and the valuation of the company. In addition, the market approach ratios analysis is included in the model as a way of calibrating the valuation results.

Note that this model uses a growth rate approach where starting values and the subsequent annualized growth rates of the variables are entered, and the model computes the future values of these variables. You can override any of the assumption cells by simply typing over the values (changing growth rates over time or using actual values rather than growth rates). In addition, some sample input assumptions have been set up (cells in green), and an example simulation was run. The following graphs illustrate the same results from the simulation, indicating that there is a 12.90% chance that the stock price at the end of 5 years will fall below $23 per share, and the total enterprise value at

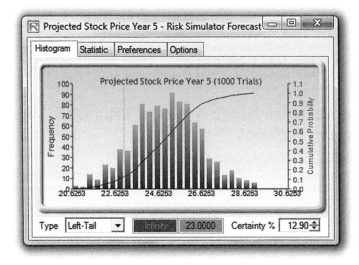

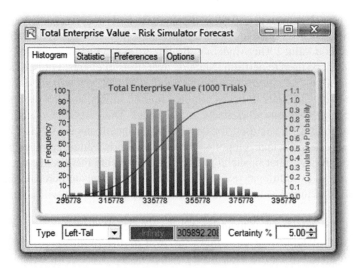

the worst-case scenario (5th percentile) Value at Risk is $309,892,000. You may over-ride these input assumptions as required to create your own valuation model.

Bankruptcy

Chapter 11 Reorganization

Chapter 11 is typically used to reorganize a business that may be a corporation, sole proprietorship, or partnership. The Chapter 11 bankruptcy case of a corporation (corporation as debtor) does not put the personal assets of the stockholders at risk, other than the value of their investment in the company's stock. A sole proprietorship (owner as debtor), in contrast, does not have an identity separate and distinct from its owner(s). Accordingly, a bankruptcy case involving a sole proprietorship includes both the business and personal assets of the owners-debtors. Like a corporation, a partnership exists separate and apart from its partners. In a partnership bankruptcy case (partnership as debtor), however, the partners' personal assets may, in some cases, be used to pay creditors in the bankruptcy case, or the partners themselves may be forced to file for bankruptcy protection.

A Chapter 11 case begins with the filing of a petition with the bankruptcy court serving the area where the debtor has a domicile or residence. A petition may be

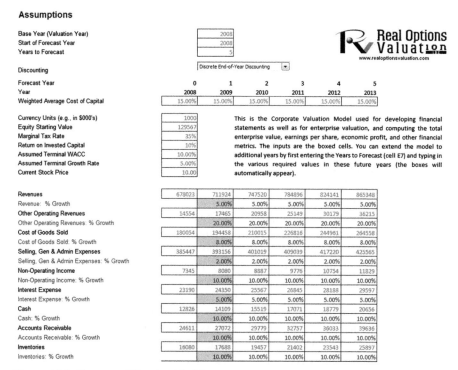

Figure 11.1 Corporate Valuation Model.

NOPLAT

EBITA	85755.00	69007.08	75352.45	82897.22	91753.69	119875.66
Adjustments (Operating Leases, Retirement Liablities, Ongoing Provisions)	2672.00	0.00	0.00	0.00	0.00	0.00
Adjusted EBITA	**88427.00**	**69007.08**	**75352.45**	**82897.22**	**91753.69**	**119875.66**
Tax on EBT	24676.00	22743.41	25834.11	29233.67	33136.98	37675.09
Tax Shield on Interest Exp	0.00	0.00	0.00	0.00	0.00	0.00
Tax Shield on Operating Lease Interest	0.00	0.00	0.00	0.00	0.00	0.00
Tax Shield on Retirement Rel. Liab.	0.00	0.00	0.00	0.00	0.00	0.00
Tax on Interest Income	0.00	0.00	0.00	0.00	0.00	0.00
Tax on Non-operating Income	0.00	0.00	0.00	0.00	0.00	0.00
Change in Deferred Taxes	0.00	0.00	0.00	0.00	0.00	0.00
Taxes on EBITA	**24676.00**	**22743.41**	**25834.11**	**29233.67**	**33136.98**	**37675.09**
NOPLAT	**63751.00**	**46263.66**	**49518.34**	**53663.55**	**58616.71**	**82200.57**

FREE CASH FLOW

NOPLAT	63751.00	46263.66	49518.34	53663.55	58616.71	82200.57
Depreciation	41321.00	38268.45	40028.18	41523.96	42795.36	43876.06
Gross Cash Flow	**105072.00**	**84532.11**	**89546.52**	**95187.51**	**101412.07**	**126076.62**
Change in Capital Expenditures	**56011.00**	**50000.00**	**50000.00**	**50000.00**	**50000.00**	**50000.00**
Change in Investment of Working Capital	13585.00	-6205.52	711.92	747.52	784.90	824.14
Change in Other Operating Assets/Liablities	23402.00	4000.00	4000.00	4000.00	4000.00	4000.00
Operating Leases	0.00	0.00	0.00	0.00	0.00	0.00
Total Investments on Working Capital	**36987.00**	**-2205.52**	**4711.92**	**4747.52**	**4784.90**	**4824.14**
Gross Investments	**92998.00**	**47794.48**	**54711.92**	**54747.52**	**54784.90**	**54824.14**
Free Cash Flow Excl. Goodwill	**12074.00**	**36737.63**	**34834.60**	**40439.99**	**46627.18**	**71252.48**
Investment in Goodwill and Intangibles	0.00	0.00	0.00	0.00	0.00	0.00
Free Cash Flow Incl. Goodwill	**12074.00**	**36737.63**	**34834.60**	**40439.99**	**46627.18**	**71252.48**
Interest Income (After Tax)	0.00	0.00	0.00	334.16	1868.21	3726.46
Decreases in Excess Marketable Securities	0.00	0.00	0.00	0.00	0.00	0.00
Foreign Exchange Translation Effects	0.00	0.00	0.00	0.00	0.00	0.00
Non-Operating Cash Flow	0.00	0.00	0.00	0.00	0.00	0.00
Extraordinary Items	1003.00	0.00	0.00	0.00	0.00	0.00
Cash Flow Available to Investors	**13077.00**	**36737.63**	**34834.60**	**40774.14**	**48495.39**	**74978.94**

ECONOMIC PROFIT

Operating Working Capital	-23008.00	-16802.48	-17514.41	-18261.93	-19046.82	-19870.97
Net Property Plant and Equipment	255123.00	266854.55	276826.37	285302.41	292507.05	298630.99
Other Assets Net of Other Liabilities	5553.00	9553.00	13553.00	17553.00	21553.00	25553.00
Value of Operating Leases	0.00	0.00	0.00	0.00	0.00	0.00
Total Invested Capital	**237668.00**	**259605.07**	**272864.96**	**284593.48**	**295013.23**	**304313.03**
Return on Invested Capital	26.82%	17.82%	18.15%	18.86%	19.87%	27.01%
Weighted Average Cost of Capital	15.00%	15.00%	15.00%	15.00%	15.00%	15.00%
Spread	11.82%	2.82%	3.15%	3.86%	4.87%	12.01%
Economic Profit (Before Goodwill)	**28100.80**	**7322.90**	**8588.60**	**10974.53**	**14364.73**	**36553.61**

Figure 11.1 (*continued*).

a voluntary petition, which is filed by the debtor, or it may be an involuntary petition, which is filed by creditors that meet certain requirements. As the principle reorganization chapter of the Bankruptcy Code, Chapter 11 permits a borrower to be protected by the bankruptcy court while the firm tries to restructure. The formulation of a plan of reorganization is the principle purpose of a Chapter 11 case. The petition includes a list of assets and liabilities, and a detailed statement outlining current financial affairs along with financial and operating plans, including the means for satisfying claims against and interest in the debtor—specifically, prior history and cause of the filing, assets and liabilities, income and expenses, treatment of creditors, liquidation analysis, projections of earnings, tax consequences, and discussion of options. If it cannot formulate such a plan, the business may be forced into Chapter 7 liquidation.

The filing of a Chapter 11 petition also triggers the provisions of Section 362 of the Bankruptcy Code. Section 362 provides for an automatic stay of all attempts to collect prepetition claims from the debtor or otherwise interfere with the debtor's property or business. The plan also sets forth certain obligations that can be impaired or forgiven to allow the business to continue operations. Taxes, delinquent rent, mortgage arrearage, and so on can be paid out over a period of time, usually five or six years, to improve the cash flow of the business.

The commencement of a Chapter 11 case creates an estate comprised of all the legal and equitable interests of the debtor in property as of the date the petition is filed. Sections 1101, 1107, and 1108 provide that a debtor may continue to operate the debtor's business as a "debtor in possession" unless the Bankruptcy Court orders the appointment of a trustee. The debtors remain in possession of their property and continue to operate the business. A creditor's committee may be appointed made up of the largest unsecured creditors to provide additional input into the reorganization process.

Priority claims, including recent tax claims, are required to be paid in full, plus interest. Secured claims are required to be paid in full, also with interest. Unsecured nonpriority claims are required to be paid a dividend at least equal to that which they would receive if it were a Chapter 7 filing. Within these limits, there are an almost infinite variety of Chapter 11 plans, each based on the debtor's own financial situation.

Chapter 7 of the Bankruptcy Code

To qualify for relief under Chapter 7 of the Bankruptcy Code, the debtor may be an individual, a partnership, or a corporation or other business entity. One of the primary purposes of bankruptcy is to discharge certain debts to give a debtor a "fresh start." A discharge releases individual debtors from personal liability for most debts and prevents the creditors owed those debts from taking any collection actions against the debtor. Secured creditors may retain some rights to seize property securing an underlying debt even after a discharge is granted. Depending on individual circumstances, if a debtor wishes to keep certain secured property, it may be decided to "reaffirm" the debt. A reaffirmation is an agreement between the debtor and the creditor that the debtor will remain liable and will pay all or a portion of the money owed, even though the debt would otherwise be discharged in the bankruptcy. In return, the creditor promises that it will not repossess or take back the collateral as long as the debtor continues to pay the debt.

Attributes of Firms While in Bankruptcy

1. Cash Buildup
   a. In the year following bankruptcy, companies tend to generate large amounts of cash if the cause of the filing was due to overleveraging their balance sheets.
   b. The result of this buildup is due to most prepetition interest and debt service not having to be repaid.
   c. Another reason cash builds is due to working capital reductions as the company rationalizes its operations through the sale of noncore assets and/or closing of marginal or unprofitable lines of businesses.
2. Trade Support
   a. At the time of the bankruptcy filing, accounts payables and most accruals go to zero, with the former balances in these accounts reclassified as prepetition liabilities.
   b. Due to the administrative expense status of shipments made to a company after it files for Chapter 11, most companies have been able to obtain some trade support after the filing.

Balance Sheets for XYZ Corporation

Effects of a Bankruptcy Filing

Balance Sheet Accounts in Millions	Last Day Before Filing	First Day After Filing	One Year After Filing	Change
Cash and equivalents	100	100	475	375
Accounts Receivable, Net	600	600	640	40
Inventories	900	900	800	(100)
Other Current Assets	80	80	110	30
Total Current Assets	*1,680*	*1,680*	*2,025*	*345*
Property Plant and Equipment	1,530	1,530	1,200	(330)
Other Assets	80	80	55	(25)
Total Assets	**3,290**	**3,290**	**3,280**	**(10)**
Accounts Payables	550	0	245	245
Accruals	300	0	115	115
Current maturities of Long Term Debt	800	0	0	0
Other Current Liabilities	80	7	20	13
Total Current Liabilities	*1,730*	*7*	*380*	*373*
				0
Pre-Petition Liabilities - Frozen	0	2,983	2,983	0
Long-Term Debt	1,110	0	0	0
Long-Term Liabilities	*150*	*0*	*0*	*0*
Total Liabilities	**2,990**	**2,990**	**3,363**	**373**
Shareholders Equity	300	300	(83)	(383)
Total Liabilities and Equity	**3,290**	**3,290**	**3,280**	**(10)**

Figure 11.2 Effects of a Bankruptcy Filing.

    c. Large bankrupt companies are quite often a vendor's best customer. So the company retains significant buying power in bankruptcy because it is difficult for the supplier to quickly replace such a large customer.

Figure 11.2 shows the effects of a bankruptcy filing on the balance sheet accounts of XYZ Corporation the day before filing for Chapter 11, the day after filing, and one year after filing. Table 11.2 provides explanations.

Debtor-in-Possession Financing

Debtor-in-possession financing, or DIP financing, is a special form of financing provided for companies in financial distress or under the Chapter 11 bankruptcy process. Usually, this security is more senior than debt, equity, and any other securities issued by a company. It gives a troubled company a new start, albeit under strict conditions. Conditions may include the following:

- The obligor must have qualified commercial accounts receivable and/or other assets (e.g., prepetition).
- The lender must have a first security position.
- Postpetition, permission of the court is needed to finance assets (usually accounts receivable).

Table 11.2 Explanations of Balance Sheet Trends Shown in Figure 11.2

Balance Sheet Account	Explanation
Assets:	
Cash (1)	Builds
Other Current Assets	Largely unaffected by the bankruptcy
Long-Term Assets	May fall due to asset sales and rationalization of business
Liabilities:	
Accounts Payable	Only those payables incurred after the Chapter 11 filing
Accruals	Only those accruals incurred after the Chapter 11 filing
Total Current Liabilities (2)	Falls
Prepetition Liabilities (3)	Frozen
Long-Term Liabilities	No new long-term liabilities are contemplated, but would need court approval

Notes:

1. Cash will build because:
   a. All prepetition accounts payable are frozen.
   b. Most prepetition accruals are frozen.
   c. All unsecured liabilities are frozen so that no interest is paid.
2. Total Current Liabilities will fall because:
   a. Only those current liabilities incurred after filing are included here.
3. Prepetition liabilities include:
   a. Prepetition accounts payable
   b. Prepetition accruals
   c. Other prepetition unsecured liabilities
   d. Secured liabilities not secured by hard assets (which could include credit facilities secured by the stock of operating subsidiaries).

In most cases, DIP financing is considered attractive because it is done only under order of the Bankruptcy Court, which is empowered by the Bankruptcy Code to afford the lender a lien on property of the bankruptcy estate and/or a priority position. The firm may possess receivables and other assets, which can be used as security for financing.

Financial institutions, including factoring houses, generally find DIP financing very attractive business because of the senior lien status provided by the court. Possibilities include receivable-backed lines of credit, factoring, equipment loans, inventory loans, and purchase order financing. As an example, the following services were offered by one financing source:[10]

- A continuous source of working capital during reorganization to enable a company to fill purchase orders and expand and accelerate production
- A verified source of funding for suppliers, thus maintaining supply support throughout the reorganization
- A positive credit relationship with a financial institution that may be utilized as a bridge to bank financing

[10] The author would like to thank 1st National Assistance Finance Association for supplying a list of its services.

- An accounts receivable management service
- Help in implementing a plan for reorganization

Developing a Debtor-in-Possession Analysis

Following is the due diligence process of a leading commercial finance institution:[11]

1. Determine why company is filing for Chapter 11.
   a. Overleverage only (i.e., allied stores)
   b. Operating performance problems
   c. Lawsuits (Texaco, Manville)
   d. To get out of leases or contracts (Ames, Columbia Gas)
   e. Lack of alternative financing to buy inventory
2. Evaluate depth and quality of management.
   a. Does management have the capacity and depth to focus on bankruptcy issues while ensuring that the management of the core business does not suffer?
3. Determine viability of the business.
   a. Will the negative publicity associated with the bankruptcy affect the company's operating performance?
   b. Will the borrower be able to emerge from Chapter 11?
   c. Asset values will be maximized if the company is a going concern; as a result there is less risk to a DIP lender.
4. Review the firm's prepetition liabilities.
   a. Review most recent historical balance sheet.
   b. Determine secured and unsecured liabilities.
   c. If prepetition liabilities are unsecured, then interest will not have to be paid in Chapter 11.
   d. If prepetition liabilities are secured, interest may have to be paid during the Chapter 11 period.
5. Review the company's prepetition assets.
   a. Look at most recent historical assets.
   b. Determine which assets are subject to a lien (encumbered) and which are not subject to a lien (unencumbered).
   c. If an asset is subject to a lien, DIP lender will not realize the benefits of its super-priority status on this asset.
   d. If an asset is not subject to a lien, DIP lender will realize the benefits of its super-priority status in this asset: The single most important ingredient in evaluating whether a DIP financing is feasible is the determination of the level of unencumbered assets of the debtor. To the extent that a substantial portion of the company's assets have not previously been pledged and that the lender designs a prudent borrowing base against the assets, the risks will be minimized. Highly liquid assets, such as inventory and accounts receivables, are preferred to assets like real estate or equipment.
6. Analyze the company's projections.
   a. Detailed projections of earnings and balance sheet flows are necessary to develop month-by-month cash flow projections. Such projections will estimate borrowing needs and assets that will be available to support outstandings at any point in time.

[11] Developed with the author when the author was providing seminars on the parent bank's behalf. Given with permission.

- For a retailer, key assumptions include revenues, cash expenses, availability of credit from suppliers, inventory required to support sales levels, and capital expenditures.

b. Reconstruction of the balance sheet:
- Due to the automatic stay that prohibits the payment of principal on all prepetition debt, all prepetition debt gives the appearance of equity and is renamed "liabilities subject to Chapter 11."
  1. This new liability account improves all leverage and tangible net worth covenants.
  2. Only true or live liabilities on the balance sheet are disclosed. Include DIP financing line, all newly created administrative expenses (postpetition accounts payable), and prepetition secured debt that is getting interest in Chapter 11.

c. Reconstruction of the income statement:
- Develop a pro forma (what if) statement from last year's performance, and eliminate interest paid on prepetition debt that no longer has to be paid. In addition, eliminate leases and contract obligations paid last year but that are now rejected as a result of debtor's rights in Chapter 11.
- Include as a reduction to earnings extra expenses associated with the bankruptcy.

d. Collateral and liquidation analysis: Determine which collateral is unencumbered and accrues to the benefit of the DIP lender. (Remember that liquid assets—inventory and accounts receivable—are preferred.)

e. Estimate liquidation value of collateral:
- The DIP loan should never be greater than a worst-case liquidation analysis of the available collateral.
- A borrowing base will be computed based on a discount to the worst-case liquidation value of the asset.
- Compare this worst-case liquidation analysis to the amount of DIP financing required at any point in time.
- In all retail situations, it is important to determine the proceeds that could be realized (after the expenses of a liquidation) in a going out of business sale.
- It is important for the lender to hire consultants to determine the liquidation values of the asset in question.

f. Audit the company's systems integrity:
- Review the company's control and monitoring systems and perform a quality audit of inventory and receivables.
- It is important that the company's reporting is reliable and accurate because borrowing bases are generated from these reports.
- For accounts receivable, the lender should be concerned with total outstandings, past-due accounts, and overall credit quality.
- For inventory, the lender should be concerned with inventory mix, age, price points, gross margin, discounting practices, and shrink history.

Repayment of the Debtor-in-Possession Loan

There are generally four ways to get repaid:

1. Cash flow from operations
2. Liquidation of the collateral
   a. If the entity is no longer viable, a liquidation of the collateral will occur.
   b. The bankrupt company will now be converted from a Chapter 11 proceeding to a Chapter 7 proceeding, in which the court presides over the liquidation of the company.

    c. The DIP lender, with its super-priority status will have first claim on the proceeds of the unencumbered assets.

    d. If the borrowing base was conservative (as it should be), the DIP lender will be repaid in full.

3. The company emerges from bankruptcy, and a new lender refinances the DIP loan.

    a. Company emerges by filing reorganization with the court.

    b. This plan is voted on by the creditors.

    c. After a negotiated settlement, creditors receive compensation for their claims.

    d. The amount of settlement for each class of creditor depends on the priorities of their respective claims (i.e., senior secured debt may be repaid in full, while senior subordinated debt may receive nothing).

    e. It should be a condition in the DIP loan agreement that the DIP lender be paid in full before the courts will confirm any plan of reorganization.

4. Refinancing of the DIP loan by a new DIP lender.

While the ability to recognize, diagnose, and respond to troubled loans is certainly a professional necessity, avoiding troubled loans in the first place is the ideal goal. Solid due diligence on the part of a knowledgeable and insightful banker has always been the best way to achieve that goal. It would be beneficial, then, to reread the back-to-basics chapters on ratios, cash flow, and financial forecasting, for example. However, the most important thing to do is to make an attempt to understand your customer's business inside and out.

12 Strategic Real Options Analysis: Managing Risk Through Flexibility

Chapter Outline

This chapter gives the reader a cursory look at and quick introduction to strategic real options analysis. It explains why only running simulations, forecasting, and optimization are not sufficient in a comprehensive risk management paradigm. Obviously, time-series forecasting and Monte Carlo simulation are used for *identifying*, *predicting*, and *quantifying* risks. The questions that should be asked are: So what? and What next? Quantifying and understanding risk is one thing, but turning this information into *actionable intelligence* is another. Real options analysis, when applied appropriately, allows you to *value* risk, creating strategies to *mitigate* risk and showing how to position yourself to *take advantage* of risk.

In the banking world of credit risk and credit engineering, strategic real options can be useful in setting up different options strategies and credit portfolios with different baskets of instruments to hedge certain types of risks (e.g., interest rate, inflation, default events), to evaluate each of the pathways or instrument combinations to determine the optimal and best strategy to execute.

This chapter provides the basics of strategic real options and how it is used in various industries. It is highly recommended that you refer to *Real Options Analysis: Tools and Techniques,* Second Edition (Wiley Finance, 2005) also by the author (J. M.), in order to learn more about the theoretical as well as pragmatic step-by-step computational details of real options analysis.

What Are Real Options?

In the past, corporate investment decisions were cut-and-dried. Buy a new machine that is more efficient, make more products costing a certain amount, and if the benefits outweigh the costs, execute the investment. Hire a larger pool of sales associates, expand the current geographical area, and if the marginal increase in forecast sales revenues exceeds the additional salary and implementation costs, start hiring. Need a new manufacturing plant? Show that the construction costs can be recouped quickly and easily by the increase in revenues the plant will generate through new and improved products, and the initiative is approved.

However, real-life business conditions are much more complicated. Your firm decides to go with an e-commerce strategy, but multiple strategic paths exist. Which path do you choose? What are your options? If you choose the wrong path, how do you get back on the right track? How do you value and prioritize the paths that exist? You are a venture capitalist firm with multiple business plans to consider. How do you value a start-up firm with no proven track record? How do you structure a mutually beneficial investment deal? What is the optimal timing to a second or third round of financing?

Business conditions are fraught with uncertainty and risks. These uncertainties hold with them valuable information. When uncertainty becomes resolved through the passage of time, managers can make the appropriate midcourse corrections through a change in business decisions and strategies. Real options incorporate this learning model, akin to having a strategic road map, whereas traditional analyses that neglect this managerial flexibility will grossly undervalue certain projects and strategies.

Real options are useful not only in valuing a firm through its strategic business options but also as a strategic business tool in capital investment decisions. For instance, should a firm invest millions in a new e-commerce initiative? How does a firm choose among several seemingly cashless, costly, and unprofitable information-technology infrastructure projects? Should a firm indulge its billions in a risky research and development initiative? The consequences of a wrong decision can be disastrous or even terminal for certain firms. In a traditional discounted cash flow model, these questions cannot be answered with any certainty. In fact, some of the answers generated through the use of the traditional discounted cash flow model are flawed because the model assumes a static, one-time decision-making process, whereas the real options approach takes into consideration the strategic managerial options certain projects create under uncertainty and management's flexibility in exercising or abandoning these options at different points in time, when the level of uncertainty has decreased or has become known over time.

The real options approach incorporates a learning model such that management makes better and more informed strategic decisions when some levels of uncertainty are resolved through the passage of time, actions, and events. The discounted cash flow analysis assumes a static investment decision and assumes that strategic decisions are made initially with no recourse to choose other pathways or options in the future. To create a good analogy of real options, visualize it as a strategic road map of long and winding roads, with multiple perilous turns and branches along the way. Imagine the intrinsic and extrinsic value of having such a road map or global positioning system when navigating through unfamiliar territory, as well as having road signs at every turn to guide you in making the best and most informed driving decisions. Such a strategic map is the essence of real options.

The answer to evaluating such projects lies in real options analysis, which can be used in a variety of settings, including pharmaceutical drug development, oil and gas exploration and production, manufacturing, start-up valuation, venture capital investment, information technology infrastructure, research and development, mergers and acquisitions, e-commerce and e-business, intellectual capital development, technology development, facility expansion, business project prioritization, enterprise-wide risk management, business unit capital budgeting, licenses, contracts, intangible asset valuation, and the like. A later section in this chapter illustrates some business cases and how real options can assist in identifying and capturing additional strategic value for a firm.

The Real Options Solution in a Nutshell

Simply defined, real options is a systematic approach and integrated solution using financial theory, economic analysis, management science, decision sciences, statistics, and econometric modeling in applying options theory in valuing real physical assets (as opposed to financial assets) in a dynamic and uncertain business environment where business decisions are flexible in the context of strategic capital investment decision making, valuing investment opportunities, and project capital expenditures.

Real options are crucial in the following situations:

- Identifying different corporate investment decision pathways or projects that management can navigate given highly uncertain business conditions.
- Valuing each of the strategic decision pathways and what it represents in terms of financial viability and feasibility.
- Prioritizing these pathways or projects based on a series of qualitative and quantitative metrics.

- Optimizing the value of strategic investment decisions by evaluating different decision paths under certain conditions or using a different sequence of pathways that can lead to the optimal strategy.
- Timing the effective execution of investments and finding the optimal trigger values and cost or revenue drivers.
- Managing existing or developing new optionalities and strategic decision pathways for future opportunities.

Issues to Consider

Strategic options do have significant intrinsic value, but this value is realized only when management decides to execute the strategies. Real options theory assumes that management is logical and competent and that management acts in the best interests of the company and its shareholders through the maximization of wealth and the minimization of risk of losses. For example, suppose a firm owns the rights to a piece of land that fluctuates dramatically in price. An analyst calculates the volatility of prices and recommends that management retain ownership for a specified time period, where within this period there is a good chance that the price of real estate will triple. Therefore, management owns a call option: an *option to wait* and defer sale for a particular time period. The value of the real estate is, therefore, higher than the value that is based on today's sale price. The difference is simply this option to wait. However, the value of the real estate will not command the higher value if prices do triple but management decides not to execute the option to sell. In that case, the price of real estate goes back to its original levels after the specified period, and then management finally relinquishes its rights.

Strategic optionality value can only be obtained if the option is executed; otherwise, all the options in the world are worthless.

Was the analyst right or wrong? What was the true value of the piece of land? Should it have been valued at its explicit value on a deterministic case where you know what the price of land is right now, and, therefore, this is its value; or should it include some types of optionality where there is a good probability that the price of land could triple in value, and, thus, the piece of land is truly worth more than it is now and should therefore be valued accordingly? The latter is the real options view. The additional strategic optionality value can only be obtained if the option is executed; otherwise, all the options in the world are worthless. This idea of *explicit* versus *implicit* value becomes highly significant when management's compensation is tied directly to the actual performance of particular projects or strategies.

To further illustrate this point, suppose the price of the land in the market is currently $10 million. Further, suppose that the market is highly liquid and volatile and that the firm can easily sell off the land at a moment's notice within the next five years, the same amount of time the firm owns the rights to the land. If there is a 50% chance the price will increase to $15 million and a 50% chance it will decrease to

$5 million within this time period, is the property worth an expected value of $10 million? If the price rises to $15 million, management should be competent and rational enough to execute the option and sell that piece of land immediately to capture the additional $5 million premium. However, if management acts inappropriately or decides to hold off selling in the hopes that prices will rise even further, the property value may eventually drop back down to $5 million. Now, how much is this property really worth? What if there happens to be an *abandonment option*? Suppose there is a perfect counterparty to this transaction who decides to enter into a contractual agreement whereby, for a contractual fee, the counterparty agrees to purchase the property for $10 million within the next five years, regardless of the market price and executable at the whim of the firm that owns the property. Effectively, a safety net has been created whereby the minimum floor value of the property has been set at $10 million (less the fee paid). That is, there is a limited downside but an unlimited upside, as the firm can always sell the property at market price if it exceeds the floor value. Hence, this strategic *abandonment option* has increased the value of the property significantly.

Logically, with this *abandonment option* in place, the value of the land with the option is definitely worth more than $10 million. The land price is stochastic and uncertain with some volatility (risk) and has some inherent probability distribution. The distribution's left tail is the downside risk, and the right tail is upside value. Having an abandonment option (in this example, a price protection of $10 million) means that you take a really sharp knife and you slice off the distribution's left tail at $10 million because the firm will never have to deal with the situation of selling the land at anything lower than $10 million. What happens is that the distribution's left-tail risk has been truncated and reduced, making the distribution now positively skewed, and the expected return or average value moves to the right. In other words, strategic real options in this case provided a *risk reduction and value enhancement strategy* to the firm. Therefore, this option has value (e.g., insurance policies require a premium or price to obtain, and you can think of this abandonment option as a price protection insurance against any downside movements), and the idea is to determine what the fair market value is, whether the option is indeed worth it, the optimal timing to execute the option, and so forth. The real options approach seeks to value this additional inherent flexibility. Real options analysis allows the firm to determine how much this safety downside insurance or abandonment option is worth (i.e., what is the fair market value of the contractual fee to obtain the option), the optimal trigger price (i.e., at what price will it be optimal to sell the land), and the optimal timing (i.e., what is the optimal amount of time to hold on to the land).

Implementing Real Options Analysis

First, it is vital to understand that real options analysis is *not* a simple set of equations or models. It is an *entire decision-making process* that enhances the traditional decision analysis approaches. It takes what has been tried-and-true financial analytics and evolves it to the next step by pushing the envelope of analytical techniques.

In addition, it is vital to understand that 50% of the value in real options analysis is simply thinking about it. Another 25% of the value comes from the number-crunching activities, while the final 25% comes from the results interpretation and explanation to management. Several issues should be considered when attempting to implement real options analysis:

- *Tools*—The correct tools are important. These tools must be more comprehensive than initially required because analysts will grow into them over time. Do not be restrictive in choosing the relevant tools. Always provide room for expansion. Advanced tools will relieve the analyst of detailed model building and let him or her focus instead on 75% of the value—thinking about the problem and interpreting the results. (Chapter Sixteen illustrates the use of Real Options Super Lattice Solver (SLS) software and how even complex and customized real options problems can be solved with great ease.)
- *Resources*—The best tools in the world are useless without the relevant human resources to back them up. Tools do not eliminate the analyst, but they enhance the analyst's ability to effectively and efficiently execute the analysis. The right people with the right tools will go a long way. Because there are only a few true real options experts in the world who actually understand the theoretical underpinnings of the models as well the practical applications, care should be taken in choosing the correct team.

  A team of real options experts is vital in the success of the initiative. A company should consider building a team of in-house experts to implement real options analysis and to maintain the ability for continuity, training, and knowledge transfer over time. Knowledge and experience in the theories, implementation, training, and consulting are the core requirements of this team of individuals. This is why training is vital. For instance, the Certified in Risk Management (CRM) certification program provides analysts and managers the opportunity to immerse themselves in the theoretical and real-life applications of simulation, forecasting, optimization, and real options (see www.realoptionsvaluation.com for details).
- *Senior Management Buy-In*—The analysis buy-in has to be top-down, where senior management drives the real options analysis initiative. A bottom-up approach in which a few inexperienced junior analysts try to impress the powers that be will fail miserably.

Types of Real Options Strategies

- *Abandonment Option*—An abandonment option provides the holder the right, but not the obligation, to sell off and abandon some project, asset, or property, at a prespecified price and term.
- *Barrier Option*—A barrier option means that the option becomes live and available for execution, and, consequently, the value of the strategic option depends on either breaching or not breaching an artificial barrier.
- *Expansion Option*—An expansion option provides management the right and ability to expand into different markets, products, and strategies, or to expand its current operations under the right conditions.
- *Chooser Option*—A chooser option implies that management has the flexibility to choose among several strategies, including the option to expand, abandon, switch, or contract, and combinations of other exotic options.
- *Contraction Option*—A contraction option provides management the right and ability to contract its operations under the right conditions, thereby saving on expenses.
- *Deferment Option (Timing Option, Option to Wait)*—This type of option is also a purchase option or an option to wait.

- *Sequential Compound Option*—A sequential compound option means that the execution and value of future strategic options depend on previous options in sequence of execution.
- *Switching Option*—A switching option provides the right and ability, but not the obligation, to switch among different sets of business operating conditions, including different technologies, markets, or products.

Execution Option Types

For all of the options listed, you can have different allowed execution times, including American, European, Bermudan, and Asian options. *American options* allow you to execute at any time before and up to and including the expiration date. *European options* allow you to execute only on a specific date, typically the expiration date itself. *Bermudan options* are a mix between European and American in that there is a blackout, or vesting period, when you cannot execute the option, but you can do so at any time after this blackout period and up to and including expiration. For example, an employee stock option usually has a 10-year maturity and a 4-year vesting period whereby the option cannot be exercised within this first 4 years and is lost if the employee leaves his or her job during this vesting period. However, once this requisite service period has passed, the option can be exercised at any time between year 4 and year 10.

Finally, *Asian options* are look-back options, where specific conditions in the option are dependent on some factor in the future. For example, United Airlines signs a purchase order today for delivery of some Airbus A380 in two years, and the price of the planes is dependent on the average market price between now and two years from now. That two-year period is in the future when the purchase order was placed, but it will be the past once the planes and final payment change hands. Thus, both parties can look back to this pricing period to obtain the final sale price of the planes. The upshot, then, is that you can have an American abandonment option or a European abandonment option, and so forth.

Industry Leaders Embracing Real Options

Industries using real options as a tool for strategic decision making started with oil and gas and mining companies and later expanded into utilities, biotechnology, and pharmaceuticals, and now into telecommunications, high-tech, and across all industries. The following examples relate how real options have been or should be used in different kinds of companies.

Automobile and Manufacturing Industry

In automobile and manufacturing, General Motors (GM) applies real options to create *switching option*s in producing its new series of autos. This option is essentially to use a cheaper resource over a given period of time. GM holds excess raw materials and has multiple global vendors for similar materials with excess contractual obligations above what it projects as necessary. The excess contractual cost is outweighed by the significant savings of switching vendors when a certain raw material becomes too expensive in a particular region of the world. By spending the additional money in contracting with vendors and meeting their minimum purchase requirements, GM has essentially paid the premium on purchasing a *switching option,* which is important especially when the price of raw materials fluctuates significantly in different regions around the world. Having an option here provides the holder a hedging vehicle against pricing risks.

Computer Industry

In the computer industry, HP-Compaq used to forecast sales in foreign countries months in advance. It then configured, assembled, and shipped the highly specific configuration printers to these countries. However, given that demand changes rapidly and forecast figures are seldom correct, the preconfigured printers usually suffered the higher inventory holding cost or the cost of technological obsolescence. HP-Compaq can create an *option to wait* and defer making any decisions too early through building assembly plants in these foreign countries. Parts can then be shipped and assembled in specific configurations when demand is known, possibly weeks in advance rather than months in advance. These parts can be shipped anywhere in the world and assembled in any configuration necessary, while excess parts are interchangeable across different countries. The premium paid on this option is building the assembly plants, and the upside potential is the savings in making wrong demand forecasts.

Airline Industry

In the airline industry, Boeing spends billions of dollars and takes several years to decide if a certain aircraft model should even be built. Should the wrong model be tested in this elaborate strategy, Boeing's competitors may gain a competitive advantage relatively quickly. Because so many technical, engineering, market, and financial uncertainties are involved in the decision-making process, Boeing can conceivably create an *option to choose* through parallel development of multiple plane designs simultaneously, knowing well the increasing cost of developing multiple designs simultaneously with the sole purpose of eliminating all but one in the near future. The added cost is the premium paid on the option. However, Boeing will be able to decide which model to abandon or continue when these uncertainties and risks become known over time. Eventually, all the models will be eliminated save one. This way, the company can hedge itself against making the wrong initial decision and benefit from the knowledge gained through parallel development initiatives.

Oil and Gas Industry

In the oil and gas industry, companies spend millions of dollars to refurbish their refineries and add new technology to create an *option to switch* their mix of outputs among heating oil, diesel, and other petrochemicals as a final product, using real options as a means of making capital and investment decisions. This option allows the refinery to switch its final output to one that is more profitable, based on prevailing market prices, to capture the demand and price cyclicality in the market.

Telecommunications Industry

In the telecommunications industry, in the past, companies like Sprint and AT&T installed more fiber-optic cable and other telecommunications infrastructure than any other company in order to create a *growth option* in the future by providing a secure and extensive network and to create a high barrier to entry, providing a first-to-market advantage. Imagine having to justify to the board of directors the need to spend billions of dollars on infrastructure that will not be used for years to come. Without the use of real options, this decision would have been impossible to justify.

Utilities Industry

In the utilities industry, firms have created an *option to execute* and an *option to switch* by installing cheap-to-build inefficient energy generator *peaker* plants to be used only when electricity prices are high and to shut down when prices are low. The price of electricity tends to remain constant until it hits a certain capacity utilization trigger level, when prices shoot up significantly. Although this occurs infrequently, the possibility still exists, and by having a cheap standby plant, the firm has created the option to turn on the switch whenever it becomes necessary to capture this upside price fluctuation.

Real Estate Industry

In the real estate arena, leaving land undeveloped creates an option to develop at a later date at a more lucrative profit level. However, what is the optimal wait time or the optimal trigger price to maximize returns? In theory, one can wait for an infinite amount of time. Real options provide the solution for the optimal timing and optimal price trigger value.

Pharmaceutical Research and Development Industry

In pharmaceutical or research and development initiatives, real options can be used to justify the large investments in what seems to be cashless and unprofitable under the discounted cash flow method but actually creates *compound expansion options* in the future. Under the myopic lenses of a traditional discounted cash flow analysis, the high initial investment of, say, a billion dollars in research and development may return a highly uncertain projected few million dollars over the next few years. Management will conclude under a net present value analysis that the project is not financially feasible. However, a cursory look at the industry indicates that research and development is performed everywhere. Hence, management must see an intrinsic strategic value in research and development. How is this intrinsic strategic value quantified? A real options approach would optimally time and spread the billion dollar initial investment over a multiple-stage investment structure. At each stage, management has an *option to wait* and see what happens as well as the *option to abandon* or the *option to expand* into the subsequent stages. The ability to defer cost and proceed only if situations are permissible creates value for the investment.

High-Tech and e-Business Industry

In e-business strategies, real options can be used to prioritize different e-commerce initiatives and to justify those large initial investments that have an uncertain future. Real options can be used in e-commerce to create incremental investment stages compared to a large one-time investment (invest a little now, wait and see before investing more) as well as create *options to abandon* and other future growth options.

Mergers and Acquisitions

In valuing a firm for acquisition, you should not only consider the revenues and cash flows generated from the firm's operations but also the strategic options that come with the firm. For instance, if the acquired firm does not operate to expectations, an *abandonment option* can be executed where it can be sold for its intellectual property and other tangible assets. If the firm is highly successful, it can be spun off into other industries and verticals, or new products and services can be eventually developed through the execution of an *expansion option*. In fact, in mergers and acquisitions, several strategic options exist. For instance, a firm acquires other entities to enlarge its existing portfolio of products or geographic location or to obtain new technology (*expansion option*), or to divide the acquisition into many smaller pieces and sell them off, as in the case of a corporate raider (*abandonment option*); sometimes it merges to form a larger organization due to certain synergies and immediately lays off many of its employees (*contraction option*). If the seller does not value its real options, it may be leaving money on the negotiation table. If the buyer does not value these strategic options, it is undervaluing a potentially highly lucrative acquisition target.

All of these cases where in the traditional discounted cash flow sense the high cost of implementation with no apparent payback in the near future seems foolish and incomprehensible, are fully justified in the real options sense when taking into account the strategic options the practice creates for the future, the uncertainty of the future operating environment, and management's flexibility in making the right choices at the appropriate time.

Real Options Example in Banking: Asset Liability Management

Asset liability management (ALM) is a financial technique that can help companies to manage the mismatch of asset and liability and/or cash flow risks. The mismatched risks are due to different underlying factors that cause the assets and liabilities to move in different directions with different magnitudes. Asset-liability risk is a leveraged form of risk. The capital of most financial institutions is small relative to the firm's assets or liabilities, so small percentage changes in assets or liabilities can translate into large percentage changes in capital.

Typically, companies such as banks, insurance companies, and pension funds (or their corporate sponsors) adopt such techniques to help them better manage their mismatched asset/liability risks (more particularly, the interest rate risks) and to ensure that their capital will not be depleted in changing demographic and economic environments.

Techniques for assessing asset-liability risk include gap analysis and duration analysis. These analyses facilitate techniques of gap management and duration matching of assets and liabilities. Both approaches worked well if assets and liabilities comprise fixed cash flows. However, the increasing use of options such as embedded prepayment risks in mortgages or callable debt, pose problems that these traditional analyses cannot address. Thus, Monte Carlo simulation techniques are more appropriate to address the increasingly complex financial markets.

Today, financial institutions also make use of *over-the-counter* (OTC) derivatives to structure hedging strategies and securitization techniques to remove assets and liabilities from their balance sheet, therefore eliminating asset-liability risk and freeing up capital for new business.

The scope of ALM activities has broadened to other nonfinancial industries, because companies now need to address all sorts of risks, including interest-rate exposures, commodity price risks, liquidity risk, and foreign exchange risk.

Embedded Options in Financial Instruments

Traditionally, ALM was used as a tool to protect the capital/surplus from movements of assets/liabilities against a certain risk (e.g., parallel shift in yield curve). In theory, ALM enables the financial institution to remove certain volatility risks. For banks and insurers, ALM can potentially lower regulatory capital requirements, as less capital is needed to protect against unforeseen risks. For pension sponsors, ALM also can reduce the plan's funding requirements and accounting costs by locking into a certain level of return.

Cash flow matching or *immunization* is one of the ALM methods in which both asset and liability cash flows are matched exactly such that any movement in the yield curve would be irrelevant for the entity. However, most financial instruments today rarely have fixed cash flows. Thus, cash flow matching would require frequent portfolio rebalancing, which is proved to be prohibitively expensive.

Due to the shortcomings of cash flow matching, *duration matching* was used to manage the mismatch risks (Figure 12.1). The typical duration matching approach is to find an optimal asset allocation portfolio in which the asset duration matches the liability duration. The asset and liability duration is defined as the amount of change in the market value of assets/liabilities when the yield curve shifts by 100 basis points. The obvious shortcomings of duration matching are that the yield curve rarely shifts in a parallel fashion and that the linear approximate (asset and liability duration) works well only on small changes to the yield curve.

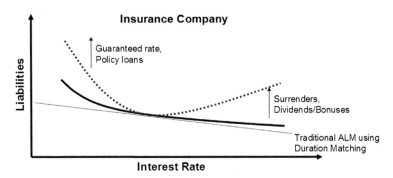

Figure 12.1 Insurance Asset Liability Management Duration Matching.

Today's financial assets and liabilities have embedded options that significantly affect the timing of cash flows, sensitivity to change in market rates, and total return. Here are some examples of embedded options in various financial institutions:

- *Insurance policies:* Guaranteed rates, cash surrender values, policy loans, dividends/bonuses
- *Banks:* Prepayment option to borrowers, overdraft, early withdrawal
- *Pension plans:* Early retirement, cash-out option, defined contribution conversion
- *Assets:* Callable options, prepayment options, abandon option (credit/bankruptcy)

Figure 12.1 illustrates the effects of compound embedded options and the sensitivity of a life insurer's liabilities to the change in interest rates.

Other variations of traditional ALM models include *convexity matching* (second derivative) and *dynamic matching* (frequent rebalancing). These variations attempt to increase the precision of the changes in market values of the assets and liabilities, compensating for the effects of the embedded options.

Traditional ALM using cash flow/duration matching is not an effective way to protect capital because those models do not recognize the risks of embedded options. Furthermore, the trading costs of rebalancing the portfolios are prohibitively expensive. The simulation approach to assets/liability models is a better way to protect capital by capturing the impact of embedded options in many possible variations and finding the optimal portfolio that can minimize the volatility of the surpluses. More advanced approaches would consider the downside risk only. Most financial institutions would like to guard against the risk of reducing capital/surpluses. An increase in capital/surpluses is actually a good thing. As a result, a slightly higher volatility in the entity's capital may be acceptable as long as the potentially higher yields can outweigh the level of downside risk undertaken.

Implementing Asset Liability Management

Six steps are taken to implement an effective ALM:

1. *Setting ALM Objectives:* First of all, the bank, insurer, or pension fund sponsor needs to decide on its ALM objectives. The objectives may be affected by the organization's desires,

goals, and positioning in relation to its stakeholders, regulators, competition, and external rating agencies. Would it be simply minimizing the volatility of surpluses? Would a higher yield be more desirable, and, if so, what is the maximum level of risk that can be undertaken?

2. *Risk Factors and Cash Flow Structure*: The ALM manager/analyst needs to capture the various risks the entity carries and take into account the complex interactions between the asset and liability cash flows. Risk factors may include market, interest rate, and credit risks, as well as contractual obligations that behave like options.

3. *Available Hedging Solutions*: While diversification can reduce nonsystematic risks, financial institutions often carry firm-specific risks that cannot be diversified easily. The organization needs to evaluate the appropriateness of various hedging solutions, including types of assets, use of hedging instruments (derivatives, interest rate options, credit options, pricing, reinsurance) and use of capital market instruments (securitization, acquisition, and sale of business lines).

4. *Modeling Risk Factors*: Modeling the underlying risk factors may not be trivial. If the ALM manager's concern is the interest rate risks, then modeling the yield curve would be critical.

5. *Setting Decision Variables:* The decision variables differ for various financial institutions. For instance, an insurer needs to set a decision on asset allocation to each qualified investment, the level of dividend/bonuses paid to policyholders, the amount of new businesses undertaking, pricing, and so on.

6. *Setting Constraints:* Typically, financial institutions are heavily regulated (reserve and capital requirements). More recently, accounting requirements (or profits) also have become increasingly important. These constraints need to be modeled to ensure that the final solution can meet the regulatory and accounting requirements.

As an example of implementing ALM, Figure 12.2 shows a typical ALM modeling flowchart for an insurance company that aims to minimize its interest rate risks.

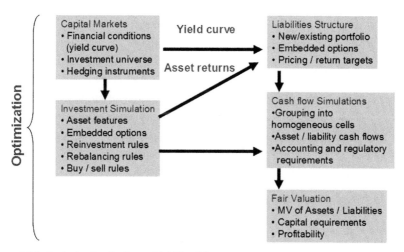

Figure 12.2 Optimization in Asset Liability Management.

Real Options Applications to Asset Liability Management

Real options have useful applications in the evaluation of various hedging strategies in an ALM context. Traditional analysis focuses on minimizing surplus volatility as a fixed strategy with periodic rebalancing (Figure 12.3). However, today's business decisions are much more dynamic, with increasingly complex hedging instruments and strategies available to management.

Each business strategy has its associated costs, risks, and benefits. Business strategies that can be implemented when needed can enhance business flexibility to guard against undesirable events, therefore enhancing their overall value to the organization (Figure 12.4). Real options can determine the risk-adjusted strategic value to the organization that can be ranked and optimized according to business objectives and available resources.

Risk Minimization (Old Way)
- All risks are undesirable

Real Options Approach (New Way)
- Downside risks are undesirable
- Missing upside potential are also undesirable
- There may be value to wait

- Minimize volatility to capital

- Formulate strategies to hedge capital depletion, while retaining upside potentials

- Limit asset allocation to match liability duration, thus reducing asset return potentials

- Value, analyze and rank /optimize alternative "protection" strategies against return/risk objectives from an organization's perspective
- Trial portfolios / proof of concept
- Redesign of products woith embedded options

Figure 12.3 New versus Old Approaches in Asset Liability Management Risk Management.

Asset-Based Strategies
- Asset allocation
- Structured products (derivatives, swaps, credit options, interest rate options etc.)
- Alpha & Beta approach to asset allocation
- Timing

Liability-Based Strategies
- Pricing margin/reserves
- Reinsurance
- Securitization
- Acquisition/sale of business lines
- Redesigning/reengineering products
- Timing

Figure 12.4 Asset versus Liability Strategies.

Part Two

Credit Administration

13 Capital Adequacy

Chapter Outline

Functions of Bank Capital

> *"Capital is an important indicator of a bank's overall condition, for financial markets, depositors, and bank regulators."[1]*

[1] The Basel Committee on Banking Supervision, which is a committee of banking supervisory authorities established by the central bank Governors of the Group of Ten countries in 1975. It consists of senior representatives of bank supervisory authorities and central banks from Belgium, Canada, France, Germany, Italy, Japan, Luxembourg, the Netherlands, Sweden, Switzerland, the United Kingdom, and the United States. It usually meets at the Bank for International Settlements in Basel, where its permanent Secretariat is located.

Credit Engineering for Bankers. DOI: 10.1016/B978-0-12-378585-5.10013-2

Bank capital fosters public confidence and provides a buffer for contingencies involving large losses, thus protecting depositors from failure. Capital funds provide time to (1) recover so losses can be absorbed out of future earnings rather than capital funds, (2) wind down operations without disrupting other businesses, and (3) ensure public confidence that the bank has positioned itself to withstand the new hardship placed on it.

Here are some additional points concerning the functions and growth of bank capital:

- Banks utilize much higher financial leverage than almost any other industry.
- Equity capital accounts for about 7% of total capital.
- Capital rules foster confidence.
- Capital must be sufficient to protect against on- or off-balance sheet risks.
- Minimum capital standards are vital to reducing systemic risk.
- Bank capital reduces risks borne by the Federal Deposit Insurance Corporation (FDIC).
- Adequate capital allows absorption of losses out of future earnings rather than capital funds.
- Regulatory functions that ensure banks comply with capital requirements.
- Other functions include supplying the working tools of the enterprise.

Perhaps the most important function of bank capital is providing protection against risks:

> *Banks must be able to demonstrate that chosen internal capital targets are well founded and these targets are consistent with the bank's overall risk profile and its current operating environment. In assessing capital adequacy, bank management needs to be mindful of the particular stage of the business cycle in which the bank is operating. Rigorous, forward-looking stress testing that identifies possible events or changes in market conditions that could adversely impact the bank should be performed. Bank management clearly bears primary responsibility for ensuring that the bank has adequate capital to support its risks.*[2]

The protective function of bank capital has been viewed not only as assuring full payoff of depositors in case of liquidation but also as contributing to the maintenance of solvency by providing a cushion so a bank threatened with losses might continue operating. Unlike most firms, only a portion of bank capital contributes to solvency. Banks are generally considered solvent as long as capital is unimpaired; that is, asset values are at least equal to adjusted liabilities,[3] and, more significantly, bank assets are diligently appraised, marked-to-market, and cushioned to a high degree against unexpected risks (risk adjusted). Bankwide risks falling under protective capital include credit, market, liquidity, operational, legal, and reputation risks.[4]

Credit risk arises from the potential that a borrower or counterparty will fail to perform on an obligation. Because most earning assets are in the form of loans, poor loan quality is the major cause of bank failure. As a result, risk exposures are assessed,

[2] Basel Committee on Banking Supervision Consultative Document Pillar 2 (Supervisory Review Process), supporting document to the New Basel Capital Accord issued January 2001 for comment by May 31, 2001.

[3] Liabilities excluding subordinated capital notes and debentures, plus capital stock.

[4] Basel Committee on Bank Supervision, Basel Switzerland.

Table 13.1 Protection Against Credit Losses for Purposes of Capital Adequacy

First Line of Defense	Second Line of Defense
Current earnings. The appropriate focal relationship is the ratio of current earnings, after taxes, provisions for loan losses and dividends, to actual loss expectations.	Reserve for loan losses and other capital accounts after the reserve has been charged and exhausted. The second line of defense of capital adequacy (from a historical perspective) holds that if the principal preconditions are satisfied, loan loss reserves and other capital accounts must aggregate to 20 times twice the level of historical loss, including loan loss, to provide a reasonable margin of safety.

whether on- or off-balance sheet, to include typical loans, receivables under derivative and foreign exchange contracts, and lending-related commitments (e.g., letters of credit and undrawn commitments to extend credit). Using statistical techniques, estimates are made of both expected losses (on average, over a cycle) and unexpected losses for each segment of the portfolio. These estimates usually drive the *credit cost along with capital allocations* to each business unit and are incorporated into each unit's "value added." As a result, the credit risk profile of each business unit becomes an important factor in assessing performance. First and second lines of protection against credit losses for purposes of capital adequacy are earnings and loan loss reserves (Table 13.1).

Market risk is based on adverse movements in market price or rate—for example, interest rates, foreign exchange rates, or equity prices. Traditionally, management and regulators focused strictly on credit risk. In recent years another group of assets have come under scrutiny: assets typically traded in financial markets. These assets form the "trading book," in contrast to the "banking book," associated with *traditionally* non-traded assets: loans (though today there is a big play in the secondary loan market). For most large banks, while the trading book is relatively small compared with the banking book, its rising prominence makes market risk an important regulatory concern.

In January 1996, rules were adopted to regulate market exposures, setting risk-based capital requirements for the trading book of banks and securities houses.[5] Basel Capital Accords require commercial banks with significant trading activity to provide regulators with value-at-risk (VaR) estimates from internal risk-measuring models because VaR estimates a bank's market risk capital requirements better than most other models. VaR addresses aggregating market exposures across disparate asset classes, helping to calculate a portfolio-level measure of market risk.

Liquidity risk stems from the possibility that an institution will be unable to meet obligations when due because assets cannot be liquidated, required funding is unavailable (referred to as "funding liquidity risk"), or specific exposures cannot be unwound without significantly lowering market prices because of weak market depth

---

[5] European Union (EU).

or market disruptions ("market liquidity risk"). Capital position has a direct bearing on an institution's ability to access liquidity, particularly during periods of crisis, which is why internal systems for measuring, monitoring, and controlling liquidity risk are frequently evolving. Weak liquidity might cause a bank to liquefy assets or acquire liabilities to refinance maturing claims. Banks typically evaluate capital adequacy in terms of their liquidity profile and the fluidity of markets in which they operate.

Operational risk encompasses the risk that inadequate information systems, operational problems, breaches in internal controls, fraud, or unforeseen catastrophes will result in unexpected losses. Frequently, operating risks account for a substantial fraction (20% or more) of large banks' total risk. Thus, assessing capital for credit and market risks, while excluding operating risks, could easily understate overall capital requirements. The requirements problem is complicated by the fact that, while operating risks are viewed as quite important, models for quantifying these risks are scarce.

Legal risk is based on the potential that unenforceable contracts, lawsuits, or adverse judgments can disrupt or otherwise negatively affect the operations or condition of a banking organization.

Reputation risk stems from the possibility that negative publicity regarding an institution's business practices, whether true or not, will cause a decline in the customer base, costly litigation, or revenue reductions.

A Historical Perspective

The purpose of this section is to provide a historical perspective to help us understand changes in capital adequacy requirements prior to and since the Basal Accords.

Traditional Asset Categories

From a historical perspective, bank assets traditionally were divided into six groups, each associated with a specific capital requirement. While these allocations may appear a bit arbitrary, they were consistent with bank policies at the time (at least before the 1988 Basel Accords) and were supposed to be ample to absorb losses. The six categories required capital levels sufficient to satisfy regulators and keep banks functional.

First Category: Required Reserves and Highly Liquid Assets: Cash, bank balances, U.S. government securities maturing within five years, bankers' acceptances, and federal funds sold. No capital was required against these essentially riskless assets. While remote market risk exists even in short-term U.S. government securities, earnings easily absorb any exposures.

Second Category: Minimum Risk Assets: Loans and investments with very low risk such as U.S. government securities with maturities over five years, government-guaranteed loans, and government agencies securities; loans secured by similar assets, by savings passbooks, cash value of life insurance, prime commercial paper; brokers loans; and other assets of similar quality.

Third Category: Portfolio Assets: Traditionally included usual banking risk assets—for example, the remaining loan portfolio free from regulatory classification, along with the remainder of investment-grade (rated Baa or above) securities (other than U.S. government bonds) maturing in more than five years.

Fourth Category: Substandard Assets: Assets with more than normal banking risk, such as obligors with a weak financial condition or unfavorable record, risky exposures backed by marginal collateral quality, or insufficient or below margin securities.

Fifth Category: "Workout" Assets: These assets included loans that auditors classified as doubtful: weak credits backed by dubious common stock, defaulted securities, or real estate assets not legally acquirable except by foreclosure.

Sixth Category: Asset Losses Along with Fixed Assets: Fixed assets are working basics but not considered bank investments in a real sense. Elaborate premises attract business but offer depositors little protection in the event of bank failure. Bank facilities can be disposed of only when a bank goes into liquidation and likely will return little value during economic downturns.

The Basel Accords

"The Basel Accord is not a static framework but is being developed and improved continuously. The Basel Committee neither ignores market participants' comments on the Accord nor denies that there may be potential for improvement. More specifically, the Committee is aware that the current treatment of credit risk needs to be revisited so as to modify and improve the Accord, where necessary, in order to maintain its effectiveness."

—Tom de Swaan

Capital rules changed with the 1988 Basel Accord. Basel was instrumental in reversing a protracted downward trend in international banks' capital adequacy, paving the way to the increased attention the financial markets paid to banks' capital quantity/quality.

"The Accord effectively contributed to enhanced market transparency, to international harmonization of capital standards, and thus, importantly, to a level playing field within the Group of Ten (G-10) countries and elsewhere. . . . Virtually all non-G-10 countries with international banks of significance have introduced, or are in the process of introducing, arrangements similar to those laid down in the Accord. These are achievements that need to be preserved."[6]

Since the 1988 Accord, banking and financial markets changed markedly, following in the wake of new innovative credit risk measurement and management tools, and sophisticated bank products. Yet, the Accords failed to keep pace with the new playing field of the 1990s and were thus ripe for revision.

Post-1988 amendments offer a lot more plasticity. Capital standards are less subject to excessive reinterpretations, dampening chances that regulatory burdens will prove unproductive. This means, the argument goes, that large spreads between regulatory perceived risks (and capital) and bank perceived risks are more easily resolved, reducing the odds of "misguided" capital allocations. For example, if a bank felt it had far more capital than needed, paring down allocations might encourage the bank to pursue riskier loans within a certain risk category (chasing higher returns on capital).

---

[6] Tom de Swaan, former chairman of the Basel Committee on Banking Supervision.

The 1988 Accord focused a great deal on credit risk.[7] Basically, the Accord provided a framework for new capital weightings according to risk: 0%, 10%, 20%, 50%, and 100%. For example, OECD-government (Organization for Economic Cooperation and Development countries) debt and cash are zero weighted; loans to banks set at 20%; loans fully secured by mortgages on residential property, 50%; claims on the private sector or on banks incorporated outside the OECD with a residual maturity of over one year, 100% (Table 13.2, left column).

The 1988 Accord has been replaced by a system using external credit ratings. Debt of an OECD country rated single "A" will risk-rate at 20%, while "AAA" debt receives zero capital weighting. Corporate debt will be marked with graduated weightings so that an "AA" rated loan will be risk-weighted at 20%, while an "A" will be at 100% (Table 13.2, right column).

Accounting, Economic, and Regulatory Defined Value

Capital adequacy is measured three ways: *book value* (GAAP), *economic (market) value,* and *regulatory defined value* (RAP). The contrasts between the three methods can be noteworthy. At times when book and economic values diverge markedly, bankers and regulators alike can walk away with a distorted view of capital coverage. Consider a money-center bank's book and market (equity) values prior to and just after the international debt crisis or at the height of the crunch in commercial real estate lending, or an S & L book net worth vis-à-vis market worth during the height of the thrift crisis and just after the government bailout. Expressed in terms of economic value to book value, we see at once that ratio falls below one. In practice, if book accounting is to have any relevance to the science (and art) of capital apportionment, then devalued assets, whether in the form of underwater mortgages or questionable loans, must be marked-to-market—and frequently.

Economic or Market Denominated Capital

The market value of capital represents the real net worth suitable for settling claims. Banks can be book solvent but insolvent when the same assets are priced in the marketplace. The situation might arise if auditors failed (by error or design) to adjust loan loss reserves to match the quality of a bank's loan portfolio or if assets were not marked-to-market following adverse interest or exchange rate movement. Remember that economic values are influenced by market-perceived *risk-adjusted* earning power, while book value follows historical cost. It is not surprising, in times of stress, to find significant differences between two methods. Banks, after all, operate in a dynamic and uncertain world.

An offshoot of market value is a concept the literature calls *fair* or *reasonable value* (known also as *intrinsic value*). While the market value of listed security can be identified at times, the stock's fair value as viewed by different investors (or, for that

---

[7] International Convergence of Capital Measurement and Capital Standards, Basel Committee on Banking Supervision, 1988.

Table 13.2 Capital Adequacy Guidelines: Basel I and II

	Old Accords: Basel I	New Accords: Basel II
0%	• Cash • Claims on central governments and central banks denominated in national currency and funded in that currency • Other claims on OECD and central governments and central banks • Claims collateralized by cash of OECD central government securities or guaranteed by OECD central governments	• AAA- to AA-rated sovereigns
0%, 10%, 20%, 50%	• At national discretion • Claims of domestic public sector entities, excluding central government, and loans guaranteed by such entities	• Not applicable
20%	• Claims on multilateral development banks and claims guaranteed by, or collateralized by, securities issued by such banks • Claims on banks incorporated in countries outside the OECD with a residual maturity of up to one year and loans with a residual maturity of up to one year guaranteed by banks incorporated in countries outside the OECD • Claims on nondomestic OECD public sector entities, excluding central government, and loans guaranteed by such entities • Cash items in process of collection	• A+- to A-rated sovereigns • AAA- to AA-rated banks • AAA- to AA-rated corporates
50%	• Loans fully secured by mortgage on residential property that is or will be occupied by the borrower or that is rented	• BBB+- to BBB-rated sovereigns • A+- to A-rated banks (risk-weighting based on that of the sovereign in which the bank is incorporated) • A+- to A-rated banks (risk-weighting based on the assessment of the individual bank) • BBB+ to BBB-rated banks • Unrated banks (risk weighting based on the assessment of the individual banks) • Loans fully secured by mortgage on residential property that is or will be occupied by the borrower or that is rented

(continued)

Table 13.2 Capital Adequacy Guidelines: Basel I and II—*Cont'd*

	Old Accords: Basel I	New Accords: Basel II
100%	• Claims on the private sector • Claims on banks incorporated outside the OECD with a residual maturity of over one year • Claims on central governments outside the OECD (unless denominated in national currency and funded in that currency) • Claims on commercial companies owned by the public sector • Premises, plant, and equipment and other fixed assets • Real estate and other investments (including nonconsolidated investment participations in other companies) • Capital instruments issued by other banks (unless deducted from capital) • All other assets	• BBB+- to BBB-rated banks (risk-weighting based on that of the sovereign in which the bank is incorporated) • BB+- to B-rated sovereigns • BB+- to B-rated banks (risk-weighting based on that of the sovereign in which the bank is incorporated) • BB+- to B-rated banks (risk-rating based on the assessment of the individual bank) • BBB+- to BBB-rated corporates • BB+- to B-rated corporates • Unrated banks (risk-weighting based on that of the sovereign in which the bank is incorporated) • Unrated corporates • Commercial mortgages
150%	Not Applicable	• Below B-rated sovereigns • Below B-rated banks (risk-weighting based on that of the sovereign in which the bank is incorporated) • Below B-rated banks (risk-weighting based on the assessment of the individual bank) • Below B-rated corporates • Securitization tranches rated below BB- and BB-bbb

Source: JP Morgan, Special Corporate Study, "Financial Institutions; The Basel's Committee's New Capital Adequacy Framework—Market Implications," p. 5, Table 3: BIS capital adequacy rules—A comparison of existing and proposed guidelines, June 8, 1999.

matter, internal auditors, management, or regulators at large) can differ. Benjamin Graham, David Dodd, and Sidney Cottle[8] define *fair value* as "that value which is justified by the facts—for example, assets, earnings, and dividends." The computed (fair) value is likely to change at least from year to year as the factors governing that value are modified.

[8] Authors and leading gurus in the investments field.

In practice, investors holding stock in the financial services look to financial strength, sustainable liquidity, and earnings quality and growth. To banks and their investors, earnings quality is practically synonymous with loan quality. Why is loan quality both a fundamental and paramount concept? Reasoning holds that investors believe that while lower-quality loans may temporarily bring in abnormally high income, in the long run this ill-advised policy will statistically result in abnormal losses negating the higher income that was temporarily booked. Also factored in are historical loan loss provisions, actual losses incurred, and the relative size of annual provisions for losses and reserves for losses, together with the tally of nonperforming assets—all disclosed in annual reports and reports published by investment houses.

Regulatory Denominated Capital (Regulatory Accounting)

The forms of banking capital were largely standardized in the Basel I Accord, issued by the Basel Committee on Banking Supervision and left untouched by the Basel II Accord. Regulators of most countries internationally have implemented these standards in local legislation. Regulatory capital deals with three capital "tiers": Tier 1 (core) capital serves as the most basic form of permanent capital; Tier 2 includes various forms of capital not qualifying as Tier 1 capital; and Tier 3 capital, a new concept, calls for capital that may be allocated only against market risks of inherently short duration.

Tier 1 Capital

Tier 1 capital (core capital) is a bank's most valuable form of capital and must comprise at least 50% of total regulatory capital. Included are common equity; qualifying noncumulative perpetual preferred shares (these instruments have the perpetual characteristics of equity and rank at the bottom of the capital structure, just ahead of common stock, but offering a fixed rather than variable rate of return); and qualifying noncontrolling interests in subsidiaries arising on consolidation from Tier 1 capital instruments. Goodwill and other intangible assets are deducted from Tier 1 capital, with the resulting figure then compared to total risk-weighted assets to determine the risk-weighted Tier 1 capital ratio.

While common equity is the most prevalent form of Tier 1 capital, it is also the most expensive. In practice, the issuing bank could be required to guarantee some level of return on capital or face constraints from existing shareholders fearful of stock dilution and so on. But the issue remains: Tier 1 is increasingly recognized as a way of balancing the often divergent concerns of *regulators*, whose overriding objective is to preserve balance sheet integrity, and *shareholders'* interests directed toward strong investment returns. For banks, the issuance of Tier 1 capital, while certainly not cheap, offers an attractive means to address the needs of two important constituencies: supervisors and investors.

Capital adequacy guidelines[9] mandate that for banks domiciled in OECD countries Tier 1 capital must amount to a minimum of 4% of total risk-weighted assets; in practice, however, most commercial banks target a Tier 1 ratio in the range of 6% to 7%. Still other banks carry significantly higher capital ratios reflecting a combination of factors like strength and sustainability of earnings, availability of hidden reserves, unrealized gains on securities, and management's conservatism toward earnings and capital retention.

A Breakdown of Tier 1 Capital Components

Common Shareholder Equity

Included are common stock, capital reserves, and retained earnings, and adjustments for the cumulative effect of foreign currency translations, less stock held in treasury. A capital instrument deemed not permanent or that has preference with regard to liquidation or payment of dividends is not considered (regulatory defined) common stock, regardless of what investors call the instrument. Regulators take special note of terms looking for common stock issues having more than one class. Preference features may be found in a class of common (stock), and, if so, that class will be pulled out of the common (stock) category. When adjustments are completed, the remaining common stock becomes the dominant form of Tier 1 capital.

Accordingly, capital guidelines discourage overreliance on nonvoting equity elements in Tier 1 capital. Nonvoting equity attributes arise in cases where a bank issued two classes of common stock, one voting and the other nonvoting. Alternatively, one class may have so-called supervoting rights entitling the holder to more votes than other classes. Here, supervoting shares may have the votes to overwhelm the voting power of other shares. Accordingly, banks with nonvoting, common equity along with Tier 1 perpetual preferred stock in excess of their voting common stock are *clearly overrelying on nonvoting equity elements in Tier 1 capital.* The important point is that, in such cases, regulators are likely to reallocate some nonvoting equity elements from Tier 1 to Tier 2 capital.

Perpetual Preferred Stock

This type of stock is defined by risk-based capital guidelines as preferred stock with no maturity date, stock not redeemable at the holder's option, and preferred issues with no other provisions requiring future redemption. Perpetual preferred qualifies as Tier 1 capital only if it can absorb losses while the bank operates and only if the bank has the inclination and legal right to defer or eliminate preferred dividends altogether.

Perpetual preferred stock allowing redemptions at the option of the financial institution may qualify as Tier 1 capital only if the redemption is subject to prior

---

[9] Established under the Basel Accord, an agreement reached under the auspices of the Bank for International Settlements.

approval of regulators. Stock that is convertible at the option of the bank into another issue of perpetual preferred stock or subordinated debt is subject to prior regulatory approval as well.

Noncumulative Preferred Stock

Banks may include perpetual preferred stock in Tier 1 only if the stock is noncumulative. Noncumulative issues must not permit accruing or payment of unpaid dividends—period. In contrast, perpetual preferred stock calling for accumulation and future payment of unpaid dividends is regulatory cumulative, regardless of what the issue says and will end up in Tier 2 supplemental capital.

Preferred issues with reset dividend rates conditional on the bank's financial condition or credit standing is excluded from Tier 1 but may be acceptable Tier 2 capital. *"The obligation under such instruments to pay out higher dividends when a bank's condition deteriorates is inconsistent with the essential precept that capital should provide both strength and loss absorption capacity to a bank during periods of adversity."*[10]

Embedded Special Features in Preferred Issues

Some preferred issues embed features that raise questions as to whether these issues are acceptable as any manner of permanent capital. In this category, regulators may see the so-called exploding rate or similar feature, where, after a specified period, the dividend rate automatically increases to a level that promotes or even triggers redemption. Higher dividend requirements could be forced on a bank trying to work out problems, thus ruling out the possibility for inclusion in Tier 1 capital.

Convertible Perpetual Preferred Stock

Convertible issues allow investors to convert bank-preferred stock into a fixed number of common stock at a preset price. Because the conversion feature reduces capital structure risk, the stock will generally qualify as Tier 1 capital (provided, of course, that it is noncumulative). However, preferred issues whereby investors are able to convert into common stock at current market prices raise concerns. If the bank is performing poorly, the conversion ratio may trigger conversion into a large number of low-priced common shares. This could result in serious common dilution. The concern here is that the threat of dilution could make the bank reluctant to sell new common stock or place the bank under strong market pressure to redeem or repurchase the convertible stock preferred. Thus, convertible preferred stock will likely not qualify as Tier 1 capital.

Minority Interest in Equity Accounts of Consolidated Subsidiaries

Minority interest in equity is included in Tier 1 capital because, as a general rule, it represents equity that is freely available to absorb losses in operating subsidiaries.

[10] Quote from the Federal Reserve Bank (FRB).

Banks are expected to avoid using minority interest as an avenue for introducing elements that do not otherwise qualify as Tier 1 capital (such as cumulative or auction-rate perpetual preferred stock) or that would, in effect, result in an excessive reliance on preferred stock within Tier 1 capital. Should a bank use minority interest in these ways, regulators might require reallocation of a portion of the bank's minority interest to Tier 2 capital. Table 13.3 provides a summary of the characteristics of Tier 1 capital.

Tier 1 Leverage Ratio

Behind Tier 1 leverage benchmarks are limits regulators like to place on an institution leveraging up its equity capital base. Dividing Tier 1 capital by average total consolidated assets brings us to Tier 1 leverage. Average total consolidated assets equals quarterly average total assets reported on the bank's recent regulatory report, less goodwill, certain other intangible assets, investments in subsidiaries or associated companies, and certain excess deferred-tax assets that are dependent on future taxable income.

The Federal Reserve has adopted minimum Tier 1 leverage as 3% for highly rated banks. For state member banks, the same holds as long as these banks operate with well-diversified risk portfolios; little unhedged interest-rate-risk exposure; solid asset quality; high liquidity; and good earnings Risk Adjusted Return On Capital (RAROC)

Table 13.3 Summary of Characteristics of Tier 1 Capital

Meaning	Tier 1 capital, often called "core" capital, represents the most basic form of permanent capital supporting a bank's operations.
Importance	Tier 1 capital is a bank's most valuable form of capital and must comprise at least 50% of total capital, as per Basel Accord guidelines.
	1. Tier 1 capital is an important focus of interest of investment analysts and rating agencies' views on a given bank's capital strength.
	2. And, like other forms of capital, Tier 1 provides operating and strategic flexibility for bank managements in pursuing performance objectives.
	3. While common equity is the most common type of Tier 1 capital, it is also the most expensive form of capital to raise
	4. Tier 1 capital is increasingly recognized as a means of balancing the often divergent interests of banking industry regulators, whose overriding objective is to preserve and/or strengthen the integrity of a bank's balance sheet, and shareholders, who are demanding high returns on their equity investments.
	5. For banks, the issuance of Tier 1 qualifying debt is an attractive means to address the needs of both of these important constituencies.
Maturity	None.
Restrictions	Minimum of 4.0% of total risk-weighted assets ("Total Capital"); most banks target 6.0% Tier 1 capital ratios.
Provisions	Noncumulative, interest deferral. Full loss absorption.

Source: Bank for International Settlements.

derived, of course)—in other words, ranked composite 1 under the CAMELS rating system.[11] Other state member banks are expected to have a minimum Tier 1 leverage ratio of 4%. Bank holding companies rated a composite 1 under the BOPEC[12] rating system and those that have implemented regulators' risk-based capital measure for market risk must maintain minimum Tier 1 leverage of 3%. Other bank holding companies are expected to have a minimum 4% Tier 1 leverage. Of course, there are exceptions, but in the final analysis, supervisors will require that regulatory capital be commensurate with both the level and nature of risks.

Tier 2 Supplemental Capital

Tier 2 capital is a measure of a bank's financial strength with regard to the second most reliable form of financial capital from a regulatory point of view. Tier 2 capital includes allowance for loan and lease losses on general reserves only (some countries, but not the United States, permit "undisclosed" reserves); nonqualifying cumulative perpetual, long-term, and convertible preferred stock; nonqualifying perpetual debt and other hybrid debt-equity instruments; intermediate-term preferred stock; and term subordinated debt, "upper" and "lower." The total of Tier 2 capital is limited to 100% of Tier 1, although amounts in excess of this limitation are permitted but do not qualify as capital. There are other limits as well. For instance, to qualify as supplementary capital, subordinated debt and intermediate-term preferred stock must have an original average maturity of at least five years.

---

[11] CAMELS is an acronym for capital adequacy, asset quality, management, earnings, liquidity, and sensitivity to market risk. The Federal Financial Institutions Examination Council (FFIEC) adopted the Uniform Financial Institution's Rating System (UFIRS) on November 13, 1979. Over the years, the UFIRS has proven to be an effective internal supervisory tool for evaluating the soundness of financial institutions on a uniform basis and for identifying those institutions requiring special attention or concern. However, a number of changes have occurred in the banking industry and in the federal supervisory agencies' policies and procedures that have prompted a review and revision of the 1979 rating system. The revisions to UFIRS include the addition of a sixth component addressing sensitivity to market risks, the explicit reference to the quality of risk management processes in the management component, and the identification of risk elements within the composite and component rating descriptions. The revisions to UFIRS are not intended to add to the regulatory burden of institutions nor require additional policies or processes. They are intended to promote and complement efficient examination processes. The revisions have been made to update the original rating system, while retaining its basic framework.

[12] While the Federal Reserve has a well-established emphasis on risk management in its supervisory processes for bank holding companies (BHC) of all sizes, which it reinforced through the introduction of a risk management rating for all BHCs in the mid-1990s, the primary components of the BHC supervisory rating system, known as BOPEC (bank subsidiaries, other subsidiaries, parent, earnings, capital) do not directly reflect this emphasis. To align more closely the ratings with the supervisory processes, the Federal Reserve has developed a revised BHC rating system that emphasizes risk management; introduces a more comprehensive and adaptable framework for analyzing and rating financial factors; and provides a framework for assessing and rating the potential impact of the parent holding company and its non-depository subsidiaries on the subsidiary depository institution(s). The subcomponents are *Board and Senior Management Oversight; Policies, Procedures, and Limits; Risk Monitoring and Management Information Systems;* and *Internal Controls.* Source: Board of Governors of the Federal Reserve System Division of Banking—Supervision and Regulation, Sr 04-18, December 6, 2004.

Upper Tier 2 subordinated debt must be less than 50% of total capital, while lower Tier 2 debt must be less than 50% of Tier 1 capital or 25% of total capital. The characteristics of Tier 2 capital are summarized in Table 13.4.

One caveat for inclusion of subordinated debt in Tier 2 capital deals with terms that permit investors to accelerate payment of the principal on the occurrence of specific events. As far as regulators are concerned, the only acceleration clauses acceptable in a subordinated debt issue are those triggered by insolvency (i.e., appointment of a receiver). Terms permitting accelerated payment other than insolvency allow investors to bail out of a troubled bank before depositors. Also, debts with accelerated payment terms that do not meet the minimum five-year maturity requirements for debt capital instruments do not qualify.

Another limitation is when an event of default is defined too broadly. A regulator's scrutiny goes into high gear when subordinated debt terms are inconsistent with safe and sound banking practice. In a case like this, the issue will likely be pulled out of regulatory denominated capital altogether. Also, there is the disquieting possibility that an event of default might allow investors to accelerate payment ahead of other

Table 13.4 Summary of Characteristics of Tier 2 Capital

Meaning	Tier 2 subordinated debt consists of two elements: "upper" and "lower."	
	Upper Tier 2 Subordinated Debt	Lower Tier 2 Subordinated Debt
Maturity	Undated in structure, but coupon step-ups allowed after 5, 7, or 10 years to provide economic maturity/ call date.	Dated. Minimum tenure of 5 years, but often at least 10 years, given required amortization starting 5 years prior to maturity.
Amortization	None, unless issued in dated form.	Typically 20% per annum in the 5 years prior to maturity.
Provisions	Interest deferral triggered at option of management, if predetermined test is breached. Loss absorption occurs under certain circumstances.	No interest deferral. No loss absorption.
Status	Junior subordinated, usually ranking below lower Tier 2.	Subordinated to senior claims; senior to upper Tier 2 capital and always senior to all equity providers.
Event of default	Failure to pay interest and/or principal when due. Acceleration limited to winding up and liquidation.	Limited to winding up and liquidation.
Lock-in	Yes, on interest, typically linked to nonpayment.	No dividends or breach of capital ratio. Interest accumulates on deferred interest and principal payments.
Restrictions	Must be less than 50% of total capital.	Must be less than 50% of Tier 1 capital or 25% of total capital.

Source: Bank for International Settlements.

issues containing cross-default clauses. This action could restrict day-to-day operations.

Other events of default, such as change of bank control or a disposal of subsidiaries, may restrict or even curtail the turnaround strategies of a troubled bank. Still other events of default, such as failure to maintain certain capital ratios or rates of return or to limit the amount of nonperforming assets or charge-offs to specific thresholds, may allow subordinated debt holders to recoup their investment before a deteriorating institution turns into a full-fledged failure.

Tier 3 Supplemental Capital

A key difference between Tier 3 and Tier 2 capital is that Tier 3 capital may only be allocated against market risks, which are inherently short term. In contrast, risk comprising the "familiar" banking book is intermediate or long term. In practice, the banking book is matched up with appropriately tenured capital instruments. The trading book, in comparison, is more liquid. Should problems arise, corrective action can be taken more quickly owing to the expected liquidity and marked-to-market nature of the underlying risks. While Tier 3 is limited in its availability to support trading book risk, a bank's ability to access this form of capital can have a positive impact on its capital planning strategies.

Assuming the trading book is large enough to accommodate the use of Tier 3 capital, a longer-dated Tier 3 issue may serve as a viable capital financing alternative for banks fully peaked on lower Tier 2 capital but reluctant to issue upper Tier 2 because of the cost or (possibly) investor resistance. For example, investors may be turned off to certain features: perpetual nature, deep subordination, unattractive setup, liquidity, and so on. Despite the relatively onerous lock-in provision, Tier 3 capital still ranks *pari passu* with lower Tier 2 capital in bankruptcy, affording it some degree of substitutability with lower Tier 2 capital. The characteristics of Tier 3 capital are summarized in Table 13.5.

Regulatory Capital Features[13]

Drawbacks

While the groundbreaking 1988 Accord established minimum capital levels for international banks, incorporating off-balance sheet exposures and a risk weighting system, some imperfections became obvious. First, applying the bank's risk weightings as they were set by the Accord did not always provide the default risk measurement precision supervisors called for. Another had to do with the problem banks had in arbitraging their regulatory capital requirements to exploit divergences between true economic risk and risks delineated by the Accord. Still another concern had to do with credit risk as the predominate focus to the exclusion of risks associated

[13] FRB.

Table 13.5 Summary of Characteristics of Tier 3 Capital

Meaning	Tier 3 capital includes certain fully paid, subordinated debt that carries unique characteristics with regard to maturity, payment of interest and principal, and structure; Tier 3 capital can only be allocated against market risk, primarily the bank's trading activities.
Maturity	No less than 2 years and 1 day in tenure.
Amortization	None.
Provisions	Interest deferral, at option of management, if predetermined test is breached; loss absorption may occur under certain circumstances.
Status	Subordinated to senior, but *pari passu* with lower Tier 2 instruments.
Events of default	Limited to winding up and liquidation.
Lock-in	Allowed for interest and principal, with regulatory approval, provided that minimum capital adequacy ratios are breached; on interest deferral, interest on interest does not accrue.
Restrictions	Tier 3 capital cannot exceed 250% of the Tier 1 capital allocated toward market.
BIS Amendment	Amount of Tier 3 that can be used by a bank is limited to 250% of the Tier 1 capital, which is allocated against market risks, although bank regulators in certain countries may apply more stringent restrictions.
S&P view	S&P indicated that it will review each Tier 3 issue individually but will likely rate such instruments three notches below senior debt.

- Their justification for this approach is that the decision about a potential default is left (to a large extent) to the bank's regulators.
- S&P argues that because the "pay or don't pay" decision is in the hands of the bank's regulators and not management (as in the case of upper Tier 2 debt instruments), Tier 3 instruments may carry greater repayment risk, particularly with regard to the timeliness of interest or principal payments.
- Thus, S&P has taken the view that the certainty of payment of interest and principal on Tier 3 obligations is *less* than that for upper Tier 2 instruments and (interestingly) even less than that for a bank's preferred shares.

Source: Bank for International Settlements.

with a broad range of bank products.[14] The Federal Reserve System Task Force on Internal Credit Risk Models had this to say about the Accord:

Supervisors have long recognized two shortcomings in the Basel Accord's risk-based capital framework. First, the regulatory measures of "capital" may not represent a bank's true capacity to absorb unexpected losses. Deficiencies in loan loss reserves, for example, could mask deteriorations in banks' economic net worth. Second, the denominator of the RBC ratios, total risk-weighted assets, may not be an accurate measure of total risk. The regulatory risk-weights do not reflect certain risks, such as interest rate and operating risks. More importantly, they

[14] Other risks were certainly a functional part of capital allocation, but with the new amendments a much more inclusive risk awareness will be required by regulators.

ignore critical differences in credit risk among financial instruments (e.g., all commercial credits incur a 100% risk-weight), as well as differences across banks in hedging, portfolio diversification, and the quality of risk management systems.[15]

As a result of such flaws, amendments calling for updates to the 1988 Accord were placed in motion. As noted earlier, the new amendments are much broader and are designed to sharpen regulatory capital's role in measuring other risks beyond credit: interest rate risk in the banking book, operational, liquidity, legal, and reputation risks; and a host of other risks not explicitly addressed in the earlier Accord.

The essence of the matter here is that new amendments call for "three pillars." The first pillar is designed to set up minimum capital requirements (already highlighted in this chapter) and to develop and expand on standardized 1988 rules *but replace the risk-weighting system with a system that uses external credit ratings* (see Table 13.2, right column). The second pillar sets up methodology dealing with *supervisory* review of capital adequacy, ensuring that a bank's capital position is consistent with its risk profile and overall strategy. The amendments encourage early supervisory intervention if a bank fails below established capital adequacy thresholds. The third pillar, market discipline, encourages high disclosure standards and augments the role of market participants (investors) so they will do more to encourage banks to hold adequate capital. Let's review here the second and third pillars in some detail.

The Second Pillar: Supervisory Review of Capital Adequacy

The second pillar establishes supervisory review explicitly as a central piece in the new capital allocation structure. The supervisory review process, rather than being a discretionary pillar, acts as a fundamental complement to both the minimum regulatory capital requirements (Pillar 1) and market discipline (Pillar 3). Supervisors are to take on an increased role, not only reviewing a bank's capital position and strategy but also ensuring capital is in accord with a bank's overall risk profile and, furthermore, that the bank is in compliance with regulatory capital minimums. If capital falls below threshold levels (e.g., supervisors want the ability to require banks that show greater degrees of risk to hold capital in excess of 8% minimum), the second pillar invites quick, early supervisory action.

Following are four basic "rules" for regulators:[16]

1. Regulators will expect banks to operate above the minimum regulatory capital ratios and require banks to hold capital in excess of the minimum.
2. Banks should have processes for assessing overall capital adequacy in relation to their risk profile, as well as strategies for maintaining capital levels.
3. Supervisors should review and evaluate a bank's internal capital adequacy assessment and strategy, as well as its compliance with regulatory capital ratios.
4. Supervisors should seek to intervene at an early stage to prevent capital from falling below prudent levels.

[15] May 1988.
[16] FRB.

With regard to establishing appropriate capital levels, a variety of "qualitative" factor fall in place in including:

1. Experience and quality of management and key personnel
2. Risk appetite and track record in managing risk
3. Nature of the markets in which a bank operate
4. Quality, reliability, and volatility of earnings
5. Quality of capital and it access to new capital
6. Diversification of activities and concentration of exposures
7. Liability and liquidity profile
8. Complexity of legal and organizational structure
9. Adequacy of risk management systems and controls
10. Support and control provided by shareholders
11. Degree of supervision by other supervisors

The Federal Reserve Bank (FRB) also has developed a framework for "a sound internal analysis of capital adequacy" (their language) calling for four fundamental elements: identifying and measuring all material risks, relating capital to the level of risk, stating explicit capital adequacy goals with respect to risk, and assessing conformity to the institution's stated objectives. Recognizing the significance of Pillar 2, we have included extracts from the FRB's four-point framework:[17]

1. *Identifying and measuring all material risks.* A disciplined risk-measurement program promotes consistency and thoroughness in assessing current and prospective risk profiles, while recognizing that risks often cannot be precisely measured. The detail and sophistication of risk measurement should be appropriate to the characteristics of an institution's activities and to the size and nature of the risks that each activity presents. At a minimum, risk-measurement systems should be sufficiently comprehensive and rigorous to capture the nature and magnitude of risks faced by the institution, while differentiating risk exposures consistently among risk categories and levels. Controls should be in place to ensure objectivity and consistency and that all material risks, both on- and off-balance sheet, are adequately addressed. Measurement should not be oriented to the current treatment of these transactions under risk-based capital regulations.

   When measuring risks, institutions should perform comprehensive and rigorous stress tests[18] to identify possible events or changes in markets that could have serious adverse effects in the future. Institutions should also give adequate consideration to contingent exposures arising from loan commitments, securitizations programs, and other transactions or activities that may create these exposures for the bank.

2. *Relating capital to the level of risk.* The amount of capital held should reflect not only the measured amount of risk but also an adequate "cushion" above that amount to take account of potential uncertainties in risk measurement. A banking organization's capital

---

[17] FRB *Trading and Capital-Markets Activities Manual*, April 2000; Capital Adequacy Section 2110.1.

[18] Author's note: As part of the evaluation process, rigorous stress testing is called for centering on unexpected downturns in market conditions that might adversely impact capital. This is particularly important in the trading area to ensure that market risk is sufficiently covered by capital. Stress testing on the market side includes material interest rate positions, repricing and maturity data, principal payments, (interest) reset dates, maturities, and the rate index used for repricing and contractual interest rate ceilings or floors for adjustable-rate instruments. This assessment is based largely on the bank's own measure of *value-at-risk*.

should reflect the perceived level of precision in the risk measures used, the potential volatility of exposures, and the relative importance to the institution of the activities producing the risk. Capital levels should also reflect that historical correlations among exposures can rapidly change. Institutions should be able to demonstrate that their approach to relating capital to risk is conceptually sound and that outputs and results are reasonable. An institution could use sensitivity analysis of key inputs and peer analysis in assessing its approach.

One credible method for assessing capital adequacy is for an institution to consider itself adequately capitalized if it meets a reasonable and objectively determined standard of financial health, tempered by sound judgment—for example, a target public-agency debt rating or even a statistically measured maximum probability of becoming insolvent over a given time horizon. In effect, this latter method is the foundation of the Basel Accord's treatment of capital requirements for market foreign-exchange risk.

3. *Stating explicit capital adequacy goals with respect to risk.* Institutions need to establish explicit goals for capitalization as a standard for evaluating their capital adequacy with respect to risk. These target capital levels might reflect the desired level of risk coverage or, alternatively, a desired credit rating for the institution that reflects a desired degree of creditworthiness and, thus, access to funding sources. These goals should be reviewed and approved by the board of directors. Because risk profiles and goals may differ across institutions, the chosen target levels of capital may differ significantly as well. Moreover, institutions should evaluate whether their long-run capital targets might differ from short-run goals, based on current and planned changes in risk profiles and the recognition that accommodating new capital needs can require significant lead time.

An institution's internal standard of capital adequacy for credit risk could reflect the desire that capital absorb "unexpected losses"—that is, some level of potential losses in excess of that level already estimated as being inherent in the current portfolio and reflected in the allowance. In this setting, an institution that does not maintain its allowance at the high end of the range of estimated credit losses would require more capital than would otherwise be necessary to maintain its overall desired capacity to absorb potential losses. Failure to recognize this relationship could lead an institution to overestimate the strength of its capital position.

4. *Assessing conformity to the institution's stated objectives.* Both the target level and composition of capital, along with the process for setting and monitoring such targets, should be reviewed and approved periodically by the institution's board of directors.

Capital compliance is, of course a large factor in the Uniform Financial Institutions Rating System (CAMELS). Recall that regulators assign CAMELS *Capital Adequacy Ratings Rating 1 and 2,* respectively, if a bank under audit exhibits a strong capital level relative to its risk profile (Rating 1) or satisfactory capital level (Rating 2). *Rating 3* is assigned to banks with a less than satisfactory capital level relative to risk. *Rating 3* implies a need for improvement, even though a bank's capital level exceeds minimum regulatory and statutory requirements. *Ratings 4 and 5* are troublesome to say the least, with *Rating 4* indicating deficient capital levels with the institution's economic soundness threatened. A *Rating 5* is given to a bank critically deficient in regulatory capital such that the institution's viability is more than just threatened. In other words, regulators reporting a CAMELS capital adequacy rating of 5 are saying that *immediate assistance from shareholders or other external sources of financial support is* required.

The Third Pillar: Market Discipline

The third pillar deals with the role market discipline plays in promoting bank capital adequacy. Basically, one could argue, a bank should disclose summary information about its *entire* capital structure, both "normal" capital—stock, subordinated notes, and so on—and the more "esoteric" capital—innovative, complex, and hybrid capital instruments. To encourage further compliance with the third pillar, banks will be required to disclose reserves for credit losses, maturity, level of seniority, step-up provisions, interest or dividend deferrals, use of special purpose vehicles (SPVs), and terms of derivatives embedded in hybrid capital instruments to mention a few. The disclosure requirements will offer a much cleaner, more unclouded view of a bank's loss-absorbing capacity.

Capital Ratios

Basel's position is that requisite capital ratios should include enough information to enable banks, regulators, and investors to improve their capital assessment abilities. Capital ratios have long been a valuable tool for evaluating the safety and soundness of banks. The informal use of ratios by bank regulators and supervisors goes back well over a century. In the United States, minimum capital ratios have been required in banking regulation since 1981, and the Basel Accord has applied capital ratio requirements to banks internationally since 1988.

Although bank regulators have relied on capital ratios formally or informally for a very long time, they have not always used the ratios in the same way. For instance, in the days before explicit capital requirements, bank supervisors would use capital ratios as rules of thumb to gauge capital adequacy; there was no illusion that the simple ratios (e.g., capital to total assets or capital to deposits) could provide an accurate measure appropriate capital levels.

As we saw earlier, the Basel Accord of 1988 applied different credit risk weights to different positions and included in the base for the capital ratio a measure of the off-balance sheet exposures of the bank. Despite these calibrations, the intent was not to determine an exact appropriate level of capital for the bank, *"but rather to provide a more flexible way of determining the minimum required level."*[19]

The degree of supervisory intervention in specific banks is now guided by a formula driven largely by the Basel ratios and by a simple leverage ratio. Banks are classified as "adequately capitalized" if they meet Basel requirements plus a leverage ratio requirement, but additional distinctions are made among levels of capital. For example, a bank is "well capitalized" if it holds a certain buffer above predetermined adequacy levels. In contrast, a bank that is falling well below the prearranged threshold, set somewhat below a minimum adequate level, is labeled "critically undercapitalized" and will likely be closed by regulators. At the lower threshold, a bank is either a de facto failure or is in imminent danger of becoming one. So, then,

---

[19] Basel Committee on Banking Supervision, 1988.

regulators choose a threshold highly correlated with failure. Some of the other ratios implicitly or explicitly linked to capital adequacy include the following:

- Return on assets
- Return on equity
- Loan loss coverage
- Net charge-offs to loans
- Equity capital to assets
- Valuation reserve to loans
- Ratio of provision for loan losses to net charge-offs. This ratio indicates whether provisions are in line with actual charge-offs.
- Ratio of nonperforming assets to total loans and other real estate loans. This ratio indicates the proportion of total loans in default and the amount of real estate that had to be foreclosed and assumed. Some banks do not include loans until they are 90 days, or even more, in default.
- Ratio of long-term subordinated debt to total capital accounts. For "all insured commercial banks," the ratio is very low, since usually large banks sell these debt issues.
- Earnings per share
- Ratio of cash and U.S. government securities to assets and deposits
- Ratio of capital accounts and equity accounts to assets and deposits
- Ratio of capital accounts to loans (risk assets)

Capital Adequacy: Establishing a Technical Framework

It should be clear at this point that many regulators have come to believe that, at a minimum, banks should have a credible internal capital allocation methodology.[20] This is small wonder, considering the global volatility in financial markets, heightened international competition, and the rapid growth of technology. Naive, ad hoc methods are of little use dealing with exposures having the potential to drain serious capital. It is reasonable to deduce that the extent to which the output of a risk model is incorporated into a bank's decision-making processes is highly suggestive of management's confidence in that model. For those banks having the most sophisticated systems for allocating capital, output from these models are embedded not only for capital adequacy but throughout the institution's risk management and incentive systems as well. For example, determining break-even prices on credit instruments, setting client exposure limits, deciding on broad portfolio concentration limits, and actively managing overall portfolio credit risk are all part of the day-to-day business of managing the capital structure.

The problem with any model is, of course, data. Sophisticated risk models require good information (though this has become less of a problem with the advent of data mining and neural network technologies). Models also tend to be limited due to their somewhat conceptual drawbacks. For example, if we look behind some models, "correct" credit data are often sparse (try asking a privately held small cap apparel manufacturer for credit information); correlations may not be easily observed or

---

[20] Federal Reserve System Task Force on Internal Credit Risk Models, May 1988.

deciphered; credit returns are often skewed; and, because of statistical problems, back-testing may be infeasible with results seriously flawed. To make matters worse, statistics, assumptions, and techniques differ across borders; thus, bank-to-bank comparisons turn out skewed with dissimilarities in required capital resulting. Alas, if we compared output from JPMorgan Chase's highly sophisticated VaR models and those employed by small regional banks, VaR measures will likely differ along with allocated capital vis-à-vis market risk.

In spite of the strong case for quantitative analysis, when all is said and done, it is Tom de Swaan's keen insight that reaches the core of what risk modeling is all about:

> *Risk models only provide an edge; a banker's experience, judgment, and common sense will never be replaced by models. . . . If credit risk models are to be used for regulatory capital purposes, they should not be judged in isolation. Supervisors should also carefully examine and supervise the qualitative factors in a bank's risk management and set standards for those factors.[21]*

As part of the process for evaluating capital adequacy, a bank should be able to identify and evaluate its risks across all its activities to determine whether its capital levels are appropriate. The process should adequately differentiate risk exposure among various risk categories, providing a complete overview of an institution's banking book risk profile. This encompasses identifying credit risk concentrations, noticing trends in the portfolio (i.e., low-quality loans, as a percentage of loan portfolio trend over time), including controls to ensure the objectivity and consistency of internal risk assessment, and, finally, providing analysis supporting the accuracy of the risk measurement process. Recent years have seen the refinement and acceptance of credit risk models as a commercial banking risk-management tool.

Exposure risk management is bound to improve in breadth and refinement across institutions, jostled in no small part by the accords reviewed in this chapter. Increased awareness will be given to the interdependencies that are now largely ignored— between atypical risks, different types of lending, and the whole business of capital adequacy. As this happens, we will see practically universal use of sophisticated risk measuring tools, whether looking at a commercial or a consumer loan, derivative, or simply transactions involving settlements.

---

[21] "Capital Regulation: The Road Ahead," *FRBNY Economic Policy Review,* October 1998, pp. 231–235.

14 Quantitative Credit and Market Risk Analysis

Analytical Techniques for Modeling Probability of Default, Loss Given Default, Economic Capital, Value at Risk, Portfolio Optimized Value at Risk, Interest Rates and Yield Curve, Delta-Gamma Hedging, Floating and Fixed Rates, Foreign Exchange Risk Hedging, Volatility, Commodity Prices, and Over-the-Counter Exotic Options

---

Chapter Outline

Credit Engineering for Bankers. DOI: 10.1016/B978-0-12-378585-5.10014-4

This chapter looks at some of the quantitative credit risk analytics required to perform credit engineering tasks, specifically the quantification of probability of default, losses given a default event, Value at Risk, and other related topics in the credit risk and market risk world.

With the new Basel II Accord, internationally active banks are now required to compute their own risk capital requirements using the internal ratings-based (IRB) approach. Not only is adequate risk capital analysis important as a compliance obligation, it provides banks with the power to optimize capital through the ability to compute and allocate risks, perform performance measurements, execute strategic decisions, increase competitiveness, and enhance profitability. This chapter discusses the various *scientific risk management* approaches required to implement an IRB method, as well as the step-by-step models and methodologies in implementing and valuing economic capital, Value at Risk (VaR), probability of default, and loss given default—the key ingredients required in an IRB approach—through the use of advanced analytics such as Monte Carlo and historical risk simulation, portfolio optimization, stochastic forecasting, and options analysis. This chapter shows the use of Risk Simulator and the Modeling Toolkit (Basel II Toolkit) software in computing and calibrating these critical input parameters. Instead of dwelling on theory or revamping what has already been written many times over, we focus solely on the practical modeling applications of the key ingredients to the Basel II Accord.

To follow along with the analyses in this chapter, we assume that the reader already has Risk Simulator, Real Options SLS, and the Basel II Modeling Toolkit installed and are somewhat familiar with the basic functions of each software program. If not, please go to www.realoptionsvaluation.com (click on the Downloads link) and watch the getting started videos, read some of the getting started case studies, or install the latest trial versions of these software programs and their extended licenses. Each topic covered starts with some basic introduction to the methodologies that are appropriate, followed by some practical hands-on modeling approaches and examples. In addition, for the best hands-on learning result, it is highly recommended that the Excel models be reviewed together with this case.

Visit www.realoptionsvaluation.com/creditenginneringbook.html or www.rov downloads.com/creditenginneringbook.html and click on the Downloads link, scroll down to the Risk Simulator software section, review the system requirements, and download and install the software. Make sure your system has all the required prerequisites listed on the webpage (e.g., Windows XP, Windows Vista, Windows 7 or later; Excel 2003, 2007, 2010, or later; and that you have administrative rights to install software). Follow the instructions on the webpage to install your free extended trial license of the software.

Probability of Default

Probability of default measures the degree of likelihood that the borrower of a loan or debt (the obligor) will be unable to make the necessary scheduled repayments on the debt, thereby defaulting on it. Should the obligor be unable to pay, the debt is in default, and the lenders of the debt have legal avenues to attempt a recovery of the debt, or at least partial repayment of the entire debt. The higher the default probability a lender estimates a borrower to have, the higher the interest rate the lender will charge the borrower as compensation for bearing the higher default risk.

Probability of default models are categorized as *structural* or *empirical*. Structural models look at a borrower's ability to pay based on market data such as equity prices, market and book values of asset and liabilities, as well as the volatility of these variables. Hence, they are used predominantly to estimate the probability of default of *companies* and *countries*, most applicable within the areas of commercial and industrial banking. In contrast, empirical models, or credit scoring models, are used to quantitatively determine the probability that a loan or loan holder will default, where the loan holder is an individual, by looking at historical portfolios of loans held, where individual characteristics are assessed (e.g., age, educational level, debt to income ratio, etc.), making this second approach more applicable to the retail banking sector.

Structural Models of Probability of Default

Probability of default models assess the likelihood of default by an obligor. They differ from regular credit scoring models in several ways. First of all, credit scoring models are usually applied to smaller credits (individuals or small businesses), whereas default models are applied to larger credits (corporation or countries). Credit scoring models are largely statistical, regressing instances of default against various risk indicators, such as an obligor's income, home renter or owner status, years at a job, educational level, debt to income ratio, and so forth. Structural default models, in contrast, directly model the default process and are typically calibrated to market variables, such as the obligor's stock price, asset value, book value of debt, or the credit spread on its bonds. Default models have many applications within financial institutions. They are used to support credit analysis and for finding the probability that a firm will default, to value counterparty credit risk limits, or to apply financial engineering techniques in developing credit derivatives or other credit instruments.

The example illustrated next uses the Merton probability of default model. This model is used to solve the probability of default of a publicly traded company with equity and debt holdings, and to take into account its volatilities in the market (Figure 14.1). It is currently used by KMV and Moody's to perform credit risk

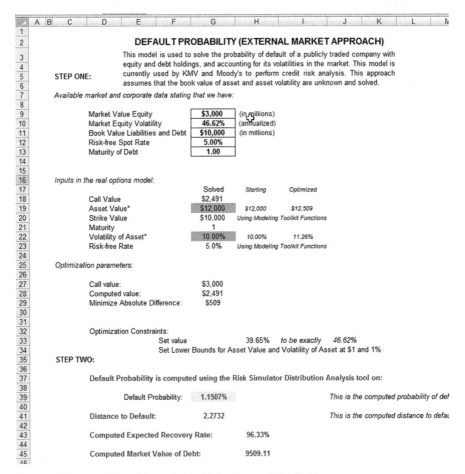

A	B	C	D	E	F	G	H	I	J	K	L	M

DEFAULT PROBABILITY (EXTERNAL MARKET APPROACH)

This model is used to solve the probability of default of a publicly traded company with equity and debt holdings, and accounting for its volatilities in the market. This model is currently used by KMV and Moody's to perform credit risk analysis. This approach assumes that the book value of asset and asset volatility are unknown and solved.

STEP ONE:

Available market and corporate data stating that we have:

Market Value Equity	$3,000	(in millions)
Market Equity Volatility	46.62%	(annualized)
Book Value Liabilities and Debt	$10,000	(in millions)
Risk-free Spot Rate	5.00%	
Maturity of Debt	1.00	

Inputs in the real options model:

	Solved	*Starting*	*Optimized*
Call Value	$2,491		
Asset Value*	$12,000	*$12,000*	*$12,509*
Strike Value	$10,000	*Using Modeling Toolkit Functions*	
Maturity	1		
Volatility of Asset*	10.00%	*10.00%*	*11.26%*
Risk-free Rate	5.0%	*Using Modeling Toolkit Functions*	

Optimization parameters:

Call value:	$3,000
Computed value:	$2,491
Minimize Absolute Difference:	$509

Optimization Constraints:

Set value   39.65%   *to be exactly*   46.62%
Set Lower Bounds for Asset Value and Volatility of Asset at $1 and 1%

STEP TWO:

Default Probability is computed using the Risk Simulator Distribution Analysis tool on:

Default Probability:	1.1507%	*This is the computed probability of def*
Distance to Default:	2.2732	*This is the computed distance to defau*
Computed Expected Recovery Rate:	96.33%	
Computed Market Value of Debt:	9509.11	

Figure 14.1 Probability of Default Model for External Public Firms.

analysis. This approach assumes that the book value of asset and asset volatility are unknown and solved in the model, and that the company is relatively stable and the growth rate of the company's assets are stable over time (e.g., not in start-up mode). The model uses several simultaneous equations in options valuation theory coupled with optimization to obtain the implied underlying asset's market value and volatility of the asset to compute the probability of default and distance to default for the firm.

Illustrative Example: Structural Probability of Default Models on Public Firms

It is assumed that at this point, the reader is well versed in running simulations and optimizations in Risk Simulator. The example model used is the Probability of Default—External Options Model and can be accessed through *Modeling Toolkit | Prob of Default | External Options Model (Public Company)*.

To run this model (see Figure 14.1), enter in the required inputs such as the market value of equity (obtained from market data on the firm's capitalization—that is, stock price times number of shares outstanding); equity volatility (computed in the *Volatility* or *LPVA* worksheets in the model); book value of debt and liabilities (the firm's book value of all debt and liabilities); the risk-free rate (the prevailing country's risk-free interest rate for the same maturity as the debt); the anticipated growth rate of the company (the expected annualized cumulative annualized growth rate of the firm's assets, which can be estimated using historical data over a long period of time, making this approach more applicable to mature companies rather than startups); and the debt maturity (the debt maturity to be analyzed, or enter *1* for the annual default probability). The comparable option parameters are shown in cells G18 to G23. All these comparable inputs are computed except for Asset Value (the market value of asset) and the Volatility of Asset. You will need to input some rough estimates as a starting point so the analysis can be run. The rule of thumb is to set the volatility of the asset in G22 to be one-fifth to half of the volatility of equity computed in G10, and the market value of asset (G19) to be approximately the sum of the market value of equity and book value of liabilities and debt (G9 and G11).

Then, an optimization needs to be run in Risk Simulator to obtain the desired outputs. To run the optimization, set Asset Value and Volatility of Asset as the decision variables (make them continuous variables with a lower limit of 1% for volatility and $1 for asset, as both these inputs can only take on positive values). Set cell G29 as the objective to minimize because this is the absolute error value. Finally, the constraint is such that cell H33, the implied volatility in the default model, is set to exactly equal the numerical value of the equity volatility in cell G10. Then run a static optimization using Risk Simulator.

If the model has a solution, the absolute error value in cell G29 will revert to zero (Figure 14.2). From here, the probability of default (measured in percent) and distance to default (measured in standard deviations) are computed in cells G39 and G41.

Then, using the resulting probability of default, the relevant credit spread required can be determined using the Credit Analysis—Credit Premium Model or some other credit spread tables (such as using the Internal Credit Risk Rating Model). The results indicate that the company has a probability of default at 0.87% with 2.37 standard deviations to default, indicating good creditworthiness (see Figure 14.2).

Illustrative Example: Structural Probability of Default Models on Private Firms

In addition, several other structural models exist for computing the probability of default of a firm. Specific models are used, depending on the need and availability of data. In the previous example, the firm is a publicly traded firm, with stock prices and equity volatility that can be readily obtained from the market. In this next example, we assume that the firm is privately held, meaning that there would be no market equity data available. The model used, therefore, essentially computes the probability

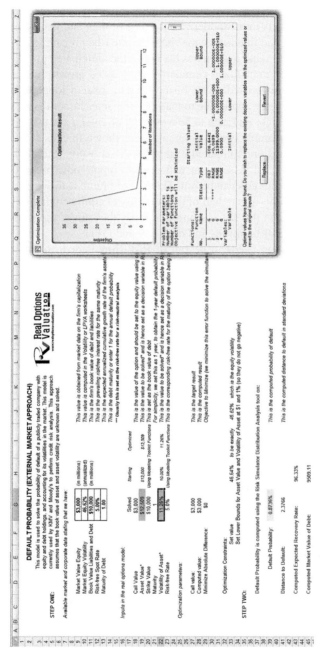

Figure 14.2 Optimized Model Results Showing Probability of Default.

CREDIT RISK DEFAULT PROBABILITY (OPTIONS APPROACH)

VALUING DEFAULT PROBABILITY AND DISTANCE TO DEFAULT BASED ON
OPTIONS MODELING OF INTERNAL DEBT

Input Assumptions

Asset Book Value	$12.0000
Debt Book Value	$10.0000
Maturity	1.0000
Risk-free Rate	7.00%
Volatility of Asset	10.00%

This is the options approach to computing the probability of default and distance to default of a company assuming that the book values of asset and debt are known, as are the asset volatilities and anticipated annual growth rates. If the book value of assets or volatility of assets are not known and the company is publicly traded, use the External Markets model instead. This model assumes these inputs are known or the company is privately held and not traded.

Probability of Default	0.6695%
Distance to Default	2.4732

Function: B2ProbabilityDefaultMertonII (Asset Value, Strike, Maturity, Riskfree, Asset Volatility)
Function: B2ProbabilityDefaultMertonDefaultDistance(Asset Value, Strike, Maturity, Asset Volatility, Riskfree Rate)

Figure 14.3 Probability of Default of a Privately Held Company.

of default or the point of default for the company when its liabilities exceed its assets, given the asset's growth rates and volatility over time (Figure 14.3). It is recommended that before using this model, the previous model on external publicly traded company is first reviewed. Similar methodological parallels exist between these two models, whereby this example builds on the knowledge and expertise of the previous example.

In Figure 14.3, the example firm with an asset value of $12M and a book value of debt at $10M with significant growth rates of its internal assets and low volatility returns a 0.67% probability of default. In addition, instead of relying on the valuation of the firm, external market benchmarks can be used if such data are available. In Figure 14.4, we see that additional input assumptions, such as the market fluctuation (market returns and volatility) and relationship (correlation between the market benchmark and the company's assets), are required. The model used is the Probability of Default—Merton Market Options Model accessible from *Modeling Toolkit | Prob of Default | Merton Market Options Model (Industry Comparable).*

MERTON MODEL OF DEBT DEFAULT PROBABILITY

VALUING THE PROBABILITY OF DEFAULT BASED ON MARKET RELATIONSHIPS

Input Assumptions

Asset Value	$100.0000
Debt Value	$50.0000
Time to Maturity	1.00
Risk-free Rate	5.00%
Volatility of Asset	20.00%
Market Volatility	10.00%
Market Return	8.00%
Correlation	0.00

This models the probability of default for both public and private companies using an index or set of comparables (the market), assuming that the company's asset and debt book values are known, as well as the asset's annualized volatility. Based on this volatility and the correlation of the company's assets to the market, we can determine the probability of default.

Probability of Default	0.0150%

Function: B2ProbabilityDefaultMertonI (Asset, Debt, Maturity, Riskfree, Asset Volatility, Market Volatility, Market Return, Correlation)

Figure 14.4 Default Probability of a Privately Held Entity Calibrated to Market Fluctuations.

Empirical Models of Probability of Default

As mentioned previously, empirical models of probability of default are used to compute an individual's default probability, applicable within the retail banking arena, where empirical or actual historical or comparable data exists on past credit defaults. The data set in Figure 14.5 represents a sample of several thousand previous loans and credit or debt issues. The data show whether each loan had defaulted or not (0 for no default, and 1 for default), as well as the specifics of each loan applicant's age, education level (1–3 indicating high school, university, or graduate professional education), years with current employer, and so forth. The idea is to model these empirical data to see which variables affect the default behavior of individuals, using Risk Simulator's *Maximum Likelihood Estimation* (MLE) tool. The resulting model will help the bank or credit issuer compute the expected probability of default of an individual credit holder with specific characteristics.

Illustrative Example on Applying Empirical Models of Probability of Default

The example file is Probability of Default—Empirical and can be accessed through *Modeling Toolkit | Prob of Default | Empirical (Individuals)*. To run the analysis, select the data set (include the headers) and make sure that the data have the same length for all variables, without any missing or invalid data points. Then, using Risk Simulator, click on *Risk Simulator | Forecasting | MLE LIMDEP*. A sample set of results are provided in the MLE worksheet, complete with detailed instructions on how to compute the expected probability of default of an individual.

The MLE approach applies a modified binary multivariate logistic analysis to model dependent variables to determine the expected probability of success of

PROBABILITY OF DEFAULT (EMPIRICAL METHOD USING MAXIMUM LIKELIHOOD MODELS ON HISTORICAL DATA)

Defaulted	Age	Education Level	Years with Current Employer	Years at Current Address	Household Income (Thousands $)	Debt to Income Ratio (%)	Credit Card Debt (Thousands $)	Other Debt (Thousands $)
1	41	3	17	12	176	9.3	11.36	5.01
0	27	1	10	6	31	17.3	1.36	4
0	40	1	15	14	55	5.5	0.86	2.17
0	41	1	15	14	120	2.9	2.66	0.82
1	24	2	2	0	28	17.3	1.79	3.06
0	41	2	5	5	25	10.2	0.39	2.16
0	39	1	20	9	67	30.6	3.83	16.67
0	43	1	12	11	38	3.6	0.13	1.24
1	24	1	3	4	19	24.4	1.36	3.28
0	36	1	0	13	25	19.7	2.78	2.15
0	27	1	0	1	16	1.7	0.18	0.09
0	25	1	4	0	23	5.2	0.25	0.94
0	52	1	24	14	64	10	3.93	2.47
0	37	1	6	9	29	16.3	1.72	3.01
0	48	1	22	15	100	9.1	3.7	5.4
1	36	2	9	6	49	8.6	0.82	3.4
1	36	2	13	6	41	16.4	2.92	3.81
0	43	1	23	19	72	7.6	1.18	4.29
0	39	1	6	9	61	5.7	0.56	2.91
0	41	3	0	21	26	1.7	0.1	0.34
0	39	1	22	3	52	3.2	1.15	0.51
0	47	1	17	21	43	5.6	0.59	1.82
0	28	1	3	6	26	10	0.43	2.17
0	29	1	8	6	27	9.8	0.4	2.24
1	21	2	1	2	16	18	0.24	2.64
0	25	4	0	2	32	17.6	2.14	3.49
0	45	2	9	26	69	6.7	0.71	3.92
0	43	1	25	21	64	16.7	0.95	9.74

The data here represents a sample of several hundred previous loans, credit, or debt issues. The data show whether each loan had defaulted or not, as well as the specifics of each loan applicant's age, education level (1-3 indicating high school, university, or graduate professional education), years with current employer and so forth. The idea is to model these empirical data to see which variables affect the default behavior of individuals, using Risk Simulator's Maximum Likelihood Models. The resulting model will help the bank or credit issuer compute the expected probability of default of an individual credit holder of having specific characteristics.

To run the analysis, select the data on the left or any other data set (include the headers) and make sure that the data have the same length for all variables, without any missing or invalid data. Then, click on Risk Simulator | Forecasting | Maximum Likelihood Models. A sample set of results are provided in the MLE worksheet, complete with detailed instructions on how to compute the expected probability of default of an individual.

Figure 14.5 Empirical Analysis of Probability of Default.

MLE Results

Log Likelihood Value	-200.507					
Variable	Coefficients	Standard Error	Z-Statistic	p-Value		Sample Inputs
	-1.7003	0.7512	-2.2634	0.0236		
Age	0.0279	0.0205	1.3588	0.1742		
Education Level	0.0728	0.1447	0.5028	0.6151		
Years with Current Employer	-0.2528	0.0391	-6.4644	0.0000		8.000
Years at Current Address	-0.0952	0.0271	-3.5064	0.0005		8.000
Household Income (Thousands)	0.0009	0.0125	0.0754	0.9399		
Debt to Income Ratio (%)	0.0750	0.0396	1.8934	0.0583		3.000
Credit Card Debt (Thousands $)	0.5521	0.1324	4.1697	0.0000		2.000
Other Debt (Thousands $)	0.0461	0.1005	0.4592	0.6461		
					Log Odds Ratio	-3.1549
					Default Probability	4.09%

Figure 14.6 MLE Results.

belonging to a certain group. For instance, given a set of independent variables (e.g., age, income, education level of credit card or mortgage loan holders), we can model the probability of default using MLE. A typical regression model is invalid because the errors are heteroskedastic and nonnormal, and the resulting estimated probability forecast will sometimes be above 1 or below 0. MLE analysis handles these problems using an iterative optimization routine. The computed results show the coefficients of the estimated MLE intercept and slopes.[1]

The coefficients estimated are actually the logarithmic odds ratios, and they cannot be interpreted directly as probabilities. A quick computation is first required. The approach is simple. To estimate the probability of success of belonging to a certain group (e.g., predicting if a debt holder will default given the amount of debt he or she holds), simply compute the estimated Y value using the MLE coefficients. Figure 14.6 illustrates that an individual with 8 years at a current employer and current address, with a low 3% debt to income ratio and $2,000 in credit card debt, has a log odds ratio of -3.1549. Then, the inverse antilog of the odds ratio is obtained by computing:

$$\frac{\exp(estimated\ Y)}{1 + \exp(estimated\ Y)} = \frac{\exp(-3.1549)}{1 + \exp(-3.1549)} = 0.0409$$

So such a person has a 4.09% chance of defaulting on the new debt. Using this probability of default, you can then use the Credit Analysis—Credit Premium Model

---

[1] For instance, the coefficients are estimates of the true population β values in the following equation $Y = \beta_0 + \beta_1 X_1 + \beta_2 X_2 + \ldots + \beta_n X_n$. The standard error measures how accurate the predicted coefficients are, and the Z-statistics are the ratios of each predicted coefficient to its standard error. The Z-statistic is used in hypothesis testing, where we set the null hypothesis (Ho) such that the real mean of the coefficient is equal to zero, and the alternate hypothesis (Ha) such that the real mean of the coefficient is not equal to zero. The Z-test is very important as it calculates if each of the coefficients is statistically significant in the presence of the other regressors. This means that the Z-test statistically verifies whether a regressor, or independent variable, should remain in the model or should be dropped. That is, the smaller the p-value, the more significant the coefficient. The usual significant levels for the p-value are 0.01, 0.05, and 0.10, corresponding to the 99%, 95%, and 90% confidence levels.

to determine the additional credit spread to charge this person given this default level and the customized cash flows anticipated from this debt holder.

Loss Given Default and Expected Losses

As shown previously, probability of default is a key parameter for computing the credit risk of a portfolio. In fact, the Basel II Accord requires that the probability of default, as well as other key parameters such as the loss given default (LGD) and exposure at default (EAD), be reported as well. The reason is that a bank's expected loss is equivalent to:

Expected Losses $=$ (Probability of Default) $\times$ (Loss Given Default)

$\times$ (Exposure at Default) or simply : $EL = PD \ x \ LGD \ x \ EAD$

PD and LGD are both percentages, whereas EAD is a value. As we have shown how to compute PD in the previous section, we now revert to some estimations of LGD. There are again several methods used to estimate LGD. The first is through a simple empirical approach where we set LGD $= 1 -$ Recovery Rate. That is, whatever is not recovered at default is the loss at default, computed as the charge off (net of recovery) divided by the outstanding balance:

LGD $= 1 -$ Recovery Rate

or

$$LGD = \frac{\text{Charge Offs (Net of Recovery)}}{\text{Outstanding Balance at Default}}$$

Therefore, if market data or historical information is available, LGD can be segmented by various market conditions, types of obligor, and other pertinent segmentations (use Risk Simulator's segmentation tool to perform this). LGD can then be easily read off a chart.

A second approach to estimate LGD is more attractive in that if the bank has available information, it can attempt to run some econometric models to create the best-fitting model under an ordinary least squares approach. By using this approach, a single model can be determined and calibrated, and this same model can be applied under various conditions, and no data mining is required. However, in most econometric models, a normal-transformation will have to be performed first. Suppose the bank has some historical LGD data (Figure 14.7). The best-fitting distribution can be found using Risk Simulator by first selecting the historical data and then clicking on *Risk Simulator | Tools | Distributional Fitting (Single Variable)* to perform the fitting routine. The example's result is a beta distribution for the thousands of LGD values. The p-value can also be evaluated for the goodness-of-fit of the theoretical distribution (i.e., the higher the p-value, the better the distributional fit; so in this example, the historical LGD fits a beta distribution 81% of the time, indicating a good fit).

Next, using the Distribution Analysis tool in Risk Simulator, obtain the theoretical mean and standard deviation of the fitted distribution (Figure 14.8). Then, transform

Past LGD   Normalized

Past LGD	Normalized
49.69%	28.54%
25.76%	18.27%
14.61%	11.84%
26.91%	18.83%
18.47%	14.33%
21.29%	15.95%
26.00%	18.39%
11.84%	9.76%
51.85%	29.41%
19.05%	14.84%
24.74%	17.76%
15.68%	12.57%
14.35%	11.66%
21.36%	15.98%
35.31%	22.65%
50.71%	28.95%
28.58%	19.63%
5.96%	3.77%
3.84%	0.38%
21.70%	16.17%
71.28%	37.64%
23.49%	17.12%
20.25%	15.36%
44.01%	26.26%
31.27%	20.87%
40.86%	24.98%
26.54%	18.65%
25.29%	18.04%
28.51%	19.60%
55.40%	30.84%
31.57%	21.00%
16.30%	12.98%
24.37%	17.57%
8.46%	6.70%
77.08%	40.52%

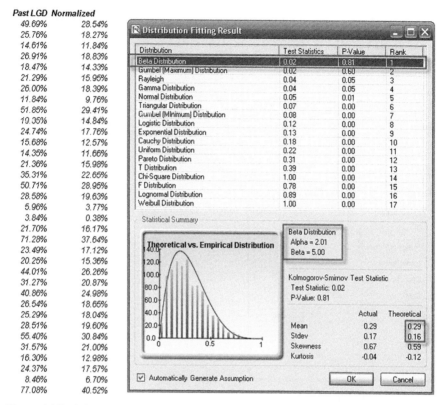

Figure 14.7 Fitting Historical LGD Data.

the LGD variable using the *B2NormalTransform* function in the Modeling Toolkit software. For instance, the value 49.69% will be transformed and normalized to 28.54%. Using this newly transformed data set, you can now run some nonlinear econometric models to determine LGD.

The following is a partial list of independent variables that might be significant for a bank, in terms of determining and forecasting the LGD value:
- Debt to capital ratio
- Profit margin
- Revenue
- Current assets to current liabilities
- Risk rating at default and one year before default
- Industry
- Authorized balance at default
- Collateral value
- Facility type
- Tightness of covenant
- Seniority of debt
- Operating income to sales ratio (and other efficiency ratios)
- Total asset, total net worth, total liabilities

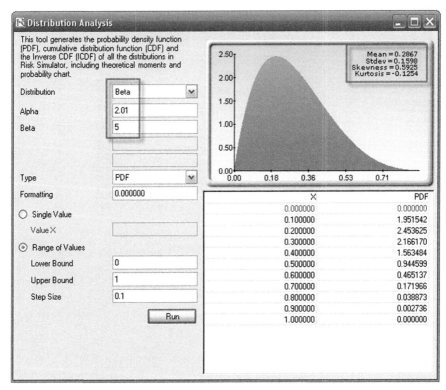

Figure 14.8 Distributional Analysis Tool.

Economic Capital and Value at Risk

Economic capital is critical to a bank as it links a bank's earnings and returns to risks that are specific to a business line or business opportunity. In addition, these economic capital measurements can be aggregated into a portfolio of holdings. Value at Risk or (VaR) is used in trying to understand how the entire organization is affected by the various risks of each holding as aggregated into a portfolio, after accounting for their cross-correlations among various holdings. VaR measures the maximum possible loss given some predefined probability level (e.g., 99.90%) over some holding period or time horizon (e.g., 10 days). The selected probability or confidence interval is typically a decision made by senior management at the bank and reflects the board's risk appetite. Stated another way, we can define the probability level as the bank's desired probability of surviving per year. In addition, the holding period is usually chosen such that it coincides with the time period it takes to liquidate a loss position.

VaR can be computed several ways. Two main families of approaches exist: structural closed-form models and Monte Carlo risk simulation approaches. We showcase both methods in this chapter, starting with the structural models.

The second, and much more powerful, approach is the use of Monte Carlo risk simulation. Instead of simply correlating individual business lines or assets in the structural models, entire probability distributions can be correlated using more advanced mathematical copulas and simulation algorithms in Monte Carlo simulation methods by using Risk Simulator. In addition, tens to hundreds of thousands of scenarios can be generated using simulation, providing a very powerful stress-testing mechanism for valuing VaR. In addition, distributional fitting methods are applied to reduce the thousands of data points into their appropriate probability distributions, allowing their modeling to be handled with greater ease.

Illustrative Example: Structural VaR Models

The first VaR example model shown is the Value at Risk—Static Covariance Method, accessible through *Modeling Toolkit | Value at Risk | Static Covariance Method*. This model is used to compute the portfolio's VaR at a given percentile for a specific holding period, after accounting for the cross-correlation effects between the assets (Figure 14.9). The daily volatility is the annualized volatility divided by the square root of trading days per year. Typically, positive correlations tend to carry a higher VaR compared to zero correlation asset mixes, whereas negative correlations reduce the total risk of the portfolio through the diversification effect (Figures 14.9 and 14.10). The approach used is a portfolio VaR with correlated inputs, where the portfolio has multiple asset holdings with different amounts and volatilities. Assets

VALUE AT RISK (VARIANCE-COVARIANCE METHOD)

Asset Allocation	Amount	Daily Volatility
Asset A	$1,000,000.00	1.20%
Asset B	$2,000,000.00	2.00%
Asset C	$3,000,000.00	1.89%
Asset D	$4,000,000.00	3.25%
Asset E	$5,000,000.00	4.20%

Correlation Matrix	Asset A	Asset B	Asset C	Asset D	Asset E
Asset A	1.0000	0.1000	0.1000	0.1000	0.1000
Asset B	0.1000	1.0000	0.1000	0.1000	0.1000
Asset C	0.1000	0.1000	1.0000	0.1000	0.1000
Asset D	0.1000	0.1000	0.1000	1.0000	0.1000
Asset E	0.1000	0.1000	0.1000	0.1000	1.0000

Horizon (Days)	10
Percentile	99.00%

Value at Risk (Daily)	$655,915.30
Value at Risk (Horizon)	$2,074,186.30

Daily Value at Risk (Positive Correlations)	$2,074,186.30
Daily Value at Risk (Zero Correlations)	$1,889,345.26
Daily Value at Risk (Negative Correlations)	$1,684,340.28

Figure 14.9 Computing Value at Risk Using the Structural Covariance Method.

Correlation Matrix	Asset A	Asset B	Asset C	Asset D	Asset E
Asset A	1.0000	0.1000	0.1000	0.1000	0.1000
Asset B	0.1000	1.0000	0.1000	0.1000	0.1000
Asset C	0.1000	0.1000	1.0000	0.1000	0.1000
Asset D	0.1000	0.1000	0.1000	1.0000	0.1000
Asset E	0.1000	0.1000	0.1000	0.1000	1.0000

Correlation Matrix	Asset A	Asset B	Asset C	Asset D	Asset E
Asset A	1.0000	0.0000	0.0000	0.0000	0.0000
Asset B	0.0000	1.0000	0.0000	0.0000	0.0000
Asset C	0.0000	0.0000	1.0000	0.0000	0.0000
Asset D	0.0000	0.0000	0.0000	1.0000	0.0000
Asset E	0.0000	0.0000	0.0000	0.0000	1.0000

Correlation Matrix	Asset A	Asset B	Asset C	Asset D	Asset E
Asset A	1.0000	-0.1000	-0.1000	-0.1000	-0.1000
Asset B	-0.1000	1.0000	-0.1000	-0.1000	-0.1000
Asset C	-0.1000	-0.1000	1.0000	-0.1000	-0.1000
Asset D	-0.1000	-0.1000	-0.1000	1.0000	-0.1000
Asset E	-0.1000	-0.1000	-0.1000	-0.1000	1.0000

Figure 14.10 Different Correlation Levels.

are also correlated to each other. The covariance or correlation structural model is used to compute the VaR given a holding period or horizon and percentile value (typically 10 days at 99% confidence). Of course, the example only illustrates a few assets or business lines or credit lines for simplicity's sake. Nonetheless, using the functions in the Modeling Toolkit, many more lines, assets, or businesses can be modeled (the function *B2VaRCorrelationMethod* is used in this example).

Illustrative Example: VaR Models Using Monte Carlo Risk Simulation

The model used is Value at Risk—Portfolio Operational and Capital Adequacy and is accessible through *Modeling Toolkit | Value at Risk | Portfolio Operational and Capital Adequacy*. This model shows how operational risk and credit risk parameters are fitted to statistical distributions, and their resulting distributions are modeled in a portfolio of liabilities to determine the VaR (e.g., 99.50th percentile certainty) for the capital requirement under Basel II requirements. It is assumed that the historical data of the operational risk impacts (*Historical Data* worksheet) are obtained through econometric modeling of the *Key Risk Indicators*.

The *Distributional Fitting Report* worksheet is a result of running a distributional fitting routine in Risk Simulator to obtain the appropriate distribution for the operational risk parameter. Using the resulting distributional parameters, we model each liability's capital requirements within an entire portfolio. Correlations can also be inputted if required, between pairs of liabilities or business units. The resulting Monte Carlo simulation results show the VaR capital requirements.

Note that an appropriate empirically based historical VaR cannot be obtained if distributional fitting and risk-based simulations were not first run. Only by running simulations will the VaR be obtained. To perform distributional fitting, follow the steps given here:

1. In the *Historical Data* worksheet (Figure 14.11), select the data area (cells *C5:L104*) and click on *Risk Simulator | Tools | Distributional Fitting (Single Variable)*.
2. Browse through the fitted distributions and select the best-fitting distribution (in this case, the exponential distribution with a particularly high p-value fit, as shown in Figure 14.12) and click OK.
3. You can now set the assumptions on the *Operational Risk Factors* with the exponential distribution (fitted results show *Lambda* = 1) in the *Credit Risk* worksheet. Note that the assumptions have already been set for you in advance. You may reset them by going to cell *F27* and clicking on *Risk Simulator | Set Input Assumption*, selecting *Exponential* distribution, entering *1* for the *Lambda* value, and clicking OK. Continue this process for the remaining cells in column F or simply perform a *Risk Simulator Copy* and *Risk Simulator Paste* on the remaining cells:
   a. Note that since the cells in column F have assumptions set, you will first have to clear them if you wish to reset and copy/paste parameters. You can do so by first selecting cells *F28:F126* and clicking on the Remove Parameter icon or select *Risk Simulator | Remove Parameter*.
   b. Then select cell *F27*, click on the Risk Simulator Copy icon or select *Risk Simulator | Copy Parameter*, then select cells *F28:F126*, and click on the Risk Simulator Paste icon or select *Risk Simulator | Paste Parameter*.
4. Next, additional assumptions can be set, such as the probability of default, using the Bernoulli distribution (column H) and *Loss Given Default* (column J). Repeat the procedure in Step 3 if you wish to reset the assumptions.
5. Run the simulation by clicking on the Run icon or clicking on *Risk Simulator | Run Simulation*.
6. Obtain the Value at Risk by going to the forecast chart once the simulation is done running and selecting *Left-Tail* and typing in *99.50*. Hit *TAB* on the keyboard to enter the confidence value and obtain the VaR of $25,959 (Figure 14.13).

Another example on VaR computation is shown next, where the model Value at Risk—Right Tail Capital Requirements is used, available through *Modeling Toolkit | Value at Risk | Right Tail Capital Requirements*.

This model shows the capital requirements per Basel II requirements (99.95th percentile capital adequacy based on a specific holding period's VaR). Without running risk-based historical and Monte Carlo simulation using Risk Simulator, the required capital is $37.01M (Figure 14.14) as compared to only $14.00M required using a correlated simulation (Figure 14.15). This difference is due to the cross-correlations between assets and business lines, and it can only be modeled using Risk Simulator. This lower VaR is preferred, since banks can now be required to hold less required capital and can reinvest the remaining capital in various profitable ventures, thereby generating higher profits.

1. To run the model, click on *Risk Simulator | Run Simulation* (if you have other models open, make sure you first click on *Risk Simulator | Change Simulation | Profile*, and select the *Tail VaR* profile before starting).
2. When simulation is complete, select *Left-Tail* in the forecast chart, enter in *99.95* in the *Certainty* box, and hit *TAB* on the keyboard to obtain the value of $14.00M VaR for this correlated simulation.

Basel II - Credit Risk and Capital Requirement (Portfolio-Based)

This model applies the Basel II requirements on capital adequacy and modeling the operational risk of probability of default of 100 loans as well as the loss given default. These values are fitted based on the bank's historical loss data (Historical Data and Distributional Fitting Report sheets) using Risk Simulator. Then, the relevant historical simulation assumptions are set in this model (Credit Risk sheet) and a Monte Carlo risk-based simulation was run in Risk Simulator to determine the expected capital required and 99.50% Value at Risk (VaR). A simulation has to be run in order to determine the VaR.

Market Factor	2.000

Weighting:	
Macro	50%
Micro	50%

Correlation	100%

Rating level	P (Default) - Long term
1	0.5%
2	1.0%
3	1.5%
4	2.0%
5	2.5%
6	3.0%
7	5.0%

Real Options Valuation

	Static	Stochastic with Risk Simulation
Expected Value of Total Capital	$11,734.54	$11,112.81
VaR 99.50% of Total Capital	$30,888.34	$25,959.60

Without running historical simulations, the 99.50% VaR cannot be obtained directly. The only recourse is to apply a theoretical distributional analysis using the fitted distributions' empirical parameters and estimating the theoretical cumulative density function value at 99.50%, and computing the relevant theoretical confidence level. This approach is at best an overestimation of the required capital (thereby requiring too much capital) and at worst, wrong.

Portfolio Losses - Risk Simulator Forecast — Histogram

Portfolio Losses (1000 Trials)

Type: Left Tail — Certainty (%): 99.50

Portfolio Losses - Risk Simulator Forecast — Statistics

Statistics	Result
Number of Trials	1000
Mean	1.11281E+004
Median	1.06799E+004
Standard Deviation	5597.8726
Variance	3133618E+007
Average Deviation	4522.4248
Maximum	3.16772E+004
Minimum	0.0000
Range	3.16772E+004
Skewness	0.4724
Kurtosis	-0.1656
25% Percentile	6678.1717
75% Percentile	1.46639E+004
Percentage Error Precision at 95% Confidence	3.121%

Bank loan	Size of loan	Rating grade	P (Default) - Long term	Operational Risk Factor	P (Default) - Now	Default?	Loss Given Default (LGD%) Static	Loss Given Default (LGD%) Stochastic	Losses Static	Losses Stochastic
1	$13,274.73	5	2.5%	2.000	5.00%	0	30.0%	30.0%	$ 199.12	$ -
2	$14,215.77	6	3.0%	2.000	6.00%	0	30.0%	30.0%	$ 255.88	$ -
3	$9,003.59	1	0.5%	2.000	1.00%	0	30.0%	30.0%	$ 27.01	$ -
4	$1,324.27	3	1.5%	2.000	3.00%	0	30.0%	30.0%	$ 11.92	$ -
5	$11,203.14	1	0.5%	2.000	1.00%	0	30.0%	30.0%	$ 33.61	$ -
6	$5,480.61	4	2.0%	2.000	4.00%	0	30.0%	30.0%	$ 65.77	$ -
7	$9,853.12	5	2.5%	2.000	5.00%	0	30.0%	30.0%	$ 147.80	$ -
8	$12,356.22	3	1.5%	2.000	3.00%	0	30.0%	30.0%	$ 111.21	$ -
9	$8,255.80	4	2.0%	2.000	4.00%	0	30.0%	30.0%	$ 99.07	$ -
10	$1,662.99	2	1.0%	2.000	2.00%	0	30.0%	30.0%	$ 9.98	$ -
11	$7,175.82	3	1.5%	2.000	3.00%	0	30.0%	30.0%	$ 64.58	$ -

Sum: $11,734.54 Static 99.50%: $30,888.34

Figure 14.11 Sample Historical Bank Loans.

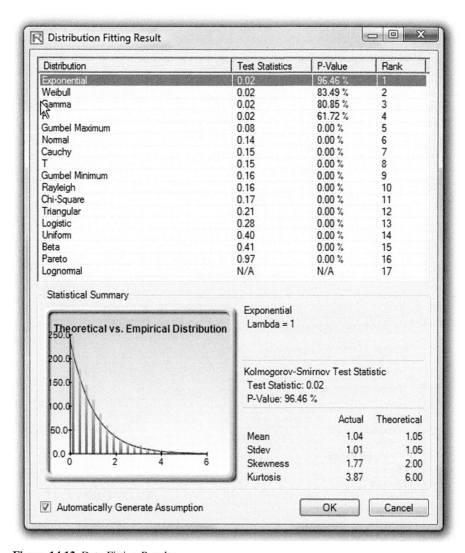

Figure 14.12 Data Fitting Results.

3. Note that the assumptions have already been set for you in advance in the model in cells *C6:C15*. However, you may reset them again by going to cell *C6* and clicking on *Risk Simulator | Set Input Assumption*, selecting your distribution of choice (or use the default *Normal Distribution* or perform a distributional fitting on historical data), and clicking *OK*. Continue this process for the remaining cells in column C. You may also decide to first *Remove Parameters* of these cells in column C and setting your own distributions. Further, correlations can be set manually when assumptions are set (Figure 14.16) or by going to *Simulation | Edit Correlations* (Figure 14.17) after all the assumptions are set.

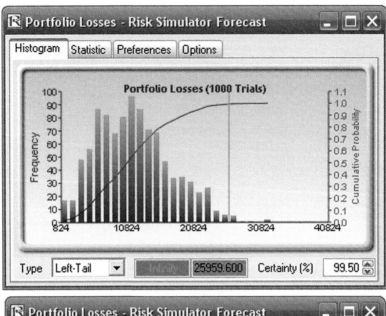

Figure 14.13 Simulated Forecast Results and the 99.50% Value at Risk Value.

If risk simulation was not run, the VaR or economic capital required would have been $37M, as opposed to only $14M. By running the simulation, all cross-correlations between business lines have been modeled, as are stress and scenario tests, and thousands and thousands of possible iterations are run. Individual risks are now aggregated into a cumulative portfolio-level VaR.

Real Options Valuation
www.realoptionsvaluation.com

TAIL VALUE AT RISK MODEL (BASEL II REQUIREMENT)

Line of Business	Mean Required Capital	99.95th Percentile	Capital Required	Allocation Weights	Minimum Allowed	Maximum Allowed	
Credit Business 1	$10.50	$36.52	$26.01	10.00%	5.00%	15.00%	3.48
Credit Business 2	$11.12	$47.52	$36.39	10.00%	5.00%	15.00%	4.27
Credit Business 3	$11.77	$48.99	$37.22	10.00%	5.00%	15.00%	4.16
Credit Business 4	$10.77	$37.34	$26.56	10.00%	5.00%	15.00%	3.47
Credit Business 5	$13.49	$49.52	$36.03	10.00%	5.00%	15.00%	3.67
Credit Business 6	$14.24	$55.59	$41.35	10.00%	5.00%	15.00%	3.91
Credit Business 7	$15.60	$60.24	$44.64	10.00%	5.00%	15.00%	3.86
Credit Business 8	$14.95	$64.69	$49.74	10.00%	5.00%	15.00%	4.33
Credit Business 9	$14.15	$61.02	$46.87	10.00%	5.00%	15.00%	4.31
Credit Business 10	$10.08	$35.37	$25.29	10.00%	5.00%	15.00%	3.51
Portfolio Total	$12.67	$49.68	$37.01	100.00%			
Total Capital Required			$14.00				

Correlation Matrix

	1	2	3	4	5	6	7	8	9	10
1										
2	-0.20									
3	-0.13	0.35								
4	-0.05	0.01	0.00							
5	0.23	0.50	0.15	0.00						
6	0.00	0.00	-0.15	0.00	0.03					
7	0.25	0.00	-0.26	0.01	0.10	-0.10				
8	0.36	-0.25	-0.60	-0.30	0.00	0.00	-0.15			
9	-0.01	-0.20	0.16	0.04	-0.01	0.01	0.00	0.00		

Figure 14.14 Right-Tail VaR Model.

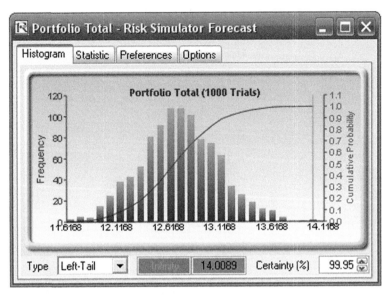

Figure 14.15 Simulated Results of the Portfolio VaR.

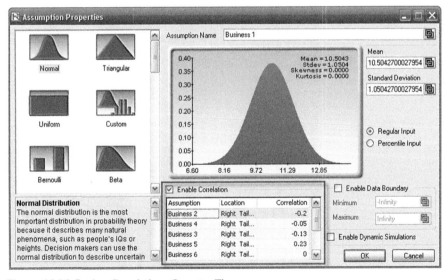

Figure 14.16 Setting Correlations One at a Time.

Efficient Portfolio Allocation and Economic Capital VaR

As a side note, by performing portfolio optimization, a portfolio's VaR can actually be reduced. In this section, we first introduced the concept of stochastic portfolio

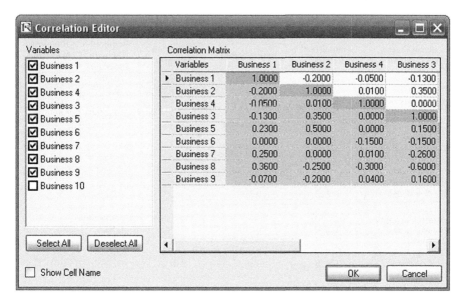

Figure 14.17 Setting Correlations Using the Correlation Matrix Routine.

optimization through an illustrative hands-on example. Then, using this portfolio optimization technique, we apply it to four business lines or assets to compute the VaR on an unoptimized versus an optimized portfolio of assets and see the difference in computed VaR. You will note that, at the end, the optimized portfolio bears less risk and has a lower required economic capital.

Illustrative Example: Portfolio Optimization and the Effects on Portfolio VaR

Now that we understand the concepts of optimized portfolios, let us go on to see what the effects are on computed economic capital through the use of a correlated portfolio VaR. This model uses Monte Carlo simulation and optimization routines in Risk Simulator to minimize the VaR of a portfolio of assets (Figure 14.18). The file used is *Value at Risk—Optimized and Simulated Portfolio VaR*, which is accessible via *Modeling Toolkit | Value at Risk | Optimized and Simulated Portfolio VaR*. In this example model, we intentionally used only four asset classes to illustrate the effects of an optimized portfolio, whereas in real life, we can extend this activity to cover a multitude of asset classes and business lines. In addition, we now illustrate the use of a left-tail VaR, as opposed to a right-tail VaR, but the concepts are similar.

First, simulation is used to determine the 90% left-tail VaR (this means that there is a 10% chance that losses will exceed this VaR for a specified holding period). With an equal allocation of 25% across the four asset classes, the VaR is determined using simulation (Figure 14.19). The annualized returns are uncertain

VALUE AT RISK WITH ASSET ALLOCATION OPTIMIZATION MODEL

Asset Class Description	Annualized Returns	Volatility Risk	Allocation Weights	Required Minimum Allocation	Required Maximum Allocation
S&P 500	7.10%	9.80%	10.00%	10.00%	40.00%
Small Cap	9.51%	14.35%	27.30%	10.00%	40.00%
High Yield	15.90%	22.50%	22.70%	10.00%	40.00%
Govt Bonds	4.50%	7.25%	40.00%	10.00%	40.00%
		Total Weight:	100.00%		

Correlation Matrix	S&P 500	Small Cap	High Yield	Govt Bonds
S&P 500	1.0000	0.7400	0.6500	0.5500
Small Cap	0.7400	1.0000	0.4200	0.3100
High Yield	0.6500	0.4200	1.0000	0.2300
Govt Bonds	0.5500	0.3100	0.2300	1.0000

Covariance Matrix	S&P 500	Small Cap	High Yield	Govt Bonds
S&P 500	0.0096	0.0104	0.0143	0.0039
Small Cap	0.0104	0.0206	0.0136	0.0032
High Yield	0.0143	0.0136	0.0506	0.0038
Govt Bonds	0.0039	0.0032	0.0038	0.0053

Starting Value	$1,000,000.00
Term (Years)	5.00

Annualized Return	8.72%	Profit/Loss	$87,151.94
Portfolio Risk	9.84%	Return to Risk Ratio	88.59%
Ending Value	$1,087,151.94		

Specifications of the optimization model:

Objective:	Maximize Return to Risk Ratio (E28)
Decision Variables:	Allocation Weights (E6:E9)
Restrictions on Decision Variables:	Minimum and Maximum Required (F6:G9)
Constraints:	Portfolio Total Allocation Weights 100% (E10 is set to 100%)

Figure 14.18 Computing Value at Risk (VaR) with Simulation.

and, thus, simulated. The VaR is then read from the forecast chart. Then optimization is run to find the best portfolio subject to the 100% allocation across the four projects that will maximize the portfolio's bang for the buck (returns to risk ratio). The resulting optimized portfolio is then simulated once again, and the new VaR is obtained (Figure 14.20). The VaR of this optimized portfolio is a lot less than the not-optimized portfolio. That is, the expected loss is $35.8M instead of $42.2M, which means that the bank will have a lower required economic capital if the portfolio of holdings is first optimized.

Illustrative Example: Risk Analysis—Interest Rate Risk

Location: www.ElsevierDirect.com (search for this book, click Companion Site button, click link in Additional Models section) *Modeling Toolkit | Risk Analysis | Interest Rate Risk*
Brief Description: Applies duration and convexity measures to account for a bond's sensitivity, how interest rate shifts can affect the new bond price and how this new bond price can be approximated using these sensitivity measures.

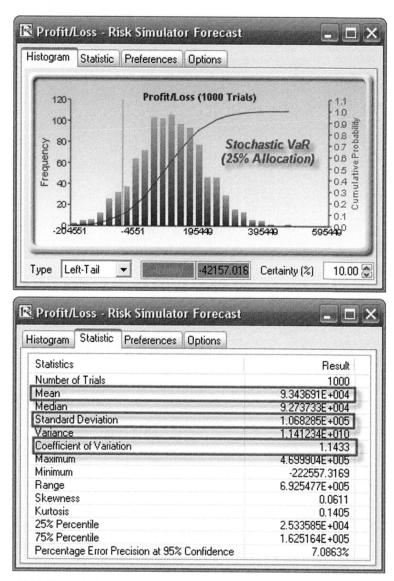

Figure 14.19 Nonoptimized Value at Risk.

Banks selling fixed income products and vehicles need to understand interest rate risks. This model uses duration and convexity to show how fixed income products react under various market conditions. To compare the effects of interest rate and credit risks on fixed income investments, this model uses modified duration and convexity (discrete discounting) to analyze the effects of a change in interest rates on the value of a bond or debt (Figure 14.21).

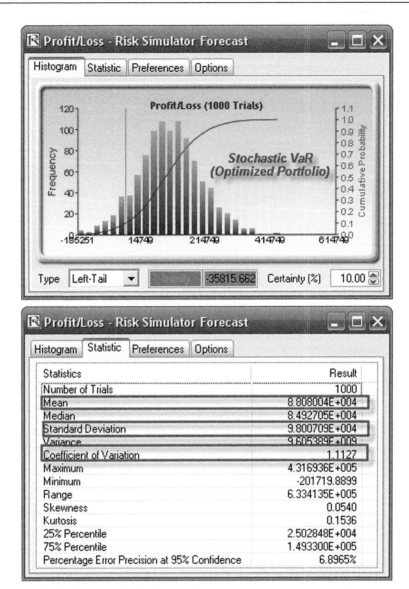

Figure 14.20 Optimal Portfolio's Value at Risk through Optimization and Simulation.

Duration and convexity are sensitivity measures that describe exposure to parallel shifts in the spot interest rate yield curve, applicable to individual fixed income instruments or entire fixed income portfolios. These sensitivities cannot warn of exposure to more complex movements in the spot curve, including tilts and bends, only parallel shifts. The idea behind duration is simple. Suppose a portfolio has a duration measure of 2.5 years. This means that the portfolio's value will decline

INTEREST RATE RISK

Face Value	$100.00
Coupon Rate	5.50%
Maturity	30.00
Current Interest Rate	5.50%
Interest Rate Shift	0.25%

Original Bond Price	$100.00
Modified Duration	14.5337
Convexity	321.0265

	Duration and Convexity	Using New Rates
New Price After Shift	$96.47	$96.46
Price Change After Shift	-3.53%	-3.54%

Cash Flow	Interest Rates	Year	Shifted Interest Rates
$5.50	5.50%	1	5.75%
$5.50	5.50%	2	5.75%
$5.50	5.50%	3	5.75%
$5.50	5.50%	4	5.75%
$5.50	5.50%	5	5.75%
$5.50	5.50%	6	5.75%
$5.50	5.50%	7	5.75%
$5.50	5.50%	8	5.75%
$5.50	5.50%	9	5.75%
$5.50	5.50%	10	5.75%

Figure 14.21 Interest Rate Risk.

about 2.5% for each 1% increase in interest rates—or rise about 2.5% for each 1% decrease in interest rates. Typically, a bond's duration will be positive, but exotic instruments such as mortgage-backed securities may have negative durations, or portfolios that short fixed income instruments or pay fixed for floating on an interest rate swap. Inverse floaters tend to have large positive durations. Their values change significantly for small changes in rates. Highly leveraged fixed income portfolios tend to have very large (positive or negative) durations.

In contrast, convexity summarizes the second-most significant piece of information, or the nonlinear curvature of the yield curve, whereas duration measures the linear or first-approximation sensitivity. Duration and convexity have traditionally been used as tools for immunization or asset-liability management. To avoid exposure to parallel spot curve shifts, an organization (such as an insurance company or defined benefit pension plan) with significant fixed income exposures might perform duration matching by structuring its assets so their duration matches the duration of its liabilities, thus allowing the two offset each other. Even more effective (but less frequently practical) is duration-convexity matching, in which assets are structured so that durations and convexities match.

Illustrative Example: Risk Hedging—Delta-Gamma Hedging

Location: www.ElsevierDirect.com (search for this book, click Companion Site button, click link in Additional Models section) *Modeling Toolkit | Risk Analysis | Delta Gamma Hedge*

Brief Description: Sets up a delta-gamma riskless and costless hedge in determining the number of call options to sell and buy, number of common stocks to buy, and the borrowing amount required to structure a perfect arbitrage-free hedge.

The delta-gamma hedge provides a hedge against larger changes in the asset value. This hedge is accomplished by buying some equity shares and a call option, which are funded by borrowing some amount of money and selling a call option at a different strike price. The net amount is a zero sum game, making this hedge completely effective in generating a zero delta and zero gamma for the portfolio. Just like in a delta hedge, where the total portfolio's delta is zero (e.g., to offset a positive delta of some underlying assets, call options are sold to generate sufficient negative delta to completely offset the existing deltas to generate a zero delta portfolio). The problem of delta-neutral portfolios is that secondary changes—larger shocks—are not hedged. Delta-gamma hedged portfolios, on the contrary, hedge both delta and gamma risk, making it much more expensive to generate. The typical problem with such a hedging vehicle is that in larger quantities, buying and selling additional options or underlying assets may change the market value and prices of the same instruments used to perform the hedge. Therefore, typically, a dynamic hedge, or continuously changing hedge portfolios, might be required.

Illustrative Example: Risk Hedging—Delta Hedging

Location: www.ElsevierDirect.com (search for this book, click Companion Site button, click link in Additional Models section) *Modeling Toolkit | Risk Analysis | Delta Hedge*

Brief Description: Sets up a delta riskless and costless hedge in determining the number of call options to sell, number of common stocks to buy, and the borrowing amount required to structure a costless hedge.

The delta hedge provides a hedge against small changes in the asset value by buying some equity shares of the asset and financing the purchase through selling a call option and borrowing some money. The net should be a zero sum game to provide a hedge where the portfolio's delta is zero. For instance, an investor computes the portfolio delta of some underlying asset and offsets this delta through buying or selling some additional instruments such that the new instruments will offset the delta of the existing underlying assets. Typically, say an investor holds some stocks or a commodity like gold in the long position, creating a positive delta for the asset. To

DELTA-GAMMA HEDGE

Asset	$100.00
Strike for Call Sold	$95.00
Strike for Call Bought	$100.00
Maturity for Call Sold	0.50
Maturity for Call Bought	0.75
Riskfree	8.00%
Volatility	20.00%
DividendRate	3.00%

Sell Calls	$9.7258
Shares to Buy	($6.9058)
Buy Calls	($9.1991)
Borrow This Amount	$6.3791
Delta-Gamma-Neutral Position Sum	$0.0000

Figure 14.22 Delta-gamma Hedging.

DELTA HEDGE

Asset	$100.00
Strike	$95.00
Maturity	0.50
Riskfree	8.00%
Volatility	20.00%
DividendRate	3.00%

Sell 1 Call	$9.7258
Shares to Buy	($71.8275)
Borrow This Amount	$62.1018
Delta-Neutral Position Sum	$0.0000

Figure 14.23 Delta Hedging.

offset this, he or she sells some calls to generate negative delta, such that the amount of the call options sold on the gold is sufficient to offset the delta in the portfolio.

Illustrative Example: Risk Hedging—Effects of Fixed versus Floating Rates (Swaps)

Location: www.ElsevierDirect.com (search for this book, click Companion Site button, click link in Additional Models section) *Modeling Toolkit | Risk Hedging | Effects of Fixed versus Floating Rates*

Brief Description: Sets up various levels of hedging to determine the impact on earnings per share.

This model illustrates the impact on financial earnings and earnings before interest and taxes (EBIT) on a hedged versus unhedged position. The hedge is done through an interest rate swap payment. Various scenarios of swaps (different combinations of fixed rate versus floating rate debt are tested and modeled) can be generated in this model to determine the impact on earnings per share (EPS) and other financial metrics. The foreign exchange cash flow hedge model (shown next) goes into more detail on the hedging aspects of foreign exchange through the use of risk simulation.

Illustrative Example: Risk Hedging—Foreign Exchange Cash Flow Model

Location: www.ElsevierDirect.com (search for this book, click Companion Site button, click link in Additional Models section) *Modeling Toolkit | Risk Hedging | Foreign Exchange Cash Flow Model*

Brief Description: This model illustrates how to use Risk Simulator for simulating foreign exchange rates to determine if the value of a hedged fixed exchange rate or a floating unhedged rate is worth more.

IMPACTS OF FIXED VERSUS FLOATING RATE INTEREST PAYMENTS

Assumptions

EBIT	$3,000,000
Shares Outstanding	$500,000
Tax Rate	40.00%
Total Debt	$8,000,000
Fixed Interest Rate	7.00%
LIBOR	6.00%
10-Year Swap Rate	5.00%

		Scenarios		
Initial Debt Structure (before swap)	Current	1	2	3
% of Total Debt in Fixed-rate Debt	50.00%	50.00%	50.00%	50.00%
% of Total Debt in Floating-rate Debt	50.00%	50.00%	50.00%	50.00%
Desired Debt Structure (after swap)				
% of Total Debt in Fixed-rate Debt	50.00%	30.00%	100.00%	0.00%
% of Total Debt in Floating-rate Debt	50.00%	70.00%	0.00%	100.00%
Change in Interest Rates	0.00%	1.00%	0.50%	0.10%
Financials				
Fixed-rate Debt	7.00%	7.00%	7.00%	7.00%
Floating-rate Debt	8.00%	9.00%	8.50%	8.10%
EBIT	3,000,000	3,000,000	3,000,000	3,000,000
Interest Expense	(600,000)	(672,000)	(560,000)	(648,000)
Net Income before Taxes	2,400,000	2,328,000	2,440,000	2,352,000
Earnings	1,440,000	1,396,800	1,464,000	1,411,200
EPS	2.8800	2.7936	2.9280	2.8224
Change in Interest Expense		72,000	(40,000)	48,000
Change in Earnings		(43,200)	24,000	(28,800)

Figure 14.24 Impacts of an Unhedged versus Hedged Position.

Cash Flow Model

Base Year	2006	Sum PV Net Benefits FC 3,809.62
Start Year	2006	Sum PV Investments FC 1,389.08
Discount Rate	15.00%	Net Present Value FC 2,420.54
Private-Risk Discount Rate	5.00%	Internal Rate of Return 54.64%
Terminal Period Growth Rate	2.00%	Return on Investment 174.25%
Tax Rate	40.00%	Profitability Index 2.74

Forex Rate (USD/FC) 0.85000

	2006	2007	2008	2009	2010	2011	2012	2013	2014	2015	
Prod A Price	FC 10.00	FC 10.50	FC 11.00	FC 11.50	FC 12.00	FC 12.00	FC 12.00	FC 12.00	FC 12.00	FC 12.00	
Prod B Price	FC 12.25	FC 12.50	FC 12.75	FC 13.00	FC 13.25	FC 13.25	FC 13.25	FC 13.25	FC 13.25	FC 13.25	
Prod C Price	FC 15.15	FC 15.30	FC 15.45	FC 15.60	FC 15.75	FC 15.75	FC 15.75	FC 15.75	FC 15.75	FC 15.75	
Prod A Quantity	50	50	50	50	50	50	50	50	50	50	
Prod B Quantity	35	35	35	35	35	35	35	35	35	35	
Prod C Quantity	20	20	20	20	20	20	20	20	20	20	
Total Revenues (Local Currency)	FC 1,231.75	FC 1,268.50	FC 1,305.25	FC 1,342.00	FC 1,378.75	FC 1,378.75	FC 1,378.75	FC 1,378.75	FC 1,378.75	FC 1,378.75	
Direct Cost of Goods Sold	FC 184.76	FC 190.28	FC 195.79	FC 201.30	FC 206.81	FC 206.81	FC 206.81	FC 206.81	FC 206.81	FC 206.81	
Gross Profit	FC 1,046.99	FC 1,078.23	FC 1,109.46	FC 1,140.70	FC 1,171.94	FC 1,171.94	FC 1,171.94	FC 1,171.94	FC 1,171.94	FC 1,171.94	
Operating Expenses	FC 157.50	FC 157.50	FC 157.50	FC 157.50	FC 157.50	FC 157.50	FC 157.50	FC 157.50	FC 157.50	FC 157.50	
Sales, General and Admin. Costs	FC 15.75	FC 15.75	FC 15.75	FC 15.75	FC 15.75	FC 15.75	FC 15.75	FC 15.75	FC 15.75	FC 15.75	
Operating Income (EBITDA)	FC 873.74	FC 904.98	FC 936.21	FC 967.45	FC 998.69	FC 998.69	FC 998.69	FC 998.69	FC 998.69	FC 998.69	
Depreciation	FC 10.00	FC 10.00	FC 10.00	FC 10.00	FC 10.00	FC 10.00	FC 10.00	FC 10.00	FC 10.00	FC 10.00	
Amortization	FC 3.00	FC 3.00	FC 3.00	FC 3.00	FC 3.00	FC 3.00	FC 3.00	FC 3.00	FC 3.00	FC 3.00	
EBIT	FC 860.74	FC 891.98	FC 923.21	FC 954.45	FC 985.69	FC 985.69	FC 985.69	FC 985.69	FC 985.69	FC 985.69	
Interest	FC 2.00	FC 2.00	FC 2.00	FC 2.00	FC 2.00	FC 3.00	FC 4.00	FC 5.00	FC 6.00	FC 7.00	
EBT	FC 858.74	FC 889.98	FC 921.21	FC 952.45	FC 983.69	FC 982.69	FC 981.69	FC 980.69	FC 979.69	FC 978.69	
Taxes	FC 343.50	FC 355.99	FC 368.49	FC 380.98	FC 393.48	FC 393.08	FC 392.68	FC 392.28	FC 391.88	FC 391.48	
Net Income	FC 515.24	FC 533.99	FC 552.73	FC 571.47	FC 590.21	FC 589.61	FC 589.01	FC 588.41	FC 587.81	FC 587.21	
Depreciation/Amort	FC 13.00	FC 13.00	FC 13.00	FC 13.00	FC 13.00	FC 13.00	FC 13.00	FC 13.00	FC 13.00	FC 13.00	
Net Working Capital	FC 0.00	FC 0.00	FC 0.00	FC 0.00	FC 0.00	FC 0.00	FC 0.00	FC 0.00	FC 0.00	FC 0.00	
Capital Expenditures	FC 0.00	FC 0.00	FC 0.00	FC 0.00	FC 0.00	FC 0.00	FC 0.00	FC 0.00	FC 0.00	FC 0.00	
Free Cash Flow	FC 528.24	FC 546.99	FC 565.73	FC 584.47	FC 603.21	FC 602.61	FC 602.01	FC 601.41	FC 600.81	FC 600.81	FC 4,709.36
Investments	FC 500.00		FC 1,500.00								
Net Free Cash Flow	FC 1,105.97	FC 546.99	FC 565.73	FC 584.47	FC 603.21	FC 602.61	FC 602.01	FC 601.41	FC 600.81	FC 600.81	FC 4,709.36

Figure 14.25 Hedging Foreign Exchange Risk Cash Flow Model.

This is a cash flow model used to illustrate the effects of hedging foreign exchange rates (Figure 14.25). The tornado sensitivity analysis illustrates that the foreign exchange rate, or forex, has the highest effects on the profitability of the project (shown in the Excel model). Suppose for the moment that the project undertaken is in a foreign country (FC), the values obtained are denominated in FC currency, and the parent company is in the United States and requires that the net revenues be repatriated back to the United States. The question we try to ask here is what is the appropriate forex rate to hedge at and the appropriate costs for that particular rate? Banks will be able to provide your firm with the appropriate pricing structure for various exchange forward rates, but by using the model here, we can determine the added value of the hedge and, thus, can decide if the value added exceeds the cost to obtain the hedge. This model is already preset for you to run a simulation on.

The *Forex Data* worksheet shows historical exchange rates between the FC and the U.S. dollar (USD). Using these values, we can create a *custom* distribution (we simply used the rounded values in our illustration), which is already preset in this example model. However, should you wish to replicate creating the simulation model, you can follow the steps given here:

1. Start a new profile (*Risk Simulator | New Profile*) and give it an appropriate name.
2. Go to the *Forex Data* worksheet, select the data in cells *K6:K490*, and click on *Edit | Copy* or *Ctrl + C*.
3. Select an empty cell (e.g., cell *K4*), click on *Risk Simulator | Set Input Assumption*, and select *Custom Distribution*.
4. Click on *Paste* to paste the data into the custom distribution, and then *Update Chart* to view the results on the chart. Then use *File | Save* to save the newly created distribution to your hard drive. Close the set assumption dialog.
5. Go to the *Model* worksheet and select the *Forex* cell (*J9*), click on *Risk Simulator | Set Input Assumption* and choose *Custom*, and then click on *Open a Distribution* and select the previously saved custom distribution.
6. You may continue to set assumptions across the entire model, and set the *NPV* cell (*G6*) as a forecast (*Risk Simulator | Set Output Forecast*).
7. *Run* the simulation with the custom distribution to denote an unhedged position. You can then rerun the simulation, but this time delete the custom distribution (use the Delete Simulation Parameter icon and *not* Excel's delete function or hitting the keyboard's delete key) and enter in the relevant hedged exchange rate, indicating a fixed rate. You may create a report after each simulation to compare the results.

From the sample analysis, we see the following:

	Mean ($000)	Stdev ($000)	% Confidence ($000)	CV (%)
Unhedged	2292.82	157.94	2021 to 2550	6.89%
Hedged at 0.85	2408.81	132.63	2199 to 2618	5.51%
Hedged at 0.83	2352.13	129.51	2147 to 2556	5.51%
Hedged at 0.80	2267.12	124.83	2069 to 2463	5.51%

From this table, several things are evident:

- The higher the hedged exchange rate, the more profitable the project (e.g., 0.85 USD/FC is worth more than 0.80 USD/FC).
- The relative risk ratio, computed as the coefficient of variation (CV, or the standard deviation divided by the mean) is the same regardless of the exchange rate, as long as it is hedged.
- The CV is lower for hedged positions than unhedged positions, indicating that the relative risk is reduced by hedging.
- It seems that the exchange rate hedge should be above 0.80, such that the hedged position is more profitable than the unhedged.
- In comparing a hedged versus unhedged position, we can determine the amount of money the hedging is worth. For instance, going with a 0.85 USD/FC means that, on average, the hedge is worth $115,990,000 (computed as $2,408.81 − $2,292.82 denominated in thousands). This means that as long as the cost of the hedge is less than this amount, it is a good idea to pursue the hedge.

Illustrative Example: Risk Hedging—Hedging Foreign Exchange Exposure

Location: www.ElsevierDirect.com (search for this book, click Companion Site button, click link in Additional Models section) *Modeling Toolkit | Risk Hedging | Hedging Foreign Exchange Exposure*

Brief Description: This model illustrates how to use Risk Simulator for simulating foreign exchange rates to determine the value of a hedged currency option position.

This model is used to simulate possible foreign exchange spot and future prices and the effects on the cash flow statement of a company under a freely floating exchange rate versus using currency options to hedge the foreign exchange exposure (Figure 14.26).

Figure 14.27 shows the effects of the VaR of a hedged versus unhedged position. Clearly the right-tailed VaR of the loss distribution is higher without the currency options hedge. Figure 14.27 shows that there is a lower risk, lower risk to returns ratio, higher returns, and less swing in the outcomes of a currency hedged position than an exposed position, with Figure 14.28 showing the simulated forecast statistics of the loss distribution. Finally, Figure 14.29 shows the hedging effectiveness—that is, how often the hedge is in the money and become usable.

Illustrative Example: Volatility—Implied Volatility

Location: www.ElsevierDirect.com (search for this book, click Companion Site button, click link in Additional Models section) *Modeling Toolkit | Volatility | Implied Volatility*

Brief Description: This model computes the implied volatilities using an internal optimization routine, given the values of a call or put option as well as all their required inputs.

This implied volatility computation is based on an internal iterative optimization, which means it will work under typical conditions (without extreme volatility values—in other words, too small or too large). It is always good modeling technique to recheck the imputed volatility using an options model to make sure the answers coincide with each other before adding more sophistication to the model. That is,

Hedging Foreign Exchange Exposure with Currency Options

Months	Jan	Feb	Mar	April	May	June	July
FX Spot Rate (HKD/USD)	7.80	7.40	7.60	7.30	7.10	7.20	7.40
FX Strike Rate (HKD/USD)	7.80	7.80	7.80	7.80	7.80	7.80	7.80
Maturity (Years)	0.5833	0.5000	0.4167	0.3333	0.2500	0.1667	0.0833
Risk Free Rate US	6.08%	6.08%	6.08%	6.08%	6.08%	6.08%	6.08%
Risk Free Rate HK	5.06%	5.06%	5.06%	5.06%	5.06%	5.06%	5.06%
Volatility	15.00%	15.00%	15.00%	15.00%	15.00%	15.00%	15.00%
Quantity of Options Hedge Position	10,000,000	10,000,000	10,000,000	10,000,000	10,000,000	10,000,000	10,000,000
Currency Put Option Value (HKD/USD)	0.3229	0.5191	0.3795	0.5533	0.7012	0.6034	0.4102
Market Value of Hedge	3,229,135	5,191,009	3,794,813	5,532,845	7,012,229	6,034,435	4,102,320
Intrinsic Value	0	4,000,000	2,000,000	5,000,000	7,000,000	6,000,000	4,000,000
Time Value	3,229,135	1,191,009	1,794,813	532,845	12,229	34,435	102,320

FINANCIAL STATEMENTS IMPACTS - MARK TO MARKET

Balance Sheet (in 000's)	Jan	Feb	Mar	April	May	June	July
Option Contract	3,229,135	5,191,009	3,794,813	5,532,845	7,012,229	6,034,435	4,102,320
Other Comp Income (SE)	4,000,000	4,000,000	2,000,000	5,000,000	7,000,000	6,000,000	4,000,000

Income Statement (in 000's)		Feb	Mar	April	May	June	July
Hedge Effectiveness gain or loss per period		(2,038,126)	603,805	(1,261,969)	(520,615)	22,206	67,884
Hedge Effectiveness sum of all periods							(3,126,816)
Market Cost of Hedge (Current Period)							3,229,135
Income from Option Exercise							4,000,000
Net Valuation of Hedging							770,865
Income from Hedging							74,770,865
Income from No Hedge							74,000,000
Loss Distribution from Hedging							3,229,135
Loss Distribution from No Hedge							4,000,000

Figure 14.26 Hedging Currency Exposures with Currency Options.

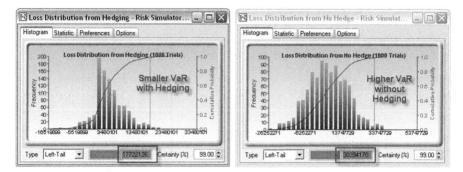

Figure 14.27 Values at Risk (VaR) of Hedged versus Unhedged Positions.

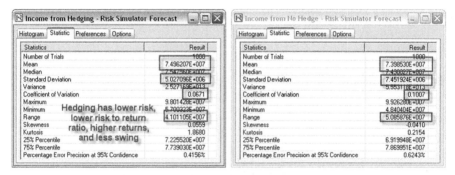

Figure 14.28 Forecast Statistics of the Loss Distribution.

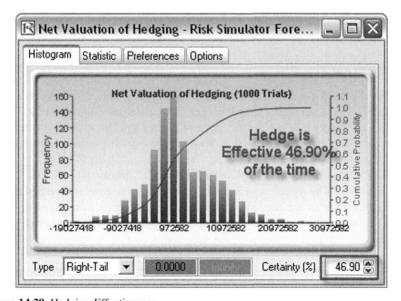

Figure 14.29 Hedging Effectiveness.

IMPLIED VOLATILITY FUNCTION

Asset	$100.00
Strike	$95.00
Maturity	0.50
Riskfree	8.00%
Volatility	25.00%
DividendRate	3.00%

Call Option	$10.9126
Put Option	$3.6764

Implied Volatility Calculation
Call Option	25.00%
Put Option	25.00%

Figure 14.30 Getting the Implied Volatility from Options.

given all the inputs in an option analysis as well as the option value, the volatility can be imputed (Figure 14.30).

Illustrative Example: Volatility—Volatility Computations

Location: www.ElsevierDirect.com (search for this book, click Companion Site button, click link in Additional Models section) *Modeling Toolkit | Volatility | Volatility Computations*
Brief Description: This model uses Risk Simulator to apply Monte Carlo simulation to compute a project's volatility measure.

Logarithmic Cash Flow Returns or Logarithmic Stock Price Returns Approach

This method is used mainly for computing the volatility of liquid and tradable assets such as stocks in financial options; however, it is sometimes used for other traded assets such as the price of oil and the price of electricity. The drawback is that dis-counted cash flow models with only a few cash flows will generally overstate the volatility, and this method cannot be used when negative cash flows occur. Therefore, this volatility approach is only applicable for financial instruments and not for real options analysis. The benefits include its computational ease, transparency, and modeling flexibility of the method. In addition, no simulation is required to obtain a volatility estimate. The approach is simply to take the annualized standard deviation of the logarithmic relative returns of the time-series data as the proxy for volatility. The Modeling Toolkit function *B2Volatility* is used to compute this volatility, where the time-series of stock prices is arranged in time-series (can be chronological or reverse chronological). See the *Log Cash Flow Returns* example model under the *Volatility* section of Modeling Toolkit for details.

Exponentially Weighted Moving Average (EWMA) Models

This approach is similar to the previously described logarithmic cash flow returns approach, using the *B2Volatility* function, to compute the annualized standard deviation of the natural logarithms of relative stock returns. The difference here is that the most recent value will have a higher weight than values further in the past. A *lambda* or weight variable is required (typically, industry standards set this at 0.94), where the most recent volatility is weighted at this lambda value, and the period before that is (1 – lambda), and so forth. See the *EWMA* example model under the *Volatility* section of Modeling Toolkit for details.

Logarithmic Present Value Returns Approach

This approach is used mainly when computing the volatility on assets with cash flows. A typical application is in real options. The drawback of this method is that simulation is required to obtain a single volatility and it is not applicable for highly traded liquid assets such as stock prices. The benefits include the ability to accommodate certain negative cash flows and the application of more rigorous analysis than the logarithmic cash flow returns approach, providing a more accurate and conservative estimate of volatility when assets are analyzed. In addition, within, say, a cash flow model, multiple simulation assumptions can be set up (we can insert any types of risks and uncertainties such as related assumptions, correlated distributions and nonrelated inputs, multiple stochastic processes, etc.), the model can distill all the interacting risks and uncertainties in these simulated assumptions, and we thus obtain the single value volatility, which represents the integrated risk of the project. See the *Log Asset Returns* example model under the *Volatility* section of Modeling Toolkit for details.

Management Assumptions and Guesses

This approach is used for both financial options and real options. The drawback is that the volatility estimates are very unreliable and are only subjective best guesses. The benefit of this approach is its simplicity; this method is very easy to explain to management the concept of volatility, both in execution and interpretation. That is, most people understand what probability is, but they have a hard time understanding what volatility is. Using this approach, we can impute one from another. See the *Probability to Volatility* example model under the *Volatility* section of Modeling Toolkit for details.

Generalized Autoregressive Conditional Heteroskedasticity (GARCH) Models

These models are used mainly for computing the volatility of liquid and tradable assets such as stocks. In financial options, this model is sometimes used for other traded assets such as the price of oil and the price of electricity. The drawbacks are that a lot of data and advanced econometric modeling expertise are required and that this approach is highly susceptible to user manipulation. The benefit is that rigorous statistical analysis is performed to find the best-fitting volatility curve, providing different volatility estimates over time. The EWMA model is a simple weighting model, whereas the GARCH model is a more advanced analytical and econometric model that requires advanced algorithms such as generalized method of moments to obtain the volatility forecasts. See the chapter on forecasting for details on how to run the various GARCH models.

See the GARCH model as well as the volatility sections for more technical details. Risk Simulator also has the data diagnostic tool and statistical analysis tool that can quickly compute the volatility of any time-series data set. Finally, in the Real Options SLS software folder, there is a *Volatility* example model that illustrates these computations in more detail.

Illustrative Example: Yield Curve—CIR Model

Location: www.ElsevierDirect.com (search for this book, click Companion Site button, click link in Additional Models section) *Modeling Toolkit | Yield Curve | CIR Model*
Brief Description: This is the CIR model for estimating and modeling the term structure of interest rates and yield curve approximation assuming the interest rates are mean-reverting.

The yield curve is the time-series relationship between interest rates and the time to maturity of the debt. The more formal mathematical description of this relationship is called the *term structure of interest rates*. The yield curve can take on various shapes. The normal yield curve means that yields rise as maturity lengthens and the yield curve is positively sloped, reflecting investor expectations for the economy to grow in the future (and, thus, an expectation that inflation rates will rise in the future). An inverted yield curve results when the opposite occurs, where the long-term yields fall below short-term yields, and long-term investors will settle for lower yields now if they think the economy will slow or even decline in the future, indicative of a worsening economic situation in the future (and, thus, an expectation that inflation will remain low in the future). Another potential situation is a flat yield curve, signaling uncertainty in the economy. The yield curve can also be humped or show a smile or a frown. The yield curve can change in shape over time through a twist or bend, a parallel shift, or a movement on one end versus another.

Because the yield curve is related to inflation rates as previously discussed, and central banks in most countries have the ability to control monetary policy to target inflation rates, inflation rates are mean-reverting in nature. This description of a yield curve also implies that interest rates are mean-reverting, as well as stochastically changing over time.

This section shows the Cox-Ingersoll-Ross (CIR) Model that is used to compute the term structure of interest rates and yield curve (Figure 14.31). The CIR model assumes a mean-reverting stochastic interest rate. The rate of reversion and long-run mean rates can be determined using Risk Simulator's statistical analysis tool. If the long-run rate is higher than the current short-term rate, the yield curve is upward sloping, and vice versa.

Illustrative Example: Yield Curve—Curve Interpolation BIM Model

Location: www.ElsevierDirect.com (search for this book, click Companion Site button, click link in Additional Models section) *Modeling Toolkit | Yield Curve | Curve Interpolation BIM*

CIR MODEL
YIELD CURVE CONSTRUCTION

Input Assumptions

Time to Maturity of the Bond or Debt (Years)	1.00
Riskfree Rate (Short Rate)	3.00%
Long-run Mean Rate	8.00%
Annualized Volatility of Interest Rate	6.00%
Market Price of Interest Rate Risk	0.00%
Rate of Mean Reversion	25.00%

Yield of Zero Coupon Bond   3.5744%

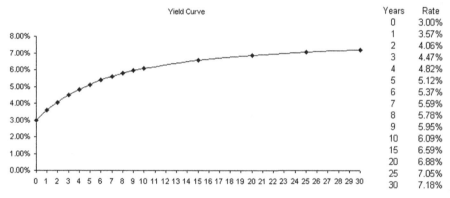

Years	Rate
0	3.00%
1	3.57%
2	4.06%
3	4.47%
4	4.82%
5	5.12%
6	5.37%
7	5.59%
8	5.78%
9	5.95%
10	6.09%
15	6.59%
20	6.88%
25	7.05%
30	7.18%

Figure 14.31 CIR Model.

Brief Description: This is the BIM model for estimating and modeling the term structure of interest rates and yield curve approximation using a curve interpolation method.

A number of alternative methods exist for estimating the term structure of interest rates and the yield curve. Some are fully specified stochastic term structure models, while others are simply interpolation models. The former are models such as the CIR and Vasicek models (illustrated in other sections in this book), while the latter are interpolation models such as the Bliss or Nelson approach. This section looks at the Bliss interpolation model (Figure 14.32) for generating the term structure of interest rates and yield curve estimation. This model requires several input parameters whereby their estimations require some econometric modeling techniques to calibrate their values. The Bliss approach is a modification of the Nelson-Siegel method by using an additional generalized parameter. Virtually any yield curve shape can be interpolated using these models, which are widely used at banks around the world.

Illustrative Example: Yield Curve—Curve Spline Interpolation and Extrapolation Model

Location: www.ElsevierDirect.com (search for this book, click Companion Site button, click link in Additional Models section) *Modeling Toolkit | Yield Curve | Spline Interpolation and Extrapolation*

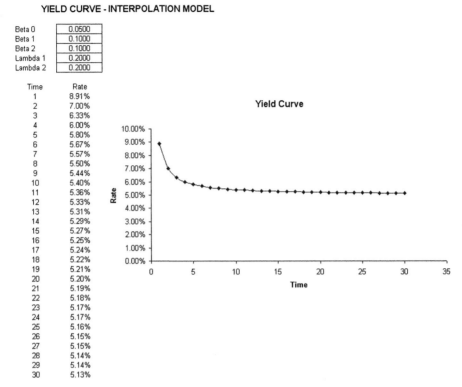

Figure 14.32 BIM Model.

Brief Description: This is the multidimensional cubic spline model for estimating and modeling the term structure of interest rates and yield curve approximation using curve interpolation and extrapolation methods.

The cubic spline polynomial interpolation and extrapolation model is used to "fill in the gaps" of missing spot yields and term structure of interest rates whereby the model can be used to both interpolate missing data points within a time-series of interest rates (as well as other macroeconomic variables such as inflation rates and commodity prices or market returns) and to extrapolate outside of the given or known range, useful for forecasting purposes. In Figure 14.33, the actual U.S. Treasury risk-free rates are shown and entered into the model as known values. The timings of these spot yields are entered as *Years* (the known *X* value inputs), whereas the known risk-free rates are the known *Y* values. Using the *B2Cubicspline* function, we can now interpolate the in-between risk-free rates that are missing as well as the rates outside of the given input dates. For instance, the risk-free Treasury rates given include 1-month, 3-month, 6-month, 1-year, and so forth, until the 30-year rate. Using these data, we can interpolate the rates for, say, 5 months or 9 months, and so forth, as well as extrapolate beyond the 30-year rate.

Years	Spot Yields
0.0833	4.55%
0.2500	4.47%
0.5000	4.52%
1.0000	4.39%
2.0000	4.13%
3.0000	4.16%
5.0000	4.26%
7.0000	4.38%
10.0000	4.56%
20.0000	4.88%
30.0000	4.84%

These are the yields that are known and are used as inputs in the Cubic Spline Interpolation and Extrapolation model

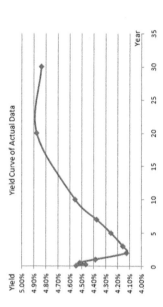

INTEREST RATE STATISTICS

Daily Treasury Yield Curve Rates

Get e-mail updates when this information changes.

This data is also available in XML format by clicking on the XML icon.

Historical Data

September 2007

Date	1 mo	3 mo	6 mo	1 yr	2 yr	3 yr	5 yr	7 yr	10 yr	20 yr	30 yr
09/04/07	4.55	4.47	4.52	4.39	4.13	4.16	4.26	4.38	4.56	4.88	4.84
09/05/07	4.41	4.36	4.41	4.28	4.03	4.05	4.16	4.29	4.46	4.82	4.78
09/06/07	4.28	4.29	4.42	4.30	4.08	4.09	4.20	4.32	4.51	4.84	4.79
09/07/07	4.03	4.07	4.20	4.10	3.90	3.92	4.03	4.17	4.38	4.73	4.70
09/10/07	3.93	3.96	4.20	4.09	3.87	3.89	4.00	4.13	4.34	4.68	4.65
09/11/07	4.13	4.11	4.27	4.16	3.95	3.97	4.07	4.19	4.37	4.68	4.65
09/12/07	4.00	4.03	4.20	4.12	3.95	3.99	4.11	4.23	4.41	4.72	4.68
09/13/07	4.04	4.08	4.27	4.20	4.08	4.11	4.22	4.33	4.49	4.79	4.75
09/14/07	3.85	4.01	4.22	4.16	4.05	4.07	4.18	4.30	4.47	4.77	4.72
09/17/07	3.82	4.15	4.31	4.23	4.08	4.11	4.21	4.32	4.48	4.76	4.72
09/18/07	3.87	4.01	4.12	4.08	4.00	4.04	4.19	4.32	4.50	4.81	4.77

Spline Interpolation and Extrapolation Results

Years	Yield	Notes
0.5	4.52%	Interpolate
1.0	4.39%	Interpolate
1.5	4.21%	Interpolate
2.0	4.13%	Interpolate
2.5	4.13%	Interpolate
3.0	4.16%	Interpolate
3.5	4.19%	Interpolate
4.0	4.22%	Interpolate
4.5	4.24%	Interpolate
5.0	4.26%	Interpolate
5.5	4.29%	Interpolate
6.0	4.32%	Interpolate
6.5	4.35%	Interpolate
7.0	4.38%	Interpolate
7.5	4.41%	Interpolate
8.0	4.44%	Interpolate
8.5	4.47%	Interpolate
9.0	4.50%	Interpolate
9.5	4.53%	Interpolate
10.0	4.56%	Interpolate
10.5	4.59%	Interpolate
11.0	4.61%	Interpolate
11.5	4.64%	Interpolate
12.0	4.66%	Interpolate
12.5	4.68%	Interpolate
13.0	4.70%	Interpolate
13.5	4.72%	Interpolate
14.0	4.74%	Interpolate

Figure 14.33 Cubic Spline Model.

FORWARD RATES
COMPUTING FORWARD RATES FROM SPOT RATES

Input Assumptions

Spot Rate 1	8.00%
Spot Rate 2	7.00%
Time of Spot Rate 1	1.00
Time of Spot Rate 2	2.00

Forward Rate   **6.00%**

Figure 14.34 Forward Rate Extrapolation.

Illustrative Example: Yield Curve—Forward Rates from Spot Rates

Location: www.ElsevierDirect.com (search for this book, click Companion Site button, click link in Additional Models section) *Modeling Toolkit | Yield Curve | Forward Rates from Spot Rates*

Brief Description: This is a bootstrap model used to determine the implied forward rate given two spot rates.

Given two spot rates (from Year 0 to some future time period), you can determine the implied forward rate between these two time periods. For instance, if the spot rate from Year 0 to Year 1 is 8%, and the spot rate from Year 0 to Year 2 is 7% (both yields are known currently), the implied forward rate from Year 1 to Year 2 (that will occur based on current expectations) is 6%. This activity is simplified by using the *B2ForwardRate* function in Modeling Toolkit (Figure 14.34).

Illustrative Example: Yield Curve—Vasicek Model

Location: www.ElsevierDirect.com (search for this book, click Companion Site button, click link in Additional Models section) *Modeling Toolkit | Yield Curve | Vasicek Model*

Brief Description: The Vasicek Model is used to create the term structure of interest rates and to reconstruct the yield curve assuming the underlying interest rates are mean-reverting and stochastic.

This model, which is used to compute the term structure of interest rates and yield curve, assumes a mean-reverting stochastic interest rate (Figure 14.35). The rate of reversion and long-run mean rates can be determined using Risk Simulator's statistical analysis tool. If the long-run rate is higher than the current short rate, the yield curve is upward sloping, and vice versa.

The yield curve is the time-series relationship between interest rates and the time to maturity of the debt. The more formal mathematical description of this relationship is called the *term structure of interest rates*. As discussed previously, the yield curve can take on various shapes. The normal yield curve means that yields rise as maturity lengthens and the yield curve is positively sloped, reflecting investor expectations for the economy to grow in the future (and, thus, an expectation that inflation rates will rise in the future). An inverted yield curve results when the opposite occurs, where the long-term yields fall below short-term yields, and long-term investors will settle for lower yields now if they think the economy will slow or even decline in the future,

VASICEK MODEL
YIELD CURVE CONSTRUCTION

Input Assumptions

Time to Maturity of the Bond or Debt (Years)	1.00
Riskfree Rate (Short Rate)	2.00%
Long-run Mean Rate	8.00%
Annualized Volatility of Interest Rate	2.00%
Market Price of Interest Rate Risk	0.00%
Rate of Mean Reversion	20.00%

Yield of Zero Coupon Bond   **2.5562%**

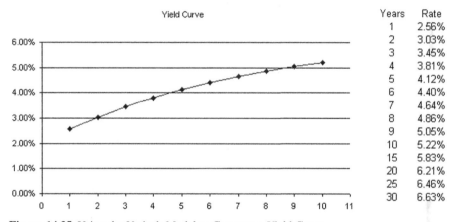

Years	Rate
1	2.56%
2	3.03%
3	3.45%
4	3.81%
5	4.12%
6	4.40%
7	4.64%
8	4.86%
9	5.05%
10	5.22%
15	5.83%
20	6.21%
25	6.46%
30	6.63%

Figure 14.35 Using the Vasicek Model to Generate a Yield Curve.

indicative of a worsening economic situation in the future (and, thus, an expectation that inflation will remain low in the future). Another potential situation is a flat yield curve, signaling uncertainty in the economy. The yield curve can also be humped or show a smile or a frown. The yield curve can change in shape over time through a twist or bend, a parallel shift, or a movement on one end versus another.

Because the yield curve is related to inflation rates as previously discussed, and central banks in most countries have the ability to control monetary policy to target inflation rates, inflation rates are mean-reverting in nature. This description of a yield curve also implies that interest rates are mean-reverting, as well as stochastically changing over time.

In a 1977 paper, a Czech mathematician, Oldrich Vasicek, proved that bond prices on a yield curve over time and various maturities are driven by the short end of the yield curve, or the short-term interest rates, using a risk-neutral martingale measure. In his work, the mean-reverting Ornstein-Uhlenbeck process was assumed, and, thus, the resulting Vasicek Model requires that a mean-reverting interest rate process be modeled (rate of mean reversion and long-run mean rates are both inputs in the Vasicek Model).

Illustrative Example: Stochastic Forecasting of Interest Rates and Stock Prices

Location: www.ElsevierDirect.com (search for this book, click Companion Site button, click link in Additional Models section) *Modeling Toolkit | Forecasting | Stochastic Processes*

Brief Description: This sample model illustrates how to simulate stochastic processes (Brownian motion random walk, mean-reversion, jump-diffusion, and mixed models).

A stochastic process is a sequence of events or paths generated by probabilistic laws. That is, random events can occur over time but are governed by specific statistical and probabilistic rules. The main stochastic processes include random walk or Brownian motion, mean-reversion, and jump-diffusion. These processes can be used to forecast a multitude of variables that seemingly follow random trends but are still restricted by probabilistic laws. We can use Risk Simulator's *Stochastic Process* module to simulate and create such processes. These processes can be used to forecast a multitude of time-series data, including stock prices, interest rates, inflation rates, oil prices, electricity prices, commodity prices, and so forth.

To run this model, simply follow these steps:

1. Select *Risk Simulator | Forecasting | Stochastic Processes*.
2. Enter a set of relevant inputs or use the existing inputs as a test case (Figure 14.36).
3. Select the relevant process to simulate.
4. Click on Update Chart to view the updated computation of a single path, or click OK to create the process.

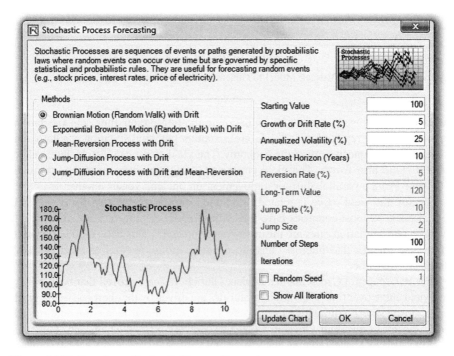

Figure 14.36 Running a Stochastic Process Forecast.

For your convenience, the analysis report sheet is included in the model. A stochastic time-series chart and forecast values are provided in the report, as well as each step's time period, mean, and standard deviation of the forecast. The mean values can be used as the single-point estimate, or assumptions can be manually generated for the desired time period. That is, finding the appropriate time period, you can create an assumption with a normal distribution with the appropriate mean and standard deviation computed. A sample chart with 10 iteration paths is included to graphically illustrate the behavior of the forecasted process.

15 Portfolio Optimization and Management of Default Risk

Chapter Outline

This chapter looks at the optimization process and methodologies in more detail in connection with using Risk Simulator. These methodologies include the use of continuous versus discrete integer optimization, as well as static versus dynamic and stochastic optimizations. The chapter then continues with several example optimization models to illustrate how the optimization process works. The first is the application of *continuous* optimization under uncertainty for a simple project (e.g., business lines, credit strategies, credit projects) selection model, where the idea is to allocate 100% of a bank's investment among several different asset classes or credit lines of business (e.g., different types of mutual funds or investment styles: growth, value, aggressive growth, income, global, index, contrarian, momentum; or business lines, credit lines, types of credit offerings, and products, etc.).

The second project deals with *discrete integer* optimization, where the idea is to look at several competing and nonmutually exclusive project choices, each with

Credit Engineering for Bankers. DOI: 10.1016/B978-0-12-378585-5.10015-6

a different return, risk, and cost profile. The job of the bank analyst here is to find the best combination of projects—defining *project* as any type of bank projects, credit lines, asset classes, and so forth—that will satisfy the bank or financial institution's budget constraints while maximizing the portfolio's total value.

The chapter continues by running a portfolio investment efficient frontier, followed by a stochastic optimization model where simulation is iteratively combined with optimization methods. Next, a case illustrates the application of optimization on selecting the optimal portfolio of correlated credit vehicles that yields the lowest portfolio Value at Risk (VaR). The chapter concludes with a detailed step-by-step set of hands-on exercises on setting up and running your own optimization routines.

Optimization Procedures

Many algorithms exist to run optimization, and many different procedures exist when optimization is coupled with Monte Carlo simulation. In Risk Simulator, there are three distinct optimization procedures and optimization types as well as different decision variable types. For instance, Risk Simulator can handle *Continuous Decision Variables* (1.2535, 0.2215, etc.), *Integer Decision Variables* (e.g., 1, 2, 3, 4 or 1.5, 2.5, 3.5, etc.), *Binary Decision Variables* (1 and 0 for go and no-go decisions), and *Mixed Decision Variables* (both integers and continuous variables). In addition, Risk Simulator can handle *Linear Optimizations* (i.e., when both the objective and constraints are all linear equations and functions) and *Nonlinear Optimizations* (i.e., when the objective and constraints are a mixture of linear and nonlinear functions and equations).

Concerning the optimization process, Risk Simulator can be used to run a *Discrete Optimization*—that is, an optimization that is run on a discrete or static model, where no simulations are run. In other words, all the inputs in the model are static and unchanging. This optimization type is applicable when the model is assumed to be known and no uncertainties exist. Also, a discrete optimization can first be run to determine the optimal portfolio and its corresponding optimal allocation of decision variables before more advanced optimization procedures are applied. For instance, before running a stochastic optimization problem and performing its protracted analysis, a discrete optimization is first run to determine if solutions to the optimization problem exist.

Dynamic Optimization is applied when Monte Carlo simulation is used together with optimization. Another name for such a procedure is *Simulation-Optimization*. That is, a simulation is first run, then the results of the simulation are applied in the Excel model, and then an optimization is applied to the simulated values. In other words, a simulation is run for N trials, and then an optimization process is run for M iterations until the optimal results are obtained or an infeasible set is found. Using Risk Simulator's optimization module, you can choose which forecast and assumption statistics to use and to replace in the model after the simulation is run. Then these forecast statistics can be applied in the optimization process. This approach is useful when you have a large model with many interacting assumptions and forecasts, and when some of the forecast statistics are required in the optimization. For example, if the standard deviation of an assumption or forecast is required in the optimization model (e.g., computing the Sharpe ratio in asset allocation and optimization problems where we have the mean divided by the standard deviation of the portfolio), then this approach should be used.

The *Stochastic Optimization* process, in contrast, is similar to the dynamic optimization procedure with the exception that the entire dynamic optimization process is repeated T times. That is, a simulation with N trials is run, and then an optimization is run with M iterations to obtain the optimal results. Then the process is replicated T times. The results will be a forecast chart of each decision variable with T values. In other words, a simulation is run, and the forecast or assumption statistics are used in the optimization model to find the optimal allocation of decision variables. Then another simulation is run, generating different forecast statistics, and these new updated values are then optimized, and so forth. Hence, the final decision variables will each have their own forecast chart, indicating the range of the optimal decision variables. For instance, instead of obtaining single-point estimates in the dynamic optimization procedure, you can now obtain a distribution of the decision variables and, thus, a range of optimal values for each decision variable, also known as a stochastic optimization.

Finally, an *Efficient Frontier* optimization procedure applies the concepts of marginal increments and shadow pricing in optimization. That is, what would happen to the results of the optimization if one of the constraints were relaxed slightly? Say, for instance, if the budget constraint is set at $1 million. What would happen to the portfolio's outcome and optimal decisions if the constraint were now $1.5 million, or $2 million, and so forth? This is the concept of the Markowitz efficient frontier in investment finance, where if the portfolio standard deviation is allowed to increase slightly, what additional returns will the portfolio generate? This process is similar to the dynamic optimization process with the exception that *one* of the constraints is allowed to change, and with each change, the simulation and optimization process is run. This process is best applied manually using Risk Simulator. It can be run either manually (rerunning the optimization several times) or automatically (using Risk Simulator's changing constraint and efficient frontier functionality). To perform the process manually, run a dynamic or stochastic optimization, then rerun another optimization with a new constraint, and then repeat that procedure several times. This manual process is important, since by changing the constraint, the analyst can determine if the results are similar or different, and, thus, whether it is worthy of any additional analysis or to determine how far a marginal increase in the constraint should be to obtain a significant change in the objective and decision variables. This is done by comparing the forecast distribution of each decision variable after running a stochastic optimization. Alternatively, the automated efficient frontier approach is shown later in the chapter.

One item is worthy of consideration: Other software products exist that supposedly perform stochastic optimization but in fact do not. For instance, after a simulation is run, then *one* iteration of the optimization process is generated, and then another simulation is run, then the *second* optimization iteration is generated, and so forth. This process is simply a waste of time and resources; that is, in optimization, the model is put through a rigorous set of algorithms, where multiple iterations (ranging from several to thousands of iterations) are required to obtain the optimal results. Hence, generating *one* iteration at a time is a waste of time and resources. The same portfolio can be solved using Risk Simulator in under a minute as compared to multiple hours using such a backward approach. Also, such a simulation-optimization approach will typically yield bad results and is not a stochastic optimization approach. Be extremely careful of such methodologies when applying optimization to your models.

The following two sections present example optimization problems. One uses continuous decision variables, and the other uses discrete integer decision variables. In either model, you can apply discrete optimization, dynamic optimization, stochastic optimization, or even manually generate efficient frontiers with shadow pricing. Any of these approaches can be used for these two examples. Therefore, for simplicity, only the model setup is illustrated, and it is up to the user to decide which optimization process to run. Also, the continuous decision variable example uses the nonlinear optimization approach (because the portfolio risk computed is a nonlinear function, and the objective is a nonlinear function of portfolio returns divided by portfolio risks), while the second example of an integer optimization is an example of a linear optimization model (its objective and all of its constraints are linear). Therefore, these two examples encapsulate all of the aforementioned procedures.

Continuous Optimization

Figure 15.1 illustrates the sample continuous optimization model. The example here uses the *11 Continuous Optimization* file found in *Risk Simulator | Example Models*. In this example, there are 10 distinct asset classes (e.g., different types of mutual funds, stocks, or assets), where the idea is to most efficiently and effectively allocate the portfolio holdings such that the best bang for the buck is obtained—that is, to generate the best portfolio returns possible given the risks inherent in each asset class. To truly understand the concept of optimization, we must delve more deeply into this sample model to see how the optimization process can best be applied.

The model shows the 10 asset classes, each of which has its own set of annualized returns and annualized volatilities. These return and risk measures are annualized values such that they can be consistently compared across different asset classes. Returns are computed using the geometric average of the relative returns, while the risks are computed using the logarithmic relative stock returns approach.

In Figure 15.1, the Allocation Weights in column E hold the decision variables, which are the variables that need to be tweaked and tested such that the total weight is constrained at 100% (cell E17). Typically, to start the optimization, we will set these cells to a uniform value, where in this case, cells E6 to E15 are set at 10% each. In addition, each decision variable may have specific restrictions in its allowed range. In this example, the lower and upper allocations allowed are 5% and 35%, as seen in columns F and G. This means that each asset class may have its own allocation boundaries. Next, column H shows the return to risk ratio, which is simply the return percentage divided by the risk percentage, where the higher this value, the higher the bang for the buck. The remaining columns show the individual asset class rankings by

ASSET ALLOCATION OPTIMIZATION MODEL

Asset Class Description	Annualized Returns	Volatility Risk	Allocation Weights	Required Minimum Allocation	Required Maximum Allocation	Return to Risk Ratio	Returns Ranking (Hi-Lo)	Risk Ranking (Lo-Hi)	Return to Risk Ranking (Hi-Lo)	Allocation Ranking (Hi-Lo)
Asset Class 1	10.54%	12.36%	10.00%	5.00%	35.00%	0.8524	9	2	7	1
Asset Class 2	11.25%	16.23%	10.00%	5.00%	35.00%	0.6929	7	8	10	1
Asset Class 3	11.84%	15.64%	10.00%	5.00%	35.00%	0.7570	6	7	9	1
Asset Class 4	10.64%	12.35%	10.00%	5.00%	35.00%	0.8615	8	1	5	1
Asset Class 5	13.25%	13.28%	10.00%	5.00%	35.00%	0.9977	5	4	2	1
Asset Class 6	14.21%	14.39%	10.00%	5.00%	35.00%	0.9875	3	6	3	1
Asset Class 7	15.53%	14.25%	10.00%	5.00%	35.00%	1.0898	1	5	1	1
Asset Class 8	14.95%	16.44%	10.00%	5.00%	35.00%	0.9094	2	9	4	1
Asset Class 9	14.16%	16.50%	10.00%	5.00%	35.00%	0.8584	4	10	6	1
Asset Class 10	10.06%	12.50%	10.00%	5.00%	35.00%	0.8045	10	3	8	1
Portfolio Total	**12.6419%**	**4.58%**	**100.00%**							
Return to Risk Ratio	**2.7596**									

Specifications of the optimization model:

Objective: *Maximize Return to Risk Ratio (C18)*
Decision Variables: *Allocation Weights (E6:E15)*
Restrictions on Decision Variables: *Minimum and Maximum Required (F6:G15)*
Constraints: *Portfolio Total Allocation Weights 100% (E17 is set to 100%)*

Additional specifications:

1. One can always maximize portfolio total returns or minimize the portfolio total risk.
2. Incorporate Monte Carlo simulation in the model by simulating the returns and volatility of each asset class and apply Simulation–Optimization techniques.
3. The portfolio can be optimized as is without simulation using Static Optimization techniques.

Figure 15.1 Continuous Optimization Model.

returns, risk, return to risk ratio, and allocation. In other words, these rankings show at a glance which asset class has the lowest risk, or the highest return, and so forth.

The portfolio's total returns in cell C17 is *SUMPRODUCT(C6:C15, E6:E15)*— that is, the sum of the allocation weights multiplied by the annualized returns for each asset class. In other words, we have $R_P = \omega_A R_A + \omega_B R_B + \omega_C R_C + \omega_D R_D$, where R_P is the return on the portfolio, $R_{A,B,C,D}$ are the individual returns on the projects, and $\omega_{A,B,C,D}$ are the respective weights or capital allocation across each project.

In addition, the portfolio's diversified risk in cell D17 is computed by taking

$$\sigma_P = \sqrt{\sum_{i=1}^{n} \omega_i^2 \sigma_i^2 + \sum_{i=1}^{n} \sum_{j=1}^{m} 2\omega_i \omega_j \rho_{i,j} \sigma_i \sigma_j}$$

Here, $\rho_{i,j}$ are the respective cross-correlations between the asset classes. Hence, if the cross-correlations are negative, there are risk diversification effects, and the portfolio risk decreases. However, to simplify the computations here, we assume zero correlations among the asset classes through this portfolio risk computation but assume the correlations when applying simulation on the returns, as will be seen later. Therefore, instead of applying static correlations among these different asset returns, we apply the correlations in the simulation assumptions themselves, creating a more dynamic relationship among the simulated return values.

Finally, the return to risk ratio, or Sharpe ratio, is computed for the portfolio. This value is seen in cell C18 and represents the objective to be maximized in this optimization exercise. To summarize, we have the following specifications in this example model:

Objective: *Maximize Return to Risk Ratio (C18)*
Decision Variables: *Allocation Weights (E6:E15)*
Restrictions on Decision Variables: *Minimum and Maximum Required (F6:G15)*
Constraints: *Total Allocation Weights Sum to 100% (E17)*

Procedure

- Open the example file (*Continuous Optimization*) and start a new profile by clicking on *Risk Simulator | New Profile* and provide it a name.
- The first step in optimization is to set the decision variables. Select cell E6, set the first decision variable (*Risk Simulator | Optimization | Set Decision*), and click on the Link icon to select the name cell (B6), as well as the lower bound and upper bound values at cells F6 and G6. Then, using *Risk Simulator Copy*, copy this cell E6 decision variable and paste the decision variable to the remaining cells in E7 to E15.
- The second step in optimization is to set the constraint. There is only one constraint here— that is, the total allocation in the portfolio must sum to 100%. So click on *Risk Simulator | Optimization | Constraints...* and select *ADD* to add a new constraint. Then select the cell E17 and make it equal (=) to 100%. Click OK when done.
- The final step in optimization is to set the objective function and start the optimization by selecting the objective cell C18 and *Risk Simulator | Optimization | Set Objective*. Then run the optimization by selecting *Risk Simulator | Optimization | Run Optimization* and

selecting the optimization of choice (*Static Optimization, Dynamic Optimization*, or *Stochastic Optimization*). To get started, select *Static Optimization*. Check to make sure the objective cell is set for C18 and select *Maximize*. You can now review the decision variables and constraints if required, or click OK to run the static optimization.

- Once the optimization is complete, you may select *Revert* to revert back to the original values of the decision variables as well as the objective, or select *Replace* to apply the optimized decision variables. Typically, *Replace* is chosen after the optimization is done.

Figure 15.2 shows the screen shots of the preceding procedural steps. You can add simulation assumptions on the model's returns and risk (columns C and D) and apply the dynamic optimization and stochastic optimization for additional practice.

Results Interpretation

The optimization's final results are shown in Figure 15.3, where the optimal allocation of assets for the portfolio is seen in cells E6:E15. Given the restrictions of each asset fluctuating between 5% and 35%, and where the sum of the allocation must equal 100%, the allocation that maximizes the return to risk ratio is seen in Figure 15.3.

A few important things must be noted when reviewing the results and optimization procedures performed thus far:

- The correct way to run the optimization is to maximize the bang for the buck or returns to risk Sharpe ratio as we have done.
- If instead we maximized the total portfolio returns, the optimal allocation result is trivial and does not require optimization to obtain. That is, simply allocate 5% (the minimum allowed) to the lowest eight assets, 35% (the maximum allowed) to the highest returning asset, and the remaining (25%) to the second-best returns asset. Optimization is not required. However, when allocating the portfolio this way, the risk is a lot higher as compared to when maximizing the returns to risk ratio, although the portfolio returns by themselves are higher.
- In contrast, one can minimize the total portfolio risk, but the returns will now be less.

Table 15.1 illustrates the results from the three different objectives being optimized. From the table, it can be seen that the best approach is to maximize the returns to risk ratio; that is, for the same amount of risk, this allocation provides the highest amount of return. Conversely, for the same amount of return, this allocation provides the lowest amount of risk possible. This approach of bang for the buck or returns to risk ratio is the cornerstone of the Markowitz efficient frontier in modern portfolio theory. That is, if we constrained the total portfolio risk levels and successively increased them over time, we would obtain several efficient portfolio allocations for different risk characteristics. Thus, different efficient portfolio allocations can be obtained for different individuals with different risk preferences.

Discrete Integer Optimization

Sometimes, the decision variables are not continuous but discrete integers (e.g., 1, 2, 3) or binary (e.g., 0 and 1). We can use such binary decision variables as on-off switches or go/no-go decisions. Figure 15.4 illustrates a project selection model

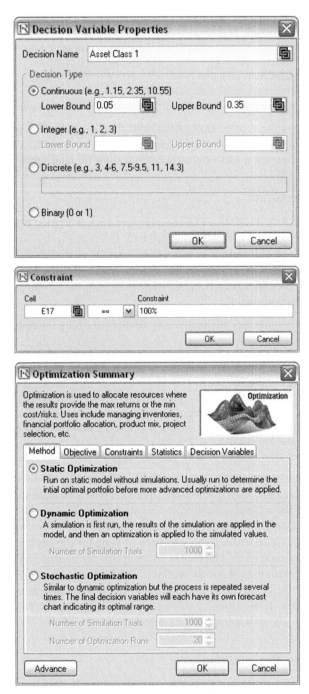

Figure 15.2 Running Continuous Optimization in Risk Simulator.

ASSET ALLOCATION OPTIMIZATION MODEL

Asset Class Description	Annualized Returns	Volatility Risk	Allocation Weights	Required Minimum Allocation	Required Maximum Allocation	Return to Risk Ratio	Returns Ranking (Hi-Lo)	Risk Ranking (Lo-Hi)	Return to Risk Ranking (Hi-Lo)	Allocation Ranking (Hi-Lo)
Asset Class 1	10.54%	12.36%	11.09%	5.00%	35.00%	0.8524	9	2	7	4
Asset Class 2	11.25%	16.23%	6.87%	5.00%	35.00%	0.6929	7	8	10	10
Asset Class 3	11.84%	15.64%	7.78%	5.00%	35.00%	0.7570	6	7	9	9
Asset Class 4	10.64%	12.35%	11.22%	5.00%	35.00%	0.8615	8	1	5	3
Asset Class 5	13.25%	13.28%	12.08%	5.00%	35.00%	0.9977	5	4	2	2
Asset Class 6	14.21%	14.39%	11.04%	5.00%	35.00%	0.9875	3	6	3	5
Asset Class 7	15.53%	14.25%	12.30%	5.00%	35.00%	1.0898	1	5	1	1
Asset Class 8	14.95%	16.44%	8.90%	5.00%	35.00%	0.9094	2	9	4	7
Asset Class 9	14.16%	16.50%	8.37%	5.00%	35.00%	0.8584	4	10	6	8
Asset Class 10	10.06%	12.50%	10.35%	5.00%	35.00%	0.8045	10	3	8	6

Portfolio Total | **12.6920%** | **4.52%** | **100.00%**

Return to Risk Ratio | **2.8091**

Specifications of the optimization model:

Objective: Maximize Return to Risk Ratio (C18)
Decision Variables: Allocation Weights (E6:E15)
Restrictions on Decision Variables: Minimum and Maximum Required (F6:G15)
Constraints: Portfolio Total Allocation Weights 100% (E17 is set to 100%)

Additional specifications:

1. One can always maximize portfolio total returns or minimize the portfolio total risk.
2. Incorporate Monte Carlo simulation in the model by simulating the returns and volatility of each asset class and apply Simulation-Optimization techniques.
3. The portfolio can be optimized as is without simulation using Static Optimization techniques.

Figure 15.3 Continuous Optimization Results.

Table 15.1 Optimization Results

Objective	Portfolio Returns	Portfolio Risk	Portfolio Returns to Risk Ratio
Maximize Returns to Risk Ratio	12.69%	4.52%	2.8091
Maximize Returns	13.97%	6.77%	2.0636
Minimize Risk	12.38%	4.46%	2.7754

where there are 12 credit strategies (these could be actual projects, lines of business in a bank, engineered credit strategies, credit hedging positions, trading positions, etc.) listed. The example here uses the *Optimization Discrete* file found on *Risk Simulator | Example Models*. Each project, like before, has its own returns (ENPV and NPV for expanded net present value and net present value—the ENPV is simply the NPV plus any strategic real options values), costs of implementation, risks, and so forth. If required, this model can be modified to include required full-time equivalences (FTE) and other resources of various functions, and additional constraints can be set on these additional resources. The inputs into this model are typically linked from other spreadsheet models. For instance, each project will have its own discounted cash flow or returns on investment model. The application here is to maximize the portfolio's Sharpe ratio subject to some budget allocation. Many other versions of this model can be created, for instance, maximizing the portfolio returns, or minimizing the risks, or adding additional constraints where the total number of projects chosen cannot exceed 6, and so forth and so on. All of these items can be run using this existing model.

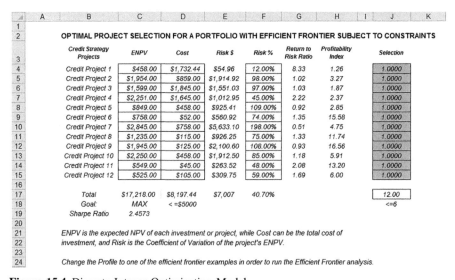

Figure 15.4 Discrete Integer Optimization Model.

Procedure

- Open the example file (*Discrete Optimization*) and start a new profile by clicking on *Risk Simulator | New Profile* and provide it a name.
- The first step in optimization is to set up the decision variables. Set the first decision variable by selecting cell J4, and select *Risk Simulator | Optimization | Set Decision*, click on the Link icon to select the name cell (B4), and select the *Binary* variable. Then, using Risk Simulator *Copy*, copy this J4 decision variable cell and paste the decision variable to the remaining cells in J5 to J15.
- The second step in optimization is to set the constraint. There are two constraints here: The total budget allocation in the portfolio must be less than $5,000 and the total number of projects must not exceed 6. So click on *Risk Simulator | Optimization | Constraints…* and select *ADD* to add a new constraint. Then, select the cell D17 and make it less than or equal (<=) to 5000. Repeat by setting cell J17 <= 6.
- The final step in optimization is to set the objective function and start the optimization by selecting cell C19 and selecting *Risk Simulator | Optimization | Set Objective*. Then run the optimization (*Risk Simulator | Optimization | Run Optimization*) after selecting the optimization of choice (*Static Optimization, Dynamic Optimization*, or *Stochastic Optimization*). To get started, select *Static Optimization*. Check to make sure that the objective cell is C19 and select *Maximize*. You can now review the decision variables and constraints if required, or click *OK* to run the static optimization.

Figure 15.5 shows the screen shots of the foregoing procedural steps. You can add simulation assumptions on the model's ENPV and Risk (columns C and F) and apply the dynamic optimization and stochastic optimization for additional practice.

Results Interpretation

Figure 15.6 shows a sample optimal selection of projects that maximizes the Sharpe ratio. In contrast, one can always maximize total revenues, but, as before, this process is trivial and simply involves choosing the highest-returning project and going down the list until you run out of money or exceed the budget constraint. Doing so will yield theoretically undesirable projects as the highest yielding projects typically hold higher risks. Now, if desired, you can replicate the optimization using a stochastic or dynamic optimization by adding in assumptions in the ENPV and/or cost and/or risk values.

Efficient Frontier and Advanced Optimization Settings

Figure 15.7 shows the efficient frontier constraints for optimization. You can get to this interface by clicking on the *Efficient Frontier* button *after* you have set some constraints. You can now make these constraints changing. That is, each of the constraints can be created to step through between some minimum and maximum value. As an example, the constraint in cell J17 <= 6 can be set to run between 4 and 8 (see Figure 15.7). That is, five optimizations will be run, each with the following constraints: J17 <= 4, J17 <= 5, J17 <= 6, J17 <= 7, and J17 <= 8. The optimal

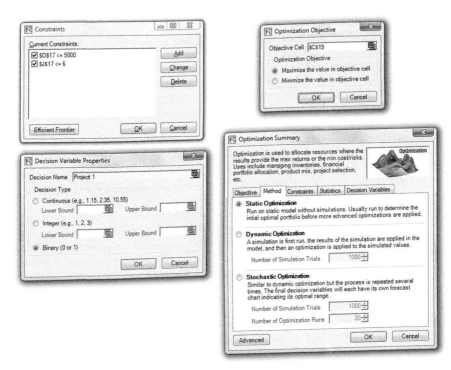

Figure 15.5 Running Discrete Integer Optimization in Risk Simulator.

results will then be plotted as an efficient frontier and the report will be generated (Figure 15.8).

Specifically, following are the steps required to create a changing constraint:

1. In an optimization model (i.e., a model with Objective, Decision Variables, and Constraints already set up), click on *Risk Simulator | Optimization | Constraints* and then click on *Efficient Frontier.*
2. Select the constraint you want to change or step (e.g., J17), enter the parameters for Min, Max, and Step Size (see Figure 15.7), and click ADD, then OK, and OK again. You should deselect the *D17 <= 5000* constraint before running.
3. Run Optimization as usual (*Risk Simulator | Optimization | Run Optimization*). You can choose static, dynamic, or stochastic. To get started, select the *Static Optimization* to run.
4. The results will be shown as a user interface (see Figure 15.8). Click on *Create Report* to generate a report worksheet with all the details of the optimization runs.

Stochastic Optimization

This example illustrates the application of stochastic optimization using a sample model with four asset classes, each with different risk and return characteristics. The

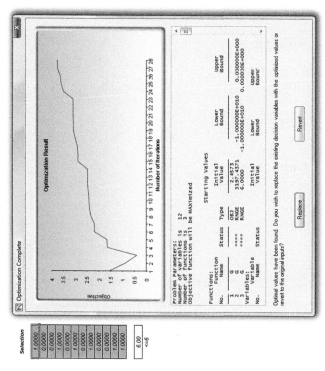

	ENPV	Cost	Risk $	Risk %	Return to Risk Ratio	Profitability Index	Selection
Project 1	$458.00	$1,732.44	$54.96	12.00%	8.33	1.26	1.0000
Project 2	$1,954.00	$859.00	$1,914.92	98.00%	1.02	3.27	0.0000
Project 3	$1,599.00	$1,845.00	$1,551.03	97.00%	1.03	1.87	0.0000
Project 4	$2,251.00	$1,645.00	$1,012.95	45.00%	2.22	2.37	1.0000
Project 5	$849.00	$458.00	$925.41	109.00%	0.92	2.85	0.0000
Project 6	$758.00	$52.00	$560.92	74.00%	1.35	15.58	1.0000
Project 7	$2,845.00	$758.00	$5,633.10	198.00%	0.51	4.75	0.0000
Project 8	$1,235.00	$115.00	$926.25	75.00%	1.33	11.74	1.0000
Project 9	$1,945.00	$125.00	$2,100.60	108.00%	0.93	16.56	0.0000
Project 10	$2,250.00	$458.00	$1,912.50	85.00%	1.16	5.91	0.0000
Project 11	$549.00	$45.00	$263.52	48.00%	2.08	13.20	1.0000
Project 12	$525.00	$105.00	$309.75	59.00%	1.69	6.00	1.0000
Total	$5,776.00	$3,694.44	$1,539	26.64%			6.00
Goal:	MAX	<=$5000	$1,539				<=6
Sharpe Ratio	3.7543						

ENPV is the expected NPV of each credit line or project, while Cost can be the total cost of administration as well as required capital holdings to cover the credit line, and Risk is the Coefficient of Variation of the credit line's ENPV.

Figure 15.6 Optimal Selection of Projects That Maximize the Sharpe Ratio.

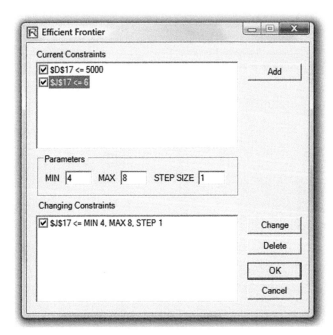

Figure 15.7 Generating Changing Constraints in an Efficient Frontier.

idea here is to find the best portfolio allocation such that the portfolio's bang for the buck, or returns to risk ratio, is maximized. That is, the goal is to allocate 100% of an individual's investment among several different asset classes (e.g., different types of mutual funds or investment styles: growth, value, aggressive growth, income, global, index, contrarian, momentum, etc.). This model is unique because it includes several simulation assumptions (risk and return values for each asset in columns C and D), as seen in Figure 15.9.

A simulation is run, then optimization is executed, and the entire process is repeated multiple times to obtain distributions of each decision variable. The entire analysis can be automated using Stochastic Optimization.

In order to run an optimization, several key specifications on the model have to be identified first:

Objective: *Maximize Return to Risk Ratio (C12)*
Decision Variables: *Allocation Weights (E6:E9)*
Restrictions on Decision Variables: *Minimum and Maximum Required (F6:G9)*
Constraints: *Portfolio Total Allocation Weights 100% (E11 is set to 100%)*
Simulation Assumptions: *Return and Risk Values (C6:D9)*

The model shows the various asset classes. Each asset class has its own set of annualized returns and annualized volatilities. These return and risk measures are annualized values such that they can be consistently compared across different asset classes. Returns are computed using the geometric average of the relative returns,

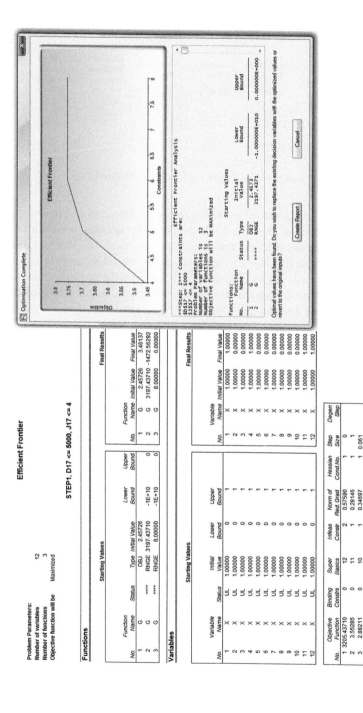

Figure 15.8 Efficient Frontier Results.

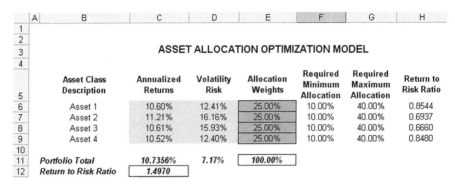

Figure 15.9 Asset Allocation Model Ready for Stochastic Optimization.

while the risks are computed using the logarithmic relative stock returns approach. Column E, the Allocation Weights, holds the decision variables, which are the variables that need to be tweaked and tested such that the total weight is constrained at 100% (cell E11). Typically, to start the optimization, we set these cells to a uniform value. In this case, cells E6 to E9 are set at 25% each. In addition, each decision variable may have specific restrictions in its allowed range. In this example, the lower and upper allocations allowed are 10% and 40%, as seen in columns F and G. This setting means that each asset class may have its own allocation boundaries.

Next, column H shows the return to risk ratio, which is simply the return percentage divided by the risk percentage for each asset, where the higher this value, the higher the bang for the buck. The remaining parts of the model show the individual asset class rankings by returns, risk, return to risk ratio, and allocation. In other words, these rankings show at a glance which asset class has the lowest risk, or the highest return, and so forth.

Running an Optimization

To run this model, simply click on *Risk Simulator | Optimization | Run Optimization*. Alternatively, and for practice, you can set up the model using the following steps:

1. Start a new profile (*Risk Simulator | New Profile*).
2. For stochastic optimization, set distributional assumptions on the risk and returns for each asset class. That is, select cell C6, set an assumption (*Risk Simulator | Set Input Assumption*), and make your own assumption as required. Repeat for cells *C7* to *D9*.
3. Select cell *E6*, define the decision variable (*Risk Simulator | Optimization | Set Decision* or click on the Set Decision D icon), and make it a Continuous Variable. Then link the decision variable's name and minimum/maximum required to the relevant cells (*B6, F6, G6*).
4. Then use the Risk Simulator copy on cell E6, select cells *E7* to *E9*, and use Risk Simulator paste (*Risk Simulator | Copy Parameter* and *Risk Simulator | Paste Parameter*, or use the copy and paste icons). Remember not to use Excel's regular copy and paste functions.
5. Next, set up the optimization's constraints by selecting *Risk Simulator | Optimization | Constraints*, selecting ADD, and selecting the cell E11 and making it equal 100% (total allocation, and do not forget the % sign).

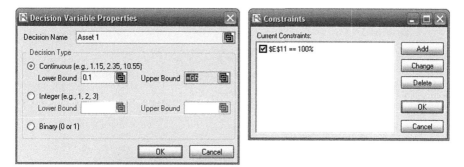

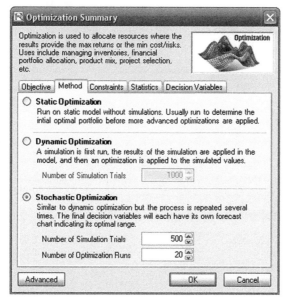

Figure 15.10 Setting Up the Stochastic Optimization Problem.

6. Select cell *C12*, the objective to be maximized, and make it the objective: *Risk Simulator | Optimization | Set Objective* or click on the O icon.
7. Run the optimization by going to *Risk Simulator | Optimization | Run Optimization*. Review the different tabs to make sure that all the required inputs in steps 2 and 3 are correct. Select *Stochastic Optimization* and let it run for 500 trials repeated 20 times (Figure 15.10 illustrates these setup steps).
8. Click OK when the simulation completes, and a detailed stochastic optimization report will be generated along with forecast charts of the decision variables.

Viewing and Interpreting Forecast Results

Stochastic optimization is performed when a simulation is first run and then the optimization is run. Then the whole analysis is repeated multiple times. The result

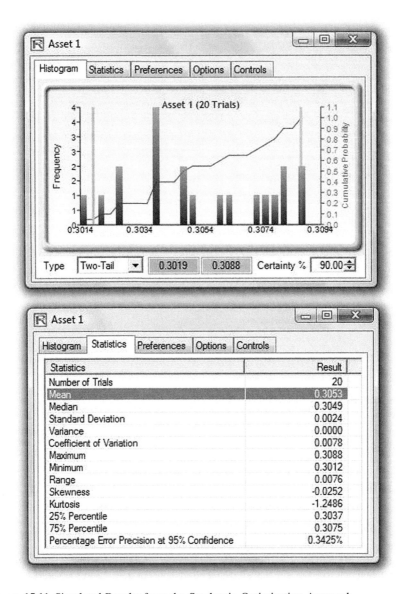

Figure 15.11 Simulated Results from the Stochastic Optimization Approach.

is a distribution of each decision variable rather than a single-point estimate (Figure 15.11). So instead of saying you should invest 30.53% in Asset 1, the optimal decision is to invest between 30.19% and 30.88% as long as the total portfolio sums to 100%. This way, the results provide management or decision makers a range of flexibility in the optimal decisions and all the while accounting for the risks and uncertainties in the inputs.

Notes

- *Super Speed Simulation with Optimization.* You can also run stochastic optimization with Super Speed simulation. To do this, first reset the optimization by resetting all four decision variables back to 25%. Next select *Run Optimization,* click on the *Advanced* button (see Figure 15.10), and select the checkbox for *Run Super Speed Simulation.* Then, in the run optimization user interface, select *Stochastic Optimization* on the *Method* tab, set it to run 500 trials and 20 optimization runs, and click OK. This approach will integrate the Super Speed simulation with optimization. Notice how much faster the stochastic optimization runs. You can now quickly rerun the optimization with a higher number of simulation trials.
- *Simulation Statistics for Stochastic and Dynamic Optimization.* Notice that if there are input simulation assumptions in the optimization model (i.e., these input assumptions are required to run the dynamic or stochastic optimization routines), the *Statistics* tab is now populated in the *Run Optimization* user interface. You can select from the droplist the statistics you want, such as average, standard deviation, coefficient of variation, conditional mean, conditional variance, a specific percentile, and so forth. Thus, if you run a stochastic optimization, a simulation of thousands of trials will first run; then the selected statistic will be computed, and this value will be temporarily placed in the simulation assumption cell; then an optimization will be run based on this statistic; and then the entire process is repeated multiple times. This method is important and useful for banking applications in computing Conditional VaR.

Illustrative Example: Portfolio Optimization and the Effects on Portfolio Value at Risk

Now that we understand the concepts of optimized portfolios, let us see what the effects are on computed economic capital through the use of a correlated credit portfolio VaR. This model uses Monte Carlo simulation and optimization routines in Risk Simulator to minimize the VaR of a portfolio of assets (Figure 15.12). The file used is *Value at Risk | Optimized and Simulated Portfolio VaR,* which is accessible via *Modeling Toolkit | Value at Risk | Optimized and Simulated Portfolio VaR.* In this example model, we intentionally used only four asset classes or credit line businesses to illustrate the effects of an optimized portfolio, whereas in real life, we can extend this process to cover a multitude of asset classes and business lines. In addition, we now illustrate the use of a left-tail VaR, as opposed to a right-tail VaR, but the concepts are similar.

First, simulation is used to determine the 90% left-tail VaR (this means that there is a 10% chance that losses will exceed this VaR for a specified holding period). With an equal allocation of 25% across the four asset classes, the VaR is determined using simulation (Figure 15.13). The annualized returns are uncertain and, thus, simulated. The VaR is then read off the forecast chart. Then optimization is run to find the best portfolio subject to the 100% allocation across the four asset classes or credit lines (in this example, we use four well-known asset classes as an example, instead of calling them generic credit lines or nameless assets) that will

VALUE AT RISK WITH ASSET ALLOCATION OPTIMIZATION MODEL

Asset Class Description	Annualized Returns	Volatility Risk	Allocation Weights	Required Minimum Allocation	Required Maximum Allocation
S&P 500	7.10%	9.80%	10.00%	10.00%	40.00%
Small Cap	9.51%	14.35%	27.30%	10.00%	40.00%
High Yield	15.90%	22.50%	22.70%	10.00%	40.00%
Govt Bonds	4.50%	7.25%	40.00%	10.00%	40.00%
		Total Weight:	*100.00%*		

Correlation Matrix	S&P 500	Small Cap	High Yield	Govt Bonds
S&P 500	1.0000	0.7400	0.6500	0.5500
Small Cap	0.7400	1.0000	0.4200	0.3100
High Yield	0.6500	0.4200	1.0000	0.2300
Govt Bonds	0.5500	0.3100	0.2300	1.0000

Covariance Matrix	S&P 500	Small Cap	High Yield	Govt Bonds
S&P 500	0.0096	0.0104	0.0143	0.0039
Small Cap	0.0104	0.0206	0.0136	0.0032
High Yield	0.0143	0.0136	0.0506	0.0038
Govt Bonds	0.0039	0.0032	0.0038	0.0053

Starting Value	$1,000,000.00
Term (Years)	5.00

Annualized Return	8.72%	**Profit/Loss**	$87,151.94
Portfolio Risk	9.84%	**Return to Risk Ratio**	88.59%
Ending Value	$1,087,151.94		

Specifications of the optimization model:

Objective:	*Maximize Return to Risk Ratio (E28)*
Decision Variables:	*Allocation Weights (E6:E9)*
Restrictions on Decision Variables:	*Minimum and Maximum Required (F6:G9)*
Constraints:	*Portfolio Total Allocation Weights 100% (E10 is set to 100%)*

Figure 15.12 Computing Value at Risk (VaR) with Simulation.

maximize the portfolio's bang for the buck (returns to risk ratio). The resulting optimized portfolio is then simulated once again and the new VaR is obtained (Figure 15.14). The VaR of this optimized portfolio is a lot less than the portfolio not optimized. That is, the expected loss is $35.8M instead of $42.2M, which means that the bank will have a lower required economic capital if the portfolio of holdings is first optimized.

Exercise: Optimization

This sample model illustrates how to use Risk Simulator for:

1. Running Static, Dynamic, and Stochastic Optimization with Continuous Decision Variables
2. Optimization with Discrete Integer Decision Variables
3. Efficient Frontier and Advanced Optimization Settings

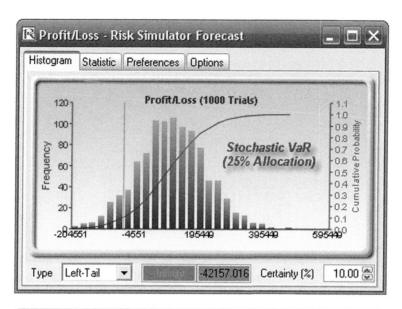

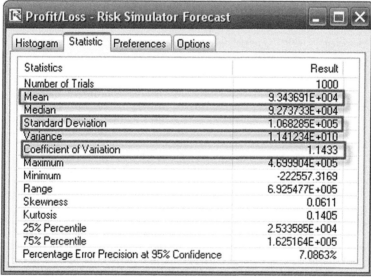

Figure 15.13 Nonoptimized Value at Risk (VaR).

Model Background

File Name: *Basic Simulation Model.xls*

Access: www.ElsevierDirect.com (search for this book, click Companion Site button, click link in Additional Models section)

Access: *Risk Simulator | Example Models | 11 Optimization Continuous*

Access: *Risk Simulator | Example Models | 12 Optimization Discrete*

Access: *Risk Simulator | Example Models | 13 Optimization Stochastic*

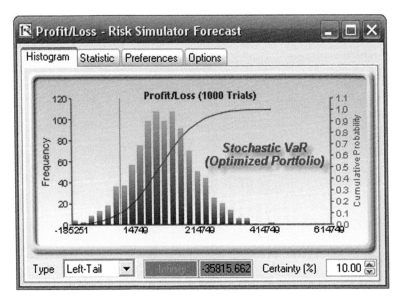

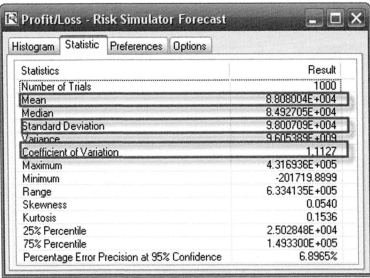

Figure 15.14 Optimal Portfolio's Value at Risk (VaR) through Optimization and Simulation.

1. Running Static, Dynamic, and Stochastic Optimization with Continuous Decision Variables

Figure 15E.A illustrates the sample continuous optimization model. In this example, there are 10 distinct asset classes (e.g., different types of mutual funds, stocks, or assets) where the idea is to most efficiently and effectively allocate the portfolio

	A	B	C	D	E	F	G	H	I	J	K	L

ASSET ALLOCATION OPTIMIZATION MODEL

Asset Class Description	Annualized Returns	Volatility Risk	Allocation Weights	Required Minimum Allocation	Required Maximum Allocation	Return to Risk Ratio	Returns Ranking (Hi-Lo)	Risk Ranking (Lo-Hi)	Return to Risk Ranking (Hi-Lo)	Allocation Ranking (Hi-Lo)
Asset Class 1	10.54%	12.36%	10.00%	5.00%	35.00%	0.8524	9	2	7	1
Asset Class 2	11.26%	16.23%	10.00%	5.00%	35.00%	0.6929	7	8	10	1
Asset Class 3	11.84%	15.64%	10.00%	5.00%	35.00%	0.7570	6	7	9	1
Asset Class 4	10.64%	12.35%	10.00%	5.00%	35.00%	0.8615	8	1	5	1
Asset Class 5	13.25%	13.28%	10.00%	5.00%	35.00%	0.9977	5	4	2	1
Asset Class 6	14.21%	14.39%	10.00%	5.00%	35.00%	0.9875	3	6	3	1
Asset Class 7	15.53%	14.25%	10.00%	5.00%	35.00%	1.0898	1	5	1	1
Asset Class 8	14.95%	16.44%	10.00%	5.00%	35.00%	0.9094	2	9	4	1
Asset Class 9	14.16%	16.50%	10.00%	5.00%	35.00%	0.8584	4	10	6	1
Asset Class 10	10.06%	12.50%	10.00%	5.00%	35.00%	0.8045	10	3	8	1

| Portfolio Total | 12.6419% | 4.58% | 100.00% |
| Return to Risk Ratio | 2.7596 |

Specifications of the optimization model:

Objective: Maximize Return to Risk Ratio (C18)
Decision Variables: Allocation Weights (E6:E15)
Restrictions on Decision Variables: Minimum and Maximum Required (F6:G15)
Constraints: Portfolio Total Allocation Weights 100% (E17 is set to 100%)

Additional specifications:

1. One can always maximize portfolio total returns or minimize the portfolio total risk.
2. Incorporate Monte Carlo simulation in the model by simulating the returns and volatility of each asset class and apply Simulation-Optimization techniques.
3. The portfolio can be optimized as is without simulation using Static Optimization techniques.

Figure 15E.A Continuous Optimization Model.

holdings such that the best bang for the buck is obtained. In other words, we want to generate the best portfolio returns possible given the risks inherent in each asset class. In order to truly understand the concept of optimization, we will have to delve more deeply into this sample model to see how the optimization process can best be applied.

The model shows the 10 asset classes, each of which has its own set of annualized returns and annualized volatilities. These return and risk measures are annualized values such that they can be consistently compared across different asset classes. Returns are computed using the geometric average of the relative returns, while the risks are computed using the logarithmic relative stock returns approach.

The Allocation Weights in column E hold the decision variables, which are the variables that need to be tweaked and tested such that the total weight is constrained at 100% (cell E17). Typically, to start the optimization, we will set these cells to a uniform value, where in this case, cells E6 to E15 are set at 10% each. In addition, each decision variable may have specific restrictions in its allowed range. In this example, the lower and upper allocations allowed are 5% and 35%, as seen in columns F and G. This means that each asset class may have its own allocation boundaries. Next, column H shows the return to risk ratio, which is simply the return percentage divided by the risk percentage; the higher this value, the higher the bang for the buck. The remaining columns show the individual asset class rankings by returns, risk, return to risk ratio, and allocation. In other words, these rankings show at a glance which asset class has the lowest risk, or the highest return, and so forth.

The portfolio's total returns in cell C17 is *SUMPRODUCT(C6:C15, E6:E15)*, that is, the sum of the allocation weights multiplied by the annualized returns for each asset class. In other words, we have $R_P = \omega_A R_A + \omega_B R_B + \omega_C R_C + \omega_D R_D$, where R_P is the return on the portfolio, $R_{A,B,C,D}$ are the individual returns on the projects, and $\omega_{A,B,C,D}$ are the respective weights or capital allocation across each project.

In addition, the portfolio's diversified risk in cell D17 is computed by taking

$$\sigma_P = \sqrt{\sum_{i=1}^{i} \omega_i^2 \sigma_i^2 + \sum_{i=1}^{n} \sum_{j=1}^{m} 2\omega_i \omega_j \rho_{i,j} \sigma_i \sigma_j}$$

Here, $\rho_{I,j}$ are the respective cross-correlations between the asset classes. Hence, if the cross-correlations are negative, there are risk diversification effects, and the portfolio risk decreases. However, to simplify the computations here, we assume zero correlations among the asset classes through this portfolio risk computation but assume the correlations when applying simulation on the returns, as will be seen later. Therefore, instead of applying static correlations among these different asset returns, we apply the correlations in the simulation assumptions themselves, creating a more dynamic relationship among the simulated return values.

Finally, the return to risk ratio, or Sharpe ratio, is computed for the portfolio. This value is seen in cell C18 and represents the objective to be maximized in this optimization exercise. The following are the specifications in this example optimization model:

Objective: *Maximize Return to Risk Ratio (C18)*
Decision Variables: *Allocation Weights (E6:E15)*
Restrictions on Decision Variables: *Minimum and Maximum Required (F6:G15)*
Constraints: *Total Allocation Weights Sum to 100% (E17)*

Procedure

1. Start Excel and open the example file *Risk Simulator | Example Models | 11 Optimization Continuous.*
2. Start a new profile with *Risk Simulator | New Profile* (or click on the New Profile icon) and give it a name.
3. The first step in optimization is to set the decision variables. Select cell *E6*, set the first decision variable (*Risk Simulator | Optimization | Set Decision*) or click on the D icon. Then click on the Link icon to select the name cell (*B6*), as well as the lower bound and upper bound values at cells *F6* and *G6*. Then, using Risk Simulator Copy, copy this cell *E6* decision variable and paste the decision variable to the remaining cells in *E7* to *E15*.
4. The second step in optimization is to set the constraint. There is only one constraint here, which is that the total allocation in the portfolio must sum to 100%. So click on *Risk Simulator | Optimization | Constraints...*, or click on the C icon, and select *ADD* to add a new constraint. Then, select the cell *E17* and make it equal ($=$) to 100%. Click when done.
   - *Exercise Question:* Would you get the same results if you set $E7 = 1$ instead of 100%?
   - *Exercise Question:* In the constraints user interface, what does the *Efficient Frontier* button mean and how does it work?

5. The final step in optimization is to set the objective function. Select cell *C18* and click on *Risk Simulator | Optimization | Set Objective* or click on the O icon. Check to make sure the objective cell is set for *C18* and select Maximize.

6. Start the optimization by going to *Risk Simulator | Optimization | Run Optimization* or click on the Run Optimization icon and select the optimization of choice (*Static Optimization, Dynamic Optimization,* or *Stochastic Optimization*). To get started, select *Static Optimization*. You can now review the objective, decision variables, and constraints in each tab if required, or click OK to run the static optimization.
   - *Exercise Question:* In the Run Optimization user interface, click on the *Statistics* tab and you see that there is nothing there. Why?

7. Once the optimization is complete, you may select *Revert* to revert back to the original values of the decision variables as well as the objective, or select *Replace* to apply the optimized decision variables. Typically, *Replace* is chosen after the optimization is done. Then review the Results Interpretation section below before proceeding to the next step in the exercise.

8. Now reset the decision variables by typing *10%* back into all cells from *E6* to *E15*. Then, select cell *C6* and *Risk Simulator | Set Input Assumption* and use the default *Normal* distribution and the default parameters. This is only an example run and we really do not need to spend time to set proper distributions. Repeat setting the normal assumptions for cells *C7* to *C15*.
   - *Exercise Questions:* Should you or should you not copy the first assumption in cell *C6* and then copy and paste the parameters to cells *C7:C15*? And if you copy and paste the assumptions, what is the difference between using Risk Simulator Copy and Paste functions as opposed to using Excel's copy and paste function? What happens when you first hit Escape before applying *Risk Simulator Paste*?
   - *Exercise Question:* Why do we need to enter *10%* back into the cells?

9. Now run the optimization *Risk Simulator | Optimization | Run Optimization*, and this time select *Dynamic Optimization* in the *Method* tab. When completed, click on *Revert* to go back to the original 10% decision variables.
   - *Exercise Question:* What was the difference between the static optimization run in Step 6 above and dynamic optimization?

10. Now run the optimization *Risk Simulator | Optimization | Run Optimization* a third time, but this time, select *Stochastic Optimization* in the *Method* tab. Then notice several things:
    - First, click on the *Statistics* tab and see that this tab is now populated. Why is this the case and how do you use this statistics tab?
    - Second, click on the *Advanced* button and select the checkbox *Run Super Speed Simulation*. Then click OK to run the optimization. What do you see? How is Super Speed integrated into stochastic optimization?

11. Access the advanced options by going to *Risk Simulator | Optimization | Run Optimization* and clicking the *Advanced* button. Spend some time trying to understand what each element means and how it is pertinent to optimization.

12. After running the stochastic optimization, a report is created. Spend some time reviewing the report and try to understand what it means, as well as reviewing the forecast charts generated for each decision variable.

Figure 15E.B shows the screen shots of the procedural steps just given. You can add simulation assumptions on the model's returns and risk (columns C and D)

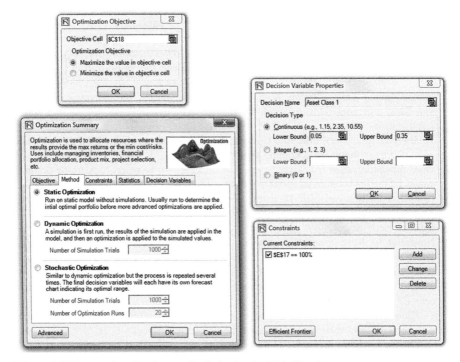

Figure 15E.B Running Continuous Optimization in Risk Simulator.

and apply the dynamic optimization and stochastic optimization for additional practice.

Results Interpretation

The optimization's final results are shown in Figure 15E.C, where the optimal allocation of assets for the portfolio is seen in cells E6:E15. That is, given the restrictions of each asset fluctuating between 5% and 35%, and where the sum of the allocation must equal 100%, the allocation that maximizes the return to risk ratio is seen in Figure 15E.C. A few important things have to be noted when reviewing the results and optimization procedures performed thus far:

- The correct way to run the optimization is to maximize the bang-for-the-buck or returns to risk Sharpe Ratio as we have done.
- If instead we maximized the total portfolio returns, the optimal allocation result is trivial and does not require optimization to obtain. That is, simply allocate 5% (the minimum allowed) to the lowest 8 assets, 35% (the maximum allowed) to the highest returning asset, and the remaining (25%) to the second-best returns asset. Optimization is not required. However, when allocating the portfolio this way, the risk is a lot higher as compared to when maximizing the returns to risk ratio, although the portfolio returns by themselves are higher.
- In contrast, one can minimize the total portfolio risk, but the returns will now be less.

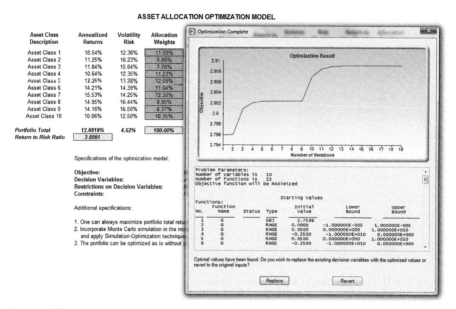

Figure 15E.C Continuous Optimization Results.

Table 15.2 Optimizing Results

Objective	Portfolio Returns	Portfolio Risk	Portfolio Returns to Risk Ratio
Maximize Returns to Risk Ratio	12.69%	4.52%	2.8091
Maximize Returns	13.97%	6.77%	2.0636
Minimize Risk	12.38%	4.46%	2.7754

Table 15.2 illustrates the results from the three different objectives being optimized. From the table it can be seen that the best approach is to maximize the returns to risk ratio; that is, for the same amount of risk, this allocation provides the highest amount of return. Conversely, for the same amount of return, this allocation provides the lowest amount of risk possible. This approach of bang for the buck or returns to risk ratio is the cornerstone of the Markowitz efficient frontier in modern portfolio theory. That is, if we constrained the total portfolio risk level and successively increased them over time, we would obtain several efficient portfolio allocations for different risk characteristics. Thus, different efficient portfolio allocations can be obtained for different individuals with different risk preferences.

2. Optimization with Discrete Integer Decision Variables

Sometimes the decision variables are not continuous, but discrete integers (e.g., 1, 2, 3) or binary (e.g., 0 and 1). In the binary situation, we can use such optimization

	A	B	C	D	E	F	G	H	I	J
1										
2										
3			ENPV	Cost	Risk $	Risk %	Return to Risk Ratio	Profitability Index		Selection
4		Project 1	$458.00	$1,732.44	$54.96	12.00%	8.33	1.26		1.0000
5		Project 2	$1,954.00	$859.00	$1,914.92	98.00%	1.02	3.27		1.0000
6		Project 3	$1,599.00	$1,845.00	$1,551.03	97.00%	1.03	1.87		1.0000
7		Project 4	$2,251.00	$1,645.00	$1,012.95	45.00%	2.22	2.37		1.0000
8		Project 5	$849.00	$458.00	$925.41	109.00%	0.92	2.85		1.0000
9		Project 6	$758.00	$52.00	$560.92	74.00%	1.35	15.58		1.0000
10		Project 7	$2,845.00	$758.00	$5,633.10	198.00%	0.51	4.75		1.0000
11		Project 8	$1,235.00	$115.00	$926.25	75.00%	1.33	11.74		1.0000
12		Project 9	$1,945.00	$125.00	$2,100.60	108.00%	0.93	16.56		1.0000
13		Project 10	$2,250.00	$458.00	$1,912.50	85.00%	1.18	5.91		1.0000
14		Project 11	$549.00	$45.00	$263.52	48.00%	2.08	13.20		1.0000
15		Project 12	$525.00	$105.00	$309.75	59.00%	1.69	6.00		1.0000
16										
17		Total	$17,218.00	$8,197.44	$7,007	40.70%				12.00
18		Goal:	MAX	< =$5000						<=6
19		Sharpe Ratio	2.4573							
20										
21		ENPV is the expected NPV of each credit line or project, while Cost can be the total cost of								
22		administration as well as required capital holdings to cover the credit line, and Risk is the								
23		Coefficient of Variation of the credit line's ENPV.								

Figure 15E.D Discrete Integer Optimization Model.

as on-off switches or go/no-go decisions. Figure 15E.D illustrates a project selection model where there are 12 projects listed. The example here uses the *Risk Simulator | Example Models | 12 Optimization Discrete* model. As before, each project has its own returns (ENPV and NPV—the ENPV is simply the NPV plus any strategic real options values), costs of implementation, risks, and so forth. If required, this model can be modified to include required FTE and other resources of various functions, and additional constraints can be set on these additional resources. The inputs into this model are typically linked from other spreadsheet models. For instance, each project will have its own discounted cash flow or returns on investment model. The application here is to maximize the portfolio's Sharpe ratio subject to some budget allocation. Many other versions of this model can be created, for instance, maximizing the portfolio returns, or minimizing the risks, or adding additional constraints where the total number of projects chosen cannot exceed 6, and so forth and so on. All of these items can be run using this existing model.

Procedure

1. Open the example file and start a new profile by clicking on *Risk Simulator | New Profile* and give it a name (Figure 15E.E shows the screen shots of these procedures).
2. The first step in optimization is to set up the decision variables. Set the first decision variable by selecting cell *J4*, and select *Risk Simulator | Optimization | Set Decision* or click on the D icon. Then, click on the Link icon to select the name cell (*B4*), and select the *Binary* variable. Then, using *Risk Simulator Copy*, copy this cell *J4* decision variable and paste the decision variable to the remaining cells in *J5* to *J15*. This is the best method if you have only

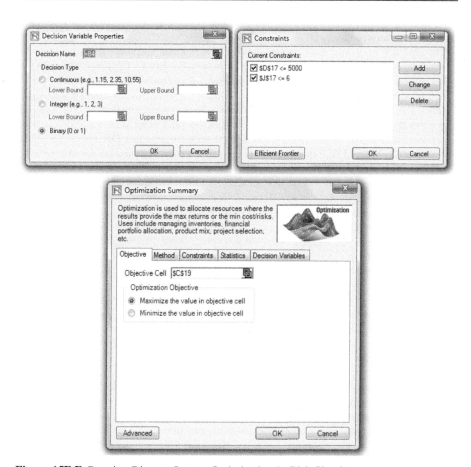

Figure 15E.E Running Discrete Integer Optimization in Risk Simulator.

several decision variables and you can name each decision variable with a unique name for identification later.

- *Exercise Question:* What is the main purpose of linking the name to cell B4 before doing the copy and paste parameters?
- *Exercise Question:* Does it matter if you hit or not hit *Escape* before pasting the parameters?

3. The second step in optimization is to set the constraint. There are two constraints here: The total budget allocation in the portfolio must be less than $5,000 and the total number of projects must not exceed 6. So, click on *Risk Simulator | Optimization | Constraints…* or click on the C icon and select *ADD* to add a new constraint. Then, select the cell *D17* and make it *D17 <= 5000*. Repeat by setting cell *J17 <= 6*.

- *Exercise Question:* Why do we use <= instead of =?
- *Exercise Question:* Sometimes when there are no feasible results or the optimization does not run, changing the equal sign to the inequality helps. Why?
- *Exercise Question:* What would you do if you wanted D17 < 5000 instead of <= 5000?

- *Exercise Question:* Explain what would happen to the binding constraints if you set only one constraint and it is D17 <= 8200 or only J17 <= 12?

4. The final step in optimization is to set the objective function and start the optimization by selecting cell *C19* and selecting *Risk Simulator | Optimization | Set Objective.* Then run the optimization using *Risk Simulator | Optimization | Run Optimization* after selecting the optimization of choice (*Static Optimization, Dynamic Optimization,* or *Stochastic Optimization*). To get started, select *Static Optimization.* Check to make sure that the objective cell is either the Sharpe ratio or portfolio returns to risk ratio and select *Maximize.* You can now review the decision variables and constraints if required, or click OK to run the static optimization. Figure 15E.F shows a sample optimal selection of projects that maximizes the Sharpe ratio.

   - *Exercise Questions:* If instead you maximized total revenues by changing the existing objective, this becomes a trivial model and simply involves choosing the highest returning project and going down the list until you run out of money or exceed the budget constraint. Doing so will yield theoretically undesirable projects as the highest yielding projects typically hold higher risks. Do you agree? What other variables can be used as objective in this model, if any?

   - *Exercise Question:* If we use coefficient of variation instead of return to risk ratio, would we maximize or minimize this variable?

   - *Exercise Questions:* How would you model a situation where, say, one project is the prerequisite for another or if two or more projects are mutually exclusive? Consider the following scenario. How do you model it?
     - You cannot do Project 2 by itself without Project 1, but you can do Project 1 on its own without Project 2.
     - Either Project 3 or Project 4 can be chosen, but not both.
     - Each project has some FTE employees required to be involved, and the company has a limited number of FTEs.

5. Now add simulation assumptions on the model's ENPV and cost variables (columns C and D) and apply dynamic optimization for additional practice.

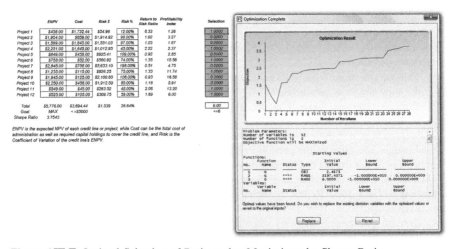

Figure 15E.F Optimal Selection of Projects that Maximizes the Sharpe Ratio.

3.   Efficient Frontier and Advanced Optimization Settings

Figure 15E.G shows the efficient frontier constraints for optimization. You can get to this interface by clicking on the *Efficient Frontier* button *after* you have set some constraints. You can now make these constraints changing. That is, each of the constraints can be created to step through between some maximum and minimum value. As an example, the constraint in cell *J17* <= *6* can be set to run between *4* and *8* (see Figure 15E.G). That is, five optimizations will be run, each with the following constraints: *J17* <= *4, J17* <= *5, J17* <= *6, J17* <= *7,* and *J17* <= *8*. The optimal results will then be plotted as an efficient frontier and the report will be generated (Figure 15E.H).

Specifically, the following illustrates the steps required to create a changing constraint:

1. In an optimization model (i.e., a model with *Objective, Decision Variables,* and *Constraints* already set up), click on *Risk Simulator | Optimization | Constraints* and click on *Efficient Frontier.*
2. Select the constraint you want to change or step, *J17,* and enter the parameters for *Min, Max, and Step Size* (see Figure 15E.G). Then click *ADD* and then OK and OK again. Also, uncheck (deselect) the first constraint of *D17* <= *5000* before running.
3. Run Optimization as usual, *Risk Simulator | Optimization | Run Optimization* or click on the Run Optimization icon. You can choose static, dynamic, or stochastic when running an efficient frontier, but to get started, choose the *Static Optimization* routine.
   - *Exercise Questions:* What happens if you run a stochastic optimization with efficient frontier? What is the step-by-step process that it goes through?
   - *Exercise Question:* What happens if you do not uncheck the first constraint?
4. The results will be shown as a user interface (see Figure 15E.H). Click on *Create Report* to generate a report worksheet with all the details of the optimization runs.
   - *Exercise Questions:* How do you interpret the efficient frontier? Is a steeper curve better or a flatter curve? Can the curve slope downwards and, if so, what does that mean?

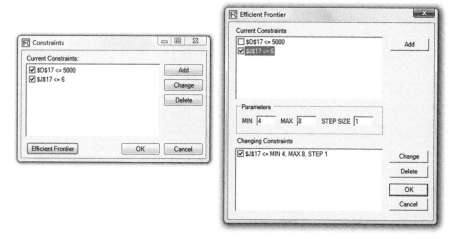

Figure 15E.G Generating Changing Constraints in an Efficient Frontier.

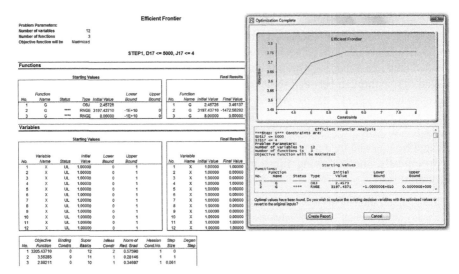

Figure 15E.H Efficient Frontier Results.

16 Options Valuation

Credit analysis is closely linked to options valuation. For instance, there are credit spread options, credit default swaps, and other exotic derivatives that are based on or triggered by credit events. In fact, in the simplest terms, the probability of default in credit risk is related to the valuation of an option. The shareholders or equity owners of a company can be seen as owning an option on paying off the existing debt of the firm, assuming the assets are high enough to justify such an action, or when the firm's asset level falls significantly below the debt threshold, a credit default event occurs.

This chapter introduces some common types of options and provides a step-by-step approach to valuing them. The methods introduced include closed-form models, partial-differential equations, and binomial lattices through the use of risk-neutral probabilities. The advantages and disadvantages of each method are discussed. In addition, the theoretical underpinnings surrounding the binomial equations are demystified here through a set of simplified discussions on how certain binomial equations are derived without the use of fancy mathematics. The next chapter follows up with a list of more exotic options.

Options Valuation: Behind the Scenes

Multiple methodologies and approaches are used in financial options analysis to calculate an option's value. These range from using closed-form equations like the Black-Scholes model and its modifications, Monte Carlo path-dependent simulation methods, lattices (e.g., binomial, trinomial, quadranomial, and multinomial lattices), and variance reduction and other numerical techniques, to using partial-differential

Credit Engineering for Bankers. DOI: 10.1016/B978-0-12-378585-5.10016-8

equations, and so forth. However, the most widely used mainstream methods are the closed-form solutions, partial-differential equations, and the binomial lattices.

Closed-form solutions are models like the Black-Scholes, which consists of equations that can be solved given a set of input assumptions. They are exact, quick, and easy to implement with the assistance of some basic programming knowledge, but they are difficult to explain because they tend to apply highly technical stochastic calculus mathematics. They are also very specific in nature, with limited modeling flexibility. Closed-form solutions are exact for European options but are only approximations for American options. Many exotic and Bermudan options cannot be solved using closed-form solutions. The same limitations apply to path-dependent simulations. Only simple European options can be solved using simulations. Many exotic, American, and Bermudan options cannot be solved using simulations.

Real options can be solved in different ways, including the use of path-dependent simulation, closed-form models, partial-differential equations, and multinomial and binomial approaches.

Binomial lattices, in contrast, are easy to implement and easy to explain. They are also highly flexible but require significant computing power and lattice steps to obtain good approximations, as we will see later in this chapter. Lattices can solve all types of options, including American, Bermudan, European, and many types of exotic options, as will be seen in later chapters. It is important to note, however, that in the limit, results obtained through the use of binomial lattices tend to approach those derived from closed-form solutions. The results from closed-form solutions may be used in conjunction with the binomial lattice approach when presenting to management a complete real options solution. In this chapter we explore these mainstream approaches and compare their results, as well as when each approach may be best used when analyzing the more common types of financial and real options.

Here is an example to illustrate the point of binomial lattices approaching the results of a closed-form solution. Let us look at a European call option as calculated using the Generalized Black-Scholes model specified as follows:

$$Call = Se^{-qT}\Phi\left[\frac{\ln(S/X) + (rf - q + \sigma^2/2)T}{\sigma\sqrt{T}}\right]$$

$$-Xe^{-rT}\Phi\left[\frac{\ln(S/X) + (rf - q - \sigma^2/2)T}{\sigma\sqrt{T}}\right]$$

Let us assume that both the stock price (S) and the strike price (X) are $100, the time to expiration (T) is one year with a 5% risk-free rate (rf) for the same duration, and the volatility (σ) of the underlying asset is 25% with no dividends (q). The

Generalized Black-Scholes calculation yields $12.3360, while using a binomial lattice yields the following results:

N = 10 steps	$12.0923
N = 20 steps	$12.2132
N = 50 steps	$12.2867
N = 100 steps	$12.3113
N = 1,000 steps	$12.3335
N = 10,000 steps	$12.3358
N = 50,000 steps	$12.3360

Notice that even in this oversimplified example, as the number of time-steps (N) gets larger, the value calculated using the binomial lattice approaches the closed-form solution. Do not worry about the computation at this point because we will detail the stepwise calculations in a moment. Suffice it to say, many steps are required for a good estimate using binomial lattices. It has been shown in past research that 100 to 1,000 time-steps are usually sufficient for a good valuation.

We can define time-steps as the number of branching events in a lattice. For instance, the binomial lattice shown as Figure 16.1 has three time-steps, starting from time 0. The first time-step has two nodes (S_0u and S_0d), while the second time-step has three nodes (S_0u^2, S_0ud, and S_0d^2), and so on. Therefore, as we have seen previously, to obtain 1,000 time-steps, we need to calculate 1, 2, 3 . . . 1001 nodes, which is equivalent to calculating 501,501 nodes. If we intend to perform 10,000 simulation trials on the options calculation, we will need approximately 5×10^9 nodal calculations, equivalent to 299 Excel spreadsheets or 4.6 GB of memory space. This is definitely a daunting task, to say the least, and we clearly see here the need for using

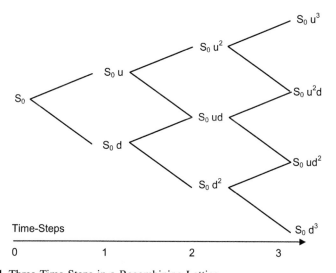

Figure 16.1 Three Time-Steps in a Recombining Lattice.

software to facilitate such calculations.[1] One noteworthy item is that the lattice in Figure 16.1 is something called a recombining lattice, where at time-step 2, the middle node (S_oud) is the same as time-step 1's lower bifurcation of S_ou and upper bifurcation of S_od.

Figure 16.2 is an example of a binomial lattice with two time-steps that is non-recombining. That is, the center nodes in time-step 2 are different (S_oud' is not the same as S_odu'). In this case, the computational time and resources are even higher due to the exponential growth of the number of nodes—specifically, 2^0 nodes at time-step 0, 2^1 nodes at time-step 1, 2^2 nodes at time-step 2, and so forth, until 2^{1000} nodes at time-step 1,000 or approximately 2×10^{301} nodes, taking your computer potentially years to calculate the entire binomial lattice!

Recombining and nonrecombining binomial lattices yield the same results at the limit, so it is definitely easier to use recombining lattices for most of our analysis. However, there are exceptions where nonrecombining lattices are required, especially when there are two or more stochastic underlying variables or when volatility of the single underlying variable changes over time. See Dr. Johnathan Mun's *Real Options Analysis,* Second Edition (Wiley 2008) for more details on the use of nonrecombining lattices with multiple volatilities, the use of multiple recombining lattices to recreate a nonrecombining lattice, and how multiple underlying assets can be solved. However, for illustration purposes, we continue with examples of a single underlying asset with constant volatility solved using recombining lattices throughout this chapter.

As you can see, closed-form solutions certainly have computational ease compared to binomial lattices. However, it is more difficult to explain the exact nature of a fancy

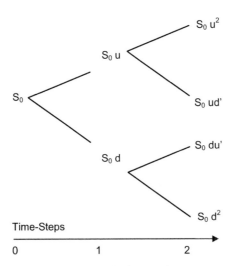

Figure 16.2 Two Time-Steps in a Nonrecombining Lattice.

---

[1] This is simply an illustration of the size and computational requirements for an exact binomial approximation where data from all the simulated trials are saved.

stochastic calculus equation than it would be to explain a binomial lattice tree that branches up and down. Because both methods tend to provide the same results at the limit anyway, for ease of exposition, the binomial lattice should be presented for management discussions. There are also other issues to contend with in terms of advantages and disadvantages of each technique. For instance, closed-form solutions are mathematically elegant but are very difficult to derive and are highly specific in nature. Tweaking a closed-form equation requires facility with sophisticated stochastic mathematics. Binomial lattices, however, although sometimes computationally stressful, are easy to build and require no more than simple algebra, as we will see later. Binomial lattices are also very flexible in that they can be tweaked easily to accommodate most types of real options problems.

Binomial Lattices

In the binomial world, several basic similarities are worth mentioning. No matter the types of real options problems you are trying to solve, if the binomial lattice approach is used, the solution can be obtained in one of two ways. The first is the use of risk-neutral probabilities, and the second is the use of market-replicating portfolios. Throughout this chapter, the former approach is used. The use of a replicating portfolio is more difficult to understand and apply, but the results obtained from replicating portfolios are identical to those obtained through risk-neutral probabilities. So while it does not matter which method is used, nevertheless, application and expositional ease should be emphasized.

Market-replicating portfolios' predominant assumptions are that there are no arbitrage opportunities and that there exist a number of traded assets in the market that can be obtained to replicate the existing asset's payout profile. A simple illustration is in order here. Suppose you own a portfolio of publicly traded stocks that pay a set percentage *dividend* per period. You can, in theory—assuming no trading restrictions, taxes, or transaction costs—purchase a second portfolio of several *non-dividend-paying* stocks, bonds, and other instruments, and replicate the payout of the first portfolio of *dividend-paying* stocks. You can, for instance, sell a particular number of shares per period to replicate the first portfolio's dividend payout amount at every time period. Hence, if both payouts are identical, even though their stock compositions are different, the value of both portfolios should then be identical. Otherwise, there will be arbitrage opportunities, and market forces will tend to make them equilibrate in value. This makes perfect sense in a financial securities world, where stocks are freely traded and highly liquid. However, in a real options world where physical assets and firm-specific projects are being valued, financial purists would argue that this assumption is hard to accept, not to mention that the mathematics behind replicating portfolios are also more difficult to apply.

Compare that to using something called a risk-neutral probability approach. Simply stated, instead of using a risky set of cash flows and discounting them at a risk-adjusted discount rate akin to the discounted cash flow models, one can instead easily risk-adjust the probabilities of specific cash flows occurring at specific times. Thus, using these risk-adjusted probabilities on the cash flows allows the analyst to discount these cash flows (whose risks have now been accounted for) at the risk-free rate. This is the essence of binomial lattices as applied in valuing options. The results obtained are identical.

Let's now see how easy it is to apply risk-neutral valuation in a binomial lattice setting. In any options model, there is a minimum requirement of at least two lattices. The first lattice is always the lattice of the underlying asset, while the second lattice is the option valuation lattice. No matter what real options model is of interest, the basic structure almost always exists, taking the form:

Inputs: S, X, σ, T, rf, b

$$u = e^{\sigma\sqrt{\delta t}} \text{ and } d = e^{-\sigma\sqrt{\delta t}} = \frac{1}{u}$$

$$p = \frac{e^{(rf-b)(\delta t)} - d}{u - d}$$

The basic inputs are the present value of the underlying asset (S), present value of implementation cost of the option (X), volatility of the natural logarithm of the underlying free cash flow returns in percent (σ), time to expiration in years (T), risk-free rate or the rate of return on a riskless asset (rf), and continuous dividend outflows in percent (b). In addition, the binomial lattice approach requires two additional sets of calculations: the up and down factors (u and d) and a risk-neutral probability measure (p). We see from the foregoing equations that the up factor is simply the exponential function of the cash flow returns volatility multiplied by the square root of time-steps or stepping time (δt). Time-steps, or stepping time, is simply the time scale between steps. That is, if an option has a one-year maturity and the binomial lattice that is constructed has 10 steps, each time-step has a stepping time of 0.1 years. The volatility measure is an annualized value; multiplying it by the square root of time-steps breaks it down into the time-step's equivalent volatility. The down factor is simply the reciprocal of the up factor. In addition, the higher the volatility measure, the higher the difference between the up and down factors. This reciprocal magnitude ensures that the lattices are recombining because the up and down steps have the same magnitude but different signs; at places along the future path these binomial bifurcations must meet.

The second required calculation is that of the risk-neutral probability, defined simply as the ratio of the exponential function of the difference between risk-free rate and dividend, multiplied by the stepping time less the down factor, to the difference between the up and down factors. This risk-neutral probability value is a mathematical intermediate and by itself has no particular meaning. One major error real options users commit is to extrapolate these probabilities as some kind of subjective or objective probabilities that a certain event will occur. Nothing is further from the truth. There is no economic or financial meaning attached to these risk-neutralized probabilities save that it is an intermediate step in a series of calculations. Armed with these values, you are now on your way to creating a binomial lattice of the underlying asset value, shown in Figure 16.3.

Binomial lattices can be solved through the use of risk-neutral probabilities and market-replicating portfolios. In using binomial and multinomial lattices, the higher the number of steps, the higher the level of granularity and, thus, the higher the level of accuracy.

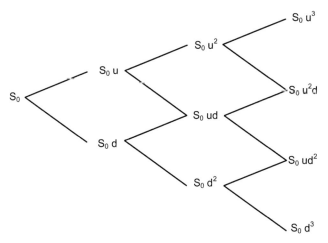

Figure 16.3 Binomial Lattice of the Underlying Asset Value.

Starting with the present value of the underlying asset at time zero (S_0), multiply it with the up (u) and down (d) factors as shown in Figure 16.3 to create a binomial lattice. Remember that there is one bifurcation at each node, creating an up branch and a down branch. The intermediate branches are all recombining. This evolution of the underlying asset shows that if the volatility is zero, in a deterministic world where there are no uncertainties, the lattice would be a straight line, and a discounted cash flow model will be adequate because the value of the option or flexibility is also zero. In other words, if volatility (σ) is zero, then the up ($u = e^{\sigma\sqrt{\delta t}}$) and down ($d = e^{-\sigma\sqrt{\delta t}}$) jump sizes are equal to one. It is because there are uncertainties and risks, as captured by the volatility measure, that the lattice is not a straight horizontal line but comprises up and down movements. It is this up and down uncertainty that generates the value in an option. The higher the volatility measure, the higher the up and down factors as previously defined, and the higher the potential value of an option as higher uncertainties exist and the potential upside for the option increases.

The Look and Feel of Uncertainty

In most financial analyses, the first step is to create a series of free cash flows, which can take the shape of an income statement or statement of cash flows. The resulting free cash flows are depicted on a time line, similar to that shown in Figure 16.4. These cash flow figures are, in most cases, forecasts of the unknown future. In this simple example, the cash flows are assumed to follow a straight-line growth curve. Similar forecasts can be constructed using historical data and fitting these data to a time-series model or a regression analysis. Whatever the method of obtaining said forecasts or the shape of the growth curve, these are single-point estimates of the unknown future. Performing a discounted cash flow analysis on these static cash flows provides an

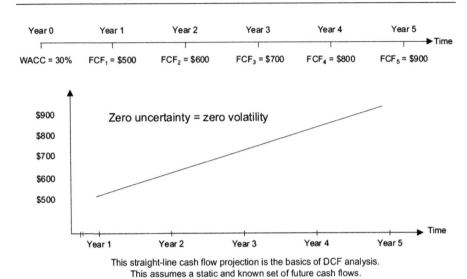

This straight-line cash flow projection is the basics of DCF analysis.
This assumes a static and known set of future cash flows.

Figure 16.4 Straight-Line Discounted Cash Flow (DCF).

accurate value of the project assuming all the future cash flows are known with certainty; that is, no uncertainty exists, and, thus, there exists zero volatility around the forecast values.

However, in reality, business conditions are hard to forecast. Uncertainty exists, and the actual levels of future cash flows may look more like those in Figure 16.5. That is, at certain time periods, actual cash flows may be above, below, or at the forecast levels. For instance, at any time period, the actual cash flow may fall within a range of figures with a certain percent probability. As an example, the first year's cash flow may fall anywhere between $480 and $520. The actual values are shown to fluctuate around the forecast values at an average volatility of 20%.[2] Certainly this example provides a much more accurate view of the true nature of business conditions, which are fairly difficult to predict with any amount of certainty.

Figure 16.6 shows two sample actual cash flows around the straight-line forecast value. The higher the uncertainty around the actual cash flow levels, the higher the volatility. The darker line with 20% volatility fluctuates more wildly around the forecast values. These values can be quantified using Monte Carlo simulation. For instance, Figure 16.6 also shows the Monte Carlo simulated probability distribution output for the 5% volatility line, where 95% of the time, the actual values will fall between $509 and $693. Contrast this to a 95% confidence range of between $399 and $920 for the 20% volatility case. This implies that the actual cash flows can fluctuate anywhere in these ranges, where the higher the volatility, the higher the range of uncertainty. A point of interest to note is that the y-axis on the time-series chart is the x-axis of the frequency distribution chart. Thus, a highly volatile cash flow will have

---

[2] The simulated actual values are based on a geometric Brownian motion with a volatility of 20% calculated as the standard deviation of the simulated natural logarithms of historical returns.

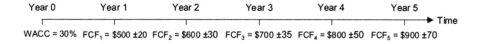

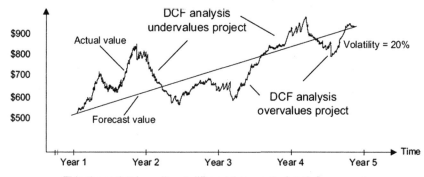

This shows that in reality, at different times, actual cash flows may be
above, below, or at the forecast value line due to uncertainty and risk.

Figure 16.5 Discounted Cash Flow with Simulation.

a wider *y*-axis range on the first chart and a wider *x*-axis range on the second chart.
The width of the frequency distribution chart is measured by the standard deviation,
a way to measure volatility. Also, the area in the frequency chart is the relevant
probability of occurrence.

Options Provide Value in the Face of Risk and Uncertainty

As seen previously, Monte Carlo simulation can be applied to quantify the levels of
uncertainty in cash flows. However, simulation does not consider the strategic
alternatives that management may have. For instance, simulation accounts for the
range and probability that actual cash flows can be above or below predicted levels but
does not consider what management can do if such conditions occur.

Consider Figure 16.7 for a moment. The area above the mean predicted levels,
assuming that management has a strategic option to expand into different markets or
products or to develop a new technology, means that executing such an option will yield
considerable value. Conversely, if management has the option to abandon a particular
technology, market, or development initiative when operating conditions deteriorate,
possessing and executing such an abandonment or switching strategy may be valuable.
This assumes that management not only has the flexibility to execute these options but
also has the willingness to follow through with these strategies when the appropriate
time comes. Often, when faced with an abandonment decision, even when it is clearly
optimal to abandon a particular project, management may still be inclined to keep the
project alive in the hopes that conditions would revert and make the project profitable
once again. In addition, management psychology and project attachment may come
into play. When the successful execution of a project is tied to some financial

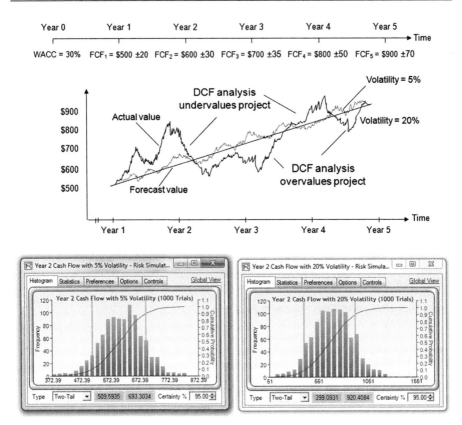

Figure 16.6 The Face of Uncertainty.

remuneration, reputation, or personal striving for merit and achievement, abandoning a project may be hard to do even when it is clearly the optimal decision.

The value of a project's real options requires several assumptions. First, a financial model can be built where the model's operating, technological, market, and other factors are subject to uncertainty and change. These uncertainties have to drive a project or initiative's value. Furthermore, there exists managerial flexibility or strategic options that management can execute along the way as these uncertainties become resolved over time, actions, and events. Finally, management must not only be able, but also willing, to execute these options when it becomes optimal to do so. That is, we have to assume that management is rational and execute strategies where the additional value generated is at least commensurate with the risks undertaken. Ignoring such strategic value will grossly underestimate the value of a project. Real options not only provide an accurate accounting of this flexibility value but also indicate the conditions under which executing certain strategies becomes optimal.

Projects that are at-the-money or out-of-the-money—that is, projects with static net present values that are negative or close to breaking even—are most valuable in terms of applying real options. Because real options analysis captures strategic value

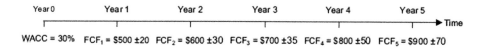

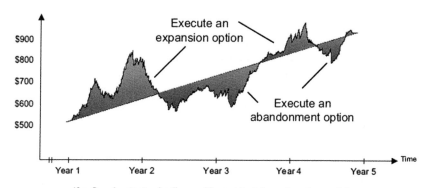

If a firm is strategically positioned to take advantage of these
fluctuations, there is value in uncertainty.

Figure 16.7 The Real Options Intuition.

that is otherwise overlooked in traditional analyses, the additional value obtained may
be sufficient to justify projects that are barely profitable.

Binomial Lattices as a Discrete Simulation of Uncertainty

As uncertainty drives the value of projects, we need to further the discussion of the
nature of uncertainty. Figure 16.8 shows a "cone of uncertainty," where we can depict

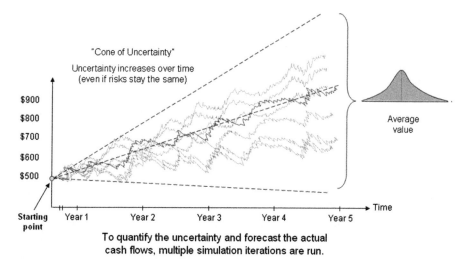

To quantify the uncertainty and forecast the actual
cash flows, multiple simulation iterations are run.

Figure 16.8 The Cone of Uncertainty.

uncertainty as increasing over time. Notice that risk may or may not increase over time, but uncertainty does increase over time. For instance, it is usually much easier to predict business conditions a few months in advance, but it becomes more and more difficult the further one goes into the future, even when business risks remain unchanged. This is the nature of the cone of uncertainty. If we were to attempt to forecast future cash flows while attempting to quantify uncertainty using simulation, a well-prescribed method is to simulate thousands of cash flow paths over time, as shown in Figure 16.8. Based on all the simulated paths, a probability distribution can be constructed at each time period. The simulated pathways were generated using a geometric Brownian motion with a fixed volatility. A geometric Brownian motion can be depicted as:

$$\frac{\delta S}{S} = \mu(\delta t) + \sigma \varepsilon \sqrt{\delta t}$$

where a percent change in the variable S (denoted $\frac{\delta S}{S}$) is simply a combination of a deterministic part ($\mu(\delta t)$) and a stochastic part ($\sigma \varepsilon \sqrt{\delta t}$). Here, μ is a drift term or growth parameter that increases at a factor of time-steps δt, while σ is the volatility parameter, growing at a rate of the square root of time, and ε is a simulated variable, usually following a normal distribution with a mean of zero and a variance of one. Note that the different types of Brownian motions are widely regarded and accepted as standard assumptions necessary for pricing options. Brownian motions are also widely used in predicting stock prices.

Notice that the volatility (σ) remains constant throughout several thousand simulations. Only the simulated variable (ε) changes every time. This is an important aspect that will become clear when we discuss the intuitive nature of the binomial equations required to solve a binomial lattice, because one of the required assumptions in options modeling is the reliance on Brownian motion. Although the risk or volatility (σ) in this example remains constant over time, the level of uncertainty increases over time at a factor of ($\sigma \sqrt{\delta t}$). That is, the level of uncertainty grows at the square root of time, and the more time that passes, the harder it is to predict the future. This is seen in the cone of uncertainty, where the width of the cone increases over time even when volatility remains constant.

Based on the cone of uncertainty, we can clearly see the similar triangular shape of the cone of uncertainty and a binomial lattice as shown in Figure 16.9. In essence, a binomial lattice is simply a discrete simulation of the cone of uncertainty. Whereas a Brownian motion is a continuous stochastic simulation process, a binomial lattice is a discrete simulation process.

At the limit, where the number of steps approach infinity, the time-steps approach zero and the results stemming from a binomial lattice approach those obtained from a Brownian motion process. Solving a Brownian motion in a discrete sense yields the binomial equations, while solving it in a continuous sense yields closed-form equations such as the Black-Scholes and its ancillary models. The next few sections show the simple intuitive discrete derivation of the Brownian motion process to obtain the binomial equations.

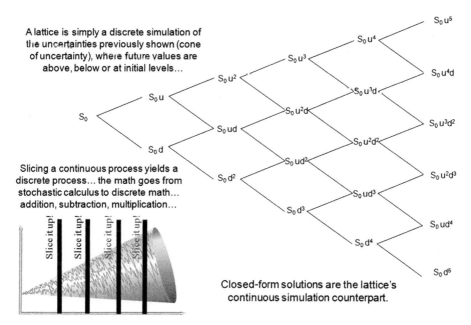

Figure 16.9 Discrete Simulation Using Binomial Lattices.

As a side note, multinomial models that involve more than two bifurcations at each node, such as the trinomial (three-branch), quadranomial (four-branch), or pentanomial (five-branch) models, require a similar Brownian motion process or other stochastic processes, such as a mean-reverting or jump-diffusion process, and, thus, are mathematically more difficult to solve. No matter how many branches are at each node, these models provide exactly the same results at the limit, the difference being that the more branches at each node, the faster the results are reached. For instance, a binomial model may require a hundred steps to solve a particular real options problem, while a trinomial model probably only requires half the number of steps. However, due to the complexity involved in solving trinomial lattices as compared to the easier mathematics required for binomial lattices, most real options problems are more readily solved using binomials.

To continue the exploration into the nature of binomial lattices, Figure 16.10 shows the different binomial lattices with different volatilities. This means that the higher the volatility, the wider the range and spread of values between the upper and lower branches of each node in the lattice. Because binomial lattices are discrete simulations, the higher the volatility, the wider the spread of the distribution. This condition can be seen on the terminal nodes, where the range between the highest and lowest values at the terminal nodes is higher for higher volatilities than the range of a lattice with a lower volatility.

At the extreme, where volatility equals zero, the lattice collapses into a straight line. This straight line is akin to the straight-line cash flow model shown in Figure 16.4. We will further show through an example that for a binomial lattice

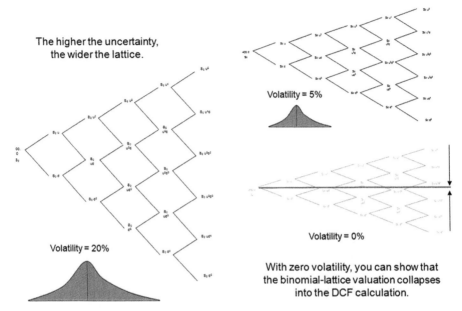

Figure 16.10 Volatility and Binomial Lattices.

calculation involving cash flows with zero volatility, the results approach those calculated using a discounted cash flow model's net present value approach. This is important because if there is zero uncertainty and risk, meaning that all future cash flows are known with absolute certainty, then there is no strategic real options value. The discounted cash flow model will suffice because business conditions are fraught with uncertainty, and, thus, volatility exists and can be captured using a binomial lattice. Therefore, the discounted cash flow model can be seen as a special case of a real options model, when uncertainty is negligible and volatility approaches zero. Therefore, discounted cash flow is not necessarily wrong at all; it only implies zero uncertainty in the future forecast of cash flows.

Granularity Leads to Precision

Another key concept in the use of binomial lattices is the idea of steps and precision. For instance, if a five-year real options project is valued using five steps, each time-step size (δt) is equivalent to one year. Conversely, if 50 steps are used, then δt is equivalent to 0.1 years per step. Recall that the up and down step sizes were $e^{\sigma\sqrt{\delta t}}$ and $e^{-\sigma\sqrt{\delta t}}$, respectively. The smaller δt is, the smaller the up and down steps, and the more granular the lattice values will be.

An example is in order. Figure 16.11 shows the example of a simple European *financial* call option. Suppose the call option has an asset value of $100 and a strike price of $100 expiring in one year. Further suppose that the corresponding risk-free rate is 5% and the calculated volatility of historical logarithmic returns is 25%. Because the

- Example of a European *financial* call option with an asset value (S) of $100, a strike price (X) of $100, a 1-year expiration (T), 5% risk free rate (rf), and 25% volatility (σ) with no dividend payments (q)
- Using the Black-Scholes equation, we obtain $12.3360

$$Call = Se^{-qT}\Phi\left[\frac{\ln(S/X)+(rf-q+\sigma^2/2)T}{\sigma\sqrt{T}}\right] - Xe^{-rf(T)}\Phi\left[\frac{\ln(S/X)+(rf-q-\sigma^2/2)T}{\sigma\sqrt{T}}\right]$$

- Using a 5-step binomial approach, we obtain $12.79
  - Step I in the binomial approach:

Given : $S = 100, X = 100, \sigma = 0.25, T = 1, rf = 0.05, q = 0$

$u = e^{\sigma\sqrt{a}} = 1.118$ and $d = e^{-\sigma\sqrt{a}} = 0.894$

$p = \dfrac{e^{(rf-q)a} - d}{u-d} = 0.517$

Figure 16.11 European Option Example.

option pays no dividends and is only exercisable at termination, a Black-Scholes equation will suffice. The call option value calculated using the Black-Scholes equation is $12.3360, which is obtained by

$$Call = S\Phi\left[\frac{\ln(S/X)+(r+\sigma^2/2)T}{\sigma\sqrt{T}}\right] - Xe^{-rf(T)}\Phi\left[\frac{\ln(S/X)+(r-\sigma^2/2)T}{\sigma\sqrt{T}}\right]$$

$$Call = 100\Phi\left[\frac{\ln(100/100)+(0.05+0.25^2/2)1}{0.25\sqrt{1}}\right]$$

$$-100e^{-0.05(1)}\Phi\left[\frac{\ln(100/100)+(0.05-0.25^2/2)1}{0.25\sqrt{1}}\right]$$

$$Call = 100\Phi[0.325] - 95.13\Phi[0.075] = 100(0.6274) - 95.13(0.5298)$$
$$= 12.3360$$

A binomial lattice can also be applied to solve this problem, as seen in the example in Figures 16.12 and 16.13. The first step is to solve the binomial lattice equations— that is, to calculate the up step size, down step size, and risk-neutral probability. This example assumes that the step size (δt) is 0.2 years (one-year expiration divided by five steps). The calculations proceed as follows:

$$u = e^{\sigma\sqrt{\delta t}} = e^{0.25\sqrt{0.2}} = 1.1183$$

$$d = e^{-\sigma\sqrt{\delta t}} = e^{-0.25\sqrt{0.2}} = 0.8942$$

$$p = \frac{e^{rf(\delta t)} - d}{u - d} = \frac{e^{0.05(0.2)} - 0.8942}{1.1183 - 0.8942} = 0.5169$$

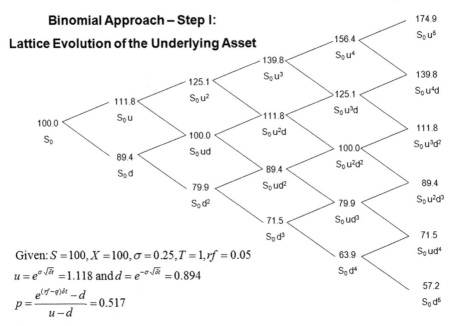

Binomial Approach – Step I:

Lattice Evolution of the Underlying Asset

Given: $S = 100, X = 100, \sigma = 0.25, T = 1, rf = 0.05$

$u = e^{\sigma \sqrt{\delta t}} = 1.118$ and $d = e^{-\sigma \sqrt{\delta t}} = 0.894$

$p = \dfrac{e^{(rf-q)\delta t} - d}{u - d} = 0.517$

Figure 16.12 European Option Underlying Lattice.

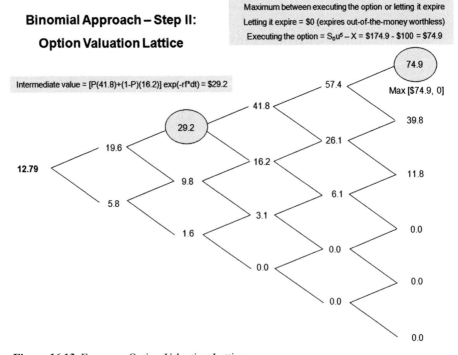

Binomial Approach – Step II:

Option Valuation Lattice

Maximum between executing the option or letting it expire
Letting it expire = $0 (expires out-of-the-money worthless)
Executing the option = $S_0 u^5 - X$ = $174.9 - $100 = $74.9

Intermediate value = [P(41.8)+(1-P)(16.2)] exp(-rf*dt) = $29.2

Max [$74.9, 0]

Figure 16.13 European Option Valuation Lattice.

Figure 16.12 illustrates the first lattice in the binomial approach. In a real options world, this lattice is created based on the evolution of the underlying asset's sum of the present values of future cash flows. However, in a financial option analysis, this is the $100 initial stock price level. This $100 value evolves over time due to the volatility that exists. For instance, the $100 value becomes $111.8 ($100 × 1.118) on the upper bifurcation at the first time period and $89.4 ($100 × 0.894) on the lower bifurcation. This up and down compounding effect continues until the end terminal node, where, given a 25% annualized volatility, stock prices can, after a period of five years, be anywhere between $57.2 and $174.9. Recall that if volatility is zero, then the lattice collapses into a straight line where at every time-step interval, the value of the stock will be $100. It is when uncertainty exists that stock prices can vary within this $57.2 to $174.9 interval.

Notice on the lattice in Figure 16.12 that the values are path-independent. That is, the value on node H can be attained through the multiplication of $S_o u^2 d$, which can be arrived at by going through paths ABEH, ABDH, or ACEH. The value of path ABEH is $S \times u \times d \times u$, the value of path ABDH is $S \times u \times u \times d$, and the value of path ACEH is $S \times d \times u \times u$, all of which yields $S_o u^2 d$.

Figure 16.13 shows the calculation of the European option's valuation lattice. The valuation lattice is calculated in two steps, starting with the terminal node and then the intermediate nodes, through a process called *backward induction*. For instance, the circled terminal node shows a value of $74.9, which is calculated through the maximization between executing the option and letting the option expire worthless if the cost exceeds the benefits of execution. The value of executing the option is calculated as $174.9 – $100, which yields $74.9. The value $174.9 comes from Figure 16.12's underlying asset lattice, and $100 is the cost of executing the option, leaving a value of $74.9.

The second step is the calculation of intermediate nodes. The circled intermediate node illustrated in Figure 16.13 is calculated using a risk-neutral probability analysis. Using the previously calculated risk-neutral probability of 0.5169, a backward induction analysis is obtained through

$$[(p)up + (1 - p)down]\exp[(-riskfree)(\delta t)]$$

$$[(0.5169)41.8 + (1 - 0.5169)16.2]\exp[(-0.05)(0.2)] = 29.2$$

Using this backward induction calculation all the way back to the starting period, the option value at time zero is calculated as $12.79.

Figure 16.14 shows a series of calculations using a Black-Scholes closed-form solution, binomial lattices with different time-steps, and Monte Carlo simulation. Notice that for the binomial lattice, the higher the number of time-steps, the more accurate the results become. At the limit, when the number of steps approaches infinity—that is, the time between the steps (δt) approaches zero—the discrete simulation in a binomial lattice approaches that of a continuous simulation model, which is the closed-form solution. The Black-Scholes model is applicable here because there are no dividend payments and the option is only executable at termination. When the number of steps approaches 1,000, the results converge. However, in

- Comparison of approaches
  - Black-Scholes: $12.3360
  - Binomial:
    - N = 5 steps $12.7946
    - N = 10 steps $12.0932
    - N = 20 steps $12.2132
    - N = 50 steps $12.2867
    - N = 100 steps $12.3113
    - N = 1,000 steps $12.3335
    - N = 10,000 steps $12.3358
    - N = 50,000 steps $12.3360
  - Simulation: (10,000 simulations: $12.3360)

Figure 16.14 More Time-Steps, Higher Accuracy.

most cases, the level of accuracy becomes sufficient when the number of steps reaches anywhere from 100 to 1,000. Notice that the third method, using Monte Carlo simulation, also converges at 10,000 simulations with 100 steps.

Figure 16.15 shows another concept of binomial lattices. When there are more time-steps in a lattice, the underlying lattice shows more granularities, and, thus, provides higher accuracy. The first lattice shows 5 steps and the second 20 steps (truncated at 10 steps due to space limitations). Notice the similar values that occur over time. For instance, the value 111.83 in the first lattice occurs at step 1 versus step 2 in the second lattice. All the values in the first lattice recur in the second lattice, but the second lattice is more granular in the sense that more intermediate values exist. As seen in Figure 16.14, the higher number of steps means a higher precision due to the higher granularity.

5 TIME STEPS

0.00	1.00	2.00	3.00	4.00	5.00
t = 0	t = 0.2	t = 0.4	t = 0.6	t = 0.8	t = 1
100.00	111.83	125.06	139.85	156.39	174.90
	89.42	100.00	111.83	125.06	139.85
		79.96	89.42	100.00	111.83
			71.50	79.96	89.42
				63.94	71.50
					57.18

20 TIME STEPS

0.00	1.00	2.00	3.00	4.00	5.00	6.00	7.00	8.00	9.00	10.00	11.00	12.00
t = 0	t = 0.05	t = 0.1	t = 0.15	t = 0.2	t = 0.25	t = 0.3	t = 0.35	t = 0.4	t = 0.45	t = 0.5	t = 0.55	t = 0.6
100.00	105.75	111.83	118.26	125.06	132.25	139.85	147.89	156.39	165.39	174.90	184.95	195.58
	94.56	100.00	105.75	111.83	118.26	125.06	132.25	139.85	147.89	156.39	165.39	174.90
		89.42	94.56	100.00	105.75	111.83	118.26	125.06	132.25	139.85	147.89	156.39
			84.56	89.42	94.56	100.00	105.75	111.83	118.26	125.06	132.25	139.85
				79.96	84.56	89.42	94.56	100.00	105.75	111.83	118.26	125.06
					75.62	79.96	84.56	89.42	94.56	100.00	105.75	111.83
						71.50	75.62	79.96	84.56	89.42	94.56	100.00
							67.62	71.50	75.62	79.96	84.56	89.42
								63.94	67.62	71.50	75.62	79.96
									60.46	63.94	67.62	71.50
										57.18	60.46	63.94
											54.07	57.18
												51.13

Figure 16.15 More Steps, More Granularity, More Accuracy.

Illustrations in Credit Analysis: Credit Default Swaps and Credit Spread Options

File Name: Credit Analysis – Credit Default Swaps and Credit Spread Options
Location: www.ElsevierDirect.com (search for this book, click Companion Site button, click link in Additional Models section) Modeling Toolkit | Credit Analysis | Credit Default Swaps and Credit Spread Options
Brief Description: Examines the basics of credit derivatives.
Requirements: Modeling Toolkit, Risk Simulator

A credit default swap (CDS) allows the holder of the instrument to sell a bond or debt at par value when a credit event or default occurs. This model computes the valuation of the CDS spread (Figure 16.16). A CDS does not protect against movements of the credit spread (only a credit spread option can do that), but it only protects against defaults. Typically, to hedge against defaults and spread movements, both CDS and credit spread options (CSO) are used. This CDS model assumes a no-arbitrage argument, and the holder of the CDS makes periodic payments to the seller (similar to a periodic insurance premium) until the maturity of the CDS or until a credit event or default occurs. Because the notional amount to be received in the event of a default is the same as the par value of the bond or debt, and time value of money is used to determine the bond yield, this model does not require these two variables as input assumptions.

In contrast, CSOs are another type of exotic debt option where the payoff depends on a credit spread or the price of the underlying asset that is sensitive to interest rate movements, such as floating or inverse floating rate notes and debt. A CSO call option provides a return to the holder if the prevailing reference credit spread exceeds the predetermined strike rate, and the duration input variable is used to translate the percentage spread into a notional currency amount. The CSO expires when there is a credit default event. Again, note that a CSO can only protect against any movements in the reference spread and not against a default event (only a CDS can do that). Typically, to hedge against defaults and spread movements, both CDSs and CSOs are used. In some cases, when the CSO covers a reference entity's underlying asset value and not the spread itself, the credit asset spread options are used instead.

Illustrations in Debt Analysis: Vasicek Debt Option Valuation

File Name: Debt Analysis – Vasicek Debt Option Valuation
Location: www.ElsevierDirect.com (search for this book, click Companion Site button, click link in Additional Models section) Modeling Toolkit | Debt Analysis | Vasicek Debt Option Valuation
Brief Description: Applies the Vasicek model of debt options assuming that interest rates are stochastic, volatile, and mean-reverting.
Requirements: Modeling Toolkit, Risk Simulator
Modeling Toolkit Function Used: *B2BondVasicekBondCallOption, B2BondVasicekBond PutOption*

Figure 16.17 shows an example of the Vasicek model on bond or debt options, where the underlying debt issue changes in value based on the level of prevailing interest rates; that is, the interest rates have a mean-reverting tendency where the interest rate at any future period approaches a long-run mean interest rate with a rate of reversion

CREDIT DEFAULT SWAP (CDS) SPREADS

Input Assumptions

Bond Yield	7.00%
Annual Coupon Rate	10.00%
Coupon Payments Per Year	2
Risk-free Yield	5.00%
Recovery Rate at Default	80.00%

Credit Default Swap Spread   **1.7690%**

Function Used: B2CreditDefaultSwapSpread

CREDIT SPREAD OPTIONS (CSO)

Input Assumptions

Credit Spread	3.00%
Strike Spread	2.90%
Duration (Spread to Currency Conversion Ratio)	1000.00
Probability of Default	2.50%
Maturity	1.00
Riskfree Rate	5.00%
Volatility	25.00%

Credit Spread Call Option   **$3.2102**
Credit Spread Put Option   **$2.2828**

B2CreditSpreadCallOption
B2CreditSpreadPutOption

Forward Asset Price at Maturity	$1,000.00
Strike Price	$900.00
Probability of Default	2.50%
Maturity	1.00
Riskfree Rate	5.00%
Volatility	25.00%

Credit Asset Spread Call Option   **$141.6406**
Credit Asset Spread Put Option   **$48.8957**

Figure 16.16 Credit Default Swaps and Credit Spread Options.

and volatility around this reversion trend. Both options are European and can be executed only at expiration. To determine other types of options, such as American and Bermudan, use the Modeling Toolkit's *Options on Debt* modules to build lattices on mean-reverting interest rates and their respective option values.

A few interesting behaviors can be determined from this model. Typically, a bond call option will have a lower value if the long-run mean interest rate is higher than the current spot risk-free rate and if the rate of reversion is high (meaning that the spot interest rates revert to this long-run rate quickly). The inverse situation is also true, where the bond call option value is higher if the long-run rate is lower than the spot

VASICEK MODEL
PRICING DEBT OPTIONS WITH MEAN-REVERTING INTEREST RATES

Input Assumptions

Face Value of Debt	$100.0000
Strike Price	$90.0000
Time to Bond Maturity (Years)	10.0000
Time to Option Expiration (Years)	5.0000
Risk-free Rate	5.00%
Long-Run Mean Reversion Level	12.00%
Rate of Mean Reversion	25.00%
Annualized Volatility	10.00%
Market Price of Risk	0.00%

Vasicek Call Option Value	$5.3606
Vasicek Put Option Value	$14.9051
Hull-White Call Option Value	$5.9859
Hull-White Put Option Value	$15.4249

Functions Used:

B2BondVasicekBondCallOption (Face Value of Debt, Strike, Bond Maturity, Option Maturity, Risk-free Rate, Long Run Rate, Reversion Rate, Volatility, MarketPrice Risk)
B2BondVasicekBondPutOption (Face Value of Debt, Strike, Bond Maturity, Option Maturity, Risk-free Rate, Long Run Rate, Reversion Rate, Volatility, MarketPrice Risk)
B2BondHullWhiteBondCallOption (Face Value of Debt, Strike, Bond Maturity, Option Maturity, Risk-free Rate, Reversion Rate, Volatility, MarketPriceRisk)
B2BondHullWhiteBondPutOption (Face Value of Debt, Strike, Bond Maturity, Option Maturity, Risk-free Rate, Reversion Rate, Volatility, MarketPriceRisk)

Figure 16.17 Vasicek Model of Pricing Debt Options and Yield with Mean-Reverting Rates.

rate and if the reversion rate is high. The opposite effects apply to the bond put option. Nonetheless, the reversion effect will be overshadowed by a high volatility of interest rate. Finally, at negligible maturities and interest rates (e.g., bond maturity of 0.01, option maturity of 0.001, spot risk-free rate of 0.001), the bond option values revert to the intrinsic value, or Face Value – Strike for bond call option, and Strike – Face Value for put option.

There is also another model for solving bond call and put options that is available through the functions *B2BondHullWhiteBondCallOption* and *B2BondHullWhiteBond PutOption*. These two Hull-White models are slightly different in that they do not require a long-run interest rate. Rather, just the reversion rate will suffice. If we calibrate the long-run rate in the Vasicek model carefully, we will obtain the same results as the Hull-White model. Typically, the Vasicek model is simpler to use.

Illustrations in Debt Analysis: Vasicek Price and Yield of Risky Debt

File Name: Debt Analysis – Vasicek Price and Yield of Risky Debt
Location: www.ElsevierDirect.com (search for this book, click Companion Site button, click link in Additional Models section) Modeling Toolkit | Debt Analysis | Vasicek Price and Yield of Risky Debt
Brief Description: The Vasicek model is used to price risky debt and to compute the yield on risky debt, where the underlying interest rate structure is stochastic, volatile, and mean-reverting (this model is also often used to compute and forecast yield curves).
Requirements: Modeling Toolkit, Risk Simulator
Modeling Toolkit Function Used: *B2BondVasicekBondPrice, B2BondVasicekBondYield*

The Vasicek stochastic model of mean-reverting interest rates (Figure 16.18) is modeled here to determine the value of a zero coupon bond and to reconstruct the term structure of interest rates and interest rate yield curve. This model assumes a mean-reverting term structure of interest rates with a rate of reversion, as well as a long-run rate that the interest reverts to in time. Use the *Yield Curve Vasicek* model

VASICEK & VAN DEVENTER MODEL
PRICING DEBT AND YIELD WITH MEAN-REVERTING INTEREST RATES

Input Assumptions

Time to Maturity of the Bond or Debt (Years)	1.00
Risk-free Rate (Short Rate)	5.00%
Long-run Mean Rate	8.00%
Annualized Volatility of Interest Rate	10.00%
Market Price of Interest Rate Risk	0.00%
Rate of Mean Reversion	1.00%

Price of Zero Coupon Bond	**$0.9527**
Yield of Zero Coupon Bond	**4.8495%**

Function call: B2BondVasicekBondPrice (Maturity,Riskfree,Longterm Rate, Volatility, Market Price of Risk, Rate of Mean Reversion)
Function call: B2BondVasicekBondYield (Maturity,Riskfree,Longterm Rate, Volatility, Market Price of Risk, Rate of Mean Reversion)

Figure 16.18 Price and Yield of Risky Debt.

to generate the yield curve and term structure of interest rates using this model. You may also use Risk Simulator to run simulations on the inputs to determine the price and yield of the zero coupon debt or to determine the input parameters, such as the long-run mean rate and rate of mean reversion (use Risk Simulator's *Statistical Analysis Tool* to determine these values based on historical data). Figure 16.17 uses a modification of this Vasicek model to price debt call and put options, versus the models described in this chapter that are used for pricing the risky bond and yield on the bond based on stochastic and mean-reverting interest rates. If multiple maturities and their respective input parameters are obtained, the entire term structure of interest rates and yield curve can be constructed, where the underlying process of these rates are assumed to be mean reverting.

17 Exotic Options, Options Engineering, and Credit Risk

Credit Engineering for Bankers. DOI: 10.1016/B978-0-12-378585-5.10017-X

The market for credit options or credit derivatives is young and wide open for creative engineering and development of exotic instruments. The process of creative engineering and innovation has to start from the fundamental theory of traded and liquid instruments such as exotic options. The only difference is that these credit derivatives use different underlying assets. Traded exotic options use stock prices, reference basket of stocks, indexes, interest rates, foreign exchange rates, and commodity prices. In contrast, credit derivatives use entity or reference credit sources, credit assets, or credit events. For instance, one default or multiple issuers' defaults will trigger the credit event, or a set of assets is used to determine the credit event (e.g., loans, liquid bonds) or other extreme events (e.g., bankruptcy, failure to pay for a certain maturity threshold and grace period, default, moratorium, repudiation, restructuring, downgrade, changes in credit spread, etc.). Regardless of the underlying asset used, these default conditions can be simulated (see Chapter Seven) and the over-the-counter (OTC) exotic options can be used to value these exotic credit derivatives. This chapter begins by introducing the two most common credit derivatives—credit default swaps and credit spread options—and continues with OTC exotic options. You can access these OTC models through the Modeling Toolkit software.

Common Credit Derivatives

Credit Default Swap

Location: www.ElsevierDirect.com (search for this book, click Companion Site button, click link in Additional Models section) Modeling Toolkit | Credit Analysis | Credit Default Swaps and Credit Spread Options

Brief Description: A credit hedging derivative that becomes valuable during a default event.

A credit default swap (CDS) allows the holder of the instrument to sell a bond or debt at par value when a credit event or default occurs. This model computes the valuation of the CDS spread. A CDS does not protect against movements of the credit spread (only a credit spread option can do that), but it only protects against defaults. Typically, to hedge against defaults and spread movements, both CDSs and credit spread options (CSOs) are used. This CDS model assumes a no-arbitrage argument, and the holder of the CDS makes periodic payments to the seller (similar to a periodic insurance premium) until the maturity of the CDS or until a credit event or default occurs. Because the notional amount to be received in the event of a default is the same as the par value of the bond or debt, and time value of money is used to determine the bond yield, this model does not require these two variables as input assumptions.

Credit Spread Option

Location: www.ElsevierDirect.com (search for this book, click Companion Site button, click link in Additional Models section) Modeling Toolkit | Credit Analysis | Credit Default Swaps and Credit Spread Options

Brief Description: A credit hedging derivative that protects against credit spreads and adverse interest rate movements.

In contrast, CSOs are another type of exotic debt option where the payoff depends on a credit spread or the price of the underlying asset that is sensitive to interest rate movements such as floating or inverse floating rate notes and debt. A CSO call option provides a return to the holder if the prevailing reference credit spread exceeds the predetermined strike rate, and the duration input variable is used to translate the percentage spread into a notional currency amount. The CSO expires when there is a credit default event. Again, note that a CSO can only protect against any movements in the reference spread and not a default event (only a CDS can do that). Typically, to hedge against defaults and spread movements, both CDSs and CSOs are used. In some cases, when the CSO covers a reference entity's underlying asset value and not the spread itself, the credit asset spread options are used instead.

OTC Exotic Options

Accruals on Basket of Assets

Location: www.ElsevierDirect.com (search for this book, click Companion Site button, click link in Additional Models section) Modeling Toolkit | Real Options Models | Accruals on Basket of Assets

Brief Description: Accruals on basket of assets instruments are essentially financial portfolios of multiple underlying assets where the holder of the instrument receives the maximum of the basket of assets or some prespecified guarantee amount.

The accruals on basket of assets instruments are exotic options in which there are several assets in a portfolio whereby the holder of the instrument receives the maximum of either the guaranteed amount or any one of the value of the assets. This instrument can be modeled as either an American option, which can be executed at any time up to and including maturity; a European option, which can be exercised only at maturity; or a Bermudan option, which is exercisable only at certain times.

Using the multiple assets and multiple phased module of the Real Options SLS software, we can model the value of an accrual option. It is highly recommended that at this point, the reader first become familiar with Chapter 16 before attempting to solve any SLS models. This model, although using the SLS software, is still listed under the exotic options category because basket accruals are considered exotic options and are solved using similar methodologies as other exotics.

American, Bermudan, and European Options with Sensitivities

File Name: Exotic Options – American, Bermudan, and European Options with Sensitivities
Location: www.ElsevierDirect.com (search for this book, click Companion Site button, click link in Additional Models section) Modeling Toolkit | Exotic Options | American, Bermudan, and European Options
Brief Description: Computation of American and European options with Greek sensitivities.

American options can be exercised at any time up to and including maturity, European options can only be exercised at maturity, and Bermudan options can be exercised only at certain times (i.e., exercisable other than during the vesting blackout period). In most instances, American $\geq$ Bermudan $\geq$ European options except for one special case: plain-vanilla call options when there are no dividends In that case, American $=$ Bermudan $=$ European call options, as it is never optimal to exercise early in a plain-vanilla call option when there are no dividends. However, once there is a sufficiently high dividend rate paid by the underlying stock, we clearly see that the relationship where American $\geq$ Bermudan $\geq$ European options apply.

European options can be solved using the Generalized Black-Scholes-Merton model (a closed for equation), as well as using binomial lattices and other numerical methods. However, for American options, we cannot use the Black-Scholes model and must revert to using the binomial lattice approach and some closed-form approximation models. Using the binomial lattice requires an additional input variable: lattice steps. The higher the number of lattice steps, the higher the precision of the results. Typically, 100 to 1,000 steps are sufficient to achieve convergence. Use the Real Options SLS software to solve more advanced options vehicles with a fully customizable lattice model. Only binomial lattices can be used to solve Bermudan options.

American Call Option on Foreign Exchange

Location: www.ElsevierDirect.com (search for this book, click Companion Site button, click link in Additional Models section) Modeling Toolkit | Real Options Models | American Call Option on Foreign Exchange
Brief Description: Computation of American and European options on foreign exchange.

A foreign exchange option (FX option or FXO) is a derivative where the owner has the right, but not the obligation, to exchange money denominated in one currency into another currency at a previously agreed on exchange rate on a specified date. The FX options market is the deepest, largest, and most liquid market for options of any kind in the world.

The valuation here uses the Garman-Kohlhagen model. You can use the *Exotic Options – Currency (Foreign Exchange) Options* model in the Modeling Toolkit software to compare the results of this Real Options SLS model. The exotic options model is used to compute the European version using closed-form models; the Real

Options SLS model—the example showcased here—computes the European and American options using a binomial lattice approach. When using the binomial lattice approach in the Real Options SLS software, remember to set the *Dividend Rate* as the foreign country's risk-free rate, *PV Underlying Asset* as the spot exchange rate, and *Implementation Cost* as the strike exchange rate.

As an example of a foreign exchange option, suppose the British pounds (GBP) versus the U.S. dollar (USD) is USD2/GBP1. Then the spot exchange rate is 2.0. Because the exchange rate is denominated in GBP (the denominator), the domestic risk-free rate is the rate in the United Kingdom, and the foreign rate is the rate in the United States. This means that the foreign exchange contract allows the holder the option to call GBP and put USD. To illustrate, suppose a U.K. firm is getting US$1M in six months, and the spot exchange rate is USD2/GBP1. If the GBP currency strengthens, the U.K. firm loses when it has to repatriate USD back to GBP, but it gains if the GBP currency weakens. If the firm hedges the foreign exchange exposure with an FXO and gets a call on GBP (put on USD), it hedges itself from any foreign exchange fluctuation risks. For discussion purposes, say the timing is short, interest rates are low, and volatility is low. Getting a call option with a strike of 1.90 yields a call value approximately 0.10 (i.e., the firm can execute the option and gain the difference of 2.00 − 1.90, or 0.10, immediately). This means that the rate now becomes USD1.90/GBP1, and it is cheaper to purchase GBP with the same USD, or the U.K. firm gets a higher GBP payoff. In situations where volatility is nonzero and maturity is higher, there is a significant value in an FXO, which can be modeled using the Real Options SLS approach.

American Call Options on Index Futures

Location: www.ElsevierDirect.com (search for this book, click Companion Site button, click link in Additional Models section) Modeling Toolkit | Real Options Models | American Call Option on Index Futures

Brief Description: Computes the value of an index option using closed-form models and binomial lattices.

The index option is similar to a regular option, but its underlying asset is a reference stock index such as the Standard & Poor's 500. The analysis can be solved using a closed-form Generalized Black-Scholes-Merton model. The model used in this chapter is similar to the closed-form model but applies the binomial lattice instead. The difference here is that Black-Scholes can solve only European options, while the binomial lattice model is capable of solving American, European, and Bermudan or mixed and customized options. Instead of using the asset value or current stock price as the input, we use the current index value. All other inputs remain the same, as in other options models. Index futures are an important investment vehicle because stock indexes cannot be traded directly, so futures based on stock indexes are the primary vehicles for trading indexes. Index futures operate in essentially the same way as other futures, and they are traded in the same way. Because indexes are based on many separate stocks, index futures are settled in cash rather than stocks. In addition, index futures allow investors to participate in the entire market without the significant cost of purchasing each underlying stock in an index. Index futures are widely used for hedging market movements and are applied in portfolios for their diversification effects.

American Call Option with Dividends

Location: www.ElsevierDirect.com (search for this book, click Companion Site button, click link in Additional Models section) Modeling Toolkit | Real Options Models | American Call Option with Dividends

Brief Description: Solves the American call option using customizable binomial lattices as well as closed-form approximation models.

The American call option with dividends model computes the call option using Real Options SLS software by applying the binomial lattice methodology. The results are benchmarked with closed-form approximation models. You can compare the results from this model with the European call option with dividends example. Note that when there are dividends, American options (which can be exercised early) are worth more than Bermudan options (options that can be exercised before termination but not during blackout periods such as vesting or contractual nontrading days), which, in turn, are worth more than European options (options that can be exercised only at maturity). This value relationship is typically true for most options. In contrast, for plain-vanilla basic call options without dividends, American options are worth the same as the Bermudan and European options, since they are never optimal to exercise early. This fact is true only for simple plain-vanilla call options when no dividends exist.

Asian Lookback Options Using Arithmetic and Geometric Averages

Location: www.ElsevierDirect.com (search for this book, click Companion Site button, click link in Additional Models section) Modeling Toolkit | Exotic Options | Asian Arithmetic

Brief Description: Solves an Asian lookback option using closed-form models, where the lookback is linked to the arithmetic average of past prices.

Asian options (also called *average options*) are options whose payoffs are linked to the average value of the underlying asset on a specific set of dates during the life of the option. An average rate option is a cash-settled option whose payoff is based on the difference between the average value of the underlying asset during the life of the option and a fixed strike. The arithmetic version means that the prices are simple averages rather than geometric averages. End-users of currency, commodities, or energy trading tend to be exposed to average prices over time, so Asian options are attractive for them. Asian options are also popular with corporations and banks with ongoing currency exposures. These options are also attractive because they tend to be less expensive—sell at lower premiums—than comparable vanilla puts or calls. This is because the volatility in the average value of an underlying asset or stock tends to be lower than the volatility of the actual values of the underlying asset or stock. Also, in situations where the underlying asset is thinly traded or there is the potential for its price to be manipulated, an Asian option offers some protection. It is more difficult to manipulate the average value of an underlying asset over an extended period of time than it is to manipulate it just at the expiration of an option.

Asset or Nothing Options

Location: www.ElsevierDirect.com (search for this book, click Companion Site button, click link in Additional Models section) Modeling Toolkit | Exotic Options | Asset or Nothing

Brief Description: Computes an asset or nothing option where, as long as the asset is above water, the holder will receive the asset at maturity.

An asset or nothing option is exactly what it implies. At expiration, if the option is in-the-money, regardless of how deep it is in-the-money, the option holder receives the stock or asset. This means that for a call option, as long as the stock or asset price exceeds the strike at expiration, the stock is received. Conversely, for a put option, the stock is received only if the stock or asset value falls below the strike price.

Barrier Options

Location: www.ElsevierDirect.com (search for this book, click Companion Site button, click link in Additional Models section) Modeling Toolkit | Exotic Options | Barrier Options
Brief Description: Values various types of barrier options such as up and in, down and in, up and out, and down and out call and put options.

Barrier options become valuable or get knocked in-the-money only if a barrier (upper or lower barrier) is breached (or not), and the payout is in the form of the option on the underlying asset. Sometimes, as remuneration for the risk of not being knocked in, a specified cash rebate is paid at the end of the instrument's maturity (at expiration) assuming that the option has not been knocked in. As an example, in an *up and in call option,* the instrument pays the specified cash amount at expiration if and only if the asset value does not breach the upper barrier (the asset value does not go above the upper barrier), thus providing the holder of the instrument with a safety net or a cash insurance. However, if the asset breaches the upper barrier, the option gets knocked in and becomes a live option. An *up and out option* is live only as long as the asset does not breach the upper barrier, and so forth.

Monitoring Periodicities means how often during the life of the option the asset or stock value will be monitored to see if it breaches a barrier. As an example, entering 12 implies monthly monitoring, 52 means weekly monitoring, 252 indicates monitoring for daily trading, 365 means monitoring daily, and 1,000,000 is used for continuous monitoring.

In general, barrier options limit the potential of a regular option's profits and, thus, cost less than regular options without barriers. For instance, if we assume no cash rebates, a Generalized Black-Scholes call option returns $6.50 as opposed to $5.33 for a barrier option (up and in barrier set at $115 with a stock price and strike price value of $100). This is because the call option will only be knocked in if the stock price goes above this $115 barrier, thereby reducing the regular option's profits between $100 and $115. This reduction effect is even more pronounced in the up and out call option, where all the significant upside profits (above the $115 barrier) are completely truncated.

Binary Digital Options

Location: www.ElsevierDirect.com (search for this book, click Companion Site button, click link in Additional Models section) Modeling Toolkit | Exotic Options | Binary Digital Options
Brief Description: Binary digital options are instruments that either get knocked in- or out-of-the-money depending on whether the asset value breaches or does not breach certain barriers.

Binary exotic options (also known as *digital, accrual,* or *fairway* options) become valuable only if a barrier (upper or lower barrier) is breached (or not), and the payout could be in the form of some prespecified cash amount or the underlying asset itself. The cash or asset exchanges hands either at the point when the barrier is breached or at the end of the instrument's maturity (at expiration), assuming that the barrier is breached at some point prior to maturity. For instance, in the *down and in cash at expiration* option, the instruments pay the specified cash amount at expiration if and only if the asset value breaches the lower barrier (the asset value goes below the lower barrier), providing the holder of the instrument a safety net or a cash insurance in case the underlying asset does not perform well. With *up and in* options, the cash or asset is provided if the underlying asset goes above the upper barrier threshold. In *up and out* or *down and out* options, the asset or cash is paid as long as the upper or lower barrier is not breached. With *at expiration* options, cash and assets are paid at maturity, whereas the *at hit* instruments are payable at the point when the barrier is breached.

Cash or Nothing Options

Location: www.ElsevierDirect.com (search for this book, click Companion Site button, click link in Additional Models section) Modeling Toolkit | Exotic Options | Cash or Nothing
Brief Description: Computes the cash or nothing option, where if in-the-money at expiration, the holder receives some prespecified cash amount.

A cash or nothing option is exactly what it implies. At expiration, if the option is in-the-money, regardless of how deep it is in-the-money, the option holder receives a predetermined cash payment. This means that for a call option, as long as the stock or asset price exceeds the strike at expiration, cash is received. Conversely, for a put option, cash is received only if the stock or asset value falls below the strike price.

Chooser Option (Simple Chooser)

Location: www.ElsevierDirect.com (search for this book, click Companion Site button, click link in Additional Models section) Modeling Toolkit | Exotic Options | Simple Chooser
Brief Description: Computes the value of an option that can become either a call or a put by a specific chooser time.

A simple chooser option allows the holder to choose if the option is a call or a put within the chooser time. Regardless of the choice, the option has the same contractual strike price and maturity. Typically, a chooser option is cheaper than purchasing both a call and a put together, but it provides the same level of hedge at a lower cost. The strike prices for both options are identical. The complex chooser option (see next) allows for different strike prices and maturities.

Chooser Option (Complex Chooser)

Location: www.ElsevierDirect.com (search for this book, click Companion Site button, click link in Additional Models section) Modeling Toolkit | Exotic Options | Complex Chooser
Brief Description: The complex chooser option allows the holder to choose if it becomes a call or a put option by a specific chooser time, while the maturity and strike price of the call and put are allowed to be different.

A complex chooser option allows the holder to choose if the option is a call or a put within the chooser time. The complex chooser option allows for different strike prices and maturities. Typically, a chooser option is cheaper than purchasing both a call and a put together. It provides the same level of hedge at a lower cost, while the strike price for both options can be different.

Commodity Options

Location: www.ElsevierDirect.com (search for this book, click Companion Site button, click link in Additional Models section) Modeling Toolkit | Exotic Options | Commodity Options
Brief Description: Models and values a commodity option where the commodity's spot and future values are used to value the option, while the forward rates and convenience yields are assumed to be mean-reverting and volatile.

This model computes the values of commodity-based European call and put options, where the convenience yield and forward rates are assumed to be mean-reverting, and each has its own volatilities and cross-correlations. This is a complex multifactor model with interrelationships among all variables.

Currency (Foreign Exchange) Options

Location: www.ElsevierDirect.com (search for this book, click Companion Site button, click link in Additional Models section) Modeling Toolkit | Exotic Options | Currency Options
Brief Description: Values a foreign exchange currency option, typically used in hedging foreign exchange fluctuations, where the key inputs are the spot exchange rate and the contractual purchase or sale price of the foreign exchange currency for delivery in the future.

A foreign exchange option (FX option or FXO) is a derivative where the owner has the right, but not the obligation, to exchange money denominated in one currency into another currency at a previously agreed on exchange rate on a specified date. The FX options market is the deepest, largest, and most liquid market for options of any kind in the world. The valuation here uses the Garman-Kohlhagen model. As an example, suppose the British pound (GBP) versus the U.S. dollar (USD) is USD2/GBP1. Then the spot exchange rate is 2.0. Because the exchange rate is denominated in GBP (the denominator), the domestic risk-free rate is the rate in the United Kingdom, and the foreign rate is the rate in the United States. This means that the foreign exchange contract allows the holder the option to call GBP and put USD. To illustrate, suppose a U.K. firm is getting US$1M in six months, and the spot exchange rate is USD2/GBP1. If the GBP currency strengthens, the U.K. firm loses if it has to repatriate USD back to GBP, but it gains if the GBP currency weakens. If the firm hedges the foreign exchange exposure with an FXO and gets a call on GBP (put on USD), it hedges itself from any foreign exchange fluctuation risks. For discussion purposes, say the timing is short, interest rates are low, and volatility is low. Getting a call option with a strike of 1.90 yields a call value approximately 0.10 (i.e., the firm can execute the option and gain the difference of 2.00 – 1.90, or 0.10, immediately). This means that the rate now becomes USD1.90/GBP1, and it is cheaper to purchase GBP with the same USD, or the U.K. firm gets a higher GBP payoff.

Double Barrier Options

Location: www.ElsevierDirect.com (search for this book, click Companion Site button, click link in Additional Models section) Modeling Toolkit | Exotic Options | Double Barriers

Brief Description: Various double barrier options are valued in this model, including up and in, up and out, with down and in, and down and out combinations, where a call or put option is knocked in- or out-of-the-money, depending on if it breaches an upper or lower barrier.

Barrier options become valuable or get knocked in-the-money only if a barrier (upper or lower barrier) is breached (or not), and the payout is in the form of the option on the underlying asset. Double barrier options have two barriers, one above the current asset value (upper barrier) and one below it (lower barrier). Either barrier has to be breached for a knock-in or knock-out event to occur. In general, barrier options limit the potential of a regular option's profits and, thus, cost less than regular options without barriers. As an example, in an *up and out, down and out call option,* the instrument is knocked out if the asset breaches either the upper or lower barriers, but it remains in effect, and the option is live at the end of maturity if the asset prices remain between these two barriers.

European Call Option with Dividends

Location: www.ElsevierDirect.com (search for this book, click Companion Site button, click link in Additional Models section) Modeling Toolkit | Real Options Models | European Call Option with Dividends

Brief Description: This model uses the customized binomial lattice approach to solve a European call option with dividends, where the holder of the option can exercise only at maturity and not before.

A European call option allows the holder to exercise the option only at maturity. An American option can be exercised at any time before, as well as up to and including, maturity. A Bermudan option is like an American and European option mixed: At certain vesting and blackout periods, the option cannot be executed until the end of the blackout period, when it then becomes exercisable at any time until its maturity. In a simple plain-vanilla call option, all three varieties have the same value, since it is never optimal to exercise early, making all three options revert to the value of a simple European option. However, this qualification does not hold true when dividends exist. When dividends are high enough, it is typically optimal to exercise a call option early, particularly before the ex-dividend date hits, reducing the value of the asset and, consequently, the value of the call option. The American call option typically is worth more than a Bermudan option, which is typically worth more than a European option, except in the special case of a simple plain-vanilla call option.

Exchange Assets Option

Location: www.ElsevierDirect.com (search for this book, click Companion Site button, click link in Additional Models section) Modeling Toolkit | Exotic Options | Exchange Assets

Brief Description: This European option allows the holder to swap out one asset for another, with predetermined quantities of each asset to be swapped at expiration.

The exchange of assets option provides the option holder the right at expiration (European version) to swap and give away *Asset 2* and, in return, receive *Asset 1*, with predetermined quantities of the first and second assets. The American option allows the swap to occur at any time before, as well as up to and including, maturity. Clearly, the more negative the correlation between the assets, the larger the risk reduction and diversification effects and, thus, the higher the value of the option. Sometimes in a real options world, where the assets swapped are not financial instruments but real physical assets, this option is called a *switching option*.

Extreme Spreads Option

Location: www.ElsevierDirect.com (search for this book, click Companion Site button, click link in Additional Models section) Modeling Toolkit | Exotic Options | Extreme Spreads
Brief Description: Computes extreme spread option values, where the vehicle is divided into two segments, and the option pays off the difference between the extreme values (min or max) of the asset during the two time segments.

Extreme spread options have their maturities divided into two segments, starting from time zero to the *first time period* (first segment) and from the first time period to *maturity* (second segment). An extreme spread call option pays the difference between the maximum asset value from the second segment and the maximum value of the first segment. Conversely, the put pays the difference between the minimum of the second segment's asset value and the minimum of the first segment's asset value. A reverse call pays the minimum from the first less the minimum of the second segment, whereas a reverse put pays the maximum of the first less the maximum of the second segments.

Foreign Equity Linked Foreign Exchange Options in Domestic Currency

Location: www.ElsevierDirect.com (search for this book, click Companion Site button, click link in Additional Models section) Modeling Toolkit | Exotic Options | Foreign Equity Linked Forex
Brief Description: Computes the option where the underlying asset is in a foreign market, the exchange rate is fixed in advance to hedge the exposure risk, and the strike price is set as a foreign exchange rate rather than a price.

Foreign equity linked foreign exchange options are options whose underlying asset is in a foreign equity market. The option holder can hedge the fluctuations of the foreign exchange risk by having a strike price on the foreign exchange rate. The resulting valuation is in the domestic currency. There are three closely related models in this and the following two sections (foreign equity linked foreign exchange option, foreign equity struck in domestic currency, and foreign equity with fixed exchange rate). Their similarities and differences can be summarized as follows:

- The underlying asset is denominated in a foreign currency.
- The foreign exchange rate is domestic currency to foreign currency.
- The option is valued in domestic currency.
- The strike prices are different where:
  - The exchange rate is the strike for the foreign equity linked foreign exchange option.
  - The domestic currency is the strike for the foreign equity struck in domestic currency option.
  - The foreign currency is the strike for the foreign equity with fixed exchange rate option.

Foreign Equity Struck in Domestic Currency
Location: www.ElsevierDirect.com (search for this book, click Companion Site button, click link in Additional Models section) Modeling Toolkit | Exotic Options | Foreign Equity Domestic Currency
Brief Description: Values the options on foreign equities denominated in foreign exchange currency while the strike price is in domestic currency.

Foreign equity struck in domestic currency is an option on foreign equities in a foreign currency but with the strike price in domestic currency. At expiration, assuming the option is in-the-money, its value will be translated back into the domestic currency. The exchange rate is the spot rate for domestic currency to foreign currency, the asset price is denominated in a foreign currency, and the strike price is in domestic currency.

Foreign Equity with Fixed Exchange Rate
Location: www.ElsevierDirect.com (search for this book, click Companion Site button, click link in Additional Models section) Modeling Toolkit | Exotic Options | Foreign Equity Fixed Forex
Brief Description: Values foreign equity options where the option is in a currency foreign to that of the underlying asset but with a risk hedging on the exchange rate.

Quanto options, also known as foreign equity options with fixed exchange rate, are traded on exchanges around the world. These options are denominated in a currency different from that of the underlying asset. They have an expanding or contracting coverage of the foreign exchange value of the underlying asset. The valuation of these options depends on the volatilities of the underlying assets and the currency exchange rate, as well as the correlation between the currency and the asset value.

Foreign Takeover Options
File Name: www.ElsevierDirect.com (search for this book, click Companion Site button, click link in Additional Models section) Exotic Options – Foreign Takeover Options
Brief Description: Computes a foreign takeover option, where the holder has the right to purchase some foreign exchange at a prespecified rate for the purposes of a takeover or acquisition of a foreign firm.

In a foreign takeover option with a foreign exchange element, if a successful takeover ensues (if the value of the foreign firm denominated in foreign currency is less than the foreign currency units required), the option holder has the right to purchase the number of foreign units at the predetermined strike price (denominated in exchange rates of the domestic currency to the foreign currency), at the option expiration date.

Forward Start Options
Location: www.ElsevierDirect.com (search for this book, click Companion Site button, click link in Additional Models section) Modeling Toolkit | Exotic Options | Forward Start
Brief Description: Computes the value of an option that technically starts in the future, with its strike price being a percentage of the asset price in the future when the option starts.

Forward start options start at-the-money or proportionally in- or out-of-the-money after some time in the future (the time to forward start). These options sometimes are used in employee stock options, where a grant is provided now, but the strike price depends on the asset or stock price at some time in the future and is proportional to the stock price. The *Alpha* variable measures the proportionality of the option being in- or out-of-the-money. *Alpha* = *1* means the option starts at-the-money or that the strike is set exactly as the asset price at the end of the time to forward start. *Alpha* < *1* means that the call option starts (*1 − Alpha*) percent in-the-money or (*1 − Alpha*) out-of-the-money for puts. Conversely, for *Alpha* > *1*, the call option starts (*Alpha* − *1*) out-of-the-money and puts start (*Alpha* − *1*) in-the-money.

Futures and Forward Options

Location: www.ElsevierDirect.com (search for this book, click Companion Site button, click link in Additional Models section) Modeling Toolkit | Exotic Options | Futures and Forward Options

Brief Description: This model applies the same generalities as the Black-Scholes model, but the underlying asset is a futures or forward contract, not a stock.

The futures option is similar to a regular option, but the underlying asset is a futures or forward contract. Be careful here, as the analysis cannot be solved using a Generalized Black-Scholes-Merton Model. In many cases, options are traded on futures. A put is the option to sell a futures contract, and a call is the option to buy a futures contract. For both, the option strike price is the specified futures price at which the future is traded if the option is exercised. A futures contract is a standardized contract, typically traded on a futures exchange, to buy or sell a certain underlying instrument at a certain date in the future at a prespecified price. The future date is called the *delivery date* or *final settlement date*. The preset price is called the *futures price*. The price of the underlying asset on the delivery date is called the *settlement price*. The settlement price normally converges toward the futures price on the delivery date. A futures contract gives the holder the obligation to buy or sell, which differs from an options contract, which gives the holder the right, but not the obligation, to buy or sell. In other words, the owner of an options contract may exercise the contract. If it is an American-style option, it can be exercised on or before the expiration date, but a European option can be exercised only at expiration. Thus, a futures contract is more like a European option. Both parties of a futures contract must fulfill the contract on the settlement date. The seller delivers the commodity to the buyer, or if it is a cash-settled future, cash is transferred from the futures trader who sustained a loss to the one who made a profit. To exit the commitment prior to the settlement date, the holder of a futures position has to offset the position either by selling a long position or by buying back a short position, effectively closing out the futures position and its contract obligations.

Gap Options

Location: www.ElsevierDirect.com (search for this book, click Companion Site button, click link in Additional Models section) Modeling Toolkit | Exotic Options | Gap Options

Brief Description: Gap options are valued with this model, where there are two strike prices with respect to one underlying asset, and where the first strike acts like a barrier that, when breached, brings the second strike price into play.

Gap options are similar to barrier options and two asset correlated options in the sense that the call option is knocked in when the underlying asset exceeds the reference *Strike Price 1*, making the option payoff the asset price less *Strike Price 2* for the underlying asset. Similarly, the put option is knocked in only if the underlying asset is less than the reference *Strike Price 1*, providing a payoff of *Strike Price 2* less the underlying asset.

Graduated Barrier Options

Location: www.ElsevierDirect.com (search for this book, click Companion Site button, click link in Additional Models section) Modeling Toolkit | Exotic Options | Graduated Barriers
Brief Description: Graduated barrier models are barrier options with flexible and graduated payoffs, depending on how far above or below a barrier the asset ends up at maturity.

Graduated, or soft, barrier options are similar to standard barrier options except that the barriers are no longer static values but a graduated range between the lower and upper barriers. The option is knocked in- or out-of-the-money proportionally. Both *upper* and *lower barriers* should be either above (for *up and in* or *up and out* options) or below (for *down and in* or *down and out* options) the starting stock price or asset value. For instance, in the *down and in* call option, the instruments become knocked-in, or live, at expiration if and only if the asset or stock value breaches the lower barrier (asset value goes below the barriers). If the option to be valued is a *down and in* call, then both the *upper* and *lower barriers* should be lower than the starting stock price or asset value, providing a collar of graduated prices. For instance, if the upper and lower barriers are $90 and $80, and if the asset price ends up being $89, a down and out option will be knocked out 10% of its value. Standard barrier options are more difficult to delta hedge when the asset values and barriers are close to each other. Graduated barrier options are more appropriate for delta-hedges, providing less delta risk and gamma risk.

Index Options

Location: www.ElsevierDirect.com (search for this book, click Companion Site button, click link in Additional Models section) Modeling Toolkit | Exotic Options | Index Options
Brief Description: Index options are similar to regular plain-vanilla options and can be solved using the Black-Scholes model, with the only difference being that the underlying asset is not a stock but an index.

The index option is similar to a regular option, but the underlying asset is a reference stock index such as the Standard & Poor's 500. The analysis can be solved using a Generalized Black-Scholes-Merton Model as well.

Inverse Gamma Out-of-the-Money Options

Location: www.ElsevierDirect.com (search for this book, click Companion Site button, click link in Additional Models section) Modeling Toolkit | Exotic Options | Inverse Gamma Out-of-the-Money Options

Brief Description: Analyzes options using an inverse gamma distribution rather than the typical normal-lognormal assumptions; this type of analysis is important for valuing extreme in- or out-of-the-money options.

This model computes the value of European call and put options using an inverse gamma distribution, as opposed to the standard normal distribution. This distribution accounts for the peaked distributions of asset returns and provides better estimates for deep out-of-the-money options. The traditional Generalized Black-Scholes-Merton Model is typically used as benchmark.

Jump Diffusion Options

Location: www.ElsevierDirect.com (search for this book, click Companion Site button, click link in Additional Models section) Modeling Toolkit | Exotic Options | Jump Diffusion
Brief Description: Sometimes the underlying asset in an option is assumed to follow a Poisson jump-diffusion process instead of a random walk Brownian motion, and applicable for underlying assets such as oil and gas commodities and price of electricity.

A jump diffusion option is similar to a regular option except that instead of assuming that the underlying asset follows a lognormal Brownian motion process, the process here follows a Poisson jump-diffusion process. That is, stock or asset prices follow jumps, which occur several times per year (observed from history). Cumulatively, these jumps explain a certain percentage of the total volatility of the asset.

Leptokurtic and Skewed Options

Location: www.ElsevierDirect.com (search for this book, click Companion Site button, click link in Additional Models section) Modeling Toolkit | Exotic Options | Leptokurtic and Skewed Options
Brief Description: Computes options where the underlying assets are assumed to have returns that are skewed and leptokurtic or have fat tails and are leaning on one end of the distribution rather than having symmetrical in returns.

This model is used to compute the European call and put options using the binomial lattice approach when the underlying distribution of stock returns is not normally distributed, is not symmetrical, and has additional slight kurtosis and skew. Be careful when using this model to account for a high or low skew and kurtosis because certain combinations of these two coefficients actually yield unsolvable results. The Black-Scholes results are typically used to benchmark the effects of a high kurtosis and positive or negatively skewed distributions compared to the normal distribution assumptions on asset returns.

Lookback with Fixed Strike (Partial Time)

Location: www.ElsevierDirect.com (search for this book, click Companion Site button, click link in Additional Models section) Modeling Toolkit | Exotic Options | Lookback Fixed Strike Partial Time
Brief Description: Computing an option where the strike price is predetermined but the payoff on the option is the difference between the highest or the lowest attained asset price against the strike.

In a fixed strike option with lookback feature (partial time), the strike price is predetermined, while at expiration, the payoff on the call option is the difference between the maximum asset price less the strike price during the time between the starting period of the lookback to the maturity of the option. Conversely, the put will pay the maximum difference between the lowest observed asset price less the strike price during the time between the starting period of the lookback to the maturity of the option.

Lookback with Fixed Strike

Location: www.ElsevierDirect.com (search for this book, click Companion Site button, click link in Additional Models section) Modeling Toolkit | Exotic Options | Lookback Fixed Strike
Brief Description: Computes the value of an option where the strike price is fixed but the value at expiration is based on the value of the underlying asset's maximum and minimum values during the option's lifetime.

In a fixed strike option with lookback feature, the strike price is predetermined, while at expiration, the payoff on the call option is the difference between the maximum asset price less the strike price during the lifetime of the option. Conversely, the put will pay the maximum difference between the lowest observed asset price less the strike price during the lifetime of the option.

Lookback with Floating Strike (Partial Time)

Location: www.ElsevierDirect.com (search for this book, click Companion Site button, click link in Additional Models section) Modeling Toolkit | Exotic Options | Lookback Floating Strike Partial Time
Brief Description: Computes the value of an option where the strike price is not fixed but floating and the value at expiration is based on the value of the underlying asset's maximum and minimum values starting from the lookback inception time to maturity as the purchase or sale price.

In a floating strike option with lookback feature (partial time), the strike price is floating. At expiration, the payoff on the call option is being able to purchase the underlying asset at the minimum observed price from inception to the end of the lookback time. Conversely, the put will allow the option holder to sell at the maximum observed asset price from inception to the end of the lookback time.

Lookback with Floating Strike

Location: www.ElsevierDirect.com (search for this book, click Companion Site button, click link in Additional Models section) Modeling Toolkit | Exotic Options | Lookback Floating Strike
Brief Description: Computes the value of an option where the strike price is not fixed but floating and the value at expiration is based on the value of the underlying asset's maximum and minimum values during the option's lifetime as the purchase or sale price.

In a floating strike option with lookback feature, the strike price is floating. At expiration, the payoff on the call option is being able to purchase the underlying asset at the minimum observed price during the life of the option. Conversely, the put will allow the option holder to sell at the maximum observed asset price during the life of the option.

Min and Max of Two Assets

Location: www.ElsevierDirect.com (search for this book, click Companion Site button, click link in Additional Models section) Modeling Toolkit | Exotic Options | Min and Max of Two Assets

Brief Description: Computes the value of an option where there are two underlying assets that are correlated with different volatilities and the differences between the assets' values are used as the benchmark for determining the value of the payoff at expiration.

Options on minimum or maximum are used when there are two assets with different volatilities. Either the maximum or the minimum value at expiration of both assets is used in the option's exercise. For instance, a call option on the minimum implies that the payoff at expiration is such that the minimum price between *Asset 1* and *Asset 2* is used against the strike price of the option.

Options on Options

Location: www.ElsevierDirect.com (search for this book, click Companion Site button, click link in Additional Models section) Modeling Toolkit | Exotic Options | Options on Options

Brief Description: Computes the value of an option on another option, or a compound option, where the option provides the holder the right to buy or sell a subsequent option at the expiration of the first option.

Options on options, sometimes known as *compound options*, allow the holder to call or buy versus put or sell an option in the future. For instance, a *put on call* option means that the holder has the right to sell a call option in some future period for a specified strike price (*strike price for the option on option*). The time for this right to sell is called the *maturity of the option on option*. The *maturity of the underlying* refers to the maturity of the option to be bought or sold in the future, starting from now.

Option Collar

Location: www.ElsevierDirect.com (search for this book, click Companion Site button, click link in Additional Models section) Modeling Toolkit | Exotic Options | Options Collar

Brief Description: Computes the call-put collar strategy—that is, to short a call and long a put at different strike prices such that the hedge is costless and effective.

The call and put collar strategy requires that one stock be purchased, one call be sold, and one put be purchased. The idea is that the proceeds from the call sold are sufficient to cover the proceeds of the put bought. Therefore, given a specific set of stock price, option maturity, risk-free rate, volatility, and dividend of a stock, you can impute the required strike price of a call if you know what put to purchase (and its relevant strike price) or the strike price of a put if you know what call to sell (and its relevant strike price).

Perpetual Options

File Name: Exotic Options – Perpetual Options

Location: www.ElsevierDirect.com (search for this book, click Companion Site button, click link in Additional Models section) Modeling Toolkit | Exotic Options | Perpetual Options

Brief Description: Computes the value of an American option that has a perpetual life where the underlying is a dividend-paying asset.

The perpetual call and put options are American options with continuous dividends that can be executed at any time and have an infinite life. Clearly a European option (only exercisable at termination) has a zero value, Hence, only American options are viable perpetual options. American closed-form approximations with 100-year maturities are typically used to benchmark the results.

Range Accruals (Fairway Options)

Location: www.ElsevierDirect.com (search for this book, click Companion Site button, click link in Additional Models section) Modeling Toolkit | Real Options Models | Range Accruals
Brief Description: Computes the value of fairway options, or range accrual options, where the option pays a specified return if the underlying asset is within a range but pays something else if it is outside the range at any time during its maturity.

A range accrual option is also called a fairway option. Here, the option pays a certain return if the asset value stays within a certain range (between the upper and lower barriers) but pays a different amount or return if the asset value falls outside this range during any time before and up to maturity. The name *fairway option* is sometimes used because the option is similar to the condition in the game of golf, where if the ball stays within the fairway (a narrow path), it is in play, and if it goes outside, a penalty might be imposed (in this case, a lower return).

Simple Chooser

Location: www.ElsevierDirect.com (search for this book, click Companion Site button, click link in Additional Models section) Modeling Toolkit | Exotic Options | Simple Chooser
Brief Description: Computes the value of an option where the holder has the ability to decide if it is a call or a put at some future time period; this option is similar to purchasing a call and a put together but costs less as a simple chooser option. Computes the value of an option that can become either a call or a put by a specific chooser time

A simple chooser option allows the holder to choose if the option is a call or a put within the chooser time. Regardless of the choice, the option has the same contractual strike price and maturity. Typically, a chooser option is cheaper than purchasing both a call and a put together but provides the same level of hedge at a lower cost. The strike prices for both options are identical. The complex chooser option (see "Chooser Option (Complex Chooser)") allows for different strike prices and maturities.

Spread on Futures

Location: www.ElsevierDirect.com (search for this book, click Companion Site button, click link in Additional Models section) Modeling Toolkit | Exotic Options | Spread on Futures
Brief Description: Computes the value of an option where the underlying assets are two different futures contracts, and their spreads (the difference between the futures) are used as a benchmark to determine the value of the option.

A spread on futures options is an option where the payoff is the difference between the two futures values at expiration. That is, the spread is *Futures 1 – Futures 2*, while the *call* payoff is the value of *Spread – Strike*, and the *put* payoff is *Strike – Spread*.

Supershare Options

Location: www.ElsevierDirect.com (search for this book, click Companion Site button, click link in Additional Models section) Modeling Toolkit | Exotic Options | Supershares
Brief Description: Computes the value of an option where it is a hybrid of a double barrier fairway option that pays a percentage proportional to the level it is in-the-money within the barriers.

Typically, supershare options are traded or embedded in supershare funds. These options are related to down and out, up and out double barrier options, where the option has value only if the stock or asset price is between the upper and lower barriers, and, at expiration, the option provides a payoff equivalent to the stock or asset price divided by the lower strike price (*S/X Lower*).

Time Switch Options

Location: www.ElsevierDirect.com (search for this book, click Companion Site button, click link in Additional Models section) Modeling Toolkit | Exotic Options | Time Switch
Brief Description: Computes the value of an option where its value depends on how many times a barrier is breached during the life of the option.

In a time switch option, the holder receives the *Accumulated Amount × Time-Steps* each time the asset price exceeds the strike price for a call option (or falls below the strike price for a put option). The time-steps are how often the asset price is checked if the strike threshold has been breached (typically, for a one-year option with 252 trading days, set *DT* as 1/252). Sometimes, the option has already accumulated past amounts or as agreed to in the option as a minimum guaranteed payment as measured by the number of time units fulfilled (which is typically set as 0).

Trading Day Corrections

Location: www.ElsevierDirect.com (search for this book, click Companion Site button, click link in Additional Models section) Modeling Toolkit | Exotic Options | Trading Day Corrections
Brief Description: Computes the value of plain-vanilla call and put options corrected for the number of trading days and calendar days left in their maturity.

An option with a trading day correction uses a typical option and corrects it for the varying volatilities. Specifically, volatility tends to be higher on trading days than on nontrading days. The *trading days ratio* is simply the number of trading days left until maturity divided by the total number of trading days per year (typically between 250 and 252). The *calendar days ratio* is the number of calendar days left until maturity divided by the total number of days per year (365). Typically, with the adjustments, the option value is lower. In addition, if the trading days ratio and calendar days ratio are identical, the results of the adjustment is zero, and the option value reverts back to the generalized Black-Scholes results. This is because the days left are assumed to be all full trading days.

Two Asset Barrier Options

Location: www.ElsevierDirect.com (search for this book, click Companion Site button, click link in Additional Models section) Modeling Toolkit | Exotic Options | Two Asset Barrier
Brief Description: Computes the value of an option with two underlying assets, one of which is a reference benchmark and the other is used to compute the value of the option payoff.

Two asset barrier options become valuable or get knocked in-the-money only if a barrier (upper or lower barrier) is breached (or not) and the payout is in the form of the option on the first underlying asset. In general, a barrier option limits the potential of a regular option's profits and, thus, costs less than regular options without barriers. A barrier option is thus a better bet for companies that are trying to hedge a specific price movement, since it tends to be cheaper. As an example, in the up and in call option, the instrument is knocked in if the asset breaches the upper barrier but is worthless if this barrier is not breached. The payoff on this option is based on the value of the first underlying asset (*Asset 1*) less the *Strike* price, while whether the barrier is breached or not depends on whether the second reference asset (*Asset 2*) breaches the *Barrier*.

Monitoring Periodicities means how often during the life of the option the asset or stock value will be monitored to see if it breaches a barrier. As an example, entering 12 implies monthly monitoring, 52 means weekly monitoring, 252 indicates monitoring for daily trading, 365 means monitoring daily, and 1,000,000 for continuous monitoring.

Two Asset Cash or Nothing

Location: www.ElsevierDirect.com (search for this book, click Companion Site button, click link in Additional Models section) Modeling Toolkit | Exotic Options | Two Asset Cash
Brief Description: Computes the value of an option that pays a prespecified amount of cash as long as the option stays in-the-money at expiration, regardless of how valuable the intrinsic value is at maturity.

Cash or nothing options pay out a prespecified amount of cash at expiration as long as the option is in-the-money, without regard to how much it is in-the-money. The two asset cash or nothing option means that *both* assets must be in-the-money before cash is paid out (for call options, both asset values must be above their respective strike prices, and for puts, both assets must be below their respective strike prices). For the up-down option, this implies that the first asset must be above the first strike price, and the second asset must be below the second strike price. Conversely, the down-up option implies that cash will be paid out only if at expiration, the first asset is below the first strike, and the second asset is above the second strike.

Two Correlated Assets Option

Location: www.ElsevierDirect.com (search for this book, click Companion Site button, click link in Additional Models section) Modeling Toolkit | Exotic Options | Two Asset Correlated
Brief Description: Computes the value of an option that depends on two assets: a benchmark asset that determines if the option is in-the-money and a second asset that determines the payoff on the option at expiration.

The two correlated asset options use two underlying assets: *Asset 1* and *Asset 2*. Typically, Asset 1 is the benchmark asset (e.g., a stock index or market comparable stock), whereby if at expiration, Asset 1's values exceed Strike 1's value, then the option is knocked in-the-money, meaning that the payoff on the call option is *Asset 2 – Strike 2* and *Strike 2 – Asset 2* for the put option (for the put, Asset 1 must be less than Strike 1). A higher positive correlation between the reference and the underlying asset implies that the option value increases because the comovement of both assets is highly positive, meaning that the higher the price movement of the reference asset, the higher the chances of it being in-the-money and, similarly, the higher the chances of the underlying asset's payoff being in-the-money. Negative correlations reduce the option value as even if the reference asset is in-the-money and the value of the option of the underlying is very little in-the-money or completely out-of-the-money. Correlation is typically restricted between –0.9999 and +0.9999. If there is a perfect correlation (either positive or negative), then there is no point in issuing such an asset, since a regular option model will suffice.

Two correlated asset options sometimes are used as a performance-based payoff option. For instance, the first or reference asset can be a company's revenues, profit margin, or an external index such as the Standard & Poor's 500, or some reference price in the market such as the price of gold. Therefore, the option is live only if the benchmark value exceeds a prespecified threshold. This European option is exercisable only at expiration. To model an American (exercisable at any time up to and including expiration) or Bermudan option (exercisable at specific periods only, with blackout and vesting periods where the option cannot be exercised), use the Real Options SLS software to model the exotic option.

Uneven Dividend Payments Option
Location: www.ElsevierDirect.com (search for this book, click Companion Site button, click link in Additional Models section) Modeling Toolkit | Exotic Options | Uneven Dividends
Brief Description: Computes the value of plain-vanilla call and put options when the dividend stream of the underlying asset comes in uneven payments over time.

Sometimes dividends are paid in various lump sums, and sometimes these values are not consistent throughout the life of the option. Accounting for the average dividend yield and not the uneven cash flows will yield incorrect valuations in the Black-Scholes paradigm.

Writer Extendible Option
Location: www.ElsevierDirect.com (search for this book, click Companion Site button, click link in Additional Models section) Modeling Toolkit | Exotic Options | Writer Extendible
Brief Description: Computes the value of various options that can be extended beyond the original maturity date if the option is out-of-the-money, providing an insurance policy for the option holder, and thereby typically costing more than conventional options.

Writer extendible options can be seen as insurance policies in case the option becomes worthless at maturity. Specifically, the call or put option can be extended automatically beyond the initial maturity date to an extended date with a new extended strike price assuming that, at maturity, the option is out-of-the-money and worthless. This extendibility provides a safety net of time for the holder of the option.

18 Credit and Debt Valuation

This chapter reviews the fundamentals of credit and debt valuation, including what credit risk premium should be charged to an obligor with a specific probability of default, the effects of credit spreads and interest rates on bond and debt valuation, simulating a credit risk spread based on industry comparables, generating an internal credit risk tiered structure, valuing the profit-cost analysis of new debt or line of credit, quantifying the market value of risky debt and its volatility, pricing risky debt assuming mean-reverting interest rates, amortizing debt and simulating prepayment risks, quantifying debt sensitivity using durations and convexity, and valuing risky debt using a markets-based options approach assuming stochastic market variables. These models are illustrated using the Modeling Toolkit software.

Illustrations in Credit Analysis

Credit Premium
Location: www.ElsevierDirect.com (search for this book, click Companion Site button, click link in Additional Models section) Modeling Toolkit | Credit Analysis | Credit Premium
Brief Description: Used to determine the credit risk premium that should be charged beyond any standard interest rates, depending on the default probability of the debt holder.

This model is used to determine the credit risk premium that should be charged above the standard interest rate given the default probability of this debt or credit's anticipated cash flows. Enter the *years* and relevant *cash flows* in the model as well as the *interest rate* and anticipated *default probability* and click *Compute* to determine the credit spread required (Figure 18.1). All values should be positive, and the default probability input can be determined using any of the Modeling Toolkit's default probability models.

For instance, in Figure 18.1, assume a regular 10-year bond with a $1,000 face value paying 10% coupon rate. Where the prevailing interest rate is 5%, a 1% default probability means that the default risk premium spread is 0.14%, making the total interest charge 5.14%.

That is, the present value of cash flows (PVCF) is the present value of future coupon payments and face value receipt at maturity, discounted at the prevailing interest rate. The sum of these values is the net present value (NPV), which is the price of the bond assuming zero default. By adding a probability of default, the cash flows are adjusted by this default rate, and a corresponding default risk premium can be determined whereby the NPV of these risk-adjusted PVCF values will equal the original no-default NPV.

The results indicate that the lower the probability of default on this debt, the lower the additional default spread (interest rate premium), and the higher the probability of default, the higher the required interest rate premium. Using this simple probability-adjusted cash flow model, we can determine the approximate simple credit spread required to obtain the same probability adjusted cash flow as another debt with no default. This is a simple cash flow model for approximation purposes and does not account for more exotic and real-life conditions such as mean-reverting interest rates, stochastic interest rates (smiles, frowns, and other shapes with localized time-dependent volatilities), credit risk migration, risk-neutral versus

Credit Risk Premium Based on Default Probability

		Increasing Default Probability Increases Risk Premium				
		Default Probability	1.00%	0.25%	0.50%	2.00%	4.00%
Standard Interest Rate	5.00%						
Default Probability	1.00%	Default Risk Premium	0.14%	0.04%	0.07%	0.29%	0.59%

NPV	1386.09

Year	Cash Flows	PVCF	Adjusted Cash Flows	Adjusted Cash Flows	Adjusted Cash Flows	Adjusted Cash Flows	Adjusted Cash Flows
1	100.00	95.24	94.42	95.03	94.83	93.59	91.94
2	100.00	90.70	90.04	90.54	90.37	89.38	88.05
3	100.00	86.38	85.87	86.26	86.13	85.36	84.33
4	100.00	82.27	81.90	82.18	82.08	81.52	80.77
5	100.00	78.35	78.11	78.29	78.23	77.86	77.35
6	100.00	74.62	74.49	74.59	74.56	74.36	74.08
7	100.00	71.07	71.04	71.06	71.05	71.01	70.95
8	100.00	67.68	67.75	67.70	67.72	67.82	67.95
9	100.00	64.46	64.61	64.50	64.54	64.77	65.08
10	1100.00	675.30	677.85	675.94	676.57	680.41	685.58

Compute!

Real Options Valuation
www.realoptionsvaluation.com

Figure 18.1 A Simple Credit Spread Premium Computation Given Default Probabilities.

empirical probabilities of default adjustments, recovery rate, changing cumulative probabilities of default, and other qualitative factors, which are addressed in later sections and models in this book. Nonetheless, this model provides a simple and highly intuitive approximation of the default spread required on a risky debt or credit issue, and it can be used as a simple benchmark against more advanced models that are discussed in later sections.

Credit Risk Analysis and Effects on Prices

Location: www.ElsevierDirect.com (search for this book, click Companion Site button, click link in Additional Models section) Modeling Toolkit | Credit Analysis | Credit Risk and Effects on Prices

Brief Description: Values the effects of credit spreads as applied to bond and debt prices.

Banks that sell or issue fixed income products and vehicles or issue debt and credit lines need to understand the effects of interest rate risks. This model is used to analyze the effects of a credit spread as applied to the price of a bond or a debt. The worse the credit rating, the higher the required credit spread and the lower the market value of the bond or debt. That is, the lower the credit rating of a debt issue, the higher the probability of default, and the higher the risk to the debt holder. This means that the debt holder will require a higher rate of return or yield on the debt in remuneration for this higher risk level. This additional yield is termed the *credit spread* (the additional interest rate above and beyond a similar debt issue with no default risk).

Using a higher yield, the price of the debt is obtained through summing the present values of future coupon payments and principal repayment cash flows, and the higher the yield, the lower the value of the bond or debt. So risk reduces the value of the bond, which means that assuming the bond does not default, the yield to maturity on the bond is higher for a risky bond than a zero-risk bond (i.e., with the same cash flows in the future, the cheaper the bond, the higher the yield on the bond, holding everything else constant). This model also allows you to determine the effects on the price of debt of a change in credit rating (Figure 18.2).

The question now is, why do we analyze credit risk based on the bond market as an example? By financial definitions, bonds are the same as debt. A bond is issued by a corporation or some government agency (debt is obtained by individuals or companies in need of external funding, that is, a bank provides a loan or credit line to these individuals or corporations). The issuer receives a discounted portion of the face value up front (for debt, the obligor receives the funds up front). A bond is purchased or held by an investor (debt is issued by a bank or financial institution and, so, they are the holders of the debt). A bond has a face value (for a debt, we call this the *principal*). A bond provides periodic payment to the bond holder (the borrower sends periodic payments back to the bank for a debt or credit line). A bond is highly sensitive to the outside market environment (inflation, bond market fluctuations, competition, economic environment) and interest rates (higher prevailing interest rates means lower bond price), and a credit line or debt is susceptible to the same pressures.

However, there are differences between a bond and regular debt or credit. A bond pays back the principal to the bond holder at maturity, whereas a debt or credit line's principal amount is typically amortized over the life of the debt. Exceptions are

CREDIT RISK ANALYSIS

Face Value	$100.00
Coupon Rate	5.50%
Maturity	10.00
Current Interest Rate	5.00%
Credit Spread	2.39%

Banks selling fixed income products and vehicles need to understand the interest rate risks. This model is used to analyze the effects of a credit spread applied to the price of a bond or debt. The worse the credit rating, the higher the required credit spread and the lower the market value of the bond or debt. This model also allows you to determine the effects of a change in credit rating.

Bond Price Original $103.86
Bond Price with Spread $86.96
Reduction in Value   -16.27%

Function Used: B2BondPriceDiscrete

Cash Flow	Interest Rates	Year	Rates with Spread
$5.50	5.00%	1	7.39%
$5.50	5.00%	2	7.39%
$5.50	5.00%	3	7.39%
$5.50	5.00%	4	7.39%
$5.50	5.00%	5	7.39%
$5.50	5.00%	6	7.39%
$5.50	5.00%	7	7.39%
$5.50	5.00%	8	7.39%
$5.50	5.00%	9	7.39%
$105.50	5.00%	10	7.39%

Credit Spreads	
AAA	0.54%
AA	0.64%
A	0.90%
BBB	1.23%
BB	2.39%
B+	2.86%
B	3.40%
B-	4.33%

Figure 18.2 Credit Risk Analysis.

amortizing bonds that provide the same payment as debt and balloon debt that provides the same payments as bonds.

Regardless of the type, both bond and debt have credit risk, prepayment risk, market risk, and other risks (e.g., sovereign and foreign exchange risk for international issues), and the cash flows can be determined up front. Hence, the valuation approaches are very similar. In addition, all the models and techniques introduced in this book for credit risk modeling, probability of default models, bond valuation, and debt options are applicable to both regular debt and corporate bonds.

External Debt Ratings and Spread

Location: www.ElsevierDirect.com (search for this book, click Companion Site button, click link in Additional Models section) Modeling Toolkit | Credit Analysis | External Debt Rating and Spreads

Brief Description: Simulates and computes the credit risk spread of a particular firm based on industry standards (EBIT and interest expenses of the debt holder) to determine the risk-based spread.

This model is used to run a simulation on a company's creditworthiness given that the earnings are uncertain. The goal is to determine the credit category this firm is in, considering its financial standing and the industry in which it operates. Assuming we have a prespecified credit category for various industries, we can then determine what interest rate to charge the company for a new loan. (See the various Credit Risk Rating Models in the Modeling Toolkit for examples on how to determine the creditworthiness of a customer or company using internal and external risk-based models and how the credit category and scoring table are obtained, as well as how to use Modeling Toolkit's probability of default models to determine the creditworthiness of an obligor.)

For instance, Figure 18.3 illustrates a manufacturing firm's earnings before interest and taxes (EBIT), as well as its current interest expenses, benchmarked against some long-term government bond rate. Using industry standards, the debt is then rated appropriately using a predefined credit ratings table, and the default spread and total interest charge are then computed.

This model is very similar to the examples described in the previous sections in that the relevant credit spread is determined for a risky debt. Previously, given a probability of default (we discuss the applications of probability of default models in the book), we can determine the relevant credit spread. In the previous section, given the credit spread, we can determine the impact in price of a bond or risky debt. In this section, we are interested in obtaining the spread on risky debt by looking at industry comparables and using other financial ratios such as a company's interest coverage. This approach is more broad-based and can be used assuming no other financial data are available.

Each of the inputs can be simulated using Risk Simulator to determine the statistical confidence of the cost of debt or interest rate to charge the client (Figure 18.4). By running a simulation, we can better estimate the relevant credit spread and its confidence interval, rather than relying on a single snapshot value of some financial ratios to determine the credit spread.

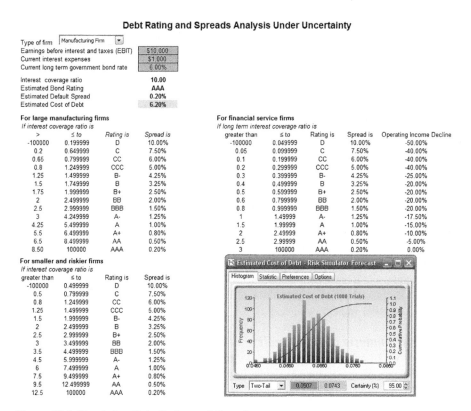

Figure 18.3 Simulating Debt Rating and Spreads.

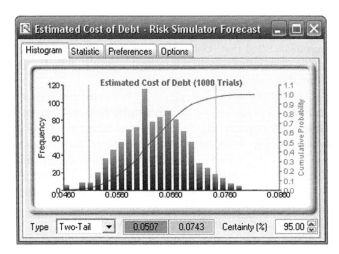

Figure 18.4 Forecast Distribution of Interest Rate with Spreads.

Internal Credit Risk Rating Model

Location: www.ElsevierDirect.com (search for this book, click Companion Site button, click link in Additional Models section) Modeling Toolkit | Credit Analysis | Internal Credit Risk Rating Model
Brief Description: This is a credit ratings model like the ones used by Moody's to determine the credit shortfall risk and alphabetical risk rating given the probability of default.

This is an internal credit rating model similar to the ones used by Moody's or other rating agencies. Obtain the required *probability of default* input from other probability of default models in the Modeling Toolkit (see the chapters on modeling probability of default), and use this model to determine the rating of this company or debt holder. To further enhance the model, the category widths of the rating table can be refined and calibrated through additional parameter-width estimates, given actual data. For instance, Figure 18.5 illustrates how a ratings table can be generated.

This model shows how the previous model, the *External Debt Rating and Spreads* example, is generated. That is, by entering the desired number of total categories for the risk ratings table and the base level (which requires calibration with actual data, and typically ranges between 1.1 and 3.0), you can develop the ratings table and determine the risk rating and credit risk shortfall, given some probability of default, recovery rate, and interest charged to a company. In some instances, the base level can be calibrated using a backcasting approach, where several base-level values are tested using various probabilities of default, and the resulting risk rating is used to benchmark against other industry standards.

Profit-Cost Analysis of New Credit

Location: www.ElsevierDirect.com (search for this book, click Companion Site button, click link in Additional Models section) Modeling Toolkit | Credit Analysis | Profit Cost Analysis of New Credit
Brief Description: Analyzes the cost and profit from a potential credit issue based on the possibilities of nonpayment by the debt holder.

INTERNAL CREDIT RISK RATING MODEL
RATING OF CREDIT RISK

Probability of Default	1.00%
Recovery Rate	25.00%
Interest Charged	7.00%

Computed Credit Shortfall Risk	0.77%
Computed Risk Rating	B

Function: CreditRiskShortfall (Probability of Default, Recovery Rate, Interest)

Assumptions for Creating of a Risk Rating Table

Total Categories	12
Base Level (Requires Calibration)	2.0000

Function: B2CreditRatingWidth (Total Categories, This Category, Base Level)

Example Internal Rating Table

Category	Width	Min	Max	Rating
1	0.0244%	0.0000%	0.0244%	AAA
2	0.0488%	0.0244%	0.0733%	AA
3	0.0977%	0.0733%	0.1709%	A
4	0.1954%	0.1709%	0.3663%	BBB
5	0.3907%	0.3663%	0.7570%	BB
6	0.7814%	0.7570%	1.5385%	B
7	1.5629%	1.5385%	3.1013%	CCC
8	3.1258%	3.1013%	6.2271%	CC
9	6.2515%	6.2271%	12.4786%	C
10	12.5031%	12.4786%	24.9817%	DDD
11	25.0061%	24.9817%	49.9878%	DD
12	50.0122%	49.9878%	100.0000%	D

Figure 18.5 Internal Credit Risk Rating Model and Risk Table Generation.

This model is used to decide if new credit should be granted to a new applicant based on the requisite costs of opening the new account, as well as other incremental costs. In addition, using the cost of funds and average time to receive payments as well as the probability of nonpayment or default (use the various probability of default models in the Modeling Toolkit to determine this), we can then determine the cost of accepting and the cost of rejecting this new line of credit, as well as the probability of breakeven (Figure 18.6). To reiterate, by using this model, a bank or credit issuing firm can decide if it is more profitable to accept or reject the application, as well as compute the probability of breakeven on this line of credit.

Illustrations in Debt Analysis

Asset-Equity Parity Model
Location: www.ElsevierDirect.com (search for this book, click Companion Site button, click link in Additional Models section) Modeling Toolkit | Debt Analysis | Asset-Equity Parity Model
Brief Description: Applies the asset-equity parity relationship to determine the market value of risky debt and its required return, as well as the market value of asset and its volatility.

CREDIT ACCEPTANCE VS. REJECTION PROFIT/COST MODEL

Inputs

Acceptance Costs

Clerical Costs Associated With Opening Account	$30
Credit Investigation Cost	$40
Collection Costs	$130
Dollars Tied Up In Receivables (Sale Price)	$100,000
Probability of Non Payment	3.00%
Incremental Cost of Production and Selling	$60,000
Average Time in Days between Sale and Payment	45
Cost of Funds	15.00%

Rejection Costs

Marginal Profit From Sale	$40,000
Probability of Payment	97.00%

Outputs

Acceptance Cost	$3,849
Rejection Cost	$38,800
Accept/Reject Credit:	ACCEPT CREDIT
Probability B/E	37.98%

Figure 18.6 Credit Acceptance and Rejection Profit and Cost Model.

This model applies the asset-equity parity assumptions, whereby given the company's book values of debt and asset and the market value of equity and its corresponding volatility, we can determine the company's market value of risky debt and the required return on the risky debt in the market and impute the market value of the company's assets and the asset's volatility. Enter the relevant inputs and click on *Compute Implied Volatility* to determine the implied volatility of the asset (Figure 18.7).

This model utilizes the basic parity assumption that the assets of a company equal any outstanding equity plus its liabilities. In publicly traded companies, the equity value and equity volatility can be computed using available stock prices, while the liabilities of the firm can be readily quantified based on financial records. However, the market value and volatility of the firm's assets are not available or easily quantified (contrary to the book value of asset, which can be readily obtained through financial records). These values are required in certain financial, options, and credit analyses and can be obtained only through this asset-equity parity model. In addition, using the equity volatility and book value of debt, we can also impute the market value of debt and the required return on risky debt.

This concept of asset-equity-options parity will be revisited later in the sections on probability of default models. Briefly, equity owners (stockholders) of a firm have the option to pay off the firm's debt to own 100% of the firm's assets. That is, assets in a public company are typically funded by debt and equity, and although debt has

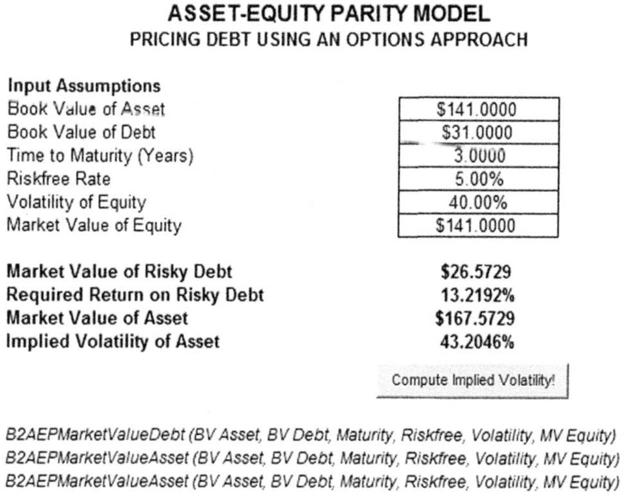

ASSET-EQUITY PARITY MODEL
PRICING DEBT USING AN OPTIONS APPROACH

Input Assumptions

Book Value of Asset	$141.0000
Book Value of Debt	$31.0000
Time to Maturity (Years)	3.0000
Riskfree Rate	5.00%
Volatility of Equity	40.00%
Market Value of Equity	$141.0000

Market Value of Risky Debt	$26.5729
Required Return on Risky Debt	13.2192%
Market Value of Asset	$167.5729
Implied Volatility of Asset	43.2046%

Compute Implied Volatility!

B2AEPMarketValueDebt (BV Asset, BV Debt, Maturity, Riskfree, Volatility, MV Equity)
B2AEPMarketValueAsset (BV Asset, BV Debt, Maturity, Riskfree, Volatility, MV Equity)
B2AEPMarketValueAsset (BV Asset, BV Debt, Maturity, Riskfree, Volatility, MV Equity)

Figure 18.7 Asset-Equity Options Model.

a higher priority for repayment (especially at default and bankruptcy situations), only equity holders can cast votes to determine the fate of the company, including the ability and option to pay off all remaining debt and own all of the firm's assets. Therefore, there is an options linkage among debt, equity, and asset levels in a company, and we can take advantage of this linkage (through some simultaneous stochastic equations modeling and optimization) to obtain the firm's market value of asset, asset volatility, market value of debt, as discussed in Chapter 14 under the probability of default section.

Cox Model on Price and Yield of Risky Debt with Mean-Reverting Rates

Location: www.ElsevierDirect.com (search for this book, click Companion Site button, click link in Additional Models section) Modeling Toolkit | Debt Analysis | Cox Model on Price and Yield of Risky Debt with Mean-Reverting Rates

Brief Description: Applies the Cox model to price risky debt and models the yield curve, assuming that interest rates are stochastic and follow mean-reverting rates.

The Cox-Ingersoll-Ross (CIR) stochastic model of mean-reverting interest rates (Figure 18.8) is used to determine the value of a zero coupon bond and to reconstruct the yield curve (term structure of interest rates). This model assumes a stochastic and mean-reverting term structure of interest rates with a rate of reversion as well as a long-run rate that the interest reverts to in time. A *Yield Curve CIR* model shown in this book is used to generate the yield curve and term structure of interest rates using this CIR model.

Such mean-reverting models imply that the underlying asset (bond or debt) is highly susceptible to fluctuations in the prevailing interest rates of the economy. To model the price of these interest-sensitive instruments, the behavior of interest rates will first need to be modeled. Interest rates are assumed to be mean-reverting—that is,

COX INGERSOLL ROSS MODEL
PRICING RISKY DEBT WITH MEAN-REVERTING INTEREST RATES

Time to Maturity of the Bond or Debt (Years)	1.0000
Risk-free Rate (Short Rate)	3.50%
Long-run Mean Rate	5.00%
Annualized Volatility of Interest Rate	20.00%
Market Price of Interest Rate Risk	5.00%
Rate of Mean Reversion	10.00%
Price of Zero Coupon Bond	**$0.9659**
Yield of Zero Coupon Bond	**3.47%**

Function: B2BondCIRBondPrice (Maturity, Riskfree, Longterm Rate, Volatility, Market Price of Risk, Rate of Reversion)
Function: B2BondCIRBondYield (Maturity, Riskfree, Longterm Rate, Volatility, Market Price of Risk, Rate of Reversion)

Sample Monte Carlo risk-simulation results when simulating the rate of mean-reversion:

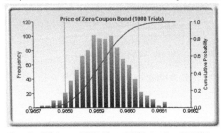 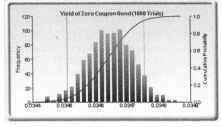

Type: Two-Tail, Lower: 0.9658, Upper: 0.9660, Certainty: 90.0000%   Type: Two-Tail, Lower: 0.0345, Upper: 0.0348, Certainty: 90.0000%

Figure 18.8 Cox Model with Underlying Mean-Reverting Interest Rates.

there is a long-run mean rate to which short-term interest rates are attracted, tends, or revert, at some rate of mean reversion. For instance, in the United States, the Federal Reserve controls interest rates in the economy (by changing the discount rate at which banks can borrow from the central bank, forcing this rate to permeate throughout to the economy; changing the required reserve ratio of bank holdings; or performing some sale or purchase of Treasury securities by the Federal Open Market Commission) in order to control the general inflation rate and economic growth. This means that there is typically a long-term economic growth rate, inflation rate, and, thus, interest rate that the Federal Reserve targets. When rates are too high, they are reduced, and vice versa, which means that interest rates, although stochastic and unpredictable in nature, are not as volatile as one would expect. This mean-reverting dampening effect is modeled here.

Finally, the interest rate volatility can be easily modeled using the Volatility models in the toolkit, and the market price of interest rate risk is the same as the market price of risk for equity. It is the prevailing interest rate for a similar type of bond or debt (with the same credit risk structure), less the risk-free rate of similar maturities.

You may also use Risk Simulator to run simulations on the inputs to determine the price and yield of debt, or to determine the input parameters such as the long-run mean rate and rate of mean reversion. Use Risk Simulator's *Statistical Analysis Tool* to determine these stochastic input parameters when calibrated on historical data. (The *Forecasting – Data Diagnostics* model has examples on how to calibrate these stochastic input parameters based on historical data.)

Debt Repayment and Amortization

Location: www.ElsevierDirect.com (search for this book, click Companion Site button, click link in Additional Models section) Modeling Toolkit | Debt Analysis | Debt Repayment and Amortization
Brief Description: Simulates interest rates on a mortgage and amortization schedule to determine the potential savings on interest payments if additional payments are made each period and when the interest rates can become variable and unknown over time.

This is an amortization model examining a debt repayment schedule. In this example, we look at a 30-year mortgage with a portion of that period based on a fixed interest rate and a subsequent period of variable rates with minimum and maximum caps. This model illustrates how the mortgage or debt is amortized and paid off over time, resulting in a final value of zero at the end of the debt's maturity (Figure 18.9). Further, this model allows for some additional periodic (monthly, quarterly, semiannually, annually) payment, which will reduce the total amount of payments, the total interest paid, and the length of time it takes to pay off the loan. Notice that, initially, the principal paid off is low but increases over time. Because of this, the initial interest portion of the loan is high but decreases over time as the principal is paid off.

As shown in Figure 18.9, the required input parameters are highlighted in boxes, and an assumption on the uncertain interest rate is set in cell D9, with a corresponding forecast cell at I12. By entering additional payments per period, you can significantly reduce the term of the mortgage (i.e., pay it off faster) and with many fewer total payments (you end up saving a lot on interest payments). A second forecast cell is set on J12 to find out the number of years it takes to pay off the loan if additional periodic payments are made.

Debt Repayment and Amortization Schedule

Mortgage at Initiation:	$550,000			Additional Payments:		$500				
Years to Maturity:	30			Once a month ▼						
Interest Rate (Fixed):	4.50%									
				Fixed Rate for the first		5		years		
Required Payment:	$2,786.77									
Variable Rate:	4.50%			*With Minimum*	*Additional*					
				Payments	*Payments*		*Savings*			
Max Rate	4.50%		Total Checks Written:	$1,003,237	$867,182		$136,055			
Likely Rate	5.50%		Total Interest Paid:	$453,237	$317,192		$136,045	22.00	years	
Min Rate	6.50%		Total Principal Paid:	$550,000	$550,000		*30 Years to payoff if paying minimum*			

Period	Start	Payment	Principal	Interest	Left	Rate	Years	Extras
1	$550,000	$2,787	$724	$2,063	$549,276	Fixed	0.08 Years	$500
2	$549,276	$2,787	$727	$2,060	$548,549	Fixed	0.17 Years	$500
3	$548,549	$2,787	$730	$2,057	$547,819	Fixed	0.25 Years	$500
4	$547,819	$2,787	$732	$2,054	$547,087	Fixed	0.33 Years	$500
5	$547,087	$2,787	$735	$2,052	$546,351	Fixed	0.42 Years	$500
6	$546,351	$2,787	$738	$2,049	$545,613	Fixed	0.5 Years	$500
7	$545,613	$2,787	$741	$2,046	$544,873	Fixed	0.58 Years	$500
8	$544,873	$2,787	$743	$2,043	$544,129	Fixed	0.67 Years	$500
9	$544,129	$2,787	$746	$2,040	$543,383	Fixed	0.75 Years	$500
10	$543,383	$2,787	$749	$2,038	$542,634	Fixed	0.83 Years	$500
11	$542,634	$2,787	$752	$2,035	$541,882	Fixed	0.92 Years	$500
12	$541,882	$2,787	$755	$2,032	$541,127	Fixed	1 Years	$500
13	$541,127	$2,787	$758	$2,029	$540,370	Fixed	1.08 Years	$500
14	$540,370	$2,787	$760	$2,026	$539,609	Fixed	1.17 Years	$500
15	$539,609	$2,787	$763	$2,024	$538,846	Fixed	1.25 Years	$500
16	$538,846	$2,787	$766	$2,021	$538,080	Fixed	1.33 Years	$500
17	$538,080	$2,787	$769	$2,018	$537,311	Fixed	1.42 Years	$500
18	$537,311	$2,787	$772	$2,015	$536,539	Fixed	1.5 Years	$500
19	$536,539	$2,787	$775	$2,012	$535,764	Fixed	1.58 Years	$500
20	$535,764	$2,787	$778	$2,009	$534,987	Fixed	1.67 Years	$500

Figure 18.9 Debt Amortization Table.

Procedure

You may either change the assumptions or keep the existing assumptions and run the simulation:

1. Click on *Risk Simulator | Change Profile,* select the *Debt Repayment and Amortization* profile, and click OK.
2. Run the simulation by clicking on *Risk Simulator | Run Simulation.*

Results Interpretation

The resulting forecast chart on the example inputs indicates that paying an additional $500 per month can potentially save the mortgage holder from $136,985 (minimum) to, at most, $200,406 (maximum), given the assumed uncertainty fluctuations of interest rates during the variable rate period. The 90% confidence level also can be obtained, meaning that 90% of the time, the total interest saved is between $145,749 and $191,192 (Figures 18.10 and 18.11).

In addition, the Payoff Year with Extra Payment forecast chart shows that given the expected fluctuations of interest rates and the additional payments made per period, there is a 90% chance that the mortgage will be paid off between 20.9 and 21.8 years, with an average of 21.37 years (mean value). The quickest payoff is 20.67 years (minimum). If interest rates are on the high end, payoff may take up to 22 years (maximum), as seen in Figures 18.12 and 18.13.

Debt Sensitivity Models

Location: www.ElsevierDirect.com (search for this book, click Companion Site button, click link in Additional Models section) Modeling Toolkit | Debt Analysis | Debt Sensitivity Models
Brief Description: Models a debt instrument's sensitivity to interest rates using duration and convexity methods, while applying various discrete and continuous discounting measures.

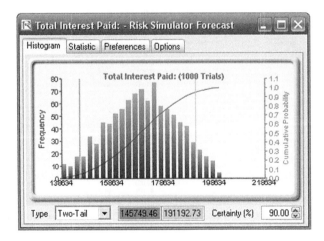

Figure 18.10 Forecast of Total Interest Paid.

Total Interest Paid: - Risk Simulator Forecast

Histogram | Statistic | Preferences | Options

Statistics	Result
Number of Trials	1000
Mean	1.690514E+005
Median	1.692578E+005
Standard Deviation	1.359216E+004
Variance	1.847468E+008
Average Deviation	1.114806E+004
Maximum	2.004062E+005
Minimum	1.369855E+005
Range	6.342076E+004
Skewness	-0.0645
Kurtosis	-0.6164
25% Percentile	1.592768E+005
75% Percentile	1.787881E+005
Percentage Error Precision at 95% Confidence	0.4983%

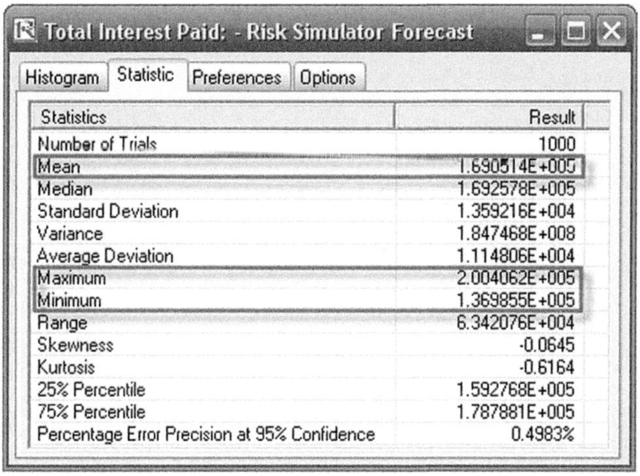

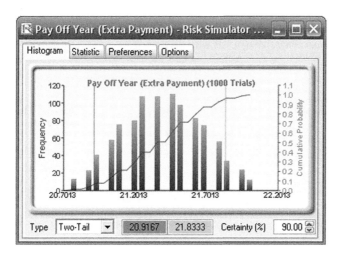

Figure 18.11 Forecast Statistics of Total Interest Paid.

Figure 18.12 Forecast of Payoff Year.

This model (Figure 18.14) is used to determine a debt's interest sensitivity while accounting for a series of cash flow payments from the debt over time (e.g., a bond's coupon payments and the final face value repayment) as interest rates are changing over time. The debt's price, yield to maturity, duration, and convexities are computed.

Duration and convexity are sensitivity measures that describe exposure to parallel shifts in the spot interest rate yield curve, applicable to individual fixed income instruments or entire fixed income portfolios. These sensitivities cannot warn of exposure to more complex movements in the spot curve, including tilts and bends,

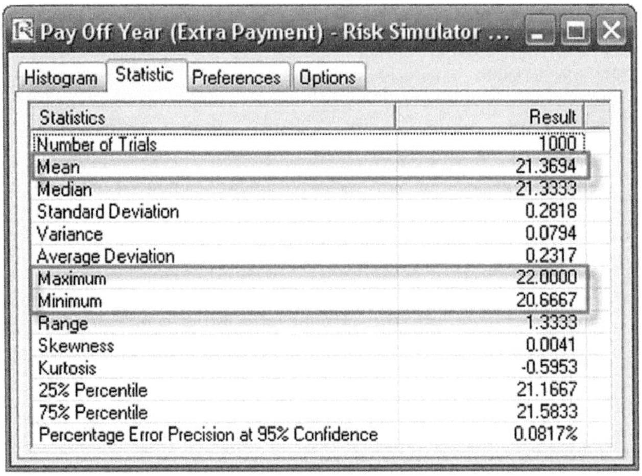

Statistics	Result
Number of Trials	1000
Mean	21.3694
Median	21.3333
Standard Deviation	0.2818
Variance	0.0794
Average Deviation	0.2317
Maximum	22.0000
Minimum	20.6667
Range	1.3333
Skewness	0.0041
Kurtosis	-0.5953
25% Percentile	21.1667
75% Percentile	21.5833
Percentage Error Precision at 95% Confidence	0.0817%

Figure 18.13 Forecast Statistics of Payoff Year.

DEBT SENSITIVITY MODELS

DURATION AND CONVEXITY ANALYSIS WITH YIELD CURVE
ANALYSIS OF INTEREST RATE SENSITIVITIES

Input Assumptions

Current Interest Rate	7.00%
Price of Bond or Debt	$1,200.00

Year	Cash Flow	Interest Rate
1.00	$100.00	5.00%
2.00	$100.00	5.00%
3.00	$100.00	5.00%
4.00	$100.00	5.00%
5.00	$1,100.00	5.00%

Results	Discrete Discounting	Continuous Discounting
PV Debt or Bond Price	$1,216.47	$1,210.23
Yield to Maturity (YTM)	0.00%	5.20%
Duration	4.2535	4.2514
Macaulay Duration	4.2480	4.2480
Modified Duration	4.0327	4.0327
Convexity	20.8013	20.8013
Convexity Using YTM	21.6495	19.7743

Figure 18.14 Debt Sensitivity Models.

only parallel shifts. The idea behind duration is simple. Suppose a portfolio has a duration measure of 2.5 years. This means that the portfolio's value will decline about 2.5% for each 1% increase in interest rates—or rise about 2.5% for each 1% decrease in interest rates. Typically, a bond's duration is positive, but exotic instruments, such as mortgage-backed securities, may have negative durations, including portfolios that short-fixed income instruments or portfolios that pay fixed for floating interest payments on an interest rate swap. Inverse floaters tend to have large positive durations. Their values change significantly for small changes in rates. Highly leveraged fixed income portfolios tend to have very large (positive or negative) durations.

While convexity summarizes the second-most significant piece of information, or the nonlinear curvature of the yield curve, duration measures the linear or first-approximation sensitivity. Duration and convexity have traditionally been used as tools for immunization or asset-liability management. To avoid exposure to parallel spot curve shifts, an organization (e.g., an insurance company or defined benefit pension plan) with significant fixed income exposures might perform duration matching by structuring assets so that their duration matches the duration of its liabilities and the two offset each other. Even more effective (but less frequently practical) is duration-convexity matching, in which assets are structured so that durations and convexities match.

The standard financial computations for duration, modified duration, and convexity are:

- Macaulay Bond Duration $= \sum_{t=1}^{n} \frac{PVCF_t}{V_B} time$

- Modified Duration $= \dfrac{Macaulay}{\left(1 + \dfrac{YTM}{number\ of\ coupons}\right)}$

- Convexity $= \dfrac{d^2 P}{di^2} = \dfrac{\sum_{t=1}^{n} \frac{CF}{(1+i)^t}(t^2 + t)}{(1+i)^2}$

where *PVCF* is the present value of cash flows (*CF*) for individual periods, *V* is the value of the bond, *time* (*t*) is the time period at which the cash flow occurs, *YTM* is the bond's yield to maturity (internal rate of return on the bond or identical interest yield by holding the bond to maturity, computed based on the value of the bond at time zero), and *i* is the interest rate used to discount and price the bond.

Merton Price of Risky Debt with Stochastic Asset and Interest

Location: www.ElsevierDirect.com (search for this book, click Companion Site button, click link in Additional Models section) Modeling Toolkit | Debt Analysis | Merton Price of Risky Debt with Stochastic Asset and Interest

Brief Description: Computes the market value of risky debt using the Merton option approach, assuming that interest rates are mean-reverting and volatile, while further assuming that the company's internal assets are also stochastic and changing over time.

The Merton model for risky debt computes the market value of debt while taking into account the book values of assets and debt in a company, as well as the volatility of interest rates and asset value over time. The interest rate is assumed to be stochastic in nature and is mean-reverting at some rate of reversion to a long-term value (Figure 18.15). Further, the model also requires as inputs the market price of risk and the correlation of the company's asset value to the market. You can set the correlation and market price of risk to zero for indeterminable conditions, while the rate of reversion and long-run interest rates can be determined and modeled using Risk Simulator's Statistical Analysis tool. Simulation on any of the inputs can also be run using Risk Simulator to determine the risk and statistical confidence of the market

MERTON MODEL OF RISKY DEBT
PRICING DEBT WITH STOCHASTIC ASSET AND STOCHASTIC INTEREST

Input Assumptions

Asset Book Value	$110.0000
Debt Book Value	$36.9940
Time to Maturity	20.00
Riskfree Rate	8.00%
Long-Run Interest Rate	8.00%
Volatility of Interest Rate	16.00%
Volatility of Asset	16.00%
Rate of Reversion of Interest Rate	15.00%
Market Price of Risk	1.00%
Correlation (Market to Asset)	0.00

Price of Debt   **$11.4392**

Figure 18.15 Merton Model of Risky Debt Assuming Stochastic Interest and Asset Movements.

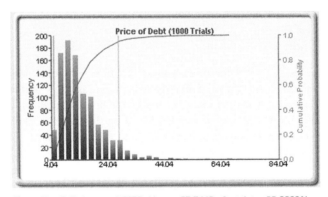

Type: Two-Tail, Lower: 4.9892, Upper: 27.7442, Certainty: 90.0000%

Figure 18.16 Forecast Distribution of Price of Risky Debt.

price of risky debt (Figure 18.16). This model is similar in nature to the Cox mean-reverting model, where both assume that the underlying debt instrument is highly sensitive to fluctuations in interest rates. The difference is that this Merton model accounts for stochastic interest rates as well as stochastic asset movements and that the market is used to calibrate the movements of the asset value (the correlation between asset and market returns is a required input).

19 Building Integrated Exposure Systems

Chapter Outline

Credit Engineering for Bankers. DOI: 10.1016/B978-0-12-378585-5.10019-3

Global exposure risk monitoring systems (GES) are the core of risk control and portfolio management, facilitating loan approvals and providing data for a wide range of credit-related products.[1] Bank managers use exposure systems to set facility limits; determine credit policy review targets and controls; and make capital allocation, pricing, and portfolio decisions. From the Basel Committee's perspective, a common cause of bank closings included failures attributed to the debt crisis, poorly managed loan portfolios, and incompetent credit risk management (including auditing and loan valuation standards):

> *Failure to identify and recognize deterioration in credit quality in a timely manner can aggravate and prolong the problem.*[2] *Unless deterioration is identified and losses recognized by the establishment of adequate allowances or charge-offs in a timely manner, a bank might well persist in highly risky lending strategies or practices and thus accumulate significant loan losses, possibly resulting in failure. From a safety and soundness perspective, therefore, it is important that both exposure data gathering capabilities and accounting principles capture and reflect realistic measurements of assets, liabilities, equity, derivative contracts, off-balance sheet commitments, and related profits and losses....Insufficient disclosure as the result of poor exposure information systems increases chances that misleading or wrong information is passed along to senior officials setting exposure limits.*

GES Structure

Global risk monitoring can be directorially structured by partitioning systems into three responsibility tiers: customer responsibility, family responsibility, and facility responsibility. Data flow begins at the customer (unit) relationship level and combines at the "family level" (parent and subsidiaries/affiliates). The process is completed at the senior coordination level—senior management, actually—where family, industry, and cross-border facility limits are set.

---

[1] Committee of European Banking Supervisors, *Guidelines on the Application of the Supervisory Review Process under Pillar 2 (CP03 revised), IG 18, 25,* January 25, 2006: "There should be effective internal control systems and reliable information systems covering all significant activities of the institution: (a) a critical component of an institution's activities is the establishment and maintenance of management information systems that cover the full range of its activities. This information is typically provided through both electronic and nonelectronic means. Institutions must be particularly aware of the organizational and internal control requirements related to processing information in an electronic form, and of the necessity to have an adequate audit trail. Management decision making could be adversely affected by unreliable or misleading information provided by systems that are poorly designed and controlled; (b) information systems, including those that hold and use data in electronic form, must be secure, independently monitored, and supported by adequate contingency arrangements."

[2] The Basel Committee on Bank Supervision.

First Tier: Customer Responsibility (Coordination) Units

First tier customer responsibility begins with relationship bankers. Line officers file comprehensive data forms on new facilities and loan renewals to ensure that no crucial information is omitted; otherwise, loan tracking will not perform efficiently. Loan information required by a large money center bank, for example, centers around the following categories of information.

Basic Information

1. Name of relationship manager
2. Location/division/credit area
3. Statements received
4. Memo distributed
5. Maximum exposure, including derivatives and letter of credit exposures
6. Amount of facility requested and facility type
7. Outstandings
8. Terms
9. Last credit committee review, including date

Company Background

1. Customer
2. Address
3. Form of organization
4. Established
5. Customer since
6. Name and address or parent (if any)
7. Name and address of guarantor (if any)
8. Industry code (SIC)
9. Geographic market area
10. Market strategy/niche
11. Major competitors
12. Industry/economic summary
13. Assessment of principal customers, suppliers, and product lines
14. Competition
15. Problems to which this company is most vulnerable
16. Fiscal sales and profits: dollar and percentage change from last year
17. Key "payback" ratios—cash flow coverage and leverage
18. Management summary principals/officers
19. S&P (or similar) debt rating
20. Name and address of accountant
21. Accounting changes or qualifications
22. Fiscal date

Other Information Supporting Facility

1. Guarantors (if any)
2. Collateral (if any)

3. Date previous credit review filed
4. Previous risk grade
5. Loan pricing
6. Risk adjusted return on capital (RAROC)
7. Documentation on file and updated
8. Subordination agreements, uniform commercial code filings, and so on
9. Total bank lines: $
10. Lead bank
11. Other lenders
12. Present rating
13. Recommended rating
14. Report including Dun and Bradstreet, TRW, and litigation records
15. Trade experience

Besides optional data banks chosen to include information as noted in the preceding lists, the Federal Reserve established minimum documentation required on bank examination reports. The following information (data) is normally entered onto computer-based loan review systems:[3]

1. Name and location of borrower
2. Notation if the borrower is an insider or a related interest of an insider
3. Business or occupation
4. Purpose of loan
5. Repayment source
6. Collateral summary and value
7. Loan officer assigned to the credit and internal rating of the credit
8. Total commitment and total outstanding balances
9. Examination date
10. Past due/nonaccrual status
11. Amounts previously classified
12. Loan disposition (pass, special mention, or adverse classification)
13. Rationale for examiner's conclusions (preferably in bullet form)
14. Name or initials of the examiner reviewing the credit
15. Any significant comments by, or commitments from, management (including management's disagreement with the disposition of the loan, if applicable)
16. Any noted documentation exceptions or loan administration policy or procedural weaknesses and any contravention of law, regulation, or policy

Second Tier: Family Responsibility (Coordination) Unit

Relationship managers transmit the information gathered (per the preceding categories: basic, company data, and other information supporting facilities) to the head office in real time—second tier. The head office group, typically referred to as Family Responsibility (Coordination) Unit, pools/decomposes family exposures (parent or holding company, subsidiaries, and affiliates). For purposes of establishing an aggregate family, total (credit) exposure is expressed as *primary* and *settlement*.

---

[3] Memo to the officer in charge of supervision at each Federal Reserve Bank, April 24, 1996. Subject: Minimum Documentation Standards for Loan Line Sheets; Richard Spillenkothen, Director.

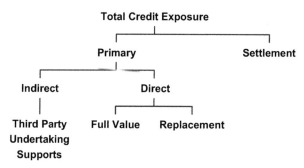

Figure 19.1 GES Perspectives: Total Credit Exposure.

Primary exposures include *direct* exposures and *indirect* exposures, with direct exposures further categorized into *full value* and *replacement* (Figure 19.1).[4]

Primary/Direct/Full Value Exposures

Examples of full value exposures include, but are not restricted to, the following:

- *Own paper borrowing:* Short-term unsecured borrowings not falling under a line of credit.
- *Lines of credit:* Short-term lines usually established with a bank letter stating the approved advances and maximum amount allowed.
- *Joint credit lines:* The parent, together with each of its subsidiaries, may borrow singly or collectively so the aggregate amount of loans outstanding does not exceed the confirmed line.
- *Overlines:* A line of credit granted to a correspondent bank's customer.
- *Revolving commitments:* Legally binding obligations to extend credit for which a fee or other compensation is received. The credit risk of loan commitments stems from the possibility that the creditworthiness of the customer will deteriorate between the time when the commitment is made and when the loan takedown occurs.
- *Term loans:* Nonrevolving commitments with maturities beyond one year. These loans generally contain periodic (annual, semiannual, or quarterly) amortization provisions.
- *Check or business credit:* Credit services provided by three basic methods: overdraft system, cash reserve system, and special draft system.
- *Commercial letters of credit (L/Cs):* A contractual agreement between an issuing bank on behalf of one of its customers, authorizing an advising or confirming bank to make payment to the beneficiary.
- *Acceptances:* Exposures arising when L/Cs mature but have not been retired.
- *Discounted bills or notes receivable (B/Rs):* Loans are reduced at the time of each collection and liquidated when all the B/Rs are collected.
- *Construction loans:* Loans for construction projects for a designated time period, with repayment contingent on the borrower obtaining permanent financing.
- *Secured loans:* Factoring, loans secured with accounts receivables, inventory, or marketable securities.

---

[4] This section serves as an example; keep in mind that GES perspectives can differ.

Primary/Direct/Replacement

Replacement exposure (or fractional exposure) represents the unhedged cost of replacing defaulted parties when banks guarantee performance under derivative contracts. In a manner of speaking, replacement exposure represents maximum loss possible on these contracts. For example, consider a simple (plain-vanilla) interest rate swap. There are two ways of looking at default risk: actual exposure and potential exposure. *Actual exposure* is the measure of the loss if the counterparty were to default. It is based on the movement in swap market rates between the inception of the agreement and the current date. *Potential exposure* is based on a forecast of how market conditions might change between the present and the swap's maturity date, including in some manner the probability of default (PD) by the counterparty. Exposures on derivatives and similar contracts are managed so they generally net out at day's end.

With traditional instruments—loans, typically—the amount the counterparty is obliged to repay is the full or principal amount of the instrument. For these instruments, the amount at risk equals the principal amount. Derivatives are different. Because they derive value from an underlying asset or index, credit risk is not equal to the principal amount of the trade but, rather, to the cost of replacing the contract if the counterparty defaults. This replacement value fluctuates over time and is made up of current replacement and potential replacement costs.

Others dealing in derivatives champion Monte Carlo simulation, probability analysis, and option valuation models as the best ways to derive potential replacement cost. Their analysis generally involves modeling the volatility of underlying variables and their effect on the value of the derivative contracts. These methods, drawing on data stored within a GES warehouse (discussed later), can be used to derive average or "expected" exposure and maximum or "worst-case" exposure.

Primary/Indirect/Third Party Undertaking, Supports

Indirect exposures include loans or obligations endorsed, guaranteed, or subject to repurchase agreements. Bank guarantees might be in the form of standby L/Cs or commercial paper backup lines. They may be negotiated to cover performance under construction contracts or serve as assurance that obligations will be honored under warranties.

Total Credit Exposure/Settlements

Settlement risk is the risk that a settlement in a transfer system fails to take place as expected. Three examples of settlement risk are foreign exchange, securities settlements, and over-the-counter derivatives. The risk that transactions cannot be settled can affect almost any type of asset (and instrument) requiring a transfer from one party to another. Settlement risk figures most prominently in currency trading because the daily settlement flows in foreign exchange clearing dwarfs just about any other exposure risk.

Since each trade involves two or more payments, daily settlement flows are likely to amount, in aggregate, to a multiple of this figure, especially on standard expiration dates. Significantly, a report prepared by the Committee on Payment and Settlement Systems (CPSS) of the central banks of the G-10 countries maintains that a bank's maximum foreign exchange settlement exposure could equal, or even surpass, the amount receivable for three days' worth of trades, so, at any point in time, the amount at risk to even a single counterparty *could exceed a bank's capital.*

Third Tier: Facility Responsibility (Portfolio and Risk Management)

The prime GES objective is to provide senior management with timely, relevant, and accurate information that is necessary to monitor and manage risk and make informed strategic decisions. Strategic decision making takes a long, rather than a day-to-day, view and is aimed at funding requirements, capital adequacy, management policies and procedures, marketing objectives, operations, and integration of asset deployment, which is, in reality, the portfolio risk management process. The elements of a portfolio risk-management process are setting portfolio objectives and risk tolerance limits; maintaining a portfolio management information system; formulating portfolio segmentation and risk diversification objectives (GES is central to accomplishing this objective); analyzing loans originated by other lenders; establishing aggregate policy and underwriting exceptions systems; subjecting portfolios to stress tests; maintaining independent controls; and analyzing portfolio risk/reward trade-offs. We review select GES and strategic decision-making topics in the remainder of the chapter.

GES and Loan Concentrations

Loans within the system are grouped so exposures with similar risk characteristics are combined. In addition to establishing strategic objectives for loan portfolios, senior management is charged with setting risk limits on lending activities. Exposure limits factor in historical loss experience, ability to absorb losses, and desired portfolio risk-adjusted return on capital. Exposure limits may be set in various ways, individually and in combination.[5] For example, limits may be set to individual loans, to geographical regions, to the volume of a particular segment of the loan portfolio, or to the structure of the portfolio as a whole. Exposure limits are set on loans to specific industries—for example, rapid growth, thinly capitalized industries—or on certain segments of the portfolio that correlate to optimal efficient (portfolio) frontiers. Risk concentrations are arguably the single most important cause of major problems in banks:[6]

1. A risk concentration is any single exposure or group of exposures with the potential to produce losses large enough (relative to a bank's capital, total assets, or overall risk level) to threaten a bank's health or ability to maintain its core operations.
2. Risk concentrations can arise in a bank's assets, liabilities, or off-balance sheet items through the execution or processing of transactions (either product or service) or through a combination of exposures across these broad categories. Because lending is the primary

---

[5] Comptroller of the Currency, Administrator of National Banks, *Loan Portfolio Management, Comptroller's Handbook,* April 1998.
[6] Ibid.

activity of most banks, credit risk concentrations are often the most material risk concentrations within a bank.

3. Credit risk concentrations, by their nature, are based on common or correlated risk factors that, in times of stress, have an adverse effect on the creditworthiness of each of the individual counterparties making up the concentration. Such concentrations are not addressed in the Pillar 1 capital charge for credit risk.

4. Banks should have in place effective internal policies, systems, and controls to identify, measure, monitor, and control their credit risk concentrations. Banks should explicitly consider the extent of their credit risk concentrations in their assessment of capital adequacy under Pillar 2. These policies should cover the different forms of credit risk concentrations to which a bank may be exposed. Concentrations include the following:
   a. Significant exposures to an individual counterparty or group of related counterparties. In many jurisdictions, supervisors define a limit for exposures of this nature, commonly referred to as a large exposure limit. Banks might also establish an aggregate limit for the management and control of all of its large exposures as a group.
   b. Credit exposures to counterparties in the same economic sector or geographic region.
   c. Credit exposures to counterparties whose financial performance is dependent on the same activity or commodity.
   d. Indirect credit exposures arising from a bank's CRM activities (e.g., exposure to a single collateral type or to credit protection provided by a single counterparty).

5. A bank's framework for managing credit risk concentrations should be clearly documented and should include a definition of the credit risk concentrations relevant to the bank and how these concentrations and their corresponding limits are calculated. Limits should be defined in relation to a bank's capital, total assets, or, where adequate measures exist, its overall risk level.

6. A bank's management should conduct periodic stress tests of its major credit risk concentrations and review the results of those tests to identify and respond to potential changes in market conditions that could adversely impact the bank's performance.

7. In the course of their activities, supervisors should assess the extent of a bank's credit risk concentrations, how they are managed, and the extent to which the bank considers them in its internal assessment of capital adequacy under Pillar 2. Such assessments should include reviews of the results of a bank's stress tests. Supervisors should take appropriate actions.

GES and Assessment of Capital Adequacy

Capital adequacy levels are tracked by exposure systems and reviewed by senior management to ensure that capital is appropriate for the nature and scale of a bank's business. Internal and outside auditors also consider the extent by which banks provide for unexpected events by setting appropriate capital levels. Basel's position is that capital ratios should be backed by enough (and accurate!) information so regulators are not faced with serious (Basel II) Pillar 2 issues. Banks are classified as "adequately capitalized" if they meet Basel requirements, but additional distinctions are made among levels of capital. Ratios implicitly or explicitly linked to capital adequacy include the following:

1. Return on assets
2. Return on equity

3. Loan loss coverage
4. Net charge-offs to loans
5. Equity capital to assets
6. Valuation reserve to loans
7. Ratio of provision for loan losses to net charge-offs
   a. This indicates whether provisions are in line with actual charge-offs.
8. Ratio of nonperforming assets to total loans and other real estate loans
   a. This ratio indicates the proportion of total loans in default and the amount of real estate that had to be foreclosed and assumed. Some banks do not include loans until they are 90 days or even more in default.
9. Ratio of long-term subordinated debt to total capital accounts
   a. For "all insured commercial banks," the ratio is very low, since usually large banks sell these debt issues.
10. Earnings per share
11. Ratio of cash and U.S. government securities to assets and deposits
12. Ratio of capital accounts and equity accounts to assets and deposits
13. Ratio of capital accounts to loans (risk assets)

Liquidity Concerns

GES is an integral part of sound funds (liquidity) control, helping to ensure that liquidity requirements are continuously monitored. Thus, senior management can then take corrective action under preestablished guidelines:[7]

1. Limits on the loan to deposit ratio
2. Limits on the loan to capital ratio
3. General limits on the relationship between anticipated funding needs and available sources for meeting those needs (e.g., the ratio of anticipated needs/primary sources shall not exceed a certain percent)
4. Quantification of primary sources for meeting funding needs
5. Limits on the dependence on individual customers or market segments for funds in liquidity position calculations
6. Flexible limits on the minimum/maximum average maturity for different categories of liabilities (e.g., the average maturity of negotiable certificates of deposit shall not be less than a preordained period)
7. Minimum liquidity provision to be maintained to sustain operations while necessary longer-term adjustments are made

Customer Relationships and Marketing

Customer information databanks include outstandings under credit lines, loan high points, fees paid for cash management services, average deposit balances, outstanding L/Cs and acceptances, profitability analyses, and affiliated data such as customers' personal loans and investments. The immediate benefits derived from information

---

[7] Federal Reserve Bank.

systems are obvious to lenders preparing client calls: Bank customers are alert to bankers taking the time to become familiar with their business. Clients exhort lenders to provide real-time information that is *accessible on laptops* and not just on loans serviced but on the aggregate account relationship, often globally. And just think: Only a short time ago, lenders had to rifle through paper files or ask colleagues in other departments to obtain customer information.

GES and Disclosure to Outsiders

Banks are, of course, charged with proper disclosure to certain outsiders, mainly regulators and auditors of impaired and past due loans. Examples of important disclosure include, but are not restricted to, the following:[8]

1. Information dealing with accounting policies and methods used to document loans and allowance for impairment
2. Disclosure regarding methods used to determine specific along with general allowances and key assumptions
3. Information on significant concentrations of credit risk
4. Loan balances when interest accruals in accordance with the terms of the original loan agreement have ceased due to deterioration in credit quality
5. Reconciliations of movements in the allowance for loan impairment ("continuity schedule") showing separately various types of allowances
6. Balances and other information when loans have been restructured
7. Contractual obligations with respect to recourse arrangements and the expected losses under those arrangements

Exception Reports

In addition to constituents forming the foundation for sound lending policies, banks often place in service GES processes that target exceptions to that policy. Before a bank grants credit, GES source information, reports, established line limits, and a host of other credit communiqués are disseminated at appropriate levels. If requisite information is missing or loan data systems are incapable of providing management with enough information and a loan is granted nonetheless, examiners will assuredly cite the "guilty" party.

Regulatory Reporting and GES

Submitting accurate, complete reports to regulators is serious business. Accordingly, regulators expect banks to develop quality systems and procedures required to prepare accurate detailed regulatory reports and maintain clear, concise records with emphasis on documenting adjustments.[9]

---

[8] Federal Reserve Bank.

[9] Exposures arising from new bank product are automatically updated on advanced GES in real time.

Consolidated Financial Statements for Bank Holding Companies (FR Y-9C)

- The FR Y-9C is the Consolidated Financial Statements for Bank Holding Companies report. In general, the panel consists of all domestic bank holding companies with total consolidated assets of $500 million or more and all multibank holding companies with debt outstanding to the general public or engaged in certain nonbanking activities. The Y-9C is filed quarterly as of the last calendar day of March, June, September, and December.

Parent Company Only Financial Statements for Large Bank Holding Companies (FR Y-9LP)

- The FR Y-9LP report is the Parent Company Only Financial Statements for Large Bank Holding Companies report. This report is filed by all domestic bank holding companies that file the FR Y-9C. If the top-tiered bank holding company files the FR Y-9C, then each bank holding company in a multitiered organization must also file a separate FR Y-9LP. The Y-9LP is filed quarterly as of the last calendar day of March, June, September, and December.

Parent Company Only Financial Statements for Small Bank Holding Companies (FR Y-9SP)

- The FR Y-9SP is the Parent Company Only Financial Statements for Small Bank Holding Companies report. The panel consists of all domestic bank holding companies with consolidated assets of less than $500 million and with only one subsidiary bank and multibank holding companies with consolidated assets of less than $500 million, without debt outstanding to the general public and not engaged in certain nonbanking activities. This report is filed semiannually at the end of June and December.

Bank Holding Company Performance Report

- The Bank Holding Company Performance Report (BHCPR) is designed to assist financial analysts and bank examiners in determining a bank holding company's financial condition and performance based on financial statements, comparative ratios, trend analyses, and percentile ranks relative to its peers. It is a computer-generated report of current and historical financial information produced quarterly for top-tier bank holding companies with consolidated assets of $500 million or more. The BHCPR is calculated for top-tier multibank holding companies engaged in a nonbank activity involving financial leverage or engaged in credit extending activities or with outstanding debt to the general public. This report is filed quarterly as of the last calendar day of March, June, September, and December.

Report of Assets and Liabilities of U.S. Branches and Agencies of Foreign Banks (FFIEC 002)

- The FFIEC 002 is the Report of Assets and Liabilities of U.S. Branches and Agencies of Foreign Banks. This report is filed quarterly as of the last calendar day of March, June, September, and December; however, supervisory agencies reserve the right to specify an alternative date at their option.

GES and Reports to the Board of Directors

The bank should establish an adequate system for monitoring and reporting risk exposures and assessing how the bank's changing risk profile affects the need for capital. The bank's senior management or board of directors should, on a regular basis, receive reports on the bank's risk profile and capital needs. These reports should allow senior management to do the following:

- Evaluate the level and trend of material risks and their effect on capital levels
- Evaluate the sensitivity and reasonableness of key assumptions used in the capital assessment measurement system
- Determine that the bank holds sufficient capital against the various risks and is in compliance with established capital adequacy goals
- Assess its future capital requirements based on the bank's reported risk profile and make necessary adjustments to the bank's strategic plan accordingly[10]

The board generally approves the *Annual Schedule for Loan Review* during the first meeting of each year. The schedule documents loan size, structure, performance, and type of loan; borrower affiliations; and portfolio concentrations. Information must be complete enough to enable the board to draw conclusions concerning the portfolio's quality along with the capital adequacy needed to cushion unexpected losses. The schedule for loan review allows sufficient time to prepare reports so information gained from the loan review is available to management. Let's review other GES actualized and accounting reports that bank board of directors typically address:[11]

1. A monthly statement of balance condition and statement of income. Those statements, according to regulators, should be in reasonable detail and should be compared to the prior month, the same month of a prior year, and to the budget. The directors should receive explanations for all large variances, which is very difficult to obtain without proper information systems.
2. Monthly statements of changes in all capital and reserve accounts. These statements should detail, again, variances.
3. Investment reports that group the securities by classifications; reflect the book value, market value, and yield; and provide a summary of purchases and sales.
4. Loan reports, which list significant past due loans, trends in delinquencies, rate reductions, non-income-producing loans, and large new loans granted since the last report.
5. Audit and examination reports. Deficiencies in those reports should produce a prompt and efficient response from the board. The reports reviewed and actions taken should be reflected in the minutes of the board of director's meetings.
6. A full report of all new executive officer borrowing at any bank.
7. A monthly listing of type and amount of borrowing by the bank.
8. An annual presentation of bank insurance coverage.

---

[10] "Core Principles for Effective Banking Supervision," Basel Committee on Banking Supervision (September 1997), and "Core Principles Methodology," Basel Committee on Banking Supervision (October 1999).

[11] Federal Reserve Bank, *Duties and Responsibilities of Directors: Examination Procedures.*

9. All correspondence addressed to the board of directors from the Federal Reserve and any other source.
10. A monthly analysis of the bank's liquidity position.
11. An annual projection of the bank's capital needs.
12. A listing of any new litigation and a status report on existing litigation and potential exposure.

Cross-Border Exposure Reporting

The expansion of international lending has made an analysis of country risk an essential element in the overall evaluation of portfolio risk and the capital assigned to protect it. Evaluating international exposures/concentrations requires lots of attention because of the possibility that adverse economic, social, or political developments in a country may prevent that country, its businesses, and other local borrowers from making timely payment of interest or principal to cross-border creditors. A constituent of country risk is "transfer risk," which arises when borrowers incur debt denominated in currencies of other countries. Government policies, general economic conditions, and changes in the international environment may prevent borrowers from obtaining foreign currencies needed to service debt. Whatever the cause, foreign currency may not be sufficiently available to permit the government and other entities of a country to service foreign debt.

Exposure Information Systems: Design

Money center banks employ robust exposure information systems that tick both around the clock and around the world. With few exceptions, officers and staff have little idea of how these recursive algorithms fit together, let alone how raw loan data is mined, warehoused, sorted, and filtered throughout the organization. (So much for JP Morgan Chase's GES—a wonderfully encyclopedic chain of systems, albeit well beyond this chapter's scope.) Nevertheless, perfectly acceptable loan exposure models can be built around a body of applications, procedures, and rules easily obtainable from the existing computer-technological literature.

Let's begin by defining the control factors required in the installation and maintenance of an exposure information system. Controls over information systems and their attendant technology can be categorized as general and application. *General controls* are controls over a computer system that, it is hoped, ensure its smooth operation. For example, general controls include backup systems and recovery capabilities, changes in software design and updates, maintenance procedures, and access security controls. *Application controls* are programmed steps within software applications and other manual procedures that control the processing of GES transactions. Banks have choices designing several different data systems, some of which follow—but by no means form the complete picture.

Data Architecture

Data architecture is a design completed early in a project that encompasses (but does not necessarily detail) all aspects of the finished product and includes the following:

- A description of the credit-related, exposure-related problem(s) the system is intended to address
- Local and global (bankwide) objectives, constraints, and critical success factors for the system
- Project participants and the role of each participant: relationship bankers, family unit responsibility, and senior level facility approvals and portfolio management described earlier
- Major system components and the interfaces, connections, or communication paths among the components
- Anticipated GES system enhancements, migration paths, and modifications
- The cadre required for developing the system on schedule and maintaining it over the long term

Data collection and management tasks present the single greatest Basel II challenge. To ensure a solid foundation for the new support systems needed to support the revised and new credit risk guidelines, financial institutions will see paybacks from developing a robust functional architecture. Here, we outline in brief several subsystems that the functional architecture for credit risk should have.

Data Supply Infrastructure

The new Capital Accord calls for one common data infrastructure to collect, aggregate, validate, and reconcile enterprise-wide credit data. Some of the requirements that this credit data architecture must satisfy include product coverage, building block, and risk mitigation data.

Exposure Computation

The Credit Exposure Module will have to be built on the common credit data infrastructure. Banks using the Advanced Internal Ratings Based (IRB) approach can supply their own exposure at default (EAD) estimates.

Risk Mitigation

Some of the techniques and mechanisms that Basel II recognizes for credit risk mitigation include netting, guarantees, credit derivatives, and collateral. Support for both on- and off-balance netting needs to be provided. Guarantees and credit derivatives and their risk transfer effects should be modeled as given in the new Accord. Finally, the collateral module should have a mechanism of applying pools of collaterals to pools of facilities. It should be flexible enough to define the eligibility criteria of various collateral types and the application of haircuts based on volatility of collateral value, maturity mismatches, currency translation risks, and exposure value volatility.

Ratings Allocation

The ratings allocation module will have to manage and store risk ratings for all three approaches[12] and also for purposes of regulatory audit under Pillar II. It should provide support for multiple ratings (internal and external) per obligor, per issue, and per country. PD, whether internally derived or externally acquired, must be captured for each rating grade or for specific obligors and facilities. User-defined logic needs to be supported in order to select the correct rating bucket in the event of multiple ratings and, thus, to determine the appropriate PD.

Risk Weight and Capital Computation

This module should provide risk-weighted assets on every exposure on a standalone basis after the application of adjustments for credit mitigation. It should support inputs from credit risk models and adjustments using collateral, credit derivatives, guarantees, and netting arrangements.

Credit Capital Reporting Facility

The solution must have a reporting infrastructure with a complete range of web-based reporting tools that will allow risk analysis to be performed along multiple dimensions. Furthermore, the reporting infrastructure must be flexible enough to support multiple reporting technologies and user reporting requirements.

Data Warehousing

A data warehouse is architecture for organizing data: a subject-oriented, integrated, time-variant, nonvolatile collection of data in support of information systems. A data warehouse stores tactical information answering "Who?" and "What?" questions. A query submitted to a data warehouse might be "What were aggregate construction loan outstandings between February 3 and April 14 for the 10 largest branches in the third lending district?" Typically, data warehouse systems contain programs that feed data from exposure positions through the bank (the global exposure environment). Three attributes of data warehouses are time-series data, data administration, and systems architecture:

1. *Time-series data:* A bank's data warehouse will support analysis of loan trends over time and compare current versus historical data.
2. *Data administration:* Another critical factor is senior management commitment to maintenance of the quality of exposure data. Data administrators—for example, unit family responsibility—proactively manage how data is applied in tracking family exposures.
3. *Systems architecture:* Databases should be able to retrieve large sets of aggregate and historical data within a quick response time, as mentioned earlier. A defining characteristic of data warehousing is separation of operational and decision support functionality.

---

[12] Recall from Chapter Ten that regulations specify that capital assigned against specific exposures is computed using one of three approaches: *standardized approach, foundation internal ratings-based (IRB) approach,* and *advanced IRB approach.*

By separating these two very different processing patterns, the data warehouse architecture enables both operational and decision support applications to focus on what they do best and, therefore, provide better performance and functionality.

Data Mining

While some institutions have constructed large data warehouses that hold vast amounts of data, database solutions are often buried under mounds of data/statistics. Data mining technology is used to unlock the intelligence hidden in the databases by making predictions such as forecasting "family" exposures or by providing raw data senior bankers use to set guidelines on, for example, exposure limits, limits on loan to deposit ratios, limits on loan to capital ratios, or general limits on the relationship between anticipated funding needs and funding sources. If banks really expect to get good paybacks from the large investments that are being made in creating data warehouses or data marts (see later in this chapter), they may need to turn to data mining technology for effective database solutions.

Characteristics associated with a data mining system include the following:

- *Response speed:* A major factor in any GES—the time it takes for the system to complete analysis or submit data at a desired level of accuracy. *Real time* is standard response speed, not the exception.
- *Compactness:* For smaller banks facing budget constraints, an exposure system's compactness can be a key budgetary issue. Compactness refers to how small bytewise the system can function without compromising portfolio objectives. In addition, compactness means the ease with which the system can be encoded into a compact portable format, whether embedded in a spreadsheet, coded into a specific computer language like Visual Basic, or carved on a silicon chip. If a system is too "bulky" to easily embed itself into a format that makes it usable where and when needed, the system itself may not be very useful.
- *Flexibility:* Another concern GES designers face—ease with which the relationships among the variables or their domains can be changed or the goals of the system modified.
- *Embeddability:* The ease with which the bank's exposure system can be coupled with the infrastructure of the organization, particularly when banks merge or divest operations. After a reorganization or merger, for example, a formally localized system may be drafted as a component within a larger system or form part of other databases. In this latter case, the localized system must be able to communicate with other components within the larger infrastructure. If the original system was outsourced, it may contain proprietary hardware/software that could result in time delays or the additional cost of renegotiated license agreements.
- *Friendliness:* Related to embeddability and tolerance of noise—ease of use, referring to how complicated a GES's mining appears to users, from line officers to senior bankers. A mining system's tolerance for data noise is a measure of its overall proficiency and accuracy.
- *Tolerance for complexity:* The degree to which a system is affected by interactions among various components of the process—for example, the prodigious GES information network. Complex processes involve many, often nonlinear, interactions between variables. A quintessential example is default prediction involving a host of nonlinear systematic and unsystematic factors: industry growth/decline rates, macroeconomic factors, financial and operating leverage, market demographics, and so on. These variables interact in complex ways, which is why default prediction is high art and science, often requiring the service of specialists like Moody's KMV.

On-Line Analytical Processing

In contrast to a data warehouse, *on-line analytical processing* (OLAP) takes a multidimensional view of aggregate data to provide quick access to strategic information for further analysis. It is a breed of software technology that allows users to gain insight from information transformed from raw data into real dimensionality.

A data warehouse stores and manages data for data access, whereas OLAP metamorphoses warehouse data into tactical information. It ranges from basic navigation and browsing (often known as "slice and dice") to calculations to more serious analyses such as time series and complex modeling. One important characteristic is multidimensional analysis: analysis reaching beyond conventional two-dimensional scrutiny to different dimensions of the same data, thus allowing for analyses across boundaries. For example, one possible query coming from a credit area VP might be "What is the effect on the covariance—family exposure—with respect to the general loan portfolio if operating segment "A" reduced its outstanding loan by $45 million, while the portfolio's standard deviation increased by "X" basis points?" Or from a producer's perspective, "What will be the change in widget production cost if metal prices increased by $.25/pound and transportation costs went down by $.15/mile?"

OLAP analytical and navigational activities include, but are not limited to, the following:

- Calculations and modeling applied across dimensions, through hierarchies, and/or across members
- Trend analysis over sequential time periods
- Slicing subsets for on-screen viewing
- Drill-down to deeper levels of consolidation
- Reach-through to underlying detail data
- Rotation to new dimensional comparisons in the viewing area

Data Marts

A *data mart* is a simple form of a data warehouse that locks onto a single subject (or functional area), such as accountants in metropolitan district XYZ who rendered clean opinions on deals that turned out bad, or the number of loan facilities Mary Smith approved this quarter over $4 million. Data marts are often built and controlled by a single department within an organization. Given its single-subject focus, a data mart typically draws data from limited sources. The information flow could come from internal operational systems, a central data warehouse, or external data. A data warehouse, in contrast, deals with multiple subject areas and is typically implemented and controlled by a central organizational unit, such as the Unit Family Coordinators reviewed earlier. Typically, a data warehouse assembles data from multiple source systems.

Data marts are generally smaller and less complex than data warehouses, so they are typically easier to build and maintain. Table 19.1 summarizes the basic differences between a data warehouse and a data mart.

Table 19.1 Differences Between a Data Warehouse and a Data Mart

	Data Warehouse	Data Mart
Realm	Senior level loan risk Management—global	Small bank letters of credit department
Fields	Multiple	Single field/subject
Data Sources	Numerous	Sparse
Normal Size	100 gigabytes to over a trillion bytes	Less than 100 gigabytes
Time to Realization	Months to years	Weeks to months

The three types of data marts are *dependent*, *independent*, and *hybrid*. Categorization is based primarily on the data source feeding into the data mart. Dependent data marts draw data from a central data warehouse that has already been created. Independent data marts, in contrast, are stand-alone systems built by drawing data directly from operational or external sources of data or both. Hybrid data marts can draw data from operational systems or data warehouses.

A dependent data mart allows an operating unit—say, a local bank's Department "D"—to combine its data in one data warehouse, providing all the advantages that arise from centralization. An independent data mart can be created without the use of a central data warehouse to, say, smaller units within department "D." A hybrid data mart allows Department "D" to combine input from sources other than a data warehouse. This capability could be useful if the department required ad hoc integration—for example, if a new loan product were added to the Department "D" product mix.

Neural Networks

A neural network is a statistical technique that calculates weights (score points) for predictor characteristics (such as age and income) by self-learning from data examples (such as good and bad loans). It can be trained to detect fraud by reviewing examples of good and fraudulent transactions on a bank's portfolio. Banks can set different thresholds on the transaction to determine the type and severity of the follow-up action they will take on the account. A key contributor to the neural network's accurate detection is its ability to factor in loan history to determine probabilities that an exposure will migrate 3, 4, or 5 credit grades. Neural networks adapt as they are inherently learning systems that adjust to changes in loan behavior patterns that match up to credit deterioration criterion. Different neural network models are in place to help financial institutions acquire, service, maintain, and manage portfolios.

Rule Induction

Rule induction is another approach for revealing patterns in the data. This approach may be applied to the same data analyzed by neural networks. The data should include both positive and negative examples—for example, a borrower table, where each record refers to another borrower and the fields are various features, such as income, profit, address, industry, key ratios, and whether the firm paid the loan on time. If the last field is selected as the dependent variable, the rule induction software will reveal if–then rules such as "If the firm's cash flow coverage ratio is between 15% and 25%, and the industry credit grade is below 5, then the probability that the loan is not paid is 0.8 (there are 1,500 customers)."

On top of revealing if–then rules, the system may find if-and-only-if rules such as "If the profit is less than 200, or the industry is food manufacturing, then the probability that the loan is not paid is 0.9, and only if these two conditions do not hold (that is, the profit is at least 200, and the field of business is not food manufacturing), then the probability that the loan is paid is 0.85." Contrary to if–then rules, if-and-only-if rules present necessary and sufficient conditions. Obviously when an if-and-only-if rule such as the preceding is discovered, we can say that we found a theory explaining almost all the cases in the data.

Either the if–then rules or the if-and-only-if rules can be used for the following purposes:

- Issuing predictions for new cases. For example, when a new customer asks for a loan, the software calculates the probability that the customer will not pay the loan by applying the rules on the customer's data.
- Revealing cases to be audited. Cases in the data that deviate from strong rules might be data errors or cases of fraud.
- Revealing interesting phenomena. Unexpected rules denote interesting phenomena in the data.

Final Thoughts

The dictionary defines *evolution* as "a gradual process in which something changes into a different and usually more complex or better form." What a fitting description of GES! Over the short term, exposure-tracking networks have evolved exponentially to become an indispensable portfolio management tool in the war chest of senior bankers. Quick-paced exchange of loan data will accelerate, particularly at small-cap banks. Indeed, GES has redefined the very nature of the banking industry. However, keep the downside in mind: Beneath the silver lining lie strata of rust—not atypical among emerging computer-driven technologies. That is, before advancing systems can deliver the goods, they require an extended period of learning by those who use them; complex software upgrades without requisite training will backfire. Even so, in these times of challenges, a GES's potential payoff is worth the price of the lottery. No matter how much time and energy an institution is prepared to invest in commercial loan tracking systems, almost any well-thought-out system will bring benefits in accuracy, productivity, security, and capital compliance. While bankers may never have to pull a GES emergency cord or face the somber task of micromanaging an imperiled loan portfolio, the investment in efficient exposure and management information systems will pay for itself in language that bankers understand: increases in shareholder value.

20 Building Risk-Adjusted Pricing Models

A bank acquires funds through deposits, borrowing, and equity, recognizing the cost of each source and the resulting average cost of funds to the total bank. The funds are allocated to assets, creating an asset mix of earning assets such as loans and nonearning assets such as a bank's premises. The price that customers are charged for the use of an earning asset represents the sum of the cost of the bank's funds, the administrative costs (e.g., salaries, compensation for nonearning assets, and other costs), and a profit objective that compensates the bank for bearing risk. If pricing adequately compensates for these costs and all risks undertaken, bank value is created. Customer value is created if the price is perceived by the customer to be fair, based on the funds and service received.[1]

As the quotation suggests, naive loan pricing hurts bank value, particularly in a tense credit environment. Conversely, well-defined pricing policies provide risk-adjusted

---

[1] R. S. Kemp and L. C. Pettit, Jr. Excerpted with permission from *The Bankers Magazine.* This excerpt was taken from the original article that appeared in the July/August 1992 issue.

Credit Engineering for Bankers. DOI: 10.1016/B978-0-12-378585-5.10020-X

returns to cover exposure risk and provide a platform to maintain and foster additional business—deposits, fee-based services, investment banking, cash management, trade finance, and trust, to mention a few. And angling the portfolio, loans are priced in line with an entire family of related accounts to position the institution for both additional business and optimal capital returns, thus neither underpricing the relationship with a diminution in risk-adjusted returns nor overpricing it only to lose the entire business to competitors.

An adept loan policy covers all aspects of the (banking) relationship, consolidating many disparate accounts, related businesses, and the multitude of other factors into a single, coherent risk/return analysis.

> *Most banks embrace the concept of relationship banking as a means of differentiating themselves from capital market or nonbank competitors. No longer is the deal a single loan, but a series of ongoing loans and services delivered to meet a wide range of customer needs. Although the most prominent element of the relationship is often the loan, the interaction of all parts of the relationship injects complexities into the pricing model. Relationship profitability becomes the primary focus, often replacing loan profitability.[2]*

Due to the nature of this highly competitive business, pricing loans has traditionally been drawn into the so-called relationship parameter. Lending serves as the foundation for broader corporate business, aiming to maximize the profitability of the entire client relationship, rather than focusing on one or two individual loans (see Chapter Nineteen). As a result, lower deal pricing may be offset by revenue-producing products in other departments (or locales), allowing institutions to earn target returns on a consolidated client basis. In other words, the loan may well serve as the cost of developing broader client relationships. Into the bargain, an effective pricing strategy means developing a price buildup methodology (Figure 20.1). The methodology works itself through all (pricing) components: obligor risk, facility structure, ancillary costs, global exposure network, and competition.

A notable difference exists between banks that follow a systematic pricing approach (see Figure 20.1) and banks that price ad hoc. The rationale for systematic loan pricing is improved risk adjusted return on equity (RAROC), superior loan yields, better margins, higher fee income, stronger earnings, more efficient credit risk management, and tight customer relationship management. Consistent pricing methodology avoids numerous questionable practices, such as failing to factor in default risk, omitting variable and fixed costs, ignoring cost of funds, and overlooking demand deposits "free" balances. These omissions (pricing errors) encourage weak credits to borrow at the same rates offered to more creditworthy borrowers. The following pricing errors deserve further attention:

1. *Meeting the competitor's price.*[3] If the lender cites competition to justify a lower price, the banker fails to understand risk, has poorly structured the credit to minimize risk, or has ignored the need for an adequate return for the bank.

---

[2] Ibid.

[3] Abstracted from Kemp and Pettit.

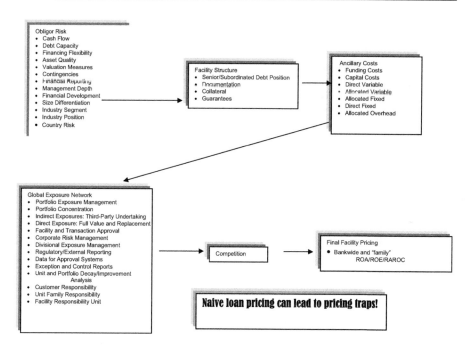

Figure 20.1 Systematic Pricing Approach: Price Buildup Methodology.

2. *Volume is more important than risk-adjusted pricing.* Volume does not, discretely, add value. Risk-based pricing transmits value. Lenders sometimes confuse volume and risk-adjusted returns, neglecting fundamentals that contribute to (bankwide) utility because they simply believe loan volume is the solution to all problems.

3. *Pricing based on marginal cost.* The problem: Deal profit is insufficient to cover overall funding costs. So how will the bank compensate stakeholders? A bank may find it difficult to survive long term with (pricing) policy grounded exclusively on marginal cost, particularly the marginal cost of a bank's cheapest funds (i.e., demand deposits).

4. *Price can compensate for default risk.* Because of competitive pressures, the lure of wider margins from riskier credits is tempting. The fact is that *no price compensates a lender for a bad loan.*

5. *Stability of price/risk relationships over time.* The quickest way to price a loan is to look at the price on the last similar successful deal with the customer. What this practice fails to recognize are the three siblings of credit risk: business, industry, and macroeconomic variability. Price is influenced by future risk, not past conditions. Also, risk premiums are not necessarily market stable—for banks or their customers.

   In volatile economic times—2001, for example—it is harder to acquire funds leading to higher-risk premiums. In less volatile times—the 1990s, for example—funds were easier to acquire, with resulting lower-risk premiums easily demonstrated by looking at returns of non-investment-grade securities. In good economic times, it is easy to sell securities at relatively low yields. Price/risk relationships are not stable over time, so loans should be priced to reflect future price/risk interrelationships associated with clients and markets.

6. *Future pricing can compensate for underpricing current risk.* Some banks justify low spreads by assuming that future client business compensates today's underperforming/

underpriced loan. In other words, as the argument goes, banks can overcharge borrowers tomorrow to make up for low rates charged today.

7. *Loan risk equal to default risk.* Lenders often measure loan risk solely as default risk. Default risk is the risk of nonpayment, whereas loan risk encompasses more than default risk. The loan risk premium must also cover the uncertainties of late payments and restructuring costs due to cyclical or other unforeseen developments. As the primary earning assets of the bank, loans play a significant role in determining the risk premiums required to cover hurdle rates associated with capital costs. Simply stated, pricing loans solely on default risk will diminish corporate value.

Few bankers argue the need to satisfactorily price deals and thus avoid value-destroying pricing traps. But how to accomplish this magic is easier said than done: Risk-adjusted or actuarial approaches to loan spreads and pricing traps represent, in a sense, reverse polarity. The process requires survival and recovery. With the right statistical estimates (no information is entirely foolproof), loan returns will generally provide enough of a margin to compensate for default risk (both for immediate loan areas and globally).

But without default and recovery estimates across a broad range of risks, risk-adjusted pricing regresses to an exercise in academia. Historical survival and recovery rates are available for a wide range of credits. When loan quality deteriorates, default rates do not increase linearly; there is little difference between a credit grade one or two, or between AAA and AA deals. But noticeable differences exist between a Baa credit and a single-B credit, where default spread widens significantly.

Beyond statistical default rates, pricing requires a profound understanding of borrowers along with the ability to judge the qualitative factors on which every risk-return relationship takes root. Bank value and its ascendant, bankwide RAROC—not loan spreads alone—govern loan policy and pricing decisions. The forces of competition and the overriding need to foster relationships apart from overall loan values have clouded the whole issue of loan pricing, creating an ever-increasing number of pitfalls for banks. Bankers are in the business of making loans, but the fiduciary responsibility of bankers is value creation as well, meaning paying special attention to all the costs of bearing risk. Pricing models focus on this, and when linked to bankwide exposure systems and risk-rating procedures, they help bankers realize value creation.

Loan Pricing Models

Pricing models include key (assumption or independent) variables—such as spreads, facility fees, fees in lieu of balances, fixed and variable service costs, and other variables—that combine to produce return on assets (ROA), return on equity (ROE), and/or RAROC (forecast or dependent variables).

Models should be able to define trade-offs among rate spreads, fees, deposit balances, fixed and variable costs, and a host of other variables to produce the appropriate return (i.e., provide correlations between assumption variables and rank correlations, between assumption variables and target forecast variables). Good pricing models include the following characteristics:

- Easy to install, use, and administer
- Available on a wide variety of platforms
- Computes risk-adjusted returns
- Computes yields-to-maturity
- Provides multiperiod analysis
- Accounts for all relevant variables
- Supports the negotiating process
- Provides full relationship profitability
- Provides comprehensive context-sensitive help

Whether the bank chooses to build its own model internally or to buy into a commercial vendor, the bank will incur costs for the model's design, evaluation, training, and systems support. However, the cost is well worth the trouble (or price) because computer-based loan pricing models, particularly the stochastic ones, markedly improve ways in which the bankers manage returns on their portfolios.

Loan pricing usually involves some combination of target return(s) (ROE, ROA, or RAROC). The basic idea is to develop a unique target price for each loan, including adjustments for identifiable risks and costs. Returns are compared to target pricing established by area or bank policy. To illustrate, consider the spreadsheet model using the net borrowed funds approach that follows this section. In calculating the loan yield, the net borrowed funds approach assumes that a company borrows its own funds first and the bank supplies the difference between the deposit and the loan amount—yield calculated on the net difference. We first consider a deterministic model and enlarge it later to factor in stochastic assumptions. Deterministic models rely on single sets of assumptions, while stochastic (i.e., simulation) models involve an entire range of results and confidence levels feasible for a given run.

Methods used for including risk in loan pricing range from simple risk spreads and allocations of loan loss reserves to complex assessment of capital allocation, estimates of default frequency, loss given default, and loss volatility. Recent developments in credit and portfolio risk measurement—particularly on the quantitative side, including sophisticated pricing modeling—are improving banks' ability to measure and price risk more accurately and are facilitating the management of capital and the allowance for loan and lease losses. However, these technologies, much of it stochastic, require accurate risk measurement at the individual loan level and robust portfolio risk management systems (covered in Chapter Fifteen). Even with these developments, the loan pricing decision is clouded, particularly at smaller banks and financial institutions in developing countries.

Banks often incorporate other revenues ascribed to the lending relationship into loan pricing decisions. The lending relationship is advanced to win other business: cash management services, foreign exchange, derivatives, custody, and demand deposit balances. Relationship pricing and profitability measures are important tools for managing credit and portfolio returns. These identify profitable business opportunities and the potential to amass lending relationships whose returns are insufficient relative to risk. However, bankers must ensure that application of relationship pricing and return are not badly chosen. Loans may be booked at unprofitable rates based on the assumption, or promise, that other profitable business will follow. When the other business fails to materialize, returns may be insufficient to compensate the bank for the credit risk. Banks should have pricing systems to accurately measure relationship returns—that is, return on risk adjusted capital, ROA, and ROE—and must exercise tight controls over all aspects of pricing.

The best way to develop an internal pricing model is to start with a very simple model and then extend it in stages in ways that appear to be most important. With this approach, the department will have a usable model early on. Moreover, you can analyze the sensitivities of the simple model to find out where key gaps are and then use this information to set priorities for expanding the model. If, instead, you try to create a large model from the start, you run the risk of running out of time or computer resources before you have anything usable. And you may end up putting a lot of work into creating an elaborate module for an aspect of the problem that turns out to be of little importance. Here are some hints:

- Identify ways to expand and improve the model.
- Add pricing variables that you think are important.
- Add objectives or criteria for evaluating outcomes.
- If you are developing an optimization pricing model, expand the number of decision options specified for a decision variable or the number of possible outcomes for a discrete chance variable.
- Expand a single decision into two or more sequential decisions, with the later decision being made after more information is revealed.
- For your dynamic model, expand the time horizon to include 10-year maturities (from 5 years, though 5-year loans may be more typical), or reduce the time steps (say, from annual to quarterly time periods).

Stochastic Net Borrowed Funds Pricing Model

Illustrative Example Stochastic Loan Pricing Model
Location: Models are available on the Elsevier Website www.ElsevierDirect.com
Brief Description: This stochastic loan pricing models will determine profit on loans, ROA, RAROC, facility hurdle rates, probabilities loan is underpriced, correlation analysis, tornado charts, pricing sensitivities (correlation analysis).

In the example, Second City Bank prices an unsecured $1,000,000 line of credit to Picnic Furniture Manufacturing Co. Details of the transaction are shown in Figure 20.2, which is the input screen for the example. The terms used in the inputting are explained in the following text.

Fees in Lieu of Balances

Compensating balance requirements, sometimes consigned to loan agreements, obligate the borrower to hold demand or low-interest deposits as additional compensation for the loan. Balances can be expressed as a component of the loan

STOCHASTIC PRICING MODEL
DEVELOPED BY PROF. MORTON GLANTZ and DR. JOHNATHAN MUN

Facility Information
Borrower Picnic Furniture Manufacturing Co
Lenders: Second City Bank
Amount: $1,000,000 Five Year Unsecured Facility
Purpose: Expansion
Bank ROA Guideline: 1.15%

Facility Information	
Enter Unsecured Line of Credit (Assumed To Be Fully Utilized)	1,000,000
Enter 12 Month Average Balances (Assume Balances Not Free)	50,000
Enter Base Rate (Prime or LIBOR) Rate	10.5%
Enter Spread Over Base	1.75%
Enter % Facility Fees (Not Connected To Balances!)	2.00%
Enter Funding Costs	8.43%
Enter Servicing: Enter % or Complete Schedule Two	2.70%
Enter Loan loss expense (Applied To Income Statement)	1.50% Function of *Expected* Risk
Enter % Equity Reserve Requirement (Function of Unexpected Risk)	9.00% Function of *Unexpected* Risk
Enter Taxes	35%
Deposit Information	
12 Month Average Balances	50,000
Enter Activity Costs as a % of Balances	4.09%
Enter Balance Requirement	8.75%
Net Borrowed Funds	950,000
Interest rate: Prime + 1.5%	12.21%
Fees In Lieu of Balances	7,673

Schedule One Types of Facility Fees
Agent Fees
Management Fees
Compensation Balances - See Schedule Two
Fees In Lieu of Balances - See Sehedule Two

Schedule Two - Servicing Costs (See Definations
Do Not Complete Schedule If % Was Entered

Direct Variable	0
Allocated Variable	0
Direct fixed	0
Allocated fixed	0
Total Servicing Costs	0

Figure 20.2 Input Screen for Stochastic Pricing Model Example.

commitment, a portion of the actual amount borrowed, or a fixed dollar amount. Fees are paid in advance or in arrears. Since it is part of the pricing mechanism, deficiency fees are charged retroactively if the agreed on balance arrangement is not honored. Deficient balances are treated as borrowed funds, and the fee is calculated like interest usually at the borrowing rate or earnings credit rate (Figure 20.3).

Compensating balances have been criticized as being an inefficient pricing mechanism because even though they raise effective borrowing costs, banks must hold idle reserves against the additional deposits and, therefore, cannot fully invest

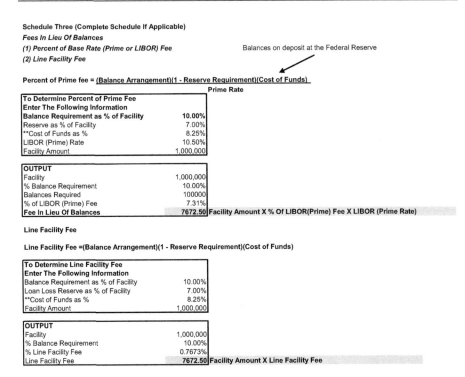

Figure 20.3 Fees in Lieu of Balances.

them in earning assets. Among banks that moved toward unbundled and explicit pricing, balance requirements obscure (loan) returns, which is one reason fees in lieu of balances or simply higher loan rates replaced balances requirements. Since balances effectively replace funds the bank would otherwise purchase, balances "earn" income at cost of funds rate. As the cost of funds fluctuates with market rates, balances are worth more if cost of funds increases and less when funding costs declines.

Fees in lieu of balances should reflect these changing rates, yet it is impracticable to reprice a loan every time the bank's funding costs change. Thus, the interest rate environment influences the setting of fees. Fees in lieu of balances are expressed as a *percent of prime fee, line fee,* or *facility fee*. Since the prime rate includes a spread over the lender's cost of funds, *percent of prime fee* in lieu of balances will keep the bankers "whole" despite fluctuations in the cost of funds. Therefore, the primary contribution of customer-supplied balances (net of effects of the reserve requirement) is reduced funding costs. As long as the balances are provided at a rate that is less than other funds available from the market, they will reduce funding costs.

The *line/facility fee* may undercompensate lenders if interest rates rise, since the fee was calculated based on a lower cost of funds. Figure 20.3 compares the percent of prime fee to the line facility fee. The result of both fee calculations are identical.

Rates

Prime Rate

At one time, approximately 90% of loans linked to prime rates. Today, most banks employ a money-market base. Prime is simply a benchmark by which rates for other borrowers are set and is the least complicated for both borrower and bank. It is a floating rate, and the pricing spread is already included in the rate. Market fluctuations during a loan's term are passed to the borrower. Additional increments added or subtracted from prime reflect a borrower's creditworthiness—the higher the credit risk, the higher the spread.

A bank's pricing decision should not be driven solely by the prime rate or any other base-rate benchmark, since the whole notion of loan pricing involves complex decision making with a multiplicity of factors at play. The myth of prime (rate) lending has come to us from the misconstrued notion that prime is the lowest rate available to the bank's best corporate customers.

In any case, a common banking practice is to price loans based with spreads over prime. The standard procedure calls for an additive—that is, borrowers are quoted something like "prime + 2," which means prime plus 200 basis points. An alternative to prime-plus pricing is prime times pricing, which calls for a multiplicative formula rather than an additive one. This pricing is expressed as Quoted rate = Multiplicative adjustment factor × Prime rate, where the adjustment factor can be greater (premium) or less than (discount). For example, if the prime is 8.5% and the adjustment factor is 1.35, then the borrower is quoted a rate of 11.475% (8.5% times 1.35).

Some banks abandoned prime because of publicity from court cases challenging this rate and associated lending practices during the early and mid-1980s. Plaintiffs claimed that banks misled customers by implying that the prime rate was the interest rate charged to their most creditworthy customers, when in fact some loans were actually made below the prime rate.

LIBOR

LIBOR, which consists of floating rates based on the London Interbank Offering Rate, is a widely quoted rate on short-term European money market credits. For some time, it has influenced the overseas lending rates of large U.S. banks, particularly when the spread between U.S. money market base rates and LIBOR rates favored the latter. Also, access to overseas sources of funds has recently made LIBOR an increasingly popular base rate among borrowers of regional and smaller banks.

Based on demand for alternative pricing structures, many corporate borrowers now have the option of tying their loan rates to the Eurodollar market. Eurodollars are U.S. dollar deposits held anywhere outside of the United States (actually, the Eurodollar market gives rise to LIBOR). LIBOR is an index or snapshot of the Eurodollar market at a particular point of time. At each business day at 11:00 a.m. London time, London's major banks are asked where Eurodollars are trading. These rates become LIBOR. After LIBOR is set, Eurodollars continue to trade freely, above and below LIBOR. LIBOR more accurately reflects the bank's marginal cost of funds than prime. However, as with prime loans, an incremental percentage above or below LIBOR is usually assessed to address the relative creditworthiness of the borrower.

For example, a manufacturer of plumbing equipment negotiates with its bank a $10 million loan that can be priced at either prime + 50 basis points or at 3-month LIBOR + 250 basis points. Assume that at current levels switching to a LIBOR-based facility reduces the borrower's loan costs by 25 basis points. Why would the prime option be higher in this case? A number of factors are in play. For example, LIBOR fluctuates along with uncertainties that are inherent in the market, while prime is an administered rate, unresponsive to whims and rumors; LIBOR fluctuates on either side of 25 basis points, while prime holds constant.

Should LIBOR options be selected simply because the rate is comparably low? Although prime-based loans carry higher pricing, their rates offer flexibility— increase (loan) exposure or pay down credit lines when cash flows permit. This is not true of LIBOR-based deals because banks cannot set pricing unilaterally but must negotiate with borrowers until parties mutually accept a structure and settle on a price.

Facility Fees

Commitment Fee

When a bank makes commitments to lend funds or issue credit facilities, customers are charged commitment fees. This per annum fee is charged (usually quarterly or at time of interest collection) from the time of acceptance of the commitment until drawdown/issuance and on the unused portion of the commitment. A commitment fee is applied to the unused amount of the available portion (the portion periodically designated available or the amount the company projects it will need during a specified period). A lower commitment fee is applied to the unavailable portion.

Commitment fees on the unused portion of the loan are usually assessed in each accounting period (monthly or yearly) by calculating the average usage rate. Because the bank must set aside capital in support of the unused credit line, commitment fees should be set high enough to generate a desirable return on capital should the credit line not be fully used and to otherwise encourage use.

Facility Fee

This fee is charged to customers for making a credit facility available. Unlike the commitment fee, the facility fee applies to the entire facility regardless of usage. Facility fees are frequently used in lieu of balance arrangements and to increase the overall yield on the facility. Facility fees and commitment fees are usually disclosed explicitly in the loan agreement. For profitability analysis and pricing, facility fees are generally amortized over the life of the loan according to FASB 91.

Prepayment Penalty Fee

This fee is charged if a loan is partially or entirely repaid before the scheduled maturity. Prepayments, if permitted at all, could be subject to potentially costly premiums. Since an existing agreement cannot be opened up and increased, customers wanting to increase outstandings must enter into new LIBOR agreements. LIBOR loan facilities more so than prime-based facilities may subject borrowers to prepayment premiums if loans are prepaid in whole or part prior to maturity. Premiums are often calculated by comparing the interest that banks would have earned if loans were not prepaid to the interest earned from reinvesting prepaid amounts at current market rates.

Agent's Fee

For its efforts and expense in packaging a credit and performing loan servicing duties, a principal bank in a multibank credit transaction charges an agent's fee. The fee may be stated as either a dollar amount or as a percentage of the facility.

Management Fee

Banks designated as managing banks in a syndicated credit collect this fee.

Miscellaneous Fees

Special financing transactions such as leveraged buyouts, acquisition financing, or tax-exempt financing often warrant charging fees for the extra costs involved in structuring the deal. *Up front fees, arrangement fees, closing fees,* and *fees certain* (to be collected whether the loan is closed or not) are common fees collected for complex deals. These fees may be flat fees or a percentage of the loan. They can be collected in advance or over the life of the loan.

Cost of Funds

Cost of funds reflects the *marginal* cost of all funds used to support loans. Conventional wisdom defines the incremental cost of funds as the rate paid on capital used for funding the loan. Some bankers believe this definition is too narrow and underestimates the true cost of funds (rate). According to some, the incremental cost of funds (rate) should be identified as the total incremental expense incurred in gathering $1 of investable funds. For example, some banks with a significant amount of demand deposits and branch networks might have higher operating costs, deposit insurance costs, and reserve requirements. These costs must be included in the cost of funds.

Service and Administrative Costs

Measuring overhead and administrative costs is more complicated than, for example, funding costs because banks traditionally have not had strong cost accounting systems. Additionally, common services with differing or ambiguous values to each user (what, for example, is the dollar value of loan review?) can be difficult to measure. An additional and often ignored cost of risk is risk-related overhead. Riskier loans tend to have higher administrative expenses because of incremental monitoring requirements together with the increased involvement of credit administration and supervisory personnel required on these deals.

Collection and loan workout areas and a portion of legal costs represent risk-related expenses, and their costs could be apportioned to loans based on the relative risks. It is unfortunate that some banks approve poorly priced loans when they cannot or are unwilling to allocate their cost base accurately.

If a bank cannot allocate costs, then it will make no distinction between the cost of lending to borrowers that require little investment in recourses and the cost of lending to borrowers that require a considerable amount of analysis and follow-up. As a result, commercial lenders have generally understood the need to reduce costs and redesign the credit process to improve efficiency, recognizing that the market will not permit a premium for inefficiency.

Service and administrative costs are based on functional-cost data, cost-accounting figures allocated to average assets, or the bank's best estimates of the costs, and usually include the following:

1. *Direct variable:* Expenses charged to the profit/cost center that are directly associated with the loan. Direct variable expense can easily be estimated either from the loan proposal or by the loan department.
2. *Allocated variable:* Allocated expenses are the expenses incurred by other cost centers in support of a product. These expenses can usually be derived from a bank's cost accounting system that includes variable support expenses for data processing, the customer phone center, and other support departments.
3. *Allocated fixed:* Direct and allocated fixed expenses are calculated according to the total capacity of each operation (cost center) rather than using the fully loaded costs. Otherwise, as volume rises, per unit fixed costs will be overstated. These calculations are usually based on an operation research and capacity/unit cost study.
4. *Direct fixed and allocated overhead:* Allocated overhead is the portion of the bank's total overhead that should be considered supportive of this particular product.

Hurdle Rate

While operating expenses factor into the pricing arithmetic, loan pricing involves three essential steps:

1. A minimum target or hurdle rate must be estimated. The appropriate hurdle rate incorporates both the funding costs and a specified profit target.
2. Estimate income, expenses, and yield associated with the loan.
3. Compare the estimated yield with the target or hurdle rate to determine loan profitability. If the yield is less than the hurdle rate, the loan should be either rejected or restructured so it meets the target.

Output Screen and Yield Calculation

The underlying algorithms used to compute loan yields should be reliable and support a bank's strategic objectives. Efficient pricing should compute yields to maturity, from inception to maturity. For example, interest rates for purchased funds can change frequently, money borrowed fluctuates over time, deposit balances vary with the borrower's cash position, administrative costs change, and so on. Changes, especially in a volatile market, affect yields and must be factored into pricing. Pricing models must respond to frequent changes in the negotiating environment and include variables affecting profitability (even factors not at issue with the customer). A lending officer cannot possibly track all pricing variables; they all fluctuate over time, which is one good reason computer-based loan pricing is *sine qua non*.

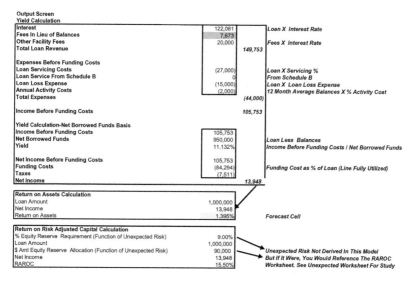

Summary: Base Case	
Borrower Picnic Furniture Manufacturing Co	
Lenders: Second City Bank	
Loan Revenue	149,753
Facility	1,000,000
Net Income	13,948
ROA	1.395%
Facility ROA Hurtle Rate	**1.15%**
Facility Internal Rate of Return (See Brady Worksheet)	
Option Pricing Generated Hurtle Rate (OptionPr Worksheet)	
RAROC	**15.50%**

In the unchanged scenario of the example pricing model, the bank's 1.395% ROA is higher than the facility ROA hurdle rate of 1.15%. The higher the ROA over the hurdle rate, the more profitable the bank will be within its desired level of risk. The estimated loan revenue consists of fees in lieu of balances and facility fees. Facility is the face value amount of the loan being borrowed. Net income is income after all funding costs and administrative expenses. ROA is net income/loan amount. Because the ROA hurdle rate is 1.15% and the actual ROA is 1.395%, the bank would accept this loan provided that the RAROC and credit grade are acceptable for the bank's loan portfolio risk profile.

Moving From Deterministic Pricing to a Stochastic Pricing Solution

Recall from Chapter Eight that deterministic models rely on single sets of assumptions that lead to limited outcomes. Risk Simulator stochastic software yield an entire range of results and confidence levels realistic for any pricing run. Risk Simulator (Monte Carlo) simulation fosters realistic loan pricing by capturing elements of uncertainty that are too complex to be solved with deterministic pricing models. Stochastic models, as we saw, necessitate a random number generator set against key variables in the pricing program to create a series of loan pricing outcomes over time, outcomes that are not deterministic in nature; that is, loan pricing (ROA, ROE, or RAROC) will change by X percent if loan spreads, or allocated variable cost of the loan, change by a specific factor. Stochastic pricing is nondeterministic. By offering a stochastic simulation, we create multiple pathways and obtain a statistical sampling of these simulations.

Before starting with simulation, we first need to identify which of the variables in the model are considered critical success factors—that is, to automatically perform a static perturbation of all the input variables in the model and rank the input assumptions from the highest impact to the least impact so we can determine which of these precedent variables have the most impact on ROA. Then, from this list, we can select the variables that are also uncertain and apply simulation assumptions on them. Do not waste time with inputs having very little impact on ROA or are simply known or contractually set in advance. The resulting static sensitivity table and tornado chart from Risk Simulator are presented as Figure 20.4 (we only set the software to show the top 10 impact variables).

Then, armed with this information, and after determining which variables are indeed known or unchanged, we set input assumptions of the critical key variables and the simulation is run. The report shown next, produced by Risk Simulator, shows a 15.0% probability that deal pricing falls below the 1.15% ROA hurdle rate set by the profit center. We are, however, 100% certain that ROA range will fall between 2.48% and 0.71%. The median return is 1.47%.

Risk Simulator also produced a statistical summary including sensitivity charts (Figure 20.5). Sensitivity charts are dynamic perturbations created after the ROA simulation run. They are dynamic perturbations in the sense that multiple assumptions are perturbed simultaneously and their interactions are captured in the fluctuations of the results. Sensitivity charts identify the impact to the forecast variable, ROA, when multiple interacting assumptions in our pricing model are simulated together.

The nonlinear rank correlation charts (Figure 20.6) indicate the rank correlations between each pricing assumption and our target forecast, and they are depicted from the highest absolute value to the lowest absolute value. Positive correlations are shown in green, while negative correlations are shown in red. Rank correlation is used instead of a regular correlation coefficient as it captures nonlinear effects between variables. In contrast, the percent variation explained computes how much of the variation in the forecast variable can be explained by the variations in each of the

Precedent Cell	Base Value: 0.0139484609812889			Input Changes		
	Output Downside	Output Upside	Effective Range	Input Downside	Input Upside	Base Case Value
Base Rate (Prime or LIBOR)	0.0071507	0.0207462	0.01	9.4%	11.5%	10.5%
Funding Costs	0.0194276	0.0084694	0.01	7.59%	9.27%	8.43%
Servicing	0.0167035	0.0121935	0.00	2.43%	2.97%	2.70%
% Facility Fees	0.0126485	0.0152485	0.00	1.80%	2.20%	2.00%
Spread Over Base	0.012811	0.015086	0.00	1.58%	1.93%	1.75%
Loan Loss Expense	0.0149235	0.0129735	0.00	1.35%	1.65%	1.50%
Enter Taxes	0.0146995	0.0131974	0.00	32%	39%	35%
Balance Requirement	0.0134497	0.0144472	0.00	9.00%	11.00%	10.00%
Facility Amount	0.0134497	0.0144472	0.00	900,000	1,100,000	1,000,000
Cost of Funds	0.0134497	0.0144472	0.00	7.43%	9.08%	8.25%
Unsecured Line of Credit	0.0143581	0.0136133	0.00	900,000	1,100,000	1,000,000
Annual Activity Costs	0.0140785	0.0138185	0.00	(1,800)	(2,200)	(2,000)
Reserve % Facility	0.013986	0.0139109	0.00	6.30%	7.70%	7.00%
Allocated Variable	0.0139485	0.0139485	0.00	0	0	0
Direct Fixed	0.0139485	0.0139485	0.00	0	0	0
Cost of Funds	0.0139485	0.0139485	0.00	7.43%	9.08%	8.25%
Direct Variable	0.0139485	0.0139485	0.00	0	0	0
Balance Requirement	0.0139485	0.0139485	0.00	9.00%	11.00%	10.00%
Loan Loss Reserve % Facility	0.0139485	0.0139485	0.00	6.30%	7.70%	7.00%
Allocated Fixed	0.0139485	0.0139485	0.00	0	0	0
LIBOR (Prime) Rate	0.0139485	0.0139485	0.00	9.45%	11.55%	10.50%
Facility Amount	0.0139485	0.0139485	0.00	900,000	1,100,000	1,000,000

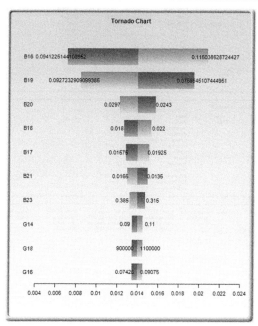

Figure 20.4 Risk Simulator's Sensitivity Table and Tornado Chart: Picnic Furniture Manufacturing Co. Loan Pricing.

assumptions by itself in a dynamic simulated environment. These charts show the sensitivity of the target forecast to the simulated assumptions.

The Nonlinear Rank Correlation (Return on Assets) and Percent Variation Explained (Return on Assets) charts demonstrate that pricing is more sensitive to loan

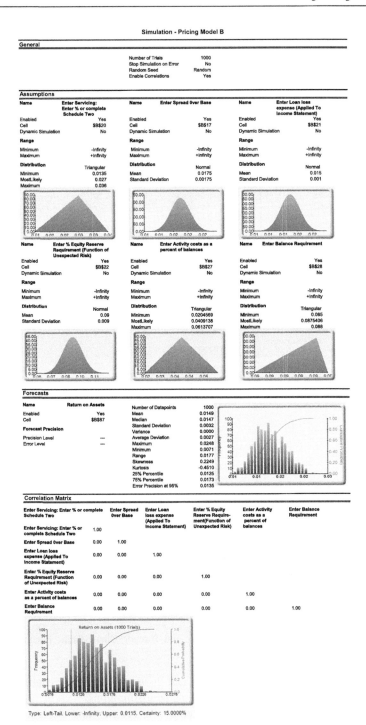

Figure 20.5 Risk Simulator's Statistical Summary for Picnic Furniture Manufacturing Co.

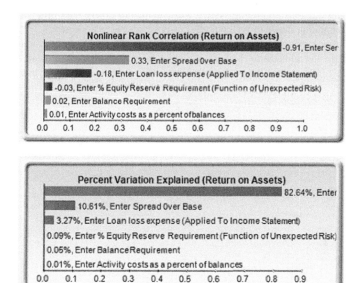

Figure 20.6 Risk Simulator's Nonlinear Rank Correlation Charts for Picnic Furniture Manufacturing Co.

servicing costs than loan spreads. This last statement is noteworthy because the bank may benefit from a substantial, profitable relationship worldwide. If a profit center were required to lower spreads over base because global relationships are immensely profitable, a pricing rebate—on the one deal—is in order. However, if loan returns are time and again unsatisfactory because the costs of managing a profit center are out of control, no compensation from head office can be expected to save the day.

Loan Pricing Lessons

Risk-adjusted pricing allows bankers to price "whole"—that is, to cover not only loan expenses but the inherent cost of credit risk associated with loss given default (LGD) and unexpected loss. Smart risk-adjusted pricing is fundamental to well-managed, optimal loan portfolios. There are few better ways to illustrate this point than to offer readers Thomas Hannagan's nine unique "lessons" in loan pricing:[4]

1. Executive involvement is critical to a successful transition to loan pricing.
2. The transition to relationship pricing must support the bank's strategy.
3. Every key aspect of configuring a loan pricing system can be accomplished.
4. Perfection is an (expensive) illusion, but logic and intuition will carry the day.

[4] Thomas A. Hannagan, "Loan and Relationship Pricing Practices: Loan Pricing Lessons," *The RMA Journal,* December 2004. Tom Hannagan is a senior client partner with Experian Decision Analytics. He specializes in advising bank management on enhanced profitability strategies in commercial lending.

5. Any loan and relationship pricing system will continue to evolve over time.
6. The implementation needs to be thoughtful; it is an educational journey.
7. The supporting logic underlying the system needs to be explained and documented.
8. Loan pricing is an addition to the bank's lending culture—not a replacement.
9. Profitability can be part of the goal setting and performance measurement process.

Index

Printed and bound by CPI Group (UK) Ltd, Croydon, CR0 4YY

08/05/2025

01864768-0004